TELLY ADDICT
COMEDY

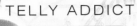

TELLY ADDICT
COMEDY

First published in the UK in 2014

© Demand Media Limited 2014

www.demand-media.co.uk

Printed and bound in Europe

ISBN 978-1-910270-08-0

Contents

Introduction

Television comedy shows have had a place in broadcasting history since the very earliest days of production. Although there are many different genres of television comedy, including the comedy-drama and sketch comedy, the situation comedy, or sitcom, has become the most common, successful and culturally significant type of television comedy over the years.

Telly Addict: Comedy highlights over fifty well-known and loved comedy shows that have given pleasure to British audiences for many years, in fact some of them for decades. The variety and diversity of comedy shows produced over the past sixty years is quite staggering. From Hancock's Half Hour, The Likely Lads, and The Fall and Rise of Reginald Perrin to Absolutely Fabulous, Blackadder and Father Ted, many have become household favourites that, despite not being newly created, are still repeated regularly on the many television networks now available with digital channels.

In addition to the numerous comedy shows themselves, many of the actors and actresses – some who launched their careers by starring in them – have also become renowned and distinguished figures. Personalities such as Rowan Atkinson, Peter Kay, Joanna Lumley and John Cleese are just some of the famous and acclaimed comedy actors and actresses who have starred in the comedy shows showcased here.

TELLY ADDICT : COMEDY

Absolutely Fabulous

Written by and starring Jennifer Saunders, the original first three series of BBC sitcom Absolutely Fabulous were broadcast from 1992 to 1995. The regular cast of Absolutely Fabulous included Jennifer Saunders as Edina Monsoon, Joanna Lumley as Patsy, Julia Sawalha as Saffron, Jane Horrocks as Bubble and June Whitfield as Mother.

The show evolved from a French & Saunders sketch called *Modern Mother and Daughter* in which a middle-aged mother, who acted like a teenager, was emotionally and financially reliant on her teenage daughter who behaved like she were the middle-aged woman in the relationship.

Absolutely Fabulous centred on the interaction between and exploits of the jet-setting PR agent Edina Monsoon (Jennifer Saunders) and her best friend, fashion magazine editor Patsy Stone (Joanna Lumley). The mother/daughter role reversal was played out by Edina's clean-living and studious daughter Saffron (Julia Sawalha). Although the series did adhere to some classic physical comedy devices, a vast amount of the comedy came from the sheer indulgence of hedonism, decadence and outrageous unladylike behaviour, with the added notable absence of any male roles. When launched in 1992 the show quickly met both popular and critical acclaim in the UK and quickly became affectionately named 'Ab Fab'.

A total of five series and thirty-nine episodes of the comedy show were broadcast, although the end of the third series was intended to be the last at the time. The original series ran from 1992 to 1996 and it was revived between 2001

and 2004. The show then returned at the end of 2011 for their 20th anniversary special three episodes, the final of which coincided with the 2012 Summer Olympics with Stella McCartney appearing in a cameo role.

Many celebrities, mainly British or American, appeared in the series and they mostly appeared as themselves. Some of the most famous include, Elton John, Whoopi Goldberg, Richard Curtis, Helena Bonham Carter, Dawn French and Naomi Campbell, to name a few.

The theme music for the show is *This Wheel's on Fire*, written by Bob Dylan and Rick Danko. Julie Driscoll and Adrian Edmondson, Saunders' husband, originally performed it. Marianne Faithfull and American soul singer P.P. Arnold sung it for the 1996 special 'Last Shout'.

Absolutely Fabulous can certainly be credited with raising the profile of women in the British comedy scene as well as catering particularly for a female audience. The British Film Institute ranks it as the seventeenth greatest British TV show of all time.

'Allo 'Allo!

Broadcast on BBC One for ten years from 1982 to 1992, 'Allo 'Allo! was originally the brainchild of David Croft and Jeremy Lloyd, and they wrote the first six seasons; David Croft also composed the theme music. The remaining seasons were written by Jeremy Lloyd and Paul Adam.

Originally 'Allo 'Allo was conceived as a spoof of the 1977-1979 BBC drama series Secret Army as well as other serious occupation dramas such ITV's Enemy at the Door.

Set at the time when France was occupied by the Nazis during World War II, the comedy show revolved around the owner of Café René, René Artois, who was the unwitting and unwilling hero of the French resistance (codename Nighthawk) and his friends. The plots centred on the misadventures of René and his eclectic mix of friends who were constantly attempting to outwit and confound the exploits of the occupying Germans who used his Café as their local headquarters and hiding place for their valuable war spoils.

The main cast of 'Allo 'Allo included Gorden Kaye as Café owner René Artois, Carmen Silvera as tone-deaf singer Edith Artois, Vicki Michelle as the lovesick waitress Yvette, Kirsten Cooke as Michelle, Rose Hill as the invalid Mother, David Janson and Richard Gibson as Herr Flick and Kim Hartman as Helga.

With most of the action taking place in the Café René, brimming with wartime stereotypes, the French resistance comedy saw sexy French resistance girls in raincoats and berets as well as limping, bespectacled Gestapo agents and dim-witted British agents.

Although René summarised the plot to date at the start of each episode, the episode plots were built on what had gone before, which meant that audiences had to follow the series to fully understand the storyline. Most members of the main cast also had a catchphrase or saying that became easily recognisable throughout the series. Perhaps most famously, with René constantly trying to keep his passionate love affairs with his waitresses secret from his wife, when caught in the arms of another woman, he famously retorted with 'You stupid woman! Can you not see that ...' Similarly, his wife Edith, whenever finding René in the embrace of one of the waitresses asked 'René! What are you doing 'olding that servant girl in your arms?'

Regardless of its incessant sexual innuendos, predictable gags and its somewhat repetitiveness, 'Allo 'Allo enjoyed the success of nine series, totalling eighty-five episodes, plus four specials. The series is one that is fondly remembered by British audiences and is therefore frequently repeated, as well as inspiring a touring theatre adaptation. It also enjoyed much international success particularly in Australia, New Zealand and North America.

In 2004 'Allo 'Allo! was voted thirteenth in Britain's Best Sitcom poll. In 2007 a reunion special was broadcast and, as well as comprising new material, it included specially recorded interviews and clips for the show's archives.

Are You Being Served?

Set in the London department store Grace Brothers, comedy show Are You Being Served? was created and written by David Croft and Jeremy Lloyd. It was originally broadcast from 1972 to 1985 and totalled ten series and sixty-nine episodes, five of which were Christmas specials.

The inspiration for the comedy show came from a brief period during the 1950s when co-creator Jeremy Lloyd worked at the clothing store Simpsons of Piccadilly. Lloyd and Croft also spent time at Rossiters of Paignton department store, which has also been credited as a major influence. The comedy show was based on the interaction and antics of the characters working on the clothing floor at department store Grace Brothers. It used its broad characters brilliantly to satirise working life as unremittingly tedious and suppressive as they all battled with management and feuded with each other.

The main cast of Are You Being Served? included John Inman as Mr Humphries, Wendy Richard as Miss Brahm, Nicolas Smith as Mr Rumbold, Mollie Sugden as Mrs Slocombe, Frank Thornton as Captain Peacock, Trevor Bannister as Mr Lucas, Arthur Brough as Mr Grainger, Harold Bennett as Young Mr Grace and Arthur English as Mr Harman.

There was, however, much controversy over the portrayal of screamingly camp menswear assistant Mr Humphries. At the time there were so few representations of gay men, it was therefore a stereotypical one. However, Mr Humphries in the series emerged as the only character with self-respect and

dignity compared to his colleagues who came across as downtrodden and full of self-loathing.

Popular in the United States, Australia and New Zealand, Are You Being Served? was perhaps one of the few British comedy shows that remains emblematic of a particular era of British humour. Very much in the same ilk as the Carry On films, the continuous stereotyping, slapstick situations and crude innuendos that characterised the show places it very accurately in that particular period in Great British comedy show history.

In 2004, Are You Being Served? was ranked at number twenty in the Britain's Best Sitcom poll and was so popular in its day that later episodes attracted up to twenty-two million viewers. In its thirteen-year run, quite incredibly, five of the original cast appeared in all sixty-nine episodes: Frank Thornton, Mollie Sugden, John Inman, Wendy Richard and Nicholas Smith. With the death of Frank Thornton in March 2013, Nicholas Smith is the only surviving member of the original cast, along with Mike Berry, who was in the eighth to tenth series.

As Time Goes By

Starring Judi Dench and Geoffrey Palmer as Lionel and Jean, As Time Goes By was created by Colin Bostock-Smith and written by Bob Larbey. It was broadcast on BBC One from 1992 to 2002 during which time nine series and sixty-seven episodes were aired.

The foundations for the show are based on the story of Lionel Hardcastle, a young man in the army and Jean Pargetter, a nurse, who are madly in love until Lionel is sent to fight the Korean War and because of a love letter that never gets delivered, they lose touch.

Thirty-eight years later they meet again. Divorcee Lionel is writing a book about his post-army life in Kenya as a coffee planter and widowed Jean runs a secretarial agency in London called Type for You. Lionel decides that he needs a secretary to help him with his book and

he chooses to contact Jean's agency. It takes a while, but gradually Jean and Lionel start to rekindle their romance and eventually get married.

In addition to Judi Dench (Jean Hardcastle) and Geoffrey Palmer (Lionel Hardcastle), other starring characters included Moira Brooker as Judith 'Judi' Deacon, Philip Bretherton as Alistair Deacon and Jenny Funnell as Sandy Edwards.

The two main lead characters outstanding performances encapsulate all the trials and tribulations of two older, set in their ways people, falling in love and then living their life together, which provides a gentle but heart-warming comedy. Alongside this is the more turbulent relationship played out by Jean's daughter Judith and Lionel's publisher Alistair. There is also Jean's efficient secretary and Judith's best friend Sandy who ends up dating

TELLY ADDICT : COMEDY

Harry, a policeman and rugby player, who also eventually get married.

The show didn't particularly break any new ground or make a unique mark with regard to British comedy shows as a genre, but it entertained millions of people for over a decade. It also gave the older generation much-deserved exposure on British television.

In 2004, As Time Goes By was voted twenty-ninth in the Britain's Best Sitcom poll. It also had much international appeal and therefore success and has been broadcast in the United States, Canada, Australia, New Zealand, Ireland, Finland and Nigeria. The series was also adapted and recorded for radio, and apart from Philip Bretherton, who missed the first series, the radio adaptation featured all of the original cast members and all episodes corresponded to the television series.

Birds Of A Feather

B AFTA-nominated Birds of a Feather was originally broadcast by the BBC from 1989 to 1998. Created by Laurence Marks and Maurice Gran, the show starred Pauline Quirke, Linda Robson and Lesley Joseph.

One of the unusual and ground-breaking aspects about the comedy show at the time was the fact that it placed the adventures (and misadventures) of a group of female lead characters at its heart.

Sisters, Sharon and Tracey Stubbs, who had been living very different lives, were suddenly brought together when their husbands (Darryl and Chris) were both convicted of armed robbery. Sharon was hard up and had lived in a council flat in Edmonton, whereas Tracey lived in an expensive house in Chigwell in Essex.

Sharon moves in with Tracey and together they face the trials and tribulations of getting used to dealing with life without the support of their husbands. They become good – if not begrudging friends – with sex-mad neighbour Dorien Green (played by Lesley Joseph), whose hobby is to cheat on her husband with much younger men, not to mention never leaving Sharon and Tracey alone.

The humour of Birds of a Feather is a brilliant combination of the relationship between the sisters, heavily influenced by the obvious culture clash between them, plus the hilarious scenes and sometimes episodes that were delivered by the man-eating Dorien.

Pauline Quirke and Linda Robson had in fact been childhood friends and trained together at drama school. This close relationship made playing the roles of the Stubbs sisters very natural and their chemistry and shared sense of timing

was a major reason why the show was so enjoyable to watch.

Sixteen years after its last episode with the BBC, Birds of a Feather returned on ITV in 2014 for its tenth series and attracted viewing figures of nearly eight million for its opening episode.

Birds of a Feather enjoyed global success and was sold to over thirty countries. In 1990 Pauline Quirke won the Best TV Comedy Newcomer and was nominated for the Best TV Comedy Actress at the British Comedy Awards. In 1993 it was nominated the Best Comedy (Programme or Series) at the BAFTA Awards, and between 1997 and 1999 Pauline Quirke was nominated for the Most Popular Comedy Performer, Most Popular Actress and Most Popular Comedy Performer at the National Television Awards. The series also won the 1999 Best Sitcom at the TV Quick Awards.

Blackadder

Originally written by Richard Curtis and Rowan Atkinson, followed by the ingenious collaboration of Richard Curtis and Ben Elton, Blackadder is the name that encompasses the total of four historical comedy series that were broadcast on the BBC between 1983 and 1989.

Each Blackadder series was set in a particular period in history – the first, The Black Adder in the late medieval era (1983); Elizabethan England in Blackadder II (1985); the turn of the 18th and 19th centuries in Blackadder the Third (1987) and World War I in Blackadder Goes Forth (1989).

The first series, The Black Adder, received very mixed reviews and was perceived by many as just not funny. The entire Blackadder concept was nearly given the chop, particularly as the first series had also cost a lot of money in the making. Thank goodness, however, for the ingenuity and sheer brilliance of the minds of Richard Curtis and Ben Elton, who rethought the overall concept and subsequently improved it beyond recognition. And the rest, as they say, is history and how pleased we are about it!

Although each series had its own unique identity and comedy flavour, there were several constants, notably Rowan Atkinson as Edmund Blackadder and Tony Robinson as Baldrick. Other regular and unmistakable actors that were intrinsic to the comedy series' success included Stephen Fry (Lord Melchett to General Melchett via the Duke of Wellington); Hugh Laurie (Prince and then Captain George); Tim McInnerny (the effeminate Lord Percy of the first two series and the highly frustrated and

uptight Captain Darling of the fourth). Although at the time still an up-and-coming actress, the portrayal of Queen Elizabeth I by Miranda Richardson was extraordinary in its characterisation and she was very much acclaimed for this, not to mention never forgotten for it either!

Fusing sophisticated literary and historical allusions with blatantly crude jokes, often in the same conversation, gave Blackadder an unmistakable winning comedy formula. It is difficult to over exaggerate the influence that Blackadder had and still has. Almost three decades after the first series was broadcast, it remains widely quoted, highly regarded and massively popular.

In 2000, Blackadder Goes Forth was ranked 16th in the British Film Institute's '100 Greatest British Television Programmes' and in 2004 in a BBC television poll, Blackadder was voted as the second best sitcom of all time and was only surpassed by Only Fools and Horses.

Bottom

Slapstick comedy show Bottom was both written by and starred the comic duo Adrian Edmondson and Rik Mayall (makers of The Young Ones) as Richie and Eddie respectively. Running from 1991 to 1995, the series totalled three series and eighteen episodes, followed by five stage shows between 1993 and 2003, and one feature film called Guest House Paradiso in 1999.

The plot of comedy show Bottom revolved simply around the pretty wretched and sex-starved lives of destitute flatmates and perverted lunatic best friends Richie Rich and Eddie Hitler, who do absolutely nothing other than hang around their filthy flat in Hammersmith abusing each other, both verbally and physically. Each episode revolved around them doing anything to try and make money without actually having to do any work. This ranged from waiting for relatives to die, stealing, gambling and swindling others. The second regular theme was their desperate plots and schemes to try and get laid, which were obviously never successful.

Although Richie and Eddie were the main stars of the show, other recurring characters appeared including Steve O'Donnell as Spud-gun; Christopher Ryan as Dave Hedgehog; Lee Cornes as Dick Head; and Roger Sloman as Mr Harrison.

The comedy show is notorious for its violent comedy slapstick as well as its chaotic and anarchistic humour. Toilet humour and jokes about parts of the body were all entwined with the

cartoon-like slapstick violence that the friends routinely inflicted on each other. Its unashamed coarse, offensive and juvenile humour did divide audiences at the time, but it has to be said that, unless very easily offended, it is hard not to find Bottom absolutely hilarious, even if it is at the same time as cringing! Bottom was definitely one of the naughtiest British comedy shows made at the time.

The comedy duo originally planned to call the series 'Your Bottom' so that viewers could say to each other phrases such as 'I saw Your Bottom on television last night'. In 2008 Bottom came in at number forty-five in the BBC's 'Britain's Best Sitcom' poll and it is regularly repeated in the UK on both Gold and Dave channels.

Bread

Broadcast from 1986 to 1991 and running for seven series, the British television sitcom Bread was written by Carla Lane and it became the biggest show in the country. The show's title comes from cockney rhyming slang bread and honey, the term for money.

Headed by the Catholic matriarch 'Ma' Boswell, the show revolved around life for a large working-class family living in a mid-terrace house near the docks in Liverpool. They faced constant unemployment and lack of money, but their guile and cunning for finding their way round the DHSS benefit system provided one of the shows most notable recurring comedy threads.

The Boswell family consisted of seven, six living under one roof and granddad who lived next door. Nellie Boswell was played by Jean Boht (rarely referred to as anything other than Mrs Boswell) and is perhaps best remembered for saying prayers before supper, putting the illicit traffic cones outside the house to save a parking space, screaming 'she is a tart' down the road at Lilo Lill, layabout ex-husband Freddie's girlfriend.

The eldest son Joey (played by Peter Howitt until series four and then Graham Bickley) was the family's patriarch and portrayed what was in the 1980s the epitome of 'cool'. Driving to the dole office in an old jag, Joey said hello to people with 'greetings', had big bouffant hair and always wore a leather jacket.

The other siblings consisted of Jack (played by Victor McGuire), a wheeler-dealer type, but hard-working nonetheless; Adrian (played by Jonathon Morris), an overly-sensitive would-be poet; the aspiring model and much-protected and mothered Aveline (played by Gilly Coman until series

four and then Melanie Hill); and the baby of the family Billy (played by Nick Conway) who was arguably the daftest of all.

Carla Lane cleverly and uniquely amalgamated long-running storylines that you would typically find in a soap opera with a traditional sitcom series format and the concept for the show came from the Boswell family that were created in the final series of The Liver Birds. Lane also employed the soap-opera style cliffhanger endings, which meant that viewers had to tune in the following week to find out what happened. The result of which was

hugely successful and popular with British audiences. The focus on a family sticking together through hard times undoubtedly appealed to a nation reeling from the Thatcher government's privatisation policies, closure of nationalised industries and the following social and economic devastation that ensued. In 1988 more than twenty-one million viewers tuned in on the day that Aveline married Protestant vicar Oswald. A radio version, stage show and feature films (including a star-studded remake planned for 2015) were also produced.

Cheers

Created and produced by James Burrows, Glen Charles and Les Charles, Cheers was an American sitcom that ran for eleven series, totalling two hundred and seventy episodes, including three double-length episodes and a triple-length finale. Cheers was broadcast between 1982 and 1993, although it was nearly cancelled due to bad ratings for its premiere. It did, however, become a highly regarded and much loved show both in America and the United Kingdom.

Set in a bar called Cheers in Boston, Massachusetts, the majority of the show took place in the front room of the bar or in the pool room or office where a group of local friends would meet regularly to socialise, drink and relax and interact with the owner and waitresses who worked there.

The original main characters consisted of Ted Danson, who played bartender and owner of Cheers, Sam Malone, who was addicted to sex and had many on and off relationships with his female opposite character Diane Chambers. Diane was played by Shelley Long, who was a sophisticated and academic student. Having been forced to take a job as a cocktail waitress due to financial problems, she was part of the series until 1987.

Nicholas Colasanto played Coach Ernie Pantusso, friend of Sam's and close friend of Diane. Unfortunately Colasanto died of a heart attack in 1985. Rhea Perlman played Carla Tortelli, a waitress whose customer service is somewhat questionable. Although a flirt with men, she carried a secret torch for Sam. George Wendt played the regular customer and sometimes employed accountant Norm Peterson. John Ratzenberger played postal worker

and 'know-it-all' regular Cliff Clavin.

Later in the series other main characters were introduced including Kelsey Grammer as Frasier Crane, a psychiatrist and regular; Woody Harrelson as not very clever bartender Woody Boyd, Bebe Neuwirth as psychiatrist and regular Lilith Sternin; Kirstie Alley portrayed the character Rebecca Howe, a strong-headed and independent character. Cheers was predominantly played out with the main characters, but the series was also supplemented by guest stars.

Written and performed by Gary Portnoy, and co-written by Judy Hart Angelo, the theme tune to Cheers, 'Where

Everybody Knows Your Name' became synonymous with the show.

Despite its fairly rocky start, Cheers went on to achieve global success and it was nominated for Outstanding Comedy Series for all eleven series broadcast. With a record at the time of one hundred and seventeen nominations, the series actually won twenty-eight Emmy Awards. Cheers also earned thirty-one Golden Globe nominations, winning six of them. In 2002 Cheers was ranked number eighteen on 'TV Guide's 50 Greatest TV Shows of All Time' and in 2013 the Writers Guild of America ranked it as the eighth best television series written.

Dad's Army

Written by Jimmy Perry and David Croft, British comedy show Dad's Army was broadcast on the BBC from 1968 to 1977 and totalled nine series and eighty episodes. A radio version, stage show and feature film were also produced. Based on the Home Guard during the Second World War, the series was and still is extremely popular all over the world and attracted audiences of some eighteen million viewers at the time.

Following the exploits of the most elderly inhabitants of Walmington-on-Sea who join the Home Guard to help in the fight against Nazi invasion, the popularity Dad's Army built and then sustained has not been equalled by any other, then or since. One of the few shows that really is regarded as a true 'classic' comedy show, certainly no other

show that was created in the 1960s still gets the honour of being repeated in primetime. It was also a benchmark in terms of comedy that really sets it apart from other contemporary comedy shows at the time.

The main characters of Dad's Army consisted of Arthur Lowe as Captain Mainwaring; John le Mesurier as Sergeant Wilson; Clive Dunn as Lance-Corporal Jones; John Laurie as Private Frazer; James Beck as Private Walker; Arnold Ridley as Private Godfrey; and Ian Lavender as Private Pike.

The humour in Dad's Army comes from the interaction of the characters rather than from the plot. The inability of Mainwaring to deal with the public school background of his Sergeant and Jones' eagerness to put his hand up for absolutely anything creates priceless

TELLY ADDICT : COMEDY

comedy regardless of what the particular context it is set in. Creators Perry and Croft drew on much of their own wartime memories for the series but never denigrated the characters in terms of bravery or patriotism, but focused the humour on the outcome of their often disorganised achievements.

Dad's Army was voted fourth in a 2004 BBC poll to find 'Britain's Best Sitcom'. In the British Film Institute's list of '100 Greatest British Television Programmes', it was placed thirteenth. The cultural influence of Dad's Army and the show's catchphrases were and still are well known due to its popularity then and now. Captain Mainwaring's 'You stupid boy!' phrase was listed by The Radio Times magazine as one of the top twenty-five greatest television put-downs.

Dinnerladies

Set in the canteen of the fictional northern HWD Components, dinnerladies was a comedy series even too modest to use a capital 'D' in its title. Created, written and co-produced by Victoria Wood, two series (sixteen episodes) were broadcast on BBC One from 1998 to 2000.

The main cast included Victoria Wood as Bren; Andrew Dunn as Tony; Anne Reid as Jean; Thelma Barlow as Dolly; Celia Imrie as Phillippa; Shobna Gulati as Anita; Maxine Peake as Twinkle; Duncan Preston as Stan; and Julie Walters as Petula. Occasional guest actors also appeared in the series, including Thora Hird, Eric Sykes and Kenny Doughty to name a few.

The canteen manager Tony does his best to keep his respect with the women, then there's the big-hearted Bren and somewhat dim and over-sensitive Anita. Best friends Dolly and Jean are like chalk and cheese and then there's Twinkle, the stroppy teenager amongst them.

Despite the bickering that goes on constantly between them, these six are fundamentally bound together by mutual respect. Some guests are tolerated - the handyman Stan for example – whilst others are seen as intruders, such as the authoritarian temporary manager, Petula, and particularly Bren's selfish mother. These characters meet the full disdainful force of the other six.

Unlike some of its other contemporary comedy shows such as The League of Gentlemen or The Office, the comedy in dinnerladies was deceptively conventional and was without unnecessary comic devices; it relied solely on the acting skills of its cast and the quality of its writing. The humour in the series mostly came from the interaction, conversation and banter between the characters. Sexual innuendos, misunderstandings and malapropisms (the use of an incorrect word in place of a word with a similar sound, resulting in a nonsensical, often humorous utterance) formed the base for much of the humour in the series.

The reception of dinnerladies was generally good and critic Tom Paulin praised the series. Viewing figures for the first series reached over twelve million and the second peaked on New Year's Eve of 1999 at just over fifteen million. It quickly created a following of avid fans when it was first broadcast, causing much disappointment when Wood decided to end the comedy show after only two series.

Drop The Dead Donkey

Broadcast on Channel 4 in the United Kingdom between 1990 and 1998, Drop the Dead Donkey was created by Andy Hamilton and Guy Jenkin. It ran for six series, totalling sixty-five episodes and was a big success for Channel 4 throughout the 1990s and remains one of its most successful home-grown series.

Drop the Dead Donkey was set in the fictional newsroom of television news company GlobeLink, who were in the process of a corporate remoulding under the charge of the new owner, multi-millionaire media tycoon Sir Royston Merchant, a somewhat unscrupulous character whose intention was to inject more sensationalism into the company's reporting. Half of the show was typical of an office-based comedy, throughout which threads of comedy were created by exploring and highlighting the tensions and relationships that are always present in the confined setting of a workplace. The other half of the comedy came from topical satire of current affairs, that was not only satirical but often dark as well.

The main cast included Robert Duncan as Gus who was not only prone to cringe worthy management speak, but also manipulation by owner Sir Royston Merchant; Haydn Gwynne as talented yet under-utilised Alex Pates; Neil Pearson as Dave the womanising, gambling researcher; Jeff Rawle as hypocritical editor George Dent; David Swift as Henry the stereotypical older newsreader; Stephen Tompkinson as Damien; Victoria Wicks as Sally; Susannah Doyle as Joy the uninspired yet ferocious PA; Hermione Norris as Octavia; and Ingrid Lacey as Helen

Cooper. With the topical satire at its heart, the series also occasionally included actual politicians of the era who were game enough to appear; Neil Kinnock and Ken Livingstone were among them.

In British comedy history, Drop the Dead Donkey is regarded by many as one of the few truly incisive satirical comedy shows of its time. With regard to the world we live in and the growing instances of sensationalist media coverage, not to mention the number of rolling twenty-four hour news channels, the comedy show still manages to retain its relevance in today's society as much as it did at the time of broadcast.

The creators and writers Andy Hamilton and Guy Jenkin were no stranger to producing winning-formula comedy scripts. They were both involved in enormously popular Not the 9 O'Clock News, Spitting Image and Who Dares Wins …?

In 1994, Drop the Dead Donkey was awarded the 'Best Comedy (Programme or Series) at the BAFTA Awards and in 1990 it won 'Best New TV Comedy' at the British Comedy Awards, followed in 1991 by the 'Best Channel 4 Comedy', and in 1994 won 'Best Channel 4 Sitcom'.

Family Guy

Created by Seth MacFarlane for the Fox Broadcasting Company, Family Guy is an American animated sitcom, but the show's humour is very much aimed at adults. It originally ran from 1999 to 2003 and was then revived in 2005 and is still very much alive and kicking today. To date there have been twelve seasons totalling two hundred and twenty-four episodes at time of writing. It has also been renewed for a thirteenth season, so Family Guy lovers, it's safe for 2014 and 2015!

Set in the fictional city of Quahog, Rhode Island, the comedy show centres on the adventures of Peter Griffin, a blundering blue-collar worker and his family: Lois, his wife, a piano teacher and housewife and their three children, Meg, Chris and Stewie. Meg is a teenager and does not fit in at school or at home; teenage son Chris is like a junior version of his father and is overweight and not blessed with a huge amount of intelligence; then Stewie is the infant son who displays strange adult mannerisms and spouts stereotypical archenemy expressions. Then there is Brian the family dog, only he is more like a human being than a canine; he drinks Martinis and engages in conversations!

There are several recurring characters in the series including the Griffin family's neighbours, paraplegic policeman Joe Swanson and his wife Bonnie and baby daughter Susie. Then there is paranoid Jewish pharmacist Mort Goldman and his wife Muriel and their highly irritating son Neil.

In addition to the episodes broadcast on television, Family Guy has been so globally successful that it has sparked

Mike Kunis   Seth MacFarlane

numerous 'other media' initiatives, not to mention the merchandise that is produced to accompany the Family Guy brand. Comic books and live performances (which featured cast members reading old episodes aloud) have all been produced. A spin-off of Family Guy called The Cleveland Show was premiered in 2009. Co-written by MacFarlane alongside Mike Henry and Richard Appel, the comedy show was conceived to be more 'family friendly' compared with Family Guy. It ran until 2013 totalling four seasons and eighty-eight episodes. There is also a Family Guy film in the making.

In 2006, the Family Guy Video Game was released for PlayStation and Xbox and by 2009 a Family Guy-based party game had been released for Xbox 360, PlayStation 3 and Wii. Six books were also published based on the Family Guy world.

Family Guy has been nominated for eleven Annie Awards and twelve Primetime Emmy Awards and has so far won three of each. Being nominated in 2009 for an Emmy Award for 'Outstanding Comedy Series', meant that it was the first time since 1961 (when The Flintstones were nominated for the award) that an animated series had had such success. In 2013, TV Guide ranked Family Guy as the ninth 'Greatest TV Cartoon of All Time'.

Father Ted

One of the most popular comedy shows of the 1990s, Father Ted was jointly written by Irish writers Arthur Matthews and Graham Linehan. It was originally broadcast from 1995 to 1998 and consisted of three series, twenty-four episodes and a Christmas Special.

Father Ted was set on a remote fictional island just off the west coast of Ireland called Craggy Island. Starring Dermot Morgan as Father Ted Crilly and fellow priests Father Dougal McGuire, played by Ardal O'Hanlon and Father Jack Hackett, played by Frank Kelly. The three Roman Catholic priests had been banished from the mainland for various past misdemeanours and they all lived together on Craggy Island in the parochial house with their housekeeper Mrs Doyle, who was played by Pauline McLynn and who quickly became a firm favourite with viewers.

The only close to sane member of the priest trio was Father Ted Crilly. Father Jack Hackett was an old soak and a rambling one at that and Father Dougal McGuire had little more noddle than a two year old.

Some would argue that although there was much awe-inspiring comedy written into Father Ted, it was also not without its share of scenes or even episodes that don't really work. Perhaps there was something a little strange about it, a little absurd. Yet some would argue unique, and at the end of the day, whatever individuals think, its popularity and success surely speaks volumes.

Despite some who think that there were aspects of the comedy show that don't always work, Father Ted turned out to be one of the most

TELLY ADDICT : COMEDY

popular sitcoms in the history of British television and certainly one of Channel 4's most successful productions ever. In 1995 Father Ted won 'Best New TV Comedy' at the British Comedy Awards with O'Hanlon being awarded 'Top TV Comedy Newcomer'. In 1996 and 1999 the show won the BAFTA award for 'Best Comedy' and Morgan won 'Best Comedy Performance'. It won the 'Top Channel 4 Sitcom Award' at the 1996 British Comedy Awards, at which McLynn also took the 'Top TV Comedy Actress' award. A year later it won the 'Best Channel 4 Sitcom Award' and in 2012 was voted by Channel 4 viewers as the number one series in Channel 4's '30 Greatest Comedy Shows'.

Apart from Father Ted being extremely popular particularly in Ireland and the United Kingdom, it was also in demand in the United States and Australia; in all of these countries the series was released on VHS at first and then DVD.

Fawlty Towers

Undoubtedly one of, if not the United Kingdom's most renowned and best loved comedy shows, Fawlty Towers was first broadcast on BBC Two in 1975 and ran for two series totalling twelve episodes until 1979. Created and written by John Cleese and his then wife Connie Booth, Fawlty Towers was voted in 2000 by the British Film Institute as the best British television series of the 20th century.

The series revolved around the antics of hotel owner Basil Fawlty (John Cleese), who was a man of limitless rudeness and who had an overzealous aversion to almost all of his hotel guests. The inspiration for the series came from 1971 when the Monty Python team were filming and stayed in a hotel in Torquay in Devon. The owner of the hotel, a Mr Donald Sinclair, was described by Cleese

later as 'the most wonderfully rude man I had ever met'. The time Cleese and Booth spent there gave them an awful lot of material that they were unconsciously gathering.

John Cleese played the neurotic, eccentric and bad-tempered owner of the fictional hotel Fawlty Towers, Basil Fawlty; Prunella Scales played his domineering wife Sybil Fawlty; Andrew Sachs played the Spanish waiter Manuel with very rudimentary command of the English language; Connie Booth played the incomprehensibly loyal chambermaid Polly Sherman; and Ballard Berkeley played Major Gowen.

Although Basil Fawlty was an inspired creation and an instant hit, the format of Fawlty Towers was not particularly unprecedented, and more or less followed the sitcom format that had developed during the 1950s and 1960s. Each and every episode, however, was side-achingly hysterical. A different storyline for each episode maybe, but each usually had Basil, teetering on the edge of insanity and hopelessly attempting to hide his ineptness from Sybil, whilst Manuel suffered numerous brutal humiliations at the hands of Basil, leaving Polly as Basil's perfect foil to his insane behaviour.

Interestingly, critics did not hold the series in such high regard at the time of its original broadcast, but by the end of the final episode it had already become an irrepressible critical success. Deciding to axe the show at the height of its popularity and after just twelve episodes was a very shrewd move on the part of Cleese and in doing so he guaranteed that the show would retain its legendary status for, in fact what turned out to be, decades to come.

Nearly forty years after the first episode was broadcast, Fawlty Towers remains a much-loved, watched and repeated comedy show. Both series were awarded a BAFTA for 'Best Situation Comedy' and in 1976 John Cleese won the BAFTA for the 'Best Light Entertainment Performance'.

Friends

An American comedy show created by David Crane and Marta Kauffman, Friends was originally broadcast from 1994 to 2004 and totalled ten series and two hundred and thirty-six episodes. The series was not only a hit with the critics, but audiences alike and it was syndicated all over the world. As well as being a commercial success, Friends also had a profound cultural impact that still continues today and it has become one of the most popular sitcoms of all time.

Set in Manhattan, a borough of New York City, the series revolved around a close circle of friends and featured the Central Park coffee house, which had such an influence that it inspired a variety of replicas all over the world. There were six friends who were the main characters throughout the series, although many others came and went and came back again.

Jennifer Aniston portrayed Rachel Green who was Monica Geller's best childhood friend and an avid follower of fashion; Courteney Cox played the bossy and competitive perfectionist Monica Geller, who was a chef and the 'mother hen' of the group; self-taught musician and idiosyncratic masseuse Phoebe Buffay was played by Lisa Kudrow; initially struggling actor, then famous for his role as Dr Drake Ramoray on American soap opera 'Days of our Lives', food lover Joey Tribbiani was played by Matt LeBlanc; Matthew Perry played Chandler Bing who worked for a multi-national company in statistical analysis and data reconfiguration; David Schwimmer portrayed Ross Geller, Monica Geller's older brother, who worked at the Museum of Natural History as a palaeontologist.

What and why Friends came about is stated perfectly by Crane, Kauffman and Bright when pitching the original idea to the television network NBC: 'It's about sex, love, relationships, careers, a time in your life when everything's possible. And it's about friendship because when you're single and in the city, your friends are your family.'

Receiving positive reviews from the very outset, Friends has been nominated for a staggering sixty-three Primetime Emmy Awards. TV Guide ranked it at number twenty-one on its list of '50 Greatest TV Shows of All Time'. In 2013 it was ranked by the Writers Guild of America at number twenty-four for the '101 Best Written TV Series of All Time'. The very last episode of the series was watched by an estimated fifty-two and a half million Americans, which made it the fourth most watched final episode in television history as well as the most viewed episode of the decade.

Gimme Gimme Gimme

Produced by Tiger Aspect Productions, written by Jonathan Harvey and developed by the aforementioned and Kathy Burke, Gimme Gimme Gimme was a BBC sitcom that ran for three series, totally nineteen episodes from 1999 to 2001. Although the first series was broadcast on BBC Two, it was immediately successful enough for the second and third series to be moved to BBC One.

The comedy show revolves around two London flatmates: thirty-year-old Tom Farrell and unattractive, middle-aged Linda La Hughes. He is gay and she is straight, and they are both as obnoxious and revolting as each other, not to mention the fact that they are both totally obsessed with men.

The series was filmed in front of a live studio audience at The London Studio on the South Bank in London. The main characters and cast included Kathy Burke as Linda La Hughes; James Dreyfus as Tom Farrell; Beth Goddard as Suze Littlewood; Brian Bovell as Jez Littlewood; Rosalind Knight as Beryl Merit; Dona Croll as Norma; Simon Shepherd as Himself; Elaine Lordan as Sugar Walls; and Jonathan Harvey as Man on sofa and Louie. Only characters Linda La Hughes and Tom Farrell appeared in all nineteen episodes. Other guest appearances included Su Pollard, Charlie Condou and Rose Keegan.

Tom and Linda rent a fairly dilapidated, poorly decorated flat in north London (69 Paradise Passage in Kentish Town) that reflects their meagre earnings. Tom is a struggling and quite frankly bad actor, but with an ego the size of any truly successful Hollywood star. Linda is an overweight

and loud-mouthed delusional woman who works as a receptionist at a media company. She would happily be a complete trollop, if only she could get any single man to go anywhere near her! Both of them get drunk a lot.

The comedy show intertwines the sad individual existences of both, as well as the relationship between them as they attempt to execute delusional ideas and then have to comfort each other when the inevitable failure follows. Also involved in their sad existences is the disgustingly in-love couple Jez and Suze, who although

seem to be sweet enough on the outside, have a slightly darker inside. The not-so-innocent ex-prostitute but retired elderly landlady Beryl lives upstairs.

At the very end of the series, Tom finally got his acting big break with a part in the television soap opera Crossroads. As Tom leaves the flat for the last time to embark on his new and promising acting career, Linda is left sitting in the flat on her own and she removes her hair, revealing to all at the very end that it had been a wig all along and nobody had known.

Happy Days

Created by Garry Marshall, Happy Days was an American comedy show that ran from 1974 to 1984. Originally broadcast on ABC, Happy Days ran for a total of eleven seasons and two hundred and fifty-five episodes.

The series was based on teenager Richie Cunningham and his family and was set in Milwaukee in Wisconsin. Marion was his mother and was cast in a traditional role of mother and housewife and his father, Howard, owned a hardware store. Younger sister Joanie completed the Cunningham family line up. Eventually becoming the family's tenant living upstairs was Arthur Fonzarelli, who became famously known as 'The Fonz' or 'Fonzie'. He was a high school dropout, but nonetheless a very smooth ladies' man. In the first season

Fonzie was very much a secondary character to Richie and his friends, Potsie Weber and Ralph Malph. The character of Fonzie, however, became so popular with the viewers, that his prominence grew in the storylines as the series developed.

Richie Cunningham was (for the first seven seasons) played by Ron Howard and Henry Winkler played Fonzie for the entire run of the show. Such was the success of Fonzie that Winkler soon appeared alongside Howard at the top of the opening credits. Following the exit of the character Richie Cunningham from the series when he left for military service, Winkler then continued to be billed at the top of the series and in fact became the central character going forward. Later on in the series other characters were also introduced, such as

Charles 'Chachi' Arcola, Fonzie's young cousin who had a romance with Joanie Cunningham.

Tom Bosley played the part of Howard Cunningham for the entire series, as did Marion Ross as his wife Marion Cunningham. Sister Joanie was played by Erin Moran and Anson Williams played Potsie Weber, with Donny Most playing the character Ralph Malph. The series also introduced other characters, some of whom recurred through different seasons. Guest stars also became a feature of the comedy show including the appearance of Tom Hanks and Robin Williams.

The success of Happy Days was such that it was syndicated by many different television networks. Two animated series were also created: The Fonz and the Happy Days Gang ran from 1980 to 1982. Its continued popularity is reflected in the fact that the Happy Days: A New Musical has been on tour in the United States since 2008. Fonzie's famous leather jacket can also be found hanging in the Smithsonian Institution. There have also been two reunion shows: one was filmed in 1992 and the other, to commemorate the series' thirtieth anniversary, in 2005.

Hancock's Half Hour

One of the most successful British comedians at the height of his popularity in the 1950s and early 1960s, Tony Hancock pushed the boundaries of British comedy at the time. Unfortunately he lost his way due to work, marital and alcohol problems and committed suicide in 1968 at the age of forty-four. It was a very sad end for one of our country's most brilliant comedians.

Hancock cemented his relationship with British radio and television audiences as a hugely popular comedian when the BBC offered him his own radio programme, Hancock's Half Hour. It was first broadcast in 1954 and a total of six series of over one hundred episodes were aired. Other well-known personalities were involved in the radio series including Sid James, Hattie Jacques, Bill Kerr and Kenneth Williams.

The series was hugely successful and it is credited as being a major contributor to the development of the genre of the sitcom as we know it today. Prior to Hancock's Half Hour, comedy radio shows had focused on a combination of sketches, musical interludes and guest appearances. This was the first time that an entire storyline was presented, developed and concluded in one half-hour episode.

Based on the underachieving existence of Anthony Aloysius St. John Hancock (Tony Hancock's full name) who was the permanently frustrated resident of the dilapidated 23 Railway Cutting, East Cheam, the BBC television version of Hancock's Half Hour began in 1956 and a total of seven series were broadcast. At the time, comedy programmes like this were broadcast live, but due to Hancock's unpredictable temperament, his shows

were prerecorded. The television episodes alternated with the radio programmes until 1959, and then the fifth television series and the final radio series were broadcast simultaneously that autumn.

Written by Ray Galton and Alan Simpson, Sid James was Hancock's co-star in the radio and television version until 1960. Hancock decided that he no longer needed James and did not like the fact that the public viewed him as part of a double act. He created one final television series called simply Hancock, which he performed alone. In fact some of Hancock's most popular and enduring episodes came out of this final series including The Blood Donor and The Radio Ham.

In 2000, the British Film Institute drew up a list of the '100 Greatest British Television Programmes'; Hancock's Half Hour was voted as number twenty-four.

Hi-de-Hi!

Broadcast on BBC One from 1980 to 1988, Hi-de-Hi! was written and created by Jimmy Perry and David Croft. It ran for nine series totalling fifty-eight episodes.

Set at a fictional holiday camp called Maplins in a fictional seaside town called Crimpton-on-Sea in Essex, Hi-de-Hi! was based loosely on the famous holiday camp Butlins. In fact the inspiration for the series came from the creators' experience when Perry was a Redcoat at Butlins in Pwllheli after being demobilised from the Army. The series revolved around the lives of the Hi-de-Hi! staff, both managers and entertainers, who were mostly has-beens and failed or struggling actors.

Part of a holiday camp empire owned by greedy and philandering entrepreneur Joe Maplin, Redcoats were replaced by Yellowcoats in Hi-de-Hi! The holiday camp guests were greeted every morning by the famous glockenspiel chimes of Gladys Pugh, Chief Yellowcoat, Sports Organiser and Radio Maplin Announcer, played by Ruth Madoc. Hi-de-Hi! became a well-known catchphrase, along with the famous line 'good morning campers'!

Simon Cadell played Professor Jeffrey Fairbrother who was the Entertainment Manager for the first five series; David Griffin then took over the role as Squadron Leader The Honourable Clive Dempster. Paul Shane played the role of Camp Host Ted Bovis who, apart from being very popular with the campers, spent most of his time trying to get the upper hand over Fairbrother and trying to scam money out of the campers. Jeffrey Holland was the Camp Comic and was played by Spike Dixon and the

relationship between Spike and Ted often produced fabulous humour. Su Pollard played Peggy Ollerenshaw, the cleaner who was ever aspiring to be promoted to a Yellowcoat. There was also the snooty ballroom dance instructors Barry and Yvonne Stuart-Hargreaves, played by Barry Howard and Diane Holland respectively.

The comedy show became hugely popular with British audiences, attracted audiences of up to thirteen million and in 1984 it won a BAFTA for 'Best Comedy Series'. In 2004 it was voted fortieth in 'Britain's Best Sitcom' and the 2008 Channel 4 poll revealed that the catchphrase 'Hi-de-Hi!' was voted as the thirty-fifth most popular comedy line quoted by viewers. There may be some aspects of the comedy of Hi-de-Hi! that now seems dated, but many of the characters were so well defined that they are still as funny now as they were when we were first introduced to them in the 1980s.

I'm Alan Partridge

Starring Steve Coogan, the BBC comedy show I'm Alan Partridge ran for two series from 1997 to 2002, totalling twelve episodes. Created and written by Peter Baynham, Steve Coogan and Armando Iannucci, the character Alan Partridge had already been introduced to British television audiences through the 1994 news parody The Day Today and then the parody chatshow Knowing Me, Knowing You with Alan Partridge (1994-1995).

The character of Alan Partridge as a narcissistic, deluded, incompetent and mostly talentless chat show host was already familiar to television audiences. I'm Alan Partridge begun by Alan being sacked from his one-time BBC chat show, leaving him clutching at his media career straws, living in the Linton Travel Tavern hotel and hosting a midnight phone-in talk show on local radio station, Radio Norwich. Choosing that particular hotel because of its equidistance between Norwich and London, the first series saw him irritate all the staff that had the unfortunate position to have to work with him. He also constantly scrabbled around looking for new ways to get back into the BBC.

No less delusional about his level of stardom and competence, the second series saw Alan move permanently to Norfolk (having at last given up hopes with the BBC) but living in a caravan and suffering a mental breakdown.

Coogan was supported by a fabulous cast including Felicity Montagu as his long-suffering personal assistant Lynn Benfield; Simon Greenall as the all-purpose worker at the Linton Travel

Tavern; and Phil Cornwell as Dave Clifton, Radio Norwich DJ who had the early morning radio programme straight after Alan's show (timed in the 'graveyard slot' of course!) Amelia Bullmore played Alan's Ukrainian girlfriend Sonja in the second series only.

The comedy show was recorded live in front of studio audiences, but it was shot in a pseudo–documentary style. The techniques employed by the producers meant that the audience watched it on monitors, allowing the actors to hear the audience reaction, but not actually be performing directly in front of them.

I'm Alan Partridge was very popular with both television audiences and critics alike. The comedy show was nominated for three BAFTAs, of which it won two. It also won a Royal Television Society award and two British Comedy Awards.

Alan Partridge well and truly lives on; a feature length film featuring him, called Alan Partridge: Alpha Papa, was released in 2013 to much critical acclaim. In addition to Coogan jumping back into his role, he was also joined by regulars Simon Greenall as Michael, Phil Cornwell as DJ Dave Clifton and Felicity Montagu as Lynn.

Just Good Friends

Created and written by John Sullivan, Just Good Friends was a British sitcom that ran on the BBC for three series from 1983 to 1986 and totalled twenty-two episodes, plus a Christmas Special. Starring Paul Nicholas as Vincent Pinner and Jan Francis as Penny Warrender, Just Good Friends was based on the story of them meeting in a pub five years after Vincent had jilted Penny at the altar.

John Sullivan had already put his hand to two extremely popular comedy shows, Citizen Smith (1977-1980) and Only Fools and Horses (1981-2003). Both of these had focused on purely male lead role characters, so Sullivan decided to turn his hand to a new series that included a woman in the starring line up, apparently having been hurt by a comment by Cheryl Hall (co-star of Citizen Smith)

about being incapable of writing a good lead female character comedy role; red rag to a bull quite obviously. The inspiration for the storyline came from an article that his wife read to him in a magazine about a fiancé being jilted at the altar on her wedding day.

Initially with a reluctant friendship after Vince and Penny had met again, their old feelings gradually returned and the series played with their love-hate, on-off relationship as it was gradually re-established. Vincent was a working-class Essex boy and Penny was the complete opposite well-to-do and pretty snobbish. The ups and downs and twists and turns of their tumultuous past and present relationship was the recurrent hook of the whole series; the main aspect that viewers evidently never got tired of.

The relationship between Vince and

Penny had British audiences captivated from the very outset, not to mention launching serious actress Jan Francis and relatively unknown actor Paul Nicholas to instant stardom. Of course, bearing in mind their different social backgrounds, the class distinction between them also played a big part, not to mention the interplay between them and their respective parents; Penny's mother famously referring to Vince as 'Thing'.

Quite unusually, not only did Sullivan write the theme tune to the series, but it was performed by Paul Nicholas himself; having starred in the 1968 production of Hair, he had also built himself an equivalent stage career in the world of musicals.

In the 2004 'Britain's Best Sitcom' poll, Just Good Friends came forty-third. It had become so very popular that its finale was broadcast on Christmas Day. This final episode saw Vince and Penny finally tie the knot – to the delight of some and total dismay of others!

Keeping Up Appearances

Created and written by Roy Clarke for the BBC, who was also author of Open All Hours and Last of the Summer Wine, Keeping Up Appearances was a British sitcom that ran for five series, totalling forty-four episodes, four of which were Christmas specials; the series ran from 1990 to 1995.

Starring Patricia Routledge as the famous suburban snob Hyacinth Bucket, who insists that everyone pronounces her name 'Bouquet', the series follows her obsessive and determined middle-class attitudes and antics as she desperately attempts to climb the social ladder at every opportunity, not to mention making her thoughts well and truly known against anything deemed cheap or common, the lowering of social standards or any sort of behaviour that she considered to be slovenly. Hyacinth Bucket (sorry, Bouquet) most definitely had illusions and delusions of grandeur!

Starring alongside her was her poor, long-suffering and hen-pecked husband Richard, who was played by Clive Swift. Next door neighbours Elizabeth and her brother Emmet (played by Josephine Tewson and David Griffin respectively) are regularly on the other end of Hyacinth's middle-class rants, so much so that they often have to hide or turn into nervous wrecks at the mere invitation of afternoon coffee with Hyacinth! When Emmit moved in with his sister in the second series, being a director of the local operatic society, it sparked a newly found passion for Hyacinth – singing - much to the distress of Emmit who is constantly being pressured to give her a leading role in one of his productions, not to mention the noise of her practising.

Other members of the cast were treated with acute social disdain including the man chasing, mini-skirt wearing Rose (played by Shirley Stelfox and then Mary Millar). Hyacinth's sister, a 'common' sibling who she was horribly ashamed of, was Daisy (played by Judy Cornwell). Daisy was married to working-class and unapologetic couch potato Onslow (played by Geoffrey Hughes). One of the fabulous and hilarious aspects to Onslow's character was the fact that he didn't really give two hoots about Hyacinth's pomposity and was one of the few who would happily try and bring her down a peg or two.

Not only was Keeping Up Appearances a great critical and audience favourite in the United Kingdom, it was also hugely popular in the United States, Canada and Australia. Patricia Routledge received two BAFTA nominations for her outstanding performance as Hyacinth Bucket. Not only is the entire series available on DVD, but it is still regularly repeated around the world on different television networks including BBC One, Gold and PBS in the United States.

Last Of The Summer Wine

Britain's longest-running comedy show, Last of the Summer Wine was initially broadcast on BBC One in 1973 and after thirty-one series and two hundred and ninety-five episodes finally came to an end in 2010. The sitcom was created and written by Roy Clarke. Although there was a change in personnel over the years of the show's characters, every single episode of Last of the Summer Wine was written by Roy Clarke.

The concept for the show revolved around the lives of a very young-at-heart group of pensioners who lived in Yorkshire and who spent their retired lives looking for adventure and playing schoolboy pranks in and around their village. Filmed in and around Holmfirth in West Yorkshire, Clarke created pension-age characters who still thought and behaved like naughty schoolboys.

Combined with the affable eccentricity of the senior citizen gang, the characters soon became widely loved by the nation's television audience.

Last of the Summer Wine was, however, quite slow to win over the hearts of the nation and it actually started life as a one-off episode in early 1973 of Comedy Playhouse (a long-running series of one-off unrelated sitcoms that aired from 1961 to 1975).

Naturally, due to the longevity of the comedy show main characters changed and new characters were introduced, particularly during the 1980s. The original cast included Michael Bates as Cyril Blamire, but the most famous central three characters of the series consisted of Peter Sallis who played Norman Clegg, Brian Wilde who played 'Foggy' Dewhurst and Bill Owen who played William 'Compo'

TELLY ADDICT : COMEDY

Simmonite. It was this trio who took the show into new dimensions of popularity and ludicrousness. And of course, no one can forget the terrifying character of Nora Batty, played by Kathy Staff.

Perhaps not ground-breaking in many respects and its gentle style and content certainly appealed to the older generations rather than the youngsters, but Last of the Summer Wine was responsible for being the very first comedy show to produce an extended Christmas special, which has now very much become the norm.

With its positive portrayal of older people and its family-friendly humour, Last of the Summer Wine has also been a global success and has been broadcast in more than twenty-five countries including the United States and Canada. To this day the comedy show is repeated regularly on television channels such as UK Gold, Yesterday and Drama. It won the 'Most Popular Comedy Programme' in 1999.

Little Britain

Written and performed by the comedy duo David Walliams and Matt Lucas, the character-based comedy sketch show Little Britain began life as a BBC Radio 4 show. The television show was first broadcast in 2003 and ran for three series and thirty-six episodes until 2006. The first two series were shown on BBC Three, the final series was then moved to BBC One.

The comedy sketches were based on exaggerated parodies of British people in many different situations and from all walks of life. This, unsurprisingly, led to a certain amount of criticism due to the fact that if certain sections of society are being cruelly mocked and imitated in a humorous way, it will undoubtedly be offensive to some, particularly those from minority groups.

Little Britain featured many different characters, the main ones of which were played by Matt Lucas and David Walliams. The narrator was Tom Baker and other regular cast playing various different characters included Steve Furst, Sally Rogers, Paul Putner, Samantha Power, Stirling Gallacher, Yuki Kushida and David Foxxe.

The most popular characters in Little Britain have had a certain linguistic if not cultural influence without a doubt. The juvenile delinquent Vicky Pollard with her now infamous catchphrase 'No but yeah but no'; Daffyd Thomas, who claimed to be 'the only gay in the village'; the Government aide Sebastian Love, who fancied the Prime Minister; the leader of the Fat Fighters club, the malicious and cruel Marjorie Dawes; the ridiculously inept transvestite Emily

Howard whose famous catchphrase was 'I'm a lady!'; and wheelchair bound Andy (really?!) and his long-suffering helper Lou.

As its popularity grew, Little Britain was certainly criticised for becoming too derogatory and vulgar, particularly in the second and third series. Despite being shown after the watershed, Little Britain became increasingly popular with children, much to the annoyance of Britain's teaching staff, who had to put up with outrageous and unacceptable copycat behaviour in the school playground!

Despite its controversial nature, however, Little Britain and its associated characters became a household name throughout Britain. It also enjoyed international success and has been broadcast in over fifteen countries worldwide including Canada, Australia, Germany, Russia, Spain, France, Portugal and the United States. In 2008 an American continuation of the show was broadcast called Little Britain USA.

In addition to the television series, the travelling Little Britain Live show was also created as well as a two–part Christmas special, Little Britain Abroad, which was broadcast in December 2006.

M★A★S★H★

Developed by Larry Gelbart and adapted from the 1970 feature film MASH, the American television satirical medical drama M★A★S★H★ was broadcast from 1972 to 1983 and comprised of eleven seasons and two hundred and fifty-six episodes. It was produced in association with 20th Century Fox Television for CBS. The original feature film was in fact itself based on the 1968 novel by Richard Hooker, MASH: A Novel About Three Army Doctors.

Although M★A★S★H★ was a sitcom, it was also labelled as a 'dramedy' or 'dark comedy' due to the dramatic subject matter frequently used. The series was based around four main characters who were personnel in a United States Army Mobile Army Surgical Hospital (hence M★A★S★H★) during the Korean War of 1950 to 1953. Many of the early storylines were also based on true stories that the production team gathered by interviewing real MASH surgeons.

Over the years of the series there were obviously many characters who joined and/or left midway through its run. There were also numerous guests and recurring characters. There were, however, four main characters in M★A★S★H★ that maintained a good level of cast consistency: Benjamin Franklin, 'Hawkeye' Pierce was played by Alan Alda; Father Mulcahy was played by William Christopher; Margaret 'Hot Lips' Houlihan was played by Loretta Swit; and Maxwell Q. Klinger by Jamie Farr. These were all stable characters throughout its eleven series run.

Although the series struggled in popularity when it was first broadcast, and was in fact nearly axed after its first

season, its second season (with a change of scheduling time) became very popular. It became one of the top ten programmes that year and then never fell out of the top twenty for its entire run. The final episode of the series was called 'Goodbye, Farewell and Amen' and it became the most watched television episode in the United States at the time of broadcast with a record-breaking one hundred and twenty-five million viewers tuning in.

The series, actors and writers enjoyed multiple award nominations and successes.

Alan Alda won the Golden Globe Award for 'Best Actor in a Television Series (Comedy or Musical) six times between 1975 and 1983. The series itself won the Directors Guild of America Award for 'Outstanding Directorial Achievement in a Comedy Series' seven times between 1973 and 1983. M★A★S★H★ was ranked as number twenty-five in the 2002 TV Guide's '50 Greatest TV Shows of All Time' and in 2013 the Writers Guild of American ranked it as the fifth best ever written television series.

Men Behaving Badly

Men Behaving Badly was a British comedy show that was first broadcast on ITV in 1992. It ran for six series totalling forty-two episodes including a Christmas special and three feature length final episodes resulting in its finale in December 1998. Written and created by Simon Nye, Men Behaving Badly was produced by Hartswood Films and Thames Television and was filmed in and around Ealing in West London.

The comedy show followed the lives of flatmates Gary Strang (played by Martin Clunes), Dermot Povey (played by Harry Enfield in the first season only), and Tony Smart (played by Neil Morrissey from the second series onwards). The boys may have been in their thirties already, but they lived their entire lives in a constant state of juvenility.

Other characters included Leslie Ash as Deborah, who was Gary and Tony's upstairs neighbour, and who Tony admired; Caroline Quentin played Gary's girlfriend Dorothy.

In the end, Men Behaving Badly became hugely popular with British television audiences, but that didn't really happen until the BBC revived the show for a third series in 1994. The first two series broadcast on ITV had not had great viewing ratings and they cancelled it at the end of the second.

Like other contemporary popular comedy shows at the time, Absolutely Fabulous (1992-2002) for example, Men Behaving Badly may have become phenomenally successful, but that was not without a good dose of controversy to accompany it. Many condoned the show's association and championing of the rise of a 'lad' culture that was growing

in society during the 1990s and believed that the behaviour and antics of Gary and Tony's lives were advocating the sexist, irresponsible, often drunken attitudes of the largely middle-class men or 'lads'. Many would argue, however, that Nye's writing was much more subtle than this and he in fact managed to push the boundaries with regard to sexual frankness (and on primetime television) but managed to do it in a funny and perceptive way, rather than being merely vulgar or flippant about it.

By the third series, the viewing figures and success of the comedy show said all there needs to be said about whether this controversy affected the show's success. It was voted the best sitcom at BBC Television's 1996 sixtieth anniversary celebrations. It won the Comedy Awards' best ITV comedy and the first National Television Award for Situation Comedy. In the 2004 BBC Two 'Britain's Best Sitcom' poll, Men Behaving Badly was ranked at number sixteen.

Monty Python

Monty Python was a British comedy group who specialised in satire, surreal humour and dark comedy. The Monty Python team, also known as The Pythons, consisted of John Cleese, Graham Chapman, Michael Palin, Terry Gilliam, Eric Idle and Terry Jones. The influence that Monty Python has had on British comedy is profound; it has been compared to the influence that The Beatles had on the world of music.

The highly influential off-the-wall sketch series, Monty Python's Flying Circus, ran for four seasons from October 1969 to December 1974 and consisted of four series totalling forty-five episodes. The series was a totally eclectic mix of observational humour, animation, innuendos and just down right silliness, and all aimed at the established and accepted norms and idiosyncrasies of life

in Britain at the time. It really did truly shatter the mould of television comedy and is still considered to be one of the most influential and pivotal comedy series ever made.

The success of their sketch show was the inspiration for their first film in 1971, And Now for Something Completely Different. This was followed by Monty Python and the Holy Grail in 1975, Life of Brian in 1979, Monty Python Live at the Hollywood Bowl in 1982, and The Meaning of Life in 1983.

To this day, Monty Python is still remembered, watched and frequently quoted. In addition to the television and film impact on the world, the group transcended many other mediums such as stage shows, albums, books and a stage musical. Of course, with the success and impact they had on British audiences, Monty Python

also helped many of the individual members of the team shoot to stardom.

In terms of how much influence Monty Python had on modern comedy cannot be overstated. The list of celebrities who they influenced is long and distinguished and includes the likes of Eddie Izzard, Rik Mayall, Sacha Baron Cohen and Vic and Bob, to name a few.

John Cleese, added to the other members of the Monty Python team, have quite simply been unique and ingenious with their 'out there' sketches and films. The Monty Python humour is perhaps not everyone's cup of tea, although anyone with a sense of humour couldn't fail to find hilarity in the brilliant team! Ingeniously, and perhaps unintentionally, they created hours of entertainment that is absolutely timeless; indeed, the surviving Pythons were back on stage for a sell-out tour in 2014.

One Foot In The Grave

Created and written by David Renwick and starring Richard Wilson, One Foot in the Grave was a BBC sitcom that ran for six series from 1990 to 2000, totalling forty-four episodes including seven Christmas and two Comic Relief specials.

Featuring the exploits of Victor Meldrew, who was magnificently played by Richard Wilson, and his forbearing, tolerant and kind-hearted wife Margaret, played by Annette Crosbie, the series followed the suburban and domestic lives of the couple. The 'normal' suburban life that they constantly strived for, was not however, ever what unfolded, as life repeatedly conspired against them. Much to Margaret's displeasure and annoyance, Victor not only seemed to be a magnet for calamity and mishap, but his incessant fury at life's imperfections caused much discord amongst the other people in their lives. Victor's infamous catchphrase 'I don't believe it!' is arguably one of the most well-known comedy phrases in the history of British comedy shows.

The other main characters who often received the brunt of Victor's disillusionment with life included Patrick and Pippa Trench, played by Angus Deayton and Janine Duvitski respectively, were the Meldrew's next door neighbours. Jean Warboys, played by Doreen Mantle, was Margaret's friend and one who annoyed Victor immensely.

The irony of the show's name and the nature of the show where comedy and tragedy were regularly intertwined throughout the series made the final episode in 2000 pretty apt really, which culminated in Victor being killed by a hit and run driver.

One of the funniest, fine and most complex comedy shows, One Foot in the Grave was enormously successful and popular with British television audiences and was only matched by Only Fools and Horses during the 1990s. Despite its fairly traditional setting and production, One Foot in the Grave was brilliant and hilarious to watch, mostly because it transcended the domestic sitcom setting by combining elements of surrealism and black humour. In fact, it reminds us that life isn't quite so bad for the majority of us after all!

Voted the tenth 'Best Sitcom Ever' in the BBC's 2004 poll, One Foot in the Grave also won a BAFTA for 'Best Comedy' in 1994 and came eightieth in the British Film Institute's '100 Greatest British Television Programmes'. It was arguably one of the last great 'traditional' British sitcoms ever to be made, as well as taking the credit for paving the way for the development and creation of a newer generation of British comedy shows such as The Office (2001-2002) and The League of Gentlemen (1999 -).

Only Fools And Horses

The award-winning BBC sitcom Only Fools and Horses, created and written by John Sullivan, was originally broadcast for seven series between 1981 and 1991 plus Christmas specials up until 2003. David Jason as Derek Trotter, 'Del Boy', was quite literally the star of the show. This was the role that turned Jason from a known and popular actor in the eyes of the British audience, to a comedy star and enduring legend; Derek Trotter and his 'Del Boyisms' infiltrated lives, and still do!

Set in a council flat in Nelson Mandela House in Peckham, South London, the adventures of wheeler-dealer Derek Trotter and his gullible brother Rodney (played by Nicholas Lyndhurst) were played out with a different set of circumstances every episode, but usually revolved around their constant 'get rich quick' schemes that, funnily enough, usually ended in some sort of calamitous flop.

Although Del Boy was the main star of the show and an inspired comic creation, each and every character involved with the Trotter shenanigans had their unique characteristics and only enhanced and complemented Del Boy's hilarious character and antics. They were all equally absurd and in their own ways pretty foolish. With the death of Granddad (played by Lennard Pearce), Uncle Albert moved into the flat in Nelson Mandela House. Played by Buster Merryfield, his most famous line throughout the series was 'When I was in the Navy …' The other close friends of the Trotters included the snooty car-dealer Boycie (played by John Challis); well-meaning but non-achieving Denzil (played by Paul Barber); and Trigger, the road-sweeper who was, to be honest, several sandwiches short of a picnic!

The only two characters who were present and had an ounce of intelligence and common sense were in fact the two female characters: one-time stripper, Raquel was Del Boy's girlfriend and was played by Tessa Peak-Jones and Rodney's sophisticated and very 'middle-class' girlfriend Cassandra, played by Gwyneth Strong. However, despite their concerted efforts, even they couldn't control or tame the impetuous exploits of the Trotter brothers.

Only Fools and Horses transcends both time and age in comedy terms. Although some of the settings, clothes, props etc. may now seem somewhat dated when watching it, the quality and hilarity of the comedy writing is undoubtedly timeless. Episodes are regularly repeated on UK Gold and occasionally BBC One.

Only Fools and Horses was voted as Britain's Best Sitcom in a BBC poll carried out in 2004. Its enduring appeal to British audiences cannot be overstated. For a comedy show that is now over twenty years old, the fact that a special sketch was made for the 2014 Sport Relief broadcast, putting Del Boy

and Rodney back on screen together for the first time in over ten years, is a testament to the comedy show that has made generations of viewers cry with laughter for years.

Open All Hours

British sitcom Open All Hours was created and written by Roy Clarke. It was first broadcast on the BBC in 1973 and ran for four series totally twenty-six episodes until 1985. It starred Ronnie Barker and David Jason; need much more be said really!

Set in Balby, near Doncaster in South Yorkshire, the series focused on a small grocer's shop owned by Albert E. Arkwright, played by Ronnie Barker. Allergic to spending money and stuck in his shop-proud ways, Arkwright was a mean yet lovable character with an unfortunate and consistent stutter. His only employee was his nephew Granville, played by David Jason, who Arkwright worked like a slave, whilst all the time Granville constantly tried to find some sort of excitement out of his mundane and hard-laboured existence. The female character was Morris Minor-driving District Nurse Gladys Emmanuel, played by Lynda Barron, who had to cope with Granville's somewhat pathetic attempts to win her heart over. Combine all of this with the acting and comedy skills of both lead characters and it made for much laughter and hilarity.

The recurring themes of Arkwright's stutter, the constant threat of the deadly till or the tension and excitement of Granville's delivery exploits are just some of the very memorable moments that made Open All Hours as successful as it was. Arkwright's catchphrase 'Granville! Feh-feh-fetch a cloth!', perfectly timed on every occasion, although predictable, nonetheless raised a laugh every time.

There were, however, some objections and controversy when the comedy show was first broadcast. Some were of the opinion that making people laugh on the

back of a character's speech impediment was not funny at all. Let's be honest, with two comedy legends like Ronnie Barker and David Jason on the screen at the same time, it should not really come as any surprise that Open All Hours became a much-loved and followed comedy show for British audiences. However, as much as the two lead characters were adored,

Arkwright would always play second fiddle to Porridge's Fletcher, as did poor Granville to Only Fools and Horses' Del Boy.

In 2013 the show returned at Christmas with a sequel entitled Still Open All Hours. Open All Hours was ranked eighth in the 2004 'Britain's Best Sitcom' poll. Rumours of a remake with David Jason still persist.

Peter Kay's Phoenix Nights

Created and written by Peter Kay, Neil Fitzmaurice and Dave Spikey, Peter Kay's Phoenix Nights was first broadcast on Channel 4 in the United Kingdom in 2001. Two series were created totalling twelve episodes and the finale was aired in September of 2002.

Peter Kay's Phoenix Nights started life as a special episode of That Peter Kay Thing that was called In The Club. The instant success and popularity of it led Peter Kay and Dave Spikey to run with the concept and create a proper sitcom from the idea. Viewed as a truly modern masterpiece of comedy, with subtle and also not so subtle tongue-in-cheek humour, Phoenix Nights (as it became known) was British comedy at its very best.

Set and filmed in Bolton in the North of England, the comedy show was based around the wheelchair-bound owner of The Phoenix Club, Brian Potter (played by Peter Kay). Potter had previously owned two clubs, but the first had flooded and the second burned down. His quest, therefore, was to make The Phoenix Club the most successful in Bolton and to most certainly outdo his arch enemy Den Perry, the owner of the rival and neighbouring club The Banana Grove.

Every episode, apart from being side-splittingly funny, saw Brian getting into all manner of sticky situations, usually ending with some sort of major incident! With superb one-liners and packed with excitement, Brian was aided and abetted by his band of friends and staff including, local entertainer Jerry 'St Clair' Dignan; the club's two bouncers, Max and Paddy; resident DJ Ray Von; Kenny 'Dalglish' Senior – the story teller; and handyman Young Kenny.

Phoenix Nights resulted in the later spin-off Max and Paddy's Road to Nowhere that was also broadcast on Channel 4. Starring Peter Kay and Paddy McGuinness as doormen who take to the open road in their prized motorhome and wreak havoc wherever they go, it ran for six episodes between November and December 2004. Phoenix Nights was nominated for several awards and it won the 'People's Choice Award' at the British Comedy Awards in 2002.

In comparison with other comedy shows that were created and produced around the turn of the century, Peter Kay's Phoenix Nights was undoubtedly one of the best and also really refreshing comedy shows of its time. Similarly to the perhaps premature end to Fawlty Towers, Peter Kay's wise decision to end Phoenix Nights after such a short run and such success means that it will be forever remembered as utterly brilliant and hilarious; Kay left no room for deterioration in terms of British audience popularity.

Porridge

Created and written by Dick Clement and Ian La Frenais, Porridge was a British comedy show broadcast on BBC One from 1974 to 1977. Starring Ronnie Barker and Richard Beckinsale as Norman Stanley Fletcher and Lennie Godber respectively, the show ran for three series totalling twenty-one episodes plus two Christmas specials. The sitcom also gave rise to a 1978 sequel called Going Straight as well as a 1979 feature length film also called Porridge.

The reason the series was called Porridge is because the term 'doing porridge' is British slang for serving time in one of Her Majesty's Prisons where traditionally porridge would have been the everyday breakfast served to inmates.

Set in Slade Prison in Cumberland, Porridge followed the prison life of 'habitual criminal' Norman Stanley Fletcher. He always tried to keep his head down, whilst at the same time striving to always get one over and win 'little victories' over the prison's powers-that-be. His cellmate Lennie Godber from Birmingham, in prison for the first time, was the recipient of Fletcher's wise words about how to survive life inside. Fletcher was not a fool, like so many comedy show main characters, but was a witty, clever and very loveable creation. Although a convicted villain, his character always portrayed a code of honour, unlike the institution he was locked up in, and he would never ever 'let the nerks grind you down'.

Throughout the series, Fletchers nemesis was Mr Mackay, played by Fulton MacKay, who was the very austere authoritarian Scottish prison guard who basically ran the prison and was always

suspicious of what Fletcher was getting up to. The actual prison governor, Mr Barrowclough (played by Brian Wilde) was the opposite: liberal and sympathetic. Fletcher often found it easy to bend Mr Barrowclough's ear or manipulate him into a situation that served his own purposes.

The inside of a prison was a surprising and eyebrow raising concept and set for a comedy show, and certainly a brave move by its creators. With its superb script and outstanding acting, it became undoubtedly one of the nation's most loved and popular comedy shows of its time. Porridge was voted number seven in the BBC poll of the '100 Greatest British Sitcoms' in 2004.

Rab C. Nesbitt

First broadcast in 1988 and created by Ian Pattison, Rab C. Nesbitt is a Scottish sitcom starring Gregor Fisher. Originally a recurring character in the BBC Two sketch series Naked Video that ran from 1986 to 1990, Rab C. Nesbitt has so far run for ten seasons totalling sixty-five episodes.

Choosing to be unemployed and drunk as a way of life, Rab C. Nesbitt lives in the Govan area of Glasgow with his wife Mary or 'Mary Doll' (played by Elaine C. Smith) and his sons Gash the eldest (played by Andrew Fairlie until 2008 and then Iain Robertson) and Burney (played by Eric Cullen until 1993). Rab's nephew Screech (played by David McKay) replaced Burney from 1994 to 1997.

Rab is rude, lazy, filthy, foul-mouthed, violent and sexist and has an opinion on absolutely anything and everything.

Wearing a string vest most of the time, his theories and views on life arguably have as many holes in them as do his vest, but that doesn't ever stop him airing them. He spends most of his life with his equally repulsive and hopeless drinking buddies in his local pub. James Aaron 'Jamesie' Cotter (played by Tony Roper) is a like-minded and self-described 'scumbag' and is Rab's long-standing friend. Jamesie's red-headed, feisty wife Ella (play by Barbara Rafferty) spends most of her time thinking about murdering him and in the meantime just generally physically abusing him at every opportunity. Other pub regulars include Andra (played by Brian Pettifer) and Dodie (first played by Alex Norton and now Iain McColl).

A highly rude and crude comedy that is soaked in Scottishness, Rab is most probably the only human on earth who

would take being called dysfunctional as a welcome compliment! In view of the fact that the comedy show thrives on covering both uncomfortable and controversial subjects, from infertility to incest, with every other imaginable contentious issue in between, Rab C. Nesbitt is certainly not a show for family entertainment and mainstream British audiences.

Despite its vile and difficult subject matter, the show of course has a following of fans and many obviously do like it. The fact that it was voted as one of the '50 Best Sitcoms' of all time in a public viewing poll reflects that fact. Whether you love it or hate it, Gregor Fisher's acting skills have to be admired and congratulated; he certainly does the very best job of portraying the grotesque good-for-nothing oaf Rab!

Red Dwarf

With a cult following, Red Dwarf is a British comedy franchise and television science fiction comedy show that consists of ten series, totalling sixty-one episodes, including a ninth mini series called Back to Earth. Created by Grant and Doug Naylor and Rob Grant, Red Dwarf was first broadcast on BBC Two between 1988 and 1993 and then again from 1997 to 1999.

Red Dwarf is a comedy show that is set in space and is the name of the damaged mining spaceship aboard which the crew live, who are apparently doomed to drift in space forever. The premise for the show is that the crew of the spaceship were killed by a radiation leak and the only survivors are left to try and return to Earth. The series revolves around their adventures that inevitably occur across the universe as they endeavour to get Red Dwarf home.

The show stars Chris Barrie as Arnold Rimmer or Ace, a holographic projection of his dead superior; Craig Charles as David Lister the spaceship's technician and only surviving human being; Danny-Jules John as Cat, a humanoid life form evolved from Lister's pet cat Frankenstein; Norman Lovett, Hatty Hayridge as Holly, the spaceship's computer; and David Ross, Robert Llewellyn as Kryten 2X4B 523P the emotionless android.

Regardless of the science fiction setting, Red Dwarf is a comedy mainly driven by the characters in it and filled with scatological science fiction aspects as well as pretty off-the-wall humour.

Red Dwarf had a fairly slow lift off to popularity and the first series didn't have very good viewing rating at all. With a steady increase over the next five

RED DWARF X

seasons, however, the ratings increased gradually and peaked at over six million. When it returned in 1999 the figures grew even higher and over eight million people tuned in to watch series eight's opening episode 'Back in the Red: Part I'. Certainly not to the taste of everyone, but those who do like Red Dwarf are nuts about it! A bit like being a 'Trekkie' for Star Trek, Red Dwarf did and still does have a cult following and the array of spin-off merchandise reflects this.

The comedy series has won numerous awards including the Royal Television Society Award for special effects, the British Science Fiction Award for Best Dramatic Presentation, as well as an International Emmy Award for the series six episode 'Gunmen of the Apocalypse'. It was for many years BBC 2's biggest comedy hit. At the time of writing, series eleven of Red Dwarf is also being written.

Rising Damp

British sitcom Rising Damp was produced by Yorkshire Television for ITV and ran for four series totalling twenty-eight episodes from 1974 to 1978. Created and adapted for television by Eric Chappell, Rising Damp was originally known as The Banana Box, which was Chappell's 1971 stage play from which he adapted the concept for the television series.

Starring Leonard Rossiter as Rigsby, Frances De La Tour as Ruth Jones, Richard Beckinsale as Alan Jones and Don Warrington as Philip Smith, Rising Damp was set in an unnamed university town in the north of the United Kingdom. Rigsby was the somewhat shabby landlord of a particularly squalid and run-down boarding house. His unfortunate tenants included the medical student Alan, Philip also a student of town and country planning and Ruth Jones, an administrator at the unnamed university.

Rigby, as a tyrannous landlord, was magnificently played by Rossiter and many a comedy scene was stolen by his performances as well as being the perfect lead for the rest of the excellent cast, and the interaction between Rigby and Alan created particularly memorable comedy moments of the series.

Being hopelessly and rather agonisingly in love with Miss Jones, (one of Britain's most fabulous female comedy characters) Rigsby did himself no justice in her eyes when she was constantly the witness to his bigotry and prejudices, which were usually directed at Alan and Philip. Miss Jones was nothing but respectable and modest, and always managed to resolutely mask any intense passion, living in the drudgery of Rigby's house with resolute sophistication.

As a comedy character Rigsby, along with his characteristic standing pose with hand on hip and wearing a shabby cardigan, was priceless; he epitomised all of the most frightful and deplorable aspects of Englishness.

The comedy and pleasure that Rising Damp radiated came more from the interaction of the four main characters, and the brilliant writing of Chappell meant that the comedy did not therefore solely rely on the show's plots or jokes.

In the 2004 poll run by the BBC, Rising Damp was the highest-ranking ITV sitcom for the '100 Best Sitcoms'. With repeats and reruns on various television networks, the joys of Rising Damp are still being introduced to a generation who weren't even twinkles in their parent's eyes when it was first broadcast! The comedy show continues to live on as a comedy show masterpiece and it is viewed by many as a high point in the acting careers of the cast involved.

Some Mothers Do 'Ave 'Em

Written and created by Raymond Allen, and co-written and starring Michael Crawford and Michele Dotrice, Some Mothers Do 'Ave 'Em was first broadcast on BBC One in 1973. Three seasons, twenty-two episodes including three Christmas specials were aired in total, with the final episode being shown on Christmas Day in 1978.

Some Mothers Do 'Ave 'Em followed the life and exploits of poor incompetent layabout Frank Spencer. Despite being consistently overenthusiastic and well-intentioned about absolutely everything he did, accident-prone Frank Spencer (played by Michael Crawford) managed to create total chaos and havoc just about anywhere he went. His poor wife Betty (played by Michele Dotrice) could only watch and weep as her husband went from one disaster to another. Dressed in a brown raincoat with black beret adorned and stereotypically pulled down to one side, combined with his phrase 'Ooh Betty …', the comic creation of Frank Spencer was complete and born.

In addition to the comedy show's hilariously funny script, Some Mothers Do 'Ave 'Em also featured many actions scenes often with crazy stunts involved and Michael Crawford performed the stunts himself. Perhaps one of the most memorable was the roller-skating episode through the streets. Filming out of the studio was quite novel at the time as most sitcoms from that period were largely staged in one particular central location.

To the surprise of many, Betty gave birth to baby daughter Jessica at the end of the second series. This allowed a further dimension to Frank's character to be explored in the third series. Apart from

TELLY ADDICT : COMEDY

showing a maturation of the characters as time had past, plus a more soft and sympathetic side to Frank, it also gave a stage for a new musical element to the comedy show as Frank sung lullabies to his daughter.

Originally being third choice for the part after Norman Wisdom and Ronnie Barker had turned the part down, Crawford was relatively unknown at the beginning of the series. By the time Some Mothers Do 'Ave 'Em had come to an end, he was (and still is) most certainly one of the nation's most loved and remembered comedy characters. Crawford's vocal abilities also led him to move into a new world of musical fame and he landed roles in stage musicals such as Andrew Lloyd Webber's The Phantom of the Opera.

Some Mothers Do 'Ave 'Em was voted number twenty-two in the BBC poll 'Britain's Best Sitcom'. The comedy show remains to this day a great success, with many viewers who were not old enough to remember it the first time round, enjoying the ridiculous and utterly hilarious Frank Spencer antics. Frank Spencer is and undoubtedly will remain a much-loved and iconic character in the history of British comedy.

South Park

Created by Trey Parker and Matt Stone for the Comedy Central television network in the United States, South Park is an animated comedy show targeted primarily at adults due to its dark and surreal humour, satire and black comedy. First broadcast in 1997 and still going strong, South Park has so far run for seventeen seasons with two hundred and forty-seven episodes broadcast at the time of writing.

South Park developed from two animated shorts that Parker and Stone created in 1992 and 1995. When the video of the latter of the two went viral on the internet it obviously gave the creators the message that their concept and creation was going to be in great demand worldwide, and so the South Park series was born.

The animated comedy show centres around the bizarre adventures in and around the small fictional town of South Park (hence the show's name) and the incessant narrative of four boys. The boys are Stan Marsh, Kyle Broflovski, Eric Cartman and Kenny McCormick.

Each episode of the show begins with a tongue-in-cheek disclaimer that says: 'All characters and events in this show - even those based on real people – are entirely fictional. All celebrity voices are impersonated … poorly. The following program contains coarse language and due to its content it should not be viewed by anyone.' That pretty much sums up the dry, witty and surreal humour that pervades every episode of the show.

The original pilot episode of South

Park was filmed using actual cut-out animation figures, but since then every episode has been made using software that imitates the cut-out technique. The principal writer and director is Parker, but both Parker and Stone also perform the majority of the voice acting for the show. Each episode is normally written and produced the week before its due to be broadcast.

Consistently enjoying the highest ratings from the very first episode in 1997, South Park has remained a firm favourite and one of Comedy Central's most successful and most highly rated shows. It is thought that South Park fans can be safe in the knowledge that the show will continue to be created and broadcast until at least 2016.

South Park has won numerous awards and accolades since its inception, including five Primetime Emmy Awards and a Peabody Award. In 2013 it was ranked by TV Guide as the tenth 'Greatest TV Cartoon of All Time'. Less than two years after the comedy show's premiere, the popularity of it was such that a feature-length film was made and released in 1999 called South Park: Longer and Uncut.

Steptoe And Son

Created and written by Ray Galton and Alan Simpson, Steptoe and Son was a British sitcom that ran from 1962 to 1974 and comprised of eight series and fifty-seven episodes. Starring Harry Corbett and Wilfrid Brambell, the first four series were broadcast by the BBC from 1962 to 1965 and then a second run of the comedy show was broadcast from 1970 to 1974.

Albert Edward Ladysmith Steptoe was played by Wilfrid Brambell and Harold Albert Kitchener Steptoe was played by Harry H. Corbett. Set in Shepherd's Bush in London, the comedy show revolved around the lives of Harold Steptoe who lived with his father Albert. They ran a rag and bone business and although Harold constantly dreamed of a better life, he was constantly obstructed by his guileful and unwashed old father.

Each episode followed a similar pattern: in their very modest and poor surroundings the father and son pair are not happy with life together and more often than not something happened to threaten their situation, but by the end they have foiled whatever it was and gone back to their status quo.

The influence and impact of Steptoe and Son with regard to the history of British television really cannot be overstated. It was so very popular with British audiences at the time that it was estimated that by the mid-1960s half the population of the United Kingdom watched the comedy show on a regular basis. The series was responsible for setting a precedent and initiating a template for the British sitcom in its true form. Steptoe and Son not only paved the way and advanced British television as a

whole, but it most certainly broke new ground with regard to British comedy in particular. For the first time ever, the British audience were confronted with a show that became a 'must see' programme in households throughout the country.

The theme tune to Steptoe and Son, 'Old Ned' was composed by Ron Grainer (1922-1981), an Australian composer who worked for most of his career in the United Kingdom and is mostly remembered for his film and television music. Apart from writing the theme tune to Steptoe and Son, he also wrote the theme music for Doctor Who.

In the 2004 BBC poll to find 'Britain's Best Sitcom', Steptoe and Son was voted number fifteen. The series was so successful that it was remade in various other countries under different guises: in the United States it was called Sanford and Son, in Sweden as Albert & Herbert, and in the Netherlands as Stiefbeen en zoon.

The Brittas Empire

Created and originally written by Andrew Norriss and Richard Fegen, The Brittas Empire enjoyed much success and a long run of seven series totalling fifty-three episodes from 1991 to 1997.

The main character is played by Chris Barrie as Gordon Brittas, who is a very well meaning yet pretty incompetent manager of Whitbury New Town Leisure Centre. Brimming with new initiatives, regulations and over complex plans, Mr Brittas, always dressed in a blue blazer, was enough to put even the most fitness mad customer off the idea of every donning trainers again. Episode after episode saw every new scheme of his reduced to rubble by the end.

The Brittas Empire was often somewhat bizarre, taking the audience through a journey of a world filled with disaster. If Mr Brittas was about, the likelihood of serious injury and chaos ensuing was almost inevitable. While Brittas is busy dreaming up new ways to make the lives of his staff more difficult, his assistant Laura does her best to keep the Leisure Centre operational.

To accompany Gordon Brittas on his ill-fated journey through life were several similarly unconventional characters: receptionist Carole kept her children in the cupboard; handyman Colin with a constantly septic hand; the over-enthusiastic coach Linda; Julie was the ill-tempered secretary; then there was Gavin and his fastidious partner Tim. To complete the chaotic and comic line-up was Helen Brittas, the poor, unfortunate and long-suffering wife of Gordon. Often turning to pills and affairs to cope with life as his wife and all that entailed, her

vulnerable mental state was only ever kept under control with the help of Deputy Manager Laura.

The style of comedy in The Brittas Empire often combined surreal or dramatic episodes with the farcical. A good example of that can be seen during the first series when, on the day of an expected and much anticipated visit by the Royal family, one visitor gets electrocuted, there is a flood in the boiler room and the doors get sealed shut. It was also quite common for death to occur, not something usually regularly seen in a traditional sitcom.

In the 2004 BBC's 'Britain's Best Sitcom' poll, The Brittas Empire came forty-seventh, which shows that it never quite made it to the core of the nation's heart. It did, however, lead to six ten-minute 'Get Fit with Brittas' specials that promoted healthy living.

The Rise And Fall Of Reginald Perrin

Starting life as a series of novels, The Fall and Rise of Reginald Perrin developed into a British sitcom in 1976, a year after the first novel in the series, The Death of Reginald Perrin, was published. Both books and sitcom were written by David Nobbs and the sitcom starred Leonard Rossiter as Reggie Perrin. There were three series of the comedy show, totalling twenty-one episodes, the last of which was broadcast in January 1979. A fourth series called The Legacy of Reginald Perrin followed in 1996, which was also written by Nobbs.

It is a common sitcom device to draw a fine line between comedy and tragedy and that is exactly what the mid-life crisis sitcom The Fall and Rise of Reginald Perrin embraced. As fantastically funny as the comedy series was, it was also a brilliant and poignant reflection of a country on the edge of crumbling, both socially and economically. Working for Sunshine Desserts as a middle-aged executive and then his own business selling completely useless items called Grot, Reggie and his wife Elizabeth struggled with the mundane existence of everyday suburban life, often turning to ridiculous daydreams as the only means of escape.

Leonard Rossiter's performance as Reginald Perrin was a brilliant combination of wit, comic hopelessness and deep internal retrospection. Following his nervous breakdown and faked suicide (depicted in a veritably moving way) and his endeavours to return to some sort of normality, his swings from being outrageous one minute to deeply reflective the next maintained an air of plausibility about the character

throughout the series.

Joining Reggie in his struggles through life were a memorable line-up of characters, including Pauline Yates as his long-suffering wife Elizabeth; cliché fanatic John Barron as C.J.; Geoffrey Palmer as Jimmy, Reggie's brother-in-law, who frequently had disasters with his catering; Trevor Adams as Tony Webster and Bruce Bould as David Harris-Jones, the overly-zealous sales managers; and Sue Nicholls as eager yet frustrated secretary Joan Greengross.

Writing a comedy show in which the main character is openly and constantly struggling with his state of mind lent itself to endless and hilarious comic possibilities – Reggie having visions of his mother-in-law as a hippopotamus for example! British audiences related to the discontentment with life that Reggie and his comrades portrayed and this escapist comedy series certainly became a national favourite at a time when other sitcoms, such as The Good Life, were tapping into the same national sentiment.

The Good Life

Created and written by Bob Larbey and John Esmonde, The Good Life was a British sitcom that was first broadcast by the BBC in 1975. Four series and thirty episodes later and the comedy show aired its final episode in the summer of 1978.

The cast line-up of Richard Briers as Tom Good, Felicity Kendal as Barbara Good, Penelope Keith as Margo Leadbetter and Paul Eddington as Jerry Leadbetter, when considered now is undoubtedly a winning formula. At the time of creation, however, it was only Richard Briers who had already established a high profile and it was in fact for him that Larbey and Esmonde wrote the comedy show; they had already written the successful sitcom Please, Sir! that was broadcast on ITV from 1968 to 1972.

Following Tom's fortieth birthday and the inevitable questioning of life that that so often brings (in real life as well in comedy), Tom and Barbara decide to leave the fast paced rat race and move to the leafy Surbiton where their intentions are to be totally self-sufficient. Surrounded by chickens, vegetables and a goat, Tom and Barbara's activities totally astound and instil horror into the middle-class, conservative neighbours, particularly Jerry and Margo Leadbetter, who share the garden fence with Tom and Barbara.

The gently satirical nature of the sitcom with regard to the suburban middle-classes was often played out at the expense of the Leadbetters - particularly Margo - who with her prim and proper ways, became a symbol of that constantly uptight suburban type.

In the 2004 poll to find 'Britain's Best Sitcom', The Good Life came in ninth and is regarded as one of the most successful sitcoms of the 'golden age' of British comedy. Ironically, the show was loved and followed by the very British middle-classes, despite the fact that their type was the brunt of the comedy every week. It was also extremely popular in the United States and was broadcast under the title Good Neighbors.

A showcase of a very fine British comedy, this gentle yet heart-warmingly funny series is still repeated today showing just how popular and fondly remembered it is. Self-sufficiency is a very topical subject now, and even after nearly forty years after The Good Life was first broadcast, people actually still use the term to describe those who reject city and corporate life and move to the country to change their lifestyle. This is what a generation of younger people did in the 1970s and it was in fact the germination period of the green movement as we know it today; it's interesting how issues and trends go round in full circle.

The League Of Gentlemen

Formed in 1995, The League of Gentlemen is a group of four British black comedy writers and actors, namely Jeremy Dyson, Mark Gatiss, Steve Pemberton and Reece Shearsmith. They were best known for their television programme, and although it is labelled as a sitcom, initially it was more like a sketch show, but with consistent elements that linked it together and made it a whole. The television series ran for three seasons, totalling nineteen episodes between 1999 and 2002.

The League of Gentlemen actually started life (as so many do) as a performance at an Edinburgh Fringe show, which first led to a Radio 4 programme. Set in the pretty grim fictional North of England town Royston Vasey, The League of Gentlemen took British comedy in a completely different direction compared with its contemporary shows such as The Office. Instead of following the trend at the time of basing comedy shows around a 'reality' setting, this show rejected this format and dug into a deep and dark gothic-inspired hole that also included elements of horror.

Linked by the common setting, the comedy show followed the everyday lives of the fictional village's mostly peculiar and weird residents. Not a village one would wish to live in going by the show. It was a place where strange, dark, horrifying and even perverted things happened behind closed doors.

Each of the writer/performers played a variety of characters and were more often than not dressed in drag

WELCOME TO
ROYSTON VASEY
YOU'LL NEVER LEAVE!

and caked in thick prosthetic make-up; all except Jeremy Dyson that is. To say the people of the town were odd is an understatement and the twisted inhabitants ranged from the wife kidnapping circus owner Papa Lazarou, whose catchphrase was 'You're my wife now', to shopkeepers Edward and Tubbs who not only put the fear of God into any visitors to the town, but also usually killed them. Dr Chinnery was a fairly mild character but a nonetheless deadly vet and Jobcentre advisor Pauline was just a nasty bully. It would be very misleading to say that visitors were welcome, even the village sign

reads, 'Welcome to Royston Vasey. You'll never leave!'

Despite its dark and sickening humour (inspired by well-known horror films such as The Wicker Man) the series was a critical success and a feature-length film was released in 2005 called The League of Gentlemen's Apocalypse. The comedy show won a BAFTA, a Royal Television Society and the Golden Rose of Montreux award. Funny, but in a very black and twisted way, The League of Gentlemen is certainly very different to any other British comedy show and certainly not for the faint-hearted.

The Likely Lads

Created and written by Dick Clement and Ian La Frenais, The Likely Lads was first broadcast by the BBC in 1964 and ran for three series until 1966. Unfortunately only eight of the original episodes have survived. Starring James Bolan as Terry Collier and Rodney Bewes as Bob Ferris, The Likely Lads followed the two's friendship and was set in the northern city of Newcastle upon Tyne.

Bob and Terry as characters were in their twenties and had grown up and been school mates together. They both ended up working in the same factory, Ellison's Electrical. Although the two were great friends and both enjoyed the normal boy hobbies of beer, football and girls, they both had very different outlooks on life: cynical Terry was quite happy with his working-class existence but Bob had great aspirations and ambitions to rise through the ranks so he could happily be a part of the great British middle class. Much of the comedy for the show came through the tension created because of the friends' very different perspectives on life. This very much reflected society in Britain in the 1970s, so was very easily related to by the viewing public.

The success of The Likely Lads turned Bewes (and his co-star James Bolam) into household names. An estimated twenty-seven million people watched the series, that's almost half the country's population!

The second show and sequel to The Likely Lads was called Whatever Happened To The Likely Lads, first broadcast in 1973 and run until 1974, it was even more popular than their first. Bewes had become firmly established as

part of many British households' comedy furniture. In 1976 a feature film called The Likely Lads followed, but it was not the box office hit that some thought it would be.

The end of The Likely Lads in 1966 saw Bob, very bored with his mundane working-class life, attempt to join the Army but he didn't get accepted because of his flat feet! Terry, however, had joined the bandwagon and did get in; he was then away with the Army for the following three years. The sequel began by Terry returning from the Army only to find that Bob is now a middle manager and living on a new suburban estate. As represented by Terry, Bob becomes torn between his new life and his old working-class habits that he had enjoyed so much with Terry.

Unfortunately Bewes and Bolam, once as good friends off the set as on it, fell out some thirty or so years ago. The on-going feud between them is one of the longest in show business, which is all strangely ironic considering their series and subsequent success was totally based around an enduring friendship!

The Muppet Show

Created and produced by puppeteer, artist, cartoonist, inventor, screenwriter, actor, film director and producer Jim Henson, The Muppet Show was a family-friendly comedy-variety television show that ran in its original form from 1976 to 1981. A total of five series and one hundred and twenty episodes were broadcast during that period and although Henson was American, the show was first shown in Britain for his ATV Associated Television franchise and all episodes were recorded at Elstree Studios just north of London.

The Muppet Show was like a weekly song and dance variety show interspersed with recurring comedy sketches. Kermit the Frog famously presented the show and was The Muppet Theatre's director. The total number of named puppets used for the show exceeded one hundred but there were certain Muppets that became adored, famous for their extraordinary personalities and antics.

Animal was a crazy drumming monster who played the drum kit for Dr Teeth and the Electric Mayhem in a frenzied fashion at all times; Beaker was Dr Busen Honeydew's lab assistant, who was always the victim of some crazy experiment, the result of which usually ended with him being eaten, blown up or knocked over; Fozzie Bear was The Muppet Theatre's comedian, apart from the fact that his jokes were always terrible; The Great Gonzo was the stuntman (or stuntmuppet) of the show and with his characteristic long nose he was so proud of his stunt work; Miss Piggy was the show's diva and certain that she was destined for super stardom.

TELLY ADDICT : COMEDY

Her feminine charm was often targeted at Kermit, not to mention her temper that always incorporated her trademark 'hi-yah' karate chop!

As well as getting to know the puppets and their characteristics, there were also recurring comedy sketches. Who doesn't fondly and nostalgically remember great comedy moments such as the Musical Chickens, Rowlf at the Piano, The Swedish Chef and Pigs in Space for example.

The Muppet Show had weekly guest stars of which no one ever appeared twice. It was part of the fun of the show every week wondering who was going to appear. Guest stars included the renowned ballet dancer Rudolph Nureyev, John Cleese, Elton John and Diana Ross, to name only a few.

The Muppet performers included Jim Henson, Frank Oz, Jerry Nelson, Dave Goelz, Richard Hunt, Louise Gold, Eren Ozker and Steve Whitmire. The Muppet Show was nominated for eleven BAFTA Awards and won two of them. It was also nominated for twenty-one Primetime Emmy Awards, of which it won four, including the 1978 award for 'Outstanding Comedy-Variety or Music Series'.

The Office

The Office was a multi award-winning comedy show that was originally broadcast in the United Kingdom in 2001. Created and written by Ricky Gervais and Stephen Merchant, it ran for only two series of six episodes plus a two-part Christmas special.

Also referred to as a mockumentary, The Office was filmed in the style of a 'fly-on-the-wall documentary' and revolved around the working life of office manager from hell David Brent and his staff at the Slough office of paper merchant Wernham Hogg. The characters spent much of their time justifying their boring jobs by lying to themselves constantly. David Brent was played by the award-winning comedy actor Ricky Gervais, weasley Gareth Keenan was played by Mackenzie Crook, not-so-lucky in love Tim Canterbury was played by Martin Freeman and Dawn Tinsley,

Tim's darling, was played by Lucy Davis.

Much of the humour in The Office came from its totally accurate portrayal of many people's experiences of everyday life working in an office and, as portrayed in the series, all in a pretty mundane place of work at that. The absurd management speak, squabbling over staplers and the staff's desperate attempts to have an exciting life outside of work, all combined to make it so very close to the truth for many, that it almost became too uncomfortable to watch!

There were some aspects of The Office that were fairly standard devices used widely in sitcoms: the workplace setting, the central character being a fool for example. All of these aspects would have been familiar to regular sitcom viewers. There was, however, something about The Office that felt new and unusual and

much of that could be attributed to how the traditional sitcom aspects were seamlessly combined with the mimicking of reality television shows, which had become so popular at the time.

The success of The Office has been quite astounding. Since it was first broadcast in the United Kingdom it has been subsequently been remade in many other countries including the United States, France, Germany, Sweden and China and the overall viewing figures are in the hundreds of millions worldwide.

In terms of awards, the UK version of The Office won two Golden Globes in 2004 and three British Academy Television Awards for Situation Comedy and Best Comedy Performance in 2001, 2002 and 2003. For the United States version of the show, it also won a Golden Globe and Emmy Award in 2006, a Screen Actors Guild Award in 2007 and an Emmy Award for Outstanding Writing for a Comedy Series in the same year.

The Royle Family

Created and written by Caroline Aherne and Craig Cash, The Royle Family was a British television sitcom that was first broadcast on the BBC in 1998. It ran initially until 2000, then between 2006 and 2012 The Royle Family Specials were produced. In total twenty-five episodes have been aired to date. At the time of writing, the latest episode was shown on Christmas Day 2012 and was called 'Barbara's Old Ring'.

The Royle Family focused on the lives of working-class Manchester-based family who were basically a related bunch of television-watching couch potatoes who spent most of their lives sitting in their filthy living room. When not glued to the television they chatted and argued, usually accompanied by considerable amounts of tea and booze.

At the head of the family with television remote control surgically attached to his side was unemployed Jim Royle (played by Ricky Tomlinson). Despite his bitter outlook on life and his total idleness, Jim was actually quite intelligent. His wife Barbara (played by Sue Johnston) worked in a bakery and although very pleasant, was downtrodden throughout the series, particularly by her daughter Denise (played by Caroline Aherne). Denise never managed to keep a job for five minutes and, having married Dave (played by Craig Cash) who she nagged constantly, controversially failed to look after her baby properly in the third series. Then there was the youngest child Antony (played by Ralf Little) who was constantly referred to by his father as 'a lazy streak of piss'. Arguably not Einstein, but ironically, Antony showed more potential in life than all of the others put

together. To complete the family line-up was Barbara's fairly nutty mother, Norma or Nana (played by Liz Smith).

The series did have many elements that were usual for the traditional family sitcom format, but the humour in The Royle Family was not based on comic plots or clever one-liners, but ingeniously reflected the type of humour and jokes that any normal family would make about each other and that so often highlight family life as it really is. As with many successful and popular comedy shows, the

comedy aspect was also balanced with an element of gloominess too. Underlying currents of neglect, despondency, disillusionment and bullying also ran through the family's living room.

The Royle Family came thirty-first in the 2000 list of the '100 greatest British television programmes', which was drawn up by the British Film Institute. In the 2004 poll to find 'Britain's Best Sitcom' it was voted nineteenth out of one hundred. The series also has several BAFTA awards to its name.

The Simpsons

Created by Matt Groening for the Fox Broadcasting Company, The Simpsons is an American animated sitcom targeted primarily at adults, although it is fair to say that many children in the world are just as addicted to the show as their parents, they may just not get all the subtleties of the humour! The Simpsons was first broadcast in 1989 and is still going strong. At the time of writing a total of twenty-five seasons, totalling five hundred and forty-five episodes have been aired.

The concept for the show came from Groening's creation of a dysfunctional family and, apart from substituting his own name for Bart, the other members were named after his own family. The Simpsons is based on an animated but middle-class American family and the satirical parody of them, American culture, society at large and many other aspects of everyday middle-class life! Set in the fictional 'Middle American' town of Springfield, the Simpson family consists of Homer (dad), Marge (mum), Bart (eldest son), Lisa (eldest daughter) and Maggie (baby daughter). The family has two pets who have both had starring roles in some episodes: the dog, Santa's Little Helper and the cat Snowball V, renamed Snowball II. Homer's catchphrase 'D'oh!' has become a widely used phrase in everyday language. In addition to the Simpson family, the show also has a large troop of equally off-the-wall characters that make up the Springfield society including teachers, family friends, and local celebrities.

The success of The Simpsons has been staggering to say the least. It has had a massive influence on many other adult-

themed animated series. Not only are the comedy show episodes watched all over the world, but the concept has given birth to an enormous array of other media and merchandise. The feature-length film, The Simpsons Movie, was released in 2007 and grossed over five hundred and twenty million dollars in box office sales. The list of other merchandise is pretty much endless and includes everything from video games and comic books to posters, t-shirts, lunchboxes, board games and trump cards.

In terms of the comedy show's fame, The Simpsons is considered to be one of the greatest series ever made in the history of television broadcasting and is the longest-running American sitcom and animated series to date. Not only does it have a star on the Hollywood Walk of Fame, but it has also won dozens of awards since its inception including thirty Annie Awards, a Peabody Award and twenty-eight Primetime Emmy Awards. In 1999 Time magazine named it as the twentieth century's best television series.

The Vicar Of Dibley

Created by Richard Curtis, written by Richard Curtis and then Gareth Carrivick and starring well-known comedy actress and writer Dawn French, The Vicar of Dibley was a British sitcom first broadcast on BBC One in 1994 and it originally ran until 2007. Including charity and Christmas special episodes, a total of twenty-five have been made and broadcast to date, including the latest 2013 Comic Relief Special. Perhaps interesting to note, at the time the series was conceived the Anglican church had not in fact lifted its ban on female vicars.

The series was set in the fictional Oxfordshire village of Dibley that consisted of a pretty eccentric rural community to say the least. Geraldine Granger, played magnificently by Dawn French, took the job of village vicar. Once the village had recovered from the initial shock of having a female vicar, Granger set about helping to improve life in the village of Dibley, helped by her down-to-earth and jovial personality.

The array of mad villagers (and fabulous supporting cast) who Granger had to live amongst included the amazingly dim verger Alice Tinker (played by Emma Chambers); local millionaire David Horton (played by Gary Waldhorn); his half-witted son Hugo Horton (played by James Fleet) and who was Alice's love interest; fastidious parish clerk Frank Pickle (played by John Bluthal; pretty rough farmer Owen Newitt (played by Roger Lloyd Pack); church flower arranger and disastrous cook Mrs Letitia Cropley (played by Liz Smith); and the elderly Jim Trott (played by Trevor Peacock).

Although when the series was first broadcast there was naturally quite a

lot of comical play on the fact that the village's new vicar was a woman (and a very buxom one at that), as the comedy show progressed the humour moved to focusing on the interaction and interplay between Granger and the absurd locals that she had to live and work with. Unlike the horrific darkness of Royston Vasey in The League of Gentlemen, however, the village of Dibley was a gentler and reassuring setting and one in which visitors were allowed to leave!

In terms of success, The Vicar of Dibley was a much-loved and followed British family comedy show and its ratings reflected this; it is one of the most successful series of the digital era. Its Christmas and New Year specials were frequently placed in the top ten programmes of the year and the series won numerous awards, including a British Comedy Award and two International Emmy Awards. In the 2004 poll to find 'Britain's Best Sitcom' it came in an honourable third place.

The Young Ones

A narchic British sitcom The Young Ones was created by Rik Mayall, Lise Mayer and Ben Elton, with material also created by Alexei Sayle. The two six-part series were broadcast on BBC Two in 1982 and ran until 1984.

Set in a run-down North London house, The Young Ones followed the anarchic and very surreal adventures of four students living together, namely Rick, Vyvyan, Mike and Neil. Rick (played by Rik Mayall) was a self-proclaimed anarchist, a bad poet, although he called himself 'The People's Poet' and an attention-seeking Cliff Richard fan; Vyvyan, often called Vyv (played by Adrian Edmondson) was a medical student who, apart from being a punk, displayed many psychopathic tendencies; Mike 'the cool person' and regular con artist (played by Christopher Ryan) was the only possible leader of the bunch and rarely got involved

in the feuds played out between the other three; Neil (played by Nigel Planer) was the hippie of the group who was reading a Peace Studies degree. It should be no surprise then that Neil was (apart from being clinically depressed) a pacifist, environmentalist and vegetarian. Constantly victimised by the others, he was regularly forced to do the everyday household chores.

Although there were elements of a traditional sitcom style about it, the series combined this with surreal humour (the use of talking animal puppets for example) violent slapstick and bizarre plots. Every episode also included a live performance by a band – Madness and Motorhead played for example.

The Young Ones had a major influence in the development of British comedy and specifically that of alternative comedy during the 1980s. It also launched the comedy and

TELLY ADDICT : COMEDY

television careers of many of those regularly involved. Mayall, Edmondson and Planer all went on to star in The Comic Strip Presents for example, and Mayall and Edmondson starred in Bottom together.

The series also featured many others who would become future British comedy household names and included the likes of Dawn French, Stephen Fry, Hugh Laurie, Ben Elton, Tony Robinson, Paul Merton, Jennifer Saunders, to name just a few.

Even though only twelve episodes of The Young Ones were made, to this day it remains a much-loved and remembered sitcom despite its alternative, aggressive and often offensive or controversial subject matter. It does, however, arguably seem very dated, such as jokes about Margaret Thatcher and her Conservative government and (following the 1981 Brixton riots) issues of police brutality. In spite of all of this The Young Ones has somehow managed to retain its infamy – everyone has heard about it! In the 2004 poll to find 'Britain's Best Sitcom' The Young Ones was voted at number thirty-one.

Till Death
Do Us Part

British sitcom Till Death Us Do Part was first aired on BBC One as a Comedy Playhouse pilot in 1965. Created and written by Johnny Speight, the comedy show ran for seven series, totalling fifty-four episodes until its finale ten years later in 1975. ITV then continued the series, called Till Death, from 1985 to 1992 and then the BBC produced the sequel In Sickness and in Health that ran from 1985 to 1992.

Starring Warren Mitchel as Alf Garnett, Dandy Nichols as his wife Else, Una Stubbs as his daughter Rita, Anthony Booth as Rita's layabout husband Mike Rawlins, plus Alfie Bass, Patricia Hayes and Joan Sims, Till Death Us Do Part was concerned with the life of the Garnett family who lived in the East End of London.

The patriarch of the family was Alf Garnett (probably one of British comedy's most recognised and loved or hated comedy characters) who was a Conservative working-class, bigoted, racist and anti-socialist character who spent his life ranting his opinionated and misinformed views in every episode of the comedy, leaving his poor long-suffering wife Else no choice but to let it all wash over her head where possible.

Till Death Us Do Part was an immediate success with British television audiences and although the comedy show was seen as highly controversial at times, it was also seen as ground-breaking with regard to the development of British television comedy at the time. The humour in the show was generated from the subject material that included a wide range of political subjects topical at the time. Every subject imaginable was

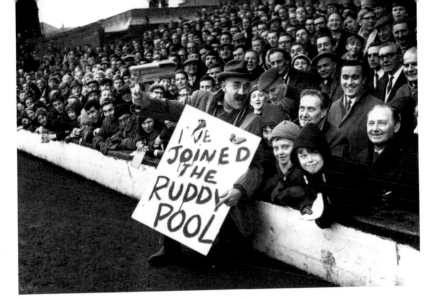

covered through the script writing and they were subjects that were timely and topical during that period.

Its sometimes controversial nature and the use of some colourful language did leave the series open for quite a lot of criticism however; Mary Whitehouse in particular took exception to the bad language used by the characters. Although these adverse campaigns were led by a minority, their influence did affect Johnny Speight and he did cast the sitcom aside after the third series. He did then return the show to British screens in the 1970s, much to the delight of British audiences.

Following the success of Till Death Us Do Part, two feature films based on the series were made. The 1969 Till Death Us Do Part film began by looking at Alf and Else Garnett in their younger days and was set during World War II. It then took their lives to the East End slum represented in the series, to them moving to the new town of Hemel Hempstead, all reflective of British life at the time. The second film was the 1972 The Alf Garnett Saga and is perhaps most memorable for portraying the infamous Alf having a trip on the drug LSD!

To The Manor Born

Created and written by Peter Spence and starring Penelope Keith and Peter Bowles, To the Manor Born was first broadcast on BBC One in 1979. This much-loved British sitcom ran for three series, totalling twenty-two episodes until its finale in 1981.

To the Manor Born was most certainly a romantic riches-to-rags concept that centred on the 1980s popular theme of England's green and pleasant land, along with the enchanting middle classes and all that that life encompassed, including the very topical theme at the time, that of social mobility. Unfortunately for the main female character, that started off as going down instead of up!

Having already become very well known for playing the famous Margo Leadbetter character in the sitcom The Good Life, Penelope Keith was brilliantly cast in To the Manor Born as an upper-class country woman called Audrey Forbes Hamilton, who was forced to move out of her cherished manor house Grantleigh due to the death of her husband and the debts that he had left behind.

Audrey sold her beloved home to the nouveau riche supermarket owner Richard DeVere (played by Peter Bowles). Despite the humiliation of becoming his tenant and in view of the fact that he didn't have a clue, Audrey took it upon herself to show Richard just how a country estate should be run, not to mention how to get him to show some sort of English country gent nobility about him.

As Richard improved, Audrey was no happier with her situation than she was to start with and much of the show's comedy

was played out through this love-hate relationship. However, the love part of that relationship did eventually blossom and, apart from Audrey seeing a way of moving back up the social ladder and getting her beloved house back, the pair finally got married in the 1981 finale. A Christmas Special was also broadcast in 2007 and showed the pair celebrating their twenty-fifth wedding anniversary.

The comedy show was popular with British audiences from the very first series and had very high viewing figures for most of its life. The finale to series one was in fact the most watched television programme in Britain in the 1970s. In the 2004 poll to find 'Britain's Best Sitcom', To the Manor Born was voted at number twenty-one. Still enduringly popular, the series is repeated regularly on digital television channels such as Gold. It may be a little dated in some respects, but due to the sitcom's strong characters, hilarious scripts and highly amusing plots, it is no wonder that viewers still find much to love and continue to enjoy the series.

Yes Minister

Created and written by Antony Jay and Jonathan Lynn, Yes Minister was a satirical British sitcom that was broadcast by the BBC from 1980 to 1984 and comprised three series of seven episodes each. The main cast of this satirical comedy about British politics starred Paul Eddington, Nigel Hawthorne and Derek Fowlds.

Yes Minister starred Member of Parliament Jim Hacker (played by Paul Eddington) who was appointed to the Cabinet as Minister for Administrative Affairs (a fictional department). His whirlwind introduction to what goes on behind closed doors in Whitehall and his constant struggle with the Civil Service and the political Whitehall engine at large was the main thrust of the comedy show.

The thorn in Hacker's side was his Permanent Secretary, Sir Humphrey Appleby (played by Nigel Hawthorne) who constantly thwarted his attempts to change things or impose authority on the department. The juxtaposing characters worked wonderfully together. On the one hand Hacker was a stereotypical MP: precious about the job, concerned with demotion and electoral defeat and although highly conscientious, still weak-willed and too easily flattered. On the other hand, Sir Appleby was highly experienced in the running of Whitehall, knew what was best for his department and was ruthless in making that happen.

In the middle of this relationship was Hacker's Principal Private Secretary Bernard Woolley (played by Derek Fowlds). Unlike the others, Woolley was actually qualified for his job, he also had a fabulous sense of humour and hadn't been in politics for so long that his conscience

was still well and truly in tact.

The comedy of Yes Minister, like many classic sitcoms, is derived from that of very simple observation and the observations made about British politics and politicians in Yes Minister then are not different from how the political system and politicians are still regarded today; that makes for a very timeless and enduring comedy series.

The series was not only a huge success and highly popular with British audiences, but also with the critics. It is regarded as one of British sitcom's finest achievements. It won several BAFTA awards and was voted at number six in the 2004 poll to find 'Britain's Best Sitcom'. It was also Margaret Thatcher's favourite television programme, and she was in office at the time. The series was also released in Australia and New Zealand. It even inspired video games that were released in 1987 for Amstrad, BBC Micro, Commodore, DOS and ZX Spectrum. The sequel to Yes Minister, Yes, Prime Minister, was broadcast from 1986 to 1988.

Comedy Quiz: Questions

1. Anthony, Barbara, Dave, Denise, Jim and Norma make up which famous family on British TV?

2. The second series of which British TV comedy featured a deadly epidemic of nosebleeds?

3. Who was the general manager of the Slough branch of a paper merchants company called Wernham-Hogg?

4. In the fourth and final series of Blackadder, how does the title character meet his death?

5. In which 1980s sitcom did a violent punk rocker, a pompous anarchist and a long-suffering hippie share a student house in North London?

6. What was the name of the ship's original computer in the TV show Red Dwarf?

7. In which town is the Phoenix Club in the TV show Peter Kay's Phoenix Nights?

8. Which Monty Python actor played the character with the catchphrase "Nudge, nudge, say no more"?

9. This Wheels On Fire was the theme tune to which sitcom?

10. What were the first names of Mr and Mrs Brittas in The Brittas Empire?

11. Which elderly character could clear a room just by uttering the

phrase "During the war"?

12. "I have a cunning plan" is a phrase associated with which down-trodden character?

13. Which of the eccentric characters in "The Vicar of Dibley" frequently answers questions with the phrase "No. No. No - yes."?

14. Which character frequently said "I didn't get where I am today."?

15. Who was frequently called a "Stupid Boy"?

16. What was Mr Humphries' catchphrase in "Are You Being Served?"?

17. Poor Margaret often heard her husband utter the phrase "I don't believe it!". To whom was she married?

18. Who was frequently accused of being a "dirty old man"?

19. Who urged people to "Go on, go on, go on, go on, go on!"?

20. Who regularly accused his wife of being a "Silly Moo"?

21. Wheelchair bound Brian Potter runs a Bolton nightclub with his sidekick Jerry "The Saint" Sinclair. What is the name of the show?

22. One of the best loved UK comedies since the early eighties follows the exploits of wheeling, dealing market trader Derek Trotter and his "plonker" brother Rodney. Which programme was this?

23. Two bachelors share a flat, Gary - who has a "sort of" girlfriend called Dorothy - and Tony, who spends most of his life lusting over Deborah who lives in the flat above. Which comedy am I referring to?

24. Three extremely bad priests live together on Craggy Island. Which show is this?

25. In which show is incompetent boss David Brent in charge of a

number of employees, who are probably frighteningly close to people you know in your own working establishment?

26. Going back to the early eighties again, four students share a house - hippy Neil, punk Vyvyan, anarchy loving Cliff Richard fan Rik and sleazy leader of the bunch Mike. What was this alternative show called?

27. This rather dark comedy is set in the village of Royston Vasey and features characters such as Tubbs, Pauline Campbell and the frightening

Papa Lazarou. What is it?

28. Which series of "Blackadder" was set in World War 1?

29. This incredibly bad chat show host, played by Steve Coogan, had his own show and catchphrase - "Knowing Me Knowing You.... Ah Haaah!" - what is the name of this hapless presenter?

30. Which sitcom broke all the rules and was the first to allow its leading character to die, thus ending the successful series, with no hope of revival?

31. When Tom Good decided to turn his back on the rat race, quit his job and, along with his wife Barbara, become self-sufficient, the Goods' life was reborn in Surbiton as 'The Good Life'. Which birthday was Tom celebrating when he made this life-changing decision in 1975?

32. What was the name of the street in which 'Open All Hours' was filmed?

33. 'Porridge' claims to be the sitcom which gave James Bond a funny line – when asked to fill a bottle while at a medical, he said 'What, from over here?' This joke came from the first episode, but what was it called?

34. True or False? Sir Humphrey Appleby ended every single episode of 'Yes, Minister' and 'Yes, Prime Minister' with the title of the programme, when speaking to Jim Hacker, the Minister (and later Prime Minister).

35. Only two series were made of 'Fawlty Towers', but its legacy will remain forever! Series 1 was originally broadcast in 1975 on the BBC. When did the second series hit the airways?

36. 'Dad's Army' was a sitcom written about the LDV (Local

Defence Volunteers) which became the largest civilian army the world has ever known. It was based in and around the fictional southern coast town of Walmington-on-Sea, but none of the filming was done on the south coast of England. Where was the series filmed?

37. What do Hugo and Alice Horton name their daughter in 'The Vicar of Dibley'?

38. Edmund Blackadder moved in highly exalted circles throughout his chequered career, mixing with royalty and generals. But is it true that a reigning British monarch is featured in all four series?

39. After many years of striving to become millionaires, the Trotter brothers finally managed it in 1996, in the last episode of the 'Only Fools and Horses' trilogy from that year. What did Del and Rodney sell at auction for over six million pounds?

40. What nationality was Rab C Nesbitt?

41. What was Tom's profession in the sitcom 'Gimme Gimme Gimme'?

42. 'The Brittas Empire' is set in a Leisure Centre in an English town, run by an enthusiastic, if incompetent Manager called Gordon Brittas – but do

IRELAND

you know which town it is in?

43. What was the surname of Adrian Edmondson's character in 'Bottom'?

44. Which 1970s popular singer starred in 'Just Good Friends'?

45. In which county did Alan Partridge take a job on a small radio station?

46. What was the name of the village featured in 'The League

of Gentlemen'?

47. What was the name of the 1950s Holiday Camp in 'Hi-De-Hi!'?

48. In which city is 'Bread' set?

49. Who lived next door to the 'Birds of a Feather'?

50. What are the bouncers called in 'Phoenix Nights'?

Comedy Quiz: Answers

1. The Royle Family

2. The League Of Gentlemen

3. David Brent (played by Ricky Gervais in The Office)

4. In battle in the First World War

5. The Young Ones

6. Holly

7. Bolton

8. Eric Idle

9. Absolutely Fabulous

10. Gordon and Helen

11. Uncle Albert in Only Fools and Horses

12. Baldrick from the Blackadder series

13. Jim, played by Trevor Peacock

14. CJ, The Fall and Rise of Reginald Perrin

15. Private Pike, Dad's Army

16. 'I'm Free!'

17. Victor Meldrew, One Foot in the Grave

18. Albert Steptoe, Steptoe and Son

19. Mrs Doyle, Father Ted

20. Alf Garnett, 'Til Death Do Us Part

21. Phoenix Nights

22. Only Fools And Horses

23. Men Behaving Badly

24. Father Ted

25. The Office

26. The Young Ones

27. The League of Gentlemen

28. Blackadder Goes Forth

29. Alan Partridge

30. One Foot in the Grave

31. 40th

32. Lister Avenue

33. New Faces, Old Hands

34. False

TELLY ADDICT : COMEDY   123

TELLY ADDICT : COMEDY

35. 1979

36. Norfolk

37. Geraldine

38. No – Edmund is the son of Richard IV in 'The Black Adder', is a member of the court of Queen Elizabeth I in 'Blackadder II' and works for the Prince Regent in 'Blackadder the Third' – during which time we also meet George III. Although we see the likes of General Haig in 'Blackadder Goes Forth' we do not actually see any reigning British monarch. Queen Victoria was seen in the special 'Blackadder's Christmas Carol'.

39. A Harrison watch

40. Scottish

41. Actor

42. Whitbury Newton

43. Hitler

44. Paul Nicholas

45. Norfolk

46. Royston Vasey

47. Maplins

48. Liverpool

49. Dorien

50. Max and Paddy

The pictures in this book were provided courtesy of the following:

Design & Artwork by Scott Giarnese

Published by Demand Media Limited

Publishers: Jason Fenwick & Jules Gammond

Written by Michelle Brachet

Smith and Keenan's
Advanced Business Law

Smith and Keenan's Advanced Business Law

Eighth Edition by Denis Keenan

Denis Keenan

LLB(Hons), FCIS, DMA, CertEd

Of the Middle Temple, Barrister-at-Law
Formerly Head of Department
of Business Studies and Law,
Mid-Essex Technical College and School of Art
(now Anglia Polytechnic University)

Pitman Publishing

Pitman Publishing
128 Long Acre, London WC2E 9AN

A Division of Longman Group UK Ltd

First published in Great Britain 1965
Eighth edition 1991
Reprinted 1992 (three times)

British Library Cataloguing in Publication Data
Keenan, Denis
  Smith and Keenan's advanced business law.
  – 8th ed.
  I. Title
  346.41

ISBN 0 273 03466 9

Typeset by BP Integraphics Ltd, Bath, Avon

Printed in England by Clays Ltd, St Ives plc

Contents

Preface to eighth edition

In this eighth edition the book has undergone its most major revision since it was first published in 1965. The aim has been to produce a more readable text in advanced business law for those categories of students who have used it since 1965. These categories are undergraduate students, students taking the examinations of professional bodies in the field of accounting and business studies and BTEC Higher National Diploma students of business law. Contemporary and classic cases are now integrated with the text, and it is also hoped that the new and more open format will be more user-friendly. In addition, the chapters have been reduced in length, comprising now 20 units to be covered over the period of a course.

The text aims to give the students at which it is aimed a solid foundation in advanced business law. The contents should be more than adequate to obtain a safe pass in the core subject areas of any of the major business-related professional bodies' examinations, and, indeed, those set internally by the polytechnics and colleges. A range of graded questions kindly supplied by these sources indicates this.

A major new addition is the inclusion of objective tests at the end of each chapter. These will give the student some practice in coping with this method of testing which is becoming increasingly popular and in addition provides the student with a chapter-by-chapter check on understanding of material studied.

May I now express my thanks to Simon Lake, Pat Bond and all those members of staff at Pitman Publishing who have been involved with the book including, especially, Giovanna Ceroni, Editor, Management and Professional Education Department, who was the production editor responsible for it, and Howard Bailey, who took charge at a later stage. My thanks are also due those who set and printed and bound the book.

In the preparation of this edition the publishers and I have had, as before, the invaluable assistance of my wife in terms of the correction of the page proofs and preparation of the indexes together with the organization of the sources of new material since the last edition.

My students continue to stimulate thoughts and ideas for improvements in the text and my thanks go also to them. The questions which they have raised since the last edition have led to a rethink in some areas and hopefully the text has been improved as a means of exposition following these changes. For the errors and omissions at the level at which the text aims I am, of course, responsible.

Maenan   Denis Keenan

April 1991

Table of cases

Table of statutes

1 | The law of contract – making the contract I

The OBJECTIVES of this chapter are to explain the requirements of a valid offer and acceptance which lead to the formation of a contract provided other essential elements, i.e. intention to create legal relations and, in most cases, consideration, are also present. Problems also arise in connection with the need for writing in some cases and the capacity of the parties.

DEFINITION OF CONTRACT

A contract may be defined as an *agreement* enforceable by the law between two or more persons to do or abstain from doing some act or acts, their intention being to create legal relations and not merely to exchange mutual promises.

In order to decide whether a contract has come into being it is necessary to establish that there has been agreement between the parties. In consequence it must in general be shown that an offer was made by one party (called the offeror) which was accepted by the other party (called the offeree).

OFFER

An offer is an announcement of a person's willingness to enter into a contract. An offer may be made to a particular person or, in some cases, to the public at large. An offer to the public at large can only be made where the contract which eventually comes into being is a unilateral one, i.e. where there is a promise on one side for an act on the other. An offer to the public at large would be made, for example, where there was an advertisement offering a reward for services to be rendered, such as finding a lost dog. **The following case is a well-known example of such an advertisement and of many other points in contract law which will be referred to in this and later chapters. Its relevance here is that it decides that where an offer is in the form of a promise for an act, the performance of the act is the acceptance and that offers of this type may be made to a particular person or to the world at large, i.e. to any unmentioned person or persons.**

Carlill v Carbolic Smoke Ball Co [1893] I QB 256

The defendants were proprietors of a medical preparation called 'The Carbolic Smoke Ball'. They inserted advertisements in various newspapers in which they offered to pay £100 to any person who contracted influenza after using the ball three times a day for two weeks. They added that they had deposited £1,000 at the Alliance Bank, Regent Street 'to show our sincerity in the matter'.

The plaintiff, a lady, used the ball as advertised, and was attacked by influenza during the course of treatment, which in her case extended from 20 November 1891 to 17 January 1892. She now sued for £100 and the following matters arose out of the various defences raised by the company.

(a) It was suggested that the offer was too vague since no time limit was stipulated in which the user was to contract influenza. The court said that it must surely have been the intention that the ball would protect its user during the period of its use, and since this covered the present case it was not necessary to go further.

(b) The suggestion was made that the matter was an advertising 'puff' and that there was no intention to create legal relations. Here the court took the view that the deposit of £1,000 at the bank was clear evidence of an intention to pay claims.

(c) It was further suggested that this was an attempt to contract with the whole world and that this was impossible in English law. The court took the view that the advertisement was an *offer* to the whole world, not an attempt to *contract* with the whole world but only with that limited portion of the public who came forward and performed the condition on the faith of the advertisement, and that, by analogy with the reward cases, it was possible to make an *offer* of this kind.

(d) The company also claimed that the plaintiff had not supplied any consideration, but the court took the view that using this inhalant three times a day for two weeks or more was sufficient consideration. It was not necessary to consider its adequacy.

(e) Finally the defendants suggested that there had been no communication of acceptance but here the court, looking at the reward cases, stated that in contracts of this kind acceptance may be by conduct.

Comment: (i) Motive was also irrelevant in this case because Mrs Carlill presumably did not use the ball with the motive of obtaining the reward, but with the motive of protection against influenza.

(ii) Most business contracts are bilateral. They are made by an exchange of promises and not, as here, by the exchange of a promise for an act. Nevertheless, *Carlill's* case has occasionally provided a useful legal principle in the field of business law. (*See*, for example, *The New Zealand Shipping Co Ltd* v *A M Satterthwaite and Co Ltd* (1974) at p. 45.)

(iii) A deposit of money from which to pay claims is not essential. In *Wood* v *Lectrik Ltd The Times* 13 January 1932 the defendants who were makers of an electric comb had advertised: 'What is your trouble? Is it grey hair? In ten days not a grey hair left. £500 Guarantee.' Mr Wood used the comb as directed but his hair remained grey at the end of ten days of use. All the comb had done was to scratch his scalp. There was no bank deposit by the company but Rowlatt J held that there was a contract and awarded Mr Wood the £500.

OFFER DISTINGUISHED FROM INVITATION TO TREAT

General

To be an offer there must be more than an indication of an *interest* in making a contract. If Fred says to Freda 'Would you like to get a reward if you find my lost dog?' we have a mere request for information and not an offer to be bound in contract.

An offer capable of being converted into an agreement by acceptance must consist of a definite promise to be bound provided that certain specified terms are accepted, and not a mere offer to *negotiate*. The distinction is sometimes expressed in judicial language by the contrast of an 'offer' with that of an 'invitation to treat' or invitation to make an offer. The distinction may be considered under the following headings.

Auctions

An advertisement stating that an auction will be held is not an offer to actually hold it. When the auction actually commences bids from those attending are the offers to buy (*Payne* v *Cave* (1789) 3 TR 148). The sale is complete when the hammer falls and until that time any bid may be withdrawn (s. 57, Sale of Goods Act 1979).

Where an auction is expressly advertised as subject to a 'reserve price' the rules stated above are not applied and there is no contract unless and until the reserve price is met and this is so even if the auctioneer knocks the goods down below the reserve price by mistake (*McManus* v *Fortescue* [1907] 2 KB 1). The auctioneer is not liable either for an apparent breach of his warranty of authority to sell because the advertising of the sale as being subject to a reserve price indicates to those attending the sale that the auctioneer's authority is limited.

However, if *dicta* in *Warlow* v *Harrison* (1859) 1 E & E 309 are correct, the addition to the advertisement of an auction sale of the two words 'without reserve' converts it into an offer, presumably to the public at large, that the sale will in fact be subject to no reserve price. If in these circumstances the sale is actually held and a prospective purchaser makes a bid, he accepts the offer of a sale 'without reserve'. The auctioneer, if he then puts a reserve price on any of the lots, is liable to an action for breach of his undertaking that the sale would be without reserve, though it should be noted that the goods in question will not have been sold unless the auctioneer's hammer has fallen.

Price lists, catalogues

The issue of a tradesman's circular or catalogue advertising goods for sale is usually regarded as a mere attempt to induce offers, not an offer itself. The same is true of advertisements to sell goods inserted in newspapers or periodicals.

Price indications

The display of an article with a price on it in a shop window, or on the shelves of a self-service store, is merely an invitation to treat. It is not an offer for sale, the acceptance of which makes a contract.

Company prospectuses/advertisements in connection with sale of securities

A prospectus/advertisement issued by a company in order to invite the public to subscribe for its shares (or debentures) is an invitation to treat so that members of the investing public offer to buy the securities when they apply for them and the company, being the acceptor, will only accept that proportion of public offers which matches the shares or debentures which the company wishes to issue. If there are more offers than shares the issue is said to be over-subscribed. Some applicants then get no shares at all or only a proportion of what they applied for. The conditions of the issue also allow the company to make a binding contract by a *partial* acceptance in this way. Normally acceptance must be absolute and unconditional. (*See* p. 8.)

The cases which follow illustrate the point that an invitation to treat is not an offer but is in general part of the process of negotiation which may lead to an offer.

Harris v Nickerson (1873) LR 8 QB 286

The defendant, an auctioneer, advertised in London newspapers that a sale of office furniture would be held at Bury St Edmunds. A broker with a commission to buy furniture came from London to attend the sale. Several conditions were set out in the advertisement, one being: 'The highest bidder to be the buyer'. The lots described as office furniture were not put up for sale but were withdrawn, though the auction itself was held. The broker sued for loss of time in attending the sale. *Held* – He could not recover from the auctioneer. There was no offer since the lots were never put up for sale, and the advertisement was simply an invitation to treat.

Comment: A sensible decision, really. The statement 'I *intend* to auction some office furniture' is not the same as an offer for sale, and in any case there seems to be no way of accepting the 'offer' in advance of the event.

Partridge v Crittenden [1968] 2 All ER 421

Mr Partridge inserted an advertisement in a publication called *Cage and Aviary Birds* containing the words 'Bramblefinch cocks, bramblefinch hens. £1.25p each.' The advertisement appeared under the general heading 'Classified Advertisements' and in no place was there any direct use of the words 'offer for sale'. A Mr Thompson answered the advertisement enclosing a cheque for £1.25 and asking that a 'bramblefinch hen' be sent to him. Mr Partridge sent one in a box, the bird wearing a closed ring. Mr Thompson opened the box in the presence of an RSPCA inspector, Mr Crittenden, and removed the ring without injury to the bird. Mr Crittenden brought a prosecution against Mr Partridge before the Chester magistrates alleging that Mr Partridge had offered for sale a brambling contrary to s.6(1) of the Protection of Birds 1954 (*see now* s. 6(1), Wildlife and Countryside Act 1981), the bird being other than a close-ringed specimen bred in captivity and being of a species which was resident in or visited the British Isles in a wild state.

The justices were satisfied that the bird had not been bred in captivity but had been caught and ringed. A close-ring meant a ring that was completely closed and incapable of being forced or broken except with the intention of damaging it: such a ring was forced over the claws of a bird when it was between three and ten days old, and at that time it was not possible to determine what the eventual girth of the leg would be so that the close-ring soon became difficult to remove. The ease with which the ring was removed in this case indicated that it had been put on at a much later stage and this, together with the fact that the bird had no perching sense, led the justices to convict Mr Partridge.

He appealed to the Divisional Court of the Queen's Bench Division where the conviction was quashed. The court accepted that the bird was a wild bird, but since Mr Partridge had been charged with 'offering for sale', the conviction could not stand. The advertisement constituted in law an invitation to treat, not an offer for sale, and the offence was not, therefore, established. There was of course a completed sale for which Mr Partridge could have been successfully prosecuted but the prosecution in this case had relied on the offence of 'offering for sale' and failed to establish such an offer.

Comment: The case shows how concepts of the civil law are sometimes at the root of criminal cases.

Pharmaceutical Society of Great Britain v Boots Cash Chemists (Southern) Ltd [1953] 1 QB 401

The defendants' branch at Edgware was adapted to the self-service system. Customers selected their purchases from shelves on which the goods were displayed and put them into a wire basket supplied by the defendants. They then took them to the cash desk where they paid the price. One section of shelves was set out with drugs which were included in the Poisons List referred to in s. 17 of the Pharmacy and Poisons Act 1933, though they were not dangerous drugs and did not require a doctor's prescription.

Section 18 of the Act requires that the sale of such drugs shall take place in the presence of a qualified pharmacist. Every sale of the drugs on the Poisons List was supervised at the cash desk by a qualified pharmacist, who had authority to prevent customers from taking goods out of the shop if he thought fit. One of the duties of the society was to enforce the provisions of the Act, and the action was brought because the plaintiffs claimed that the defendants were infringing s. 18. *Held* – The display of goods in this way did not constitute an offer. The contract of sale was not made when a customer selected goods from the shelves, but when the company's employee at the cash desk accepted the customer's offer to buy what had been chosen. There was, therefore, supervision in the sense required by the Act at the appropriate moment in time.

Comment: (i) It was held in *Esso Petroleum Ltd* v *Customs and Excise Commissioners* [1976] 1 All ER 117 by the House of Lords that an indication of the price at which petrol is to be sold at a filling station is also only an invitation to treat; (ii) the relevant provisions of the Pharmacy and Poisons Act 1933 are now enacted in ss. 2 and 3 of the Poisons Act, 1972; (iii) although a trader can *refuse to sell* at his wrongly advertised price he may find himself facing prosecution under ss. 20 and 21 of the Consumer Protection Act 1987 where the price ticket shows a lower price than that at which he is prepared to sell.

Negotiations for the sale of land

A sale of land, which includes, obviously, house purchase, involves the adjustment of many matters of detail, e.g. the searching of land registers to see whether the seller is the owner and can give the purchaser a title. The court is therefore likely to regard communications between the parties to a sale at an early stage of negotiations as being invitations to treat and not offers.

In addition, if a sale of land has been completed and the seller refuses to convey the land to the purchaser, the latter may be able to get a decree of specific performance from the court if damages are not regarded by the purchaser as the remedy required. Such a decree, which is particularly applicable to a contract for the sale of land, obliges the seller to actually perform the contract by conveying the land to the purchaser or be in contempt of court. Before requiring the seller to take such an important step the court will need clear evidence of an intention to be bound in contract and also that the contract be in writing (*see further* p. 65).

The following case is illustrative of these rules relating to negotiations for the sale of land.

Harvey v Facey [1893] AC 552

The plaintiffs sent the following telegram to the defendant: 'Will you sell us Bumper Hall Pen? Telegraph lowest cash price.' The defendant telegraphed in reply: 'Lowest price for Bumper Hall Pen £900.' The plaintiffs then telegraphed: 'We agree to buy Bumper Hall Pen for £900 asked by you. Please send us your title deeds in order that we may get early possession.' The defendant made no reply. The Supreme Court of Jamaica granted the plaintiffs a decree of specific performance of the contract. On appeal the Judicial Committee of the Privy Council held that there was no contract. The second telegram was not an offer, but was in the nature of an invitation to treat at a minimum price of £900. The third telegram could not therefore be an acceptance resulting in a contract.

Comment: The matter of invitation to treat and offer in the context of the sale of land produced the most interesting case of *Gibson v Manchester City Council* [1979] 1 All ER 972. The City Treasurer wrote to Mr Gibson saying that the Council 'may be prepared' to sell the freehold of his council house to him at £2,725 less 20 per cent, i.e. £2,180. The letter said that Mr G should make a formal application which he did. Following local government elections three months later the policy of selling council houses was reversed. The Council did not proceed with the sale to Mr Gibson. He claimed a binding contract existed. The House of Lords said that it did not. The Treasurer's letter was only an invitation to treat. Mr G's application was the offer, but the Council had not accepted it. In the Court of Appeal Lord Denning had said that there was an 'agreement in fact' which was enforceable. It was not always necessary to stick to the strict rules of offer and acceptance in order to produce a binding agreement. The House of Lords would not accept this and Lord Denning's view has not as yet found a place in the law.

ACCEPTANCE GENERALLY

Once the existence of an offer has been proved the court must be satisfied that the offeree has accepted otherwise there is no contract. The problems arising are considered under the following headings.

Acceptor ignorant of offer and motive

If B has found A's lost dog and, not having seen an advertisement by A offering a reward for its return, returns it out of goodness of heart, B will not be able to claim the reward. However, as long as the acceptor is aware of the making of the offer his motive in accepting it is immaterial.

The following case is an illustration of this point which is that so long as the acceptor knows the offer exists the reasons for accepting it are of no importance in deciding whether a contract has come into being.

Williams v Carwardine (1833) 5 C & P 566

The defendant published a handbill by the terms of which he promised to pay the sum of £20 to any person who should give information leading to the discovery of the murderer of Walter Carwardine. Two persons were tried for the murder at Hereford Assizes and were acquitted. Shortly afterwards the plaintiff, who was living with Williams, was severely beaten by him and, believing that she was going to die and to ease her conscience, she gave information leading to the conviction of Williams for the murder. In an action to recover the reward the jury found that the plaintiff was not induced to give the information by the reward offered, but by motives of spite and revenge. *Held* – She was nevertheless entitled to the reward, for she had seen the handbill and had given information. Patteson J said: 'We cannot go into the plaintiff's motives.'

   Comment: The point about motive is also made in *Carlill*'s case at p. 2.

Effect of acceptance 'subject to contract'

Acceptance must be absolute and unconditional. One important form of conditional assent is an acceptance 'subject to contract'. The law has placed special significance on these words and they are always construed as meaning that the parties do not intend to be bound until a formal contract is prepared and signed.

   The case which follows is an illustration of the rule that this phrase, which is used in sales of land and agreements for leases, indicates that the contract is merely in the stage of negotiation.

Winn v Bull (1877) 7 Ch D 29

The defendant had entered into a written agreement with the plaintiff for the lease of a house, the term of the lease and the rent being agreed. However, the written agreement was expressly made 'subject to the preparation and approval of a formal contract.' It appeared that no other contract was made between the parties. The plaintiff now sued for specific performance of the agreement. *Held* – There was no binding contract between the parties because, although certain covenants are normally implied into leases, it is also true that many and varied express covenants are often agreed between the parties. The words 'subject to contract' indicated that the parties were still in a state of negotiation, and until they entered into a formal contract there was no agreement which the court could enforce.

   Comment: (i) It is, of course, a matter of construction what effect the phrase has in each particular set of circumstances before the court. For example, in *Alpenstow Ltd* v *Regalian Properties Ltd* [1985] 2 All ER 966 Nourse J decided that a contract had come into being because the phrase was not used at the beginning of the negotiations but only in letters exchanged some four or five months after they had opened and agreement had been reached.

   (ii) The effect of acceptances 'subject to contract' has been widely criticized because of the widespread practice in a buoyant housing market of what is called 'gazumping'. Under this practice the seller of a house agrees to sell to a purchaser 'subject to contract' by which he is not bound. This allows the seller to sell to another purchaser who is prepared to pay more. If he finds such a purchaser he can tell the first potential purchaser that he refuses to sell because there is no enforceable contract. (But *see now* the Law of Property (Miscellaneous Provisions) Act 1989 at p. 67.)

Counter offer

A counter offer is a rejection of the original offer and has the effect of cancelling the original offer. However, the communication must amount to a counter offer. Thus where it appears that the offeree is merely seeking further information before making up his mind, his request for information will not destroy the offer.

The cases which follow provide an illustration of these rules, i.e. that as regards rejection of an offer, a distinction must be made between a counter offer and a request for information.

Hyde v Wrench (1840) 3 Beav 334

The defendant offered to sell his farm for £1,000. The plaintiff's agent made an offer of £950 and the defendant asked for a few days to think about it after which the defendant wrote saying he could not accept it, whereupon the plaintiff wrote purporting to accept the offer of £1,000. The defendant did not consider himself bound, and the plaintiff sued for specific performance. *Held* – The plaintiff could not enforce this 'acceptance' because his counter offer of £950 was an implied rejection of the original offer to sell at £1,000.

Stevenson v McLean (1880) 5 QBD 346

The defendant offered to sell to the plaintiffs a quantity of iron 'at £2.00 net cash per ton till Monday.' On Monday the plaintiffs telegraphed asking whether the defendant would accept £2.00 for delivery over two months, or if not what was the longest limit the defendant would give. The defendant received the telegram at 10.1 a.m. but did not reply, so the plaintiffs, by telegram sent at 1.34 p.m., accepted the defendant's original offer. The defendant had already sold the iron to a third party, and informed the plaintiffs of this by a telegram despatched at 1.25 p.m. arriving at 1.46 p.m. The plaintiffs had therefore accepted the offer before the defendant's revocation had been communicated to them. If, however, the plaintiffs' first telegram constituted a counter offer, then it would amount to a rejection of the defendant's original offer. *Held* – The plaintiffs' first telegram was not a counter offer, but a mere inquiry for information as to the availability of credit which did not amount to a rejection of the defendant's original offer, so that the offer was still open when the plaintiffs accepted it.

It should be noted, however, that the counter offer may be accepted by the original offeror. The above principles of contract law are of increasing importance because of the modern commercial practice of making quotations and placing orders with conditions attached, so that the terms and conditions of the contract which may eventually be made may not be those which the original offeror put forward, since these may have been changed as a result of a 'battle of forms' between the parties.

That a process involving exchange of terms may continue for some time until an act by one of the parties can be regarded as an acceptance of the other's terms is illustrated by the following case.

Butler Machine Tool Co Ltd v Ex-Cell-O Corporation (England) Ltd
[1979] 1 All ER 965

In this case it appeared that on 23 May 1969 Butler quoted a price for a machine tool of
£75,535, delivery to be within 10 months of order. The quotation gave terms and conditions
which were stated expressly to prevail over any terms and conditions contained in the
buyer's order.

One of the terms was a price variation clause which operated if costs increased before
delivery. Ex-Cell-O ordered the machine on 27 May 1969, their order stating that the
contract was to be on the basis of Ex-Cell-O's terms and conditions as set out in the order.
These terms and conditions did not include a price variation clause but did contain additional
items to the Butler quotation, including the fact that Ex-Cell-O wanted installation of the
machine for £3,100 and the date of delivery of 10 months was changed to 10–11 months.

Ex-Cell-O's order form contained a tear-off slip which said: 'Acknowledgement: please
sign and return to Ex-Cell-O. We accept your order on the terms and conditions stated
therein – and undertake to deliver by . . . date . . . signed.' This slip was completed and signed
on behalf of Butler and returned with a covering letter to Ex-Cell-O on 5 June 1969.

The machine was ready by September 1970, but Ex-Cell-O could not take delivery until
November 1970 because they had to rearrange their production schedule. By the time Ex-
Cell-O took delivery, costs had increased and Butler claimed £2,892 as due under the price
variation clause. Ex-Cell-O refused to regard the variation clause as a term of the contract.

The Court of Appeal, following a traditional analysis, decided that Butler's quotation of 23
May 1969 was an offer and that Ex-Cell-O's order of 27 May 1969 was a counter offer
introducing new terms and that Butler's communication of 5 June 1969 returning the slip
was an acceptance of the counter offer: so that the contract was on Ex-Cell-O's terms and
not Butler's, in spite of the statement in Butler's original quotation.

Thus there was no price variation clause in the contract and Ex-Cell-O need not pay the
£2,892.

Comment: (i) Most commonly the parties will exchange terms relating to delivery dates,
rights of cancellation, the liability of the supplier for defects, fluctuations in price (as here),
and arbitration clauses to settle differences. (ii) Title retention clauses (see p. 280) may also
be exchanged in this way. For example, in *Sauter Automation v Goodman (HC) (Mechanical
Services)* (1986) 5 Current Law, para. 353, Sauter tendered to supply the control panel of a
boiler. The tender contained a title retention clause. Goodman accepted on the basis of
their standard contract which did not contain retention arrangements. Sauter did not
formally accept what was in effect a counter offer by Goodman but they did deliver the panel
which was deemed acceptance. Goodman went into liquidation but the court held that
Sauter could not recover the panel or the proceeds of its sale. The contract was on
Goodman's terms. Goodman's terms did not contain a retention arrangement. Sauter were
left to prove in the liquidation of Goodman with little, if any, prospect of getting paid.

Acceptance in the case of tenders

It is essential to understand what is precisely meant by 'accepting' a tender since
different legal results are obtained according to the wording of the invitation to

tender. If the invitation by its wording implies that the potential buyer *will* require the goods, acceptance of a tender sent in response to such an invitation results in a binding contract under which the buyer undertakes to buy all the goods specified in the tender from the person who has submitted it. On the other hand, if the invitation by its wording suggests that the potential buyer *may* require the goods, acceptance of a tender results in a standing offer by the supplier to supply the goods set out in the tender as and when required by the person accepting it. The use of the word 'may' or a phrase such as 'if and when required or demanded' indicates a vagueness in the requirements of the purchaser which prevents a contract for the whole of the goods coming into being. Under the standing offer each time the buyer orders a quantity there is a contract confined to that quantity; but if the buyer does not order any of the goods set out in the tender, or a smaller number than the supplier quoted for, there is no breach of contract. If the person submitting the tender wishes to revoke his standing offer he may do so except in so far as the buyer has already ordered the goods under the tender. These must be supplied or the tenderer is in breach of contract.

Take the two examples which follow:

(a) Tenders are invited for the supply of 10,000 tonnes of coal to Boxo plc, delivery to take place as demanded between January and December 199 – .
(b) Tenders are invited for the supply of coal not exceeding 10,000 tonnes to Boxo plc if and when demanded between January and December 199 – .

Acceptance in the case of (a) above will produce a binding contract. Acceptance in (b) above will lead to a standing offer.

The following case shows the practical effect of a standing offer.

Great Northern Railway v Witham (1873) LR 9 CP 16

The company advertised for tenders for the supply for one year of such stores as they might think fit to order. The defendant submitted a tender in these words: 'I undertake to supply the company for twelve months with such quantities of (certain specified goods) as the company may order from time to time.' The company accepted the tender, and gave orders under it which the defendant carried out. Eventually the defendant refused to carry out an order made by the company under the tender, and this action was brought. *Held* – The defendant was in breach of contract. A tender of this type was a standing offer which was converted into a series of contracts as the company made an order. The defendant might revoke his offer for the remainder of the period covered by the tender, but must supply the goods already ordered by the company.

Inchoate contracts

A contract will not be enforced unless the parties have expressed themselves with reasonable clarity on the matter of essential terms. A situation may, therefore, exist in which there is sufficient assent to satisfy the basic requirements of offer and acceptance and yet the contract is incomplete (or inchoate) as to certain of its terms. The court will not make up a contract for the parties and enforce it so that the contract will remain unenforceable unless:

(a) the vague term is meaningless and can be ignored; or
(b) the contract itself provides a method of clarifying the contract; or
(c) the court can complete the contract by reference to a trade practice or course of dealing between the parties.

The context in which the problem often arises is that one of the parties to an agreement fails to carry it out and when sued for breach of the agreement defends himself by saying that he would have liked to perform it but because of the vagueness of an essential term he cannot do so.

The following cases give practical examples of the approach of the courts to this problem.

Scammell (G) and Nephew Ltd v Ouston [1941] AC 251

Ouston wished to acquire a new motor van for use in his furniture business. Discussions took place with the company's sales manager as a result of which the company sent a quotation for the supply of a suitable van. Eventually Ouston sent an official order making the following stipulation. 'This order is given on the understanding that the balance of the purchase price can be had on hire-purchase terms over a period of two years.' This was in accordance with the discussions between the sales manager and Ouston, which had taken place on the understanding that hire purchase would be available. The company seemed to be content with the arrangement and completed the van. Arrangements were made with the finance company to give hire-purchase facilities, but the actual terms were not agreed at that stage. The appellants also agreed to take Ouston's present van in part exchange, but later stated that they were not satisfied with its condition and asked him to sell it locally. He refused and after much correspondence he issued a writ against the appellants for damages for non-delivery of the van. The appellants' defence was that there was no contract until the hire-purchase terms had been ascertained. *Held* – The defence succeeded: it was not possible to construe a contract from the vague language used by the parties.

Comment: If there is a trade custom, business procedure or previous dealings between the parties, which assist the court in construing the vague parts of an agreement, then the agreement may be enforced. Here there was no such evidence.

Nicolene Ltd v Simmonds [1953] 1 All ER 822

The plaintiffs alleged that there was a contract for the sale by them of 3,000 tons of steel reinforcing bars and that the defendant seller had broken his contract. When the plaintiffs claimed damages the seller set up the defence that, owing to one of the sentences in the letters which constituted the contract, there was no contract at all. The material words were 'We are in agreement that the usual conditions of acceptance apply.' In fact there were no usual conditions of acceptance so that the words were meaningless but the seller nevertheless suggested that the contract was unenforceable since it was not complete. *Held* – by the Court of Appeal – that the contract was enforceable and that the meaningless clause could be ignored. Lord Denning said: 'In my opinion a distinction must be drawn between a clause which is meaningless and a clause which is yet to be agreed. A clause which is meaningless can often be ignored, whilst still leaving the contract good: whereas a clause which has yet to be agreed may mean that there is no contract at all, because the parties have not agreed on all the essential terms . . . In the present case there was nothing yet to be agreed. There was nothing left to further negotiation. All that happened was that the parties agreed that "the normal conditions of acceptance apply". The clause was so vague and uncertain as to be incapable of any precise meaning. It is clearly severable from the rest of the contract. It can be rejected without impairing the sense or reasonableness of the contract as a whole, and it should be so rejected. The contract should be held good and the clause ignored. The parties themselves treated the contract as subsisting. They regarded it as creating binding obligations between them; and it would be most unfortunate if the law should say otherwise. You would find defaulters all scanning their contracts to find some meaningless clause on which to ride free.'

Foley v Classique Coaches Ltd [1934] 2 KB 1

F owned certain land, part of which he used for the business of supplying petrol. He also owned the adjoining land. The company wished to purchase the adjoining land for use as the headquarters of their charabanc business. F agreed to sell the land to the company on condition that the company would buy all their petrol from him. An agreement was made under which the company agreed to buy its petrol from F 'at a price to be agreed by the parties in writing and from time to time'. It was further agreed that any dispute arising under the agreement should be submitted 'to arbitration in the usual way'. The agreement was acted upon for three years. At this time the company felt it could get petrol at a better price, and the company's solicitor wrote to F repudiating the contract. *Held* – Although the parties had not agreed upon a price, there was a contract to supply petrol at a reasonable price and of reasonable quality, and although the agreement did not stipulate the future price, but left this to the further agreement of the parties, a method was provided by which the price could be ascertained without such agreement, i.e. by arbitration. An injunction was therefore granted requiring the company to take petrol from F as agreed.

Comment: If the contract is completely silent on a term the court may fill in a gap by implying a reasonable term. Thus in a contract for the sale of goods where no price at all is agreed, a reasonable price must be paid (s. 8(2), Sale of Goods Act, 1979). However, where, as in *Foley*, there is an agreement for the sale of goods 'at a price to be agreed', the contract is not silent on the matter of price and the court cannot use s. 8(2) of the 1979 Act.

Hillas & Co Ltd v Arcos Ltd [1932] 1 All ER Rep 494

The plaintiffs had entered into a contract with the defendants under which the defendants were to supply the plaintiffs with '22,000 standards of soft wood (Russian) of fair specification over the season 1930.' The contract also contained an option allowing the plaintiffs to take up 100,000 standards as above during the season 1931. The parties managed to perform the contract throughout the 1930 season without any argument or serious difficulty in spite of the vague words used in connection with the specification of the wood. However, when the plaintiffs exercised their option for 100,000 standards during the season 1931, the defendants refused to supply the wood, saying that the specification was too vague to bind the parties, and the agreement was therefore inchoate as requiring a further agreement as to the precise specification. *Held* – by the House of Lords – that the option to supply 100,000 standards during the 1931 season was valid. There was a certain vagueness about the specification, but there was also a course of dealing between the parties which operated as a guide to the court regarding the difficulties which this vagueness might produce. Since the parties had not experienced serious difficulty in carrying out the 1930 agreement, there was no reason to suppose that the option could not have been carried out without difficulty had the defendants been prepared to go on with it. Judgment was given for the plaintiffs.

Comment: As we have seen in these cases, the defendant is trying to avoid damages for failing to perform the contract by saying 'I would like to perform the contract but I don't know what to do'. If there are, for example, previous dealings, then he does know what to do and the defence fails.

THE COMMUNICATION OF ACCEPTANCE

An acceptance is not effective to produce a contract merely because the offeree decides that he will accept it. His decision must in most cases be accompanied by some external sign of assent. This takes place by the communication of the acceptance to the offeror, either by the offeree or someone authorized by the offeree to do it.

An acceptance may be made in various ways. It may be made in writing or orally but it must in general be communicated. This provides some protection against inertia selling as where a firm sends a book to a person, A, at his home stating that if no reply is received within seven days it will be assumed that A has accepted the offer to sell the book and is bound in contract. Silence cannot amount to acceptance in this way.

However, the matter is also covered by the Unsolicited Goods and Services Act 1971 (as amended by the Unsolicited Goods and Services (Amendment) Act 1975). Under this legislation a person who receives, for example, unsolicited goods is entitled to treat them as if they had been given to him unless the sender takes them back within six months, or, if the recipient gives notice to the sender that he wants them taken back, within 30 days of the notice being given. The Acts apply to both business and private transactions.

The following case provides an illustration of the rule that silence cannot normally amount to acceptance.

Felthouse v Bindley (1862) 11 CB (NS) 869

The plantiff had been engaged in negotiations with his nephew John regarding the purchase of John's horse, and there had been some misunderstanding as to the price. Eventually the plaintiff wrote to his nephew as follows: 'If I hear no more about him I consider the horse is mine at £30.75p.' The nephew did not reply but, wishing to sell the horse to his uncle, he told the defendant, an auctioneer who was selling farm stock for him, not to sell the horse as it had already been sold. The auctioneer inadvertently put the horse up with the rest of the stock and sold it. The plaintiff now sued the auctioneer in conversion, the basis of the claim being that he had made a contract with his nephew and the property in the animal was vested in him (the uncle) at the time of the sale. *Held* – The plaintiff's action failed. Although the nephew intended to sell the horse to his uncle, he had not communicated that intention. There was, therefore, no contract between the parties, and the property in the horse was not vested in the plaintiff at the time of the auction sale.

Comment: (i) The general principle laid down in this case, i.e. that an offeree who does not wish to accept an offer should not be put to the trouble of refusing it is quite acceptable. However, it is difficult to support the decision on its own facts. John wanted to accept the offer and intended to accept it and since the uncle by his letter waived any right to receive an acceptance, there appears on the facts to be no reason why there should not have been a contract.

(ii) It should also be noted that the communication of acceptance must be authorized. In *Powell* v *Lee* (1908) 99 LT 284 Powell offered his services to the managers of a school as headmaster. The secretary to the managers told P that he had been selected, which was true. The secretary had no authority, actual or otherwise, to do this. The managers later selected another candidate as headmaster. P's action for breach of contract failed.

Waiver of communication

There are some cases in which the offeror is regarded as having waived communication of the acceptance. This occurs, for example, in the case of unilateral contracts, such as a promise to pay money in return for some act to be carried out by the offeree. Performance of the act operates as an acceptance and no communication is required (*Carlill* v *Carbolic Smoke Ball Co* (1893) – *see* p. 2). In addition, acceptance need not necessarily be communicated if the post is used (*see below*).

Mode of communication prescribed by offeror

The offeror may stipulate the mode of acceptance, e.g. to be by letter so that there will be written evidence of it. In such a case, however, the offeror could still waive his right to have the acceptance communicated in a given way and agree to the substituted method.

In addition, an acceptance made in a different way may be effective if there is no prejudice to the offeror, as where the method used is as quick and as suitable as the method prescribed.

Thus although the method of communication of acceptance may be prescribed

by the offeror, very clear words are required to make the court treat that method as essential, as the following case shows.

Yates Building Co v R J Pulleyn & Sons (York) (1975) 119 SJ 370

An option to purchase a certain plot of land was expressed to be exercisable by notice in writing by or on behalf of the intending purchaser to the intending vendor 'such notice to be sent by registered or recorded delivery post'. *Held* – by the Court of Appeal – that the form of posting described was directory rather than mandatory, or, alternatively, permissive rather than obligatory, and in consequence the option was validly exercised by a letter from the intending purchaser's solicitors to the intending vendor's solicitors sent by ordinary post and arriving well within the option period.

Oral acceptances

If the offeror has not stipulated a method of acceptance the offeree may choose his own method, though where acceptance is by word of mouth it is not enough that it be spoken, it must actually be heard by the offeror. As regards the use of the telephone and teleprinter, these are methods of instantaneous communication and it has been held that the contract is not complete unless the offeror hears the acceptance.

Thus where instantaneous methods of communication over long distances are used actual communication is necessary as the following case illustrates.

Entores Ltd v Miles Far Eastern Corporation [1955] 2 QB 327

The plaintiffs, who conducted a business in London, made an offer to the defendants' agent in Amsterdam by means of a teleprinter service. The offer was accepted by a message received on the plaintiffs' teleprinter in London. Later the defendants were in breach of contract and the plaintiffs wished to sue them. The defendants had their place of business in New York and in order to commence an action the plaintiffs had to serve notice of writ on the defendants in New York. The Rules of Supreme Court allow service out of the jurisdiction when the contract was made within the jurisdiction. On this point the defendants argued that the contract was made in Holland when it was typed into the teleprinter there, stressing the rule relating to posting. *Held* – Where communication is instantaneous, as where the parties are face to face or speaking on the telephone, acceptance must be received by the offeror. The same rule applied to communications of this kind. Therefore the contract was made in London where the acceptance was received.

Comment: (i) The suggestion was made that the doctrine of estoppel may operate in this sort of case so as to bind the offeror, e.g. suppose X telephones his acceptance to Y, and Y does not hear X's voice at the moment of acceptance, then Y should ask X to repeat the message, otherwise Y may be estopped from denying that he heard X's acceptance and will be bound in contract, presumably because the failure of communication is to some extent the fault of Y, the offeror.

If this is so, the estoppel provides another example of a situation in which acceptance need not actually be communicated.

(ii) The House of Lords approved the *Entores* decision in *Brinkibon* v *Stahag Stahl* [1982] 1 All ER 293. The plaintiff wanted leave to serve a writ out of the jurisdiction, as in *Entores*. The message accepting an offer had been sent by telex from London to Vienna. The House of Lords held that the writ could not be served because the contract was made in Vienna and not London. The *Entores* decision presumably applies to acceptances by fax.

Use of the post and telemessages

If the post is a proper and reasonable method of communication between the parties, then acceptance is deemed complete immediately the letter of acceptance is posted, even if it is delayed or is lost or destroyed in the post so that it never reaches the offeror.

The better view is that in English law an acceptance cannot be recalled once it has been posted, even though it has not reached the offeror at the time of recall.

A telemessage is presumably effective as an acceptance when it is given to the Telecom operator. *Cowan* v *O'Connor* (1880) 20 QBD 640 decided that this was so with the old telegram.

The following case confirms the legal position in regard to letters.

Household Fire Insurance Company v Grant (1879) 4 Ex D 216

The defendant handed a written application for shares in the company to the company's agent in Glamorgan. The application stated that the defendant had paid to the company's bankers the sum of £5, being a deposit of 5p per share on an application for one hundred shares, and also agreed to pay 95p per share within 12 months of the allotment. The agent sent the application to the company in London. The company secretary made out a letter of allotment in favour of the defendant and posted it to him in Swansea. The letter never arrived. Nevertheless the company entered the defendant's name on the share register and credited him with dividends amounting to 25p. The company then went into liquidation and the liquidator sued for £94.75 the balance due on the shares allotted. *Held* – by the Court of Appeal – that the defendant was liable. Acceptance was complete when the letter of allotment was posted, the Post Office being regarded as the agent of the parties to receive the acceptance.

Comment: (i) The rule is clearly one based on convenience rather than principle and, indeed, Bramwell, L J, in a dissenting judgment, regarded actual communication as essential. If the letter of acceptance does not arrive, he said, an unknown liability is imposed on the offeror. If actual communication is required the status quo is preserved, i.e. the parties have not made a contract.

(ii) If the statements of the parties appear to exclude the rule then the court will not apply it and there will be no contract unless the letter is received. Thus in *Holwell Securities* v *Hughes* [1974] 1 All ER 161 Dr Hughes gave the plaintiffs an option to purchase his premises, the agreement providing that the option was to be exercised 'by notice in writing'. The plaintiffs exercised the option by a letter which was not received by Dr Hughes and it was held that there was no contract because 'notice' meant that the letter must be received.

(iii) It should also be noted that the letter of acceptance must be properly stamped and addressed. If not there is no communication until the letter arrives.

Communication of cross offers

There is some controversy as to whether agreement can result from cross offers. Suppose after discussions between X and Y regarding the sale of X's watch, X by letter offers to sell his watch to Y for £50 and Y by means of a second letter which crosses X's letter in the post offers to buy X's watch for £50. Can there be a contract? The matter was discussed by an English court in *Tinn v Hoffman* (1873) 29 LT 271 and the court's decision was that no contract could arise. However, the matter is still undecided and it is possible to hold the view that a contract could come into being where it appears that the parties have intended to create a legally binding agreement on the same basis.

TERMINATION OF OFFER

It is now necessary to consider the ways in which an offer may be terminated or negatived.

Revocation – generally

The general rule is that an offer may be revoked, i.e. withdrawn, at any time before acceptance. If there is an option attached to the offer as where the offeror agrees to give seven days for acceptance, the offeror need not keep the offer open for seven days but can revoke it without incurring legal liability unless the offeree has given some consideration for the option. Where consideration, e.g. a payment of, or a promise to pay, money, has been given by the offeree the offeror may still revoke his offer and sell the property which was the subject-matter of the offer to someone else. He will, however, be liable to an action for damages for breach of option. It was thought at one time that where the option to buy property was not supported by consideration, the offer could be revoked merely by its sale to another. However, in modern law it is necessary for the offeror to communicate the revocation to the offeree himself or by means of some other person. (*See Stevenson v McLean* (1880) at p. 9 and *Dickinson v Dodds* (1876) below, the facts of which make this point.)

To be effective revocation must be communicated to the offeree before he has accepted the offer. When revocation is by letter the question arises as to whether it is effective when delivered or when the offeree has read it. The latter solution seems unreasonable because the offeree may delay reading the letter until he has accepted the offer. A better solution would be to regard revocation as effective when the offeree has had a reasonable time or opportunity to read the letter after delivery. Indeed, in *Eaglehill Ltd* v *J Needham (Builders) Ltd* (1972) (*see further* p. 466), the House of Lords, when discussing notice of dishonour of a bill of exchange, said that an offer would be revoked when the letter of revocation 'was opened in the ordinary course of business or would have been so opened if the ordinary course of business was followed.'

Communication may be made directly by the offeror or may reach the offeree by some other reliable source. It is not enough in, for example, a sale of goods merely to sell the goods to someone else.

The following cases provide a useful illustration of the operation of the rules of communication of acceptance and the communication of revocation of offer.

Byrne *v* Van Tienhoven (1880) 5 CPD 344

On 1 October the defendants in Cardiff posted a letter to the plaintiffs in New York offering to sell them tin plate. On 8 October the defendants wrote revoking their offer. On 11 October the plaintiffs received the defendants' offer and immediately telegraphed their acceptance. On 15 October the plaintiffs confirmed their acceptance by letter. On 20 October the defendants' letter of revocation reached the plaintiffs who had by this time entered into a contract to resell the tin plate. *Held* – (i) that revocation of an offer is not effective until it is communicated to the offeree; (ii) the mere posting of a letter of revocation is not communication to the person to whom it is sent. The rule is not, therefore, the same as that for acceptance of an offer. Therefore the defendants were bound by a contract which came into being on 11 October.

Dickinson *v* Dodds (1876) 2 Ch D 463

The defendant offered to sell certain houses by letter stating, 'This offer to be left over until Friday, 9 am.' On Thursday afternoon the plaintiff was informed by a Mr Berry that the defendant had been negotiating a sale of the property with one Allan. On Thursday evening the plaintiff left a letter of acceptance at the house where the defendant was staying. This letter was never delivered to the defendant. On Friday morning at 7 a.m. Berry, acting as the plaintiff's agent, handed the defendant a duplicate letter of acceptance explaining it to him. However, on the Thursday the defendant had entered into a contract to sell the property to Allan. *Held* – Since there was no consideration for the promise to keep the offer open, the defendant was free to revoke his offer at any time. Further, Berry's communication of the dealings with Allan indicated that Dodds was no longer minded to sell the property to the plaintiff and was in effect a communication of Dodds' revocation. There was therefore no binding contract between the parties.

Comment: This decision could cause hardship because it may mean that the offeree will have to accept as revocation all kinds of rumour from people who may not necessarily appear to be reliable and well informed. It would be nice to think that in modern law the third party would have to be apparently reliable and likely to know the true state of affairs as where he is the offeror's agent but there is no actual clear statement in this case that this is so.

Revocation – unilateral contracts

Where the offer consists of a promise in return for an act, as where a reward is offered in a newspaper for the return of lost property, the offer, although made to the whole world, can be revoked as any other offer can. It is thought to be enough that the same publicity be given to the revocation in the same newspaper as was given to the offer, even though the revocation may not be seen by all the persons who saw the offer. A more difficult problem arises when an offer which requires a certain act to be carried out is revoked after some person has begun to perform the act but before he has completed it. For example, X offers £1,000 to anyone who can successfully swim the Channel and Y, deciding he will try to obtain the money, starts his swim from Dover. Can X revoke his offer, e.g. from a helicopter, when Y is half way across the Channel? The better view is that he cannot on the grounds that an offer of the kind made by X is two offers in one, namely:

(a) to pay £1,000 to a successful swimmer; and
(b) something in the nature of an implied offer not to revoke for a reasonable time once performance has been embarked upon so that a person trying to complete the task has a reasonable chance of doing so

A similarly fair result can be achieved by regarding Y as accepting the offer when he enters the water, making effective revocation impossible thereafter. However, Y would not qualify for the prize of £1,000 unless and until he had provided the consideration by actually swimming the Channel. It would have been necessary to consider the application of one or other of these solutions in *Carlill's* case (*see* p. 2) if the company had revoked the offer *after* Mrs Carlill had started to use the ball.

The matter also came before the Court of Appeal in *Errington* v *Errington* [1952] 1 All ER 149. In that case a father bought a house for his son and daughter-in-law to live in. He paid the deposit but the son and daughter-in-law made the mortgage payments after the father gave the building society book to the daughter-in-law, saying 'Don't part with this book. The house will be your property when the mortgage is paid.' The son left his wife who continued to live in the house. It was held by the Court of Appeal that neither the father nor the plaintiff, his widow, to whom the house was left by will, could eject the daughter-in-law from the property. As Lord Denning said: 'The father's promise was a unilateral contract – a promise of the house in return for their act of paying the instalments. It could not be revoked by him once the couple entered on the performance of the act ... ' The Court went on to decide that the son and daughter-in-law would be fully entitled to the house once they had made all the mortgage repayments.

Lapse of time

If a time for acceptance has been stipulated then the offer lapses when the time has expired. If no time has been stipulated then acceptance must be within a reasonable time, and this is a *matter of fact* for the judge to decide on the circumstances of the case. **The following case provides an example.**

Ramsgate Victoria Hotel Co v Montefiore (1866) LR I Exch 109

The defendant offered by letter dated 8 June 1864 to take shares in the company. No reply was made by the company, but on 23 November 1864 they allotted shares to the defendant. The defendant refused to take up the shares. *Held* – His refusal was justified because his offer had lapsed by reason of the company's delay in notifying their acceptance. He also recovered a part-payment of 1/– (5p) a share.

Comment: Much depends upon the subject matter of the contract and the conditions of the market in which the offer is made. Offers to take shares in companies are normally accepted quickly because prices fluctuate day by day on investment exchanges, and the same would be true of an offer to sell perishable goods. An offer to sell a farm might well not lapse so soon. The form in which the offer is made is also relevant so that an offer by cable could well lapse quickly.

Conditional offers

An offer may terminate on the happening of a given event if it is made subject to a condition that it will do so. Thus, an offer to buy goods may terminate if the goods offered for sale are seriously damaged before acceptance. Such a condition may be made expressly in the contract but may also be implied from the circumstances.

Thus, as the following case illustrates, there is an implied condition in an offer to buy goods that the offer is not capable of acceptance after the goods are damaged in a serious way.

Financings Ltd v Stimson [1962] 3 All ER 386

On 16 March 1961, the defendant saw a motor car on the premises of a dealer and signed a hire-purchase form provided by the plaintiffs (a finance company), this form being supplied by the dealer. The form was to the effect that the agreement was to become binding only when the finance company signed the form. It also carried a statement to the effect that the hirer (the defendant) acknowledged that before he signed the agreement he had examined the goods and had satisfied himself that they were in good order and condition, and that the goods were at the risk of the hirer from the time of purchase by the owner. On 18 March the defendant paid the first instalment and took possession of the car. However, on 20 March the defendant, being dissatisfied with the car, returned it to the dealer though the finance company were not informed of this. On the night of 24–25 March the car was stolen from the dealer's premises and was recovered badly damaged. On 25 March the finance company signed the agreement accepting the defendant's offer to hire the car. The defendant did not regard himself as bound and refused to pay the instalments. The finance company sold the car, and now sued for damages for the defendant's breach of the hire-purchase agreement. *Held* – The hire-purchase agreement was not binding on the defendant because:

(a) he had revoked his offer by returning the car, and the dealer was the agent of the finance company to receive notice;

(b) there was an implied condition in the offer that the goods were in substantially the same condition when the offer was accepted as when it was made.

Effect of death

The effect of the death of a party or potential party would appear to vary according to the type of contract in question, whether the death is that of the offeror or offeree and whether death takes place before or after acceptance.

Death of offeror before acceptance

If the contract envisaged by the offer involves a personal relationship, such as an offer to act as an agent, then the death of the offeror prevents acceptance. If the contract envisaged by the offer is not one involving the personality of the offeror, there are two points of view. In *Dickinson* v *Dodds* (1876) (*see* p. 19) Mellish LJ in an *obiter dictum* expressed the opinion: 'that if a man who makes an offer dies the offer cannot be accepted after he is dead.' However, the decision in *Bradbury* v *Morgan* (1862) (*see below*) suggests that the offer can be accepted until the offeree is notified of the offeror's death. The matter is, therefore, unresolved pending a further decision.

Bradbury v Morgan (1862) 1 H & C 249

The defendants were the executors of J. M. Leigh who had entered into a guarantee of his brother's account with the plaintiffs for credit up to £100. The plaintiffs, not knowing of the death of J. M. Leigh, continued to supply goods on credit to the brother, H. J. Leigh. The defendants now refused to pay the plaintiffs in respect of such credit after the death of J. M. Leigh. *Held* – The plaintiffs succeeded, the offer remaining open until the plaintiffs had knowledge of the death of J. M. Leigh.

Comment: This was a continuing guarantee which is in the nature of a standing offer accepted piecemeal whenever further goods are advanced on credit. Where the guarantee is not of this nature, it may be irrevocable. Thus in *Lloyds* v *Harper* (1880) 16 Ch D 290, the defendant, while living, guaranteed his son's dealings as a Lloyds underwriter in consideration of Lloyds admitting the son. It was held that, as Lloyds had admitted the son on the strength of the guarantee, the defendant's estate was still liable under it, because it was irrevocable in the defendant's lifetime and was not affected by the defendant's death. It continued to apply to defaults committed by the son after the father's death.

Death of offeree before acceptance

Once the offeree is dead there is no offer which can be accepted and his executors cannot, therefore, accept the offer in his stead. The offer being made to a living person can only be accepted by that person and assumes his continued existence. The rule applies whether the proposed contract involves a personal relationship or not. (*Re Cheshire Banking Co, Duff's Executors' Case* (1886) 32 Ch D 301.)

Death of parties after acceptance

Death after acceptance has normally no effect unless the contract is for personal services when it is discharged. Thus if X sells his car to Y and before the car is delivered X dies, it would be possible for Y to sue X's personal representatives for breach of contract if they were to refuse to deliver the car. But if X agrees to play the piano at a concert and dies two days before the performance, the contract is discharged and his personal representatives are not expected to play the piano in his stead.

OFFER AND ACCEPTANCE NOT IDENTIFIABLE

Before leaving the topic of formation of contract it should be noted that the court may from time to time infer the existence of a contract from the words and acts of the parties in a situation where there has been *no offer and acceptance*. An example is provided by a collateral contract, so called because it is associated with another contract from which it derives and is subordinate to.

The following case is a good practical illustration of the operation of this rule in company law.

Rayfield v Hands [1958] 2 All ER 194

The articles of a private company provided by Art. 11 that 'Every member who intends to transfer his shares shall inform the directors who will take the said shares ... at a fair price.' The plaintiff held 725 fully-paid shares of £1 each, and he asked the directors to buy them but they refused. *Held* – The directors were bound to take the shares. Having regard to what is now s. 14(1) of the Companies Act 1985, the provisions of Art. 11 constituted a binding contract between the directors, as members, and the plaintiff, as a member, in respect of his rights as a member. The word 'will' in the article did not import an option in the directors. Vaisey J did say that the conclusion he had reached in this case may not apply to all companies, but it did apply to a private company, because such a company was an intimate concern closely analogous with a partnership.

Comment: (i) Although the articles placed the obligation to take shares of members on the directors, Vaisey J construed this as an obligation falling upon the directors in their capacity as members. Otherwise the contractual aspect of the provision in the articles would not have applied.

(ii) The leading case is *Clarke v Dunraven* [1896] AC 59 where it was held that competitors in a regatta had made a contract not only with the club which organized the race but also with each other, so that one competitor was able to sue another for damages when his boat was fouled and sank under a rule which said that each competitor was liable 'to pay all damages' that he might cause.

GRADED QUESTIONS

Essay mode

1. (a) Explain, giving illustrations, the postal rules as they affect offer and acceptance where contracts are concluded through using the post as the method of communication.

   (b) On Friday 27th November 1987 Buyer sends a telex to Seller offering to buy 1,000 tons of sugar at the current market price. The telex is received in Seller's offices after a short delay at 5.00 p.m. Since the telex operator has gone home for the weekend, Seller posts a letter in the last post on Friday, accepting the offer. This reaches Buyer at 2.30 p.m. on Monday 30th November. Meanwhile, at 9.30 a.m. on 30th November, Buyer sends a further telex to Seller withdrawing his offer. This reaches Seller and is read by him immediately at 9.45 a.m. on 30th November. Seller now seeks your advice.

   Advise Seller.

   (Institute of Chartered Secretaries and Administrators. English Business Law. June 1988)

2. On 1st December Noel advertised his motor-car for sale in the magazine *Car Mart*. The advertisement read as follows:

   FOR SALE

   1982 Morgan Countryman. Offers around £10,000.
   Write to PO Box 100, Car Mart Magazine.

   On 2nd December Guy posts a letter to the address in the advertisement in which he states the following:

   'I've always wanted a Morgan and I will be happy to give you £10,000 for the car. Please telephone me on 8th December between 8 pm and 9 pm to let me know whether this is enough, failing which, I will assume that you've agreed to sell the vehicle to me.'

   Noel receives the letter on 6th December and writes the following entry in his diary:

   '8th December – Ring Guy at 8 pm to agree sale of car.'

   Noel forgets to make the telephone call. On 9th December Guy meets an acquaintance of Noel's who says that Noel has decided to sell the car to Guy. In

the meantime Noel has received a higher offer of £12,000 from Donald and writes a letter to Guy advising him that he has had a better offer for the car.
Advise Guy.

(The Institute of Legal Executives. Part II: Law of Contract. June 1990)

3. (a) In the law of contract explain what is meant by:
   (i)   an offer;
   (ii) an invitation to treat;
   (iii) a statement of intention.

   (10 marks)

   (b) A advertised his car for sale in a newspaper for £5,000. B wrote offering to buy the car for £4,500. A replied by return of post stating that he would accept £4,750. Having received no reply from B, A wrote again saying he would accept his offer of £4,500.

   Advise A.

   (10 marks)

(The Chartered Association of Certified Accountants. Level 1: Paper 1.4 (E). June 1988)

Objective mode

Four alternative answers are given. Select ONE only. Circle the answer which you consider to be correct. Check your answers by referring back to the information given in the chapter and against the answers at the back of the book.

1. John decides that he will sell his antique desk at auction and so he sends it to the auctioneers with a reserve price of £2,000. Martin the auctioneer notes this in the catalogue and informs those attending that there is a reserve. Michael puts in a bid for £1,800 and the desk is knocked down to him. Martin then informs Michael that a mistake has been made and he cannot have the desk because John refuses to sell it for £1,800.

   A Michael is not entitled to the desk because the sale was made on the basis of a mistake and the contract is void.
   B Michael is entitled to the desk because the amount of the reserve price was not communicated to him and he is not therefore bound by the reserve.
   C Michael knew that there was a reserve and as the auctioneer mistakenly sold the desk for less, Michael is not entitled to it.
   D Michael is entitled to the desk. His offer of £1,800 has been accepted and, as an agent, Martin is able to bind his principal John.

2. Eric wants to sell his car and advertises it in the local newspaper at £8,000 giving

his telephone number. Fred sees the advertisement and, being interested in buying a car at about that price, rings Eric and makes an appointment to see the car. Fred likes the car but not the price. He makes Eric an offer of £7,500. Eric nevertheless insists on £8,000.

On the following Monday Fred gets a telephone call from Eric during which Eric offers his car for sale to Fred at £7,800 saying that Fred can have until noon on Friday to think about it.

On Wednesday evening Fred meets his brother Tom in the local. Tom tells him that Eric's son-in-law bought the car on Wednesday morning for £8,000. Fred gulps down his pint and goes over to the public telephone. He rings Eric and says: 'I accept your offer of £7,800 for the car. I will be along in a minute with a cheque.' Eric replies: 'You are too late it is sold.'

Fred thinks Eric is in breach of contract and proposes to sue him for damages. As regards the legal position of Eric and Fred:

A There is no contract between them because Eric's offer was revoked before Fred accepted it.

B There is a contract between them because Eric did not revoke the offer himself.

C There is a contract between them because Eric promised to keep the offer open until Friday and Fred accepted before then.

D There is no contract between them because Eric's offer had lapsed when Fred accepted it.

3. In contract the rules relating to the use of the telephone state that:

A An acceptance is always effective when it is spoken into the telephone by the offeree.

B An acceptance is effective only if it is heard by the offeror.

C An acceptance can be effective when spoken into the telephone even though the offeror does not hear it.

D An acceptance is effective only if it is heard by the offeror and he acknowledges to the offeree that he has heard it.

4. Smart, a young salesman employed by Speedytype Ltd, a company manufacturing electric typewriters, visits Wiley, a partner in Wiley and Fox, solicitors, with a view to selling a new electric typewriter to the firm.

In the course of conversation Smart, being desperate to make his first sale for several days, offers the machine at £30 less than the normal selling price. Wiley says that he will consult Miss Dragon, the head of the typing pool, and let Smart have an answer by letter in a few days.

On returning to the area sales office Smart realizes that although he has authority to give special prices he might have been unduly generous in his offer to Wiley. Accordingly he consults Allick, the area sales manager, who is not prepared to sell the typewriter at the price at which Smart has offered it. Smart rings Wiley immediately but is unable to speak to him or any of the other partners in the firm – even Miss Dragon is not available. Smart therefore writes a letter to Wiley revoking the offer and posts it immediately by first-class mail.

When Wiley arrives at his office on the following day he notices that among the incoming mail is a franked envelope bearing the slogan 'Speedytype Ltd for Electric Typewriters'. It occurs to him that the envelope might contain a retraction of the offer made by Smart and decides not to open it immediately. Instead he dictates a letter to his secretary accepting the offer and tells her to post it before lunch. After lunch Wiley, having ascertained that his secretary has posted his letter, opens the letter from Smart and discovers that it is indeed a revocation of the offer made the previous day. Nevertheless Wiley rings Allick, the area sales manager of Speedytype Ltd, and asks for delivery of the typewriter. Allick replies 'We cannot possibly sell at that price. Surely you received our letter this morning?' 'Yes' says Wiley, 'it came first delivery but I had already posted my acceptance before I had a chance to open all my mail.' Wiley intends to sue Speedytype for breach of contract. Will he succeed?

Which one of the following decisions is the court likely to make?

A That Wiley accepted Smart's offer when his secretary posted the letter of acceptance and Speedytype is bound to sell the machine at Smart's price.

B That Smart's letter of revocation took effect after Wiley had had a reasonable time in which to read it after delivery. Since such an opportunity occurred before Wiley accepted Speedytype is not bound.

C That Smart's offer was withdrawn when the letter of revocation was delivered so that Wiley's acceptance was not effective and Speedytype is not bound.

D That Smart's offer was withdrawn when the letter of revocation was posted so that Wiley's acceptance is ineffective and Speedytype is not bound.

5. On 1 November Adder, an accountant, receives through the post at his office a large volume entitled *Tax Made Easy*. Accompanying the volume is a note from the publishers, Messrs Galley & Co, stating that the volume will greatly assist Adder in his work and that if he does not reply within seven days Messrs Galley & Co will assume that he wishes to purchase the volume and they will expect to receive a remittance of £12.

Adder does not wish to purchase the book but forgets to reply to Galley & Co. At the end of the month he receives an invoice for £12 from the publishers.

Is Adder obliged to pay for the book?

Which one of the following statements is correct?

A Adder must pay for the book since he did not tell Galley & Co within seven days that he did not want it.

B Adder cannot be made to pay for the book but must return it to Galley & Co.

C Adder must pay for the book because it is a business not a private transaction.

D Adder cannot be made to pay for the book and need only make it available for Galley & Co to repossess.

6. Laura, a keen amateur photographer, wrote to Rex, who had just given up photography because of an eye injury, asking: 'Would you be prepared to sell me

your Olympus camera?' Rex replied by letter saying: 'Would you be prepared to pay a fair price, say £350?'

Laura thought £350 was a reasonable price but she had to sell her own camera in order to raise the money. She wrote to Rex saying: 'I accept your offer to let me have the Olympus at £350 but could you give me until the end of the month to pay?'

In fact before Laura posted her letter Rex had sold the camera to Dan who had offered him £400.

As regards the legal position of Laura and Rex:

A Rex is in breach of contract because Laura accepted his offer when she posted her letter of acceptance.

B Rex is not in breach of contract but he would have been if Laura's acceptance had not been a conditional counter offer.

C Rex is not bound because he never made Laura an offer.

D Rex is not bound because when Laura accepted his offer it had been revoked by the sale of the camera to Dan.

7. The Midshires Hospital placed a newspaper advertisement inviting tenders to supply the hospital with fruit and vegetables. Miss Avan Apple, a local greengrocer, applied for a form on which to tender.

Under the tender she agreed to supply 'such quantities of fruit and vegetables as may be required from 1 January to 31 December 199 – '. Miss Apple offered to supply such produce at ten per cent below the current market price at the time orders were made. Her tender was accepted.

The hospital ordered a quantity of produce in February and Miss Apple supplied it according to the terms agreed. No further order was received until September. Since Miss Apple had received only one previous order during the period of the tender she refused to deliver the second order.

Which one of the following statements represents the legal position?

A Miss Apple is in breach of contract. A contract to supply fruit and vegetables throughout the year came into being when Midshires accepted her tender.

B Miss Apple is not in breach of contract. The Midshires acceptance did not give rise to any contractual relationship.

C Miss Apple is in breach of contract in respect of her failure to supply the produce ordered in September but she can tell Midshires that she will not fulfil any further orders.

D Miss Apple is in breach of contract in respect of her failure to supply the produce ordered in September and her tender, being a standing offer, can be accepted by Midshires' orders until the end of the year since a standing offer cannot be revoked.

8. Dora lost her dog and advertised a reward of £50 to the finder. This appeared in the local paper and Clarence saw it. He later found the dog and returned it to Dora who thanked him profusely. She then said: 'There's a reward you know,' and

Clarence replied: 'Yes I know, but I would have brought it home anyway. I could see from its collar where it lived and I am a great lover of dogs and hate to see them lost.' Dora who was a bit short of cash said to Clarence: 'Oh well, you will not want the reward then,' and slammed the door. Clarence who is also short of cash would like the reward.

Which one of the following statements represents the legal position?

A Clarence is not entitled to the reward because his main reason for bringing the dog back was his love of dogs and not the reward.

B Clarence is not entitled to the reward because all newspaper advertisements are invitations to treat and not offers.

C Clarence is not entitled to the reward because he did not tell Dora he was looking for the dog and so never accepted her offer of a reward.

D Clarence is entitled to the reward. He saw the offer and accepted by conduct, motive being irrelevant.

Answers to questions set in objective mode appear on p. 551.

2 | The law of contract – making the contract II

The OBJECTIVES of this chapter are to continue the study of those elements of contract law which go to making *a mere agreement* into *a contract* which is at least *potentially* binding on the parties. Consideration and the intention to create legal relations are looked at here.

CONSIDERATION

Consideration is essential to the formation of any contract not made by deed. What has each party promised or agreed to do? If the answer is nothing there is no enforceable contract unless made by deed.

Definition and related matters

The definition given by Sir Frederick Pollock is to be preferred:

'An act of forbearance of one party *or the promise thereof* is the price for which *the promise* of the other is bought and the promise thus given for value is enforceable.'

This definition, which was adopted by the House of Lords in *Dunlop* v *Selfridge* [1915] AC 847, is preferred because it properly describes executed consideration by including acts and forbearances and executory consideration by referring to the fact that a promise to do something in the future also amounts to consideration.

Executed and executory consideration

Consideration may be *executory* where the parties exchange promises to perform acts in the future. For example, C promises to deliver goods to D and D promises to pay for the goods. Or it may be *executed* where one party promises to do something in return for the act of another rather than for the mere promise of future performance of an act. Here the performance of the act is required before there is any liability on the promise. Where X offers a reward for the return of his lost dog, X is buying the act of the finder and will not be liable until the dog is found and returned. (And *see Carlill*'s case at p. 2.)

A more commercial example is to be found in the request by a seller of goods to 'send cash with order'. The seller *promises* to deliver goods in return for the *act* of payment by the buyer.

Let us look at this a little further.

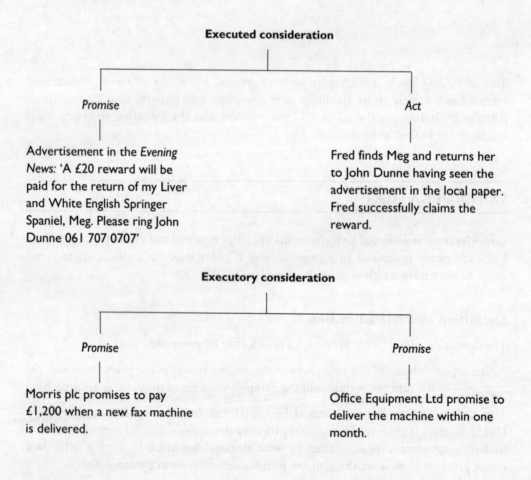

Executed consideration

Promise

Advertisement in the *Evening News*: 'A £20 reward will be paid for the return of my Liver and White English Springer Spaniel, Meg. Please ring John Dunne 061 707 0707'

Act

Fred finds Meg and returns her to John Dunne having seen the advertisement in the local paper. Fred successfully claims the reward.

Executory consideration

Promise

Morris plc promises to pay £1,200 when a new fax machine is delivered.

Promise

Office Equipment Ltd promise to deliver the machine within one month.

CONSIDERATION IN RELATION TO FORMATION OF CONTRACT

The main rules governing consideration in formation of contract are set out below.

Past consideration

Sometimes the act which one party to a contract puts forward as consideration was performed before any promise of reward was made by the other. Where this is so the act in question is regarded as past consideration and will not support a contractual claim. This somewhat technical rule seems to be based on the idea that the act of one party to an alleged contract can only be regarded as consideration if it was carried out in respect of some promise of the other. Where this is not so the act is regarded as gratuitous, being carried out before any promise of reward was made.

The following case provides a practical example of the operation of this rule.

Re McArdle [1951] 1 All ER 905

Certain children were entitled under their father's will to a house. However, their mother had a life interest in the property and during her lifetime one of the children and his wife came to live in the house with the mother. The wife carried out certain improvements to the property and, after she had done so, the children signed a document addressed to her saying: 'In consideration of your carrying out certain alterations and improvements to the property . . . at present occupied by you, the beneficiaries under the Will of William Edward McArdle hereby agree that the executors, the National Provincial Bank Ltd . . . shall repay to you from the said estate when so distributed the sum of £488 in settlement of the amount spent on such improvements . . . 'On the death of the testator's widow the children refused to authorize payment of the sum of £488, and this action was brought to decide the validity of the claim. *Held* – Since the improvements had been carried out before the document was executed, the consideration was past and the promise could not be enforced.

Exceptions to the rule

There are some exceptions to the rule about past consideration. These are set out below.

(a) Where services are rendered at the express or implied request of the promisor in circumstances which raise an implication of a promise to pay. This exception is not entirely a genuine one since the promisor is assumed to have given an implied undertaking to pay at the time of the request, his subsequent promise being regarded as deciding merely the actual amount to be paid. In this situation the act which follows the request but precedes the settling of the reward is more in the nature of executed consideration which, as we have seen, will support a contract. Anyway it is presumably true to say that if Mrs McArdle had been requested by her relatives to do the work the consideration would not have been regarded as past and her claim would have succeeded.

The following case provides an example of the position where the service is performed at the defendant's request in circumstances where the parties understand that payment will follow.

Re Casey's Patents, Stewart v Casey [1892] 1 Ch 104

Patents were granted to Stewart and another in respect of an invention concerning appliances and vessels for transporting and storing inflammable liquids. Stewart entered into an arrangement with Casey whereby Casey was to introduce the patents. Casey spent two years 'pushing' the invention and then the joint owners of the patent rights wrote to him as follows: 'In consideration of your service as the practical manager in working both patents we hereby agree to give you one-third share of the patents.' Casey also received the letters patent. Some time later Stewart died and his executors claimed the letters patent from Casey, suggesting that he had no interest in them because the consideration for the promise to give him a one-third share was past. *Held* – The previous request to render the services raised an implied promise to pay. The subsequent promise could be regarded as fixing the value of the services so that Casey was entitled to one-third share of the patent rights.

(b) Under s. 27 of the Bills of Exchange Act 1882 an antecedent (or previous) debt or liability which is a form of past consideration will support a bill of exchange or cheque (*see further* p. 457). This is essential particularly in the case of cheques, many of which are based upon this form of past consideration. Thus if S sells goods to B a debt comes into being payable in legal tender (i.e. bank notes or coins – *see further* p. 199) when the contract is made, so when B decides to pay S by cheque the cheque is based upon a previous or antecedent debt or liability and is for past consideration. However, this idea would not have helped Mrs McArdle if she had been paid by a cheque which was not paid. She could not have sued upon the cheque because what she had done did not create a previous or antecedent debt or liability.

(c) Under s. 29 of the Limitation Act 1980 a person who owes another a debt, or that person's agent if properly authorized, can make a written acknowledgment of the existence of the debt to the creditor or his agent. This extends the time for which the creditor can sue for his debt though once the debt is statute barred, e.g. because it was incurred more than six years previously, it cannot be revived in this way (*see further* p. 228). It appears at first sight as if this is an exception to the rule about past consideration because the acknowledgment is supported by a past debt. However, the exception is not wholly genuine because the 1980 Act simply states that *no consideration of any kind* need be looked for.

Consideration must move from the promisee and the doctrine of privity of contract

If A wishes to sue successfully upon a promise made by B, it is essential for A (as the recipient of the promise – the promisee) to show that he gave consideration to B (the promisor). The concept is based upon a fundamental assumption of English law that a contract is a bargain. If a person furnishes no consideration he takes no part in a bargain: if he takes no part in a bargain he takes no part in a contract.

There has been much discussion as to whether the doctrine is based on consideration or whether it is a matter of privity, i.e. not being a party to the contract. It is now settled that consideration is the crucial matter in English law. Thus, if A and B contract to benefit C, C cannot sue because he has not supplied consideration and also because he is not a party. However, it is also clear that if A contracts with B and C to benefit C, C still cannot sue unless he has supplied consideration or unless the contract is by deed where consideration is not required. In all cases B, or his executors, can sue on behalf of C.

Thus for all practical purposes the concepts are similar but not quite identical. The rule about privity of contract states that a person cannot sue unless he is a party to the contract. The rule about consideration moving from the promisee takes matters a step further as regards contracts not made by deed by stating that even if a person is a party to a contract he cannot sue upon it unless he has provided consideration.

The following cases provide a practical illustration of the rules.

Dunlop v Selfridge [1915] AC 847

The appellants were motor tyre manufacturers and sold tyres to Messrs Dew & Co who were motor accessory dealers. Under the terms of the contract Dew & Co agreed not to sell the tyres below Dunlop's list price, i.e. £4.05 per tyre, and as Dunlop's agents, to obtain from other traders a similar undertaking. In return for this undertaking Dew & Co were to receive discounts, some of which they could pass on to retailers who bought tyres. Selfridge & Co accepted two orders from customers for Dunlop covers at a lower price. They obtained the covers through Dew & Co and signed an agreement not to sell or offer the tyres below list price. It was further agreed that £5 per tyre so sold should be paid to Dunlop by way of liquidated damages. Selfridge's supplied one of the two tyres ordered below list price, i.e. at £3.65 per tyre. They did not actually supply the other, but informed the customer that they could only supply it at list price. The appellants claimed an injunction and damages against the respondents for breach of the agreement made with Dew & Co, claiming that Dew & Co were their agents in the matter. *Held* – There was no contract between the parties. Dunlop could not enforce the contract made between the respondents and Dew & Co because they had not supplied consideration. Even if Dunlop were undisclosed principals, there was no consideration moving between them and the respondents. The discount received by Selfridge was part of that given by Dunlop to Dew & Co. Since Dew & Co were not bound to give any part of their discount to retailers the discount received by Selfridge operated only as consideration between themselves and Dew & Co and could not be claimed by Dunlop as consideration to support a promise not to sell below list price. (*See now* Resale Prices Act 1976, s. 26 – see pp. 38 and 181.)

Beswick v Beswick [1967] 2 All ER 1197

A coal merchant agreed to sell the business to his nephew in return for a weekly consultancy fee of £6.50 payable during his lifetime, and after his death an annuity of £5 per week was to be payable to his widow for her lifetime. After the agreement was signed the nephew took over the business and paid his uncle the sum of £6.50 as agreed. The uncle died on

3 November 1963, and the nephew paid the widow one sum of £5 and then refused to pay her any more. On 30 June 1964, the widow became the administratrix of her husband's estate, and on 15 July 1964 she brought an action against the nephew for arrears of the weekly sums and for specific performance of the agreement for the future. She sued in her capacity as administratrix of the estate and also in her personal capacity. Her action failed at first instance and on appeal to the Court of Appeal, it was decided amongst other things that:

(i)   specific performance could in a proper case be ordered of a contract to pay money;

(ii) 'property' in s. 56(1) of the Law of Property Act 1925 included a contractual claim not concerned with realty and that therefore a third party could sue on a contract to which he was a stranger. The widow's claim in her personal capacity was therefore good (per Denning MR and Danckwerts LJ);

(iii) the widow's claim as administratrix was good because she was not suing in her personal capacity but on behalf of her deceased husband who had been a party to the agreement;

(iv) no trust in her favour could be inferred.

There was further appeal to the House of Lords, though not on the creation of a trust, and there it was held that the widow's claim as administratrix succeeded, and that specific performance of a contract to pay money could be granted in a proper case. However, having decided the appeal on these grounds their Lordships went on to say that the widow's personal claim would have failed because s. 56 of the Law of Property Act 1925 was limited to cases involving realty. The 1925 Act was a consolidating not a codifying measure, so that if it contained words which were capable of more than one construction, effect should be given to the construction which did not alter the law. It was accepted that when the present provision was contained in the Real Property Act 1845, it had applied only to realty. Although s. 205(1) of the 1925 Act appeared to have extended the provision to personal property, including things in action, it was expressly qualified by the words: 'unless the context otherwise requires', and it was felt that Parliament had not intended to sweep away the rule of privity by what was in effect a sidewind.

Comment: It is unlikely that s. 56 does have a very wide application. The subsection says that a person may take the benefit of an agreement although he is not 'named as a party'. The legislation does not say that he need not *be* a party. There are those who take the view, therefore, that s. 56(1) is designed to cover the situation where there is a covenant over land in favour of, say, 'the owner of Whiteacre', so that the owner of Whiteacre could benefit from the covenant, provided he could be ascertained, even though he was not named in the instrument creating the covenant. If this interpretation is correct then s. 56(1) of the 1925 Act has little effect on the law of contract generally.

The remedies of the promisee

If A makes a contract with B for the benefit of C then, if the contract is not made by deed and C has not given or promised any consideration, C cannot sue A for breach.

B can of course, but what are his remedies? **The following case and comment are illustrative of the legal position**.

Jackson v Horizon Holidays [1975] 3 All ER 92

Mr Jackson sued successfully on a contract *he made* with the defendants to provide a holiday which, in the event, was not of the high standard described in the brochure. He received damages for his own loss and disappointment and also for that of his family since the contract was *also made for their benefit*.

Comment: This judgment by Lord Denning has been much criticized since it infringes a very old rule of English contract law which states that if A contracts with B in return for B's promise to do something for C, then if B repudiates the contract, C has no enforceable claim, and A is restricted to an action for nominal damages by reason of his having suffered no loss. The judgment was criticized by the House of Lords in *Beswick* (*see above*) and again in *Woodar Investment Development* v *Wimpey Construction (UK)* [1980] 1 All ER 571 and must therefore be regarded with caution. The problem was rather neatly overcome in *Beswick* because the House of Lords, unusually, granted specific performance. However, four Law Lords said that if damages had been awarded they would have been nominal only, though Lord Pearce would have awarded substantial damages. It was suggested in *Woodar* that if *Jackson* could be justified it might be on the basis that the booking of a holiday for a family and/or the ordering of meals for oneself and others in restaurants may be a special case so that the person who makes the booking or gives the order can obtain damages in respect of loss suffered by other persons in the party. If damages are so recovered then according to Lord Denning in *Jackson* the recipient must hand the relevant shares over to the other members of the party and if he does not they could sue him in quasi-contract rule (*see further* p. 226).

Exceptions to the rule of privity

There are, however, some exceptions to the rule, the most important of which in examination terms are as follows.

Agency

A principal may sue on a contract made by an agent. This exception is perhaps more apparent than real because in fact the principal is the contracting party who has merely acted through the instrumentality of the agent.

Cheques and bills of exchange

The holder for value of a cheque or bill of exchange can sue prior parties. Thus if A buys goods from B and pays by cheque which B then endorses over to C, his son, as a birthday present, then C can sue A although no consideration moved from him to A.

C cannot sue B because as between immediate parties absence of consideration makes a claim impossible (*see further* p. 458).

Price restrictions

Under the Resale Prices Act 1976, s. 26, the supplier of goods is given a statutory cause of action so that he may enforce against a person not a party to the contract of sale a condition as to resale price. However, the resale price agreement must have been approved under the provisions of the Resale Prices Act 1976, otherwise there can be no enforcement of it.

The section has an effect upon the decision in *Dunlop* v *Selfridge* (1915) (*see above*) in the sense that although the rules relating to privity of contract at common law are still valid, Dunlop may now have had a statutory cause of action in the particular circumstances. The object of s. 26 is to allow a manufacturer to bring a cut-price retailer before an ordinary court of law which was not possible before 1956 unless the retailer had bought the goods direct from the manufacturer. Consequently, manufacturers not having access to the ordinary courts of law often brought the retailer before a secret and possibly unjust trade association tribunal which might put the retailer quite unreasonably on a stop list so that he was denied supplies.

However, it is unlikely that the court would have approved Dunlop's arrangements, and in fact most minimum resale price maintenance agreements were regarded as void by the courts and cannot be enforced against anyone. Books are one of the few items approved for this purpose (*see Net Book Agreement* [1962] 3 All ER 751).

It is worth noting that a *maximum* resale price can be enforced against a third party without approval of the court provided the third party receives the goods with notice of the restriction. This is provided for by s. 26 of the 1976 Act.

Land law

The position in land law is that benefits and liabilities attached to or imposed on land may in some circumstances follow the land into the hands of other owners. **The following cases provide an illustration of this exception**.

Smith and Snipes Hall Farm Ltd v River Douglas Catchment Board
[1949] 2 All ER 179
In 1938 the defendants entered into an agreement with 11 persons owning land adjoining a certain stream that, on the landowners paying some part of the cost, the defendants would improve the banks of the stream and maintain the said banks for all time. In 1940 one landowner sold her land to Smith, and in 1944 Smith leased the land to Snipes Hall Farm Ltd. In 1946, because of the defendants' negligence, the banks burst and the adjoining land was flooded. *Held* – The plaintiffs could enforce the covenant in the agreement of 1938 even

though they were strangers to it. The covenants were for the benefit of the land and affected its use and value and could therefore be transferred with it.

Tulk v Moxhay (1848) 2 Ph 774

The plaintiff was the owner of several plots of land in Leicester Square and in 1808 he sold one of them to a person called Elms. Elms agreed, for himself, his heirs and assigns, 'to keep the Square Gardens open as a pleasure ground and uncovered with buildings'. After a number of conveyances, the land was sold to the defendant who claimed a right to build on it. The plaintiff sued for an injunction preventing the development of the land. The defendant, whilst admitting that he purchased the land with notice of the covenant, claimed that he was not bound by it because he had not himself entered into it. *Held* – An injunction to restrain building would be granted because there was a jurisdiction in equity to prevent, by way of injunction, acts inconsistent with a restrictive covenant on land, so long as the land was acquired with notice of that covenant, and the defendant retains land which can benefit from the covenant.

Comment: Such notice may now be constructive where the covenant is registered under s. 2(5) of the Land Charges Act 1972.

Bankers' commercial credits and performance bonds

Bankers commercial credits also present problems in the field of privity. It is common practice for an exporter, E, to ask the buyer of the goods, B, to open with his banker a credit in favour of E, the credit to remain irrevocable for a specified time. B agrees with his banker that the credit should be opened and in return promises to pay the banker and usually gives him a lien over the shipping documents. The banker will also require a commission for his services. B's banker then notifies E that a credit has been opened in his favour and E can draw upon it on presentation of the shipping documents.

It will be seen that E and B's banker are not in privity of contract. It might be thought that this could give rise to problems in the unlikely event that the banker did not pay. However, this is not so. In fact the buyer/customer of the bank cannot stop payment. In *Malas (Hamzeh)* v *British Imex* [1958] 1 All ER 262 the plaintiffs, who were buyers of goods, applied to the court for an injunction restraining the sellers, who were the defendants in the case, from drawing under a credit established by the buyers' bankers. The Court of Appeal refused to grant this injunction and Jenkins LJ said: 'The opening of a confirmed letter of credit constitutes a bargain between the banker and the vendor of the goods which imposes on the banker an absolute obligation to pay . . . ' Sellers LJ said that there could well be exceptions where the court would exercise a jurisdiction to grant an injunction, as where there was a fraudulent transaction. However, in other situations the binding nature of the bankers' commercial credit is an exception to privity of contract.

There are similar developments rendering performance bonds enforceable by commercial custom, so that where a bank guarantees performance of an export contract by the supplier the bank must pay the buyer if the contract is not performed.

Economic value

Consideration must be real, which means capable of estimation in terms of economic value. **This matter has not received much attention in the courts but the following case is an example of its application.**

White v Bluett (1853) 23 LJ Ex 36

This action was brought by White who was the executor of Bluett's father's estate. The plaintiff, White, alleged that Bluett had not paid a promissory note given to his father during his lifetime. Bluett admitted that he had given the note to his father, but said that his father had released him from it in return for a promise not to keep on complaining about the fact that he had been disinherited. *Held* – The defence failed and the defendant was liable on the note. The promise not to complain was not real consideration to support his release from the note.

Comment: This case is the only major illustration of the principle and, although included in formation of contract, actually related to the discharge of one contract by another.

Adequacy of consideration

Provided that the consideration satisfies the test of economic value the court will not normally concern itself with its adequacy. Thus the amount of the consideration offered need not be what the average person would think to be satisfactory. A person who is making a contract is usually able to offer as little as he thinks the other party will accept in return for the promise of that party.

Why is this? Basically because the courts do not exist to repair bad bargains and though consideration must be present, the parties themselves must attend to its value. Under this principle it would be possible to enforce a contract to purchase a Rolls-Royce for a penny; both a Rolls-Royce and a penny are consideration. Obviously inadequate consideration gives rise to suspicion of fraud, duress or undue influence, and possibly unsoundness of mind, but if these are not proved the contract is good. Thus in *Thomas* v *Thomas* (1842) 2 QB 851 the plaintiff's husband had expressed the wish that the plaintiff, if she survived him, should have the use of his house. He left a will of which his brothers were executors. The will made no mention of the testator's wish that his wife should be given the house. The executors knew of the testator's wish and agreed to allow the widow to occupy the house on payment of £1 per year for as long as she remained a widow. The plaintiff remained in possession of the house until the death of one of the executors, Samuel Thomas. The other executor then turned her out. She sued him for breach of contract. It was held that the plaintiff's promise to pay £1 a year was consideration and need not be adequate. The action for breach of contract succeeded.

The following case is also an illustration of the rule of nominal consideration though set in a somewhat complicated commercial situation.

Chappell & Co Ltd v Nestlé Co Ltd [1959] 2 All ER 701

The plaintiffs owned the copyright in a dance tune called 'Rockin' Shoes', and the defendants were using records of this tune as part of an advertising scheme. A record company made the records for Nestlé who advertised them to the public for 7½p each but required in addition three wrappers from their 7½p bars of chocolate. When they received the wrappers they threw them away. The plaintiffs sued the defendants for infringement of copyright. It appeared that under the Copyright Act of 1956 a person recording musical works for retail sale need not get the permission of the holder of the copyright, but had merely to serve him with notice and pay 6¼ per cent of the retail selling price as royalty. The plaintiffs asserted that the defendants were not retailing the goods in the sense of the Act and must therefore get permission to use the musical work. The basis of the plaintiff's case was that retailing meant selling entirely for money, and that as the defendants were selling for money plus wrappers, they needed the plaintiffs' consent. The defence was that the sale was for cash because the wrappers were not part of the consideration. *Held* – The plaintiffs succeeded because the wrappers were part of the consideration and the question of their adequacy did not arise.

Comment: (i) Presumably the wrappers could have formed the whole consideration.

(ii) The statutory licence to copy records sold by retail was granted by s. 8 of the Copyright Act 1956. This was repealed by the Copyright, Designs and Patents Act 1988, Sched. I, para. 21, and permission to reproduce is now required even by those retailing the records. However, the fact was that the wrappers were part of the consideration and the House of Lords ruling as to adequacy survives as a relevant example.

Forbearance to sue

Although there were once arguments to the contrary, it is now accepted that forbearance to sue may be adequate consideration. It is not necessary to show that the action would have succeeded but merely that if it had been brought to trial it might have done. Thus the court would be unlikely to accept that a bookmaker could supply consideration by forgoing a claim against a client for stake money. Such an action, being based upon an illegal transaction, could have no hope of success.

The person who forbears to sue may actually promise not to do so or merely forbear in fact. A promise is not essential provided the evidence is that there was some causal connection between the forbearance and the acts of the parties.

The following case is an illustration of implied forbearance.

Horton v Horton [1960] 3 All ER 649

The parties were husband and wife. In March 1954, by a separation agreement under seal, the husband agreed to pay the wife £30 a month. On the true construction of the deed the husband should have deducted income tax before payment but for nine months he paid the money without deductions. In January 1955 he signed a document, not under seal, agreeing that instead of 'the monthly sum of £30' he would pay a monthly sum as 'after deduction of income tax should amount to the clear sum of £30'. For over three years he paid this clear sum but then stopped payment. To an action by his wife he pleaded that the later agreement was unsupported by consideration and that the wife could sue only on the earlier deed. *Held* – by the Court of Appeal – that there was consideration to support the later agreement. It was clear that the original deed did not implement the intention of the parties. The wife therefore might have sued to rectify the deed and the later agreement represented a compromise of this possible action. Whether such an action would have succeeded was irrelevant; it sufficed that it had some prospect of success and that the wife believed in it.

Existing duties and consideration – the rule of sufficiency

Whether the performance of an existing duty can amount to consideration is a matter which is often considered under the heading of 'sufficiency of consideration'. To many people the difference between the words 'adequacy' and 'sufficiency' is either small or non-existent. However, to lawyers the two words encompass very different ideas. Adequacy is concerned with the amount of economic value to be supplied or promised. Sufficiency is concerned with the question whether there is any consideration at all. Three main situations should be noted. They are set out below.

Discharge of a public duty

The discharge of a public duty imposed by law is not consideration. However, where the contractual duty is not precisely coincident with the public duty but is in excess of it, performance of the contractual duty may provide consideration.

The cases which follow provide illustrations of these rules.

Collins v Godefroy (1831) I B & Ad 950

The plaintiff was subpoenaed to give evidence for the defendant in an action to which the defendant was a party. The plaintiff now sued for the sum of six guineas which he said the defendant had promised him for his attendance. *Held* – The plaintiff's action failed because there was no consideration for the promise. Lord Tenterden said: 'If it be a duty imposed by law upon a party regularly subpoenaed to attend from time to time to give evidence, then a promise to give him any remuneration for loss of time incurred in such attendance is a promise without consideration.'

Glasbrook Bros v Glamorgan County Council [1925] AC 270

The question had arisen as to how best to protect a coal mine during a strike. The police authorities thought it enough to provide a mobile force but the colliery manager wanted a stationary guard. It was ultimately agreed to provide the latter at a rate of payment which involved the sum of £2,200. The company refused to pay and when sued pleaded the absence of consideration. The House of Lords gave judgment for the plaintiffs. The police were bound to afford protection but they had a discretion as to the form it should take, and an undertaking to provide more protection than in their discretion they deemed necessary was consideration for the promise of reward.

Comment: This case was applied in *Harris v Sheffield United Football Club* [1987] 2 All ER 838 where Boreham J held that the provision of policemen at a football ground to keep law and order was the provision of special services by the police. The police authority is under a duty to protect persons and property against crime or threatened crime for which no payment is due. However, the police have no public duty to protect persons and property against the mere fear of possible future crime. The claim of the police authority for some £70,000 for police services provided at the defendants' football ground over 15 months was allowed. The judge's decision was affirmed by the Court of Appeal.

Ward v Byham [1956] 2 All ER 318

An unmarried mother sued to recover a maintenance allowance by the father of the child. The defence was that, under s. 42 of the National Assistance Act 1948, the mother of an illegitimate child was bound to maintain it. However, it appeared that in return for the promise of an allowance the mother had promised:

(i) to look after the child well and ensure that it was happy; and
(ii) to allow it to decide whether it should live with her or the father.

Held – There was sufficient consideration to support the promise of an allowance because the promises given in (i) and (ii) above were in excess of the statutory duty, which was merely to care for the child.

Comment: 'Is a promise to make a child happy real consideration?' (see *White v Bluett* (1853) at p. 40). This point is not taken in the above case and shows the considerable power which judges have to find or not to find contractual obligations.

Discharge of contractual duties under a contract with the same party

The performance of a contractual duty already owed to the defendant is not consideration. However, the carrying out of some additional act beyond what has already been contracted for does provide consideration. **The following cases make the point**.

Stilk v Myrick (1809) 2 Camp 317

A sea-captain, being unable to find any substitutes for two sailors who had deserted, promised to divide the wages of the deserters among the rest of the crew if they would work the ship home shorthanded. *Held* – The promise was not enforceable because of absence of consideration. In sailing the ship home the crew had done no more than they were already bound to do. Their original contract obliged them to meet the normal emergencies of the voyage of which minor desertions were one.

Comment: It must be said that the decision in *Stilk* took a nasty knock in *Williams v Roffey Bros and Nicholls (Contractors) Ltd, The Times*, 8 December 1989. The defendants in that case were building contractors. They made a contract to refurbish a block of 27 flats and engaged Mr Williams to carry out carpentry work for £20,000. This turned out to be too low to enable Mr Williams to operate at a profit and after completing some of the flats and receiving interim payments of £16,000 he got into financial difficulties. The defendants, concerned that the job might not be finished on time and that they would in that event have to pay money under a penalty clause in the main contract, made an oral promise to pay Mr Williams a further sum of £10,300 to be paid at the rate of £575 for each flat on which work was completed. Mr Williams was not paid in full for this work and later brought this claim for the additional sum promised. The Court of Appeal *held* that he was entitled to it because where a party to a contract agrees to make an additional payment to secure its performance on time this may provide sufficient consideration contractually to support the extra payment if the agreement to pay is obtained without economic duress or fraud (*see further* p. 126) and where it ensures the completion of the contract to the paying party's satisfaction and benefit as by avoiding a penalty which was the position here. Apparently *Stilk* survives only where the person making the promise receives no benefit for it. It would seem to have been possible to find benefit in *Stilk* so that it may well be overruled on its own facts though the Court of Appeal would only say that the principle had been 'refined'.

Hartley v Ponsonby (1857) 7 E & B 872

A greater remuneration was promised to a seaman to work the ship home when the number of deserters was so great as to render the ship unseaworthy. *Held* – This was a binding promise because the sailor had gone beyond his duty in agreeing to sail an unseaworthy ship. In fact the number of desertions was so great as to discharge the remaining seamen from their original contract, leaving them free to enter into a new bargain.

Discharge of an obligation under a contract with a third party

The actual performance of an outstanding contractual obligation may be sufficient to support a promise of a further payment by a third party. **The following cases are a selection from a number which illustrate the point**.

Shadwell v Shadwell (1860) 9 CB (NS) 159

The plaintiff was engaged to marry a girl named Ellen Nicholl. In 1838 he received a letter from his uncle, Charles Shadwell, in the following terms: 'I am glad to hear of your intended marriage with Ellen Nicholl and, as I promised to assist you at starting, I am happy to tell you that I will pay you one hundred and fifty pounds yearly during my life and until your income derived from your profession of Chancery barrister shall amount to six hundred guineas, of which your own admission will be the only evidence that I shall receive or require.' The plaintiff duly married Ellen Nicholl and his income never exceeded 600 guineas during the 18 years his uncle lived after the marriage. The uncle paid 12 annual sums and part of the thirteenth but no more. On his death the plaintiff sued his uncle's executors for the balance of the 18 instalments to which he suggested he was entitled. *Held* – The plaintiff succeeded even though he was already engaged to Ellen Nicholl when the promise was made. His marriage was sufficient consideration to support his uncle's promise, for, by marrying, the plaintiff had incurred responsibilities and changed his position in life. Further the uncle probably derived some benefit in that his desire to see his nephew settled had been satisfied.

Comment: An engagement to marry is no longer binding as a contract – Law Reform (Miscellaneous Provisions) Act 1970, s.1 – but the rule can still be applied in other situations (*see The New Zealand Shipping case below*).

The New Zealand Shipping Co Ltd v A M Satterthwaite & Co Ltd [1974] 1 All ER 1015

In this case the makers of an expensive drilling machine entered into a contract for the carriage of the machine by sea to New Zealand. The contract of carriage (the bill of lading) exempted the carriers from full liability for any loss or damage to the machine during carriage and also purported to exempt any servant or agent of the carrier, including independent contractors employed from time to time by the carrier. The machine was damaged by the defendants, who were stevedores, in the course of unloading, and the question to be decided was whether the defendant stevedores, who had been employed by the carrier to unload the machine, could take advantage of the exemption clause in the bill of lading since they were not parties to the contract. It was decided by the Privy Council that they could. The stevedores provided consideration and so became parties to the contract when they unloaded the machine. (*Carlill v Carbolic Smoke Ball Co* (1893) (see p. 2) applied.) The performance of services by the stevedores in discharging the cargo was sufficient consideration to constitute a contract, even though they were already under an obligation to the carrier to perform those services because the actual performance of an outstanding contractual obligation was sufficient to support the promise of an exemption from liability given by the makers of the drill to the shippers, who were in effect, third parties to the contract between the carrier and the stevedores. (*Shadwell v Shadwell* (1860) (see *above*) applied.)

Comment: It is not easy to see when and where the relevant offers and acceptances were made in this case, but as we have already noted, a court can construe a contract from the circumstances without a precise application of the offer and acceptance formula (*see Rayfield v Hands* (1958) at p. 23).

CONSIDERATION IN RELATION TO THE DISCHARGE OF A CONTRACT

All that has so far been said in regard to consideration relates to the *formation* of a contract. As we have seen, there must be offer, acceptance, consideration and intention to create legal relations in order to bring a contract into existence. The rules are rather different where a contract is to be *discharged*. There are a number of ways in which a contract may be discharged, all of which will be dealt with later. However, the one with which we are now concerned is *discharge by agreement* under which contract A is to be discharged by a new contract, B, the question being to what extent does contract B require consideration? The attitude of the common law is different from that of equity, as we shall see.

COMMON LAW: THE RULE OF ACCORD AND SATISFACTION

At common law if A owes B £10 and wishes to discharge (bring to an end) that obligation by paying B £9 he must:

(a) obtain the agreement (accord) of B; and
(b) provide B with some consideration (satisfaction) for giving up his right to £10 unless the release is under seal.

This is the common law doctrine of accord and satisfaction. The doctrine is an ancient one and an early example of it is to be found in the judgment of Brian CJ in *Pinnel*'s case (1602). Pinnel sued Cole in debt for what would now be £8.50 which was due on a bond on 11 November 1600. Cole's defence was that at Pinnel's request he had paid him £5.12 on 1 October and that Pinnel had accepted this payment in full satisfaction of the original debt. Although the court found for Pinnel on a technical point of pleading, it was said that:

(a) payment of a lesser sum on the day due in satisfaction of a greater sum cannot be any satisfaction for the whole; but
(b) payment of a smaller sum at the creditor's request before the due day is good consideration for a promise to forgo the balance for it is a benefit to the creditor to be paid before he was entitled to payment and a corresponding detriment to the debtor to pay early.

The first branch of the rule in *Pinnel*'s case was much criticized but was approved by the House of Lords in *Foakes* v *Beer* (1884) (*see below*) and the doctrine then hardened because of the system of binding precedent.

Foakes v Beer (1884) 9 App Cas 605

Mrs Beer had obtained a judgment against Dr Foakes for debt and costs. Dr Foakes agreed to settle the judgment debt by paying £500 down and £150 per half-year until the whole was paid, and Mrs Beer agreed not to take further action on the judgment. Foakes duly paid the amount of the judgment plus costs. However, judgment debts carry interest by statute, and while Dr Foakes had been paying off the debt, interest amounting to £360 had been accruing on the diminishing balance. In this action Mrs Beer claimed the £360. *Held* – she could do so. Her promise not to take further action on the judgment was not supported by any consideration moving from Dr Foakes.

Comment: Since the development of equitable estoppel in the *High Trees* case (see p. 51), there is no reason why a part-payment should not be enough to discharge the contract. Perhaps *Foakes* will in future be confined to cases where the acceptance of the part-payment results from threats as in *D & C Builders* v *Rees* (1965) (*see below*).

Some qualifications to the rule

The practical effect of the rule that payment of a smaller sum will not do is reduced under the common law by the following, each of which seems to include an element of consideration, however small.

(a) *Where there is a dispute as to the sum owed.* If the creditor accepts less than he thinks is owed to him the debt will be discharged. Thus A says that B owes him £11. B says it is only £9. A agrees to compromise by taking £10. Even if it can be proved that A is really owed £11 he cannot recover the £1. He has compromised his claim.

(b) *Where the creditor agrees to take something different in kind*, e.g. a chattel, the debt is discharged by substituted performance. Thus, if A gives B a watch worth £5 and B is agreeable to taking it, then the debt of £10 will be discharged. **In this connection it should be noted that a cheque for a smaller sum no longer constitutes substituted performance as the following case illustrates.**

D & C Builders Ltd v Rees [1965] 3 All ER 837

D & C Builders, a small company, did work for Rees for which he owed £482 13s 1d. There was at first no dispute as to the work done but Rees did not pay. In August and October 1964, the plaintiffs wrote for the money and received no reply. On 13 November 1964, the wife of Rees (who was then ill) telephoned the plaintiffs, complained about the work, and said, 'My husband will offer you £300 in settlement. That is all you will get. It is to be in satisfaction.' D & C Builders, being in desperate straits and faced with bankruptcy without the money, offered to take the £300 and allow a year to Rees to find the balance. Mrs Rees replied: 'No, we will never have enough money to pay the balance, £300 is better than nothing.' The plaintiffs then said: 'We have no choice but to accept.' Mrs Rees gave the defendants a cheque and insisted on a receipt 'in completion of the account'. The plaintiffs, being worried about their financial position, took legal advice and later brought an action for the balance. The defence was bad workmanship and also that there was a binding settlement. The question of settlement was tried as a preliminary issue and the judge, following *Goddard* v *O'Brien* (1882), decided that a cheque for a smaller amount was a good discharge of the debt, this being the generally accepted view of the law since that date. On appeal it was *held* (per the Master of the Rolls, Lord Denning) that *Goddard* v *O'Brien* was wrongly decided. A smaller sum in cash could be no settlement of a larger sum and 'no sensible distinction could be drawn between the payment of a lesser sum by cash and the payment of it by cheque.'

In the course of his judgment Lord Denning said of *High Trees* (*see below*):

> It is worth noting that the principle may be applied, not only so as to suspend strict legal rights but also so as to preclude the enforcement of them. This principle has been applied to cases where a creditor agrees to accept a lesser sum in discharge of a greater. So much so that we can now say that, when a creditor and debtor enter on a course of negotiation, which leads the debtor to suppose that on payment of the lesser sum, the creditor will not enforce payment of the balance, and on the faith thereof the debtor pays the lesser sum and the creditor accepts it as satisfaction: then the creditor will not be allowed to enforce payment of the balance when it would be inequitable to do so . . . But he is not bound unless there has been truly an accord between them.

In the present case there was no true accord. The debtor's wife had held the creditors to ransom and there was no reason in law or equity why the plaintiffs should not enforce the full amount of the debt.

(c) *The payment of a smaller sum before the larger is due* gives the debtor a good discharge. This is the second branch of the rule in *Pinnel*'s case and makes valid the giving of a discount for early payment.

(d) *Payment at a different place* gives the debtor a good discharge. A creditor may accept the payment of a smaller sum provided the debtor hands over the money at a different place from the one originally agreed. The question of adequacy of consideration does not arise and the court will assume some benefit to the creditor.

The exceptions to the rule

(a) *If a debtor makes an arrangement with his creditors* to compound his debts, e.g. by paying them 85p in the £1, he is satisfying a debt for a larger sum by the payment of a smaller sum. Nevertheless, it is a good discharge, the consideration being the agreement by the creditors with each other and with the debtor not to insist on their full rights. These arrangements would more usually be made today under the Insolvency Act 1986. Section 260 of that Act states that such an arrangement binds every creditor if it is approved by a meeting of creditors at which three-quarters in value vote in favour of the arrangement. Therefore, s. 260 really provides an exception to the rule of accord and satisfaction.

(b) *Payment of a smaller sum by a third party* operates as a good discharge. **The following case illustrates this.**

Welby v Drake (1825) 1 C & P 557

The plaintiff sued the defendant for the sum of £9 on a debt which had originally been £18. The defendant's father had paid the plaintiff £9 and the plaintiff had agreed to take that sum in full discharge of the debt. *Held* – The payment of £9 by the defendant's father operated to discharge the debt of £18.

Comment: The basis of the decision may be found both in the law of contract and in the tort of deceit, since it would be a fraud on the third party to sue the original debtor. 'If the father did pay the smaller sum in satisfaction of this debt, it is a bar to the plaintiff's now recovering against the son: because by suing the son, he commits fraud on the father, whom he induced to advance his money on the faith of such advance being a discharge of his son from further liability' (per Lord Tenterden CJ). Also, of course, the creditor breaks his contract with the third party.

EQUITY: THE RULE OF PROMISSORY ESTOPPEL

There has always been some dissatisfaction with the common law rule of accord and satisfaction. After all, if A owes B £10 and B agrees to take £9, as he must before there can be any question of discharging the obligation on A to pay £10, why should B be allowed afterwards to break his promise to take £9 and succeed in an action against A simply because A gave him no consideration?

It was to deal with this sort of situation that the equitable rule of promissory estoppel was propounded, first by Lord Cairns in *Hughes* v *Metropolitan Railway* (1877) and later by Denning J (as he then was), in the *High Trees* case (1947) (*see below*). It was affirmed by the House of Lords in *Tool Metal Manufacturing Co Ltd* v *Tungsten Electric Co Ltd* (1955) (*see below*).

The rule of estoppel is basically a rule of evidence under which the court, surprisingly enough, is not prepared to listen to the truth. It occurs at common law out of physical conduct. Suppose A and B go into a wholesaler's premises and A asks for goods on credit. The wholesaler, who knows that B is creditworthy, but has no knowledge of A, is not prepared to give credit until A says, 'Do not worry, you will be paid, B is my partner.' If B says nothing and A receives the goods on credit and does not pay, then B could be sued for the price, even though he can produce evidence that he was not in fact A's partner. This evidence will not be admitted because the wholesaler relied on a situation of partnership created by B's *conduct*, *and* the statement is concerned with *existing fact* which is essential at common law (*see Jorden* v *Money* (1854) 5 HL Cas 185).

Promissory estoppel in equity is very little different except that the estoppel arises from a *promise*, not *conduct*. The common law does not recognize an estoppel arising out of a promise, or a statement about *future conduct* but equity does.

Ingredients of promissory estoppel

As a result of the above decisions and others (as indicated) the rule of promissory estoppel has the following ingredients:

(a) It arises from a promise made with the intention that it should be acted upon. The promise must be clear and unambiguous to the effect that strict legal rights will not be enforced.

(b) It was once thought that the person who had received the promise must do something to show that he had relied on it. If A, a landlord, said B could pay only half his usual rent while he was unemployed, it was thought that B would have to show, for example, that he had spent what should have been the rent money on travelling expenses to find work in the district. Reliance upon the promise in this way is not, it would appear, a necessary requirement (*Alan* v *El Nasr* (1972) – *see below*).

(c) It relates only to variation or discharge of contract by agreement and does not affect the requirement of consideration on formation of contract (*Combe* v *Combe* (1951) – *see below*).

(d) So far as the rule has been developed in cases, it merely suspends rights but does not totally preclude enforcement of the original contract after reasonable notice has been given (*Tool Metal Manufacturing Co Ltd* v *Tungsten Electric Co Ltd* (1955) – *see below*).

(e) The promise must be freely given and not extorted by threats, for if it is then it is not inequitable to allow the promisor to go back on his promise (*D & C Builders Ltd* v *Rees* (1965) – *see p. 47*).

(f) Of considerable importance is a *dictum* by Lord Denning in *D & C Builders* v *Rees* (1965) – (*see p. 48*) that the rule could be developed to the point at which it operated, not merely to suspend rights, but to prevent enforcement of them. If this point is reached, then if A owes B £10 and B agrees to take £9, A will be discharged from his obligation to pay £10 without the need for consideration.

Such a situation would involve a virtual overruling of *Foakes* v *Beer* (1884) (*see* p. 46) and would put an end to the first branch of the rule in *Pinnel*'s case which is that payment of a lesser sum on the day due in satisfaction of a greater sum cannot be any satisfaction for the whole. Although in the past a number of *dicta* by Lord Denning have been incorporated into the *ratio* of subsequent decisions, the position outlined here has not yet been reached.

Promissory estoppel – the case law

The following cases which have already been referred to are illustrative of the various aspects of the rule.

Hughes v Metropolitan Railway (1877) 2 App Cas 439

A landlord gave six months notice to his tenant to carry out certain repairs and said that if the tenant failed to do the repairs the lease would be forfeited. During the period of six months the landlord started negotiations with the tenant with a view to selling the lease to the tenant. The tenant did not do any repairs while the negotiations were in progress. However, the negotiations broke down during the six month period and before the end of it the landlord claimed to forfeit the lease for failure to repair. The House of Lords *held* that he could not do so. The landlord had by his conduct led the tenant into thinking that he would not enforce forfeiture at the end of the six month period. The tenant had relied on this by not doing the repairs. However, the six month period began to run again from the breakdown in negotiations.

Central London Property Trust Ltd v High Trees House Ltd [1947] KB 130

In 1937 the plaintiffs granted to the defendants a lease of 99 years of a new block of flats at a rent of £2,500 per annum. The lease was under seal. During the period of the war the flats were by no means fully let owing to the absence of people from the London area. The defendant company, which was a subsidiary of the plaintiff company, realized that it could not meet the rent out of the profits then being made on the flats, and in 1940 the parties entered into an agreement which reduced the rent to £1,250 per annum, this agreement being put into writing but not sealed. The defendants continued to pay the reduced rent from 1941 to the beginning of 1945, by which time the flats were fully let, and they continued to pay the reduced rents thereafter. In September 1945, the receiver of the plaintiff company investigated the matter and asked for arrears of £7,916, suggesting that the liability created by the lease still existed, and that the agreement of 1940 was not supported by any consideration. The receiver then brought this action to establish the legal position. He claimed £625, being the difference in rent for the two quarters ending 29 September and 29 December 1945. *Held* – (a) A simple contract can in equity vary a deed (i.e. the lease), though it had not done so here because the simple contract was not supported by consideration. (b) As the agreement for the reduction of rent had been acted upon by the defendants, the plaintiffs were estopped in equity from claiming the full rent from 1941 until early 1945 when the flats were fully let. After that time they were entitled to do so because the second agreement was only operative during the continuance of the conditions which gave rise to it. To this extent the limited claim of the receiver succeeded.

Comment: The rule established by the case, in its developed state, seems to be that where a person has indicated by a promise that he is not going to insist upon his strict rights, as a result of which the other party acts on the belief induced by the other's promise, which may mean no more than making the reduced payments as in this case, then the law, although it does not give a cause of action in damages if the promise is broken, will require it to be honoured to the extent of refusing to allow the promisor the right to act inconsistently with it, even though the promise is not supported by consideration. The doctrine has been called 'equitable estoppel', 'quasi-estoppel' and 'promissory estoppel', in order to distinguish it from estoppel at common law. At common law estoppel arises when the defendant by his conduct suggests that certain existing facts are true. Here the estoppel was based on a promise, not conduct, and the promise related to future conduct, not to existing facts.

Tool Metal Manufacturing Co Ltd v Tungsten Electric Co Ltd [1955] 2 All ER 657

The appellants were the registered proprietors of British letters patent. In April 1938 they made a contract with the respondents whereby they gave the latter a licence to manufacture 'hard metal alloys' in accordance with the inventions which were the subject of patent. By the contract the respondents agreed to pay 'compensation' to the appellants if in any one month they sold more than a stated quantity of metal alloys.

Compensation was duly paid by the respondents until the outbreak of war in 1939, but thereafter none was paid. It was found as a fact that in 1942 the appellants agreed to suspend the enforcement of compensation payments pending the making of a new contract. In 1944 negotiations for such new contracts were begun but broke down. In 1945 the respondents sued the appellants for breach of contract and the appellants counter-claimed for payment of compensation as from 1 June 1945. As regards the arguments on the counter-claim, it was eventually *held* by the Court of Appeal that the agreement of 1942 operated in equity to prevent the appellants demanding compensation until they had given reasonable notice to the respondents of their intention to resume their strict legal rights and that such notice had not been given.

In September 1950 the appellants themselves issued a writ against the respondents claiming compensation as from 1 January 1947. The respondents pleaded the equity raised by the agreement of 1942 and argued that reasonable notice of its termination had not been given. When this action reached the House of Lords it was *held* – affirming *Hughes* v *Metropolitan Railway Co* and the *High Trees* case – that the agreement of 1942 operated in equity to suspend the appellants' legal rights to compensation until reasonable notice to resume them had been given. However, the counter-claim in the first action in 1945 amounted to such notice, and since the appellants were not now claiming any compensation as due to them before 1 January 1947, the appellants succeeded in this second action and were awarded £84,000 under the compensation clause.

W J Alan & Co v El Nasr Export and Import Co [1972] 2 All ER 127

A contract for the sale of coffee provided for the price expressed in Kenyan shillings to be paid by irrevocable letter of credit. The buyers procured a confirmed letter expressed in sterling and the sellers obtained part payment thereunder. While shipment was in progress sterling was devalued and the sellers claimed such additional sum as would bring the price up to the sterling equivalent of Kenyan shillings at the current rate. Orr J held that the buyers were liable to pay the additional sum as the currency of account was Kenyan shillings. On appeal by the buyers it was *held* – allowing the appeal – that the sellers by accepting payment in sterling had irrevocably waived their right to be paid in Kenyan currency or had accepted a variation of the sale contract, and that a party who has waived his rights cannot afterwards insist on them if the other party has acted on that belief differently from the way in which he would otherwise have acted: and the other party need not show that he has acted to his detriment. In the course of his judgment Lord Denning MR said:

> . . . if one party, by his conduct, leads another to believe that the strict rights arising under

the contract will not be insisted on, intending that the other should act on that belief, and he does act on it, then the first party will not afterwards be allowed to insist on the strict legal rights when it would be inequitable for him to do so … There may be no consideration moving from him who benefits by the waiver. There may be no detriment to him acting on it. There may be nothing in writing. Nevertheless, the one who waives his strict rights cannot afterwards insist on them. His strict rights are at any rate suspended so long as the waiver lasts. He may on occasion be able to revert to his strict legal rights for the future by giving reasonable notice in that behalf, or otherwise making it plain by his conduct that he will thereafter insist on them … I know that it has been suggested in some quarters that there must be a detriment. But I can find no support for it in the authorities cited by the judge. The nearest approach to it is the statement by Viscount Simonds in the *Tool Metal* case that the other must have been led 'to alter his position' which was adopted by Lord Hodson in *Emmanuel Ayodeji Ajayi* v *R T Briscoe (Nigeria) Ltd* [1964] 3 All ER 556. But that only means that he must have been led to act differently from what he otherwise would have done. And, if you study the cases in which the doctrine has been applied, you will see that all that is required is that one should have 'acted on the belief induced by the other party'. That is how Lord Cohen put it in the *Tool Metal* case and it is how I would put it myself.

Comment: Since, as in *High Trees*, a tenant who only pays one-half of his rent can hardly be said to have 'acted to his detriment', the better view is that acting to one's detriment is not a requirement of equitable estoppel. It is a requirement of common law estoppel.

Combe v Combe [1951] 1 All ER 767

The parties were married in 1915 and separated in 1939. In February 1943, the wife obtained a decree nisi of divorce, and a few days later the husband entered into an agreement under which he was to pay his wife £100 per annum, free of income tax. The decree was made absolute in August 1943. The husband did not make the agreed payments and the wife did not apply to the court for maintenance but chose to rely on the alleged contract. She brought this action for arrears under that contract. Evidence showed that her income was between £700 and £800 per annum and the defendant's was £650 per annum. Byrne J, at first instance, *held* that, although the wife had not supplied consideration, the agreement was nevertheless enforceable, following the decision in the *High Trees* case, as a promise made to be acted upon and in fact acted upon. *Held* – by the Court of Appeal – (a) that the *High Trees* decision was not intended to create new actions where none existed before, and that it had not abolished the requirement of consideration to support simple contracts. In such cases consideration was a cardinal necessity. (b) In the words of Birkett LJ the rule was 'a shield not a sword', i.e. a defence to an action, not a cause of action. (c) The rule applied to the modification of existing agreements by subsequent promises and had no relevance to the formation of a contract. (d) It was not possible to find consideration in the fact that the wife forbore to claim maintenance from the court, since no such contractual undertaking by her could have been binding even if she had given it. Therefore this action by the wife must fail because the agreement was not supported by consideration.

DISCHARGE OF CONTRACT BY PERFORMANCE: RELEVANCE OF *HIGH TREES* CASE

The rule of equitable estoppel has relevance in discharge of a contract by performance (*see* p. 194). Although the agreed date of delivery must usually be complied with in a contract of sale, the buyer may waive the condition relating to the date of delivery and accept a later date. Such a waiver may be binding on him whether made with or without consideration. It was held by Lord Denning in *Charles Rickards Ltd* v *Oppenhaim* (1950) (*see* p. 198) that the binding nature of a waiver without consideration might be based on the *High Trees* case (*see* p. 51) (i.e. a promissory estoppel to accept a later delivery date). Alternatively, the seller may rely on s. 11(2) of the Sale of Goods Act 1979 which states: 'Where a contract of sale is subject to any condition to be fulfilled by the seller, the buyer may waive that condition'.

INTENTION TO CREATE LEGAL RELATIONS

The law will not necessarily recognize the existence of a contract enforceable in a court of law simply because of the presence of mutual promises. It is necessary to establish also that both parties made the agreement with the intention of creating legal relations so that if the agreement was broken the party offended would be able to exercise legally enforceable remedies. The subject can be considered under two headings as follows.

Cases where the parties have not expressly denied their intention to create legal relations

Advertisements

Most advertisements are statements of opinion and as such are not actionable. Thus unless the advertisement makes false statements of specific verifiable facts, which is rare, the court will not enforce the claims made for the product on a contractual basis. However, where a company deposits money in the bank against possible claims then the court is likely to hold that legal relations were contemplated (*Carlill* v *Carbolic Smoke Ball Co* (1893)), though a deposit is not essential (*Wood* v *Lectrik Ltd* (1932) – *see* pp. 2 and 3).

Family agreements

Many of these cannot be imagined to be the subject of litigation but some may be.

The question is basically one of construction and the court looks at the words and the surrounding circumstances. The two basic divisions of family agreements are set out below.

(a) *Husband and wife*. With regard to agreements between husband and wife, it is difficult to draw precise conclusions. However, the following situations have appeared in decided cases.

    (i) Where husband and wife were living together in amity when the agreement was made, then the agreement is not enforceable as a contract because legal proceedings are an inappropriate method of settling purely domestic disputes. **The following case illustrates this**.

Balfour v Balfour [1919] 2 KB 571

The defendant was a civil servant stationed in what was then called Ceylon (now Sri Lanka). In November 1915, he came to England on leave with his wife, the plaintiff in the present action. In August 1916, the defendant returned alone to Ceylon because his wife's doctor had advised her that her health would not stand up to a further period of service abroad. Later the husband wrote to his wife suggesting that they should remain apart, and in 1918 the plaintiff obtained a decree nisi. In this case the plaintiff alleged that before her husband sailed for Ceylon he had agreed, in consultation with her, that he would give her £30 per month as maintenance, and she now sued because of his failure to abide by the said agreement. The Court of Appeal *held* that there was no enforceable contract because the parties did not intend to create legal relations. The provision for a flat payment of £30 per month for an indefinite period with no attempt to take into account changes in the circumstances of the parties did not suggest a binding agreement. Duke LJ seems to have based his decision on the fact that the wife had not supplied any consideration.

    (ii) Where husband and wife were living together but not in amity or were separated altogether when the agreement was made, the court may enforce it. **The following illustration from case law shows this.**

Merritt v Merritt [1970] 2 All ER 760

After a husband had formed an attachment for another woman and had left his wife a meeting was held between the parties on 25 May 1966, in the husband's car. The husband agreed to pay the wife £40 per month maintenance and also wrote out and signed a document stating that in consideration of the wife paying all charges in connection with the matrimonial home until the mortgage repayments had been completed, he would agree to transfer the property to her sole ownership. The wife took the document away with her and in the following months paid off the mortgage. The husband did not subsequently transfer the property to his wife and she claimed a declaration that she was the sole beneficial owner and asked for an order that her husband should transfer the property to her forthwith. The husband's defence was that the agreement was a family arrangement not intended to create legal relations. *Held* – by the Court of Appeal – (a) that the agreement, having been made when the parties were not living together in amity, was enforceable (*Balfour* v *Balfour* (1919) *above* distinguished); and (b) that the contention that there was no consideration to support the husband's promise could not be sustained. The payment of the balance of the mortgage was a detriment to the wife and the husband had received the benefit of being relieved of liability to the building society; (c) therefore the wife was entitled to the relief claimed.

> (iii) If the words used by the parties are uncertain, then the agreement will not be enforced, the uncertainty leading to the conclusion that there was no intention to create legal relations. Thus in *Gould* v *Gould* [1969] 3 All ER 728 a contractual intention was negatived where a husband on leaving his wife undertook to pay her £15 per week 'so long as I can manage it'. The uncertainty of this term ruled out a legally binding agreement.

Agreements of a non-domestic nature made between husband and wife are enforceable, e.g. in *Pearce* v *Merriman* [1904] 1 KB 80 it was held that a husband may be his wife's tenant and as such could be made to pay the rent.

> (b) *Other family and personal relationships*. The question of intention to create legal relations arises for consideration here as well but it seems that the less close the relationship between the parties the more likely it is that the court *will presume* that legal relations were intended. **The following case is an illustration of this point**.

Simpkins v Pays [1955] 3 All ER 10

The defendant and the defendant's grand-daughter made an agreement with the plaintiff, who was a paying boarder, that they should submit in the defendant's name a weekly coupon, containing a forecast by each of them, to a Sunday newspaper fashion competition. On one occasion a forecast by the grand-daughter was correct and the defendant received a prize of £750. The plaintiff sued for her share of that sum. The defence was that there was no intention to create legal relations but that the transaction was a friendly arrangement binding in honour only. *Held* – There was an intention to create legal relations. Far from being a friendly domestic arrangement, the evidence showed that it was a joint enterprise and that the parties expected to share any prize that was won.

Comment: A family agreement which went the other way was *Julian* v *Furby* (1982) 132 NLJ 64. J was an experienced plasterer who helped F, his son-in-law, and his wife (J's favourite daughter) to buy, alter and finish a house for them. They later quarrelled and J. sued for £4,440. This included materials supplied and F was prepared to pay for these but not for J's labour which, it was understood, would be free. It was *held* by the Court of Appeal that there was never an intention to create a legal relationship between the parties in regard to labour which J and F jointly provided in refurbishing the house.

> However, in these cases also *uncertainty* as to the terms of the agreement normally leads to the conclusion that there was no contractual intention. **The following case shows this**.

Jones v Padavatton [1969] 2 All ER 616

In 1962 the plaintiff, Mrs Jones, who lived in Trinidad, made an offer to the defendant, Mrs Padavatton, her daughter, to provide maintenance for her at the rate of £42 a month if she would leave her job in Washington in the United States and go to England and read for the Bar. Mrs Padavatton was at that time divorced from her husband, having the custody of the child of that marriage. The agreement was an informal one and there was uncertainty as to its exact terms. Nevertheless the daughter came to England in November 1962, bringing the child with her, and began to read for the Bar, her fees and maintenance being paid for by Mrs Jones. In 1964 it appeared that the daughter was experiencing some discomfort in England, occupying one room in Acton for which she had to pay £6 17s 6d per week. At this stage Mrs Jones offered to buy a large house in London to be occupied by the daughter and partly by tenants, the income from rents to go to the daughter in lieu of maintenance. Again there was no written agreement but the house was purchased for £6,000 and conveyed to Mrs Jones. The daughter moved into the house in January 1965, and tenants arrived, it still being uncertain what precisely was to happen to the surplus rent income (if any) and what rooms the daughter was to occupy. No money from the rents was received by Mrs Jones and no accounts were submitted to her. In 1967 Mrs Jones claimed possession of the house from her daughter, who had by that time married again, and the daughter counter-claimed for £1,655 18s 9d, said to been paid in connection with running the house. At the hearing the daughter still had, as the examinations were then structured, one subject to pass in Part I and also the whole of Part II remained to be taken. *Held* – by the Court of Appeal:

(a) That the arrangements were throughout family agreements depending upon the good faith of the parties in keeping promises made and not intended to be rigid binding agreements. Furthermore, the arrangements were far too vague and uncertain to be enforceable as contracts. (Per Danckwerts and Fenton Atkinson L JJ.)

(b) That although the agreement to maintain while reading for the Bar might have been regarded as creating a legal obligation in the mother to pay (the terms being sufficiently stated and duration for a reasonable time being implied), the daughter could not claim anything in respect of that agreement which must be regarded as having terminated in 1967, five years being a reasonable time in which to complete studies for the Bar. The arrangements in relation to the home were very vague and must be regarded as made without contractual intent. (Per Salmon LJ.)

The mother was therefore entitled to possession of the house and had no liability under the maintenance agreement. The counter-claim by the daughter was left to be settled by the parties.

Other cases

There may well be other areas where intention to create legal relations is doubtful but which have not been the subject of cases in court. Again, the matter is one of fact for the court. However, in the case of clubs and societies many of the relationships which exist and promises which are made are enforceable only as moral obligations.

They are merely *social agreements*. For example, the decision in *Lens* v *Devonshire Club The Times*, 4 December 1914, would suggest that if a person competes for a prize at a local golf club and is the winner, he or she may not be able to sue for the prize which has been won if it is not otherwise forthcoming.

However, in *Peck* v *Lateu The Times*, 18 January 1973, two ladies attended bingo sessions together and had an arrangement to pool their winnings. One of them won an additional 'Bonanza' prize of £1,107 and claimed it was not covered by the sharing arrangements. Pennycuick VC *held* – that there was an intention to create legal relations and to share all prizes won. The plaintiff was entitled to a share in the prize.

It should also be borne in mind that quotations and estimates may be passed from one person to another without any intention that they should be legally binding *at that stage*.

Cases where the parties expressly deny any intention to create legal relations

By contrast with family arrangements, agreements of a commercial nature are *presumed* to be made with contractual intent. Furthermore, the test applied by the court is an *objective* one so that a person cannot escape liability simply because *he did not* have a contractual intention. The presumption is a strong one and it was held in *Edwards* v *Skyways Ltd* [1964] 1 All ER 494 that the use of the words *ex gratia* in regard to an airline pilot's contractual redundancy payment did not displace the presumption, so that the airline had to make the payments and did not have a discretion whether to make them or not.

However, the Court of Appeal has held more recently that a court need not necessarily presume intention to create legal relations just because the parties are in business.

Kleinwort Benson Ltd v Malaysian Mining Corporation, Berhand [1989] 1 All ER 785

In this case the High Court had decided that a letter of comfort (as they are called) stating that it was the policy of Malaysian Mining to ensure that its subsidiary MMC Metals Ltd was 'at all times in a position to meet its liabilities' in regard to a loan made by Kleinworts to MMC had contractual effect. This meant that Kleinworts was entitled to recover from Malaysian the amount owed to it by the insolvent MMC, which went into liquidation after the tin market collapsed in 1985. Malaysian appealed to the Court of Appeal which reversed the High Court ruling. The problem has always been to decide whether a letter of comfort of the usual kind contains a legal obligation or only a moral one. In the High Court Mr Justice Hirst decided that there was a legal obligation: the Court of Appeal decided that it was only a moral one. The letter, said the Court of Appeal, stated the policy of Malaysian. It gave no contractual warranty as to the company's future conduct. In these circumstances there was no need to apply the presumption of an intention to create legal relations just because the transaction was in the course of business as laid down in *Edwards* v *Skyways* [1964] (*above*).

Comment: The wording of the letter of comfort must be looked at and if it appears to create a moral obligation only, then it has no contractual force. It is of course no bad thing for those in business to honour moral obligations but as Lord Justice Ralph Gibson said, moral responsibilities are not a matter for the courts.

Some agreements where the court would normally assume an intention to create legal relations may be expressly taken outside the scope of the law by the parties agreeing to rely on each other's honour. This is a practice which appears to be allowable to pools companies who are especially subject to fraudulent entries but should not be allowed to spread into other areas of *standardized* contracts, i.e. contracts where the consumer has no choice of supplier as where he requires electrical services laid on which can only be provided by a state corporation.

There is no such objection where businessmen reach agreements at arm's length, and if the parties expressly declare, or clearly indicate, that they do not wish to assume contractual obligations, then the law accepts and implements their decision.

The following cases illustrate these points.

Jones v Vernon's Pools Ltd [1938] 2 All ER 626

The plaintiff said that he had sent to the defendants a football coupon on which the penny points pool was all correct. The defendants denied having received it and relied on a clause printed on every coupon. The clause provided that the transaction should not 'give rise to any legal relationship . . . or be legally enforceable . . . but . . . binding in honour only'. *Held –* that this clause was a bar to any action in a court of law.

Comment: This case was followed by the Court of Appeal in *Appleson* v *Littlewood Ltd* [1939] 1 All ER 464 where the contract contained a similar clause.

Rose and Frank Co v Crompton (J R) & Brothers Ltd [1925] AC 445

In 1913 the plaintiffs, an American firm, entered into an agreement with the defendants, an English company, whereby the plaintiffs were appointed sole agents for the sale in the USA of paper tissues supplied by the defendants. The contract was for a period of three years with an option to extend that time. The agreement was extended to March 1920, but in 1919 the defendants terminated it without notice. The defendants had received a number of orders for tissues before the termination of the contract, and they refused to execute them. The plaintiffs sued for breach of contract and for non-delivery of the goods actually ordered. The agreement of 1913 contained an 'Honourable Pledge Clause' drafted as follows: 'This arrangement is not entered into nor is this memorandum written as a formal or legal agreement and shall not be subject to legal jurisdiction in the courts of the United States of America or England . . . 'Held – by the House of Lords – that the 1913 agreement was not binding on the parties, but that in so far as the agreement had been acted upon by the defendants' acceptance of orders, those orders were binding contracts of sale. Nevertheless the agreement was not binding for the future.

Statutory provisions

Sometimes an Act of Parliament renders an agreement unenforceable. Thus under s. 1 of the Law Reform (Miscellaneous Provisions) Act 1970, a contract of engagement, which is, in effect, an agreement to marry, is not enforceable at law since there is a statutory presumption that there was no intention to create legal relations. Thus actions for breach of promise are no longer possible.

In addition, under s. 29 of the Post Office Act 1969, the acceptance of ordinary letters and packets for transmission does not give rise to a contract between the post office and the sender.

Finally, under s. 18 of the Trade Union and Labour Relations Act 1974, collective agreements between trade unions and employers (or employers' associations) concerning industrial conditions such as hours, wages, holidays, procedures in disputes and so on, are presumed *not* to be intended to be legally enforceable unless they are in writing and contain a provision to that effect.

GRADED QUESTIONS

Essay mode

1. (a) It is often said that although consideration need not be 'adequate' it must be 'legally sufficient'. Explain and illustrate this statement.

   (b) The employees of Machine Tools Ltd have been called out on an unofficial strike during a period in which the firm has a major export order to fulfil. Their contracts contain a 'no-strike' clause under which they have undertaken to submit disputes to arbitration. Cecil, who is in no way connected with Machine Tools Ltd and who is a member of the 'Break the Unions' campaign, offers to pay the employees an additional £20 per week if they return to work immediately. The employees do so and complete the order on time. Cecil later refuses to pay.

   Advise the employees as to whether they are entitled to the promised sum.
   (Institute of Chartered Secretaries and Administrators. English Business Law. June 1989)

2. The many exceptions to the doctrine of privity of contract suggest that the doctrine is unpopular, inconvenient and should be abolished.'
Discuss.
   (The Institute of Legal Executives. Part II: Law of Contract. June 1990)

3. Three sisters, Mary, Jane and Susan, agree to form a syndicate for the purpose of making a weekly entry in a football pools competition. Mary and Jane know nothing about football, and they give Susan £1 each weekly, letting her fill in and send off the coupon. Susan always fills it in in her own name. After two months, Susan wins £21,000, which she now refuses to share.

   Advise Mary and Jane.

   (North Staffordshire Polytechnic. BA(Hons) Business Studies)

Objective mode

Four alternative answers are given. Select ONE only. Circle the answer which you consider to be correct. Check your answers by referring back to the information given in the chapter and against the answers at the back of the book.

1. In which of the following situations will the consideration most probably be regarded as being past?

   A An offer of a reward is made by John, and Dinah, having satisfied the conditions of the offer, claims the reward.

   B Norman asks Jack to help him negotiate a partnership agreement. Jack does so successfully. Norman then agrees to pay Jack £1,000 for his assistance.

   C Jim helps his neighbour and friend Julie to lay a lawn. Three days later Julie promises Jim £50 for his work.

   D Hank agrees to deliver some goods which Jake asked for. No price was agreed for the work at the time but afterwards Hank sent an invoice to Jake for £50.

2. Archie is the author of a number of best-selling novels. Bertie is Archie's publisher. Archie is a supporter of a charity called Redpeace which has as its objects the protection of the environment. Archie wanted to add to the funds of Redpeace so he wrote a novel and Bertie published it.

   It was agreed between Archie and Bertie that Redpeace would receive the total royalty of 20p a copy for every book sold.

   The novel has sold one million copies but Bertie refuses to pay anything to Redpeace.

   Which of the following statements is correct?

   A Redpeace can bring a successful action against Bertie and so can Archie.

   B Only Redpeace can bring a successful action against Bertie.

   C Only Archie can bring a successful claim against Bertie.

   D Neither Archie nor Redpeace has any claim against Bertie.

3. In December Mr Smith, who owned a number of unfurnished houses, decided to give his son John a start in his married life by granting him a lease of one of the houses which had recently been vacated by a previous tenant. Under the

agreement John received a lease for two years at a rent of £1 per annum and he and his wife took possession.

Mr Smith died in March of the following year leaving all his houses to his wife Vera and appointing two of the partners in a firm of accountants as his executors. Unfortunately Vera had never approved of her son's marriage and she and John were not on speaking terms. Vera now refuses to honour the agreement made by her husband with John and threatens to bring a court action in order to have John and his wife evicted from the house. She claims that the agreement to pay a rent of only £1 annually was manifestly inadequate and no real consideration at all.

Ignoring matters relating to security of tenure under legislation relating to landlord and tenant which one of the following decisions is the court likely to make if Vera proceeds with her action?

A That John and his wife may continue in possession of the house provided they are prepared to agree an economic rent with Vera.

B That John and his wife must vacate the house immediately.

C That John and his wife must find other accommodation as soon as they can.

D That John and his wife are entitled to remain in the house for the rest of the two year period at the rent agreed with Mr Smith.

4. Lucre, the managing director of a manufacturing company, arranges for a party of overseas buyers to spend the weekend at his country estate in the hope of obtaining export orders for the company. As part of the entertainment Lucre makes a personal agreement with Rodger under which Rodger is to give the guests a two-hour trip in his private plane on the Saturday afternoon. A fee of £500 is agreed by Rodger and the arrangement regarding the air trip is mentioned by Lucre in all the letters of invitation.

On the preceding Thursday Rodger tells Lucre that the fee which has been agreed is not enough and that he will not turn up on the Saturday. Lucre discusses the matter with his sales manager, Sellars, and both agree that it is too late to make other arrangements and that Rodger must somehow be persuaded to carry out the contract.

Later that day Sellars rings Rodger saying 'I will give you £100 of my own money if you agree to show up on Saturday.' Rodger agrees to do so, and Sellars leaves immediately for a weekend business trip to the continent without discussing the matter with Lucre.

On Friday morning Lucre rings Rodger saying 'I think I can afford to pay you a little more. Would an extra £100 be all right?' Rodger replies 'Yes that's enough. See you Saturday.' Rodger turns up on Saturday and carries out a two-hour flight as agreed.

Lucre returns to the office on Monday and in the course of conversation with Sellars learns of the extra payment which Sellars has promised to Rodger. Lucre and Sellars are furious at being treated in this way and Lucre sends Rodger a cheque for £500 with a note saying 'Sellars and I are disgusted by your behaviour in this matter. The enclosed cheque is in final settlement. You will get no more from either of us.'

Two weeks later Lucre and Sellars each receive a letter from Rodger saying that unless he receives £100 from them both he will sue for the money.

Which one of the following statements correctly represents the legal position?

A Only Lucre is liable to pay the extra £100 to Rodger.

B Only Sellars is liable to pay the extra £100 to Rodger.

C Sellars is not bound to pay the extra £100 to Rodger nor is Lucre.

D Lucre and Sellars must both pay £100 to Rodger.

5. Kate had run up a debt on her Sparks and Mencers credit card to the extent of £800, including interest. Sparks and Mencers were threatening Kate with a civil action to recover the amount due. Kate's father Peter wrote to Sparks informing them that Kate was only 19 and out of work and was not likely to be able to pay. He said that he did not like credit being offered to young people but in order to protect Kate's future credit he was enclosing a cheque for £650 in full settlement and if this was not acceptable Sparks could return the cheque. The cheque was duly cleared and Sparks have now sent Kate an account for £150 informing her that interest is accruing at 2.5% per month.

Which of the following statements represents the legal position?

A This is a case of promissory estoppel: by accepting part payment Sparks are estopped from insisting on their right to the balance owing.

B Part payment of a debt does not discharge the debt. Payment by Peter is no different from payment by Kate.

C Peter's offer to pay £650 is made by a third party; by cashing his cheque Sparks accepted his offer and can not sue for the balance.

D Silence cannot be imposed as a condition of acceptance. Sparks have not accepted Peter's offer and can sue for the balance of £150.

6. On 1 October Mr Golightly, the office manager of Twitchett Ltd, was authorized to purchase a calculating machine for the accounts department. On 5 October he saw Sharp, a sales representative of Addom Ltd, who manufactured what Mr Golightly regarded as a suitable machine. After some discussion Mr Golightly selected an Addom Mark I and delivery was arranged for 1 November.

On 12 October Sharp rang Mr Golightly and said 'We have just received an export order for 100 Addom Mark II machines. This is an important order for us and I wondered whether you would be prepared to accept delivery of your machine on 1 December. I am asking a number of people who have placed small orders to help our production side out in this way.' Mr Golightly agreed to delivery on 1 December 1978.

On 12 November Mr Golightly attended a sale of office machinery and bought a second-hand Addom Mark I for his company. On the same day he rang Sharp saying 'I have bought a good second-hand machine and shall not require the new one. I am very sorry about this but it is your fault in a way because you could not deliver on time.' Sharp replied: 'But you agreed to take delivery later. I am afraid that we altered our production arrangements on the strength of promises from customers like yourself and we shall sue you for damages if you do not accept the machine.' Mr Golightly replied: 'But you gave us nothing for that promise so we are not bound to accept.'

The machine was delivered on 1 December, but was returned by Mr Golightly. Which of the following statements correctly represents the legal position?

A Twitchett Ltd are entitled to reject the machine because Addom Ltd were in breach of contract and Twitchett's waiver requires consideration.

B Twitchett are entitled to reject the machine: time of delivery is of the essence of the contract and cannot be waived.

C Twitchett are not entitled to reject the machine. They have waived Addom's breach and the waiver does not require consideration.

D Twitchett are not entitled to reject the machine because they were in breach themselves by buying a second-hand machine.

7. In domestic agreements there is:

A A rebuttable presumption that there is an intention to create legal relations.

B An irrebuttable presumption that there is no intention to create legal relations.

C A rebuttable presumption that there is no intention to create legal relations.

D No presumption either way.

8. Harold has promised to pay his wife Jane £100 a month. In which one of the following cases will the promise not be enforceable by Jane?

A It was intended as extra housekeeping money.

B Jane and Harold's marriage having broken down, it was part of a separation agreement between them.

C It was intended as payment for the typing by Jane of a series of articles by Harold for a magazine.

D It was the rent for an office which Harold leases from Jane.

Answers to questions set in objective mode appear on p. 551.

3 | The law of contract – making the contract III

The OBJECTIVES of this chapter are to conclude the study of those elements of contract law which go to making a *mere agreement* into *a binding contract*. *Formalities (or the need for writing)* and the requirement that the parties should have *capacity in law* to make the contract are considered here.

FORMALITIES

In most cases a contract made orally (or by parol, which is an alternative expression) is usually just as effective as a written one. Exceptionally, however, written formalities are required as follows.

Contracts which must be made by deed

A lease of more than three years should be made by deed otherwise no legal estate is created (*see* s. 52 and s. 54, Law of Property Act 1925). If there is no deed then there is in equity a contract for a lease. This is an estate contract under s. 2(3), Law of Property Act 1925. It is enforceable against third parties who acquire the freehold from the landlord only if it has been registered at the Land Registry. Registration gives notice to the whole world. Failure to register makes the contract void against a later purchaser of the freehold from the landlord for a consideration, even though in fact the purchaser *knows* the lease exists (s. 199(1), Law of Property Act 1925). The purchaser could turn out the tenant if the lease was not registered. However, where it is registered the tenant is protected.

As regards the form of a deed the Law of Property (Miscellaneous Provisions) Act 1989 is now relevant. Section 1 requires, as before, that a deed must be in writing but gets rid of the requirement for sealing where a deed is entered into by an individual. Instead the signature of the individual making the deed must be witnessed and attested. There is no longer any need for the little red wafer! Attestation consists of a statement that the deed has been signed in the presence of the witness.

The section also provides that it must be made clear on the face of the document that it is intended to be a deed. How can this be done? The usual form to satisfy this requirement and attestation is: 'signed as a deed by *xy* in the presence of *ab*'.

As far as companies are concerned s. 36A of the Companies Act 1985 provides that while a company may continue to execute documents by affixing its common seal it need not have such a seal. Any document signed by a director and the secretary of the company or by two directors and said to be executed by the company will be regarded as if the seal had been affixed. If the document is intended to be a deed then this must be made clear on the face of the document and it will then be a deed on delivery, which is presumed, in the absence of a contrary intention, to occur when it is signed.

Contracts which must be in writing

For example, the following simple contracts are required by statute to be in writing otherwise they are affected in various ways:

(a) Regulated consumer credit agreements, including hire-purchase agreements, under which the amount of credit does not exceed £15,000 and the customer is not a company (Consumer Credit Act 1974, s. 61). If these agreements are not in appropriate written form they cannot be enforced by the dealer, unless the court thinks it is fair in the circumstances to allow him to enforce the contract (*see further* p. 347).

(b) Contracts of marine insurance, which must be embodied in a written policy otherwise the contract is not effective, being inadmissible in evidence unless embodied in a written policy signed on behalf of the insurer (Marine Insurance Act 1906, s. 22).

(c) Contracts for the sale or other disposition of land are required by statute to be in writing otherwise they are invalid, i.e. there is no contract. Section 2(1) of the Law of Property (Miscellaneous Provisions) Act 1989 provides that a contract for the sale or other disposition of an interest in land can only be made in writing and only by incorporating all the terms which the parties have expressly agreed in one document or, where contracts are exchanged, in each contract. The document must be signed by each party.

There are some exceptions to the above requirements as follows:
(i) leases for *less* than three years where the tenant takes possession can be granted orally;
(ii) sales at public auctions are excluded and the contract is regarded as made when the auctioneer's hammer falls. There is thus no requirement of writing at all at auction sales.

Since the document must now contain all the terms agreed by the parties and be signed by both parties solicitors and conveyancers are no longer at risk that pre-contract correspondence signed by only one party might amount to a contract itself as was a possibility before. The practice of heading correspondence 'subject to contract' can now be brought to an end.

Contracts which must be evidenced in writing

Here we are concerned with contracts of guarantee where the Statute of Frauds 1677 requires writing which, though not essential to the formation of the contract, is needed as evidence if a dispute about it comes before a court. The court will not enforce the guarantee in the absence of written evidence.

The provision in the Statute of Frauds applies to guarantees and not to indemnities. It is therefore necessary to distinguish between these two. In a contract of indemnity the person giving the indemnity makes himself primarily liable by using such words as 'I will see that you are paid'.

In a contract of guarantee the guarantor expects the person he has guaranteed to carry out his obligations and the substance of the wording would be: 'If he does not pay you, I will'. An indemnity does not require writing because it does not come within the Statute of Frauds: a guarantee requires a memorandum.

An additional distinction is that it is an essential feature of a guarantee that the person giving it is totally unconnected with the contract except by reason of his promise to pay the debt. Thus a *del credere* agent who, for an extra commission, promises to make good losses incurred by his principal in respect of the unpaid debts of third parties introduced by the agent, may use the guarantee form 'if they do not pay you I will' but no writing is required. Such a promise is enforceable even if made orally because even where a person does promise to be liable for the debt of another that promise is not within the Statute of Frauds where it is, as here, an incident of a wider transaction, i.e. agency.

The following case illustrates the distinction between guarantees and indemnities.

Mountstephen v Lakeman (1871) LR 7 QB 196

The defendant was chairman of the Brixham Local Board of Health. The plaintiff, who was a builder and contractor, was employed in 1866 by the Board to construct certain main sewage works in the town. On 19 March 1866, notice was given by the Board to owners of certain homes to connect their house drains with the main sewer within 21 days. Before the expiration of the 21 days Robert Adams, the surveyor of the Board, suggested to the plaintiff that he should make the connection. The plaintiff said he was willing to do the work if he would see him paid. On 5 April 1866, i.e. before the expiration of the 21 days, the plaintiff commenced work on the connections. However, before work commenced it appeared that the plaintiff had had an interview with the defendant at which the following conversation took place:

Defendant: 'What objection have you to making the connections?'

Plaintiff: 'I have none, if you or the Board will order the work or become responsible for the payment.'

Defendant: 'Go on Mountstephen and do the work and I will see you paid.'

The plaintiff completed the connections in April and May 1866, and sent an account to the Board on 5 December 1866. The Board disclaimed responsibility on the ground that they never entered into any agreement with the plaintiff nor authorized any officer of the Board to agree with him for the performance of the work in question. *Held* – that Lakeman had undertaken a personal liability to pay the plaintiff and had not given a guarantee of the liability to pay the plaintiff and had not given a guarantee of the liability of a third party, i.e. the Board. In consequence Lakeman had given an indemnity which did not need to be in writing under s. 4 of the Statute of Frauds. The plaintiff was therefore entitled to enforce the oral undertaking given by the defendant.

Comment: Section 4 of the Statute of Frauds 1677 provides that 'No action shall be brought ... whereby to charge the defendant upon any special promise to answer for the debt default or miscarriage of another person ... unless the agreement upon which such action shall be brought or some memorandum or note thereof shall be in writing and signed by the party to be charged therewith or some other person thereunto by him lawfully authorized'. It was held in *Birkmyr* v *Darnell* (1805) 1 Salk 27 that the words 'debt default or miscarriage of *another person*' meant that the section applied only where there was some person other than the surety who was primarily liable.

The memorandum in writing to satisfy the court need not exist when the contract is made but must be in existence when an action, if any, is brought for breach of the guarantee. A guarantee cannot be proved orally – writing is required as evidence. The memorandum must identify the parties, normally by containing their names. The material terms must be included, e.g. that it is a guarantee of a bank overdraft facility limited to £50,000. The memorandum must also contain the signature of the party to be charged or his agent properly authorized to sign. However, the law is not strict on this point and initials or a printed signature will do. The 'party to be charged' is the proposed defendant and there may be cases where one party has a sufficient memorandum to commence an action whereas the other may not since the memorandum does not contain the other party's signature. This could happen where the memorandum was in a letter written by Bloggs to Snooks. The letter would presumably be signed by Bloggs but not by Snooks. It would therefore be a good memorandum for an action by Snooks but not by Bloggs. Section 3 of the Mercantile Law Amendment Act 1856 dispenses with the need to set out the consideration in the memorandum but it must exist. It is normally the extension of credit by A to B in consideration of C's guarantee of B's liability if B fails to pay.

CAPACITY TO CONTRACT

Adult citizens have full capacity to enter into any kind of contract but certain groups of persons and corporations have certain disabilities in this connection. The most important groups for our purposes are dealt with below.

MINORS

The Family Law Reform Act 1969, s. 1, reduced the age of majority from 21 to 18 years. Contracts made by minors were governed by the common law (including parts of sale of goods legislation) as amended by the Infants Relief Act 1874 and the Betting and Loans (Infants) Act 1892. The Minors' Contracts Act 1987 repealed the relevant parts of the 1874 and 1892 Acts so that minors' contracts are now governed by the rules of common law (including the Sale of Goods Act 1979) as amended by the Minors' Contracts Act 1987.

Valid contracts

These are as follows:

(a) *Executed contracts for necessaries.* These are defined in s. 3(3) of the Sale of Goods Act 1979 as 'Goods suitable to the condition in life of the minor and to his actual requirements at the time of sale and delivery.' If the goods are deemed necessaries the minor may be compelled to pay a reasonable price which will usually, but not necessarily be, the contract price. The minor is not liable if the goods, though necessaries, have not been delivered. This, together with the fact that he is only required to pay a reasonable price, illustrates that a minor's liability for necessaries is only quasi-contractual.

If the goods (or services) have a utility value, such as clothing, and are not merely things of luxury, e.g. a diamond tiara, then they are basically necessaries. Whether the minor will have to pay a reasonable price for them then depends upon:

   (i) the minor's income which goes with his condition in life. If he is wealthy then quite expensive goods and services may be necessaries for him provided they are useful;

   (ii) the supply of goods which the minor already has is also relevant. If the minor is well supplied with the particular articles then they will not be necessaries even though they are useful and are well within his income.

All of these points are neatly illustrated by the following case.

Nash v Inman [1908] 2 KB 1

The plaintiff was a Savile Row tailor and the defendant was a minor undergraduate at Trinity College, Cambridge. The plaintiff sent his agent to Cambridge because he had heard that the defendant was spending money freely, and might be the sort of person who would be interested in high-class clothing. As a result of the agent's visit, the plaintiff supplied the defendant with various articles of clothing to the value of £145 0s 3d during the period October 1902 to June 1903. The clothes included 11 fancy waistcoats. The plaintiff now sued the minor for the price of the clothes. Evidence showed that the defendant's father was in a good position, being an architect with a town and country house, and it could be said that the clothes supplied were suitable to the defendant's position in life. However, his father proved that the defendant was amply supplied with such clothes when the plaintiff delivered the clothing now in question. *Held* – The plaintiff's claim failed because he had not established that the goods supplied were necessaries.

(b) *Contracts for the minor's benefit*. These include contracts of service, appren–ticeship and education.
The following case illustrates this.

Roberts v Gray [1913] 1 KB 520

The defendant wished to become a professional billiards player and entered into an agreement with the plaintiff, a leading professional, to go on a joint tour. The plaintiff went to some trouble in order to organize the tour, but a dispute arose between the parties and the defendant refused to go. The plaintiff now sued for damages of £6,000. *Held* – The contract was for the minor's benefit, being in effect for his instruction as a billiards player. Therefore the plaintiff could sustain an action for damages for breach of contract, and damages of £1,500 were awarded.

However, trading contracts of minors are not enforceable no matter how beneficial they may be to the minor's trade or business. The theory behind this rule is that when a minor is in trade his capital is at risk and he might lose it, whereas in a contract of service there is no likelihood of capital loss.
The following case provides an example of this rule.

Mercantile Union Guarantee Corporation v Ball [1937] 2 KB 498

The purchase on hire-purchase terms of a motor lorry by a minor carrying on business as a haulage contractor was *held* not to be a contract for necessaries or for the minor's benefit, but a trading contract by which the minor could not be bound.

Comment: It would be possible for the owner to recover the lorry, without the assistance of s. 3 of the Minors' Contracts Act 1987 (*see below*), because a hire-purchase contract is a contract of bailment not a sale. Thus ownership does not pass when the goods are delivered.

Contracts not binding unless ratified

These are as follows:
(a) *Loans*. These are not binding on the minor unless he ratifies the contract of loan

after reaching 18 which he may now legally do. No fresh consideration is now required on ratification.

(b) *Contracts for non-necessary goods.* Again, these are not binding on the minor unless he ratifies the contract after reaching 18 as he may now legally do. Once again, no fresh consideration is required on ratification.

It should be noted that in spite of the fact that the contracts in (a) and (b) above are not enforceable against the minor, he gets a title to any property which passes to him under the arrangement and can give a good title to a third party as where, for example, he sells non-necessary goods on to someone else (who takes in good faith and for value). This was decided in *Stocks* v *Wilson* [1913] 2 KB 235. Furthermore, any money or property transferred by the minor under the contract can only be recovered by him if there has been a total failure of consideration (*see below*).

Contracts binding unless repudiated

These are usually contracts by which the minor acquires an interest of a permanent nature in the subject-matter of the contract. Such contracts bind the minor unless he takes active steps to avoid them, either during his minority or within a reasonable time thereafter. Examples of voidable contracts are shares in companies, leases of property and partnerships.

The following case material illustrates these points.

Steinberg v Scala (Leeds) Ltd [1923] 2 Ch 452

The plaintiff, Miss Steinberg, purchased shares in the defendant company and paid certain sums of money on application, on allotment and on one call. Being unable to meet future calls, she repudiated the contract whilst still a minor and claimed:

(a) rectification of the Register of Members to remove her name therefrom, thus relieving her from liability on future calls; and

(b) the recovery of the money already paid.

The company agreed to rectify the register but was not prepared to return the money paid.

Held – The claim under (b) above failed because there had not been total failure of consideration. The shares had some value and gave some rights, even though the plaintiff had not received any dividends and the shares had always stood at a discount on the market.

Comment: In *Davies* v *Beynon-Harris* (1931) 47 TLR 424 a minor was allowed to avoid a lease of a flat without liability for future rent or damages but was not allowed to recover rent paid. However, in *Goode* v *Harrison* (1821) 5 B & Ald 147 a partner who was a minor took no steps to avoid the partnership contract while a minor or afterwards. He was held liable for the debts of the firm incurred after he came of age.

CONSEQUENCES OF THE DEFECTIVE CONTRACTS OF MINORS

We must now have a look at what happens where there has been some performance of a contract with a minor which is either not binding unless ratified or binding unless repudiated.

Recovery by minor of money paid

Where a minor has paid money under these defective contracts he cannot recover it unless total failure of consideration can be proved, i.e. that the minor has not received any benefit at all under the contract. The court is reluctant to say that no benefit has been received. This can be seen in the context of a contract not binding unless ratified in *Pearce* v *Brain* (*see below*) and in the context of a contract binding unless repudiated in *Steinberg* v *Scala* (*see above*).

Pearce v Brain [1929] 2 KB 310

Pearce, a minor, exchanged his motor cycle for a motor car belonging to Brain. The minor had little use out of the car, and had in fact driven it only a short distance when it broke down because of serious defects in the back axle. Pearce now sued to recover his motor cycle, claiming that the consideration had wholly failed. *Held* – (a) That a contract for the exchange of goods, whilst not a sale of goods, is a contract for the supply of goods, and that if the goods are not necessaries, the contract is voidable (type A) if with a minor. (b) The car was not a necessary good; the court considered that the minor had received a benefit under the contract, albeit small, and that he could not recover the motor cycle, i.e. the consideration had not wholly failed.

  Comment: In *Corpe* v *Overton* (1833) 10 Bing 252 a minor agreed to enter into a partnership and deposited £100 with the defendant as security for the due performance of the contract. The minor rescinded the contract before the partnership came into being. *Held* – he could recover the £100 because he had received no benefit, having never been a partner. There had been total failure of consideration.

Effect of purchase by minor of non-necessary goods

As we have seen, the minor acquires a title to the goods and can give a good title to a third party who takes them bona fide and for value (*Stocks* v *Wilson* [1913] 2 KB 235). The tradesman who sold the goods to the minor cannot recover them from the third party.

  However, as regards recovery from the minor, if he still has the property, s. 3 of the Minors' Contracts Act 1987 provides that the court can order restitution, for example, of non-necessary goods to the tradesman, where the minor is refusing to pay for them. As we know, he cannot be sued for the price.

The question of recovery in any particular case is left to the court which must regard it as just and equitable to allow recovery, though a restitution order can be made whether the minor is fraudulent, as where he obtained the goods by overstating his age, *or not*. Fraud is no longer a requirement for restitution. Money will be virtually impossible to recover because it will normally be mixed with other funds and not identifiable. However, the minor could be made under s. 3 to offer up any goods acquired in exchange for the non-necessary goods. The tradesman recovers the goods in the state he finds them and cannot ask for compensation from the minor if they are, for example, damaged.

Thus if Ann, a minor, buys a gold necklace and does not pay for it the seller can recover the necklace from Ann. If Ann exchanges the necklace for a gold bangle the seller can recover the gold bangle from Ann. If Ann sells the necklace for £500 it is not clear whether the seller can get restitution of the money unless it has been kept separate from Ann's other funds or can be identified in a fund containing other money of Ann's, for example, a bank account into which she has paid her salary. Section 3 says that the seller can recover the article passing under the contract 'or any property representing it'. It is at least arguable that Ann's general funds do not solely represent the necklace in the way that the bangle does. Judicial interpretation is required.

Guarantees

Section 2 of the Minors' Contracts Act 1987 provides that a guarantee by an adult of a minor's transaction shall be enforceable against the guarantor even though the main contractual obligation is not enforceable against the minor. Thus if a bank makes a loan to a minor or allows a minor an overdraft and an adult gives a guarantee of that transaction, then although the loan or overdraft cannot be enforced against the minor, the adult guarantor can be required to pay.

MENTAL DISORDER AND DRUNKENNESS

Where the property and affairs of a mental patient are placed under the management of the court by order under Part VII of the Mental Health Act 1983, the mental patient has no capacity to contract as regards that property. However, the other party is bound should the patient's representatives wish to regard him as bound.

Apart from the above, the position is governed by the common law as follows:

(a) A contract made by a person who by reason of mental disease or drunkenness is incapable of understanding what he is doing is valid unless he can prove:
   (i) that he did not understand the nature of the contract; and
   (ii) that the other party knew this to be the case.

(b) A contract made by such a person is binding on him if he afterwards ratifies it at any time when the state of his mind is such that he can understand what he is doing.
(c) Where necessaries are sold and delivered to a person who by reason of mental incapacity or drunkenness is incompetent to contract, he is bound to pay a reasonable price (Sale of Goods Act 1979, s. 3(2)).
(d) Necessaries are 'goods suitable to the condition in life of such person and to his actual requirements at the time of the sale and delivery' (s. 3(3), 1979 Act). Therefore the principle of 'necessaries' is applied to persons with mental incapacity and drunkards in the same way as it is to minors.

The following cases illustrate the rules set out above.

Imperial Loan Co v Stone [1892] QB 599

This was an action on a promissory note. The defendant pleaded that at the time of making the note he was insane and that the plaintiff knew he was. The jury found that he was in fact insane but could not agree on the question of whether the plaintiff knew it. The judge entered judgment for the defendant. *Held* – that he was wrong. The defendant in order to succeed must convince the court on both issues.

Comment: In *Hart* v *O'Connor* [1985] 2 All ER 880 the Privy Council refused to set aside an agreement to sell farmland in New Zealand because although the seller was of unsound mind, his affliction was not apparent. The price paid was not unreasonable. If it had been the Privy Council said that the contract could have been set aside for equitable fraud as an unconscionable bargain.

Matthews v Baxter (1873) LR 8 Exch 132

Matthews agreed to buy houses from Baxter. He was so drunk as not to know what he was doing. Afterwards, when sober, he ratified and confirmed the contract. It was *held* that both parties were bound by it.

Comment: A contract with a drunken person must in effect always be voidable by him because presumably the fact that he is drunk will be known to the other party. This is not so in regard to unsoundness of mind which might not be known to the other party.

CORPORATIONS

Regardless of the method by which it is formed, a company on incorporation becomes a *legal person*, acquires an identity quite separate and distinct from its members, and carries on its activities through agents. **The following case is a classic example of what is known as the corporate entity theory.**

Salomon v Salomon & Co [1897] AC 22

Salomon carried on business as a leather merchant and boot manufacturer. In 1892 he formed a limited company to take over the business. The memorandum of association was signed by Salomon, his wife, daughter and four sons. Each subscribed for one share. The company paid £39,000 to Salomon for the business and mode of payment was to give Salomon £10,000 in debentures, secured by a floating charge, 20,000 shares of £1 each and £9,000 in cash. The company fell on hard times and a liquidator was appointed. The debts of the unsecured creditors amounted to nearly £8,000, and the company's assets were approximately £6,000. The unsecured creditors claimed all the remaining assets on the ground that the company was a mere alias or agent for Salomon. *Held* – The company was a separate and distinct person. The debentures were perfectly valid and therefore Salomon was entitled to the remaining assets in part payment of the secured debentures held by him.

The *ultra vires* rule – generally

As regards powers, charter corporations have the same powers as ordinary persons and may act legally even though the transaction concerned is not provided for in the charter. However, if a charter corporation does act beyond its powers the Crown may forfeit the charter or a member of the corporation may ask the court to restrain it by injunction from doing acts which are *ultra vires* (i.e. beyond its powers).

The following case is an illustration of a member's injunction to prevent a charter corporation from acting *ultra vires*. A member of a registered company has the same right. However, if a statutory corporation such as British Coal were to act *ultra vires* the Attorney-General would have to ask the court for an injunction on behalf of the public, since these statutory corporations are public corporations and no individual member of the public is able to complain to the court about them. The Attorney-General must do it on behalf of us all.

Jenkin v Pharmaceutical Society [1921] 1 Ch 392

The defendant society was incorporated by Royal Charter in 1843 for the purpose of advancing chemistry and pharmacy and promoting a uniform system of education of those who should practise the same, and also for the protection of those who carried on the business of chemists and druggists. *Held* – The expenditure of the funds of the society in the formation of an industrial committee, to attempt to regulate hours of work and wages and conditions of work between employer and employee members of the society, was *ultra vires* the charter, because it was a trade union activity which was not contemplated by the Charter of 1843. Further, the expenditure of money on an insurance scheme for members was also not within the powers given in the charter, for it amounted to converting the defendant society into an insurance company. The plaintiff, a member of the society, was entitled to an injunction to restrain the society from implementing the above schemes.

Ultra vires rule – statutory and registered companies

The powers of statutory corporations are contained in the statute setting them up and these powers are sometimes increased by subsequent statutes or by delegated legislation. Acts beyond these powers are *ultra vires* and *void*, i.e. of no effect.

The powers of registered companies are determined by the objects clause of the memorandum of association and an act in excess of the powers given in this clause is *ultra vires* and *void*, i.e. of no effect.

The following case provides a classic illustration of the operation of the *ultra vires* rule at common law and before the intervention of Parliament (*see below*).

Ashbury Railway Carriage & Iron Co v Riche (1875) LR 7 HL 653

The company was formed for the purposes (stated in the memorandum of association) of making and selling railway wagons and other railway plant and carrying on the business of mechanical engineers and general contractors. The company bought a concession for the construction of a railway system in Belgium from Antwerp to Tournai and entered into an agreement whereby Messrs Riche were to construct the railway line. Messrs Riche commenced the work and the company paid over certain sums of money in connection with the contract. The Ashbury company later ran into difficulties, and the shareholders wished the directors to take over the contract in a personal capacity and indemnify the shareholders. The directors thereupon repudiated the contract on behalf of the company and Messrs Riche sued for breach of contract. *Held* – The directors were able to repudiate because the contract to construct a railway system was *ultra vires* and void. On a proper construction of the objects, the company had power to supply materials for the construction of railways but had no power to engage in the actual construction of them. Further, the subsequent assent of all the shareholders could not make the contract binding, for a principal cannot ratify the *ultra vires* contracts of his agent.

By way of explanation of the decision in the above case it should be said that the *ultra vires* rule was brought in by the courts in earlier times to protect shareholders. It was thought that if a shareholder X bought shares in a company which had as its main object publishing and allied activities then X would not want the directors of that company to start up a different kind of business because he wanted his money in publishing.

In more recent times it has been noted that shareholders are not so fussy about the kind of business the directors take the company into so long as it makes money to pay dividends and raises the price of the company's shares on the stock market thus giving a capital gain. In these days of the conglomerates it is doubtful whether any investor invests in a company because of only one facet of its trading.

The people most affected by the *ultra vires* rule in more recent times were those who had supplied goods or services to a company for a purpose not covered by its objects clause. If the company was solvent no doubt such creditors would be paid but if it went into insolvent liquidation they would not even be able to put in a claim. Other creditors might get some part of their debts paid, say 20p in the £1 if the company had any funds, but the *ultra vires* suppliers would get nothing. For this reason it became usual to put in the objects clause of the memorandum a large number of objects and powers, and to include a special clause stating that each clause of the objects clause contained a separate and independent object which could be carried on separately from any of the others. The House of Lords decided in *Cotman* v *Brougham* [1918] AC 514 that this type of clause was legal, and this greatly relieved the problem of *ultra vires* by giving the directors legitimate access to many kinds of business listed in the objects clause.

Also the decision of the Court of Appeal in *Bell Houses* v *City Wall Properties Ltd* [1966] 2 All ER 674 states that the objects clause can be drafted in such a way as to allow the company to carry on any additional business which the members or directors choose.

In this way the limitations which are placed by the common law on a company's business activities by the *ultra vires* rule have been much reduced, though of course the control over the activities of the directors by the members has also been lessened. In fact with a large number of clauses in the objects clause as one finds in the typical memorandum, and with sub-clauses such as those approved in *Cotman* and *Bell Houses*, the modern company's contractual capacity approaches that of a natural person. The *ultra vires* rule as a method of controlling the activities of the boards of companies has been largely abandoned as the twentieth century has progressed. In addition there has been massive statutory intervention by Parliament to make the *ultra vires* rule ineffective (*see below*).

Companies Act 1985

Section 35, as inserted by the Companies Act 1989, now represents the United Kingdom's response to Article 9 of the First Directive (No 68/151) issued by the European Community for the harmonization of company law in the member states of the EC. It is intended largely to eliminate the effect of the *ultra vires* rule on the claims of creditors, though it has perhaps less impact today since fewer transactions are likely to be *ultra vires* at common law.

However, on the assumption that the narrow scope of a particular company's objects clause may lead to a transaction being *ultra vires* at common law a review of the provisions is worthwhile.

The company's capacity

Section 35(1) of the Companies Act 1985 states: 'The validity of an act done by a company shall not be called into question on the ground of lack of capacity by reason of anything in the company's memorandum'. The immediate effect of this would be to put right the sort of problem which was raised in *Ashbury*. Something in its memorandum, i.e. its objects clause, confined it to making things for railways but not a whole railway system. Mr Riche's action would now have been successful and he would have got a remedy from the court, i.e. damages for breach of contract. In addition the drafting techniques approved in *Cotman* and *Bell Houses* will continue to be useful in converting long objects clauses into a series of independent objects and allowing the members or directors to choose new businesses for the company. These clauses will undoubtedly continue in use for many years to come.

Exceptions to s. 35(1)

(a) A shareholder may ask for an injunction to prevent the directors entering into an *ultra vires* contract, but if the contract has been made the court cannot grant an injunction to stop it proceeding.

(b) Directors are as before placed under a specific duty to observe the limitations on their powers in the memorandum and the articles and can be sued by the company for any loss caused by a transaction which is outside the company's constitution (s. 35A(5)). However, the *ultra vires* act can be ratified by a special resolution of the members, and if it is desired to exempt the directors from liability for damage then another special resolution is required. It was not possible for the members to ratify in this way before the present legislation (*see* the *Ashbury* decision).

(c) Where the transaction is with a director of the company or its holding company or a person connected with him, e.g. a spouse, then it is voidable (i.e. the company can have it set aside). However, the members may ratify it by special resolution where the problem is that the transaction is beyond the company's capacity.

Power of the directors to bind the company

Section 35A(1) of the Companies Act 1985 states: 'In favour of a person dealing with a company in good faith, the power of the board of directors to bind the company, or authorize others to do so shall be deemed to be free of any limitation under the company's constitution'.

Actual knowledge of the contents of the memorandum or articles is not in itself bad faith. Those who have read these documents but have misinterpreted them will be all right. If we look at the *Ashbury* situation it would have been possible for businessmen to misinterpret the objects clause which actually allowed the company to enter into 'general contracting' but the court took a restrictive view and said that this covered only general contracting in the field of making things for railways. Those who have actual knowledge of the company's or directors' lack of authority and act in bad faith will not be all right as in *International Sales and Agencies Ltd* v *Marcus* [1982] 3 All ER 551 where a sole effective director used the company's power to draw cheques to issue cheques to pay the private loan of a director who had died insolvent. He was aided and abetted by the lender who knew all about the circumstances and who along with the sole effective director was acting contrary to the company's interests. The cheques were held to be invalid and could not be enforced against the company.

Exceptions to s. 35A(1)

The section does not apply:

(a) If the act of the directors is illegal. Thus it would not authorize the issue of shares at a discount because this is forbidden by the Companies Act 1985.

(b) It would not help in a situation in which the directors had used their powers for an improper purpose provided this is known to the other party. Thus in *Rolled Steel Products (Holdings) Ltd* v *British Steel Corporation* [1985] 3 All ER 401 a managing director and major shareholder of a company called Scottish Sheet Steel gave a guarantee of that company's debts to British Steel. British Steel wanted additional security and the managing director gave one on behalf of Rolled Steel which was another company of which he was managing director and major shareholder. The companies were not connected in any way and British Steel knew that the managing director was not acting for the benefit of Rolled Steel and that therefore he was using his legitimate power to give guarantees on behalf of Rolled Steel for an improper purpose. The guarantee by Rolled Steel was not enforceable against it. If British Steel had not been aware of the improper purpose, it would have been.

(c) The company cannot sue on the transaction but only the third party. The section says: 'In favour of a person dealing with a company . . .'. However, the members can ratify the transaction by special resolution if the company's lack of capacity is the problem or by an ordinary resolution if only the directors' powers are in issue.

(d) As before if the party dealing with the company is a director of the company or its holding company or connected person, e.g. a spouse, the director concerned cannot rely on s. 35A. The transaction is voidable by the company, but as already mentioned the company can ratify it by special or ordinary resolution as the case may be.

The single line clause

Section 3A of the Companies Act 1985 states that a company may alter its objects (or be registered with objects) which merely state that the company is to 'carry on business as a general commercial company'. This means that it can carry on any trade or business whatsoever. All necessary powers will be implied.

If a company does register with or change its objects clause to this new formula it will have effectively opted out of the *ultra vires* rule even for internal purposes of shareholder injunctions.

Rule of constructive notice

At one time knowledge of the contents of a company's constitution was assumed by the courts to be in the minds of all of us even if we had not seen or read it. This was because the memorandum and articles are registered with the Registrar of Companies and the register can be inspected.

Under more recent provisions added by the Companies Act 1989 to the Companies Act 1985 the rule of constructive notice of the contents of the company's memorandum and articles and also company documents kept by the Registrar is abolished.

GRADED QUESTIONS

Essay mode

1. (a) What do you understand by the expression 'contractual capacity'? Illustrate your answer with examples.

                                                                            (10 marks)

   (b) G, aged 17, entered into the following agreements:
       (i)   a contract with a tailor to supply him with a new suit of clothes for £150;
       (ii) a partnership agreement;
       (iii) a loan of £2,000 at 10% interest, to be repaid in two years.
       Advise G which of the agreements are binding upon him.

                                                                            (10 marks)
                                                                            (20 marks)

(Chartered Association of Certified Accountants. Level 1: Paper 1.4. June 1988)

Objective mode

Four alternative answers are given. Select ONE only. Circle the answer which you consider to be correct. Check your answers by referring back to the information given in the chapter and against the answers at the back of the book.

1. Which of the following contracts is required to be made by deed?

   A A lease of more than three years.
   B A lease of less than three years.
   C A contract of guarantee.
   D Rental property subject to a mortgage.

2. Fred decided that he must move to Canada and Alan enters into a verbal contract to buy his house in Derbyshire for £150,000. Fred and Alan agree all the terms of the contract, including a completion date. Before anything is put into writing Alan changes his mind. Is the contract:

   A Invalid.
   B Voidable.

C Illegal.

D Unenforceable.

3. Compost Ltd, who are manufacturers of various kinds of health foods, are anxious to expand the export side of the business. Some years ago the company initiated a similar sales drive abroad but unfortunately incurred a number of bad debts which were not recovered because of the difficulties experienced by the company in bringing actions in foreign courts.

Vend, the sales manager of Compost, decides to enter into negotiations with Schloss, who is a general agent with branches in England and Boravia. Schloss agrees for an extra commission to introduce Compost's products in Boravia on terms that he will reimburse Compost if any of the customers he introduces fails to pay for goods received. This agreement is made on the telephone and Schloss agrees to send written confirmation as soon as possible. Shortly afterwards Braunbrot, who is the buyer for Gesundheit, a chain of health food shops in Boravia, rings up Vend and says 'Schloss tells me that you are prepared to supply us with some items at a very competitive price. You will be receiving our order this week.' A large order from Gesundheit arrives and the goods are despatched by Compost. Unfortunately Braunbrot does not regard the packaging as sufficiently attractive and complains to Schloss. As a result of this complaint, Schloss rings Vend and says 'Braunbrot does not think much of your packaging and for that matter neither do I. You will get no more orders from him and what is more I will no longer act as your agent here. There is no point now in writing to you regarding our agreement.'

Three months later, Vend learns that Gesundheit have become insolvent and cannot pay for the goods which they received. Vend rings Schloss immediately and asks him to pay Gesundheit's debt as agreed. Schloss refuses to make any payment and Compost are intending to sue him and claim against his assets in England.

The contract between Schloss and Compost is:

A A guarantee and enforceable.

B An indemnity and unenforceable.

C A guarantee and unenforceable.

D An indemnity and enforceable.

With reference to the following information answer questions 4 and 5:

Dabbler who was training to be a commercial artist, left art school on his seventeenth birthday without having completed the course and decided to go into business as a dealer in antiques and bric-à-brac. For this purpose he entered into an agreement with Jasper to rent for one year a small shop and obtained £1,000 worth of stock on credit from another dealer, Peddler, with whom he was friendly.

After trading for two months Dabbler found that because of inexperience he was unable to buy articles at a price which would give a reasonable margin of profit, and he therefore decided to give up business and informed Jasper that he would no longer require the shop. Dabbler has not paid any rent to Jasper and still owes Peddler £1,000; he also refuses to hand over the remainder of the original stock on the ground that he might start another business.

4. As regards the agreement to rent the shop:

   A Dabbler is liable to occupy the shop for one year and pay the rent.
   B Dabbler is not bound to occupy the shop for one year but must pay the rent.
   C Dabbler need not stay in occupation of the shop but must pay two months rent.
   D Dabbler need not stay in occupation of the shop and cannot be made to pay any rent.

5. As regards the stock supplied by Peddler:

   A Dabbler is liable to pay Peddler in full and may then retain the stock.
   B Dabbler is only bound to pay Peddler for the goods he has sold and can retain the rest without payment.
   C The debt cannot be enforced against Dabbler who may also retain the remainder of the stock.
   D The debt cannot be enforced against Dabbler but he is required by law to return the remainder of the stock to Peddler.

6. The Chartered Institute of Hod Carriers was incorporated by Royal Charter for the purpose of advancing the science of hod carrying and promoting a uniform system of education of those who should practise the same. The Institute has announced a scheme under which it intends to set up a chain of launderettes in the hope that the profits will render an increase in subscriptions unnecessary.

   Peregrine, who is a member of the Institute, is outraged by the Council's scheme which he regards as seriously affecting the image of the profession. He asks your advice as to the legal position of the Institute.

   Peregrine should be advised:

   A That the scheme is valid and can be implemented without risk to the Institute.
   B That the scheme is *ultra vires* and cannot effectively be implemented because all relevant contracts will be void.
   C That the scheme is *ultra vires* and can be implemented effectively and without risk because all relevant contracts are enforceable.
   D That the scheme although *ultra vires* can be effectively implemented so far as contract law is concerned but the Institute may forfeit its Charter.

7. Under s. 35 of the Companies Act 1985, what is the position of a person who innocently enters into an *ultra vires* contract with the company and decided on by the sales director as part of a corporate project which the board had authorized him to carry out?

   A The contract is void and no action can be taken on it.

B The contract is deemed to be within the contractual capacity of the company and the third party can sue upon it.

C The third party can only sue the director in person for exceeding his powers.

D The contract is unenforceable but the third party can retain any property received under it.

8. Lord Seaworthy is 95 years of age and a wealthy retired Rear Admiral. He suffers from periods of mental incapacity and his family has been advised to place his property and affairs under the management of the court but no steps have been taken to achieve this.

Lord Seaworthy recently visited London with his grandson but during the visit managed to slip away on his own for three hours. He was subsequently found standing under one of the fountains in Trafalgar Square re-enacting a naval battle with a number of paper boats. It now appears that he had visited the Boat Show and purchased a cabin cruiser worth £125,000 after telling the salesman it would look well on his mantelpiece.

The manufacturers of the cabin cruiser, having delivered Lord Seaworthy's purchase, are now pressing for payment. Lady Seaworthy is resisting the claim on the grounds of her husband's mental incapacity. What advice should she receive?

A That Lord Seaworthy must pay in full.

B That Lord Seaworthy must pay a reasonable price.

C That the contract is voidable by Lord Seaworthy.

D That the contract is void and not binding on Lord Seaworthy.

Answers to questions set in objective mode appear on p. 551.

4 | The law of contract – reality of consent I

The OBJECTIVE of this chapter is to begin a study of the various factors which can affect an agreement once it has been formed. We begin by dealing with the law relating to mistake which affects the true consent of one or both of the parties so that one or both of them may ask to be released from contractual obligations.

INTRODUCTION

A contract which is regular in all respects may still fail because there is no real consent to it by one or both of the parties. There is no *consensus ad idem* or meeting of the minds. Consent may be rendered unreal by mistake, misrepresentation, duress and undue influence. There are also instances of inequality of bargaining power where it would be inequitable to enforce the resulting agreement.

It is particularly important to distinguish between mistake and misrepresentation because a contract affected by mistake is void, whereas a contract affected by misrepresentation is only voidable. As between the parties themselves, this makes little difference since in both cases goods sold and money paid can be recovered. However, the distinction can be vital so far as third parties are concerned. If A sells goods to B under circumstances of mistake and B resells them to C, then C gets no title and A can recover the goods from him or sue him for damages in conversion. If, on the other hand, the contract between A and B was voidable for misrepresentation, then if B sold the goods to C who took them bona fide and for value before A had rescinded his contract with B, then C would get a good title and A would have a remedy only against B. For the position where A has rescinded *see Car & Universal Finance Co* v *Caldwell* (1964) and *Newtons of Wembley Ltd* v *Williams* (1964) at p. 295.

AGREEMENT MISTAKE IN GENERAL

Mistake, to be operative, must be of *fact* and not of *law*. Furthermore, the concept has a technical meaning and does not cover, for example, errors of judgment as to value. Thus, if A buys an article thinking it is worth £100 when in fact it is worth only £50, the contract is good and A must bear the loss if there has been no misrepresentation by the seller. This is what is meant by the maxim *caveat emptor* (let the buyer beware). An interesting example of how the judiciary can interpret what some might think to be mistakes of law as mistakes of fact is provided by *Solle* v *Butcher* at p. 94.

The various categories of mistake will now be considered, beginning with the rather special case where a document is signed by mistake.

DOCUMENTS MISTAKENLY SIGNED

If a person signs a contract in the mistaken belief that he is signing a document of a different nature, there may be a mistake which avoids the contract. He may be able to plead *non est factum* ("it is not my deed'). This is a defence open to a person who has signed a document by mistake. Originally it was a special defence to protect those who could not read who had signed deeds which had been incorrectly read over to them. At one time the defence was available only where the mistake referred to the *kind* of document it was and not merely its contents. Now the defence is available to a person who has signed a document having made a *fundamental* mistake as to the kind of document it is or as to its contents. Furthermore, the defendant must prove that he made the mistake despite having taken all reasonable care. If he is negligent he will not usually be able to plead the defence.

The following case provides an illustration of the above rules.

Saunders v Anglia Building Society [1970] 3 All ER 961

Mrs Gallie, a widow aged 78 years, signed a document which Lee, her nephew's friend, told her was a deed of gift of her house to her nephew. She did not read the document but believed what Lee had told her. In fact the document was an assignment of her leasehold interest in the house to Lee, and Lee later mortgaged that interest to a building society. In an action by Mrs Gallie against Lee and the building society it was *held* at first instance – (a) that the assignment was void and did not confer a title on Lee; (b) although Mrs Gallie had been negligent she was not estopped from denying the validity of the deed against the building society for she owed it no duty. The Court of Appeal, in allowing an appeal by the building society, held that the plea of *non est factum* was not available to Mrs Gallie. The transaction intended and carried out was the same, i.e. an assignment.

The appeal to the House of Lords was brought by Saunders, the executrix of Mrs Gallie's estate. The House of Lords affirmed the decision of the Court of Appeal but took the opportunity to restate the law relating to the avoidance of documents on the ground of mistake as follows.

(a) The plea of *non est factum* will rarely be available to a person of full capacity who signs a document apparently having legal effect without troubling to read it, i.e. negligently.

(b) A mistake as to the identity of the person in whose favour the document is executed will not normally support a plea of *non est factum* though it may do if the court regards the mistake as fundamental (Lord Reid and Lord Hodson). Neither judge felt that the personality error made by Mrs Gallie was sufficient to support the plea.

(c) The distinction taken in *Howatson* v *Webb* [1908] 1 Ch 1 that the mistake must be as to the class or character of the document and not merely as to its contents was regarded as illogical. Under the *Howatson* test, if X signed a guarantee for £1,000 believing it to be an insurance policy he escaped all liability on the guarantee, but if he signed a guarantee for £10,000 believing it to be a guarantee for £100 he was fully liable for £10,000. Under *Saunders* the document which was in fact signed must be 'fundamentally different', 'radically different', or 'totally different'. The test is more flexible than the character/contents one and yet still restricts the operation of the plea of *non est factum*.

Comment: (i) The charge of negligence might be avoided where a person was told he was witnessing a confidential document and had no reason to doubt that he was. Many such documents are witnessed each day and the witnesses would never dream of asking to read them nor would they think themselves negligent because they had not done so. Surely the *Saunders* decision is not intended to turn witnesses into snoopers. Thus the decision in the old case of *Lewis* v *Clay* (1898) 77 LT 653 would probably be the same under modern law. In that case Clay was asked by Lord William Neville to witness a confidential document and signed in holes in blotting paper placed over the document by Neville. In fact he was signing two promissory notes and two letters authorizing Lewis to pay the amount of the notes to Lord William Neville. The court *held* that the signature of Clay in the circumstances had no more effect than if it had been written for an autograph collector or in an album and he was bound by the bills of exchange.

(ii) As between the immediate parties to what is always in effect a fraud, there is, of course, no difficulty in avoiding the contract or transaction mistakenly entered into. The rules set out above are relevant only where the contract or transaction mistakenly entered into has affected a third party, as where he has taken a bill of exchange bona fide and for value on which the defendant's signature was obtained under circumstances of mistake (*Foster* v *Mackinnon* (1869) LR 4 CP 704) or has lent money on an interest in land obtained by a fraudulent assignment under circumstances of mistake (*Saunders* v *Anglia Building Society*

(1970) *see above*). The principles set out in *Saunders'* case apply also to those who sign blank forms as well as to those who sign completed documents without reading them (*United Dominions Trust Ltd* v *Western* [1975] 3 All ER 1017).

UNILATERAL MISTAKE

Unilateral mistake occurs when one of the parties, X, is mistaken as to some fundamental fact concerning the contract and the other party, Y, knows, or ought to know, this. This latter requirement is important because if Y does not know that X is mistaken the contract is good.

   The following case provides an example of this rule.

Higgins (W) Ltd v Northampton Corporation [1927] 1 Ch 128

The plaintiff entered into a contract with the corporation for the erection of dwelling houses. The plaintiff made an arithmetical error in arriving at his price, having deducted a certain rather small sum twice over. The corporation sealed the contract, assuming that the price arrived at by the plaintiff was correct. *Held* – The contract was binding on the parties. Rectification of such a contract was not possible because the power of the court to rectify agreements made under mistake is confined to common not unilateral mistake. Here, rectification would only have been granted if fraud or misrepresentation had been present.

   Comment: (i) Since this case was decided the courts have moved away from the idea that rectification of a contract for unilateral mistake is permissible only if there is some form of sharp practice (see *Thomas Bates & Sons Ltd* v *Wyndham's (Lingerie) Ltd* (1981) at p. 97). Even so, rectification would not have been granted in this case because Northampton Corporation were not aware of the plaintiff's error which is still a requirement for rectification.

   (ii) The rule of unilateral mistake does not seem to apply to mistakes as to the value of the contract. If you go into a junk shop and recognize a genuine Georgian silver teapot marked at £10 then your contract of purchase, if made, would be good in law, although it would be obvious that the seller had made a mistake and that the buyer was aware of it. This is the rule of *caveat venditor* (let the seller beware) and applies provided the seller intends to offer the goods at his marked price.

The cases are mainly concerned with mistake by one party as to the *identity* of the other party. Thus a contract may be void for mistake if X contracts with Y thinking that Y is another person, Z, and if Y knows that X is under that misapprehension. Proof of Y's knowledge is essential but since in most cases Y is a fraudulent person, the point does not present great difficulties.

   The following case and comment shows how the rules are applied.

Cundy v Lindsay (1878) 3 App Cas 459

The respondents were linen manufacturers with a business in Belfast. A fraudulent person named Blenkarn wrote to the respondents from 37 Wood Street, Cheapside, ordering a quantity of handkerchiefs but signed his letter in such a way that it appeared to come from Messrs Blenkiron, who were a well-known and solvent house doing business at 123 Wood Street. The respondents knew of the existence of Blenkiron but did not know the address. Accordingly the handkerchiefs were sent to 37 Wood Street. Blenkarn then sold them to the appellants, and was later convicted and sentenced for the fraud. The respondents sued the appellants in conversion claiming that the contract they had made with Blenkarn was void for mistake, and that the property had not passed to Blenkarn or to the appellants. *Held* – The respondents succeeded; there was an operative mistake as to the party with whom they were contracting.

Comment: It is, however, essential that at the time of making the apparent contract the mistaken party regarded the identity of the other party as vital and that he intended to deal with some person other than the actual person to whom in fact he addressed the offer, as in *Cundy* v *Lindsay* (1878) (*see above*). The mistake must be as to *identity*, not *attributes*, e.g. creditworthiness. As between the parties the result is much the same since a mistake as to attributes may make the contract *voidable*, but the difference may vitally affect the interests of third parties. Thus in *King's Norton Metal Co Ltd* v *Edridge, Merrett and Co Ltd* (1897) 14 TLR 98 where the facts were similar to *Cundy*, a fraudulent person called Wallis ordered goods from the plaintiffs using notepaper headed Hallam & Co. The notepaper said that Hallam & Co had agencies abroad and generally represented the company as creditworthy. The plaintiffs sold Hallam & Co some brass rivet wire on credit. The goods were never paid for but Wallis sold the goods on to Edridge Merrett who paid for them and were innocent of the way in which Wallis had obtained them. The plaintiffs sued Edridge Merrett in conversion saying that the contract between them and Hallam/Wallis was void for mistake so that Edridge Merrett did not become owners of the wire because Hallam/Wallis had not. The Court of Appeal *held* that the contract between King's Norton and Edridge was voidable for fraud but not void for mistake. The plaintiffs could not show a confusion of entities. There was no other Hallam or Wallis in their business lives with whom they could have been confused.

There were difficulties where the parties contracted face to face because in such a case the suggestion could always be made that whatever the fraudulent party was saying about his identity, the mistaken party must be regarded as intending to contract with the person in front of him, whoever he was. Thus in this situation, the court might find on the facts of the case that the contract was voidable for fraud or sometimes void for mistake.

However, the position is now a little clearer as a result of the decision in *Lewis* v *Averay* (1971) (*see below*) where it was said that if the parties contracted face to face the contract will normally be voidable for fraud but rarely void for mistake. However, much depends upon the facts of the case and if the court is convinced on the evidence that identity was vital then even a 'face to face' contract will be regarded as void for mistake, as *Ingram* v *Little* (1961) (*see below*) shows.

Lewis v Averay [1971] 3 All ER 907

Mr Lewis agreed to sell his car to a rogue who called on him after seeing an advertisement. Before the sale took place the rogue talked knowledgeably about the film world giving the impression that he was the actor Richard Green in the 'Robin Hood' serial which was running on TV at the time. He signed a dud cheque for £450 in the name of 'R. A. Green' and was allowed to have the log book and drive the car away late the same night when he produced a film studio pass in the name of 'Green'. *Held* – by the Court of Appeal – that Mr Lewis had effectively contracted to sell the car to the rogue and could not recover it or damages from Mr Averay, a student, who had bought it from the rogue for £200. The contract between Mr Lewis and the rogue was voidable for fraud but not void for unilateral mistake.

Comment: It is thought that the contract would be void for mistake in a case such as this if the dishonest person assumed a disguise so that he appeared physically to be the person he said he was.

Ingram and others v Little [1961] 1 QB 31

The plaintiffs, three ladies, were the joint owners of a car. They wished to sell the car and advertised it for sale. A fraudulent person, introducing himself as Hutchinson, offered to buy it. He was taken for a drive in it and during conversation said that his home was at Caterham. Later the rogue offered £700 for the car but this was refused, though a subsequent offer of £717 was one which the plaintiffs were prepared to accept. At this point the rogue produced a cheque book and one of the plaintiffs, who was conducting the negotiations, said that the deal was off and that they would not accept a cheque. The rogue then said that he was P. G. M. Hutchinson, that he had business interests in Guildford, and that he lived at Stanstead House, Stanstead Road, Caterham. One of the plaintiffs checked this information in a telephone directory and, on finding it to be accurate, allowed him to take the car in return for a cheque. The cheque was dishonoured, and in the meantime the rogue had sold the car to the defendants and had disappeared without trace. The plaintiffs sued for the return of the car, or for its value as damages in conversion, claiming that the contract between themselves and the rogue was void for mistake, and that the property (or ownership) had not passed. At the trial judgment was given for the plaintiffs, Slade J finding the contract void. His judgment was *affirmed* by the Court of Appeal, though Devlin LJ dissented, saying that the mistake made was as to the creditworthiness of the rogue, not as to his identity, since he was before the plaintiffs when the contract was made. A mistake as to the substance of the rogue would be a mistake as to quality and would not avoid the contract. Devlin LJ also suggested that legislation should provide for an apportionment of the loss incurred by two innocent parties who suffer as a result of the fraud of a third.

Comment: The distinctions drawn in some of these cases are fine ones. It is difficult to distinguish *Ingram* from *Lewis*. As we have seen, the question for the court to answer in these cases is whether or not the offeror at the time of making the offer regarded the identity of the offeree as a matter of vital importance. The general rule seems to be that where the parties are face to face when the contract is made identity will not be vital and the contract voidable only. *Ingram* would appear to be the exceptional case.

Effect of unilateral mistake in equity

If the plaintiff is asking for an equitable remedy, such as rescission of the contract or specific performance of it, then equitable principles will apply. As far as unilateral mistake is concerned, equity follows the principles of the common law and regards a contract affected by unilateral mistake as void and will therefore rescind it or refuse specific performance of it. Rectification of the contract is also available (*See* p. 95).

The following case is an example of the refusal of an equitable remedy in circumstances of unilateral mistake.

Webster v Cecil (1861) 30 Beav 62

The parties had been negotiating for the sale of certain property. Later Cecil offered by letter to sell the property for £1,250. Webster was aware that his offer was probably a slip because he knew that Cecil had already refused an offer of £2,000, and in fact Cecil wished to offer the property at £2,250. Webster accepted the offer and sued for specific performance of the contract. The court refused to grant the decree.

Comment: This is not merely a case of mistake as to the value of the contract because here Webster knew that Cecil did not intend to offer the property at £1,250. The rule of let the seller beware applies where the seller is mistaken as to value but at least intends to offer the goods at his marked price.

BILATERAL IDENTICAL (OR COMMON) MISTAKE

This occurs where both parties are mistaken and each makes the same mistake. There is no general rule that common mistake affects a contract and in practice only common mistakes as to the existence of the subject matter of the contract or where the subject matter of the contract already belongs to the buyer will make the contract void at common law. The principles applied are considered below.

(a) *Cases of res extincta*. Here there is a common mistake as to the existence of the subject matter of the contract. Thus, if S agrees to sell his car to B and unknown to both the car had at the time of the sale been destroyed by fire, then the contract will be void because A has innocently undertaken an obligation which he cannot possibly fulfil. **The following case is an illustration of the application of *res extincta* which shows as well that the goods may actually exist but if they are not in the condition envisaged by the parties the rule will be applied.**

Couturier v Hastie (1856) 5 HLC 673

Messrs Hastie dispatched a cargo of corn from Salonica and sent the charterparty and bill of lading to their London agents so that the corn might be sold. The London agents employed Couturier to sell the corn and a person named Callander bought it. Unknown to the parties the cargo had become overheated, and had been landed at the nearest port and sold, so that when the contract was made the corn was not really in existence. Callander repudiated the contract and Couturier was sued because he was a *del credere* agent, i.e. an agent who, for an extra commission, undertakes to indemnify his principal against losses arising out of the repudiation of the contract by any third party introduced by him. *Held* – The claim against Couturier failed because the contract presupposed that the goods were in existence when they were sold to Callander.

(b) *Cases of res sua.* These occur where a person makes a contract about something which already belongs to him. Such a contract is void at common law. **The application of the rule is illustrated by the following case.**

Cochrane v Willis (1865) LR 1 Ch App 58

Cochrane was the trustee in bankruptcy of Joseph Willis who was the tenant for life of certain estates in Lancaster. Joseph Willis had been adjudicated bankrupt in Calcutta where he resided. The remainder of the estate was to go to Daniel Willis, the brother of Joseph, on the latter's death, with eventual remainder to Henry Willis, the son of Daniel. Joseph Willis had the right to cut the timber on the estates during his life interest, and the representative of Cochrane in England threatened to cut and sell it for the benefit of Joseph's creditors. Daniel and Henry wished to preserve the timber and so they agreed with Cochrane through his representatives to pay the value of the timber to Cochrane if he would refrain from cutting it. News then reached England that when the above agreement was made Joseph was dead, and therefore the life interest had vested in (i.e. become owned by) Daniel. In this action by the trustee to enforce the agreement it was *held* that Daniel was making a contract to preserve something which was already his and the court found, applying the doctrine of *res sua*, that the agreement was void for an identical or common mistake.

(c) *Other cases – mistakes as to quality.* These occur when the two parties have reached agreement but have made an identical mistake as to some fact concerning the quality of the subject matter of the contract. Suppose, for example, that X sells a particular drawing to Y for £5,000 and all the usual elements of agreement are present, including offer and acceptance and consideration, and the agreement concerns an identified article. Nevertheless, if both X and Y think that the drawing is by a well-known Victorian artist when it is in fact only a copy worth £25, then the agreement is made in circumstances of common mistake.

At common law a mistake of the kind outlined above has no effect on the contract and the parties would be bound in the absence of fraud or misrepresentation. **The following cases illustrate how reluctant the courts have been to recognize a general rule of common mistake.**

Bell v Lever Bros Ltd [1932] AC 161

Lever Bros had a controlling interest in the Niger Company. Bell was the chairman, and a person called Snelling was the vice-chairman of the Niger Company's Board. Both directors had service contracts which had some time to run. They became redundant as a result of amalgamations and Lever Bros contracted to pay Bell £30,000 and Snelling £20,000 as compensation. These sums were paid over and then it was discovered that Bell and Snelling had committed breaches of duty against the Niger Company during their term of office by making secret profits of £1,360 on a cocoa pooling scheme. As directors of the Niger Company, Bell and Snelling attended meetings at which the selling price of cocoa was fixed in advance. Both of them bought and sold on their own account before the prices were made public. They could therefore, have been dismissed without compensation. Lever Bros sought to set aside the payments on the ground of mistake. *Held* – The contract was not void because Lever Bros had got what they bargained for, i.e. the cancellation of two service contracts which, though they might have been terminated, were actually in existence when the cancellation agreement was made. The mistake was as to the quality of the two directors and such mistakes do not avoid the contracts. The case is one of common mistake because although Bell and Snelling admitted that they were liable to account to the company for the profit made from office, they convinced the court that they had forgotten their misdemeanour of insider dealing when they made the contract for compensation. They thought they were good directors who were entitled to that compensation.

Comment: The case also decided that an employee was not under a duty to disclose to his employer his own misconduct or breaches of duty towards his employer. However, employee/directors do have a duty to disclose their *own* breaches of contract to their companies. This is because their fiduciary position as directors overrides the ordinary employer/employee relationship. However, in the *Bell* case the directors concerned kept the compensation and were not required to disclose their wrongdoing to Lever Bros because they were not directors of Lever Bros but only of Niger. However, a director of, say, company A is under a duty to disclose his wrongdoing, if any, towards company A where he receives his compensation from company A itself. Failure so to disclose will allow the company to claim back a golden handshake of the kind given to Bell and Snelling.

It is worth mentioning that an employee is under a duty to disclose breaches of duty/ misconduct of subordinate employees, even though he is not under a duty to disclose to his employer his own misconduct or breaches of duty. This follows from the decision of the Court of Appeal in *Sybron Corporation* v *Rochem Ltd* [1983] 2 All ER 707.

Leaf v International Galleries [1950] 1 All ER 693

In 1944 the plaintiff bought from the defendants a drawing of Salisbury Cathedral for £85. The defendants said that the drawing was by Constable. Five years later the plaintiff tried to sell the drawing at Christies and was told that this was not so. He now sued for rescission of the contract, no claim for damages being made. The following points of interest emerged from the decision of the Court of Appeal. (a) It was possible to restore the status quo by the mere exchange of the drawing and the purchase money so that rescission was not prevented by inability to restore the previous position. (b) The mistake made by the parties in assuming the drawing to be a Constable was a mistake as to quality and did not avoid the contract. (c) The statement that the drawing was by Constable could have been treated as a warranty giving rise to a claim for damages, but it was not possible to award damages because the appeal was based on the plaintiff's right to rescind. (d) The court, therefore, treated the statement as a representation and, finding it to be innocent, refused to rescind the contract because of the passage of time since the purchase.

Comment: (i) Although this case was decided after *Solle* v *Butcher* (*see below*), there was presumably no need for the equitable relief of rescission in regard to the common mistake. After all, Leaf had paid only £85 for the drawing and the court may have regarded the contract as a speculation, each party taking a risk as to the authenticity of the drawing.

(ii) Mr Leaf might well have recovered damages if he had sued for these under what is now s. 13 of the Sale of Goods Act 1979 (sale by description – goods described as by Constable) (*see further* p. 248).

Effect of identical bilateral (or common) mistake in equity

The position in equity is as follows.

(a) *Cases of res extincta and res sua.* Equity treats these in the same way as the common law, regarding the agreement as void. The equitable remedy of specific performance is not available for such an agreement which may also be rescinded. **The following case is an example of the equitable approach**.

Cooper v Phibbs (1867) LR 2 HL 149

Cooper agreed to take a lease of a fishery from Phibbs, his uncle's daughter who became apparent owner of it on her father's death. Unknown to either party the fishery already belonged to Cooper. This arose from a mistake by Cooper's uncle as to how the family land was held. The uncle innocently thought he owned the fishery and before he died told Cooper so, but in fact it was owned by Cooper himself. Cooper now brought this action to set aside the lease and for delivery up of the lease. *Held* – The lease must be set aside on the grounds of common or identical bilateral mistake; however, since equity has the power to give ancillary relief, Phibbs was given a lien on the fishery for the improvements she had made to it during the time she believed it to be hers. This lien could be discharged by Cooper giving Phibbs the value of the improvements.

(b) *Other cases.* Equity will apparently regard an agreement affected by common mistake as voidable even though the case is not one of *res extincta* or *res sua*.

The following case is at the root of the equitable approach. The court may order that the contract be set aside on terms, i.e. the court may require the parties to consider first conditions imposed by the court to achieve a fairer solution to the problem.

Solle v Butcher [1950] I KB 671

Butcher had agreed to lease a flat in Beckenham to Solle at a yearly rental of £250, the lease to run for seven years. Both parties had acted on the assumption that the flat, which had been substantially reconstructed so as to be virtually a new flat, was no longer controlled by the Rent Restriction legislation then in force. If it were so controlled the maximum rent payable would be £140 per annum. Nevertheless Butcher would have been entitled to increase that rent by charging 8 per cent of the cost of repairs and improvements which would bring the figure up to about £250 per annum, the rent actually charged, if he had served a statutory notice on Solle before the new lease was executed. No such notice was in fact served. Actually they both for a time mistakenly thought that the flat was decontrolled when this was not the case. Solle realized the mistake after some two years, and sought to recover the rent he had overpaid and to continue for the balance of the seven years as a statutory tenant at £140 per annum. Butcher counter-claimed for rescission of the lease in equity. It was *held* by a majority of the Court of Appeal that the mistake was one of fact and not of law, i.e. the fact that the flat was not within the provisions of the Rent Acts, and this was a bilateral mistake as to quality which would not invalidate the contract at common law. However, on the counter-claim for rescission, it was held that the lease could be rescinded. In order not to dispossess Solle, the court offered him the following alternatives:

(a) to surrender the lease entirely: or
(b) to remain in possession as a mere licensee until a new lease could be drawn up after Butcher had had time to serve the statutory notice which would allow him to add a sum for repairs to the £140 which would bring the lawful rent up to £250 per annum.

Comment: (i) It is impossible to say at the present time what are the limits of this case. Equitable remedies are discretionary and it is not certain whether it applies to a contract for the sale of goods, nor whether it requires some form of sharp practice before it is implemented.

(ii) In *Grist* v *Bailey* [1966] 2 All ER 875 a house was sold cheaply because the parties thought that vacant possession could not be obtained as there was a tenant in it who was protected by the Rent Acts and could not be got out. This was not the case and the tenant gave up possession. Even so the plaintiff asked for specific performance while the defendant asked the court to rescind the contract. The contract was set aside on the terms that the defendant would give the plaintiff the opportunity to purchase the property 'at a proper price for vacant possession'. Naturally, perhaps, specific performance was not granted.

(c) *Rectification*. If the parties are agreed on the terms of their contract but because, for example, of drafting or typing errors certain terms are set out incorrectly, the court may order equitable rectification of the contract so that it properly represents what the parties agreed. Thus if A orally agrees to give B a lease of premises for 99 years and in the subsequent written contract the term is expressed as 90 years by mistake, then if A will not co-operate to change the lease, B may ask the court to rectify it by substituting a term of 99 years for 90 years. In order to obtain rectification it must be proved:

(i) that there was complete agreement on all the terms of the contract or at least a continuing intention to include certain terms in it which in the event were not included. It is not necessary to show that the term was intended to be legally binding prior to being written down;

(ii) that the agreement continued unchanged until it was reduced into writing. If the parties disputed the terms of the agreement then the written contract may be taken to represent their final position;

(iii) that the writing does not express what the parties had agreed. If it does then there can be no rectification.

The following cases illustrate the application of the above principles. Of particular importance is the *Thomas Bates* case because it shows that rectification is available also for unilateral mistake.

Joscelyne v Nissen [1970] I All ER 1213

The plaintiff, Mr Joscelyne, sought rectification of a written contract made on 18 June 1964, under which he had made over his car hire business to his daughter, Mrs Margaret Nissen. It had been expressly agreed during negotiations that in return for the car hire business Mrs Nissen would pay certain expenses including gas, electricity and coal bills but the agreement on these matters was not expressly incorporated in the written contract. Furthermore, the parties had agreed that no concluded contract was to be regarded as having been made until the signing of a formal written document.

Mrs Nissen failed to pay the bills and the plaintiff brought an action in the Edmonton County Court claiming amongst other things a declaration that Mrs Nissen should pay the gas, electricity and coal bills and alternatively that the written agreement of 18 June 1964 should be rectified to include a provision to that effect. The county court judge allowed the claim for rectification although there was no binding antecedent contract between the parties on the issue of payment of the expenses. The Court of Appeal, after considering different expressions of judicial views upon what was required before a contractual instrument might be rectified by the court, *held* that the law did not require a binding antecedent contract, provided there was some outward expression of agreement between the contracting parties. Rectification could be made even though there was no binding contract until the written agreement which was to be rectified was entered into.

Frederick Rose (London) Ltd v William Pim & Co Ltd [1953] 2 All ER 739

The plaintiffs received an order from an Egyptian firm for feveroles (a type of horsebean). The plaintiffs did not know what was meant by feveroles and asked the defendants what they were and whether they could supply them. The defendants said that feveroles were horsebeans and that they could supply them, so the plaintiffs entered into a written agreement to buy horsebeans from the defendants which were then supplied to the Egyptian firm under the order. In fact there were three types of horsebeans: feves, feveroles and fevettes, and the plaintiffs had been supplied with feves, which were less valuable than feveroles. The plaintiffs were sued by the Egyptian firm and now wished to recover the damages they had had to pay from the defendants. In order to do so they had to obtain rectification of the written contract with the defendants in which the goods were described as 'horsebeans'. The word 'horsebeans' had to be rectified to 'feveroles', otherwise the defendants were not in breach. *Held* –

(a) Rectification was not possible because the contract expressed what the parties had agreed to, i.e. to buy and sell horsebeans. Thus the supply of any of the three varieties would have amounted to fulfilment of the contract.

(b) The plaintiffs might have rescinded for misrepresentation but they could not restore the status quo, having sold the beans.

(c) The plaintiffs might have recovered damages for breach of warranty, but the statement that 'feveroles are horsebeans and we can supply them' was oral, and warranties in a contract for the sale of goods of £10 and upwards had in 1953 to be evidenced in writing. This is not the case today.

(d) The defence of mistake was also raised, i.e. both buyer and seller thought that all horsebeans were feveroles. This was an identical bilateral or common mistake, but since it was not a case of *res extincta* or *res sua* it had no effect on the contract.

Comment: This case is quite complex on its facts but to put the rule in a simpler context, if A and B orally agreed on the sale of A's drawing of Salisbury Cathedral, thought by A and B to be by John Constable, but in fact by Fred Constable an unknown Victorian artist, and then put that into a written contract, that contract could not be rectified simply because A and B thought that the drawing was by John Constable, because the written contract would be the same as the oral one, as in the above case. The approach is after all logical enough. You cannot sensibly ask the court to make the written agreement conform with the one actually made when it already does!

Thomas Bates & Sons Ltd v Wyndham's (Lingerie) Ltd [1981]
1 All ER 1077

The plaintiff granted in 1956 a lease to the defendants with an option for renewal. This lease had a clause under which the rent on renewal was to be agreed by the parties or by arbitration. The option was exercised in 1963 for a seven-year lease, and again in 1970 for a 14-year lease at a rent of £2,350 per annum for the first five years and thereafter subject to rent review every five years. This lease, which was drafted by the plaintiffs' managing director, did not contain an arbitration clause. The defendants knew that it did not. At the end of the first five-year period the plaintiffs suggested that a new rent should be agreed. The defendants would not agree and took the view that the rent of £2,350 should continue for the whole 14 years unless there was an agreement between the parties to the contrary. Deputy Judge Michael Wheeler QC, sitting in the High Court, ordered rectification and the Court of Appeal affirmed that decision. The clause inserted by the court allowed the rent to be settled by arbitration if the parties did not agree.

Comment: At one time it was thought that rectification was available only for a common mistake by both parties. However, as appears from this case, rectification can be given for unilateral mistake. The principles on which it is granted appear in the judgment of Buckley LJ, who said: 'First, that one party, A, erroneously believed that the document sought to be rectified contained a particular term or provision, or possibly did not contain a particular term or provision, which, mistakenly, it did contain; second that the other party, B, was aware of the omission or the inclusion and that it was due to a mistake on the part of A; third that B has omitted to draw the mistake to the notice of A. And I think there must be a fourth element involved, namely that the mistake must be calculated to benefit B.' The general principle upon which the judgment is based would appear to be one of equitable estoppel.

NON-IDENTICAL BILATERAL (OR MUTUAL) MISTAKE

If X offers to sell car A and Y agrees to buy, thinking X means car B, there is a bilateral mistake which is non-identical. It will be remembered that in the previous category the mistake was bilateral but both parties had made an identical mistake. Confusion of this non-identical bilateral kind generally exists in the mind of one party only and may therefore have no effect on the contract (*see below*).

Effect of non-identical bilateral (or mutual) mistake at common law

The contract is not necessarily void because the court will try to find the 'sense of promise'. This usually occurs where, although the parties are at cross purposes, the contract actually *identifies* their agreement.

If the parties are at cross purposes and the contract does *not identify* their agreement it is void.

Effect of non-identical bilateral (or mutual) mistake in equity

Equity also tries to find the sense of the promise as identified by the contract, thus following the law. However, equitable remedies are discretionary and even where the sense of the promise as identified by the contract can be ascertained equity will not necessarily grant specific performance if it would cause hardship to the defendant.

The following cases illustrate the 'sense of the promise' approach.

Wood v Scarth (1858) 1 F & F 293

The plaintiff was suing for damages for breach of contract alleging that the defendant had entered into an agreement to grant the plaintiff a lease of a public house, but had refused to convey the property. It was shown in evidence that the defendant intended to offer the lease at a rent, and also to include a premium on taking up the lease of £500. The defendant had told his agent to make this clear to the plaintiff, but the agent had not mentioned it. After discussions with the agent the plaintiff wrote to the defendant proposing to take the lease 'on the terms already agreed upon' to which the defendant replied accepting the proposal. There was a mutual or non-identical bilateral mistake. The defendant thought that he was agreeing to lease the premises for a rent plus a premium, and the plaintiff thought he was taking a lease for rental only because he did not know of the premium. The plaintiff had sued for specific performance in 1855, and the court in the exercise of its equitable jurisdiction had decided that specific performance could not be granted in view of the mistake, as to grant it would be unduly hard on the defendant. However, in this action the plaintiff sued at common law for damages, and damages were granted to him on the ground that in mutual or non-identical mistake the court may find the sense of the promise and regard a contract as having been made on these terms. Here it was quite reasonable for the plaintiff to suppose that there was no premium to be paid. Thus a contract came into being on the terms as understood by the plaintiff, and he was entitled to damages for breach of it. The contract clearly identified the agreement made.

Comment: This case shows that equitable remedies are discretionary and not available as of right as damages at common law are. Also note the benefits of the Judicature Acts 1873 – 75. In this case, which pre-dates those Acts, the action for specific performance was brought in Chancery in 1855 and the action at common law for damages in 1858. Common law and equitable remedies could not be granted in one and the same action until the Judicature Acts were passed.

Raffles v Wichelhaus (1864) 2 HC 906

The defendants agreed to buy from the plaintiffs 125 bales of cotton to arrive 'ex Peerless from Bombay'. There were two ships called Peerless sailing from Bombay, one in October and one in December. The defendants thought they were buying the cotton on the ship sailing in October, and the plaintiffs meant to sell the cotton on the ship sailing in December. In fact the plaintiffs had no cotton on the ship sailing in October. The defendants refused to take delivery of the cotton when the second ship arrived and were now sued for breach of contract. *Held* – Since there was a mistake as to the subject matter of the contract there was in effect no contract between the parties, or at least no contract which clearly identified the agreement made. The plaintiff's action failed.

GRADED QUESTIONS

Essay mode

1. (a) Certain types of mistake in the formation of a contract affect its validity. Examine those types of mistake which do *not* affect the validity of a contract.

   (b) Anthony, a collector, buys a porcelain dish from Charles, believing it to be an eighteenth-century Chinese work. Charles has in no way represented the piece as having any particular age. If Anthony subsequently discovers the porcelain dish to be a modern copy, will he be able to avoid the contract if –
   (i) Charles did not know of Anthony's mistake;
   (ii) Charles did know, but took no steps to enlighten him.

      (The Institute of Company Accountants. Part 3: Law Relating to Business. November 1988)

2. 'In general, contracts entered into under a common mistake or mutual mistake are still binding upon the parties.' To what extent does this statement represent the law?

      (The Institute of Legal Executives. Part II: Law of Contract. October 1989)

3. Brian agrees to buy a computer from Stella. Explain how the mistakes in each of the following circumstances would affect the contract.

   (a) Brian believes that he is obtaining credit over six months whereas Stella believes that it is a cash sale.

      (5 marks)

   (b) Brian believes that he is buying from David and not from Stella.

      (5 marks)

   (c) Both Brian and Stella believe that the contract price of £4,000 represents the true value of the computer but, because of a latent defect in its manufacture, the computer is only worth £2,000.

      (5 marks)

   (d) Stella offered to sell the computer for £400. Brian believed that a mistake had been made and that £4,000 was intended but, nevertheless, accepted the offer.

      (5 marks)

      (Total: 20 marks)

      (The Chartered Institute of Management Accountants. Business Law. November 1987)

Objective mode

Four alternative answers are given. Select ONE only. Circle the answer which you consider to be correct. Check your answers by referring back to the information given in the chapter and against the answers at the back of the book.

1. John agreed to buy Geoffrey's vintage 3-litre Lagonda motor car for £20,000. Unknown to John and Geoffrey a fire in David's garage, where the car was stored, the day before the contract had been made had destroyed the car. What is the legal position?

   A John must pay the contract price since the risk of loss passes to the buyer when the contract is made.

   B John must pay but can sue David for negligence as a bailee.

   C John need not pay for the goods as the contract is void since the goods had perished when the agreement was made.

   D John need not pay for the goods as the contract is voidable because the goods had perished when the agreement was made.

2. Which of the following is a mutual mistake which renders the contract void?

   A A mistake whereby both parties to the contract believe that the subject matter is a genuine Picasso drawing whereas in fact it is a fake.

   B A mistake whereby X believes he is buying a 1930 Picasso drawing entitled 'Le vierge' whereas Y believes he is selling a 1932 drawing by Picasso entitled 'Le vierge'.

   C A mistake whereby X believes he is contracting by post with Y Ltd with whom he has done business before whereas in fact X is contracting with a fraudulent person W.

   D A contract for the sale of a dog called Meg whereby both parties believe mistakenly that the dog is alive at the time of the contract.

3. John Smith bought a Rolex watch from Golds the jewellers. When asked to pay he told the manager that he was James Smith, a well-known American businessman whose takeover exploits were often reported in the British press. The manager took a cheque from John Smith and the latter departed with the watch. The cheque was dishonoured and Golds are trying to recover the watch from Dennis who bought it from John Smith in good faith and for value. What is the legal position?

   A The contract is void for common mistake. The watch belongs to Golds.

   B The contract is void for unilateral mistake of identity. The watch belongs to Golds.

   C The contract is voidable for mutual mistake. Golds may claim the watch.

   D The contract is voidable for fraud but John Smith has passed on a good title to Dennis.

4. Fusty, an antique dealer, discovered that he was a beneficiary under the will of his deceased maiden aunt, Virginia. She left him the contents of her house including an oil painting of a dog signed 'J. Hargreaves' which he knew she had received as a gift from the Hargreaves family in the 1930s. John Hargreaves was a minor Victorian artist specializing in animal studies whose paintings began to

increase in value during the 1960s. Knowing this, Fusty put the painting up for sale in his shop at £600. Garner saw the painting and offered £500 for it. Fusty refused stating that the painting was by John Hargreaves and had belonged to his aunt Virginia who had received it as a gift from the Hargreaves family in the 1930s. On the basis of this assurance Garner paid £600 for the painting and took delivery of it.

Last month Garner held a party at his house at which Dabster, who was an expert on Victorian paintings employed by Christby's, was a guest. Dabster told Garner that the painting was a copy valued at £100 and executed in the 1920s probably by the painter's son Joseph Hargreaves, who was a good amateur artist.

What is the legal position?

A The contract between Garner and Fusty is void for common mistake.
B The contract between Garner and Fusty is void for mutual mistake.
C The contract between Garner and Fusty is void for misrepresentation and Garner can ask for rescission of the contract.
D Garner's only remedy is to sue Fusty for damages under the Sale of Goods Act 1979.

5. In October 1984 Jake, the son of a restaurant owner, Purvey, was in financial difficulties. Knowing that his father had consistently refused to help him pay his debts, Jake asked Dibbs plc, a finance company, for a loan of £1,000 without security. Dibbs plc were prepared to lend Jake the money provided that Purvey gave an indemnity in respect of the loan and Jake agreed that a form of indemnity should be sent to Purvey for his signature.

Jake managed to intercept all the mail received by Purvey during the following week and extracted the form of indemnity from an envelope franked in the name of Dibbs plc. Jake placed the form on Purvey's desk along with a number of other business documents, marking the place for signature with a cross. Later that day Purvey, who was running late for a luncheon appointment, signed all the documents without bothering to read any of them. Jake then extracted the indemnity and posted it to Dibbs plc, and later Purvey's secretary posted the rest of the mail. In due course Jake received the loan from Dibbs plc and used it to take a holiday in France.

Jake and his father have now been adjudicated bankrupt and Dibbs plc approach you in your capacity as Purvey's trustee in bankruptcy asking your advice as the liability of his estate with regard to the indemnity. What advice would you give?

A That Purvey is not liable on the indemnity because he did not intend to sign it.
B That Purvey is liable on the indemnity because he was negligent in not checking what he was signing.
C That Purvey is liable on the indemnity because those who sign documents cannot deny liability on them.

D That Purvey is not liable on the indemnity because the bank should have ensured that he received independent advice.

6. The equitable contribution to the existence of a mistake in a contract is to:

A Treat all forms of mistake in the same way as the common law.
B Ignore the concept of mistake altogether.
C Treat all forms of mistake differently from the common law.
D Treat all forms of mistake in the same way as the common law except for common mistake.

7. Bloggs and Snooks orally agreed that Snooks would purchase from Bloggs a painting which both of them thought to be by John Constable. The contract was drawn up in writing the same day. Two weeks later Snooks discovered that the painting was by James Constable, a minor artist. Snooks is proposing to ask the court to rectify the written agreement. What is the legal position?

A Snooks will obtain rectification for common mistake.
B Snooks will not obtain rectification because he has left it too late.
C Snooks will obtain rectification for mutual mistake.
D Snooks will not obtain rectification because there is no literal difference between the oral and written contract.

8. John's house 'The Grange' was advertised as being for sale by auction and on the basis of the auction particulars which were available to all wishing to attend the auction. Joe was interested in the property because he had seen John using an adjacent field to graze half a dozen sheep and Joe thought he would do the same with a few rare breeds. Joe got a copy of the auction particulars which made it quite clear that the field in question was not part of the sale since it did not belong to John: he had only rented it from the adjacent owner. Joe did not read the particulars having convinced himself the field would be included in the sale. 'The Grange' was sold to Joe who made the highest bid but at a bit less than 'The Grange' might have fetched at a private sale. The relevant formalities were completed and then Joe discovered that the field was not included in the sale. John intends to ask the court for specific performance but Joe is resisting this. What is the legal position?

A Specific performance will be granted on the assumption of a contract only to buy 'The Grange'.
B Specific performance will not be granted because there is a common mistake.
C Specific performance will be granted on the assumption of a contract to buy 'The Grange' and the adjacent field.
D Specific performance will not be granted because the parties are at cross purposes and there is an irreconcilable mutual mistake.

Answers to questions set in objective mode appear on p. 551.

5 | The law of contract – reality of consent II

The OBJECTIVES of this chapter are to continue a study of further situations in which a contract can be affected by lack of proper consent. Topics considered to complete the study of consent problems are misrepresentation, duress, undue influence and economic duress, and unconscionable bargains.

MISREPRESENTATION

Misrepresentation is an expression used to describe a situation in which there is no genuineness of consent to a contract by one of the parties. The effect of misrepresentation on a contract is less serious than that of mistake because the contract becomes *voidable and not void*. This means that the party misled can ask the court to rescind the contract, i.e. to put the parties back into the positions they held before the contract was made. Thus in a sale of goods the goods would be returned to the seller and the money to the buyer.

However, the effect on third parties is more fundamental because if A sells goods to B under circumstances of misrepresentation by B and before A has a chance to rescind the contract B sells the goods to C, who takes them for value without notice of the misrepresentation, C has a good title and A cannot recover the goods or sue him in conversion. For the position where A has rescinded *see Car & Universal Finance Co Ltd* v *Caldwell* (1964) and *Newtons of Wembley Ltd* v *Williams* (1964) at p. 295. His remedy is against B and the type of remedy available will depend upon the nature of B's misrepresentation, i.e. whether it was fraudulent, negligent or innocent.

MEANING OF REPRESENTATION

A representation is an inducement only and its effect is to lead the other party merely to make the contract. A representation must be a statement of some specific existing and verifiable fact or past event. It becomes a misrepresentation, of course, when it is false.

Thus there are five ingredients as follows.

There must be a statement

In consequence silence or non-disclosure has no effect except in the following circumstances.

(a) *Failure to disclose a change in circumstances.* Where the statement was true when made but became false before the contract was made there is a duty on the party making the statement to disclose the change and if he does not do so his silence can amount to an actionable misrepresentation. **An illustration is provided by the following case.**

With v O'Flanagan [1936] 1 All ER 727

The defendant was a medical practitioner who wished to sell his practice. The plaintiff was interested and in January 1934, the defendant represented to the plaintiff that the income from the practice was £2,000 a year. The contract was not signed until May 1934, and in the meantime the defendant had been ill and the practice had been run by various other doctors who substituted for the defendant while he was ill. In consequence the receipts fell to £5 per week, and no mention of this fact was made when the contract was entered into. The plaintiff now claimed rescission of the contract. *Held* – He could do so. The representation made in January was of a continuing nature and induced the contract made in May. The plaintiff had a right to be informed of a change of circumstances, and the defendant's silence amounted to a misrepresentation.

(b) *Where the contract is uberrimae fidei* (of utmost good faith), such as a contract of insurance (*see further* p. 120).

(c) *Where there is a confidential or fiduciary relationship between the parties*, as where they are solicitor and client. Here the equitable doctrine of constructive fraud may apply to render the contract voidable.

Although this branch of the law is closely akin to undue influence, which will be considered later, there is a difference in the sense that in undue influence the person with special influence, such as a solicitor over his client, is often the prime mover in seeking the contract. Constructive fraud, however, could apply where the client was the prime mover in seeking a contract with his solicitor. In such a case if the solicitor remains silent as regards facts within his knowledge material, say, to the contract price, then the client could rescind the contract for constructive fraud.

(d) *Where statute requires disclosure*, as does the Financial Services Act 1986 under which a number of specified particulars must be disclosed in an advertisement/prospectus issued by a company to invite the public to subscribe for shares or debentures. The particulars must give all such information as investors and their professional advisers would reasonably require and reasonably expect to find in the advertisement/prospectus for the purpose of making an informed assessment as to whether to buy the securities.

(e) *In cases of concealed fraud*, following the case of *Gordon v Selico Co Ltd*, *The Times*, 26 February 1986. In that case a flat in a block of flats which had recently been converted by a developer was taken by the plaintiff on a 99-year lease. Soon after he moved in dry rot was discovered. Goulding J, who was later upheld by the Court of Appeal, decided that deliberate concealment of the dry rot by the developer could amount to fraudulent misrepresentation whereupon damages were awarded to the plaintiff. Silence can, therefore, amount to misrepresentation in the case of concealed fraud.

Specific existing and verifiable fact or past event

The representation must be a statement of some specific, existing and verifiable fact or past event, and in consequence the following are excluded.

(a) *Statements of law.* Everyone is presumed to know the law which is equally accessible to both parties and on which they should seek advice and not rely on the statements of the other party. Thus, if A has allowed B, a tradesman, to have goods on credit and C has agreed orally to indemnify A in respect of the transaction, then if A enters into a second contract with B under which A is to receive two-thirds of the price of the goods from B in full settlement on B's representation that C's indemnity is unenforceable at law because it is not in writing, then the second contract would be good because A cannot deny that he knows the law because of the maxim 'ignorance of the law is no excuse'.

(b) *Statements as to future conduct or intention.* These are not actionable, though if the person who makes the statement has no intention of carrying it out, it may be regarded as a representation of fact, i.e. a misrepresentation of what is really in the mind of the maker of the statement. **The following is an illustration from case law.**

Edgington v Fitzmaurice (1885) 29 Ch D 459

The plaintiff was induced to lend money to a company by a representation made by its directors that the money would be used to improve the company's buildings and generally expand the business. In fact the directors intended to use the money to pay off the company's existing debts as the creditors were pressing hard for payment. When the plaintiff discovered that he had been misled, he sued the directors for damages for fraud. The defence was that the statement that they had made was not a statement of a past or present fact but a mere statement of intention which could not be the basis of an action of fraud.

Held – The directors were liable in deceit. Bowen LJ said: 'There must be a misstatement of an existing fact: but the state of a man's mind is as much a fact as the state of his digestion. It is true that it is very difficult to prove what the state of a man's mind at a particular time is, but if it can be ascertained, it is as much a fact as anything else. A misrepresentation as to the state of a man's mind is, therefore, a misstatement of fact.'

(c) *Statements of opinion.* Again these are not normally actionable unless it can be shown that the person making the statement held no such opinion whereupon the statement may be considered in law to be a misstatement of an existing fact as to what was in the mind of the maker of the statement at the time. However, in *Bissett* v *Wilkinson* [1927] AC 177 it was held that a vendor of land was not liable for stating that it could support 2,000 sheep, because he had no personal knowledge of the facts, the land having never been used for sheep farming. The buyer knew this so that it was understood by him that the seller could only be stating his opinion.

Nevertheless the expression of an opinion may involve a statement of fact. Suppose A writes a reference for B to help B get a house to rent and A says to C the prospective landlord: 'B is a very desirable tenant'. A is doing two things: first he is giving his opinion of B, but also he is making a statement of fact by saying that he *believes* B to be a very desirable tenant. If in fact therefore A actually believes B to be a bad tenant he is lying as to what is in his mind. **This can be an actionable misrepresentation as the following case illustrates.**

Smith v Land and House Property Corporation (1884) 28 Ch D 7

The plaintiffs put up for sale on 4 August 1882 the Marine Hotel, Walton-on-the-Naze, stating in the particulars that it was let to 'Mr Frederick Fleck (a most desirable tenant) at a rental of £400 for an unexpired term of 27½ years.' The directors of the defendant company sent the Secretary, Mr Lewin, to inspect the property and he reported that Fleck was not doing much business and that the town seemed to be in the last stages of decay. The directors, on receiving this report, directed Mr Lewin to bid up to £5,000, and in fact he bought the hotel for £4,700. Before completion Fleck became bankrupt and the defendant company refused to complete the purchase, whereupon the plaintiffs sued for specific performance. It was proved that on 1 May 1882 the March quarter's rent was wholly unpaid, that a distress was then threatened, i.e. the landlord was threatening to remove property from the hotel for sale to pay the rent, and that Fleck paid £30 on 6 May, £40 on 13 June, and the remaining £30 shortly before the sale. No part of the June quarter's rent had been paid. The chairman of the defendant company said that the hotel would not have been purchased but for the statement in the particulars that Fleck was a most desirable tenant. *Held* – Specific performance would not be granted. The description of Fleck as a most desirable tenant was not a mere expression of opinion, but contained an implied assertion that the vendors knew of no facts leading to the conclusion that he was not. The circumstances relating to the unpaid rent showed that Fleck was not a desirable tenant and there was a misrepresentation. Bowen LJ said:

It is material to observe that it is often fallaciously assumed that a statement of opinion cannot involve the statement of a fact. In a case where the facts are equally well known to both parties, what one of them says to the other is frequently nothing but an expression of opinion. The statement of such opinion is in a sense a statement of a fact about the condition of the man's own mind, but only of an irrelevant fact, for it is of no consequence what the opinion is. But if the facts are not equally known to both sides, then a statement of opinion by the one who knows the facts best involves very often a statement of a material fact, for he impliedly states that he knows facts which justify his opinion.

(d) *Sales talk, advertising, 'puffing' (or what is called these days 'hype').* Not all statements in this area amount to representations. The law has always accepted that it is essential in business that a seller of goods or services should be allowed to make some statements about them in the course of dealing without necessarily being bound by everything he says. Thus, if a salesman confines himself to statements of opinion such as 'This is the finest floor polish in the world' or 'This is the best polish on the market', there is no misrepresentation. However, the nearer a salesman gets to a statement of specific verifiable fact, the greater the possibility that there may be an action for misrepresentation. Thus a statement such as 'This polish has as much wax in it as Snooks' wax polish' may well amount to a misrepresentation if the statement is not in fact true.

The statement must induce the contract

It must therefore:

(a) have been relied upon by the person claiming to have been misled who must not have relied on his own skill and judgment;
(b) have been material in the sense that it affected the plaintiff's judgment;
(c) have been known to the plaintiff. The plaintiff must always be prepared to prove that an alleged misrepresentation had an effect on his mind, a task which he certainly cannot fulfil if he was never aware that it had been made.

Thus in *Re Northumberland and Durham District Banking Co ex parte Bigg* (1858) 28 LJ Ch 50 a person who bought shares in a company asked to have the purchase rescinded because the company had published false reports as to its solvency. Although these reports were false, the claimant failed because, among other things, he was unable to show that he had read any of the reports or that anyone had told him what they contained;

(d) have been addressed to the person claiming to have been misled.

The following case is an illustration of the common law approach.

Peek v Gurney (1873) LR 6 HL 377

Peek purchased shares in a company on the faith of statements appearing in a prospectus issued by the respondents who were directors of the company. Certain statements were false and Peek sued the directors. It appeared that Peek was not an original allottee, but had purchased the shares on the market, though he had relied on the prospectus. *Held* – Peek's action failed because the statements in the prospectus were only intended to mislead the original allottees. Once the statements had induced the public to be original subscribers, their force was spent.

Comment: (i) The decision has a somewhat unfortunate effect because at those times when public issues are over-subscribed it is most likely that persons who did not receive an allotment or an adequate allotment as subscribers will try to purchase further shares within a short time on the Stock Exchange. These people will clearly be relying on the prospectus, but under this decision would have no claim in respect of false statements in it.

(ii) This decision and the one in *Re Northumberland* (*above*) would appear to be affected, at least on their own facts, by the Financial Services Act 1986. As regards who can sue under an inaccurate prospectus s.150(1) states: ' . . . any person who has acquired any of the securities in question and suffered loss in respect of them . . . '. This would seem to include all subscribers whether they have relied on the prospectus (or listing particulars) or not. It seems therefore that a subscriber need not be aware of the error or even have seen the listing particulars. The subsection would also seem to cover subsequent purchasers after the first issue thus overruling *Peek* v *Gurney* (*above*), at least on its own facts.

(iii) A claim in tort for damages for negligent misstatement should also be available under *Hedley Byrne* (*see* p. 115) in that those who publicly advertise a prospectus must surely in the modern context foresee that it will be relied upon by subscribers *and* by those who purchase from subscribers on the stock market for a reasonable time after the issue of the prospectus.

Knowledge that statement is untrue

If the person to whom the false statement was made knew that it was untrue then he cannot sue in respect of it because he has not been misled. However, **it is not an acceptable defence to an action for misrepresentation that the representee was given the means of discovering that the statement was untrue, as the following case illustrates.**

Redgrave v Hurd (1881) 20 Ch D 1

The plaintiff was a solicitor who wished to take a partner into the business. During negotiations between the plaintiff and Hurd the plaintiff stated that the income of the business was £300 a year. The papers which the plaintiff produced showed that the income was not quite £200 a year, and Hurd asked about the balance. Redgrave then produced further papers which he said showed how the balance was made up, but which only showed a very small amount of income making the total income up to about £200. Hurd did not examine these papers in any detail, but agreed to become a partner. Later Hurd discovered the true position and refused to complete the contract. The plaintiff sued for breach and Hurd raised the misrepresentation as a defence, and also counter-claimed for rescission of the contract. *Held* – Hurd had relied on Redgrave's statements regarding the income and the contracts could be rescinded. It did not matter that Hurd had the means of discovering their untruth; he was entitled to rely on Redgrave's statement.

Comment: Relief is not barred simply because there is an unsuccessful attempt by the person misled to discover the truth where the misrepresentation is fraudulent.

Did the statement influence the representee's decision?

The law requires that a misrepresentation must have operated on the mind of the representee. **If it has not, as where the representee was not influenced by it, there is no claim as the following case illustrates**.

Smith v Chadwick (1884) 9 App Cas 187

This action was brought by the plaintiff, who was a steel manufacturer, against Messrs Chadwick, Adamson and Collier, who were accountants and promoters of a company called the Blochairn Iron Co Ltd. The plaintiff claimed £5,750 as damages sustained through taking shares in the company which were not worth the price he had paid for them because of certain misrepresentations in the prospectus issued by the defendants. The action was for fraud. Among the misrepresentations alleged by Smith was that the prospectus stated that a Mr J.J. Grieves MP was a director of the company, whereas he had withdrawn his consent the day before the prospectus was issued. *Held* – That the statement regarding Mr Grieves was untrue but was not material to the plaintiff, because the evidence showed that he had never heard of Mr Grieves. His action for damages failed.

TYPES OF ACTIONABLE MISREPRESENTATION AND REMEDIES IN GENERAL

Innocent misrepresentation

A purely innocent misrepresentation is a false statement made by a person who had reasonable grounds to believe that the statement was true, not only when he made it but also at the time the contract was entered into. As regards reasonable grounds, the representer's best hope of proving this will be to show that he himself had been induced to buy the goods by the same statement, particularly where he is not technically qualified to verify it further (*see Humming Bird Motors Ltd* v *Hobbs* (1986) and *Oscar Chess Ltd* v *Williams* (1957), pp. 113 and 139). The party misled can ask the court to rescind the contract but has no right to ask for damages. However, the court may at its discretion award damages instead of rescission, provided the remedy of rescission is still available and has not been lost, e.g. by delay (Misrepresentation Act 1967, s. 2(2)). Rescission in effect cancels the contract and the court may in some cases regard this as a drastic remedy, particularly where there has been misrepresentation on a trivial matter, such as the quality of the tyres on a car. Suppose the seller of a car in a private sale says: 'the previous owner fitted new tyres at 26,000 miles'. If that statement is false but the seller was told this by the previous owner, then the court could award damages instead of rescission, thus leaving the contract intact but giving the party misled monetary compensation. Statements by dealers, however, are often taken to be terms of the contract (*see* p. 138).

Negligent misrepresentation

A negligent misrepresentation is a false statement made by a person who had no reasonable grounds for believing the statement to be true. The party misled may sue for rescission (*see below*) and/or damages and the requirement to prove that the statement was not made negligently but that there were reasonable grounds for believing it to be true is on the maker of the statement (or representer) (Misrepresentation Act 1967, s. 2(1)).

The subsection recognizes only a claim for damages and says nothing about rescission. However, in *Mapes* v *Jones* (1974) 232 EG 717 a property dealer contracted to lease a grocer's shop to the plaintiff for 21 years but in fact did not have sufficient interest in the property himself to grant such a lease, the maximum period available to him being 18 years. Despite constant requests no lease was supplied as originally promised and the plaintiff shut the shop and elected to treat the contract as repudiated. Willis J *held* that the plaintiff was entitled to rescission for misrepresentation under s. 2(1) of the 1967 Act. He also found that the defendant's delay in completion was a breach of condition allowing the plaintiff to repudiate the contract.

The following case provides a practical example of the application of s. 2(1).

Gosling v Anderson, *The Times*, 8 February 1972

Miss Gosling, a retired schoolmistress, entered into negotiations for the purchase of one of three flats in a house at Minehead owned by Mrs Anderson. Mr Tidbury, who was Mrs Anderson's agent in the negotiations, represented to Miss Gosling by letter that planning permission for a garage to go with the flat had been given. Mrs Anderson knew that this was not so. The purchase of the flat went through on the basis of a contract and a conveyance showing a parking area but not referring to planning permission which was later refused. Miss Gosling now sought damages for misrepresentation under s. 2(1) of the Misrepresentation Act 1967. *Held* – The facts revealed a negligent misrepresentation by Mr Tidbury made without reasonable grounds for believing it to be true. Mrs Anderson was liable for the acts of her agent and must pay damages under the Act of 1967.

Comment: (i) This action was against Mrs Anderson who was the other party to the contract. It was decided in *Resolute Maritime Inc and Another* v *Nippon Kaiji Kyokai and Others* [1983] 2 All ER 1 that no action is available against an agent such as Mr Tidbury under s. 2(1) of the Misrepresentation Act 1967. Section 2(1) of the 1967 Act begins: 'Where a person has entered into a contract after a misrepresentation has been made to him by another party thereto . . . ' Thus the subsection only applies when the representee has entered into a contract after a misrepresentation has been made to him by another party to the contract. Where an agent acting within the scope of his authority makes a representation under s. 2(1), the principal is liable to the third party misled, but not the agent. The agent will be liable to the third party only if he is guilty of fraud, or, under the rule in *Hedley Byrne* v *Heller* (1963) (*see* p. 115) for negligence at common law. Here the principal will be liable vicariously *along with the agent* for the latter's fraud or negligence if the agent is acting within the scope of his authority.

(ii) As regards proving reasonable grounds, an expert will be expected to verify his statements in a professional way. However, those without relevant technical knowledge will often find that the court will accept a statement as made innocently if the maker of the statement had been induced to purchase the goods himself by the same statement.

Thus in *Humming Bird Motors* v *Hobbs* [1986] RTR 276 H was a young man whom the judge found to be an amateur doing a bit of 'wheeling and dealing' in the motor trade. He bought a car from a dealer who told him that the mileage recorded, 34,900 miles, was correct. H sold the car on to the plaintiffs making the same statement, i.e. that the recorded mileage was, to the best of his knowledge and belief, correct. The plaintiffs discovered that the vehicle had done 80,000 miles and tried to claim damages for negligent misrepresentation. The Court of Appeal decided that H was not negligent; he was an amateur and was merely repeating what he himself believed.

Fraudulent misrepresentation

A fraudulent misrepresentation is a false representation of a material fact made knowing it to be false, or believing it to be false, or recklessly not caring whether it be true or false. Mere negligence is not enough. An element of dishonesty is required. For example, if Mr Tidbury in the *Gosling* case had *known* that there was no planning permission for the garage but had nevertheless gone on to state that there was, then the element of dishonesty would have been present and he would have been guilty of fraud. The party misled may sue for rescission and/or damages. As regards the action for damages, the plaintiff sues not on the contract but on the tort of deceit.

The following is the main case dealing with the definition of fraud.

Derry v Peek (1889) 14 App Cas 337

The Plymouth, Devonport and District Tramways Company had power under a special Act of Parliament to run trams by animal power, and with the consent of the Board of Trade (now the Department of Trade and Industry) by mechanical or steam power. Derry and the other appellants were directors of the company and issued a prospectus, inviting the public to apply for shares in it, stating that they had power to run trams by steam power, and claiming that considerable economies would result. The directors had assumed that the permission of the Board of Trade would be granted as a matter of course, but in the event the Board of Trade refused permission except for certain parts of the tramway. As a result the company was wound up and the directors were sued for fraud. The court decided that the directors were not fraudulent but honestly believed the statement in the prospectus to be true. As Lord Herschell said: 'Fraud is proved when it is shown that a false representation has been made (a) knowingly, or (b) without belief in its truth, or (c) recklessly, careless whether it be true or false.'

Comment: (i) This case gave rise to the Directors' Liability Act 1890 which made directors of companies liable to pay compensation for negligent misrepresentation in a prospectus, subject to a number of defences. The latest provisions are in the Financial Services Act 1986 (*see below*).

(ii) It will be noticed from this case that the mere fact that no grounds exist for believing a false statement does not of itself constitute fraud. There must also be an element of dishonesty which was not present in this case.

COMPENSATION UNDER THE FINANCIAL SERVICES ACT 1986

Under this Act, where the directors of a company publish an advertisement or prospectus containing false statements made innocently they may have to pay a form of damages called compensation.

There are a number of special defences available under the Act. For example, a director may deny responsibility for the prospectus, as where he ceased to be a director before it was issued. Assuming, however, that he does admit responsibility for the prospectus, the defences are that:

(a) he had reasonable grounds for believing the statement to be true;
(b) the statements were made on the authority of an expert who was thought to be competent;
(c) the statements were a copy of an official document; or
(d) that he published a correction or took reasonable steps to see that one was published and he reasonably believed it had been.

Experts, such as accountants, are also liable under the Act for false statements in their reports which are included in the prospectus. Again, the defence of lack of responsibility is available, as where the expert has not consented to the inclusion of his report in the prospectus. However, given that he accepts responsibility for the inclusion of his report, he has a defence if he can show that he had reasonable grounds for believing the statement to be true. Presumably, he could sustain this defence by showing, amongst other things, that the false statement came from an official document. Furthermore, whether or not a professional person has reasonable grounds will almost always depend upon the steps taken to *verify* the statement. If these are reasonable the professional person will not be liable even if the statement is wrong.

AGENT'S BREACH OF WARRANTY OF AUTHORITY

Under the law of agency where an agent misrepresents himself as having authority he does not possess, the third party will not obtain a contract with the principal and if he suffers loss as a consequence he may sue the agent for breach of warranty of authority, the action being for damages and brought in *quasi-contract*. Quasi-contract is based on the idea that a person should not obtain a benefit or unjust enrichment or cause injury to another with impunity merely because there is no obligation in contract or another established branch of law which will operate to make him account. The law may in these circumstances provide a remedy by implying a *fictitious promise* to account for the benefit of the enrichment or to compensate for damage caused.

NEGLIGENCE AT COMMON LAW

The tort remedy in general

Where the parties concerned were not in a *pre-contractual relationship* when the statement was made, s. 2(1) of the Misrepresentation Act 1967 will not apply. However, an action for damages for negligence will lie in tort, provided the false statement was made negligently.

The following case in the House of Lords finally affirmed this rule.

Hedley Byrne & Co Ltd v Heller & Partners Ltd [1963] 2 All ER 575

The appellants were advertising agents and the respondents were merchant bankers. The appellants had a client called Easipower Ltd who was a customer of the respondents. The appellants had contracted to place orders for advertising Easipower's products on television and in newspapers, and since this involved giving Easipower credit, they asked the respondents, who were Easipower's bankers, for a reference as to the creditworthiness of Easipower. The respondents said that Easipower Ltd was respectfully constituted and considered good, although they said in regard to the credit: 'These are bigger figures than we have seen' and also that the reference was given 'in confidence and without responsibility on our part'. Relying on this reply, the appellants placed orders for advertising time and space for Easipower Ltd, and the appellants assumed personal responsibility for payment to the television and newspaper companies concerned. Easipower Ltd went into liquidation and the appellants lost over £17,000 on the advertising contracts. The appellants sued the respondents for the amount of the loss, alleging that the respondents had not informed themselves sufficiently about Easipower Ltd before writing the statement, and were therefore liable in negligence. *Held* – In the present case the respondents' disclaimer was

adequate to exclude the assumption by them of the legal duty of care, but, in the absence of
the disclaimer, the circumstances would have given rise to a duty of care in spite of the
absence of a contract or fiduciary relationship.

Comment: (i) The House of Lords stated that the duty of care arose where there was 'a
special relationship' requiring care. This arises where the defendant has special knowledge
and/or expertise and offers information in the full *knowledge* that it will be relied upon by the
plaintiff. (For further developments in professional liability *see* p. 537.)

(ii) The ease with which the duty to take care placed upon the bank was excluded in this
case by the disclaimer was disappointing. However, such a disclaimer of negligence liability
would, these days, have to satisfy the test of 'reasonableness' under the Unfair Contract
Terms Act 1977 (*see* p. 154). It would seem that such a disclaimer would fall short of the
reasonable expectations of those in business who naturally and reasonably expect that a
bank will have taken proper care before giving a reference of this kind.

(iii) In this connection it was held in *Smith* v *Eric S. Bush* [1987] 3 All ER 179 that it was
unreasonable to allow a surveyor to rely on a general disclaimer of negligence where he had
been asked by a building society to carry out a reasonably careful visual inspection of the
property for valuation purposes (paid for by the would-be purchaser) when the valuer knew
that the purchaser would be likely to rely on his report and not get another one. The house
was purchased but, because of defects, turned out to be unfit for habitation. The surveyors
when sued could not escape liability for damages on the basis of disclaimer.

The case suggests that in so far as such disclaimers are still used by professional persons
they may not be effective, at least as regards ordinary consumers of professional services.

Use of the tort remedy in contract cases

In *Esso Petroleum* v *Mardon* [1976] 2 All ER 5 the court *held* that the principle in *Hedley
Byrne* could apply even where the parties concerned were in a pre-contractual
relationship and in addition that the person who had made the statement need not
necessarily be in business to give advice, provided it is reasonable for one party to
rely on the other's skill and judgment in making the statement. Mr Mardon was
awarded damages for a negligent misstatement by a senior sales representative of
Esso in regard to the amount of petrol he could expect to sell per year from a petrol
station which he was leasing from Esso. The facts of *Mardon* pre-dated the 1967 Act
and the court could not use it. The decision is obviously important but where the
facts have occurred since 1967 the Misrepresentation Act is likely to prove more
popular to plaintiffs who have been misled *into making contracts*, since they can ask
the representer to show he was not negligent. In *Hedley Byrne* claims the burden of
proof is on the plaintiff to prove negligence.

There is a very obvious use, however, for the tort of negligence claim even where
the careless misstatement has induced a contract. The tort claim allows an action for
a misleading *opinion or falsely stated intention*, whereas misrepresentation in all its
forms requires a misstatement of *fact*, not opinion or intention. The use of *Hedley
Byrne* would today make the legal gymnastics seen in *Edgington* v *Fitzmaurice* (1885)
(*see* p. 107) and *Smith* v *Land and House Property Co* (1884) (*see* p. 108) unnecessary.

Use of tort remedy for inaccurate company securities advertisements

As regards actions against directors and experts in respect of statements in an advertisement for the sale of securities or in a prospectus, there is as we have seen a statutory claim under the Financial Services Act 1986 and under *Hedley Byrne* at common law. The claim against directors under *Hedley Byrne* is specifically preserved by the Financial Services Act 1986 in s. 150(4). A claim under the Misrepresentation Act 1967 is against 'the other party to the contract', i.e. the company or issuing house, and not against directors or agents.

It will be recalled in *Esso Petroleum Co Ltd* v *Mardon* (1976) (*see above*) that the court *held* that it was too restrictive to limit the duty in *Hedley Byrne* to persons who carried on or who held themselves out as carrying on the *business* of giving information or advice. The acceptance of these views means that the duty can apply more widely and brings in company directors in terms that they could be liable on a personal basis for negligence.

In any case, it is a requirement as part of admission of the shares to a full Stock Exchange or USM (Unlisted Securities Market) listing, that the advertisement or prospectus shall state that the directors have taken reasonable care to ensure that the facts stated in it are true and accurate, that there are no misleading omissions and that, accordingly, all the directors take responsibility for the prospectus.

In view of this statement, it is likely that a duty of care is owed only by the individuals involved in the making of the statements and not by the company as such. If this is so, no claim can be made against the company. This would accord with the general principle of capital maintenance inherent in the prospectus remedies, i.e. it is difficult to get one's money back from the company and easier to get compensation from directors or experts, leaving capital contributed with the company.

In view of this it would seem that an action for rescission of the contract (*see below*) against the company will not in the company law context be a likely remedy. In any case it is very quickly lost as we shall see.

REMEDY OF RESCISSION

As we have seen, this remedy is available to a party misled by innocent, negligent or fraudulent misrepresentation. It restores the status quo, i.e. it puts the parties back to the position they were in before the contract was made. However, the remedy may be lost:

(a) *By affirmation.* If the injured party affirms the contract he cannot rescind. He will affirm if with full knowledge of the misrepresentation he expressly affirms the contract by stating that he intends to go on with it or if he does some act from which an implied intention may properly be deduced. In the company situation this could, for example, be attending a company meeting to complain about an inaccurate prospectus.

The following case is a general commercial example of the application of the affirmation rule.

Long v Lloyd [1958] 2 All ER 402

The plaintiff and the defendant were haulage contractors. The plaintiff was induced to buy the defendant's lorry by the defendant's misrepresentation as to condition and performance. The defendant advertised a lorry for sale at £850, the advertisement describing the vehicle as being in 'exceptional condition'. The plaintiff telephoned the defendant the same evening when the defendant agreed that his advertisement was a little ambiguous and said that the lorry was 'in first class condition'. The plaintiff saw the lorry at the defendant's premises at Hampton Court on a Saturday. During a trial run on the following Monday the plaintiff found that the speedometer was not working, a spring was missing from the accelerator pedal, and it was difficult to engage top gear. The defendant said there was nothing wrong with the vehicle except what the plaintiff had found. He also said at this stage that the lorry would do 11 miles to the gallon.

The plaintiff purchased the lorry for £750, paying £375 down and agreeing to pay the balance at a later date. He then drove the lorry from Hampton Court to his place of business at Sevenoaks. On the following Wednesday, the plaintiff drove from Sevenoaks to Rochester to pick up a load, and during that journey the dynamo ceased to function, an oil seal was leaking badly, there was a crack in one of the road wheels, and he used 8 gallons of petrol on a journey of 40 miles. That evening the plaintiff told the defendant of the defects, and the defendant offered to pay half the cost of a reconstructed dynamo, but denied any knowledge of the other defects. The plaintiff accepted the offer and the dynamo was fitted straightaway. On Thursday the lorry was driven by the plaintiff's brother to Middlesbrough, and it broke down on the Friday night. The plaintiff, on learning of this, asked the defendant for his money back, but the defendant would not give it to him. The lorry was subsequently examined and an expert said that it was not roadworthy. The plaintiff sued for rescission. *Held* – at first instance, by Glyn-Jones J – that the defendant's statements about the lorry were innocent and not fraudulent because the evidence showed that the lorry had been laid up for a month and it might have deteriorated without the defendant's precise knowledge. The Court of Appeal affirmed this finding of fact and made the following additional points.

(a) The journey to Rochester was not affirmation because the plaintiff was merely testing the vehicle in a working capacity.

(b) However, the acceptance by the plaintiff of the defendant's offer to pay half the cost of the reconstructed dynamo, and the subsequent journey to Middlesbrough, did amount to affirmation, and rescission could not be granted to the plaintiff.

Comment: (i) Damages could now be obtained for negligent misrepresentation under the Misrepresentation Act 1967, s. 2(1), for how could the seller say he had reasonable grounds for believing that the lorry was in exceptional condition or first class condition?

(ii) It seems remarkable that Glyn-Jones J did not find fraud. However, fraud must be proved according to the criminal standard, i.e. beyond a reasonable doubt, and not according to the civil standard which is on balance of probabilities. Fraud is therefore difficult to prove and in this case there was presumably a reasonable doubt in the mind of the judge on the issue of fraud.

(iii) The Court of Appeal would not accept that the statement that the lorry was in first class condition was a term of the contract (see further p. 135) but decided that it was only a misrepresentation.

   (b) *By lapse of time.* This is a form of implied affirmation and applies as follows:
      (i) In innocent and negligent misrepresentation the position is governed by equity and the passage of a reasonable time, even without knowledge of the misrepresentation, may prevent the court from granting rescission: *Leaf v International Galleries* (1950) – *see* p. 93.
      (ii) In fraudulent misrepresentation the position is governed by s. 32 of the Limitation Act 1980 and lapse of time has no effect on rescission where fraud is alleged as long as the action is brought within six years of the time when the fraud was, or with reasonable diligence, could have been discovered.
   (c) *Where status quo cannot be restored.* Rescission is impossible if the parties cannot be restored to their original positions as where goods sold under a contract of sale have been consumed. **The following case provides a further example**.

Clarke v Dickson (1858) 27 LJQB 223

In 1853 the plaintiff was induced by the misrepresentation of the three defendants, Dickson, Williams and Gibbs, to invest money in what was in effect a partnership to work lead mines in Wales. In 1857 the partnership was in financial difficulty and with the plaintiff's assent it was converted into a limited company and the partnership capital was converted into shares. Shortly afterwards the company commenced winding-up proceedings and the plaintiff, on discovery of the falsity of the representations, asked for rescission of the contract. *Held* – Rescission could not be granted because capital in a partnership is not the same as shares in a company. The firm was no longer in existence, having been replaced by the company, and it was not possible to restore the parties to their original positions.

Comment: It should be noted that in addition to the problem of restoration, third-party rights, i.e. creditors, had accrued on the winding-up of the company and this is a further bar to rescission (see *below*).

   (d) *Where a third party has acquired rights in the subject matter of the contract.* Thus if X obtains goods from Y by misrepresentation and pawns them with Z, Y cannot rescind the contract on learning of the misrepresentation in order to recover the goods from Z. Nor can he sue Z in conversion (*Lewis v Averay* (1971) – *see* p. 90).

CONTRACTS *UBERRIMAE FIDEI* (UTMOST GOOD FAITH)

Silence does not normally amount to misrepresentation. However, an important exception to the rule occurs in the case of certain contracts where from the circumstances of the case one party alone possesses full knowledge of all the material facts and in which therefore the law requires him to show utmost good faith. He must make full disclosure of all the material facts known to him otherwise the contract may be rescinded. The contracts concerned are as follows.

At common law

Contracts of insurance provide the only true example of a contract *uberrimae fidei*. There is a duty on the person taking up the insurance to disclose to the insurance company all facts of which he is aware which might affect the premium or acceptance of the risk. Failure to do so renders the contract voidable at the option of the insurance company. This could happen, for example, where a person seeking insurance did not disclose that he had been refused insurance by another company.

In addition, most proposals for insurance require the proposer to sign a declaration in which he warrants that the statements he has made are true and agrees that they be incorporated into the contract as terms. Where this is so any false statement which the proposer makes will be a ground for avoidance of the contract by the insurance company, even though the statement was not material in terms of the premium.

Thus the duty of disclosure in insurance contracts may be widened by the terms of the contract itself as the following case illustrates.

Dawsons Ltd v Bonnin [1922] 2 AC 413

Dawsons Ltd insured their motor lorry against loss by fire with Bonnin and others, and signed a proposal form which contained the following as Condition 4: 'Material misstatement or concealment of any circumstances by the insured material to assessing the premium herein, or in connection with any claim, shall render the policy void.' The policy also contained a clause saying that the 'proposal shall be the basis of the contract and shall be held as incorporated therein'. Actually the proposal form was filled up by an insurance agent, and although he stated the proposer's address correctly as 46 Cadogan Street, Glasgow, he also stated that the vehicle would usually be garaged there, although there was no garage accommodation at the Cadogan Street address and the lorry was garaged elsewhere. Dawsons' secretary, who signed the proposal, overlooked this slip made by the agent. The lorry was destroyed by fire and Dawsons claimed under the policy. *Held* – on appeal, by the House of Lords – the statement was not material within the meaning of Condition 4. However, the basis clause was an independent provision, and since the statement, though nor material, was untrue, the policy was void for breach of condition. Viscount Cave said: 'The meaning and effect of the basis clause, taken by itself, is that any untrue statement in the proposal, or any breach of its promissory clauses, shall avoid the policy, and if that be the contract of the parties, the question of materiality has not to be considered.'

Comment: (i) The Unfair Contract Terms Act 1977 does not apply to contracts of insurance. This resulted from a deal between the insurance companies and the government under which the insurance companies agreed to abide by voluntary statements of practice. These have no legal effect but some moral force. If the insurance company follows these statements of practice then certainly in consumer, i.e. non-business, insurance the worst effect of the basis clause should be eliminated.

(ii) However, even if we get rid of the basis clause problem, the rules of disclosure of material matters by the person seeking insurance remains a difficulty. It is based upon s. 18(2) of the Marine Insurance Act 1906. This should not have been used as a basis for *all* insurances. Those seeking marine insurance are well aware of the risks they seek to insure. Those seeking, for example, domestic fire insurance are not. The Law Commission Report entitled *Non-Disclosure and Breach of Warranty* places a heavy burden on insurance companies to phrase their questions so as to elicit the kind and amount of information they want and not to leave it, as at present, to the person seeking insurance to make uninformed guesses as to what might be material to the insurers. The common law has already taken steps in this direction in *Hair* v *Prudential Assurance* [1983] 2 Lloyd's Rep 667, the court deciding in that case that if a person seeking insurance answered honestly all the questions put to him by the proposal for insurance he should not be required to disclose any other matters. The questions should reveal all material issues.

By statute

As regards contracts to take shares in a company, there is a duty on the directors or its promoters, under the Financial Services Act 1986, to disclose various matters essential to an informed assessment as to whether an investor should purchase the securities. These provisions, and those in earlier statutes which preceded them, had to be put into the law by Parliament because the judiciary had always refused to regard the sale of securities by a company as a contract *uberrimae fidei*. They did not, therefore, require the advertisement or prospectus under which the shares were issued necessarily to disclose all the material facts.

In equity-fiduciary relationships

In contracts between members of a family, partners, principal and agent, solicitor and client, guardian and ward, and trustee and beneficiary, the relationship of the parties requires that the most ample disclosure should be made. The duties of disclosure arising from the above fiduciary relations recognized by equity are not situations of *uberrimae fidei*. In contracts *uberrimae fidei* it is the nature of the contract, i.e. insurance, which requires disclosure regardless of the relationship of the parties. In the fiduciary situation it is the relationship of parties and not the particular contract which gives rise to the need to disclose.

The following case is an illustration in a family situation.

Gordon v Gordon (1819) 3 Swan 400

Two brothers made an agreement for division of the family estates. The elder supposed he was born before the marriage of his parents and was therefore illegitimate. The younger knew that their parents had been married before the birth of the elder brother and the elder brother was therefore legitimate and his father's heir. He did not communicate this information to his elder brother. Nineteen years afterwards the elder brother discovered that he was legitimate and the agreement was set aside following this action brought by him. He would have had no case if at the time of the agreement both brothers had been in honest error as to the date of their parents' marriage.

DURESS

Duress will affect all contracts and gifts procured by its use. Duress, which is a common law concept, means actual violence or threats of violence to the person of the contracting party or those near and dear to him. The threats must be calculated to produce fear of loss of life or bodily harm.

Threats of violence

A contract will seldom be procured by actual violence but threats of violence are more probable. The threat must be illegal in that it must be a threat to commit a crime or tort. Thus to threaten an imprisonment, which would be unlawful if enforced, constitutes duress, but not, it is said, if the imprisonment would be lawful. However, the courts are unlikely to look with favour on a contract obtained by threatening to prosecute a criminal. A contract procured by a threat to sue for an act which was not a crime, e.g. trespass, would not be affected by duress.

The following case provides an example of the avoidance of a contract made under duress by threats of violence.

Welch v Cheesman (1973) 229 EG 99

Mrs Welch lived with the defendant, C, for many years in a house which she owned. C was a man given to violence, and after he threatened her Mrs Welch sold the house to him for £300. C died and his widow claimed the house which was worth about £3,000. Mrs Welch brought this action to set aside the sale of the house to C on the grounds of duress and she succeeded.

Threats to property

In *Skeate* v *Beale* (1840) 11 Ad & EL 983 a tenant owed £19 10s in old money and agreed to pay £3 7s 6d immediately and the remaining £16 2s 6d within a month if his landlord would withdraw a writ of distress under which he was threatening to sell the tenant's goods. The tenant later disputed what he owed and the landlord tried to set up the agreement and sued for the remaining £16 2s 6d. It was held that the landlord was entitled to £16 2s 6d under the agreement which was not affected by duress since the threat was to sell the tenant's goods. However, more recently the courts have been moving away from the view that threats to property cannot invalidate contracts. In *The Siboen and The Sibotre* [1976] Lloyd's Rep 293 it was said that duress could be a defence if a person was forced to make a contract by the threat of having a valuable picture slashed or his house burnt down.

Duress probably renders a contract *voidable*

This, at least, is the view expressed in Cheshire & Fifoot's *Law of Contract* (a leading text on contract law), though other writers have argued that the effect of duress is to render a contract void. However, the judgments of the Privy Council in *Barton* v *Armstrong* [1975] 2 All ER 465 and *Pao On* v *Lau Yiu Long* [1979] 3 All ER 65 suggest that duress has the same effect as fraud, i.e. it renders a contract voidable. The issue is an important one for third parties, since if B procures goods from A by duress and sells the goods to C, who has no knowledge of the duress, A will be able to recover the goods from C if the contract is void, but will not be able to do so if it is voidable. On the authorities to date, therefore, A would have no claim against C.

UNDUE INFLUENCE AND ASSOCIATED EQUITABLE PLEAS

The doctrine of undue influence was developed by equity. The concept of undue influence is designed to deal with contracts *or gifts* obtained without free consent by the influence of one mind over another.

If there is no special relationship between the parties undue influence may exist, but must be proved by the person seeking to avoid the contract.

Where a confidential or fiduciary relationship exists between the parties, the party in whom the confidence was reposed must show that undue influence was not used, i.e. that the contract was the act of a free and independent mind. It is desirable, though not essential, that independent advice should have been given.

There are several confidential relationships which are well established in the law, namely parent and child, solicitor and client, trustee and beneficiary, guardian and ward and religious adviser and disciple. In these cases there is a presumption of undue influence by the parent, the solicitor, the trustee and so on. There is no presumption of such a relationship between husband and wife, nor, according to the Court of Appeal in *Mathew* v *Bobbins* (1980) 256 EG 603 between employer and employee. However, a presumption of undue influence may be made between husband and wife where there are special circumstances such as the lack of sufficient mental capacity in either party to resist the influence of the other leading to gifts of property which are quite out of character with the donor's normal inquiring disposition when disposing of property (*Simpson* v *Simpson*, *The Times*, 11 June 1988). The fiduciary relationship between parent and child ends usually, but not necessarily, on reaching 18 or on getting married. **The following case illustrates this.**

Lancashire Loans Ltd v Black [1934] 1 KB 380

A daughter married at 18 and went to live with her husband. Her mother was an extravagant woman and was in debt to a firm of moneylenders. When the daughter became of age, her mother persuaded her to raise £2,000 on property in which the daughter had an interest, and this was used to pay off the mother's debts. Twelve months later the mother and daughter signed a joint and several promissory note of £775 at 85 per cent interest in favour of the moneylenders, and the daughter created a further charge on her property in order that the mother might borrow more money. The daughter did not understand the nature of the transaction, and the only advice she received was from a solicitor acting for the mother and the moneylenders. The moneylenders brought this action against the mother and daughter on the note. *Held* – The daughter's defence that she was under the undue influence of her mother succeeded, in spite of the fact that she was of full age and married with her own home.

A further illustration of a situation of presumed undue influence in the case of religious influence appears below.

Allcard v Skinner (1887) 36 Ch D 145

In 1868 the plaintiff joined a Protestant institution called the sisterhood of St Mary at the Cross, promising to devote her property to the service of the poor. The defendant Miss Skinner was the Lady Superior of the Sisterhood. In 1871 the plaintiff ceased to be a novice and became a sister in the order, taking her vows of poverty, chastity and obedience. By this time she had left her home and was residing with the sisterhood. The plaintiff remained a sister until 1878 and, in compliance with the vow of poverty, she had by then given property to the value of £7,000 to the defendant. The plaintiff left the order in 1879 and became a Roman Catholic. Of the property she had transferred, £1,671 remained in 1885 and the plaintiff sought to recover this sum, claiming that it had been transferred in circumstances of undue influence. *Held* – The gifts had been made under pressure of an unusually persuasive nature, particularly since the plaintiff was prevented from seeking outside advice under a rule of the sisterhood which said, 'Let no sister seek the advice of any extern without the superior's leave.' However, the plaintiff's claim was barred by her delay because, although the influence was removed in 1879, she did not bring her action until 1885.

However, there may be a presumption of undue influence even though the relationship between the parties is not in the established categories outlined above. In *Re Craig Dec'd* [1970] 2 All ER 390 Ungoed-Thomas J ruled that presumption of undue influence arose on proof:

(a) of a gift so substantial or of such a nature that it could not on the face of it be accounted for on the grounds of the ordinary motives on which ordinary men acted, and

(b) of a relationship of trust and confidence such that the recipient of the gift was in a position to exercise undue influence over the person making it. **This principle was applied in the following case.**

Hodgson v Marks [1970] 3 All ER 513

Mrs Hodgson, who was a widow of 83, owned a freehold house in which she lived. In 1959 she took in a Mr Evans as a lodger. She soon came to trust Evans and allowed him to manage her financial affairs. In June 1960, she transferred the house to Evans, her sole reason for so doing being to prevent her nephew from turning Evans out of the house. It was orally agreed between Mrs Hodgson and Evans that the house was to remain hers although held in the name of Evans. Evans later made arrangements to sell the house without the knowledge or consent of Mrs Hodgson. The house was bought by Mr Marks and Mrs Hodgson now asked for a declaration that he was bound to transfer the property back to her. The following questions arose:

(a) whether Evans held the house in trust for Mrs Hodgson. It was *held* – by Ungoed-Thomas J – that he did. The absence of written evidence of trust as required by s. 53 of the Law of Property Act 1925 was not a bar to Mrs Hodgson's claim. The section does not apply to implied trusts of this kind;

(b) whether Evans had exercised undue influence. It was *held* that he had and that a presumption of undue influence was raised. Although the parties were not in the established categories, Evans had a relationship of trust and confidence with Mrs Hodgson of a kind which raised a presumption of undue influence.

However, Mrs Hodgson lost the case because Mr Marks was protected by s. 70 of the Land Registration Act 1925, which gives rights to a purchaser of property for value in respect of interests in that property of which the purchaser is not aware. In this case Mr Marks bought the house from Mr Evans, the house being in the name of Evans and he had no reason to suppose that Mrs Hodgson had any interest in it.

Comment: (i) Mrs Hodgson's appeal to the Court of Appeal in 1971 succeeded and she got her house back, the court holding that in spite of s. 70 a purchaser must pay heed to the possibility of rights in all *occupiers*. Mrs Hodgson was obviously in occupation with Mr Evans and inquiries should have been made by the purchaser as to her rights in the property.

(ii) The application of the presumption in a relationship which was not one of the established ones is also illustrated by *Goldsworthy v Brickell* [1987] 1 All ER 853, where a contract to grant a tenancy of a farm advantageous to the defendant in that, for example, it did not allow the landlord, G, to make any rent increases, was set aside. The defendant, B, who had become the tenant, was a neighbour of G's. G was 85 and had come to rely implicitly on the advice of B. Undue influence was presumed although neighbours are not within the established categories where undue influence is generally presumed.

Effect of undue influence on third parties

A contract between A and B procured by undue influence cannot be avoided by rescission against third parties who acquire rights for value without notice of the facts. Where this has happened the party suffering the undue influence, say, A, will have to rely on tracing the proceeds of sale into the original purchaser's, i.e. B's, assets. The contract may be avoided and the property recovered from third parties for value with notice of the facts and also against volunteers (i.e. persons who have given no consideration) even though they were unaware of the facts.

Effect of undue influence on the parties to the contract

Undue influence renders the contract voidable so that it may be rescinded. However, since rescission is an equitable remedy, there must be no delay in claiming relief after the influence has ceased to have effect. Delay in claiming relief in these circumstances may bar the claim since delay is evidence of affirmation. This is illustrated by the case of *Allcard* v *Skinner* (*above*)

ECONOMIC DURESS

Apart from the old concepts of duress and undue influence, the courts are developing in modern times wider rules to protect persons against improper pressure and inequality of bargaining power as it affects contracts. This development was perhaps best described by Lord Denning in *Lloyds Bank* v *Bundy* [1974] 3 All ER 757 where he said, having discussed duress and various forms of undue pressure in contract:

> Gathering all together, I would suggest that through all these instances there runs a single thread. They rest on 'inequality of bargaining power'. By virtue of it, the English law gives relief to one who, without independent advice, enters into a contract on terms which are very unfair or transfers property for consideration which is grossly inadequate, where his bargaining power is grievously impaired by reason of his own needs or desires, or by his own ignorance or infirmity coupled with undue influence or pressures brought to bear on him by or for the benefit of the other.

Economic duress is within this concept. Suppose A agrees to build a tanker for B by an agreed date at an agreed price and B enters into a contract with C under which the tanker is to be chartered to C from the agreed completion date or shortly afterwards. If A then threatens not to complete the contract by the agreed date unless B pays more and B makes an extra payment because he does not want to be liable in breach of contract to C, then the agreement to pay more is affected by economic duress. (*See* the judgment of Mocatta J in *North Ocean Shipping Co Ltd* v *Hyundai Construction Co Ltd. The Atlantic Baron* [1978] 3 All ER 1170.)

The decision of the House of Lords in *Universe Tankships Inc of Monrovia* v *International Transport Workers' Federation* [1982] 2 All ER 67 is instructive in that it affirms the existence of the doctrine of economic duress. In that case a ship called the *Universe Sentinel*, which was owned by Universe Tankships, was 'blacked' by the respondent trade union, the ITF, which regarded the ship as sailing under a flag of convenience. ITF was against flag-of-convenience ships and refused to make tugs available when the ship arrived at Milford Haven to discharge her cargo. The blacking was lifted after Universe Tankships had made an agreement with ITF regarding improvements in pay and conditions of the crew and had paid money to ITF which included a contribution of $6,480 to an ITF fund known as The Seafarers' International Welfare Protection and Assistance Fund. Universe Tankships sued for the return of the $6,480 on the basis of economic duress, and the House of Lords *held* that they were entitled to recover it. It appears from the judgments that the effect of economic duress is to make the contract voidable and to provide a ground for recovery of money paid as money had and received to the plaintiff's use – a form of quasi-contractual claim.

The decision in *Universe Tankships* was applied by the Court of Appeal in *B & S Contracts & Design* v *Victor Green Publications* [1984] IGR 419 where A agreed to erect stands for B who was doing a presentation at Olympia. A's employees threatened to strike unless they received extra money which they had demanded and to which they were not entitled. A said that the contract could not proceed unless these extra sums were paid by B as an increase in the contract price. B paid the extra sums to get the work done and then recovered them in this action. The money was paid under economic duress.

It should also be noted that where extra contractual payments have been arranged under circumstances of economic duress they cannot be recovered in a claim before a court. Thus in *Atlas Express* v *Kafco* [1989] 1 All ER 641 Atlas, a national road carrier, made a contract to deliver cartons of basketware to Woolworths stores for Kafco who were a small company importing and distributing the basketware. A price of £1.10 per carton was agreed but the first load had fewer cartons than had been anticipated and Atlas told Kafco that they would not carry any more without a minimum payment per trip regardless of the number of cartons carried. Kafco could not find another carrier quickly and, being worried about their contract with Woolworths if the latter did not get their supplies, Kafco agreed to the new terms but later refused to pay the new rate, only the per carton rate. The High Court *held* that the claim of Atlas for the minimum rate must be dismissed. The circumstances amounted to economic duress and there was no proper consent by Kafco.

UNCONSCIONABLE BARGAINS

The court will, in what it regards as an appropriate case, set aside a contract which is affected by improper pressure by one party or where there is inequality of bargaining power. However, mere inequality is not in itself enough: the court will look at all the circumstances of the case.

The following case and comment illustrates the legal position.

Lloyds Bank v Bundy [1974] 3 All ER 757

The defendant and his son's company both banked with the plaintiffs, the defendant having been a customer for many years. The company's affairs deteriorated over a period of years and at the son's suggestion the bank's assistant manager visited the defendant and said that the bank could not continue to support an overdraft for the company unless the defendant entered into a guarantee of the account. The defendant received no independent advice, nor did the bank's assistant manager suggest that he should do so. The defendant charged his house as security for the overdraft and shortly afterwards the company went into receivership. The bank obtained possession of the house from the defendant in the county court, where the assistant branch manager in evidence said that he thought that the defendant had relied upon him implicitly to advise him about the charge.

The defendant appealed to the Court of Appeal in an attempt to set aside the guarantee and the security and it was *held* – allowing the defendant's appeal – that in the particular circumstances a special relationship existed between the defendant and the bank's assistant manager, as agent for the bank, and the bank was in breach of its duty of fiduciary care in procuring the charge which would be set aside for undue influence. The defendant, without any benefit to himself, had signed away his sole remaining asset without taking independent advice.

Comment: (i) While the majority of the Court of Appeal (Cairns LJ and Sir Eric Sachs) were content to decide the appeal on the conventional ground that a fiduciary relationship existed between the bank and its customer, which is to suggest that a new fiduciary relationship has come into being, Lord Denning took the opportunity to break new ground by deciding that in addition to avoiding the contract on the grounds of fiduciary relationship, Mr Bundy could also have done so on the basis of 'inequality of bargaining power'. Although inequality of bargaining power obviously includes undue influence, Lord Denning made it clear that the principle does not depend on the will of one party being dominated or overcome by the other. This is clear from that part of the judgment where he says: 'One who is in extreme need may knowingly consent to a most improvident bargain, solely to relieve the straits in which he finds himself.' This approach is, of course, at variance with the traditional view of undue influence which was that it was based on dominance resulting in an inferior party being unable to exercise independent judgment or on a relationship of trust and confidence.

(ii) It should be noted that cases such as this which introduce into the law a requirement that a contract must be fair may eventually develop to the point where adequacy of consideration is required in contract. This is not the case at the present time.

(iii) In *National Westminster Bank plc v Morgan* [1983] 3 All ER 85 the Court of Appeal set aside a charge over a wife's share in the matrimonial home after she executed it without legal advice in order to secure a loan from the bank to clear a building society mortgage, and after the bank manager had assured her that the charge would not be used to secure her husband's business advances, whereas it did in fact extend to such advances. However, the bank had no intention of using the charge other than to secure the advance to clear the building society mortgage; nor did it.

The above decision, which moved in the direction of saying that banks would have to ensure that all their customers had independent legal advice before taking out a bank mortgage was reversed by the House of Lords in *National Westminster Bank plc v Morgan* [1985] 1 All ER 821. Undue influence, the House of Lords said, was the use by one person of a power over another person to take a certain course of action generally to his or her disadvantage. A bank manager need not advise independent legal advice in a situation such as this. The manager in this case had stuck to explaining the legal effect of the charge which, though erroneous as to the terms of the charge, correctly represented his intention and that of the bank. The security represented no disadvantage to Mrs Morgan. It was exactly what she wanted to clear the building society loan on her home. The House of Lords also rejected the view that a court would grant relief where there was merely an inequality of bargaining power. Their Lordships rejected that view which was expressed by Lord Denning in *Bundy*. The courts will not, said the House of Lords, protect persons against what they regard as a mistake merely because of inequality of bargaining power. This is a much harder line.

(iv) In *Bundy*, therefore, the Court of Appeal *held* that the bank in not advising the person giving the security to get independent advice exercised undue influence and for this reason set the security aside. In *Morgan* the House of Lords *held* that no presumption of undue influence existed. In *Cornish v Midland Bank* [1985] 3 All ER 513 the Court of Appeal decided that the proper way to deal with these cases was not through undue influence but by using the law of negligence, though only where the bank had given wrong advice.

In *Cornish* the plaintiff had signed a second mortgage on a farmhouse jointly owned with her husband in order to secure £2,000 which her husband had borrowed from the bank. She did so because the bank clerk involved said that the mortgage was like a building society mortgage. It was not because unlike a building society mortgage it covered all future borrowing by the husband. The bank later tried to enforce the security. Eventually the Court of Appeal *held* that the bank was liable in negligence for the wrong advice of its clerk who made a negligent misstatement causing damage, i.e. that £2,000 was the borrowing limit when it was not. The mortgage was not set aside for undue influence so that the bank was entitled to the proceeds of the sale of the farmhouse but had to pay the plaintiff £11,231 damages plus interest for negligence. Thus, although it would be good practice for a bank to advise independent advice, it is not necessary for it to do so. The security will be good and there is no presumption of undue influence. However, if an employee of the bank *actually* gives negligent advice or fails to explain the consequences of the charge and/or fails to advise the taking of independent advice (*see Midland Bank plc v Perry, The Times*, 28 May 1987), the bank will be able to enforce the security but will be liable in damages under the ruling in *Hedley Byrne v Heller & Partners* (1963) (*see* p. 115).

Further examples of inequality of bargaining power may be found in *Clifford Davis Management* v *WEA Records* [1975] 1 All ER 237 where A, an experienced manager, obtained a contract with a pop star, B, who had little or no business experience, under which B gave A the copyright in all his compositions for a period of years. It was *held* that B could avoid the contract because A had exploited his superior bargaining power.

NO GENERAL RULE THAT ALL CONTRACTS MUST BE FAIR

There is no rule of law which states that a fair price must be paid in *all* transactions and some unfair contracts will be held binding provided the parties were of equal bargaining strength. In *Burma Oil Ltd* v *The Governor of the Bank of England, The Times*, 4 July 1981, Burma was in financial difficulties and sold a large holding of shares which it had in British Petroleum to the government at a price below the Stock Exchange price. Burma then brought an action to set the contract aside. The court refused to do so. Although there was authority to set aside a transaction where one party had acted without independent advice, or where the bargaining strength of one party was grievously impaired, neither of those situations existed in this case. The relationship was purely commercial and the contract for the sale of shares must stand.

GRADED QUESTIONS

Essay mode

1. (a) Adam, when negotiating for the sale of his business as a school outfitter, told Barry, a prospective purchaser, that his customers included all the schools within five miles. He also made exaggerated statements regarding annual turnover and profits.

   Adam urged Barry to check the accounts. He did not. If he had, he would have discovered the truth.

   Two days before Barry bought the business the largest school in the area informed Adam that they had decided that from next term uniforms would no longer be compulsory. Only after the contract for the sale of the business was signed did Barry become aware of the true position.

   Advise Barry.   (15 marks)

   (b) What circumstances may lead to the loss of the right of rescission?

                                                                            (5 marks)

   (North Staffordshire Polytechnic. BA Business Studies. Business Law)

2. Frank is an antique dealer and a world-famous authority on eighteenth-century French furniture. Clive, who has just bought an old house and wishes to buy antique furniture for it, admires a set of dining chairs in Frank's antique shop. Frank tells him that the chairs are 'undoubtedly eighteenth century' and 'might well have come from Versailles itself'. Clive pays £8,000 for the chairs and takes them home. Two days later Clive is polishing one of the chairs and sees a label underneath the seat which says: 'Made by Arnold Sidebotham, Leeds, 1927'. Clive finds this label on all the chairs and establishes very quickly that the label is correct. Arnold Sidebotham did make the chairs in 1927. The chairs are worth about £425.

Frank's error is honest. He had bought the chairs in a sale at an old country house and did not bother to examine them closely.

What remedies does Clive have against Frank?

(The Institute of Company Accountants. Law Relating to Business. May 1989)

3. To what extent have the courts been prepared to recognize that a contract can be vitiated by economic duress?

(The Institute of Legal Executives. Part II: Law of Contract. June 1990)

Objective mode

Four alternative answers are given. Select ONE only. Circle the answer which you consider to be correct. Check your answers by referring back to the information given in the chapter and against the answers at the back of the book.

1. A representation:

    A Always consists of a statement inducing a contract.

    B Is a term of a contract.

    C Can never consist in a false opinion.

    D May be a statement inducing a contract or in some cases non-disclosure or a false opinion.

2. A person may sue upon a misrepresentation at common law:

    A If he knew it was untrue.

    B If he was given information which showed it to be untrue which he did not read.

    C If it was not material to his decision to make the contract.

    D If it was not addressed to him.

3. A negligent misstatement is a false statement made:

    A Dishonestly.

    B Without reasonable grounds for believing it to be true.

    C Knowing it to be false.

D Without caring whether it is true or false.

4. Rescission is an equitable remedy which:

    A Is available only for innocent misrepresentation.

    B Puts the parties in the position they would have been in if the contract had been performed.

    C Is available only for fraudulent misrepresentation.

    D Puts the parties in the position they would have been in if the contract had not been made.

5. A presumption of undue influence does not exist between:

    A Solicitor and client.

    B Trustee and beneficiary.

    C Religious adviser and disciple.

    D Employer and employee.

With reference to the following information answer questions 6, 7 and 8.

Mrs Pelfer, a wealthy widow and property owner aged 72, became interested in the beliefs of a religious sect called the Brothers and Sisters of Charity. She went to see Brother Reynard, who was the leader of the sect and asked what she might do to assist in the work. Brother Reynard suggested that she should first join the sect and decide over a period of time where she might best make her contribution. Mrs Pelfer became a member of the sect and attended regular prayer meetings which were held at Brother Reynard's home. On one such occasion Brother Reynard suggested to Mrs Pelfer that the sect ought to have its own premises and asked her if she would sell one of her properties, Warren Manor, to the sect at less than market price.

Mrs Pelfer at first refused but six months later she sold the property to Brother Reynard for half its market value having been told repeatedly by him that in doing so she would be assured of a place in Heaven on her death. The conveyance and other legal formalities were carried out for her by Proctor who was also solicitor to the sect.

Two months after conveying Warren Manor to Brother Reynard Mrs Pelfer, who has not received any money in respect of the sale either from Brother Reynard or Proctor, was received into the Church of England and now wishes to recover the property.

6. The contract for the sale of Warren Manor is:

    A Valid.

    B Voidable.

    C Void.

    D Unenforceable.

7. Mrs Pelfer will be able to recover her property because the contract of sale of Warren Manor is affected by:

   A Mistake.
   B Duress.
   C Misrepresentation.
   D Undue influence.

8. Which of the following cases has been relevant to you in reaching your decisions?

   A *Hodgson* v *Marks* (1970).
   B *Peek* v *Gurney* (1873).
   C *Smith* v *Chadwick* (1884).
   D *Allcard* v *Skinner* (1887).

Answers to questions set in objective mode appear on p. 551.

6 | The law of contract – contractual terms

The OBJECTIVES of this chapter are to consider the contents of the contract by explaining the types of terms, express or implied, which may be found in a contract and the rules which decide whether an exclusion clause which excludes liability for breach of contract and other civil damage is valid.

INDUCEMENTS AND TERMS GENERALLY

Even where it is clear that a valid contract has been made it is still necessary to decide precisely what it is the parties have undertaken to do in order to be able to say whether each has performed or not performed his part of the agreement.

In order to decide upon the terms of the contract it is necessary to find out what was said or written by the parties. Furthermore, having ascertained what the parties said or wrote, it is necessary to decide whether the statements were mere inducements (or representations) or terms of the contract, i.e. part of its actual contents. The distinction in diagrammatic form together with an indication of remedies appears in Fig. 6.1 at p. 136.

The distinction is less important than it was since the passing of the Misrepresentation Act 1967. Before the Act became law there was often no remedy for a misrepresentation which was not fraudulent, and in such a case the plaintiff's only hope of obtaining a remedy was to convince the court that the defendant's statement was not a mere inducement but a term of the contract of which the defendant was in breach and for which damages might be obtained. As we have seen, under the Misrepresentation Act 1967 the new form of negligent misrepresentation which did not exist before will now give rise in many cases to an action for damages even in respect of a mere misrepresentation or inducement.

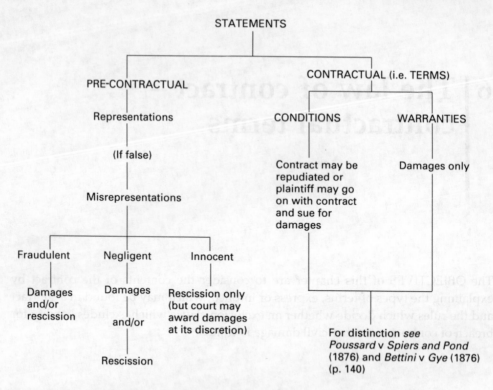

Fig. 6.1   Pre-contractual and contractual statements.

INDUCEMENTS AND TERMS DISTINGUISHED

Nevertheless, it is still necessary to consider the main tests applied by the courts in order to distinguish between a mere misrepresentation and a term of the contract, bearing in mind always that the question whether a statement is an inducement or a term and, if a term, whether a condition or warranty *is a matter of fact for the judge.* Fact decisions of this sort vary widely according to the circumstances of each case, so that it is virtually impossible to predict with absolute accuracy what the outcome of a particular case will be. However, by way of illustration the following headings contain the major guidelines which are applied.

The statements and intentions of the parties

The court will always be concerned to implement the intentions of the parties as they appear from statements made by them. Thus in *Gill & Duffus SA* v *Société pour l'Exportation des Sucres SA* [1985] 1 Lloyd's Rep 621 the defendants agreed to sell sugar to Gill. A term of the contract (not specified as a condition or warranty) said that the defendants were to name a port at which the sugar was to be loaded by November 14 'at latest'. The defendants did not nominate a port by that time and so

Gill refused to take any sugar from the defendants and regarded the contract as cancelled. The defendants then tried to make a nomination of a port but Gill refused to accept it saying that they had repudiated the contract because of the defendants' breach of condition (or repudiatory breach). Following a decision unfavourable to them at arbitration, Gill appealed. Leggatt J said that there were no words in the English language by which a deadline could be appointed more concisely, more precisely, or with more finality than 'at latest'. They meant what they said and the judge had no doubt that the intention of the parties as gathered from the contract itself would be best carried out by treating the promise not as a mere warranty but as a condition precedent by the failure to perform which the other party was relieved of liability. Gill's contention was accepted. There was a repudiatory breach of condition. Where in a contract the parties have indicated that a particular undertaking is to be a term of the contract, the courts will in general abide by the wishes of the parties. However, the court will not slavishly follow the parties' statements and where, for example, the parties appear to have regarded a trivial matter as a vital term of the agreement, the court may still take the view that it is not.

Thus so far as a written contract is concerned, the court may disregard a statement by the parties that a particular undertaking is a condition and say instead that it is a warranty. So far as wholly oral contracts are concerned, the court may ignore the statements of the parties and decide that a particular undertaking is a condition, a warranty, or a mere inducement.

Thus in *L Schuler AG* v *Wickham Machine Tool Sales* [1973] 2 All ER 39 the plaintiffs entered into a contract for four years with the defendants giving them the sole right to sell panel presses in England. A clause of the contract provided that it should be a condition of the agreement that the defendants' representative should visit six named firms each week to solicit orders. The defendants' representatives failed on a few occasions to do so and the plaintiffs claimed to be entitled to repudiate the agreement on the basis that a single failure was a breach of condition giving them an absolute right to treat the contract as at an end. The House of Lords said that such minor breaches by the defendants did not entitle the plaintiffs to repudiate. The House of Lords construed the clause on the basis that it was so unreasonable that the parties could not have intended it as a condition, giving Schuler a right of repudiation but rather as a warranty. Thus Schuler were themselves in breach of contract leaving Wickham with a claim for damages against Schuler.

This case is also an example of the court trying to give redress in regard to an unconscionable bargain and to correct unscrupulous commercial conduct.

The nature of the statement

A statement is likely to be an inducement rather than a term if the person making the statement asks the other party to check or verify it, e.g. 'The car is sound but I should get an engineer's report on it.'

In addition a statement is likely to be a term rather than a mere inducement if it is made with the intention of preventing the other party from looking for defects and succeeds in doing this, e.g. 'The car is sound, you need not look it over.'

The importance of the statement

If the statement is such that the plaintiff would not have made the contract without it, then the statement will be a term of the contract and not a mere inducement. **The following case illustrates this point.**

Bannerman v White (1861) 10 CB (NS) 844

The defendant was intending to buy hops from the plaintiff and he asked the plaintiff whether sulphur had been used in the cultivation of the hops, adding that if it had he would not even bother to ask the price, by which he meant he would not make the contract. The plaintiff said that no sulphur had been used, though in fact it had. It was *held* that the plaintiff's assurance that sulphur had not been used was a term of the contract and the defendant was justified in raising the matter as a successful defence to an action for the price.

The timing of the statement

A statement made during preliminary negotiations tends to be an inducement. Where the interval between the making of the statement and the making of the contract is distinct then the statement is almost certain to be an inducement. Thus in *Routledge* v *McKay* [1954] 1 All ER 855 the plaintiff and defendant were discussing the possible purchase and sale of the defendant's motor cycle. Both parties were private persons. The defendant, taking the information from the registration book, said, on 23 October, that the cycle was a 1942 model. On 30 October a written contract of sale was made. The actual date of the cycle was later found to be 1930. The buyer's claim for damages for breach of warranty failed in the Court of Appeal. In this case the interval between the negotiations and the contract was well marked and the statement was not a term. However, the interval is not always so well marked and in such cases there is a difficulty in deciding whether the statement is an inducement or term.

Oral statements later put into writing

If the statement was oral and the contract was afterwards reduced to writing, then the terms of the contract tend to be contained in the written document and all oral statements tend to be pre-contractual inducements. Even so the court may still consider the apparent intentions of the parties and decide that they had made a contract which was part oral and part written (*see Evans* v *Merzario* (1976) at p. 149).

Special skill and knowledge or lack of same

Where one of the parties has special knowledge or skill with regard to the subject matter of the contract, then the statements of such a party will normally be regarded as terms of the contract. In addition it will be difficult for an expert to convince the court that a person with no particular knowledge or skill in regard to the subject matter has made statements which constitute terms of the contract. **The following case and comment illustrate this**.

Oscar Chess Ltd v Williams [1957] I All ER 325

In May 1955, Williams bought a car from the plaintiffs on hire-purchase terms. The plaintiffs took Williams' Morris car in part exchange. Williams described the car as a 1948 model and produced the registration book, which showed that the car was first registered in April 1948, and that there had been several owners since that time. Williams was allowed £290 on the Morris. Eight months later the plaintiffs discovered that the Morris car was a 1939 Model there being no change in appearance in the model between 1939 and 1948. The allowance for a 1939 model was £175 and the plaintiffs sued for £115 damages for breach of warranty that the car was a 1948 model. Evidence showed that some fraudulent person had altered the registration book but he could not be traced, and that Williams honestly believed that the car was a 1948 model. *Held* – The contract might have been set aside in equity for misrepresentation but the delay of eight months defeated this remedy. This mistake was a mistake of quality which did not avoid the contract at common law and in order to obtain damages the plaintiffs must prove a breach of warranty. The Court was unable to find that Williams was in a position to give such a warranty, and suggested that the plaintiffs should have taken the engine and chassis number and written to the manufacturers, so using their superior knowledge to protect themselves in the matter. The plaintiffs were not entitled to any redress. Morris LJ dissented, holding that the statement that the car was a 1948 model was a fundamental condition.

Comment: (i) No doubt Mr Williams would have been liable for innocent and not negligent misrepresentation under the Misrepresentation Act 1967 for he had reasonable grounds to believe that the car was a 1948 Morris. He was merely repeating an earlier deception made when he bought the vehicle.

(ii) Since the remedy of rescission had been lost by reason of delay the court would not even now grant that remedy or damages at the court's discretion, which the court can do but only if the remedy of rescission is still available. The reluctance of the court to say that statements by non-dealers are contractual terms for breach of which damages can be recovered leads to an unfair result as in this case. After all, Mr Williams obtained £115 more for his Morris than it was worth.

(iii) A contrast is provided by *Dick Bentley Productions Ltd v Harold Smith (Motors) Ltd* [1965] 2 All ER 65 where a dealer sold a Bentley to a customer, the instruments showing that it had done only 30,000 miles since a replacement engine was fitted when in fact it had done 100,000 miles since that time. The seller was held liable for breach of condition whereas in *Oscar Chess* the seller who was not a dealer was not.

CONDITIONS AND WARRANTIES

Having decided that a particular statement is a term of the contract and not a mere inducement, the court must then consider the importance of that statement in the context of the contract as a whole. Not all terms are of equal importance. Failure to perform some may have a more serious effect on the contract than failure to perform others. The law has applied special terminology to contractual terms in order to distinguish the vital or fundamental obligations from the less vital, the expression *condition* being applied to the former and the expression *warranty* to the latter. A condition is a fundamental obligation which goes to the root of the contract. A warranty on the other hand is a subsidiary obligation which is not so vital that a failure to perform it goes to the root of the contract.

This distinction is important in terms of remedies. A breach of condition is called a repudiatory breach and the injured party may elect either to repudiate the contract or claim damages and go on with the contract.

It should be noted that the plaintiff must go on with the contract and sue for damages if he has affirmed the contract after knowledge of a breach of condition. He may do this expressly as where he uses the goods, or by lapse of time as where he simply fails to take any steps to complain about the breach for what in the court's view is an unreasonable period of time. A breach of warranty is not repudiatory and the plaintiff must go on with the contract and sue for damages.

Whether a term is a condition or warranty is basically a matter for the court which will be decided on the basis of the commercial importance of the term. As we have seen, the words used by the parties are, of course, relevant, but are not followed slavishly by the court which may still decide differently from the parties on the basis of the commercial importance of the term.

It should be noted that the word *warranty* is sometimes used in a different way, e.g. by a manufacturer of goods who gives a *warranty* against faulty workmanship offering to replace parts free. The term *warranty* is used by the manufacturer as equivalent to a guarantee. We are concerned here with its use as a term of a contract.

A useful illustration of the distinction between a condition and a warranty is provided by the following two cases.

Poussard v Spiers and Pond (1876) 1 QBD 410

Madame Poussard had entered into an agreement to play a part in an opera, the first performance to take place on 28 November 1874. On 23 November Madame Poussard was taken ill and was unable to appear until 4 December. The defendants had hired a substitute, and discovered that the only way in which they could secure a substitute to take Madame Poussard's place was to offer that person the complete engagement. This they had done, and they refused the services of Madame Poussard when she presented herself on 4 December. The plaintiff now sued for breach of contract. *Held* – The failure of Madame Poussard to perform the contract as from the first night was a breach of condition, and the defendants were within their rights in regarding the contract as discharged.

Comment: This case merely illustrates the availability of repudiation for serious breach of contract. Madame Poussard was not liable to pay damages for breach because unlike the defendants in *Gill & Duffus SA* (see p. 136) she could not help the breach, the contract being also frustrated (see p. 201).

Bettini v Gye (1876) 1 QBD 183

The plaintiff was an opera singer. The defendant was the director of the Royal Italian Opera in London. The plaintiff had agreed to sing in Great Britain in theatres, halls and drawing rooms for a period of time commencing on 30 March 1875, and to be in London for rehearsals six days before the engagement began. The plaintiff was taken ill and arrived on 28 March 1875, but the defendant would not accept the plaintiff's services, treating the contract as discharged. *Held* – The rehearsal clause was subsidiary to the main purposes of the contract, and its breach constituted a breach of warranty only. The defendant had no right to treat the contract as discharged and must compensate the plaintiff, but he had a counter-claim for any damage he had suffered by the plaintiff's late arrival.

Comment: This case is also concerned with the availability of repudiation and the court decided that the breach was not sufficiently serious. The court suggested that if Gye wanted redress he should cross-claim for damages against Bettini. If and when he did and there is no report suggesting that he did, the matter of Bettini's illness excusing his breach would have had to be raised. Presumably it would have been a defence even though in this case the contract was not discharged by frustration.

INNOMINATE TERMS

In modern law there are also terms which the parties call conditions and where the breach has *in fact* had a serious result on the contract. The court will then agree that the breach should be treated as a breach of condition and the contract can be repudiated. There are also terms which the parties call warranties and where the breach has *in fact* not been serious. The court will then agree that the breach shall be treated as a breach of warranty and the contract cannot be repudiated. The parties must go on with it though the person injured by the breach has an action for damages.

These are what are called *innominate terms* which the parties may have called conditions or warranties. The effect of these on the contract will depend upon how serious the breach has turned out to be *in fact*. If the breach has turned out to be serious the court will then treat the term as a condition, even if called a warranty by the parties, so that the contract can be repudiated. If *in fact* the breach has not had a serious effect on the contract the court will treat it as a breach of warranty, even if called a condition by the parties, so that the parties must proceed with the contract, though the injured party will have an action for damages.

Thus if Dodgy Motors advertises a car for sale as having done 32,000 miles this statement is likely to be a warranty giving an action for damages only if in fact the car has done, say, 34,000 miles. If, however, the car had done 60,000 miles the court would be likely to regard the statement as a condition allowing repudiation of the contract (and *see Cehave NV v Bremer Handelsgesellschaft mbH* (1975) at p. 243).

IMPLIED TERMS

Before leaving the topic of the contents of the contract it must be appreciated that in addition to the express terms inserted by the parties, the contract may contain and be subject to implied terms. Such terms are derived from custom or statute, and in addition a term may be implied by the court where it is necessary in order to achieve the result which in the court's view the parties obviously intended the contract to have.

Customary implied terms

A contract may be regarded as containing customary terms not specifically mentioned by the parties. **The following case provides an illustration.**

Hutton v Warren (1836) 150 ER 517

The plaintiff was the tenant of a farm and the defendant the landlord. At Michaelmas 1833, the defendant gave the plaintiff notice to quit on the Lady Day following. The defendant insisted that the plaintiff should cultivate the land during the period of notice which he did. The plaintiff now asked for a fair allowance for seeds and labour of which he had had no benefit having left the farm before harvest. It was proved that by custom a tenant was bound to farm for the whole of his tenancy and on quitting was entitled to a fair allowance for seeds and labour. *Held* – The plaintiff succeeded. 'We are of opinion that this custom was, by implication, imported into the lease. It has long been settled, that in commercial transactions, extrinsic evidence of custom and usage is admissible to annex incidents to written contracts in matters with respect to which they are silent. The same rule has also been applied to contracts in other transactions of life, in which known usages have been established and prevailed; and this has been done upon the principle of presumption that, in such transactions, the parties did not mean to express in writing the whole of the contract by which they intended to be bound, but to contract with reference to those known usages' (per Parke B).

Comment: Michaelmas Day is 29 September and is a quarter day for payment of rent as well as a Christian feast. Lady Day is 25 March. It is also a quarter day for the payment of rent and is so called because it is a Christian feast.

Statutory implied terms

In a contract for the sale of goods or hire purchase the Sale of Goods Act 1979 and the Supply of Goods (Implied Terms) Act 1973, ss. 8–11 (as amended by Sch. 4, Part 1, para. 35 to the Consumer Credit Act 1974, and s. 17 of the Supply of Goods and Services Act 1982), deal with the matter of implied terms. These Acts are considered in Chapter 10.

Judicial implied terms

Implication according to parties' intentions

The court may imply a term into a contract whenever it is necessary to do so in order that the express terms decided upon by the parties shall have the effect which was presumably intended by them. This is often expressed as the giving of 'business efficacy' to the contract, the judge regarding himself as doing merely what the parties themselves would *in fact* have done in order to cover the situation if they had addressed themselves to it.

This is illustrated by the following case.

The Moorcock (1889) 14 PD 64

The appellants in this case were in possession of a wharf and a jetty extending into the River Thames, and the respondent was the owner of the steamship *Moorcock*. In November 1887, the appellants and the respondents agreed that the ship should be discharged and loaded at the wharf and for that purpose should be moored alongside the jetty. Both parties realized that when the tide was out the ship would rest on the river bed. In the event the *Moorcock* sustained damage when she ceased to be waterborne owing to the centre of the vessel settling on a ridge of hard ground beneath the mud. There was no evidence that the appellants had given any warranty that the place was safe for the ship to lie in, but it was *held* – by the Court of Appeal – that there was an implied warranty by the appellants to this effect, for breach of which they were liable in damages. Per Bowen LJ:

> Now, an implied warranty, or as it is called, a covenant in law, as distinguished from an express contract or express warranty, really is in all cases founded on the presumed intention of the parties, and upon reason. The implication which the law draws from what must obviously have been the intention of the parties, the law draws with the object of giving efficacy to the transaction and preventing such a failure of consideration as cannot have been within the contemplation of either side; and I believe if one were to take all cases, and they are many, of implied warranties or covenants in law, it will be found that in all of them the law is raising an implication from the presumed intention of the parties with the object of giving to the transaction such efficacy as both parties must have intended that at all events it should have. In business transactions such as this, what the law desires to effect by the implication is to give such business efficacy to the transaction as must have been intended at all events by both parties who are business men; not to

impose on one side all the perils of the transaction, or to emancipate one side from all chances of failure, but to make each party promise in law as much, at all events, as it must have been in the contemplation of both parties that he should be responsible for in respect of those perils or chances.

Comment: (i) This statement of the law is to the effect that the court cannot imply a term because it is reasonable to do so but only when it is commercially necessary to do so. Lord Denning, particularly, in *Liverpool City Council* v *Irwin* [1977] (*see below*) put forward the view that the court could imply a term whenever it was reasonable to do so even if it was not necessary to do so to make the contract work in a commercial sense. This view is still not entirely accepted by the judiciary in general.

(ii) Although the court most often implies covenants or terms which are *positive*, i.e. the party concerned *has to do something*, *negative* covenants can be implied. Thus in *Fraser* v *Thames Television Ltd* [1983] 2 All ER 101 the members of a group called Rock Bottom brought an action alleging that Thames had broken an agreement with them about a TV series, an implied term of which was that Thames would not use the idea for the series, which was based on the history of the group and its subsequent struggles, unless the members of the group were employed as actresses in the series. Hirst J implied this negative term on the grounds that it was necessary to give business efficacy to the agreement between the parties.

Implication as a matter of law

Sometimes, however, the courts imply a term which is quite complex so that the parties would not, *in fact*, have addressed themselves to it. Here the judge is saying *as a matter of law* how the contract should be performed. This is illustrated by *Liverpool City Council* v *Irwin* [1977] AC 239 where the House of Lords *held* that it was an implied term of a lease of a maisonnette in a block of properties owned by the Council that the landlord should take reasonable care to keep the common parts of the block in a reasonable state of repair, although the obligation to do so would *not* have been accepted by the landlord.

When *Irwin's* case was in the Court of Appeal, Lord Denning, in deciding that there should be an implied term regarding maintenance, rejected the business efficacy test as the only test, saying that the court could imply a term whenever it was *just and reasonable* to do so, whether or not the term was strictly *necessary* to the performance of the contract or not. Although the House of Lords implied a term relating to maintenance, they did not go along with the view of Lord Denning that the test should be reasonableness regardless of necessity. The Court of Appeal returned to the 'necessary' approach in *Mears* v *Safecar Security* [1982] 2 All ER 865 and refused to imply a term into a contract of service that payment should be made to an employee during sickness. Stephenson LJ was of opinion that the term could not be implied because, although it might be *reasonable* to imply a term relating to sick-pay, it was not *necessary* in a contract of employment. The term relating to maintenance in *Irwin* was in sense not absolutely vital to performance of the contract in that the tenants could have walked up the stairs, even in the dark, to their flats if lift and light maintenance had not been carried out, but it was much closer to being necessary to performance of the contract than was the sick-pay term in *Mears*.

EXCLUSION CLAUSES

A contract may contain express terms under which one or both of the parties excludes or limits liability for breach of contract or negligence. Although such express terms are permissible, both the courts and Parliament have been reluctant to allow exclusion clauses to operate successfully where they have been imposed on a weaker party, such as an ordinary consumer, by a stronger party, such as a person or corporation in business to supply goods or services.

The judges have protected consumers of goods and services against the effect of exclusion clauses in two main ways, i.e. by deciding that the exclusion clause never became part of the contract, and by construing (or interpreting) the contract in such a way as to prevent the application of the clause.

Was the clause part of the contract?

The court will require the person wishing to rely on an exclusion clause to show that the other party agreed to it at or before the time when the contract was made, otherwise it will not form part of the agreement. In this connection:

(a) *Where a contract is made by signing a written document* the signer will in general be bound by everything which the document contains, even if he has not read it, unless the signature was induced by misrepresentation as to the effect of the document. An exception is the rule of *non est factum* provided the signer is not negligent.

   The effect of signing a document containing an exclusion clause is illustrated by the following case.

L'Estrange v Graucob (F) [1934] 2 KB 394

The defendant sold to the plaintiff, Miss L'Estrange, who owned a cafe in Llandudno, a cigarette slot machine, inserting in the sales agreement the following clause: 'Any express or implied condition, statement or warranty, statutory or otherwise, is hereby excluded.' The plaintiff signed the agreement but did not read the relevant clause, apparently because she thought it was merely an order form, and she now sued in respect of the unsatisfactory nature of the machine supplied which often jammed and soon became unusable. *Held* – The clause was binding on her, although the defendants made no attempt to read the document to her nor call her attention to the clause. 'Where a document containing contractual terms is signed, then in the absence of fraud, or I will add, misrepresentation, the party signing it is bound, and it is wholly immaterial whether he has read the document or not' (per Scrutton LJ).

Comment: The ruling in this case would appear to apply even where the party signing cannot understand the document, as where a signer cannot read or does not understand the language in which the document is written (*The Luna* [1920] P 22). This would not, of course, apply if the person relying on the clause *knew* that the other party could not read (*Geir* v *Kujawa* [1971] Lloyd's Rep 364). It will, of course, be realized that s. 6(3) of the Unfair Contract Terms Act 1977 would now apply so that the clause could only be effective if reasonable.

The following case illustrates the effect of misrepresenting the effect of an exclusion clause in a signed document.

Curtis v Chemical Cleaning and Dyeing Co [1951] I All ER 631

The plaintiff took a wedding dress, with beads and sequins, to the defendant's shop for cleaning. She was asked to sign a receipt which contained the following clause: 'This article is accepted on condition that the company is not liable for any damage howsoever arising.' The plaintiff said in evidence: 'When I was asked to sign the document I asked why? The assistant said I was to accept any responsibility for damage to beads and sequins. I did not read it all before I signed it'. The dress was returned stained, and the plaintiff sued for damages. The company relied on the clause. *Held* – The company could not rely on the clause because the assistant had misrepresented the effect of the document so that the plaintiff was merely running the risk of damage to the beads and sequins.

(b) *Where the terms are contained in an unsigned document,* the person seeking to rely on an exclusion clause must show that the document was an integral part of the contract which could be expected to contain terms. However, if the document is contractual in the sense outlined above the clause will apply even though the plaintiff did not actually know about the exclusion clause in the sense that he had not read it. Communication may be constructive so long as the document adequately draws the attention of a reasonable person to the existence of terms and conditions.

An example of constructive communication appears in the following case.

Thompson v LMS Railway [1930] I KB 41

Thompson, who could not read, asked her niece to buy her an excursion ticket to Manchester from Darwin and back on the front of which were printed the words, 'Excursion. For conditions see back'. On the back was a notice that the ticket was issued subject to the conditions in the company's timetables, which excluded liability for injury however caused. Thompson was injured and claimed damages. *Held* – Her action failed. She had constructive notice of the conditions which had, in the court's view, been properly communicated to the ordinary passenger.

Comment (i) The railway ticket was regarded as a contractual document (Contrast *Chapelton below.*)

(ii) The injuries, which were caused when the train on returning to Darwin at 10 p.m. did not draw all the way into the station so that the plaintiff fell down a ramp, would not have been the subject of an action at law today because the Unfair Contract Terms Act 1977 outlaws exclusion clauses relating to death and personal injury. Thus, on its own facts, this case is of historical interest only, though still relevant on the question of constructive notice.

The following case provides a contrast on the issue of constructive communication

Chapelton v Barry Urban District Council [1940] 1 All ER 356

The plaintiff Chapelton wished to hire deckchairs and went to a pile owned by the defendants, behind which was a notice stating: 'Hire of chairs 2d per session of three hours.' The plaintiff took two chairs, paid for them, and received two tickets which he put into his pocket after merely glancing at them. One of the chairs collapsed and he was injured. A notice on the back of the ticket provided that 'The council will not be liable for any accident or damage arising from hire of chairs'. The plaintiff sued for damages and the council sought to rely on the clause in the ticket. *Held* – The clause was not binding on Chapelton. The board by the chairs made no attempt to limit the liability, and it was unreasonable to communicate conditions by means of a mere receipt.

Comment: The defendants would now have had to face an additional problem, i.e. was the clause reasonable?

> This rule of constructive communication will not necessarily be applied if the term in the contract is particularly burdensome for the other party. In such a case the law may require that the burdensome clause is actually brought to the attention of the other party. This results from the decision of the Court of Appeal in *Interfoto Picture Library Ltd* v *Stiletto Visual Programmes Ltd* [1988] 1 All ER 348. In that case Interfoto sent some transparencies to Stiletto for them to make a selection. The delivery note, which is a contractual document, contained a clause that if the transparencies were not returned within 14 days Stiletto would pay £5 per day for each transparency retained after that. Stiletto delayed returning the transparencies for some three weeks and ran up a bill of some £3,783. When they were sued for this sum the court said that it could not be recovered by Interfoto because the clause was not specifically drawn to the attention of Stiletto. The court awarded damages of £3.50 per transparency per week but would not apply the clause.
>
> (c) *As regards previous dealings*, where the defendant has not actually given the plaintiff a copy of conditions or drawn his attention to them when making a particular contract, the doctrine of constructive notice will not apply, at least in consumer transactions, in order to enable the defendant to rely on previous communications in previous dealings, unless, perhaps, the dealings have been frequent. Thus in *Hollier* v *Rambler Motors* [1972] 1 All ER 399 it appeared that

the plaintiff had had his car repaired five times in five years (i.e. infrequently) by the defendants and had signed a form containing a clause stating 'the company is not responsible for damage caused by fire to customers' cars on the premises'. On the occasion in question the plaintiff was not required to sign a form when leaving his car for repair. In the event the car was damaged by fire caused by the defendants' negligence. In an action by the plaintiff the defendants pleaded the clause. It was *held* by the Court of Appeal that the plaintiff succeeded and that the clause did not apply. Previous dealings were not incorporated and in any case as a matter of construction the wording was not sufficiently plain to exclude negligence. However, where the parties are, for example, large corporations, terms used in previous dealings between the parties themselves *or in the trade generally* may be incorporated.

Thus in *British Crane Hire Corporation Ltd* v *Ipswich Plant Hire Ltd* [1974] 1 All ER 1059 the defendants hired a crane from the plaintiffs who were the owners. The agreement was an oral one, though after the contract was made the defendants received a printed form from the plaintiffs containing conditions. One of these was that the hirer of the crane was liable to indemnify the owner against all expenses in connection with its use. Before the defendants signed the form the crane sank into marshy ground, though this was not the fault of the defendants. The plaintiffs were put to some cost in repairing the crane and now sued the defendants for an indemnity under the contract. The defendants argued that the indemnity had not been incorporated into the oral contract of hire. It was held that the bargaining power of the defendants was equal to that of the plaintiffs and the defendants knew that printed conditions in similar terms to those of the plaintiffs were *in common use in the business*. The conditions had therefore been incorporated into the oral contract on the basis of the common understanding of the parties and the plaintiffs' claim for an indemnity succeeded.

(d) *Any attempt to introduce an exclusion clause after the contract has been made is ineffective* because the consideration for the clause is then past. **An illustrative case and comment appears below.**

Olley v Marlborough Court Ltd [1949] 1 All ER 127

A husband and wife arrived at a hotel as guests and paid for a room in advance. They went up to the room allotted to them; on one of the walls was the following notice: 'The proprietors will not hold themselves responsible for articles lost or stolen unless handed to the manageress for safe custody.' The wife closed the self-locking door of the bedroom and took the key downstairs to the reception desk. There was inadequate and therefore negligent staff supervision of the keyboard. A third party took the key and stole certain of the wife's furs. In the ensuing action the defendants sought to rely on the notice as a term of the contract. *Held* – The contract was completed at the reception desk and no subsequent notice could affect the plaintiff's rights.

Comment: (i) It was said in *Spurling* v *Bradshaw* [1956] 1 WLR 461 that if the husband and wife had seen the notice on a previous visit to the hotel it would have been binding on them, though this is by no means certain in view of cases such as *Hollier* (see p. 147) which suggest that in consumer transactions previous dealings are not necessarily incorporated unless perhaps the dealings have been frequent.

(ii) A further illustration is provided by *Thornton v Shoe Lane Parking Ltd* [1971] 1 All ER 686 where the Court of Appeal decided that the conditions exempting the company from certain liabilities on a ticket issued by an automatic barrier at the entrance to a car park were communicated too late. The contract was made when the plaintiff put his car on the place which activated the barrier. This was before the ticket was issued.

(e) *An exclusion clause may be made ineffective by an inconsistent oral promise.* **The following case illustrates this point**.

J Evans & Son (Portsmouth) Ltd *v* Andrea Merzario Ltd [1976] 2 All ER 930

The plaintiffs imported machines from Italy. They had contracted with the defendants since about 1959 for the transport of these machines. Before the defendants went over to the use of containers the plaintiffs' machines had always been crated and carried under deck. When the defendants went over to containers they orally agreed with the plaintiffs that the plaintiffs' goods would still be carried under deck. However, on a particular occasion a machine being transported for the plaintiffs was carried in a container on deck. At the start of the voyage the ship met a swell which caused the container to fall off the deck and the machine was lost. The contract was expressed to be subject to the printed standard conditions of the forwarding trade which contained an exemption clause excusing the defendants from liability for loss or damage to the goods unless the damage occurred whilst the goods were in their actual custody and by reason of their wilful neglect or default, and even in those circumstances, the clause limited the defendants' liability for loss or damage to a fixed amount. The plaintiffs claimed damages against the defendants for loss of the machine alleging that the exemption clause did not apply. It was *held* by the Court of Appeal that it did not apply. The printed conditions were repugnant to the oral promise for, if they were applicable, they would render that promise illusory. Accordingly, the oral promise was to be treated as overriding the printed conditions and the plaintiffs' claim succeeded, the exemption clause being inapplicable.

Comment: The court may also regard these oral promises as collateral contracts (see *also* p. 23), i.e. in this case a collateral contract to carry the machine under deck, that collateral contract not having an exclusion clause in it.

(f) *The doctrine of privity of contract may also prevent the application of an exclusion clause.* Thus, if A, the owner of a road haulage company, excludes his own and his employees' liability for damage to the goods of his business customers by a properly communicated clause, an employee who causes damage to the goods will be liable, although his employer will not be, provided the clause is reasonable under the Unfair Contract Terms Act 1977, because the employee has not supplied consideration for the contract which is between his employer and the customers.

Reference should, however, be made to the case of *NZ Shipping* v *A M Satterthwaite* (*see* p. 45) where by application of the rules relating to acceptance in unilateral contracts and the performance of existing contractual duties owed to a third party the court was able to hold that a stevedore could take the benefit of an exclusion clause in the shipping company's contract of carriage.

CONSTRUCTION OF EXCLUSION CLAUSES

Rules of construction (i.e. interpretation) of contract may, when applied, prevent the application of an exclusion clause. The major rules of construction are as follows.

The *contra proferentem* rule

Under this rule if there is any ambiguity or room for doubt as to the meaning of an exclusion clause the courts will construe it in a way unfavourable to the person who put it into the contract. An example of the application of this rule is to be seen in *Hollier* v *Rambler Motors* (p. 147) because the Court of Appeal, having decided that previous dealings were not incorporated, went on to use the rule by saying that the wording in the form was not sufficiently plain to exclude negligence. That ambiguity had therefore to be construed against the defendants who put it into the contract. Those who wish to exclude liability for negligence must use clear words, said the House of Lords in *Smith* v *South Wales Switchgear* [1978] 1 All ER 18.

A further illustration of the application of the *contra proferentem* rule appears below.

Alexander v Railway Executive [1951] 2 All ER 442

Alexander was a magician who had been on a tour together with an assistant. He left three trunks at the parcels office at Launceston station, the trunks containing various properties which were used in an 'escape illusion'. The plaintiff paid 5d for each trunk deposited and received a ticket for each one. He then left saying that he would send instructions for their dispatch. Some weeks after the deposit and before the plaintiff had sent instructions for the dispatch of the trunks, the plaintiff's assistant persuaded the clerk in the parcels office to give him access to the trunks, though he was not in possession of the ticket. The assistant took away several of the properties and was later convicted of larceny. The plaintiff sued the defendants for damages for breach of contract, and the defendants pleaded the following term which was contained in the ticket and which stated that the Railway Executive was 'not liable for loss mis-delivery or damage to any articles where the value was in excess of £5 unless at the time of the deposit the true value and nature of the goods was declared by the depositor and an extra charge paid'. No such declaration or payment had been made. *Held –*

The plaintiff succeeded because, although sufficient notice had been given constructively to the plaintiff of the term, the term did not protect the defendants because they were guilty of a breach of a fundamental obligation in allowing the trunks to be opened and things to be removed from them by an unauthorized person.

Comment: (i) Devlin J said that a deliberate delivery to the wrong person did not fall within the meaning of 'mis-delivery', and this may be regarded as the real reason for the decision, as it involved the application of the *contra proferentem* rule.

(ii) Note also that the receipt or ticket for the goods deposited was held to be a contractual document. (Contrast *Chapelton* at p. 147.)

The repugnancy rule

This rule says in effect that the exemption clause is in direct contradiction to the main purpose of the contract and is therefore repugnant to it. Where such repugnancy exists the exemption clause can be struck out. Thus, if A makes a contract to supply oranges to B but includes a clause which allows him to supply any sort of fruit, the clause is repugnant to the main purpose of the contract and could be struck out. Thus, A would be liable in breach of contract if he supplied B with apples and could not rely on the clause to excuse his breach of contract.

An illustration from case law appears below.

Pollock v Macrae [1922] SC (HL) 192

The defendants entered into a contract to build and supply marine engines. The contract had an exclusion clause which was designed to protect them from liability for defective materials and workmanship. The engines supplied under the contract had so many defects that they could not be used. The House of Lords struck out the exclusion clause as repugnant to the main purpose of the contract which was to build and supply workable engines. The plaintiff's claim for damages was allowed to proceed.

The four corners rule

Under this rule exemption clauses only protect a party when he is acting within the four corners of the contract. Thus he is liable for damage which occurs while he is deviating from the contract and he would not be protected by the exclusion clause.

An illustration from case law appears below.

Thomas National Transport (Melbourne) Pty Ltd and Pay v May and Baker (Australia) Pty Ltd [1966] 2 Lloyd's Rep 347

The owners of certain packages containing drugs and chemicals made a contract with carriers under which the packages were to be carried from Melbourne to various places in Australia. The carriers employed a subcontractor to collect the parcels and take them to the carriers' depot in Melbourne. When the subcontractor arrived late at the Melbourne depot it was locked and so he drove the lorry full of packages to his own house and left it in a garage there. This was in accordance with the carriers' instructions to their subcontractors in the event of late arrival at the depot. There was a fire and some of the packages were destroyed. The cause of the fire was unknown. However, the alleged negligence of the carriers consisted in their instruction to the subcontractors to take the goods home. The court said it was unthinkable that valuable goods worth many thousands of pounds should be kept overnight at a driver's house, regardless of any provision for their safety. The owners sued the carriers who pleaded an exemption clause in the contract of carriage. *Held* – by the High Court of Australia – that the plaintiffs succeeded. There had been a fundamental breach of contract. The intention of the parties was that goods would be taken to the carriers' depot and not to the subcontractor's house, in which case the carriers could not rely on the clause.

Comment: The decision, which was partly based on fundamental breach of contract (*see below*), is perhaps better founded on the four corners rule, i.e. the exclusion clause is available only so long as the contract is being performed in accordance with its terms.

THE DOCTRINE OF FUNDAMENTAL BREACH

This doctrine was usually invoked where a plaintiff sought a remedy on a contract containing exemption clauses which had been adequately communicated. The doctrine said, in effect, that where one party had fundamentally broken his contract, that is done something fundamentally different from what he had contracted to do, an exclusion clause could not protect him, and that this was a *rule of law* and *not a rule of construction*, so that the court had no discretion in the matter.

After some years of differing judicial opinion regarding this the House of Lords eventually affirmed that there was no rule by which exclusion clauses had become inapplicable to exclude liability for a fundamental breach of contract. It was in each case a question of construction whether in fact the clause covered the breach which had taken place.

The case which affirmed that this was the legal position appears below.

Photo Production Ltd v Securicor Transport Ltd [1980] 1 All ER 556

The plaintiff company had contracted with the defendant security company for the defendant to provide security services at the plaintiff's factory. A person employed by the defendant lit a fire in the plaintiff's premises while he was carrying out a night patrol. The fire got out of control and burned down the factory. The trial judge was unable to establish from the evidence precisely what the motive was for lighting the fire – it may have been deliberate or merely careless. The defendant relied on an exclusion clause in the contract which read:

Under no circumstances shall the company (Securicor) be responsible for any injurious act or default by any employee of the company unless such act or default could have been foreseen and avoided by the exercise of due diligence on the part of the company as his employer . . .

It was accepted that Securicor were not negligent in employing the person who lit the fire. He came to them with good references and there was no reason for them to suppose that he would act as he did. It was *held* by the House of Lords that the exclusion clause applied so that Securicor were not liable. All the judges in the House of Lords were unanimous in the view that there was no rule of law by which exclusion clauses became inapplicable to fundamental breach of contract, which this admittedly was. Although the Unfair Contract Terms Act 1977 was not in force at the time this action was brought and therefore could not be applied to the facts of this case, the existence of the Act and its relevance was referred to by Lord Wilberforce who said that the doctrine of fundamental breach had been useful in its time as a device for avoiding injustice. He then went on to say:

But . . . Parliament has taken a hand; it has passed the Unfair Contract Terms Act 1977. This Act applies to consumer contracts and those based on standard terms and enables exception clauses to be applied with regard to what is just and reasonable. It is significant that Parliament refrained from legislating over the whole field of contract. After this Act, in commercial matters generally, when the parties are not of unequal bargaining power, and when risks are normally borne by insurance . . . there is everything to be said . . . for leaving the parties free to apportion the risks as they think fit . . .

Comment: (i) In *Harbutt's Plasticine Ltd* v *Wayne Tank & Pump Co Ltd* [1970] 1 All ER 225 Lord Denning accepted that the principle which said that no exclusion clause could excuse a fundamental breach was not a rule of law when the injured party carried on with (or affirmed) the contract. Where this was so rules of construction must be used and the exclusion clause might have to be applied. However, if the injured party elected to repudiate the contract for fundamental breach and, as it were, pushed the contract away, the exclusion clause went with it and could never apply to prevent the injured party from suing for the breach. The same, he said, was true where the consequences were so disastrous (as they were in *Photo Production*) that one could assume that the injured party had elected to repudiate. The *Photo Production* case overrules *Harbutt*, as does s.9(1) of the Unfair Contract Terms Act 1977. This provides that if a clause, as a matter of construction, is found to cover the breach and if it satisfies the reasonableness test, it can apply and be relied on by the party in breach, even though the contract has been terminated by express election or assumed election following the disastrous results of the breach.

(ii) The House of Lords also allowed a Securicor exemption clause to apply in circumstances of fundamental breach in *Ailsa Craig Fishing Co Ltd* v *Malvern Fishing Co Ltd* [1983] 1 All ER 101. In that case the appellants' ship sank while berthed in Aberdeen harbour. It fouled the vessel next to it which was owned by Malvern. The appellants sued Malvern. Securicor were the second defendants. Securicor had a contract with the appellants to protect the ship. The accident happened as a result of a rising tide. At the time the Securicor patrolman had left his post to become involved in New Year celebrations. Although there were arguments by counsel to the contrary, the House of Lords *held* that the exclusion clause covered the circumstances of the case provided the words were given their natural and plain meaning. It therefore applied to limit the liability of Securicor and the appellants failed to recover all their loss.

(iii) The Unfair Contract Terms Act 1977 gives its strongest protection to those who deal as consumers. The contracts in *Photo Productions* and *Ailsa Craig* were non-consumer contracts where both parties were in business. It by no means follows that in a consumer transaction (*see below*) the court would have allowed a defendant to rely on 'Securicor' type of clause. It might well be regarded as unreasonable in that context.

THE APPROACH OF PARLIAMENT TO EXCLUSION CLAUSES

Parliament has tried to prevent the widespread use of exclusion clauses by the passing of various statutes, the main one being the Unfair Contract Terms Act 1977.

The strongest protection is given by the Act to persons who deal as consumers (C), though those dealing otherwise than as consumers, e.g. where the goods are bought for use in a business, are covered. To be a consumer one must be dealing as a *private buyer* with a *person in business* (B). Thus a contract between a *private buyer* and a *private seller* is not a consumer deal.

However, in *R & B Customs Broker Co Ltd* v *United Dominions Trust Ltd* [1988] 1 All ER 847 the Court of Appeal decided that when a business buys goods it may still take advantage of consumer law applying to an ordinary member of the public if the transaction concerned is not a regular one. The facts of the case were that R & B Customs bought a car for the use of a director. The contract excluded an implied term under s.14(3) of the Sale of Goods Act 1979 that the goods be fit for the purpose. Such an exclusion does not operate if the sale is between a person in business and a consumer. It was *held* that R & B Customs must be treated as a consumer. The purchase of the car was not a frequent transaction and unless regularity could be established the transaction could not be regarded as an integral part of the business and was not therefore in the course of business.

Clauses rendered ineffective by the Unfair Contract Terms Act

These are as follows:

(a) Any exclusion clause contained in a contract or notice by which B tries to exclude or restrict his liability for death or personal injury resulting from negligence is wholly ineffective (ss.2 and 5). However, in *Thompson* v *Lohan* [1987] 2 All ER 631 A hired plant together with operatives to B. The contract contained a clause stating that B was liable for the negligence of the operatives who were A's employees. This clause was held by the Court of Appeal not to be contrary to s. 2 of the Unfair Contract Terms Act. It was not designed to restrict or exclude liability to those who might be injured by the negligence of the operatives but merely decided whether A or B was to bear the liability.

(b) A manufacturer's guarantee cannot exclude or restrict the manufacturer's liability for loss or damage arising from defects in goods if used by a consumer which results from negligence in manufacture or distribution (s. 5). The section is concerned with actions either in negligence or on the collateral contract (*see further* p. 23) which the guarantee can create against the manufacturer who is not the seller of the goods to the customer. The section is not concerned with a contractual relationship between the seller and the customer which is covered by ss. 6 and 7. Thus a manufacturer's 12-month guarantee for a vacuum cleaner which said that the goods would, if defective, be replaced or repaired free of charge but ended with a phrase such as: 'This guarantee is in lieu of, and expressly excludes, all liability to compensate for loss or damage howsoever caused' would not prevent a claim by the purchaser against the manufacturer if he/she was electrocuted by the cleaner (*see Donoghue* v *Stevenson* (1932), p. 267).

(c) A clause under which B tries to exclude his liability, whether by guarantee or otherwise, to C for breach of the implied terms in the Sale of Goods Act 1979 (on a sale) or the Supply of Goods (Implied Terms) Act 1973 (as amended) (on a hire-purchase transaction), e.g. that the goods are fit for the purpose or of merchantable quality, is wholly ineffective, as is a clause which tries to exclude against the consumer the implied terms in the Supply of Goods and Services Act 1982 in a contract of pure hiring, e.g. of a car, or a contract for work and materials, as in the repair of a car (ss. 6(2) and 7(2), Unfair Contract Terms Act 1977).

Section 6 also applies to non-business liability. However, since the implied terms requiring merchantable quality and fitness for the purpose do not apply to non-business transactions, only s. 13, Sale of Goods Act 1979 (sale by description) can be implied. However, s.13 cannot be excluded in a non-business transaction with a consumer.

EXCLUSION CLAUSES APPLICABLE IF REASONABLE

General

These are as follows:

(a) Any clause by which B tries to exclude or restrict his liability for loss arising from negligence other than death or personal injury (s. 2(2)).

(b) Any clause by which B tries to exclude or restrict his liability to a non-consumer for breach of the implied terms in the Sale of Goods Act 1979, the

Supply of Goods (Implied Terms) Act 1973, and the Supply of Goods and
Services Act 1982 relating, for example, to contracts of hiring and work and
materials (s. 6(3) and 7(3)).

(c) Any clause by which B tries to exclude his liability for breach of contract if the
contract is with a consumer or, in the case of a non-consumer contract, the
agreement is on B's written standard terms (s. 3(1) and (2)(a)). There is no
definition of 'written standard terms' in the 1977 Act, but it obviously covers
cases in which the seller requires that all (or nearly all) of his customers
purchase goods on the same terms with no variation from one contract to
another. This section applies also to cases where the clause purports to allow B
to render a substantially different performance, as where a tour operator tries
to reserve the right to vary the accommodation or itinerary or reserves the
right to render no performance at all (s.3(2)(b)).

(d) As regards *indemnity clauses in consumer transactions*, B may agree to do work
for C only if C will indemnify B against any liability which B may incur during
performance of the contract, e.g. an injury to X caused by B's work (s. 4). B
may, for example, be a builder who takes an indemnity from C, the owner of a
property on which B is to do work in regard to any injuries which B's work
might cause to third parties. Such an indemnity will be unenforceable by B
unless reasonable. Such clauses are unlikely to be found reasonable and B will
have to cover himself by insurance. The section does not cover non-consumer
situations and the indemnity found in *British Crane Hire* (*see* p. 148) would still
be enforceable (and *see Thompson* v *Lohan* (1987) at p. 154).

Inducement liability

Any clause purporting to exclude liability for misrepresentation applies only if
reasonable, whether the transaction is with a consumer or a non-consumer (s. 3,
Misrepresentation Act 1967, as substituted by s. 8(1) of the Unfair Contract Terms
Act 1977). Thus an estate agent would not be able to exclude his liability for falsely
representing the state of a house unless the court felt that it was reasonable for the
agent to exclude his liability, as it might be if the property was very old and there
had been no survey.

Section 3 also applies to non-business liability. A private seller cannot exclude his
liability for misrepresentation unless he can show that the exclusion clause
concerned satisfied the test of reasonableness.

**An example of the application of the inducement liability rules is provided by
the following case.**

Walker v Boyle [1982] 1 All ER 634
The vendor of a house was asked in a pre-contract enquiry whether the boundaries of the
land were the subject of any dispute. The vendor asked her husband to deal with the
enquiries. He said that there were no disputes. There were, in fact, disputes but the husband

did not regard them as valid because he believed that he was in the right and his view could not be contradicted. His answers were nevertheless wrong and misleading. Contracts were later exchanged. These contracts were on the National Conditions of Sale (19th Edition) produced under the aegis of the Law Society. Condition 17(1) excluded liability for misleading replies to preliminary enquiries. The purchaser later heard of the boundary disputes and claimed in the High Court for rescission of the contract and the return of his deposit. Dillon J held that condition 17(1) did not satisfy the requirements of reasonableness as set out in s. 3 of the Misrepresentation Act 1967 (as substituted by s. 8(1) of the Unfair Contract Terms Act 1977). The plaintiff therefore succeeded.

Comment: (i) The National Conditions of Sale have been revised and as regards misrepresentation, the contract now only attempts a total exclusion of the purchaser's remedies if the misrepresentation is not material or substantial in terms of its effect and is not made recklessly or fraudulently.

(ii) The provisions relating to inducement liability were also applied in *South Western General Property Co Ltd* v *Marton, The Times,* 11 May 1982; the court *held* that conditions of sale in an auction catalogue which tried to exclude liability for any representations made, if these were incorrect, were not fair and reasonable. The defendant had relied upon a false statement that some building would be allowed on land which he bought at an auction, even though the facts were that the local authority would be most unlikely to allow any building on the land. The clauses excluding liability for misrepresentation did not apply and the contract could be rescinded.

REASONABLENESS

The burden of proof

The burden of proving that the clause is reasonable lies upon the party claiming that it is – usually B, the person in business (s.11(5)).

Meaning of reasonableness

Although the matter is basically one for the judge, the following guidelines appear in the 1977 Act.

(a) The matter of reasonableness must be decided on the circumstances as they were when the contract was made (s.11(1)).

(b) Where a clause limits the amount payable regard must be had to the resources of the person who included the clause and the extent to which it was possible for him to cover himself by insurance (s.11(4)). The object of this rule is to encourage companies to insure against liability in the sense that failure to do so will go against them if any exclusion clause which they have is before the court. However, in some cases it may be right to allow limitation of liability, e.g. in the case of professional persons such as accountants where monetary loss may be caused to a horrendous amount following negligence and be beyond their power to insure against.

(c) Where the contract is for the supply of goods, i.e. under a contract of sale, hire purchase, hiring, or work and materials, the criteria of reasonableness are laid down by s. 11(2) and Sch. 2 of the 1977 Act. They are:

(i) strength of the bargaining position of the parties. Thus if one party is in a strong position and the other in a weaker in terms of bargaining power, the stronger party may not be allowed to retain an exclusion clause in the contract;

(ii) availability of other supplies. Again, if a seller is in a monopolistic position so that it is not possible for the buyer to find the goods readily elsewhere, the court may decide that an exclusion clause in the contract of a monopolistic seller shall not apply.

(iii) inducements to agree to the clause. If the goods have been offered for sale at £10 without an exemption clause but at £8 with the inclusion of the clause, the court may see fit to allow the clause to apply at the lower price because there has been a concession by the seller in terms of the price;

(iv) buyer's knowledge of the extent of the clause. If the clause had been pointed out to the buyer and he is fully aware that it reduces the liability of the seller, then this will be relevant in deciding whether the seller should be allowed to rely on the clause. If a buyer is reasonably fully informed and aware of the seller's intentions as regards exclusion of liability, then the buyer may have to accept the clause;

(v) customs of trade and previous dealings. If, for example, exclusion clauses are usual in the trade or have been used by the parties in previous dealings, then the court may decide that an exclusion clause should apply. It should be noted that previous dealings do not seem relevant in consumer transactions, unless quite regular, but they are in this area where one is considering a non-consumer situation;

(vi) whether the goods have been made, processed or adapted to the order of the buyer. Obviously if the seller has been required by the buyer to produce goods in a certain way, then it may well be fair and reasonable for the seller to exclude his liability in respect of faults arising out of, for example, the buyer's design which he insisted was used. It would probably be reasonable to exclude the implied term under the Sale of Goods Act 1979 that the goods were fit for the purpose (*see further* p. 251).

Although the above criteria are strictly speaking confined to exclusion of statutory implied terms in, for example, the Sale of Goods Act 1979, they are being applied in other situations. For example, Judge Clarke in the *Woodman* case (*see below*) felt it was right to use them where what was at issue was a negligent service. The Supply of Goods and Services Act 1982 has not changed the law regarding the exclusion of liability of a supplier of services. Services are not specifically mentioned in the 1977

Act but they fall within the ambit of ss. 2 and 3 which deal with negligence and breach of contract respectively.

The test of reasonableness: the case law

The following is a selection of case law on the 1977 Act to illustrate its application.

Mitchell (George) (Chesterhall) Ltd v Finney Lock Seeds Ltd [1983] 1 All ER 108

This case is a landmark. It was the last case heard by Lord Denning in the Court of Appeal. In it he gave a review of the development of the law relating to exclusion clauses in his usual clear and concise way. The report is well worth reading in full. Only a summary of the main points can be given here.

George Mitchell ordered 30lb of cabbage seed and Finney supplied it. The seed was defective. The cabbages had no heart; their leaves turned in. The seed cost £192 but Mitchell's loss was some £61,000, i.e. a year's production from the 63 acres planted. Mitchell carried no insurance. When sued Finney defended the claim on the basis of an exclusion clause limiting their liability to the cost of the seed or its replacement. In the High Court Parker J found for Mitchell. Finney appealed to the Court of Appeal. The major steps in Lord Denning's judgment appear below.

(a) *The issue of communication – was the clause part of the contract?* Lord Denning said that it was. The conditions were usual in the trade. They were in the back of Finney's catalogue. They were on the back of the invoice. 'The inference from the course of dealing would be that the farmers had accepted the conditions as printed – even though they had never read them and did not realize that they contained a limitation on liability ...'

(b) *The wording of the clause.* The relevant part of the clause read as follows: 'In the event of any seeds or plants sold or agreed to be sold by us not complying with the express terms of the contract of sale or with any representation made by us or by any duly authorized agent or representative on our behalf prior to, at the time of, or in any such contract, or any seeds or plants proving defective in varietal purity we will, at our option, replace the defective seeds or plants, free of charge to the buyer or will refund all payments made to us by the buyer in respect of the defective seeds or plants and this shall be the limit of our obligation. We hereby exclude all liability for any loss or damage arising from the use of any seeds or plants supplied by us and for any consequential loss or damage arising out of such use or any failure in the performance of or any defect in any seeds or plants supplied by us for any other loss or damage whatsoever save for, at our option, liability for any such replacement or refund as aforesaid.'

Lord Denning said that the words of the clause did effectively limit Finney's liability. Since the Securicor cases (see *Photo Production* and *Ailsa Craig*, pp. 152–3) words were to be given their natural meaning and not strained. A judge must not proceed in a hostile way towards the wording of exclusion clauses as was, for example, the case with the word 'misdelivery' in *Alexander* v *Railway Executive* (1951) (*see* p. 150).

(c) *The test of reasonableness.* Lord Denning then turned to the new test of reasonableness which could be used to strike down an exclusion clause, even though it had been communicated, and in spite of the fact that its wording was appropriate to cover the circumstances. On this he said: 'What is the result of all this? To my mind it heralds a revolution in our approach to exemption clauses; not only where they exclude liability altogether and also where they limit liability; not only in the specific categories in the Unfair Contract Terms Act 1977, but in other contracts too ... We should do away with the multitude of cases on exemption clauses. We should no longer have to go through all kinds of gymnastic contortions to get round them. We should no longer have to harass our students with the study of them. We should set about meeting a new challenge. It is presented by the test of reasonableness.'

(d) *Was the particular clause fair and reasonable?* On this Lord Denning said: 'Our present case is very much on the borderline. There is this to be said in favour of the seed merchant. The price of this cabbage seed was small: £192. The damages claimed are high: £61,000. But there is this to be said on the other side. The clause was not negotiated between persons of equal bargaining power. It was inserted by the seed merchants in their invoices without any negotiation with the farmers. To this I would add that the seed merchants rarely, if ever, invoked the clause ... Next, I would point out that the buyers had no opportunity at all of knowing or discovering that the seed was not cabbage seed: whereas the sellers could and should have known that it was the wrong seed altogether. The buyers were not covered by insurance against the risk. Nor could they insure. But as to the seed merchants the judge said [Lord Denning here refers to Parker J at first instance]: "I am entirely satisfied that it is possible for seedsmen to insure against this risk ... " To that I would add this further point. Such a mistake as this could not have happened without serious negligence on the part of the seed merchants themselves or their Dutch suppliers. So serious that it would not be fair to enable them to escape responsibility for it. In all the circumstances I am of the opinion that it would not be fair or reasonable to allow the seed merchants to rely on the clause to limit their liability.'

Oliver and Kerr LJJ also dismissed the appeal.

The suppliers asked for leave to appeal to the House of Lords but the Court of Appeal refused. However, the House of Lords granted leave and affirmed the decision of the Court of Appeal in 1983 (*see* [1983] 2 All ER 737).

Comment: This is in effect an application of s. 6(3) of the Unfair Contract Terms Act 1977. It was actually brought under the Sale of Goods Act 1979 which contained transitional provisions and s. 55(3) of the 1979 Act plus para. 11 of Sch. 1 applied to this contract. For contracts made after 31 January 1978 the Unfair Contract Terms Act 1977, s. 6(3) would apply.

Section 2(2) came up for consideration in two County Court cases which were brought under the Act. In *Woodman* v *Photo Trade Processing Ltd*, heard in the Exeter County Court in May 1981, Mr Woodman took to the Exeter branch of Dixons Photographic for processing a film which carried pictures of a friend's wedding. The film was of special value because Mr Woodman had been the only photographer at the wedding, and he had said he would give the pictures as a wedding present. Unfortunately, the film was lost and when Dixons were sued they relied on an exclusion clause which, it appeared, was standard practice throughout the trade and had been communicated. The clause read as follows: 'All photographic materials are accepted on the basis that their value does not exceed the loss of the material itself. Responsibility is limited to the replacement of film. No liability will be accepted consequential or otherwise, however caused.' His Honour Judge Clarke found in the County Court that the customer had no real alternative but to entrust his film to a firm that would use such an exclusion clause and that, furthermore, Dixons could have foreseen that the film might be irreplaceable and although they could argue that the exclusion clause enabled them to operate a cheap mass-production technique, it could not be regarded as reasonable that all persons, regardless of the value of their film, should be required to take their chance of the system losing them. The judge therefore granted compensation of £75 to Mr Woodman and held that the exclusion clause was unreasonable.

In *Waldron-Kelly* v *British Railways Board*, which was heard in the Stockport County Court in 1981, the plaintiff delivered a suitcase to Stockport railway station so that it could be taken to Haverfordwest station. The contract of carriage was subject to the British Railways Board general conditions 'at owner's risk' for a price of £6.00. A clause exempted the Board from any loss, except that if a case disappeared then the Board's liability was to be assessed by reference to the weight of the goods, which in this case was £27.00 and not to their value, which in this case was £320.00. The suitcase was lost whilst it was in the control of British Rail. In the County Court Judge Brown *held* that the plaintiff succeeded in his contention that the exclusion clause was unreasonable and therefore of no effect. The judge held that in the case of non-delivery of goods the burden of proof to show what had happened to the goods was on the bailee. British Rail had failed to show that the loss was not their fault, and in any case the fault and loss were not covered by the exclusion clause because it did not satisfy the test of reasonableness.

Further, in *Stag Line Ltd* v *Tyne Ship Repair Group Ltd* [1984] 2 Lloyd's Rep 211 Staughton J, in finding that exclusion clauses inserted into the contract by the defendants were not fair and reasonable, said:

> The courts would be slow to find clauses in commercial contracts made between parties of equal bargaining power to be unfair or unreasonable, but a provision in a contract, which deprived a ship owner of any remedy for breach of contract or contractual negligence unless the vessel were returned to the repairer's yard for the defect to be remedied would be unfair and unreasonable because it would be capricious; the effectiveness of the remedy would depend upon where the ship was when the casualty occurred and whether it would be practical or economic to return the vessel to the defendants' yard.

Also in *Rees-Hough Ltd* v *Redland Reinforced Plastics Ltd* [1984] Construction Industry Law Letters, His Honour Judge Newey QC decided that it was not fair and reasonable for the defendants to rely on an exclusion clause in their standard terms and conditions of sale. They had sold pipes to the plaintiffs which were not fit for the purpose for which the defendants knew they were required, nor were they of merchantable quality under the Sale of Goods Act 1979 (*see further* p. 251) and the clause excluded liability for this. Clearly, then it is difficult to apply exclusion clauses which try to prevent liability for supplying defective goods.

Where there is no contract, as in the *Hedley Byrne* situation where a bank used a 'without responsibility' disclaimer, s.2(2) of the Act applies the reasonable test to the disclaimer (*see further* pp. 537–8).

PROVISIONS AGAINST EVASION OF LIABILITY

General

If an attempt is made to exclude or restrict liability in contract X by a clause in a secondary contract Y, then the clause in Y is ineffective (s. 10). For example, C buys a television set from B. There is an associated maintenance contract. The sale of a television would be within s. 6 of the 1977 Act and so there could be no exclusion of B's implied obligations. Any attempt to exclude or restrict these obligations in the maintenance contract would also fail. If the transaction was a non-consumer one the 'reasonable' test would have to be applied.

Nor can the Act be excluded by a clause which states that the contract is to be governed by the law of another country which does not outlaw exclusion clauses, at least if it is part of an evasion scheme, or if the contract is with a United Kingdom consumer and the main steps in the making of the contract took place in the UK (s. 27).

The Act does not apply to insurance contracts, nor to contracts for the transfer of an interest in land (s. 1(2) and Sch.1, para. 1(a) and (b)). House purchase is therefore excluded though inducement liability cannot be excluded unless reasonable (*see* p. 156). Nor does it apply to certain contracts involving the supply of goods on an international basis because these are covered by conventions. Furthermore, it should be noted that a written arbitration agreement will not be treated as excluding or restricting liability for the purposes of the 1977 Act and such an agreement is valid. (Section 13(2).)

Fair Trading Act 1973

Under s.13 of this Act the Director-General of Fair Trading can in the course of investigating consumer trade practices deal in particular with 'terms and conditions on which or subject to which goods or services are supplied'. This, of course, concerns exemption clauses being used in consumer transactions. If after investigation the Director-General feels that a particular practice in terms of exemption clauses should cease he will make a report to the Minister who may introduce a statutory instrument to stop the practice. For example, the Consumer Transactions (Restrictions on Statements) Order 1976 (No. 1813) as amended by SI 1978/127 makes it a criminal offence to sell or supply goods and purport that the implied terms in sale of goods and hire-purchase legislation can be excluded in a consumer sale since this might suggest to the customer that he has no rights so that he will not bother to try to enforce them.

GRADED QUESTIONS

Essay mode

1. (a) The Unfair Contract Terms Act 1977 has placed considerable restrictions on the ability of a business to exclude or restrict its liability through the use of contract terms or notices.

   Explain and illustrate this statement.

   (b) Microbyte manufactures personal computers which are sold through dealers to the general public. Its managing director knows that there is a risk that some of the components which are bought in from outside suppliers for use in the computers will be faulty. He seeks your advice on how Microbyte should attempt to ensure through its conditions of purchase that any liability which is associated with such faults is passed on to the component suppliers.

   Advise the managing director.

   (The Institute of Chartered Secretaries and Administrators. English Business Law. June 1989)

2. When parties enter into a contract it is virtually impossible for them to include express terms to cover every eventuality. If a dispute later arises it may then be necessary for terms to be implied into the contract.

   Explain:

   (a) when these implied terms will be introduced:
   (i) by the courts, and
   (ii) by statute   (12 marks)

   (b) the extent to which it is possible to exclude or vary these terms at the time of contracting.

       (8 marks)
       (Total: 20 marks)
   (The Chartered Institute of Management Accountants. Business Law. May 1987)

3. (a) In the law of contract what is the effect of:
      (i) A mutual mistake?
      (ii) A common mistake?   (10 marks)
   (b) Albert advertised his car for sale in a local newspaper. He was visited by Brian
       who expressed an interest in buying the vehicle. The sale price of the car was
       £2,000 and Brian offered to pay for it by cheque. Albert was reluctant to accept
       a cheque, upon which Brian produced a driving licence which indicated,
       falsely, that Brian was the well-known footballer, Dan.
           Albert decided to let Brian have the car, but the cheque has now been
       dishonoured. Meanwhile Brian has sold the car to Cedric and has
       subsequently disappeared with the proceeds of the sale.
           Advise Albert.   (10 marks)
                                                                         (20 marks)

(The Chartered Association of Certified Accountants. Paper 1.4 (E). June 1990)

4. 'If there is one thing more than another which public policy requires, it is that men
   of full age and competent understanding shall have the utmost liberty of
   contracting and that their contracts when entered into freely and voluntarily shall
   be held sacred and shall be enforced by courts of justice' (per Sir George Jessel in
   Printing and Numerical Registering Co v *Sampson* (1875).

       Discuss the extent to which state and judicial intervention in the use of
   exclusion clauses has rendered the above statement obsolete.

(The Polytechnic, Huddersfield. BA and BA(Hons) Business Studies)

Objective mode

Four alternative answers are given. Select ONE only. Circle the answer which you
consider to be correct. Check your answers by referring back to the information
given in the chapter and against the answers at the back of the book.

1. On Monday Tom and Jerry who are workmates were discussing the sale to Jerry
   of Tom's car. Tom said that he had fitted new tyres at 30,000 miles but this was not
   true, Tom having forgotten that they were fitted at 25,000 miles. On Friday
   afternoon Jerry agreed to buy Tom's car. In the above circumstances Tom's
   statement about the tyres will be regarded as:

   A A condition of the contract.
   B A warranty.
   C A misrepresentation.
   D As a non-actionable hyping of the car.

2. Fred offered his car for sale to Joe saying that it had done 30,000 miles. Joe bought
   it. In fact it had done 31,000 miles.
       Fred's statement in the offer about the mileage was a:

A Warranty.
B Condition.
C Non-actionable hyping of the car.
D Misrepresentation.

3. A judge will imply a term into a contract:

A Only if the parties intended it.
B If the parties intended it and as a matter of law even if they did not.
C Only as a matter of law and regardless of the intentions of the parties.
D If the parties intended it or as a matter of law but only if it is commercially necessary to do so.

4. Jane took a dress into a dry cleaning company for cleaning. She signed a document without reading it. It said the company exempted itself from damage accidental or negligent. The dress was returned torn on the hem. What is the legal position?

A Such an exclusion clause can never be binding because of the Unfair Contract Terms Act 1977.
B The clause is not binding because it was not actually communicated to Jane.
C The clause was constructively communicated to Jane but will not be binding unless reasonable.
D The clause is binding merely because it was constructively communicated to Jane.

5. Jack, a plumber, took his video into Electrics Ltd for repair. Jack had taken his video into Electrics only once in the past six years. On that occasion he had been given a document stating that the company was not liable for damage caused to customers' equipment while on the premises of the company. The video was damaged beyond repair when it was knocked off a shelf by a football during a lunch-time game between three employees of Electrics in the warehouse. Jack has been told that he cannot claim because of the previous communication of the exclusion clause.

The legal position is that

A Jack is bound by the previous notice and cannot claim.
B Jack is not bound by the previous notice because the Unfair Contract Terms Act 1977 outlaws clauses of this kind.
C Jack is not bound by the clause but only because the previous notice does not specifically exclude negligent damage.
D Jack is not bound by the notice because his previous dealing with Electrics is not regular and also because the clause, even if reasonable, does not exclude negligent damage.

6. Mary parked her car in the customers' car park of Garrod's store, at the cost of £2. At the entrance to the car park there were two notices. One, placed on the right of

the entrance read: 'No liability is accepted for death of, or injury to, a customer'. The other, placed on the left of the entrance but not visible because two Garrod's vans were parked in front of it, read: 'Cars parked at owner's risk'.

While she was parking the car in one of the spaces provided, two employees of Garrod's who were cleaning the upper windows of the store, negligently dropped a bucket of water through the windscreen of Mary's car causing facial injury to Mary and completely ruining some other goods which Mary had just bought from another store.

Advise Mary.

A Mary has no claim because the two notices taken together are effective to exclude Garrod's liability.

B Mary can claim for her facial injury only because the notice she has seen is outlawed by the Unfair Contract Terms Act 1977. The other clause relating to property damage is constructively communicated and effective.

C Mary can claim for all the damage because the notice she saw contains a clause outlawed by the Unfair Contract Terms Act 1977 and the other notice was not communicated.

D Mary can claim for her facial injuries because the notice she saw is outlawed by the Unfair Contract Terms Act 1977. She may be able to claim for the property damage but only if the court decides that the clause on the second notice was unreasonable.

7. Booker, the accountant of Bloggs Ltd, a small manufacturing company, wished to appoint a successor to Scribe, a clerk in charge of wages and salaries who was leaving to take up another appointment. After interviewing a number of applicants Booker decided to appoint Dodger who had some ten years' previous experience in a similar post.

Dodger agreed to accept the appointment with effect from 1 February and gave his employer two months' notice. He also undertook as part of the agreement to spend up to four Saturday mornings during the period of notice at the offices of Bloggs Ltd so that Scribe, who was leaving on 31 January, could introduce him to the company's procedures. Two dates in December and two in January were agreed between Scribe and Dodger but by the end of December Dodger had presented himself on only one occasion.

On 4 January Booker rang Dodger and asked him why he had not attended at the company's offices as agreed. Dodger replied that Saturday was inconvenient because he played for a local football team which always trained for one hour on Saturday morning prior to an afternoon match. Dodger did, however, agree to attend on the first date in January but said that he could not make the second, adding 'I have been doing similar work for ten years and I already understand most of your procedures from my visit in December.' Booker replied that this arrangement was not suitable and concluded 'You need not bother to turn up on 1 February. I would not dream of taking an unreliable person such as yourself into employment here.'

Dodger's employer refused to accept the withdrawal of his resignation and he was out of work for two months.

What is the legal position?

(*Note*: Statute law relating to unfair dismissal is not relevant here and should be ignored.)

A Booker was legally entitled to repudiate the contract and Dodger has no remedy against them.

B Booker should have honoured the contract and taken Dodger into employment. Each party may sue the other for loss

C Dodger may make Booker take him into employment.

D Neither party has a claim against the other because the employment never began.

8. Rudy, a former employee of the Russian government who sought and obtained political asylum in England, has set up in business as a bookseller. Rudy speaks English quite well but cannot read the language as yet. His pride compels Rudy to conceal this from everyone. Rudy ordered a number of textbooks for sale to students at a local college from Hawker who was a representative of Booker Ltd the publishers with whom he had not previously done business. Hawker gave Ruby a sold note containing the following clause: 'All goods are sold subject to their being in stock when the order reaches head office.'

The books which Rudy ordered have not been delivered and since the first college term has now commenced it is likely that the students will purchase their textbooks from another retailer in a neighbouring town who has stocks on his shelves.

Rudy proposes to sue Booker Ltd for breach of contract but he has been told by Hawker that he will have no claim in view of the clause set out in the sold note. Hawker says the clause is part of the contract and that the books will be despatched shortly when they come into Booker Ltd's stock.

Given that the exclusion clause appears to be reasonable what is the legal position?

A Booker will be liable because Rudy cannot read English.

B Booker will be liable because the sold note is not a contractual document.

C Booker will not be liable because the sold note is a contractual document and its contents were constructively communicated to Rudy.

D Booker will be liable because they did not get Rudy to sign the sold note.

Answers to questions set in objective mode appear on p. 551.

7 | Contracts in restraint of trade and restrictive practices

The OBJECTIVES of this chapter are to consider transactions which are made void by the judiciary or by Parliament not because they are illegal in the sense that any morally blameworthy conduct is involved but because if enforced they would produce unsatisfactory results in society. There is in view of examination requirements a concentration on contracts in restraint of trade and restrictive practices legislation together with the impact of European Community law.

CONTRACTS IN RESTRAINT OF TRADE GENERALLY

Such contracts are prima facie void and will only be binding if reasonable. Thus the contract must be reasonable between the parties which means that it must be no wider than is necessary to protect the interest involved in terms of the area and time of its operation. It must also be reasonable as regards the public interest. Finally, the issue of reasonableness is a matter of law for the judge on the evidence presented to him which would include, for example, such matters as trade practices and customs.

One of the leading cases on public interest as an ingredient making a contract in restraint of trade void appears below.

Wyatt v Kreglinger and Fernau [1933] 1 KB 793
In June 1923, the defendants wrote to the plaintiff, who had been in their service for many years, intimating that upon his retirement they proposed to give him an annual pension of £200, subject to the condition that he did not compete against them in the wool trade. The plaintiff's reply was lost and he did not appear ever to have agreed for his part not to engage in the wool trade, but he retired in the following September and received the pension until

June 1932 when the defendants refused to make any further payments. The plaintiff sued them for breach of contract. The defendants denied any contract existed and also pleaded that if a contract did exist, it was void as being in restraint of trade. The Court of Appeal gave judgment for the defendants and although there was no unanimity with regard to the *ratio decidendi*, it appeared to two judges that the contract was injurious to the interests of the public, since to restrain the plaintiff from engaging in the wool trade was to deprive the community of services from which it might derive advantage.

Comment: the basis of this decision seems to be that if a contract did exist it was supported only by an illegal consideration moving from Wyatt, i.e. an agreement not to engage in the wool trade. If he had been entitled to a pension as part of his original contract of service then no doubt the pension arrangements would have been severed (see p. 179) and enforced.

VOLUNTARY CONTRACTUAL RESTRAINTS OF TRADE ON EMPLOYEES GENERALLY

Here the contract is entered into voluntarily by the parties and as regards employees it should be noted that there are only two things an employer can protect:

(a) *Trade secrets*. A restraint against competition is justifiable if its object is to prevent the exploitation of trade secrets learned by the employee in the course of his employment. In this connection it should be noted that the area of the restraint must not be excessive. Furthermore, a restraint under this heading may be invalid because its duration is excessive.

   An example of the application of the above principles is set out below.

Forster & Sons Ltd v Suggett (1918) 35 TLR 87
The works manager of the plaintiffs who were mainly engaged in making glass and glass bottles was instructed in certain confidential methods concerning, amongst other things, the correct mixture of gas and air in the furnaces. He agreed that during the five years following the termination of his employment he would not carry on in the United Kingdom, or be interested in, glass bottle manufacture or any other business connected with glass-making as conducted by the plaintiffs. It was *held* that the plaintiffs were entitled to protection in this respect and that the restraint was reasonable.

(b) *Business connection*. Sometimes an employer may use a covenant against *solicitation* of persons with whom the employer does business. The problem of area is less important in this type of covenant, though its duration must be reasonable. The burden on the employer increases as the duration of the restraint is extended, though in rare situations a restraint for life may be valid.

   Illustrative case law is set out below.

Home Counties Dairies v Skilton [1970] 1 All ER 1227

Skilton, a milk roundsman employed by the plaintiffs, agreed, amongst other things, not for one year after leaving his job 'to serve or sell milk or dairy produce' to persons who within six months before leaving his employment were customers of his employers. Skilton left his employment with the plaintiffs in order to work as a roundsman for Westcott Dairies. He then took the same milk round as he had worked when he was with the plaintiffs. *Held* – by the Court of Appeal – that this was a flagrant breach of agreement. The words 'dairy produce' were not too wide. On a proper construction they must be restricted to things normally dealt in by a milkman on his round. 'A further point was taken that the customer restriction would apply to anyone who had been a customer within the last six months of the employment and had during that period ceased so to be, and it was said that the employer could have no legitimate interest in such persons. I think this point is met in the judgment in *G W Plowman & Sons Ltd v Ash* [1964] 2 All ER 10 where it was said that a customer might have left temporarily and that his return was not beyond hope and was therefore a matter of legitimate interest to the employer' (per Harman LJ).

Comment: It was *held* by the Court of Appeal in *John Michael Design v Cooke* [1987] 2 All ER 332 after referring to *Plowman v Ash* that a restraint in a contract of employment preventing an employee (A) from competing with his former employer (B) could be enforced by an injunction even to prevent the former employee from doing business with a customer (C) of his former employer who had made it clear that he would not do business with (B) again. There was always the possibility that (C) would change his mind.

Fitch v Dewes [1921] 2 AC 158

A solicitor at Tamworth employed a person who was successively his articled clerk and managing clerk. In his contract of service, the clerk agreed, if he left the solicitor's employment, never to practise as a solicitor within seven miles of Tamworth Town Hall. *Held* – The agreement was good because during his service the clerk had become acquainted with the details of his employer's clients, and could be restrained even for life from using that knowledge to the detriment of his employer.

Comment: (i) Although the restraint was for life, it did cover a rather small area in which at the time there were comparatively few people. It is unlikely that such a restraint would be regarded as valid today, particularly in a more densely populated area.

(ii) The Privy Council stated quite clearly in *Deacons v Bridge* [1984] 2 All ER 19 that a restraint such as this would only be applied in unusual circumstances. The decision seems confined to its own facts though the statements of principle in the case by the House of Lords are more enduring.

CONTRACTUAL RESTRAINTS ON EMPLOYEES THROUGH THE PERIOD OF NOTICE

In recent times the court has had to consider the validity of contracts of service with restrictively long periods of notice which have sometimes been given to able and ambitious executives. Typically such contracts provide that if the employee leaves he must give notice of, say, one year and during that time the employer can suspend him from work but agrees to give him full pay and other benefits. The contract will normally also provide that the employer may exclude the employee from the workplace so that he cannot after serving his notice obtain any further information which might be of benefit to the new employer nor can he work for the new employer during the period of notice without being in breach of contract. He can either do nothing or pursue his hobbies. This is why the period of notice has been called 'garden leave'.

Such a contract was considered by the Court of Appeal in *Provident Financial Group plc* v *Whitegates Estate Agency* [1989] IRLR 84. The court did not decide that such a contract was void but said it would be cautious about granting an injunction to stop an employee from working for the new employer during the period of notice. However, the court would be prepared to hear a claim for damages by the employer.

NON-CONTRACTUAL RESTRAINTS ON EMPLOYEES: CONFIDENTIAL INFORMATION

The position is different where the employee has no restraint of trade clause in his contract. Thus in *Faccenda Chicken Ltd* v *Fowler* [1986] 1 All ER 617, Mr Fowler was sales manager for Faccenda Chicken Ltd for seven years and set up a van sales operation whereby refrigerated vans travelled around certain districts offering fresh chicken to retailers and caterers. He left the company and set up his own business selling chickens from refrigerated vans in the same area. Eight of the company's employees went to work for him. Each of the salesmen in the company knew the names and addresses of the customers, the route and timing of deliveries, and the different prices quoted to different customers.

The company unsuccessfully brought an action for damages in the High Court, alleging wrongful use of confidential sales information and were also unsuccessful in a counter-claim for damages for breach of contract by abuse of confidential information in Mr Fowler's action against them for outstanding commission.

It is generally the case that rather more protection in terms of preventing an employee from approaching customers can be obtained by an express term which is reasonable in terms of its duration. In the absence of an express term, it is clear from this decision of the Court of Appeal that confidential information of an employer's business obtained by an employee in the course of his service may be used by that employee when he leaves the job unless, as the Court of Appeal decided, it can be classed as a trade secret or is of such a confidential nature that it merits the same protection as a trade secret. For example, there would have been no need for a term in the contract of service in *Forster* (*see* p. 170). The court could have prevented use of the secret process for a period without this. It should, however, be noted that in

Faccenda the Court of Appeal did say that if the employees had written down lists of customers, routes, etc., as distinct from having the necessary information in their memories, and presumably being unable to erase it, short of amnesia, they might have been restrained for a period from using the lists. This follows the case of *Robb* v *Green* [1895] 2 QB 315 where the manager of a firm dealing in live game and eggs copied down the names of customers before leaving and then solicited these for the purposes of his own business after leaving the employment of the firm. He was restrained from soliciting the customers.

EMPLOYEE RESTRAINTS ARISING FROM AGREEMENTS BETWEEN MANUFACTURERS AND TRADERS

The courts are concerned to prevent an employer from obtaining by indirect means restraint protection which he could not have obtained in an express contract with the employee.

The following case is an illustration of the operation of this principle.

Kores Manufacturing Co Ltd v Kolok Manufacturing Co Ltd [1958] 2 All ER 65

The two companies occupied adjoining premises in Tottenham and both manufactured carbon papers, typewriter ribbons and the like. They made an agreement in which each company agreed that it would not, without the written consent of the other, 'at any time employ any person who during the past five years shall have been a servant of yours'. The plaintiffs' chief chemist sought employment with the defendants, and the plaintiffs were not prepared to consent to this and asked for an injunction to enforce the agreement. *Held* – by the Court of Appeal –

(a) a contract in restraint of trade cannot be enforced unless:
   (i) it is reasonable as between the parties; and
   (ii) it is consistent with the interests of the public;
(b) the mere fact that the parties are dealing on equal terms does not prevent the court from holding that the restraint is unreasonable in the interests of those parties;
(c) the restraint in this case was grossly in excess of what was required to protect the parties and accordingly was unreasonable in the interests of the parties.
(d) The agreement therefore failed to satisfy the first of the two conditions set out in (a) above and was void and unenforceable.

Comment: The restrictive agreement which was at the root of *Kores Manufacturing Co* v *Kolok Manufacturing Co Ltd* was not covered by the Restrictive Trade Practices Act which is not concerned with agreements between traders in regard to their employees and was decided on common-law principles. These principles are that the agreement must be reasonable between the parties and reasonable in the public interest. Both of these points arose in *Kores*, the Court of Appeal holding that the agreement was unreasonable as between the parties and also that it was contrary to the public interest, though the *ratio* is based on the fact that the agreement was unreasonable as between the parties.

RESTRAINTS IMPOSED ON THE VENDOR OF A BUSINESS

Such a restraint will be void unless it is required to protect the business sold and not to stifle competition.

It should be noted, however, that the protection of the business sold may in rare situations involve a world-wide restraint.

Illustrative case law appears below.

British Reinforced Concrete Co v Schelff [1921] 2 Ch 563
The plaintiffs carried on a large business for the manufacture and sale of BRC Road Reinforcements. The defendant carried on a small business for the sale of 'Loop Road Reinforcements'. The defendant sold his business to the plaintiffs and agreed not to compete with them in the manufacture or sale of road reinforcements. It was *held* that the covenant was void. All that the defendant transferred was the business of selling the reinforcements called 'Loop'. It was therefore only with regard to that particular variety that it was justifiable to curb his future activities.

Nordenfelt v Maxim Nordenfelt Guns and Ammunition Co [1894] AC 535
Nordenfelt was a manufacturer of machine guns and other military weapons. He sold the business to a company, giving certain undertakings which restricted his business activities. This company was amalgamated with another company and Nordenfelt was employed by the new concern as managing director. In his contract Nordenfelt agreed that for 25 years he would not manufacture guns or ammunition in any part of the world, and would not compete with the company in any way. *Held* – The covenant regarding the business sold was valid and enforceable, even though it was world-wide, because the business connection was world-wide and it was possible in the circumstances to sever this undertaking from the rest of the agreement (*see* p. 179). However, the further undertaking not to compete in any way with the company was unreasonable and void.

RESTRICTIONS ON SHAREHOLDER-EMPLOYEES

The courts will generally allow wider restraints in the case of vendors of businesses than in the case of employees. However, what is the position where the employee is also a shareholder and therefore also a proprietor of the business? **The following case is the first of its kind to come before the courts**.

Systems Reliability Holdings plc v Smith [1990] IRLR 377

In 1986 Mr Smith commenced work with a company called Enterprise Computer Systems (ECS). He was a computer engineer engaged upon the reconfiguration of IBM mainframe computers. He became highly skilled in the modification and rebuilding of the latest generation of IBM's 3090 computer. His skill was instrumental in making ECS a leading company providing computer services. He was dismissed on 1 February 1990.

While he was employed by ECS Mr Smith had purchased shares totalling 1.6 per cent of the holding in the company. After his dismissal Systems Reliability Holdings plc acquired all the shares in ECS and Mr Smith received £247,000 for his 1.6 per cent holding. The share sale agreement had a restrictive covenant. Mr Smith had seen and initialled the agreement in final draft form. The covenant said: 'None of the specifically restricted vendors will during the restricted period directly or indirectly carry on or be engaged or interested . . . in any business which competes with any business carried on at the date of this agreement . . . by the company or any of its subsidiaries.'

Mr Smith was one of the specifically restricted vendors and the restricted period was in effect one of 17 months from the date of the sale. There was a further covenant which provided that: 'None of the vendors will at any time after the date of this agreement disclose or use for his own benefit or that of any other person any confidential information which he now possesses concerning the business or affairs or products of or services supplied by the company or any of the subsidiaries or of any person having dealings with the company or any of its subsidiaries.'

Soon after his dismissal and the share sale Mr Smith set up in business supplying computer services. Systems Reliability asked for an injunction to enforce the restrictive covenant in the share sale agreement.

The High Court *held* that a restrictive covenant imposed upon the defendant as part of the plaintiffs' acquisition of the shares in the company in which he was formerly employed was entirely reasonable and would be enforced against him notwithstanding that his shareholding in the company had amounted to only 1.6 per cent of the total. The present case was a true vendor and purchaser situation in which the defendant had received £247,000 for his 1.6 per cent shareholding. There was no public policy to prevent the defendant taking himself out of competition for what was a comparatively short period of 17 months as required under the agreement which on the evidence was entirely reasonable, or to prevent the imposition of a world-wide restriction which was also reasonable given that the business was completely international. The covenant would therefore be enforced.

Comment: As we have seen the courts have traditionally allowed wider restraints on competition to be placed on the vendors of businesses than on employees. In Mr Smith we have a mix of the two and the court applied the wider vendor/purchaser approach.

It must, of course, be significant that Mr Smith got £247,000 for a comparatively small shareholding and it must remain doubtful whether the court would apply the vendor/purchaser test to an employee whose shareholding was merely nominal. Presumably, here the tighter employer/employee test of reasonableness would apply.

The matter is one of some importance because the number of employee/shareholders has increased rapidly over the past few years.

RESTRICTIONS ACCEPTED BY DISTRIBUTORS OF MERCHANDISE

A manufacturer or wholesaler may refuse to make merchandise available for distribution to the public unless the distributor accepts certain conditions restricting his liberty of trading. This is the main purpose of the solus agreement used by petrol companies. Such agreements are void unless reasonable.

There is an important distinction here between a garage proprietor who borrows money on mortgage of his own property from a petrol company and agrees to sell only that company's products for a period of time. The rule relating to unreasonable restraints of trade applies to the mortgage. However, if the petrol company is the owner of the land and garage premises and grants a lease to a tenant who will run the garage then the rule relating to unreasonable restraints of trade does not apply to an agreement in the lease to take the petrol company's products.

The following cases provide an illustration.

Esso Petroleum Co Ltd v Harper's Garage (Stourport) Ltd [1967] 1 All ER 699

The defendant company owned two garages with attached filling stations, the Mustow Green Garage, Mustow Green, near Kidderminster, and the Corner Garage at Stourport-on-Severn. Each garage was tied to the plaintiff oil company, the one at Mustow Green by a solus supply agreement only with a tie clause binding the dealer to take the products of the plaintiff company at its scheduled prices from time to time. There was also a price-maintenance clause which was no longer enforceable and a 'continuity clause' under which the defendants, if they sold the garage, had to persuade the buyer to enter into another solus agreement with Esso. The defendants also agreed to keep the garage open at all reasonable hours and to give preference to the plaintiff company's oils. The agreement was to remain in force for four years and five months from 1 July 1963, being the unexpired residue of the ten-year tie of a previous owner. At the Corner Garage there was a similar solus agreement for 21 years and a mortgage under which the plaintiffs lent Harpers £7,000 to assist them in buying the garage and improving it. The mortgage contained a tie covenant and forbade redemption for 21 years. In August 1964, Harpers offered to pay off the loan but Esso refused to accept it. Harpers then turned over all four pumps at the Corner Garage to VIP, and later sold VIP at Mustow Green. The plaintiff company now asked for an injunction to restrain the defendants from buying or selling fuels other than Esso at the two garages during the subsistence of the agreements. *Held* – by the House of Lords – that the rule of public policy against unreasonable restraints of trade applied to the solus agreements and the mortgage. The shorter period of four years and five months was reasonable so that the tie was valid but the other tie for 21 years in the solus agreement and the mortgage was invalid, so that the injunction asked for by the plaintiffs could not be granted.

Comment: The House of Lords appears to have been influenced by the report of the Monopolies Commission on the Supply of Petrol to Retailers in the United Kingdom (Cmnd 1965, No. 264) which recommended the period of five years.

Cleveland Petroleum Co Ltd v Dartstone Ltd [1969] 1 All ER 201

The owner of a garage and filling station at Crawley in Sussex leased the property to Cleveland and they in turn granted an underlease to the County Oak Service Station Ltd. The underlease contained a covenant under which all motor fuels sold were to be those of Cleveland. There was power to assign in the underlease and a number of assignments took place so that eventually Dartstone Ltd became the lessees, having agreed to observe the covenants in the underlease. They then challenged the covenant regarding motor fuels and Cleveland asked for an injunction to enforce it. The injunction was granted. Dealing in the Court of Appeal with *Harper's* case Lord Denning MR said

> ... It seems plain to me that in three at least of the speeches of their Lordships a distinction is taken between a man who is already in possession of the land before he ties himself to an oil company and a man who is out of possession and is let into it by an oil company. If an owner in possession ties himself for more than five years to take all his supplies from one company, that is an unreasonable restraint of trade and is invalid. But if a man, who is out of possession, is let into possession by the oil company on the terms that he is to tie himself to that company, such a tie is good.

Comment: (i) The essential distinction is, as we have seen, that where the restraint on the use of the land is contained in a conveyance or lease the common law rules of restraint of trade do not apply. The person who takes over the property under a conveyance or lease has given nothing up. In fact he has acquired rights which he never had before even though subject to some limitations.

(ii) In *Alec Lobb (Garages) Ltd v Total Oil GB Ltd* [1985] 1 All ER 303 the plaintiff company borrowed from the defendant to develop a site. As part of the loan arrangements, the plaintiff agreed to buy the defendant's petrol for 21 years. Since the company was already in occupation of the garage and filling station when the agreement was made, it was subject to the doctrine of restraint of trade being a *contract* and not a *lease*. The High Court said that 21 years was too long and that the restraint was unenforceable. The Court of Appeal rejected that view and with it the opinion of the Monopolies Commission that it was not in the public interest that a petrol company should tie a petrol filling station for more than five years in the circumstances of this case.

Therefore, the *Lobb* case seems to show that the courts may not be prepared to help the so-called weaker party, i.e. the garage owner, as they were in the past. In the *Lobb* case the Court of Appeal said that each case must depend on its own facts. In fact the longer restriction seems on the facts of the case to have been justified. The loan by Total was a rescue operation greatly benefiting Lobb and enabling it to continue in business. There were also break clauses in the arrangement at the end of seven and 14 years if Lobb wished to use them. In view of the ample consideration offered by Total, the restraint of 21 years was not, according to the Court of Appeal, unreasonable and was therefore valid and enforceable.

INVOLUNTARY RESTRAINTS OF TRADE

We have so far considered, subject to an exception in the case of confidential information, restrictions against trading contained in contracts. However, the doctrine is not confined to these voluntary restraints. It extends to involuntary restraints imposed by trade associations or professional bodies upon their members. Such restraints are void unless reasonable.

The following case provides an example.

Pharmaceutical Society of Great Britain v Dickson [1968] 2 All ER 686

The Society passed a resolution to the effect that the opening of new pharmacies should be restricted and be limited to certain specified services, and that the range of services in existing pharmacies should not be extended except as approved by the Society's council. The purpose of the resolution was clearly to stop the development of new fields of trading in conjunction with pharmacy. Mr Dickson, who was a member of the Society and retail director of Boots Pure Drug Company Ltd, brought this action on the grounds that the proposed new rule was *ultra vires* as an unreasonable restraint of trade. A declaration that the resolution was *ultra vires* was made and the Society appealed to the House of Lords where the appeal was dismissed, the following points emerging from the judgment.

(a) Where a professional association passes a resolution regulating the conduct of its members the validity of the resolution is a matter for the courts even if binding in honour only, since failure to observe it is likely to be construed as misconduct and thus become a ground for disciplinary action.

(b) A resolution by a professional association regulating the conduct of its members is *ultra vires* if not sufficiently related to the main objects of the association. The objects of the society in this case did not cover the resolution, being 'to maintain the honour and safeguard and promote the interests of the members in the exercise of the profession of pharmacy'.

(c) A resolution by a professional association regulating the conduct of its members will be void if it is an unreasonable restraint of trade.

CONSEQUENCES WHERE THE CONTRACT IS CONTRARY TO PUBLIC POLICY: SEVERANCE

Where a contract is rendered void by the judiciary it is enforceable only in so far as it contravenes public policy. Thus lawful promises may be severed and enforced. A contract of service which contains a void restraint is not wholly invalid and the court will sever and enforce those aspects of it which do not offend against public policy. Thus an employee who has entered into a contract of service which contains a restraint which is too wide can recover his wages or salary.

The court will not add to a contract or in any way redraft it but will merely strike out the offending words. What is left must make sense without further additions otherwise the court will not sever the void part in order to enforce what is good. For example, A agrees 'not to set up a competing business within ten miles' in a covenant when he sells his business. If we suppose that five miles would be reasonable the court will not in fact substitute 'five' and then enforce the covenant because this would mean making a contract for the parties.

It is important also to note that the court will not delete the invalid part of a restraint clause if it is the major part of the restraints imposed.

Thus in *Attwood* v *Lamont* [1920] 3 KB 571 the heads of each department in a business of a general outfitter were required to sign a contract agreeing, amongst other things, after leaving the business not to be engaged in 'the trade or business of a tailor, dressmaker, general draper, milliner, hatter, haberdasher, gentlemen's, ladies' or children's outfitters, at any place within a radius of ten miles of the employers' place of business at Regent House, Kidderminster . . .' Lamont, who was employed as cutter and head of the tailoring department, left and began to compete, doing business with some of his former employer's customers. The employer then tried to enforce the above restraint which was drawn too wide in terms of the various departments covered, since Lamont had never been concerned with departments other than the tailoring department. The court refused to sever the tailoring covenant from the rest because that would have meant severing almost the whole of the restraint in order to leave the restraint regarding tailoring.

A contrast is provided by *Goldsoll* v *Goldman* [1915] 1 Ch 292. In that case the defendant sold imitation jewellery and when he sold his business he agreed 'not for two years to deal in real or imitation jewellery in any part of the United Kingdom'. The court was prepared to sever the words 'real or' in order to make the restraint valid and restrict the defendant from competing in imitation jewellery. Only two words needed to be deleted and this was a very small part of the restraint as a whole.

PUBLIC POLICY: THE CONTRIBUTION OF PARLIAMENT

Some contracts are prohibited by statute in terms that they are illegal, the word 'unlawful' being used in the statute concerned. In this context 'statute' includes the orders, rules and regulations that ministers of the Crown and other persons are authorized by Parliament to issue.

The statutory prohibitions with which we are concerned may be express or implied.

Implied statutory prohibition

In these cases the statute itself does not say expressly that contracts contravening its provisions are necessarily illegal. The statute may affect the formation of a particular contract as where a trader does business without taking out a licence. In some cases the statute may affect the manner of performance of the contract as where a trader is required to deliver to a purchaser a written statement such as an invoice containing, for example, details of the chemical composition of the goods.

In either case whether failure to comply with a statutory provision renders the contract illegal is a matter of construction of the statute and is for the judge to decide.

If, in the opinion of the judge, the Act was designed to protect the public then the contract will be illegal. Thus in *Cope* v *Rowlands* (1836) 2 M & W 149 an unlicensed broker in the City of London was held not to be entitled to sue for his fees because the purpose of the licensing requirements was to protect the public against possibly shady dealers. Furthermore, in *Anderson Ltd* v *Daniel* [1924] 1 KB 138 a seller of artificial fertilizers was *held* unable to recover the price of goods which he had delivered because he had failed to state in an invoice the chemical composition of the fertilizers which was required by Act of Parliament.

On the other hand, if in the opinion of the judge the purpose of the legislation was mainly to raise revenue or to help in the administration of trade, contracts will not be affected. Thus in *Smith* v *Mawhood* (1845) 14 M & W 452 it was held that a tobacconist could recover the price of tobacco sold by him even though he did not have a licence to sell it and had not painted his name on his place of business. The purpose of the statute involved was not to affect the contract of sale but to impose a fine on offenders for the purpose of revenue. In addition, in *Archbolds (Freightage) Ltd* v *Spanglett Ltd* [1961] 1 QB 374 a contract by an unlicensed carrier to carry goods by road was held valid because the legislation involved was only designed to help in the administration of road transport.

Express statutory prohibition

In a book of this nature it would be inappropriate to deal in detail with all statutes which render contracts illegal but a modern example is found in the Resale Prices Act 1976, s. 1. One particular type of agreement, namely an agreement between a number of manufacturers for the collective enforcement of conditions regulating the price at which goods may be sold, is prohibited and made unlawful.

Such agreements were not usually regarded as illegal at common law but the doctrine of privity of contract prevented enforcement of the resale price agreement by a manufacturer against a retailer (*see*, for example, *Dunlop* v *Selfridge* (1915), p. 35).

Consequently, manufacturers not having access to the ordinary courts of law often brought the retailer before a secret and possibly unjust trade association tribunal which might put the retailer quite unreasonably on a stop list so that he was denied supplies.

Under Part 1 of the Resale Prices Act 1976 *collective* agreements by two or more persons regulating the price at which goods may be resold are unlawful. There is no criminal penalty but the Crown may institute civil proceedings in the High Court and obtain, for example, an injunction to prevent the practice.

It is important to note that *individual* agreements between one manufacturer and his retailers are sanctioned by s. 26 of the Resale Prices Act 1976 so that such a manufacturer now has access to the ordinary courts of law to enforce his agreement. The action may be for damages or an injunction, though it is important to note that s. 26 only applies if the resale price agreement has been approved by the Restrictive Practices Court under the Resale Prices Act 1976. In fact very few such agreements have been approved, although an example is the *Net Book Agreement* [1962] 3 All ER 751 under which publishers can enforce resale price maintenance agreements in respect of books.

In that case the court thought that abolition of resale price maintenance would lead to fewer stockholding booksellers (because, for example, supermarkets would stock and sell more cheaply the best-selling books) and fewer new titles, particularly of slow-selling but useful books on specialist topics which would not be stocked by supermarkets. All of this the court thought would be detrimental to the public interest. The case was decided under earlier legislation before there was a separate Act concerned with resale price maintenance.

WAGERING CONTRACTS: INSURANCE AND DEALING IN DIFFERENCES

In essence for a wager to exist it must be possible for one party to win and one party to lose and there must be two persons or two groups opposed to each other in their views as to a future event. Thus, where X, Y and Z each put £5 into a fund to be given to the party whose selected horse wins a given race, there is no wager. The only commercial importance of the concept of wagering and the only reason why it is introduced in a book of this nature relates to insurance and dealing in differences (*see below*). A contract is not a wager if the person to whom the money is promised on the occurrence of the event has an interest in the non-occurrence of that event, e.g. where a person has paid a premium to insure his house against destruction by fire. Such an interest is called an *insurable interest* and is not a wager. However, to insure someone else's property would be a wager and not a valid contract of insurance.

The Gaming Act 1845 renders wagering contracts void so that there is no action for the bet or for the winnings. However, it should be noted that if the bet or the winnings have actually been paid over they cannot be recovered. Payment operates as waiver of the Act and the payment over of the money confers a good title to that money upon the person to whom it is paid.

It has become more common in recent times for persons to deal in differences, i.e. to bet on the future rises or falls in selected stock exchange indexes. No securities are bought or sold, the only transaction being the payment by one party to the other of the eventual difference in the indexes according to the accuracy or otherwise of the gambler's predictions.

It was decided in *City Index Ltd* v *Leslie, The Times*, 3 October 1990, that such a contract was validated by s. 63 of the Financial Services Act 1986 so long as it was made 'by way of business'. The plaintiffs offered clients a differences service and recovered £34,580 plus interest from the defendant whose predictions of rise and fall had not been successful.

CONTRACTS AFFECTED BY THE RESTRICTIVE TRADE PRACTICES ACT 1976

Under the Act of 1976 collective agreements between two or more persons designed to fix prices and/or regulate supplies of *goods* must be registered with the Director General of Fair Trading. They are then presumed void unless the parties can prove to the Restrictive Trade Practices Court that the agreement is in the public interest. This might be done, for example, where the parties can show that the agreement is designed to maintain the export trade. If the parties attempt to operate the agreement in spite of the fact that it has not been approved by the Restrictive Practices Court, the Director General of Fair Trading may ask for an injunction to prevent the operation of the agreement. However, it is rare that such action has to be taken because in most cases the firms concerned have not attempted to operate an agreement if it has been rejected by the court.

This Act also allows the Director General of Fair Trading to investigate restrictive practices in regard to services. If necessary the matter can be brought before the Restrictive Trade Practices Court which has a jurisdiction in respect of restrictive agreements relating to services.

An example is provided by *Agreement between the Members of the Association of British Travel Agents, The Times*, 25 June 1983. In that case it appeared that under the ABTA agreement no tour operator could sell foreign package tours through a non-ABTA agent. The Director General of Fair Trading thought that that was contrary to the public interest under the Restrictive Trade Practices Act of 1976 and took the agreement to the Restrictive Practices Court. However, the court decided that the agreement was valid because (a) the accounting discipline imposed by ABTA in terms of financial statements and returns from their agents and operators was valuable in terms of the public interest, and (b) there were ABTA arrangements under which members of the Association would cope with those who had booked holidays with an operator or agent who had collapsed because of insolvency. This again was very much in the public interest.

The Restrictive Practices Court may approve modifications to a registered agreement or may make an order under s. 4(1) of the Restrictive Trade Practices Act 1976 on the application of the Director General of Fair Trading, allowing the Director to approve modifications where the variation is not a substantial one (*see re Building Employers' Confederation's Application* [1985] ICR 167).

THE RESALE PRICES ACT 1976

This Act is concerned with arrangements (or agreements) under which a supplier *imposes* upon a buyer a restriction in regard to the price at which the buyer must resell the goods he has bought under that arrangement or agreement.

Resale price maintenance agreements are presumed void under the 1976 Act unless the supplier can prove to the Restrictive Practices Court that the restriction is in the public interest. This might be done, for example, by showing that after-sales service would be reduced or non-existent unless the resale price maintenance agreement was enforced (and *see* the *Net Book Agreement* (1962) at p. 183). We have already seen that if a *minimum* resale price maintenance agreement is approved by the Restrictive Practices Court it can be enforced regardless of the doctrine of Privity of Contract under s. 26 of the Resale Prices Act 1976.

A *maximum* resale price can be enforced under s. 26 against a third party if the goods have been acquired by that third party with notice of the restriction. Maximum resale price arrangements do not require the approval of the court.

THE FAIR TRADING ACT 1973

This Act gives wide powers to the Office of Fair Trading under the Director General of Fair Trading by reason of which it can deal with monopolies, mergers, restrictive practices, and the protection of consumers against trading practices which are considered unfair. A recent example is a report by the Director on the 'timeshare' industry which reveals that undesirable techniques are used by some organizations to induce people to buy and make unduly hasty decisions about this. The report contains recommendations to the government for changes in the law to control these matters. The Office of Fair Trading is perhaps best known for its duty to vet mergers between parties having a large share of the relevant market and to recommend to the Department of Trade and Industry whether they should be referred to the

Monopolies and Mergers Commission. The government is not bound to take the advice of the Office of Fair Trading regarding reference. The Office of Fair Trading has, however, a much wider brief under the following main pieces of legislation: the Consumer Credit Act 1974 (*see* p. 347); the Competition Act 1980 (*see below*); and, as we have seen, the Restrictive Trade Practices Act 1976 and also the Resale Prices Act 1976.

As regards consumer protection and surveillance of traders it works with local Trading Standards Consumer Protection departments and advice agencies and gives information on consumer rights. It can obtain assurances of future obedience of the law from traders under the Fair Trading Act 1973 and under the Consumer Credit Act 1974 it vets the fitness of traders offering credit and resolves disputes over the accuracy of information on people which is given by credit reference agencies.

The competition legislation brings monopolies and mergers and other trade practices which restrict, distort or prevent competition in the UK under the surveillance and control of the Office of Fair Trading.

THE COMPETITION ACT 1980

The main significance of this Act is that it brings within the scope of investigation the practices of single firms which are neither monopolies in a statutory sense nor in collusion with other enterprises for the purposes of the Restrictive Trade Practices Act 1976.

The Act provides a two-stage inquiry process. First of all the Director General of Fair Trading can, under s. 3 of the Act, initiate a preliminary inquiry into a practice of a firm or firms and is required to report publicly his findings as to whether it constitutes an anti-competitive practice and if so, whether he feels it is right to refer the matter for investigation to the Monopolies and Mergers Commission. A company may volunteer undertakings in regard to the abandonment of its restrictive or monopolistic practices to the Director General at this stage and he may accept them instead of taking the matter to the Monopolies and Mergers Commission.

If the matter goes to the Commission, the Commission must assess and report whether the practice is anti-competitive and, in addition, whether it has operated or may be expected to operate against the public interest. Where the conclusion of the Commission is adverse the Secretary of State may make an order under s. 10 requiring the company to desist from or amend the practice concerned, or ask the Director General of Fair Trading to seek undertakings from the company.

A number of s. 3 investigations have been made by the Office of Fair Trading. For example, there was an investigation into certain practices within the Raleigh Group. The report of the Director General found certain anti-competitive practices by the company regarding the supply of their products to discount stores. These operated against the public interest. Accordingly, the company gave the Director General an undertaking not to refuse to supply certain makes of bicycle to discount stores and certain other retail outlets.

Section 13 provides for prices to be investigated by the Director General at the direction of the Secretary of State if the price is a matter 'of major public concern'. There are no follow-up powers by which any recommendations could be enforced.

Section 11 allows public bodies to be referred to the Monopolies and Mergers Commission for a review of efficiency and costs, sometimes known for short as an efficiency audit. Section 12 allows the relevant minister to order the body concerned to prepare a plan to put matters right. A number of reports have been published, e.g. one dealing with the London and South Eastern commuter services of British Rail. A more recent example is the investigation into the efficiency of London Underground Ltd.

THE EUROPEAN COMMUNITY APPROACH TO RESTRICTIVE PRACTICES

Under Articles 85 and 86 of the Treaty of Rome all agreements between firms which operate to prevent or restrict competition in the Market are void. Under s. 5 of the Restrictive Trade Practices Act 1976 the Director General of Fair Trading and the Restrictive Practices Court are to take Articles 85 and 86 into account:

(a) on the issue of registration of a particular agreement; and
(b) if the agreement comes before the court for adjudication.

Restrictive trading agreements and the Treaty of Rome generally

We have already considered the position under English domestic law with regard to restrictive trading agreements. Some consideration must now be given to the position under Community law.

Policy and source of law

The provisions of the Treaty, which have been part of our law since January 1973, are based, as UK law is, on the protection of the public interest. The basis of the competition policy is to be found in Articles 85 and 86 of the Treaty. These ban practices which distort competition between members of the Community (Art. 85), and prohibit the abuse of a monopolistic position by an organization within the Market (Art. 86). There is an additional aim of raising living standards.

Relationship with UK law

On the matter of relationship, national legislation on restrictive trade practices and monopolies applies alongside Community law unless it conflicts with Community law as interpreted by the Commission or the European Court of Justice. Therefore, if a restrictive agreement or merger threat affects only the UK market, the matter will remain subject exclusively to UK legislation. If such agreement affects trade between two or more Member States then to that extent national law is excluded by Community law. Furthermore, if there is an overlap between Community and national law, Community law predominates. Therefore, once an agreement with inter-Market effect has been exempted by the Commission under Art. 85, it will from then on be immune from attack under United Kingdom restrictive practices or resale prices legislation. If the agreement had already been regarded as invalid under that legislation the invalidation will cease to be effective if the Commission exempts it under Art. 85. Additionally, if the restrictive practice has been approved by a UK court its approval will lapse if the agreement turns out to infringe the provisions of Art. 85. This is why it is important for UK restrictive practices courts to decline or postpone exercising jurisdiction where the Treaty applies and the Commission has already initiated proceedings.

Application of Articles 85 and 86, Treaty of Rome

It is perhaps inappropriate in a non-specialist book of this nature to go through the many illustrative cases on the above articles of the Treaty of Rome which have been heard by the European Court of Justice. However, by way of illustration and to show the application of the Articles in English cases before English courts we can consider the following.

Article 85

Of interest here is the case of *Cutsforth* v *Mansfield Inns* [1986] 1 All ER 577. C supplied coin-operated machines to 57 Humberside public houses owned by Northern County Breweries. M acquired Northern and requested all the tenants of the old Northern public houses to operate equipment supplied by M's list of nominated suppliers. M refused to put C on that list. This was *held* to be an infringement of Art. 85 and an injunction was granted preventing M from interfering with C's agreements with the tenants of the 57 public houses and from taking any action to limit the freedom of those tenants to order machines from C. M was not infringing Art. 86 because they were not in a dominant position in the market.

Article 86

An illustration of the use of Art. 86 in an English court of law is provided by *Garden Cottage Foods Ltd* v *Milk Marketing Board* [1982] 2 All ER 292. Garden Cottage (the company) was a middle-man transferring butter from the Board to traders in the bulk market in Europe and the UK taking a cut of the price. In March 1982 following some packaging problems which the company appeared to have overcome, the

Board refused to supply direct. It said that supplies must be obtained from one of four independent distributors nominated by the Board.

These distributors were the company's competitors. The company would have to pay more to them for its supplies than if it bought direct from the Board. Therefore it could not compete on price, and would be forced out of business.

The company alleged that the Board was in breach of Art. 86 of the Treaty of Rome. This provides: 'Any abuse by one or more undertakings of a dominant position when in the Common Market or in a substantial part of it, shall be prohibited as incompatible with the Common Market in so far as it may affect trade between Member States . . . '

The Court of Appeal, and later the House of Lords (*see Garden Cottage Foods Ltd* v *Milk Marketing Board* [1983] 2 All ER 770), decided that there had been a breach of Art. 86.

As regards remedies the court was asked to grant an injunction restraining the Board from refusing to maintain normal business relations contrary to Art. 86. The case was dealt with on that basis. However, the House of Lords was of the opinion that the remedy of damages was available for breach of the Treaty but there is still some uncertainty about this. UK courts have not as yet clarified precisely what remedies are available in this area.

GRADED QUESTIONS

Essay mode

1. Explain the controls over anti-competitive practices which were introduced by the Competition Act 1980. How are these controls related to the competition rules of the European Economic Community?

   (*The Institute of Chartered Secretaries and Administrators. English Business Law. December 1989*)

2. International Instruments Ltd employ Ronald as a sales manager and Geoffrey as a computer software designer.
   (i) In Ronald's contract of employment there is a provision that should he wish to leave the company he will give one year's notice; and that he will not for a period of one year after leaving their employment solicit or approach any former customer of theirs nor will he work in the very specialized industry in which International Instruments Ltd are market leaders anywhere in the European Community.
   (ii) In Geoffrey's contract of employment there is a provision that he will give one year's notice of intention to leave the company should he wish to do so.
   Both Ronald and Geoffrey leave the company suddenly and without giving

notice. Ronald goes to work for another company Amalgamated Instruments Ltd who are engaged in approximately the same area of business as International Instruments Ltd although at the moment they have no products which are in direct competition; however International Instruments suspect that Ronald is about to approach former customers and may well have been recruited with a view to leading an assault on International Instruments Ltd's market share with new products which Amalgamated Instruments are preparing to bring out.

Geoffrey has decided to leave computing to set up his own Woodland Craft Centre. His sudden departure has caused major disruption and it will be some months before a suitable replacement can be obtained.

Advise International Instruments Ltd on their rights and remedies against Ronald and Geoffrey.

(The Institute of Legal Executives. Part II: Commercial Law. June 1990)

3. Four years ago Victor joined the firm of Sparks, an electrical retail business, as a TV and radio repair man. Sparks agreed to train Victor, including sending him on a day-release course at a local college to gain a diploma in TV engineering. When entering into his contract of employment, Victor agreed to abide by a term stating that if he were to leave Sparks he would not engage in any activity related to the manufacture, sale, service or repair of any radio, TV, or other domestic electrical appliances for a period of three years within a radius of five miles of Sparks' shop.

Victor has now had a disagreement with Sparks, and wishes to leave. He has been offered a job as a technical sales assistant at a local electrical discount warehouse.

Advise Victor on the legal principles involved in determining whether Sparks may prevent him from taking this job, with reference to appropriate case law.

(North Staffordshire Polytechnic. BA Business Studies. Business Law)

Objective mode

Four alternative answers are given. Select ONE only. Circle the answer which you consider to be correct. Check your answers by referring back to the information given in the chapter and against the answers at the back of the book.

With reference to the following information answer questions 1 to 5.

Upon entering the service of Pans plc (who manufacture kitchenware) as sales manager, Egon undertook by his contract that if, for any reason, he should leave that service he would never:
by clause (a) solicit any of the company's customers;
by clause (b) divulge to anyone details of certain secret processes;
by clause (c) set up in competition with the company.
Egon, who is now considering leaving Pans' employment, shows you a copy of the contract and wishes to know to what extent if he does leave he will be bound by the terms set out in (a) to (c) above.

1. Which one of the following areas of law is relevant?

   A Treaty of Rome.
   B Restrictive trade practices.
   C Restraint of trade.
   D Failure of consideration.

2. Which of the following statements is a correct application of the relevant law to clauses (a), (b) and (c)?

   A Clauses (a), (b) and (c) are unenforceable.
   B Clauses (a) and (c) are enforceable; clause (b) is unenforceable.
   C Clauses (a) and (b) are enforceable; clause (c) is unenforceable.
   D Clauses (a) and (b) are unenforceable; clause (c) is enforceable.

3. Which one of the following cases is relevant in reaching a correct conclusion in regard to clause (a)?

   A *Forster* v *Suggett* (1918).
   B *Home Counties Dairies* v *Skilton* (1970).
   C *Robb* v *Green* (1895).
   D *Kores Manufacturing Co Ltd* v *Kolok Manufacturing Co Ltd* (1958).

4. Which one of the following cases is relevant in reaching a correct conclusion in regard to clause (b)?

   A *Robb* v *Green* (1895).
   B *Home Counties Dairies* v *Skilton* (1970).
   C *Forster* v *Suggett* (1918).
   D *Kores Manufacturing Co Ltd* v *Kolok Manufacturing Co Ltd* (1958).

5. Which one of the following cases is relevant in reaching a correct conclusion in regard to clause (c)?

   A *Faccenda Chicken Ltd* v *Fowler* (1986).
   B *Nordenfelt* v *Maxim Nordenfelt Guns and Ammunition Co* (1894).
   C *Esso Petroleum Co Ltd* v *Harper's Garage (Stourport) Ltd* (1967).
   D *Wyatt* v *Kreglinger and Fernau* (1933).

With reference to the following information answer questions 6 and 7?

In order to ensure that its petrol and allied products are sold exclusively by certain garages and filling stations, Chronic Petroleum Ltd includes 'ties' to that effect for a period of five years in the supply agreements with those retail outlets. A competing oil company, Wizz Petroleum Ltd, offers Green, the owner of a garage which is a Chronic outlet, an interest-free loan of £40,000 if Green will breach his 'tie' with Chronic and sell exclusively the products of Wizz.

Green needs the cash urgently to develop the site and is keen to accept the offer made by Wizz.

Advise Green as to the legal implications involved.

6. Which of the following statements is a correct application of the law?

   A Chronic Petroleum will be able to enforce its tie against Green and prevent the arrangement with Wizz.
   B Green can go ahead with the arrangement with Wizz since the tie with Chronic is unenforceable.
   C Chronic's tie is unenforceable without the approval of the Monopolies and Mergers Commission.
   D Both the ties of Chronic and Wizz are illegal. Green would not be bound by either of them.

7. Which one of the following cases is relevant in reaching the correct conclusion in question 6 above?

   A *Cleveland Petroleum v Dartstone* (1968).
   B *Attwood v Lamont* (1920).
   C *Goldsoll v Goldman* (1915).
   D *Esso Petroleum v Harper's Garage (Stourport) Ltd* (1967).

8. Roach Ltd is a company whose business is the importing of fish through the port of Grimstoft. Tranter (Transport) Ltd is an associated company operating refrigerated vans to distribute fish to various parts of the country including the city of Midchester. This arrangement has enabled Roach Ltd to quote keener prices and provide a better delivery service than could be done by using other transport contractors.

   Some months ago the members of the Midchester Fish Merchants Association, representing wholesalers in the Midchester Wholesale Fish Market, passed the following resolution: 'That all fish consigned to the Midchester Wholesale Fish Market be transported only in vehicles officially nominated by the Chairman of the Association and members of the Association shall not accept fish from any vehicle not so nominated.'

   Shortly afterwards the Chairman of the Association nominated Carters Ltd as sole transporters and a letter outlining the new arrangement was sent to all importers sending fish to the Midchester Market.

   In consequence Roach Ltd cannot now send fish to Midchester Fish Market except by using transport provided by Carters Ltd. This involves additional costs which will necessitate an increase in the price for which the fish can be sold. Roach Ltd threatened to sue the Midchester Fish Merchants Association and the Association thereupon registered the agreement with the Registrar of Restrictive Practices who intends to place the matter before the Restrictive Practices Court as soon as possible.

   The court's view of the agreement is likely to be:

   A That it is unenforceable under the Resale Prices Act 1976.
   B That it is enforceable and not contrary to law.

    C That it is unenforceable under the Restrictive Trade Practices Act 1976.

    D That it is unenforceable under the Competition Act 1980.

Answers to questions set in objective mode appear on p. 551.

8 | Discharge of contract

The OBJECTIVES of this chapter are to consider the four methods by which a contract can be discharged or terminated together with an explanation of the rules relating to the limitation of actions which, while they do not properly speaking discharge a contract, may prevent an action being brought upon it.

The discharge of a contract means in general that the parties are freed from their mutual obligations. A contract may be discharged in four ways: *lawfully* by agreement, by performance or by frustration, and *unlawfully* by breach.

DISCHARGE BY AGREEMENT

Obviously, what has been created by agreement may be ended by agreement. Discharge by agreement may arise in the following ways.

Out of the original agreement

Thus the parties may have agreed at the outset that the contract should end automatically on the expiration of a fixed time. This would be the case, for example, with a lease of premises for a fixed term. Alternatively, the contract may contain a provision entitling one or both parties to terminate it if they wish. Thus a contract of employment can normally be brought to an end by giving reasonable notice. This area of the law is, of course, subject to statutory minimum periods of notice laid down by s. 49 of the Employment Protection (Consolidation) Act 1978. They are one week after one month's service, two weeks after two years' service and an additional week for each year of service up to 12 weeks after 12 years' service. Section 49 provides that the employee must, once he has been continuously employed for one month, give at least one week's notice to his employer to terminate his contract of employment. This is regardless of the number of years of service. Individual contracts may provide for longer periods of notice both by employer and employee.

Out of a new contract

If the contract is *executory*, i.e. a promise for a promise, and there has been no performance, the mutual release of the parties provides the consideration and is called bilateral discharge. The only difficulty here is in relation to the form of the release. The position is as follows:

(a) written contracts may be rescinded or varied by oral agreement;
(b) deeds may be rescinded or varied orally;
(c) contracts required to be evidenced in writing may be totally discharged by oral agreement but variations must be in writing.

If the contract is executed as where it has been performed or partly performed by one party, then the other party who wishes to be released must provide consideration for that release unless it is effected by deed. This is referred to as unilateral discharge. In other words, the doctrine of accord and satisfaction applies. This matter has already been dealt with and is really an aspect of the law relating to consideration (*see* p. 46).

DISCHARGE BY PERFORMANCE GENERALLY

A contract may be discharged by performance, the discharge taking place when both parties have performed the obligations which the contract placed upon them. Whether performance must comply exactly with the terms of the contract depends on the following.

CONSTRUCTION OF THE CONTRACT AS ENTIRE

According to the manner in which the court construes the meaning, the contract may be an entire contract. Here the manner of performance must be complete and exact. An illustration is provided by the following case.

Bolton v Mahadeva [1972] 2 All ER 1322
Bolton installed a central heating system in the defendant's house. The price agreed was a lump sum of £560. The work was not done properly and it was estimated that it would cost

£179 to put the system right. The Court of Appeal decided that the lump sum payment suggested that the contract was entire and since Bolton had not performed his part of it properly and in full he could not recover anything for what he had done.

Comment. The case of *Cutter v Powell* (1795) 6 Term Rep 320 is sometimes used to illustrate the point about entire contracts. The facts of the case were that a seaman agreed to serve on a ship from Jamaica to Liverpool for the sum of 30 guineas (£31.50 today) to be paid on completion of the voyage. He died when the ship was nineteen days short of Liverpool. The court *held* that the contract was entire and his widow was not entitled to anything on behalf of his estate. While the case is valid as an illustration it has been overtaken on its own facts by more recent law. The Merchant Shipping Act 1970 now provides for the payment of wages for partial performance in such cases and the Law Reform (Frustrated Contracts) Act 1943 would also have assisted the widow to recover because the seaman had conferred a benefit on the master of the ship prior to his death (which would now frustrate the contract) giving the widow the right to sue the master of the ship for the benefit of the seaman's work up to the time of his death.

There is obviously some hardship when the entire contract rule is applied because some work is done by A for B which B does not pay for and certain other approaches have been worked out by the judiciary as follows.

SUBSTANTIAL PERFORMANCE

If the court construes the contract in such a way that precise performance of every term by one party is not required in order to make the other party liable to some extent on it, then the plaintiff may recover for work done, though the defendant may, of course, counter-claim for any defects in performance. In this connection it should be noted that in construing a contract to see whether a particular term must be fully performed or whether substantial performance is enough, the court will refer to the difference between conditions and warranties. A condition must be wholly performed whereas substantial performance of a warranty is often enough. (*Poussard v Spiers and Pond* (1876) and *Bettini v Gye* (1876) – *see* pp. 140–1.)

An example of construction in favour of substantial performance appears below.

Hoenig v Isaacs [1952] 2 All ER 176

The defendant employed the plaintiff who was an interior decorator and furniture designer to decorate a one-room flat owned by the defendant. The plaintiff was also to provide furniture, including a fitted bookcase, a wardrobe and a bedstead, for the total sum of £750. The terms of the contract regarding payment were as follows: 'Net cash as the work proceeds and the balance on completion'. The defendant made two payments to the plaintiff of £150 each, one payment on the 12 April and the other on 19 April. The plaintiff claimed that he had completed the work on 28 August, and asked for the balance, i.e. £450. The defendant asserted that the work done was bad and faulty, but sent the plaintiff a sum of £100 and moved into the flat and used the furniture. The plaintiff now sued for the balance of £350, the defence being that the plaintiff had not performed his contract, or in the alternative that he had done so negligently, unskilfully and in an unworkmanlike manner.

The Official Referee assessed the work that had been done, and found that generally it was properly done except that the wardrobe door required replacing and that a bookshelf was too short and this meant that the bookcase would have to be remade. The defendant claimed that the contract was entire and that it must be completely performed before the plaintiff could recover. The Official Referee was of opinion that there had been substantial performance, and that the defendant was liable for £750 less the cost of putting right the above mentioned defects, the cost of this being assessed at £55 18s 2d. The court accordingly gave the plaintiff judgment for the sum of £294 1s 10d.

Comment: The Official Referee is a judge designated to consider cases referred to him by a court because they involve consideration of documents and accounts to assess what damages should be payable.

ACCEPTANCE OF PARTIAL PERFORMANCE

If, for example, S agrees to deliver three dozen bottles of brandy to B and delivers two dozen bottles only, then B may exercise his right to reject the whole consignment. But if he has accepted delivery of two dozen bottles he must pay for them at the contract rate (s. 30(1), Sale of Goods Act 1979).

However, the mere conferring of a benefit on one party by another is not enough; there must be evidence of acceptance of that benefit by the party upon whom it was conferred. The acceptance must arise following a genuine choice.

The following case provides an example of a situation in which there was no genuine choice.

Sumpter v Hedges [1898] 1 QB 673

The plaintiff entered into a contract with the defendant under the terms of which the plaintiff was to erect some buildings for the defendant on the defendant's land for a price of £565. The plaintiff did partially erect the buildings up to the value of £333, and the defendant paid him for that figure. The plaintiff then told the defendant that he could not finish the job because he had run out of funds. The defendant then completed the work by using materials belonging to the plaintiff which had been left on the site. The plaintiff now sued for work done and materials supplied, and the court gave him judgment for materials supplied, but would not grant him a sum of money by way of a *quantum meruit* (an action for reasonable payment for work done), for the value of the work done prior to his abandonment of the job. The reason given was that, before the plaintiff could sue successfully on a *quantum meruit*, he would have to show that the defendant had voluntarily accepted the work done, and this implied that the defendants must be in a position to refuse the benefit of the work as where a buyer of goods refuses to take delivery. This was not the case here; the defendant had no option but to accept the work done, so his acceptance could not be presumed from conduct. There being no other evidence of the defendant's acceptance of the work, the plaintiff's claim for the work failed.

Comment: In practice this form of injustice to the builder is avoided because a building contract normally provides for progress payments as various stages of construction are completed, thus making it a divisible agreement.

FULL PERFORMANCE PREVENTED BY THE PROMISEE

Here the party who cannot further perform his part of the contract may bring an action on a *quantum meruit* against the party in default for the value of work done up to the time when further performance was prevented. **The following case provides an illustration.**

De Barnardy v Harding (1853) 8 Exch 822
The plaintiff agreed to act as the defendant's agent for the purpose of preparing and issuing certain advertisements and notices designed to encourage the sale of tickets to see the funeral procession of the Duke of Wellington. The plaintiff was to be paid a commission of 10 per cent upon the proceeds of the tickets actually sold. The plaintiff duly issued the advertisements and notices, but before he began to sell the tickets the defendant withdrew the plaintiff's authority to sell them and in consequence the plaintiff did not sell any tickets and was prevented from earning his commission. The plaintiff now sued upon a *quantum meruit* and his action succeeded.

TIME OF PERFORMANCE

Section 41 of the Law of Property Act 1925 provides that stipulations as to the time of performance in a contract are not construed to be of the essence of the contract and therefore need not be strictly complied with, unless equity would have regarded them as such. There are the following exceptional situations in which time was of the essence even in equity.
  (a) The contract fixes a date and makes performance on that date a condition.
  (b) The circumstances indicate that the contract should be performed at the agreed time. Thus, in the sale of a business, equity will generally take the view

that the contract should be completed on time so that uncertainties regarding a change of owner should not be prolonged and affect adversely the goodwill of the business. Commercial contracts, such as contracts for the sale of goods where a time is fixed for delivery, are also in this category. **The following case shows that in a commercial or business contract the time fixed for delivery is of the essence. This includes early delivery!**

Bowes v Shand (1877) 2 App Cas 455

The action was brought for damages for non-acceptance of 600 tons (or 8,200 bags) of Madras rice. The sold note stated that the rice was to be shipped during 'the months of March and/or April 1874'. 8,150 bags were put on board ship on or before 28 February 1874, and the remaining 50 bags on 2 March 1874. The defendants refused to take delivery because the rice was not shipped in accordance with the terms of the contract. *Held* – The bulk of the cargo was shipped in February and therefore the rice did not answer the description in the contract and the defendants were not bound to accept it.

Comment: A buyer can reject in these circumstances even though there is nothing wrong with the goods and he merely wants to reject because the market price has fallen.

(c) Where the time of performance was not originally of the essence of the contract or has been waived but one party has been guilty of undue delay, the other party may give notice requiring that the contract be performed within a reasonable time. **An illustration from case law appears below**.

Chas Rickards Ltd v Oppenhaim [1950] 1 KB 616

The defendant ordered a Rolls-Royce chassis from the plaintiffs, the chassis being delivered in July 1947. The plaintiffs found a coachbuilder prepared to make a body within six or at the most seven months. The specification for the body was agreed in August 1947, so that the work should have been completed in March 1948. The work was not completed by then but the defendant still pressed for delivery. On 29 June 1948, the defendant wrote to the coachbuilders saying that he would not accept delivery after 25 July 1948. The body was not ready by then and the defendant bought another car. The body was completed in October 1948, but the defendant refused to accept delivery and counter-claimed for the value of the chassis which he had purchased. *Held* – Time was of the essence of the original contract, but the defendant had waived the question of time by continuing to press for delivery after the due date. However, by his letter of 29 June he had again made time of the essence, and had given reasonable notice in the matter. Judgment was given for the defendant on the claim and counter-claim.

Comment: That a waiver of a date of delivery without consideration is binding can be based on promissory estoppel (as in *High Trees* – see p. 51) said Denning LJ in *Rickards*, or on s. 11(2) of the Sale of Goods Act 1979 which states: 'Where a contract of sale is subject to any condition to be fulfilled by the seller, the buyer may waive that condition.' This section was used to justify a waiver without consideration by McCardie J in *Hartley* v *Hymans* [1920] 3 KB 475.

This is an example of the doctrine of promissory estoppel being used by a plaintiff, i.e. as a sword not a shield, because a seller may tender delivery after the originally agreed date relying on the buyer's promise to accept such delivery by reason of his waiver. If the buyer then refuses to accept the delivery the seller can claim damages and is in essence suing upon the waiver which is unsupported by consideration.

TENDER

With regard to the manner of performance, the question of what is good tender arises. Tender is an offer of performance which complies with the terms of the contract. If goods are tendered by the seller and refused by the buyer the seller is freed from liability, given that the goods are in accordance with the contract as to quantity and quality. As regards the payment of money, this must comply with the following rules.

(a) It must be in accordance with the rules relating to legal tender. By s. 1(2) and (6) of the Currency and Bank Notes Act 1954 a tender of a note or notes of the Bank of England expressed to be payable to bearer on demand is legal tender for the payment of any amount. A tender of notes of a bank other than the Bank of England is not legal tender, though the creditor may waive his objection to the tender if he wishes. As regards coins, s. 2 of the Coinage Act 1971, as amended by the Currency Act 1983, provides that coins made by the Mint shall be legal tender as follows:

   (i) Certain gold coins for payment of any amount. We are referring here to the gold sovereign. These are legal tender if struck after 1837. Even though the sovereign contains just under ¼ ounce of gold it is valid only for £1 although it is worth much more as a collector's item.

   (ii) Coins of cupro-nickel or silver of denominations of more than 10 pence, i.e. 20p, 50p, £1 and £2 coins are legal tender for payment of any amount not exceeding £10.

   (iii) Coins of cupro-nickel or silver of denominations of not more than 10 pence (in practice, the 5p and 10p coins) are legal tender for payment of any amount not exceeding £5.

   (iv) Coins of bronze, i.e. the 2p and 1p coins are legal tender for payment of any amount not exceeding 20 pence.

   There is power of proclamation to call in coins which then cease to be legal tender or to make other coins legal tender.

(b) There must be no request for change.

(c) Tender by cheque or other negotiable instrument or by charge card or credit card is not good tender unless the creditor does not object. It should be noted that if a proper tender of money is refused the debt is not discharged, but if the money is paid into court the debtor has a good defence to an action by his creditor and the debt does not bear interest.

In connection with payment by credit card or charge card the consumer normally discharges his obligation to the seller by payment in this way. If the card company cannot pay the seller as where that company is insolvent the seller has no redress against the consumer subject always to the terms of the contract (*Re Charge Card Services* [1988] 3 All ER 702).

APPROPRIATION OF PAYMENTS

In connection with performance it is important to consider the rules governing appropriation of payments. Certain debts are barred by the Limitation Act 1980 and money which has been owed for six years under a simple contract or 12 years under a specialty contract without acknowledgment may not be recoverable by an action in the courts. Where a debtor owes several debts to the same creditor and makes a payment which does not cover them all, there are rules governing how the money should be appropriated. These are as follows.

(a) The debtor can appropriate either expressly by saying which debt he is paying or by implication as where he owes £50 and £20 and sends £20.
(b) If the debtor does not appropriate the creditor can appropriate to any debt, *even to one which is statute-barred* (*see further* p. 228). However, if the statute-barred debt is £50 and the creditor appropriates a payment of £25 to it the balance of the debt is not revived and cannot be sued for (*Mills v Fowkes* (1839) 5 Bing NC 455).
(c) Where there is a current account there is a presumption that the creditor has not appropriated payments to him to any particular item. The major example is a bank current account. Appropriation here is on a chronological basis, i.e. the first item on the debit side of the account is reduced by the first item on the credit side: a first in first out principle. This follows from the rule in *Clayton's Case* (1816) 1 Mer 572. **The following case provides an illustration.**

Deeley v Lloyds Bank Ltd [1912] AC 756
A customer of the bank had mortgaged his property to the bank to secure an overdraft limited to £2,500. He then mortgaged the same property to the appellant for £3,500, subject to the bank's mortgage. It is the normal practice of bankers, on receiving notice of a second

mortgage, to rule off the customer's account, and not to allow any further withdrawals since these will rank after the second mortgage. In this case the bank did not open a new account but continued the old current account. The customer thereafter paid in sums of money which at a particular date, if they had been appropriated in accordance with the rule in *Clayton's* case, would have extinguished the bank's mortgage. Even so the customer still owed the bank money, and they sold the property for a price which was enough to satisfy the bank's debt but not that of the appellant. *Held* – The evidence did not exclude the rule in *Clayton's* case, which applied, so that the bank's mortgage had been paid off and the appellant, as second mortgagee, was entitled to the proceeds of the sale.

Comment: The operation of *Clayton's Case* is normally prevented by the bank stating in the mortgage that it is a continuing security given on a running account varying from day to day and excluding the repayment of the borrower's liability which would otherwise take place as credits are paid in.

DISCHARGE BY FRUSTRATION GENERALLY

If an agreement is impossible of performance from the outset it is void. This is at the root of s. 6 of the Sale of Goods Act 1979 which provides that where there is a contract for the sale of specific goods and the goods, without the knowledge of the seller, have perished at the time when the contract is made, it is void. However, some contracts are possible of performance when they are made but it subsequently becomes impossible to carry them out in whole or in part and they are then referred to as frustrated.

The judges developed the doctrine of discharge by frustration, which applies, as the House of Lords decided in *Davis Contractors Ltd* v *Fareham UDC* [1956] 2 All ER 145 in the restricted set of circumstances where there has been such a change in the significance of the obligation that the thing undertaken would, if performed, be a different thing than that contracted for. The subject is considered under the following heads.

CONTRACTS FOR PERSONAL SERVICE

Such a contract is discharged by the death of the person who was to perform it; thus if A agrees to play the piano at a concert and dies before the date on which the performance is due, his personal representatives will not be expected to go along and play in his stead.

Incapacity of a person who has to perform a contract may discharge it. However, temporary incapacity is not enough unless it affects the contract in a fundamental manner (*Poussard* v *Spiers and Pond* (1876) – *see* p. 140).

The doctrine of frustration will usually only apply where there is no fault by either party. Where performance of the contract is prevented by the fault of one party, that party is in breach of contract and that is the proper approach to the problem.

The following cases provide examples.

Storey v Fulham Steel Works (1907) 24 TLR 89

The plaintiff was employed by the defendant as manager for a period of five years. After he had been working for two years he became ill, and had to have special treatment and a period of convalescence. Six months later he was recovered, but in the meantime the defendant had terminated his employment. The plaintiff now sued for breach of contract, and the defendants pleaded that the plaintiff's period of ill-health operated to discharge the contract. *Held* – The plaintiff's illness and absence from duty did not go to the root of the contract, and was not so serious as to allow the termination of the agreement.

Norris v Southampton City Council [1982] IRCR 141

Mr Norris was employed as a cleaner. He was convicted of assault and reckless driving and was sentenced to a term of imprisonment. His employers wrote dismissing him and Mr Norris complained to an industrial tribunal that his dismissal was unfair. The tribunal held that the contract of employment was frustrated and that the employee was not dismissed and therefore not entitled to compensation. The Employment Appeal Tribunal to which Mr Norris appealed laid down that frustration could only arise where there was no fault by either party. Where there was a fault, such as deliberate conduct leading to an inability to perform the contract, there was no frustration but a repudiatory breach of contract. The employer had the option of whether or not to treat the contract as repudiated and if he chose to dismiss the employee he could do so, regarding the breach as repudiatory. The question then to be decided was whether the dismissal was fair. The case was remitted to the Industrial Tribunal for further consideration of whether there was unfair dismissal on the facts of the case.

GOVERNMENT INTERFERENCE

In times of national emergency the government may often requisition property or goods in the national interest. This will have the effect of frustrating relevant contracts. **The following case illustrates this point.**

Re Shipton, Anderson & Co and Harrison Bros' Arbitration [1915] 3 KB 676

A contract was made for the sale of wheat lying in a warehouse in Liverpool. Before the seller could deliver the wheat, and before the property in it had passed to the buyer, the government requisitioned the wheat under certain emergency powers available in time of war. *Held* – Delivery being impossible by reason of lawful requisition by the government, the seller was excused from performance of the contract.

DESTRUCTION OF THE SUBJECT MATTER OF THE CONTRACT

Physical destruction of the subject matter of the contract operates to frustrate it. **The following case illustrates this point.**

Taylor v Caldwell (1863) 3 B & S 826

The defendant agreed to let the plaintiff have the use of a music hall for the purpose of holding four concerts. Before the first concert was due to be held the hall was destroyed by fire without negligence by any party, and the plaintiff now sued for damages for wasted advertising expenses. *Held* – The contract was impossible of performance and the defendant was not liable.

Comment: A modern example of the rule is to be found in *Vitol SA v Esso Australia, The Times*, 1 February 1988, where the buyers of petroleum were discharged from the contract by frustration when the vessel and cargo were destroyed by a missile attack in the Gulf.

NON-OCCURRENCE OF AN EVENT

Where the taking place of an event is vital to the contract its cancellation or postponement will, in the absence of a contrary provision, frustrate it. However, if the main purpose of the contract can still be achieved there will be no frustration. **The following cases provide examples of these rules.**

Krell v Henry [1903] 2 KB 740

The plaintiff owned a room overlooking the proposed route of the Coronation procession of Edward VII, and had let it to the defendant for the purpose of viewing the procession. The procession did not take place because of the King's illness and the plaintiff now sued for the agreed fee. *Held* – The fact that the procession had been cancelled discharged the parties from their obligations, since it was no longer possible to achieve the real purpose of the agreement.

Herne Bay Steamboat Co v Hutton [1903] 2 KB 683

The plaintiffs agreed to hire a steamboat to the defendant for two days, in order that the defendant might take paying passengers to see the naval review at Spithead on the occasion of Edward VII's Coronation. An official announcement was made cancelling the review, but the fleet was assembled and the boat might have been used for the intended cruise. The defendant did not use the boat, and the plaintiffs employed her on ordinary business. The action was brought to recover the fee of £200 which the defendant had promised to pay for the hire of the boat. *Held* – The contract was not discharged, as the review of the fleet by the Sovereign was not the foundation of the contract. The plaintiffs were awarded the difference between £200 and the profits derived from the use of the ship for ordinary business on the two days in question.

   Comment: It may be thought that it is difficult to reconcile this case with *Krell* (*see above*). However, whatever the legal niceties may or may not be, there is clearly a difference in fact. To cruise round the fleet assembled at Spithead, even though the figure of the Sovereign (miniscule to the viewer, anyway) would not be present, is clearly more satisfying as the subject matter of a contract than looking through the window at ordinary London traffic.

COMMERCIAL PURPOSE DEFEATED

Physical destruction of the subject matter is not essential to frustration. It extends to situations where although there is no physical destruction the essential commercial purpose of the contract cannot be achieved – a rule referred to as 'frustration of the common venture'. **The following case provides an illustration.**

Jackson v Union Marine Insurance Co (1874) LR 10 CP 125

The plaintiff was the owner of a ship called *Spirit of the Dawn* which had been chartered to go with all possible dispatch from Liverpool to Newport, and there load a cargo of iron rails for San Francisco. The plaintiff had entered into a contract of insurance with the defendants, in order that he might protect himself against the failure of the ship to carry out the charter. The vessel was stranded in Caernarfon Bay whilst on its way to Newport. It was not refloated for over a month, and could not be fully repaired for some time. The charterers hired another ship and the plaintiff now claimed on the policy of insurance. The insurance company suggested that since the plaintiff might claim against the charterer for breach of contract there was no loss, and the court had to decide whether such a claim was possible. *Held* – The delay consequent upon the stranding of the vessel put an end, in the commercial sense, to the venture, so that the charterer was released from his obligations and was free to hire another ship. Therefore, the plaintiff had no claim against the charterer and could claim the loss of the charter from the defendants.

SITUATIONS IN WHICH THE DOCTRINE DOES NOT APPLY

It is now necessary to consider the three situations where the application of the rules relating to frustration are limited.

Express provision in the contract

In such a case the provisions inserted into the contract by the parties will apply. Thus in some of the coronation seat cases, e.g. *Clark* v *Lindsay* (1903) 19 TLR 202, the contracts provided that if the procession was postponed the tickets would be valid for the day on which it did take place or that the parties should get their money back with a deduction for the room owner's expenses. These took effect to the exclusion of the principles of frustration.

Self-induced events

The rules relating to frustration did not apply where the event making the contract impossible to perform was the voluntary act of one of the parties. **The following case provides an example**.

Maritime National Fish Ltd v Ocean Trawlers Ltd [1935] AC 524

The respondents were the owners and the appellants the charterers of a steam trawler, the *St Cuthbert*. The *St Cuthbert* was fitted with, and could only operate with an otter trawl. When the charter party was renewed on 25 October 1932, both parties knew it was illegal to operate with an otter trawl without a licence from the minister. The appellants operated five trawlers and applied for five licences. The minister granted only three and said that the appellants could choose the names of three trawlers for the licences. The appellants chose three but deliberately excluded the *St Cuthbert* though they could have included it. They were now sued by the owners for the charter fee, and their defence was that the charter party was frustrated because it would have been illegal to fish with the *St Cuthbert*. It was *held* that the contract was not frustrated, in the sense that the frustrating event was self-induced by the appellants and that therefore they were liable for the hire.

Comment: An otter trawl is a type of net which can, because of its narrow mesh, pick up small immature fish. Its use is restricted for environmental reasons.

Leases and contracts for the sale of land

Judicial opinion has been divided as to whether leases and contracts for the sale of land can be frustrated since these create an interest in land which survives any frustrating event. **The following cases and comment set out the present position**.

Cricklewood Property and Investment Trust Ltd v Leighton's Investment Trust Ltd [1945] AC 221

In May 1936, a building lease was granted between the parties for 99 years, but before any building had been erected war broke out in 1939 and government restrictions on building materials and labour meant that the lessees could not erect the buildings as they intended, these buildings being in fact shops. Leighton's sued originally for rent due under the lease and Cricklewood, the builders, said the lease was frustrated. The House of Lords *held* that the doctrine of frustration did not apply because the interruption from 1939 to 1945 was not sufficient in duration to frustrate the lease, and so they did not deal specifically with the general position regarding frustration of leases, basing their judgment on the question of the degree of interruption. In so far as they did deal with the general position this was *obiter*, but Lord Simon thought that there could be cases in which a lease would be frustrated, and the example that he quoted was a building lease where the land was declared a permanent open space before building took place; here he thought that the fundamental purpose of the transaction would be defeated. Lord Wright took much the same view on the same example. Lord Russell thought frustration could not apply to a lease of real property, and Lord Goddard CJ took the same view. Lord Porter expressed no opinion with regard to leases generally and so this case does not finally solve the problem.

Comment: (i) Even if the courts were prepared to apply the doctrine of frustration, it would not often apply to leases, particularly long leases. In a lease for 99 years a tenant temporarily deprived of possession as by requisition of the property would hardly ever be put out of possession long enough to satisfy the test of frustration (*see below*).

(ii) In *National Carriers v Panalpina (Northern)* [1981] 1 All ER 161 the House of Lords were of the opinion that a lease could be frustrated. The plaintiffs leased a warehouse to the defendants for 10 years. The Hull City Council closed the only access to it because a listed building nearby was in a dangerous condition. The access road was closed for 20 months. The defendants refused to pay the rent for this period. The House of Lords said that they must. A lease could be frustrated, they said, but 20 months out of 10 years was not enough to frustrate it in the particular circumstances of this case. Once again, therefore, the decision of the House of Lords on the matter of frustration of leases was *obiter*.

(iii) In *Amalgamated Investment and Property Co Ltd v John Walker & Sons Ltd* [1976] 3 All ER 509 Buckley LJ was prepared to presume that the doctrine of frustration could be applied to contracts for the sale of land, though once again this decision was *obiter* because he did not have to apply the doctrine in this case. Walker sold a warehouse to Amalgamated, both parties believing that the property was suitable and capable of being re-developed. After the contract was made the Department of the Environment included it in a list of buildings of architectural and historic interest so that development became more difficult. The Court of

Appeal *held* that the contract was not frustrated. The listing merely affected the value of the property and the purchaser always took the risk of this in terms of a listing order or, indeed, compulsory purchase. The contract could be completed according to its terms and specific performance was granted to Walkers. Nor was the contract voidable under *Solle* v *Butcher* (1950) (*see* p. 94) because the mistake did not exist at the date of the contract.

THE LAW REFORM (FRUSTRATED CONTRACTS) ACT 1943

This important statute has laid down the conditions which will govern the rights and duties of the parties when certain contracts are frustrated.

Before 1943

The common-law doctrine of frustration did not make the contract void *ab initio* (from the beginning) but only from the time when the frustrating event occurred. Thus money due and not paid could be claimed and money paid before the frustrating event was not recoverable. **A somewhat startling application of these rules appears below.**

Chandler v Webster [1904] 1 KB 493

The defendant agreed to let the plaintiff have a room for the purpose of viewing the Coronation procession on 26 June 1902 for £141 15s. The contract provided that the money be payable immediately. The procession did not take place because of the illness of the King and the plaintiff, who had paid £100 on account, left the balance unpaid. The plaintiff sued to recover the £100 and the defendant counter-claimed for £41 15s. It was *held* by the Court of Appeal that the plaintiff's action failed and the defendant's counter-claim succeeded because the obligation to pay the rent had fallen due before the frustrating event.

Comment: This case is included only to show how important the Law Reform (Frustrated Contracts) Act 1943 really is!

After 1943

The position under the Act is as follows:

(a) Money paid is recoverable.
(b) Money payable ceases to be payable.
(c) The parties may recover expenses in connection with the contract or retain the relevant sum from money received, if any.
(d) It is also possible to recover on a *quantum meruit* (a reasonable sum of money as compensation) where one of the parties has carried out acts of part performance before frustration, provided the other party has received what the Act calls 'a valuable benefit' under the contract other than a money

payment 'before the time of discharge', i.e. to the time of the frustrating event. There are difficulties in regard to the expression 'valuable benefit', particularly where the work is destroyed, since the Act is not clear as to whether a sum can be recovered by the person conferring the benefit where there has been destruction of his work. In *Parsons Bros* v *Shea* (1965) 53 DLR (2d) 86 a Newfoundland court, in dealing with an identical provision under the Newfoundland Frustrated Contracts Act 1956, *held* that the carrying out of modifications to a heating system in a hotel subsequently destroyed by fire could not be regarded as conferring any 'benefits' upon the owner. However, in *BP Exploration* v *Hunt (No. 2)* [1982] 1 All ER 125 the plaintiffs were engaged to develop an oil field on the defendant's land and were to be paid by oil from the wells. After the wells came on stream but before BP had received all the oil which the development contract provided they should have, the wells were nationalized by the Libyan government which gave the defendant some compensation. The contract was obviously frustrated but Goff J, who was later affirmed by the Court of Appeal and the House of Lords, gave BP a sum of 35 million dollars as representing the 'benefit' received by the defendant prior to the frustrating event.

Clearly, here there was a surviving benefit conferred before the frustrating event and at the time of it, e.g. the value of the oil already removed by Mr Hunt before nationalization and, of course, his claim for compensation against the Libyan government. None of these things would have been available to him before BP's discovery and extraction of oil on his land. Since the benefit conferred up to the time of frustration clearly survived the frustrating event, i.e. the nationalization, the case does not resolve the problems posed by *Parsons Bros* v *Shea* (*above*) where the benefit did not survive the frustrating event.

However, it is the better view that there is no need for the benefit conferred to survive the frustrating event. The court can make an award provided benefit was once conferred. The fact that it did not survive the frustrating event can be taken into account by the court when assessing (and probably reducing) how much it gives to the plaintiff.

DISCHARGE BY BREACH

This occurs where a party to a contract fails to discharge it lawfully but instead breaches one or more of the terms of the contract. There are several forms of breach of contract as follows:

(a) Failure to perform the contract is the most usual form as where a seller fails to deliver goods by the appointed time or where, although delivered, they are not up to standard as to quality or quantity.

(b) Express repudiation which arises where one party states that he will not perform his part of the contract.

(c) Some action by one party which makes performance impossible.

Any breach which takes place before the time for performance has arrived is called an *anticipatory breach*. Thus the situations described in (b) and (c) above are anticipatory breaches.

Where the breach is anticipatory the aggrieved party may sue at once for damages. Alternatively, he can wait for the time for performance to arrive and see whether the other party is prepared at that time to carry out the contract.

The following cases provide illustrations of these points.

Hochster v De la Tour (1853) 2 E & B 678

The defendant agreed in April 1852 to engage the plaintiff as a courier for European travel, his duties to commence on 1 June 1852. On 11 May 1852, the defendant wrote to the plaintiff saying that he no longer required his services. The plaintiff commenced an action for breach of contract on 22 May 1852, and the defence was that there was no cause of action until the date due for performance, i.e. 1 June 1852. *Held* – The defendant's express repudiation constituted an actionable breach of contract.

Omnium D'Enterprises and Others v Sutherland [1919] 1 KB 618

The defendant was the owner of a steamship and agreed to let her under a charter to the plaintiff for a period of time and to pay the second plaintiffs a commission on the hire payable under the agreement. The defendant later sold the ship to a purchaser, free of all liability under his agreement with the plaintiffs. *Held* – The sale by the defendant was a repudiation of the agreement and the plaintiffs were entitled to damages for breach of the contract.

Comment: The charterer would have no claim against the purchaser of the vessel because restrictive covenants do not pass with chattels (which a ship is) but only with land. Compare *Dunlop* v *Selfridge* (1915) (see p. 35) and *Tulk* v *Moxhay* (1848) (see p. 39).

White and Carter (Councils) Ltd v McGregor [1961] 3 All ER 1178

The respondent was a garage proprietor on Clydebank and on 26 June 1957, his sales manager, without specific authority, entered into a contract with the appellants whereby the appellants agreed to advertise the respondent's business on litter bins which they supplied to local authorities. The contract was to last for three years from the date of the first advertisement display. Payment was to be by instalments annually in advance, the first instalment being due seven days after the first display. The contract contained a clause that, on failure to pay an instalment or other breach of contract, the whole sum of £196 4s became due. The respondent was quick to repudiate the contract for on 26 June 1957, he wrote to the appellants asking them to cancel the agreement, and at this stage the appellants had not taken any steps towards carrying it out. The appellants refused to cancel the agreement and prepared the advertisement plates which they exhibited on litter bins in November 1957, and continued to display them during the following three years. Eventually the appellants demanded payment, the respondent refused to pay, and the appellants brought an action against him for the sum due under the contract. *Held* – The appellants were entitled to recover the contract price since, although the respondents had repudiated the contract, the appellants were not obliged to accept the repudiation. The contract survived and the appellants had now completed it. The House of Lords said that there was no duty to mitigate loss until there was a breach which the appellants had accepted and they had not accepted this one.

Comment: Although the respondent's agent had no actual authority, he had made a similar contract with the appellants in 1954, and it was not disputed that he had apparent authority to bind his principal.

It is worth pointing out that there was in this case no evidence that the appellants could have mitigated their loss. No evidence was produced to show that the demand for advertising space exceeded the supply so it may be that the appellants could not have obtained a new customer for the space on the litter bins intended for the respondent. Thus White & Carter may have had a 'legitimate interest' in continuing with the contract. Perhaps if evidence that mitigation was possible had been produced the House of Lords would have applied the principles of mitigation to the case, or held that White & Carter had no 'legitimate interest' in continuing the agreement. This view is supported by a decision of the Court of Appeal in *Attica Sea Carriers Corporation* v *Ferrostaal Poseidon Bulk Reederei GmbH* [1976] 1 Lloyd's Rep 250 where the charterer of a ship agreed to execute certain repairs before he redelivered it to the owner and to pay the agreed hire until that time. He did not carry out the repairs but the owner would not take redelivery of the ship until they had been done and later sued for the agreed hire. It was *held* that the owner was not entitled to refuse to accept redelivery and to sue for the agreed hire. The cost of the repairs far exceeded the value which the ship would have if they were done and the owner had therefore no legal interest in insisting on their execution and the payment of the hire. The court held that he should have mitigated his loss by accepting redelivery of the unrepaired ship so that his only remedy was damages and not for the agreed hire.

This line was followed also in the case of *Clea Shipping Corporation* v *Bulk Oil International, The Alaskan Trader* [1984] 1 All ER 129. A vessel had been chartered by the plaintiff owners to the defendants, the hire charge having been paid in advance. However, the ship broke down and required extensive repairs. The charterers thereupon gave notice that they intended to end the contract. However, the plaintiffs decided to keep the agreement open and undertook the repairs and then informed the defendants that the vessel was at their disposal. The plaintiffs said they were exercising their right of election conferred upon the innocent party in such circumstances to keep the contract open, thus entitling them to keep the hire money instead of suing for damages. Lloyd J denied the existence of an unfettered right of election for an innocent party to keep the contract running in such circumstances. He found that, in the absence of a 'legitimate interest' in the contract's perpetuation by the party faced with repudiation, the party concerned could, though innocent, be forced to accept damages in lieu of sums falling due under the contract subsequent to the actionable event. This restraint is founded on general equitable principles, to be based on what is reasonable on the facts of each case.

ANTICIPATORY BREACH AND SUPERVENING EVENTS

It may be dangerous to wait for the time of performance to arrive since the contract may, for example, have become illegal thus providing the party who was in anticipatory breach with a good defence to an action. **The following case provides an example of this risk.**

Avery v Bowden (1855) 5 E & B 714

The defendant chartered the plaintiff's ship *Lebanon* and agreed to load her with a cargo at Odessa within 45 days. The ship went to Odessa and remained there for most of the 45 day period. The defendant told the captain of the ship that he did not propose to load a cargo and that he would do well to leave, but the captain stayed on at Odessa, hoping that the defendant would change his mind. Before the end of the 45 day period the Crimean War broke out so that performance of contract would have been illegal as a trading with the enemy. *Held* – The plaintiff might have treated the defendant's refusal to load a cargo as an anticipatory breach of contract but his agent, the captain, had waived that right by staying on at Odessa, and now the contract had been discharged by something which was beyond the control of either party.

Comment: A modern application of the above rule can be seen in *Fercometal Sarl* v *Mediterranean Shipping Co Ltd* [1988] 2 All ER 742. The plaintiffs chartered a ship to the defendants. The charterparty (i.e. the contract) provided that if the ship was not ready to load during the period 3–9 July the defendants could cancel the contract. On 2 July the defendants said that they were not going on with the contract anyway but the plaintiff did not accept that breach and provided the ship, but this was not ready to load until 12 July and the defendants said again that they would not go on with the contract. The plaintiffs sued for damages and failed. They could have based an action on the first breach but had not done so. Their action on the second 'breach' failed because the ship was not ready to load.

EFFECT OF BREACH ON CONTRACT

Not every breach entitles the innocent party to treat the contract as discharged. It must be shown that the breach affects a vital part of the contract, i.e. that it is a breach of condition rather than a breach of warranty (contrast *Poussard* v *Spiers* (*see* p. 140) with *Bettini* v *Gye* (*see* p. 141) or that the other party has no intention of performing his contract as in *Hochster* v *De la Tour* (*see above*) or has put himself in a position where it is impossible to perform it as in *Omnium D'Enterprises and Others* v *Sutherland* (*see above*).

OTHER MATTERS RELEVANT TO BREACH

Two further points arise in connection with breach of contract. The first is that the concept of contributory negligence does not apply. In *Basildon District Council* v *JE Lesser (Properties) Ltd* [1985] 1 All ER 20 the plaintiff sued for breach of contract in regard to the building of dwellings which had become unfit for habitation without repair. There was a defence that the damages payable should be reduced on the basis that the council's officers were guilty of contributory negligence. It was said that they should have noticed the lack of appropriate depth in foundations on seeing the building contractors' original drawings. It was decided by the High Court that the defence of contributory negligence did not apply in contract but only in tort.

It should be noted, however, that the obligation in the above case was entirely contractual. If the plaintiff could have sued, either in contract or in tort, as where the damage arises from a breach of contract and a tort, then even if the injured party decides to sue for breach of contract only the damages can be reduced if he is contributorily negligent (*see Forsikrings Vesta* v *Butcher*) [1988] 2 All ER 43.

Secondly, the Drug Trafficking Offences Act 1986 in s. 24 brings in what is called a 'laundering' offence under which anyone knowingly assisting with the retention, control or investment of drug trafficking proceeds could be liable to a maximum of 14 years' imprisonment. Banks, building societies, accountants, solicitors and other advisers are given protection by the Act if they disclose their suspicions about their client's finances if these seem to be connected with drug trafficking. However, the Act ensures that they cannot be sued for breach of contract if they pass on to the appropriate authorities their suspicions that any funds or investments may be connected with drug trafficking.

GRADED QUESTIONS

Essay mode

1. (a) How true is it to say that for a contract to be discharged by performance, that performance must be precise and exact?
   (b) Geoff agreed to paint Terry's house at an agreed price. When Geoff had finished the work Terry discovered that, although most of the painting was satisfactory, Geoff had forgotten to put a coat of gloss paint on one of the doors. Geoff was now ill and could not complete the work. Terry refused to pay him the contract price, claiming that the contract had not been completely executed and that therefore Geoff was entitled to be paid only a reasonable sum for the work he had actually undertaken. This, Terry claimed, was much less than the contract price.
   Advise Geoff.

   (The Institute of Company Accountants. Law Relating to Business. November 1989)

2. Miller decides to stage a big band concert and engages a number of eminent musicians, paying each of them 10% of the agreed fee at the time the separate contracts are made. Four days before the concert he is informed that four of the musicians will not be appearing. Shaw cannot get a visa to enter the country and Armstrong claims that his fee is not large enough. Dorsey has injured his fingers chopping firewood, whilst James says that he is incapacitated with a heavy cold. Miller believes that the concert will be a failure and decides to cancel it.

   Advise Miller as to

   (a) the effect of each incident on the contracts, whether he may recover the advance payment from any of these four musicians, and whether he has any further claim for compensation against any of them;

   (16 marks)

   (b) his legal position with respect to the other members of the band who are willing to appear, and to the public who have bought tickets for the concert.

   (4 marks)

   (Total: 20 marks)

   (The Chartered Institute of Management Accountants. Business Laws. May 1987)

3. In what ways may a contract be discharged?

   (The Chartered Association of Certified Accountants. Paper 1.4(E). June 1988

4. Distinguish between the various types of misrepresentation, and show what remedies are available to the injured party. Are there any limitations on these remedies?

(North Staffordshire Polytechnic. BA(Hons) Business Studies. Business Law)

Objective mode

Four alternative answers are given. Select ONE only. Circle the answer which you consider to be correct. Check your answers by referring back to the information given in the chapter and against the answers at the back of the book.

With reference to the following information answer questions 1 and 2.

Hatcher, an interior designer specializing in offices, was employed by Tally Ltd to design the interior of a small branch accounts office at Grantchester. The terms of payment were contained in a letter from Hatcher to Tally Ltd which set out the work to be done and concluded:

'The foregoing, complete, for the sum of £5,000 net. Terms of payment are net cash as the work proceeds and balance on completion.'

Hatcher commenced work in January and received £1,250 from Tally Ltd in February and a similar sum in April. The work was completed on 30 June and Tally Ltd moved staff and equipment into the new office on 1 July and full use was made of all the facilities provided by Hatcher. On 10 July Hatcher asked for payment of the balance of £2,500 but Tally Ltd replied complaining of bad workmanship but sent a further £500 saying that no more would be paid until the work had been completed to their satisfaction. In fact two doors were badly warped and will have to be replaced and a row of bookshelves which are shorter than specified will have to be remade. These defects can be put right for about £100 but Hatcher cannot do the work since he has now gone to America to carry out another contract. Nevertheless he is demanding payment of £2,000.

1. Which one of the following legal concepts is relevant?

   A The doctrine of frustration.
   B Anticipatory breach.
   C Entire contracts.
   D Accord and satisfaction.

2. Which one of the following statements is correct?

   A Hatcher is entitled to £2,000.
   B Hatcher is entitled to £2,000 less a deduction for defects.
   C Hatcher is entitled to a reasonable price.
   D Hatcher is not entitled to anything.

With reference to the following information answer questions 3 and 4.

For some years past it has been the practice of Pathfinders Ltd, travel agents, to advertise their package tours on the screens of certain cinemas in London and the Midlands during January and February. The necessary contracts have been made annually by local branch managers on receipt of a letter from head office describing the particular tours to be advertised in their areas. Having considered its advertising policy for 1991 Pathfinders Ltd decided to abandon cinema advertising in favour of an increased television campaign and during September 1990 letters were sent to branch managers outlining the new policy and instructing them not to make advertising contracts with local cinemas for 1991.

However, in July 1990 Earlybird, the manager of Pathfinder's Midchester branch, had entered into contracts on behalf of his company with the managers of certain cinemas belonging to a large chain and also with Luxor Cinemas, a small but successful chain operating only in the Midlands. The contracts were to run a series of advertisements on package holidays in France, Italy and Germany which Earlybird understood to be his company's policy for 1991, his information having been received unofficially from Clara, his girlfriend, who worked at head office.

As soon as he received the official letter from head office Earlybird rang Stoney, the manager of the local Luxor cinema and told him to cancel the contract. Stoney refused saying that he had already prepared the necessary frames of film in accordance with Earlybird's specification and that these would be run as agreed in January and February 1991. Earlybird wrote to head office informing them of the situation and they wrote to Luxor Cinemas saying that they did not regard themselves as bound by the unauthorized arrangements made by Earlybird, and would not pay for the advertising which they did not now require. Luxor Cinemas refused to accept this arrangement and ran the advertisements as agreed. They have now submitted an invoice for the agreed charge and Pathfinders Ltd are refusing to pay. What is the legal position?

3. One of the following legal concepts is relevant. Select:

  A Remoteness of damage.
  B Novation.
  C Frustration of contract.
  D Anticipatory breach of contract.

4. As regards the advertising arrangements made by Earlybird:

  A Pathfinders can be made to pay the full cost of the advertising.
  B Pathfinders can be required to pay only a reasonable price.
  C Pathfinders are liable to pay Luxor the cost of preparation of the frames of films and no more.
  D Pathfinders need pay nothing.

5. Frustration arises where:

   A An event occurs after a contract has been made rendering its performance difficult to perform.

   B A party expressly undertakes to do something which he then finds he cannot achieve.

   C A contract is impossible to perform when it is made.

   D A contract becomes impossible to perform after it has been entered into.

6. Which of the following statements about an active misrepresentation is true?

   A It always involves the making of an express false statement whether made innocently, negligently or fraudulently.

   B It is a type of breach of contract.

   C It usually involves a misstatement of fact but may sometimes involve a false opinion.

   D It cannot occur in contracts of utmost good faith.

Answers to questions set in objective mode appear on p. 551.

9 | Remedies and limitation of actions

The OBJECTIVES of this chapter are to consider the various remedies which exist both in common law and equity to redress losses arising from contractual relationships and the rules which cover the recovery of monetary compensation through damages together with the time limits which are placed on the bringing of claims.

DAMAGES GENERALLY

This is the main remedy for breach of contract and the rules of law relating to an award of damages are considered below.

LIQUIDATED DAMAGES

In some cases the parties foreseeing the possibility of breach may attempt in the contract to assess in advance the damages payable. Such a provision for *liquidated* damages will be valid if it is a genuine pre-estimate of loss and not a *penalty* inserted to make it a bad bargain for the defendant not to carry out his part of the contract. The court will not enforce a penalty but will award damages on normal principles used in the assessment of unliquidated damages (*see below*).

Certain tests are applied in order to decide whether or not the provision is a penalty. Obviously, extravagant sums are generally in the nature of penalties. Where the contractual obligation lying on the defendant is to pay money then any provision in the contract which requires the payment of a larger sum on default of payment is a penalty because the damage can be accurately assessed. Where the sum provided for in the contract is payable on the occurrence of any one of several events it is probably a penalty for it is unlikely that each event can produce the same loss. If the sum agreed by the parties is regarded as liquidated damages it will be enforced even though the actual loss is greater or smaller.

The following cases provide illustrations of the above rules.

Ford Motor Co (England) Ltd v Armstrong (1915) 31 TLR 267

The defendant was a retailer who received supplies from the plaintiffs. As part of his agreement with the plaintiffs the defendant had undertaken:

(a) not to sell any of the plaintiffs' cars or spares below list price;

(b) not to sell Ford cars to other dealers in the motor trade;

(c) not to exhibit any car supplied by the company without their permission.

The defendant also agreed to pay £250 for every breach of the agreement as being the agreed damage which the manufacturer will 'sustain'. The defendant was in breach of the agreement and the plaintiffs sued. It was *held* by the Court of Appeal that the sum of £250 was in the nature of a penalty and not liquidated damages. The same sum was payable for different kinds of breach which were not likely to produce the same loss. Furthermore its size suggested that it was not a genuine pre-estimate of loss.

Comment: A contrast is provided by *Dunlop v New Garage & Motor Co Ltd* [1915] AC 79 where the contract provided that the defendants would have to pay £5 for every tyre sold below the list price. The House of Lords *held* that this was an honest attempt to provide for a breach and was recoverable as liquidated damages. Privity problems did not arise here because the wholesalers were Dunlop's agents (*see further* p. 35).

Cellulose Acetate Silk Co Ltd v Widnes Foundry Ltd [1933] AC 20

The Widnes Foundry entered into a contract to erect a plant for the Silk Co by a certain date. It was also agreed that the Widnes Foundry would pay the Silk Co £20 per week for every week they took in erecting the plant beyond the agreed date. In the event the plant was completed 30 weeks late, and the Silk Co claimed for their actual loss which was £5,850. *Held* – The Widnes Foundry were only liable to pay £20 per week as agreed.

UNLIQUIDATED DAMAGES

Assessment

Unliquidated damages are intended as compensation for the plaintiff's loss and not as punishment for the defendant. Thus where no loss has been suffered, as where a seller fails to deliver the goods but the buyer is able to purchase elsewhere at no extra cost, the court will award *nominal* damages, i.e. an award of a small sum, e.g. £2, to reflect the view that any loss or damage is purely technical. An additional example arises in actions for loss of earnings arising from a breach of contract where damages are reduced after taking into account the plaintiff's liability to taxation.

Exemplary or punitive damages which exceed the actual loss suffered by an amount intended to punish the offending party are not awarded for breach of contract. The intention is that the plaintiff should be placed in the same situation as if the contract had been performed.

Thus in an action by an employee for wrongful dismissal the court will base its award on 'net' wages, i.e. after deduction of income tax and national insurance contributions. An award based on 'gross' wages or salary would make the employee better off than if the contract had continued.

The following cases and comment illustrate the judicial approach.

Beach v Reed Corrugated Cases Ltd [1956] 2 All ER 652

This was an action brought by the plaintiff for wrongful dismissal by the defendants. The plaintiff was the managing director of the company and he had a 15-year contract from 21 December 1950 at a salary of £5,000 per annum. His contract was terminated in August 1954 when he was 54 years old and the sum of money that he might have earned would have been £55,000, but the general damages awarded to him were £18,000 after the court had taken into account income tax, including tax on his private investments.

It should be noted that the award of damages itself is not subject to tax.

Comment: (i) In a later case and on similar reasoning it was held that what the plaintiff would have paid by way of national insurance contributions must also be deducted (*see* Cooper v Firth Brown Ltd [1963] 2 All ER 31).

(ii) In *C & P Haulage v Middleton* [1983] 3 All ER 94 C & P let Mr Middleton have a licence for six months renewable of premises from which he conducted a business as a self-employed engineer. He lived in a council house and would have used his own garage there, but the council objected. There was a quarrel between the parties and M was evicted from the premises before the licence term expired. This was a breach of contract by C & P. M stopped a cheque which was payable to C & P because of his grievance. They sued him on it. He counter-claimed for damages because of his eviction. In fact the council had let him use his own garage for the remainder of the six months' term. *Held* – by the Court of Appeal – that since he had paid no rent for the premises in which he had worked following his eviction, he was no worse off than if the contract had been properly carried out. It was not the function of the court to put a plaintiff in a better position than he would have been if the contract had not been broken. Only nominal damages were awarded.

(iii) Damages have been awarded for the loss of a chance. This is not prevented by the rule that the plaintiff must not be better off. Thus in *Chaplin v Hicks* [1911] 2 KB 786 the plaintiff who had won earlier stages of a beauty contest was, by error of the defendant organizer, not invited to the final. Although it was by no means certain that she would have won, the plaintiff was awarded £100 damages.

Type of loss recoverable

Damages can include compensation for financial loss, personal injury and damage to property. Also there may be included a sum by way of compensation for disappointment, vexation and mental distress.

The following case provides an illustration of the mental distress awards.

Jarvis v Swans Tours Ltd [1973] 1 All ER 71

Swans promised the plaintiff a 'Houseparty' holiday in Switzerland. Some of the more important things promised were a welcome party on arrival: afternoon tea and cake, Swiss dinner by candlelight, fondue party, yodeller evening and farewell party. Also the hotel owner was said to speak English.

Among the matters which the plaintiff complained about were that the hotel owner could not speak English. This meant he had no one to talk to since although there were 13 people present during the first week he was on his own for the second week. The cake for tea was potato crisps and dry nutcake. The yodeller evening consisted of a local man who came in his overalls and sang a few songs very quickly. The Court of Appeal *held* that the plaintiff was entitled to an award of £125 damages. (Incidentally the holiday had cost £63.)

Remoteness

Apart from the question of *assessment*, the matter of *remoteness of damage* arises. The consequence of a breach of contract may be far reaching and the law must draw a line somewhere and say that damages incurred beyond a certain limit are too remote to be recovered. Damages in contract must therefore be proximate.

The modern law regarding remoteness of damage in contract is based upon the case of *Hadley* v *Baxendale* (*see below*), as further explained in *The Heron II* (*see below*). These cases are authority for the statement that damages in contract will be too remote to be recovered unless they arise naturally, i.e. in the usual course of things, or if they do not arise naturally they are such that the defendant, as a reasonable man, *ought* to have had them in contemplation as likely to result. Damage which does not arise naturally and which would not have been in the contemplation of the reasonable man can only be recovered if the defendant was made aware of it *and* agreed to accept the risk of the loss.

The following cases illustrate the above rules.

Hadley v Baxendale (1854) 9 Exch 341

The plaintiff was a miller at Gloucester. The driving shaft of the mill being broken, the plaintiff engaged the defendant, a carrier, to take it to the makers at Greenwich so that they might use it in making a new one. The defendant delayed delivery of the shaft beyond a reasonable time, so that the mill was idle for much longer than should have been necessary.

The plaintiff now sued in respect of loss of profits during the period of additional delay. The court decided that there were only two possible grounds on which the plaintiff could succeed. (a) That in the usual course of things the work of the mill would cease altogether for want of the shaft. This the court rejected because, to take only one reasonable possibility, the plaintiff might have had a spare. (b) That the special circumstances were fully explained, so that the defendant was made aware of the possible loss. The evidence showed that there had been no such explanation. In fact the only information given to the defendant was that the article to be carried was the broken shaft of a mill, and that the plaintiff was the miller of that mill. *Held* – The plaintiff's claim failed, the damage being too remote.

Comment: The loss here did not arise *naturally* from the breach because there might have been a spare. The fact that there was no spare was not within the contemplation of the defendant and he had not even been told about it, much less accepted the risk. The defendant did not know that there was no spare nor as a reasonable man ought have known there was not.

The Heron II (Koufos v Czarnikow) [1967] 3 All ER 686

Shipowners carrying sugar from Constanza to Basra delayed delivery at Basra for nine days during which time the market in sugar there fell and the charterers lost more than £4,000. It was *held* that they could recover that sum from the shipowners because the very existence of a 'market' for goods implied that prices might fluctuate and a fall in sugar prices was likely or in contemplation.

Comment: The existence of a major sugar market at Basra made it within the *contemplation* of the defendants that the plaintiff might sell the sugar and not merely use it in a business.

Horne v Midland Railway Co (1873) LR 8 CP 131

The plaintiff had entered into a contract to sell 4,595 pairs of boots to the French Army at a price above the market price. The defendants were responsible for a delay in the delivery of boots, and the purchasers refused to accept delivery, regarding time as the essence of the contract. The plaintiff's claim for damages was based on the contract price, namely 4s per pair, but it was held that he could only recover the market price of 2s 9d per pair unless he could show the defendants were aware of the exceptional profit involved, and that they had undertaken to be liable for its loss.

Comment: In *Simpson v London & North Western Rail Co* (1876) 1 QBD 274 the plaintiff entrusted samples of his products to the defendants so that they could deliver them to Newcastle for an agricultural exhibition. The goods were marked 'Must be at Newcastle on Monday certain'. The defendants did not get them to Newcastle on time and were held liable for the plaintiff's prospective loss of profit arising because he could not exhibit at Newcastle. They had agreed to carry the goods knowing of the special instructions of the customer.

Victoria Laundry Ltd v Newman Industries Ltd [1949] 2 KB 528

The defendants agreed to deliver a new boiler to the plaintiffs by a certain date but failed to do so, being 22 weeks late, with the result that the plaintiff lost (a) normal business profits during the period of delay, and (b) profits from dyeing contracts which were offered to them during the period. It was *held* that (a) but not (b) were recoverable as damages.

Comment: The general loss of profit in this case arises naturally from the breach and no further 'contemplation' or 'notice' test need be applied. The loss of profit on the dyeing contracts was not *known* to the defendants nor as reasonable men *ought* they to have had it in *contemplation*.

MITIGATION OF LOSS

The injured party has a duty to *mitigate* or minimize his loss, i.e., he must take all reasonable steps to reduce it. Thus a seller whose goods are rejected must attempt to get the best price for them elsewhere and the buyer of goods which are not delivered must attempt to buy as cheaply as possible elsewhere. Loss arising from failure to take such steps cannot be recovered.

The following case also provides an illustration.

Brace v Calder [1895] 2 QB 253

The defendants, a partnership consisting of four members, agreed to employ the plaintiff as manager of a branch of the business for two years. Five months later the partnership was dissolved by the retirement of two of the members and the business was transferred to the other two who offered to employ the plaintiff on the same terms as before but he refused the offer. The dissolution of the partnership constituted a wrongful dismissal of the plaintiff and he brought an action for breach of contract seeking to recover the salary that he would have received had he served the whole period of two years. It was *held* that he was entitled only to nominal damages since it was unreasonable to have rejected the offer of continued employment.

However, the plaintiff is not under a duty to mitigate his loss before there has been a breach of contract which the plaintiff has accepted as a breach. No doubt this is logical but it can produce startling results (*see White and Carter (Councils) Ltd* v *McGregor* (1961), p. 209). More recently the requirement of a 'legitimate interest' in keeping the contract going has made the position more equitable (*see*, for example, *Clea Shipping*, p. 210).

PROVISIONAL DAMAGES FOR PERSONAL INJURIES

The Administration of Justice Act 1982 makes provision for a court to award provisional damages for contractual claims for personal injuries. Thus in an action for a fracture to the hip caused to a passenger in an accident involving a negligently driven bus the court can make an order for damages payable at once for the fracture and an award of provisional damages in case in the future chronic arthritis affects the injured passenger. If it does, but not otherwise, the provisional damages may also be recovered without another visit to the court to prove the damage.

INTEREST ON DEBT AND DAMAGES

Under the provision of s. 15 and Sch. 1 of the Administration of Justice Act 1982, which inserted s. 35A of the Supreme Court Act 1981, the court has power to award interest on debt or damages at the end of the trial or where judgment is obtained in default, i.e. where there is no defence and no trial. Interest may also be awarded where the defendant settles after service of writ but before judgment. Interest is not available where a person settles *before* service of writ no matter how long he has kept the other party waiting. The interest payable is at such rate as the court thinks fit or as rules of court may provide. The rate currently payable on judgment debts under s. 17 of the Judgments Act 1838 which is likely to be a guideline is 15 per cent per annum (SI 1985/437). The interest is tax-free (s. 74 Administration of Justice Act 1982).

EQUITABLE REMEDIES

Damages are the common law remedy for breach of contract. However, in some situations equity will provide more suitable remedies and these will now be considered.

A decree for specific performance

This is an equitable remedy which is sometimes granted for breach of contract, where damages are not an adequate remedy or where specific performance is regarded by the court as a more appropriate remedy (*see Beswick* v *Beswick* (1967), p. 35). It is an order of the court and constitutes an express instruction to a party to a contract to perform the actual obligations which he undertook in a contract. For all practical purposes the remedy is now confined to contracts for the sale of land, though it may be a more appropriate remedy in the case of a contract to pay an annuity because the exact value of the annuity will depend on how long the annuitant lives and this cannot be known at the time of the breach (*see Beswick* v *Beswick* (1967), p. 35). It is not normally granted in the case of contracts for the sale of goods because other goods of a similar kind can be purchased and the difference assessed in money damages. In addition, it should be noted that specific performance will not be granted if the court cannot adequately supervise its enforcement. Thus contracts of a personal nature, such as employment, which rely on a continuing relationship between the parties will not generally be specifically enforced because the court cannot supervise performance on the day-to-day basis which would be necessary. However, if constant supervision by the court is not required, a decree of specific performance may be made of a personal service undertaking. Thus in *Posner* v *Scott-Lewis* [1986] 3 All ER 51 Mervyn-Davies J decided that the tenants of a block of flats could enforce by specific performance an undertaking in their leases that the defendant landlords would employ a resident porter to keep the communal areas clear. The court had only to ensure that the appointment was made. The plaintiffs were not asking the court to supervise the porter's day-to-day work. Furthermore, specific performance will not be awarded either to or against a minor because a minor's contracts cannot in general be enforced against him and those which can, i.e. beneficial contracts (*see* p. 70), are in the nature of contracts of personal service. Equity requires equality or mutuality as regards its remedies and this does not exist in the case of minors' contracts.

An injunction

This is an order of the court used in this context to direct a person not to break his contract. The remedy has a somewhat restricted application in the law of contract and will be granted to enforce a negative stipulation in a contract where damages would not be an adequate remedy. Being an equitable remedy it is only ordered on the same principles as specific performance, so that it will not normally be awarded where damages are an adequate remedy (*see Garden Cottage Foods Ltd* v *Milk Marketing Board* (1982), p. 186). Its main use in the contractual situation has been as an indirect means of enforcing a contract for personal services but a clear negative stipulation is required. The court will not imply one.

   The following cases illustrate the application of these rules.

Warner Brothers Pictures Incorporated v Nelson [1937] 1 KB 209

The defendant, the film actress Bette Davis, had entered into a contract in which she agreed to act exclusively for the plaintiffs for 12 months. She was anxious to obtain more money and so she left America, and entered into a contract with a person in England. The plaintiffs now asked for an injunction restraining the defendant from carrying out the English contract. *Held* – An injunction would be granted. The contract contained a negative stipulation not to work for anyone else, and this could be enforced. However, since the contract was an American one, the court limited the operation of the injunction to the area of the court's jurisdiction, and although the contract stipulated that the defendant would not work in any other occupation, the injunction was confined to work on stage or screen.

Comment: (i) Even where, as here, there is a negative stipulation, the court will not grant an injunction if the pressure to work for the plaintiffs is so severe as to be for all practical purposes irresistible. In this case it was said that Bette Davis could still earn her living by doing other work.

(ii) The idea that persons such as Bette Davis or others subjected to injunctions of negative stipulations would take other work was challenged by the Court of Appeal in *Warren* v *Mendy* [1989] 3 All ER 103 on the grounds of 'realism and practicality'. The Court of Appeal said that it was unrealistic to suppose that such persons would take up other work, i.e. that boxers would become clerks and actresses secretaries. Thus the making of an injunction of a negative stipulation in this sort of case was in general terms likely to operate as a decree of specific performance. This means that it is in modern law less likely that such injunctions will be granted or that the Warner Brothers case will be followed though it is not overruled.

Whitwood Chemical Co v Hardman [1891] 2 Ch 416

The defendant entered into a contract of service with the plaintiffs and agreed to give the whole of his time to them. In fact he occasionally worked for others, and the plaintiffs tried to enforce the undertaking in the service contract by injunction. *Held* – An injunction could not be granted because there was no express negative stipulation. The defendant had merely stated what he would do, and not what he would not do, and to read into the undertaking an agreement not to work for anyone else required the court to imply a negative stipulation from a positive one. No such implication could be made.

Comment: It is because of the fact that the granting of an injunction of a negative stipulation is so close to specific performance that it is restricted to cases where the negative stipulation is express.

Mareva injunction

This remedy, which can be of assistance to a party suing for breach of contract, has developed considerably over recent times. In general terms a court will not grant an injunction to prevent a person disposing of his property merely to assist a person suing, for example, for a debt, to recover his money. However, the Mareva injunction is an exception to that general rule and is granted to restrict removal of assets outside the jurisdiction, often by a foreign defendant, where this is a real and serious possibility. The injunction takes its name from the second case in which it was awarded, i.e. *Mareva Compania Naviera SA* v *International Bulk Carriers SA* [1975] 2 Lloyds Rep 509. However, the power of the High Court to issue Mareva injunctions is now recognized by s. 37 of the Supreme Court Act 1981 which makes it clear that the power applies to domestic as well as foreign defendants. It is clearly a valuable addition to existing contractual remedies, particularly when business is now so often conducted on an international scale.

Rescission

This is a further equitable remedy for breach of contract. The rule is the same when the remedy is used for breach as it is when it is used for misrepresentation. If the contract cannot be completely rescinded it cannot be rescinded at all; it must be possible to restore the status quo.

Refusal of further performance: a self-help remedy

If the person suffering from the breach desires merely to get rid of his obligations under the contract, he may refuse any further performance on his part and set up the breach as a defence if the party who has committed the breach attempts to enforce the contract against him.

CLAIMS FOR RESTITUTION: QUASI-CONTRACT

Quasi-contract is based on the idea that a person should not obtain a benefit or an unjust enrichment as against another merely because there is no obligation in contract or another established branch of the law which will operate to make him account for it. The law may in these circumstances provide a remedy by implying a fictitious promise to account for the benefit or enrichment. This promise then forms the basis of an action in quasi-contract.

In practice the following two areas are important.

Claims on a *quantum meruit*

This remedy means that the plaintiff will be awarded as much as he has earned or deserved. The remedy can be used contractually or quasi-contractually as follows.

(a) *Contractually*. Here it may be used to recover a reasonable price or remuneration where there is a contract for the supply of goods or services but the parties have not fixed any precise sum to be paid. This area is also covered by statute law in the case of a sale of goods by s. 8 of the Sale of Goods Act 1979, and in the case of a supply of goods, e.g. a new distributor in a car repair contract, or the mere supply of a service by s. 15 of the Supply of Goods and Services Act 1982.

(b) *Quasi-contractually*. A claim on this basis may be made where, for example, work has been done under a void contract. The plaintiff cannot recover damages for breach because no valid contract exists, but he may in some circumstances recover on a *quantum meruit*. **The following case illustrates this point.**

Craven-Ellis v Canons Ltd [1936] 2 All ER 1066

The plaintiff was employed as managing director by the company under a deed which provided for remuneration. The articles provided that directors must have qualification shares, and must obtain these within two months of appointment. The plaintiff and other directors who appointed him never obtained the required number of shares so that the deed was invalid. However, the plaintiff had rendered services, and he now sued on a *quantum meruit* for a reasonable sum by way of remuneration. *Held* – he succeeded on a *quantum meruit*, there being no valid contract.

Total failure of consideration: actions for money had and received

Of particular importance here is the action for total failure of consideration. A total failure will result in the recovery of all that was paid. A common reason for total failure of consideration arises where A, who has no title, sells goods to B and B has to give up the goods to the true owner. B can then recover the whole of the consideration from A, his action being based upon the quasi-contractual claim of money had and received.

It should be noted that the action is based on failure of consideration and not its absence. Thus money paid by way of a gift cannot be recovered in quasi-contract.

The following case is an illustration of an action for total failure of consideration.

Rowland v Divall [1923] 2 KB 500

In April 1922, the defendant bought an 'Albert' motor car from a man who had stolen it from the true owner. One month later the plaintiff, a dealer, purchased the car from the defendant for £334, repainted it, and sold it for £400 to Colonel Railsdon. In September 1922, the police seized the car from Colonel Railsdon and the plaintiff repaid him the £400. The plaintiff now sued the defendant for £334 on the grounds that there had been a total failure of consideration since the plaintiff had not obtained a title to the car. *Held* – The defendant was in breach of s. 12 of the Sale of Goods Act, which implies conditions and warranties into a sale of goods relating to the seller's right to sell, and there had been a total failure of consideration in spite of the fact that the car had been used by the plaintiff and his purchaser. The plaintiff contracted for the property in the car and not the mere right to possess it. Since he had not obtained the property, he was entitled to recover the sum of £334 and no deductions should be made for the period of use.

Comment: (i) Although the court purported to deal with this case as a breach of s.12(1) of the Act, it would appear that in fact they operated on common-law principles and gave complete restitution of the purchase price because of total failure of consideration arising out of the seller's lack of title. The condition under s. 12(1) had by reason of the plaintiff's use of the car and the passage of time become a warranty when the action was brought, and if the court had been awarding damages for breach of warranty it would have had to reduce the sum of £334 by a sum representing the value to the plaintiff of the use of the vehicle which he had had.

(ii) The drawback to making an allowance to the seller for use is that he gets an allowance for a car which is not his and the owner might sue the buyer in damages for conversion so that he would have to pay an allowance and damages to the true owner in conversion. In other words pay for use twice.

(iii) It is also relevant to say that the court felt an allowance for use should not be made because the plaintiff had paid the price for the car to become its *owner*, and not merely to have *use* of it. So why should he be subject to an allowance for use when that is not what he wanted or bargained for? As Bankes LJ said: ' . . . he did not get what he paid for – namely a car to which he would have title.'

LIMITATION OF ACTIONS

Contractual obligations are not enforceable for all time. After a certain period the law bars any remedy in the main because evidence becomes less reliable with the passage of time. Time is the greatest enemy of the truth! The Limitation Act 1980 lays down the general periods within which an action may be brought. They are as follows.

(a) An action on a simple contract may be brought within six years from the date when the cause of action accrued.
(b) An action upon a contract made by deed may be brought within 12 years from the date when the cause of action accrued.

However, where the plaintiff's claims include a claim for damages in respect of personal injuries, the period is three years.

However, a person may suffer personal injury the extent of which only comes to light more than three years after the breach of contract which caused it. For example, A is a passenger on B's coach and B's careless driving causes an accident as a result of which A suffers injury consisting of bruising of the face. Four years later A goes blind as a result of the accident. Under the Limitation Act 1980 A has three years from his knowledge of the blindness to sue B and the court's permission is not required. The court may extend this period at its discretion, though in this case application must be made to the court for the extension.

A right of action 'accrues' from the moment when breach occurs, not from the date when the contract was made. Thus if money is lent today for four years the creditor's right to recover it will not expire until 10 years from today.

If when the cause of action accrues the plaintiff is under a disability by reason of minority or unsoundness of mind, the period will not run until the disability is ended or until his death, whichever comes first. Once the period has started to run subsequent insanity has no effect.

If the plaintiff is the victim of fraud or acts under a mistake, the limitation period will not begin to run until the true state of affairs is discovered or should with reasonable diligence have been discovered.

The following case was decided on the above rules of the common law which are now in the Limitation Act 1980.

Lynn v Bamber [1930] 2 KB 72

In 1921 the plaintiff purchased some plum trees from the defendant and was given a warranty that the trees were 'Purple Pershores'. In 1928 the plaintiff discovered that the trees were not 'Purple Pershores' and sued for damages. The defendant pleaded that the claim was barred by the current Limitation Act. *Held* – The defendant's fraudulent misrepresentation and fraudulent concealment of the breach of warranty provided a good answer to this plea, so that the plaintiff could recover.

Comment: (i) The present jurisdiction is s. 32 of the Limitation Act 1980.

(ii) In *Peco Arts Inc v Hazlitt Gallery Ltd* [1983] 3 All ER 193 the plaintiffs bought from the defendants in November 1970 what purported to be an original drawing in black chalk on paper *Etude pour le Bain Turc* by J.A.D. Ingres for the price of $18,000. In 1976 it was revalued by an expert for insurance purposes. No doubts were cast upon its authenticity. However, on a valuation in 1981 it was discovered that the drawing was a reproduction. The plaintiffs claimed rescission and recovery of the purchase price plus interest on the grounds of mutual, common or unilateral mistake of fact. The trial was adjourned on the first day because the parties wished to simplify the issues. After this the only defence was the Limitation Act 1980, i.e. that the plaintiffs' claim was statute barred. It was held that it was not and judgment was given for the plaintiffs. Webster J decided that a prudent buyer in the position of the plaintiffs would not normally have obtained an independent authentification but would have relied on the defendants' reputation, as the plaintiffs had done. Further, the plaintiffs were entitled to conclude that the drawing was an original as the valuers who had examined it in 1976 had not questioned its authenticity. There was no lack of diligence on the part of the plaintiffs. Accordingly, the action was not time barred and there would be judgment for the plaintiffs.

(iii) The *Peco* case does not decide what the effect of the mistake was, and to that extent does not go contrary to *Leaf* (see p. 93) and *Bell* (see p. 93). These matters were not contested by the defendants. In *Leaf* the court was deciding how soon an action must be brought for rescission for *innocent misrepresentation*. The issue here was how soon must an action be brought where the plaintiff claimed relief for the consequences of an operative mistake.

The Limitation Act does not truly discharge a contract, which is why it has been dealt with separately here. The Act merely makes the contract unenforceable in a court of law and if the defendant does not plead the statutes of limitation, the judge will enforce the contract. In addition, where the contractual claim is not for damages but for a debt or other liquidated (i.e. ascertained) demand, time for making a claim can be extended by a subsequent payment of money not appropriated by the debtor, because, as we have seen, the creditor can appropriate it, or by the debtor or his duly authorized agent making a written acknowledgment of the debt to the creditor or his agent. Time begins to run again from the date of the acknowledgment. However, once a debt is statute-barred it cannot be revived in this way (s. 29, Limitation Act 1980).

Equitable remedies, i.e. specific performance or an injunction, are not covered by the ordinary limitation periods but will usually be barred much earlier under general equitable rules. An equitable remedy must be sought promptly and, according to the nature of the contract, a short delay of weeks or even days may bar the remedy.

GRADED QUESTIONS

Essay mode

1. (a) Explain the difference between liquidated damages and penalties in the law of contract. What criteria do the courts use to determine whether a provision stipulating for the payment of a particular sum is a penalty? Why is the distinction between liquidated damages and penalties important?

   (b) Digger agrees to hire a crane to Contractor for a period of twelve months at a rate of £2,000 per month. The terms of the contract provide that: 'Contractor may terminate this agreement on giving one month's notice in writing. If this option is exercised, Contractor will pay £16,000 to Digger by way of agreed compensation.' After eight months, Contractor gives Digger one month's notice in writing terminating the agreement. He now wishes to know whether he is bound to pay Digger £16,000.
   Advise Contractor.

   (*Institute of Chartered Secretaries and Administrators. English Business Law. December 1988*)

2. R is an accountant. He agrees with S, a garage proprietor, that he will assist S with his annual tax return if S will service his car for him. He also agrees with T, a landscape gardener, that he will advise T on the installation of a computerized financial management system if T, in return, will carry out some landscaping work at the house of R's daughter, U.

   R assists S and advises T, but both refuse to carry out their side of the agreements. Because his car has not been serviced R is late for an important meeting with a client after the car breaks down on the way to the meeting. As a result of this the client switches his work, worth some £5,000 per annum, to another accountant. U is very anxious to have the landscaping work done on her garden and because T has a reputation for doing good quality work she is keen that it is done by T.

   Advise R and U as to the nature of the contractual remedies, if any, which may be available to them.

   (20 marks)

   (*The Chartered Institute of Certified Accountants. Paper 1.4: Law. June 1989*)

3. (a) What principles of law are applied by the courts in determining what damages should be awarded to a plaintiff who has successfully established that the defendant was in breach of his contractual obligations?

   (b) Fred is a commercial traveller who regularly uses George's garage for servicing his company vehicle. On one occasion he is told that his car will be ready for 11 a.m. the next day and he therefore arranges to visit his most important client Bert at noon. He arrives at the garage at 11 a.m. to be told by George that the service is not yet finished because a mechanic has not turned in. The car is not therefore usable. Fred abandons his plan to visit Bert because of the non-availability of his vehicle. Bert is annoyed and transfers his custom to another supplier. Fred, having lost his most lucrative account, is dismissed by his employer. Fred's family suffer the trauma of the drastic reduction in income. Is George liable for all these consequences of his breach of contract?

   (The Polytechnic, Huddersfield. BA and BA (Hons) Business Studies: Business Law)

Objective mode

Four alternative answers are given. Select ONE only. Circle the answer which you consider to be correct. Check your answers by referring back to the information given in the relevant chapter and against the answers at the back of the book.

With reference to the following information answer questions 1, 2 and 3.

Kitchener Ltd agree to supply and fit an electric cooking range in a new restaurant belonging to Cook and situated near a major junction on the M99. The contract provided that the range should be delivered and fitted during the period 29 to 30 May so that the restaurant could open on 3 June. Cook has provided restaurant facilities from older premises on the site, serving on average 750 meals a week. These premises were, to the knowledge of Kitchener Ltd, to be demolished during the week ending 27 May.

Unknown to Kitchener Ltd Cook had organized as part of the opening ceremony of the new restaurant a beauty contest which was to take place on the forecourt of the restaurant, and had also entered into a contract to supply meals to the canteen of a local factory from 5 June.

Kitchener Ltd, who had taken orders in excess of production capacity, were unable to supply and fit the range until 27 June. Cook opened the restaurant on 1 July and the beauty contest which was held on that date was won by Gloria who received a prize of £200. Unfortunately Freda, who was one of the eight girls entered for the contest, did not attend, Cook having failed to notify her of the revised date. The supply of meals to the factory commenced on 3 July.

Cook intends to sue Kitchener Ltd for damages for loss of profit and Freda is suing Cook for damages for his breach of contract in failing to notify her of the revised date of the contest.

1. As regards Cook's claim for loss of profit:

   A He will only recover damages for the estimated loss of profit on ordinary customers between 3 June and 1 July.
   B He will recover damages for loss of profit on ordinary customers and the meals he was unable to supply to the factory.
   C He will recover only for the loss of profit on factory meals.
   D He will not recover anything because Kitchener Ltd did not accept the risk of any loss.

2. One of the following cases is relevant to Cook's claim. Select:

   A *Hochster* v *De la Tour* (1853).
   B *Brace* v *Calder* (1895).
   C *Warren* v *Mendy* (1989).
   D *Victoria Laundry* v *Newman Industries* (1949).

3. As regards Freda's claim:

   A She will recover something by way of damages from Cook even though she might not have won the contest.
   B She will not recover any damages from Cook.
   C She can try to get restitution of part of the prize from Gloria.
   D She can ask for specific performance to make Cook hold the beauty contest again.

With reference to the following information answer questions 4 and 5.

Layouts Ltd agree to design and install new equipment at a factory belonging to Bloggo Ltd within twenty weeks from the receipt of the final approval of drawings. A clause in the contract provided that if this period was exceeded Layouts Ltd would pay Bloggo Ltd the sum of £200 per week for every week in excess of the twenty weeks. This is a fair estimate of the likely loss.

In the event Layouts Ltd, who had made a number of similar contracts with other companies, found that they were unable to carry out the work in time and the installation of the equipment designed for Bloggo Ltd was eventually completed thirty weeks after final approval of drawings.

The ten-week delay has in fact resulted in a loss of profit to Bloggo Ltd of £4,000 and Bloggo Ltd are now claiming this sum by way of damages. Layouts Ltd are standing by the contractual arrangement under which they see their liability as limited to £2,000.

4. Which one of the following legal concepts will apply to the case?

   A *Quantum meruit.*
   B Quasi-contract.
   C Frustration of contract.
   D Liquidated damages and penalties.

5. Which of the following decisions is the court likely to make?

   A That Bloggo Ltd are entitled to recover the sum of £4,000.
   B That Bloggo Ltd are entitled to recover £2,000 as agreed.
   C That Bloggo Ltd are not entitled to recover anything since the clause is a penalty.
   D That Bloggo Ltd cannot recover anything because the contract is frustrated since Layouts Ltd could not find it possible to perform it.

6. Under the Unfair Contract Terms Act 1977 what is the effect of a notice disclaiming liability for death or personal injury?

   A Void.
   B Voidable.
   C Valid.
   D Unenforceable.

Answers to questions set in objective mode appear on p. 551.

10 | The sale of goods I

The OBJECTIVES of this chapter are to consider the principles and rules laid down by case law and statute – mainly the Sale of Goods Act 1979 – in regard to this highly important type of business transaction in terms of the definition of goods, contracts of sale and related transactions, and conditions and warranties both express and implied. The remaining principles and rules will be dealt with in subsequent chapters.

The law relating to the sale of goods is to be found in the Sale of Goods Act 1979. This is a consolidating measure bringing together a number of previous Acts but in particular the Sale of Goods Act 1893. Certain provisions of the Factors Act 1889 are also relevant, as are rules of the common law not dealt with by legislation. All section references are to the Sale of Goods Act 1979 unless otherwise stated.

DEFINITION: CONTRACT OF SALE OF GOODS

A contract of sale of goods is a contract whereby the seller transfers or agrees to transfer the property in goods to the buyer for a money consideration called the price (s. 2(1)). The definition covers:

(a) *A contract of sale* in which the property in goods is transferred from seller to buyer.
(b) *An agreement to sell* in which the transfer of property takes place at a future time or on fulfilment of certain conditions (s. 2(5)). A contract for the sale of goods yet to be manufactured is an agreement to sell because the property in the goods cannot pass until they are manufactured and ascertained.

Unless the contract otherwise provides, the property in goods which are the subject of a contract of sale passes to the buyer when the contract is made. English law does not require actual delivery of the goods, and the contract of sale operates as the conveyance.

Property is defined as the general property in goods and not merely a special property (s. 61), and therefore to say that the property passes to the buyer normally means that he gets ownership and not mere possession. A contract which does not pass ownership at all, e.g. a contract to rent a TV set, is outside the definition (*but see* Supply of Goods and Services Act 1982, p. 334).

However, under s. 12(3) A may transfer goods to B on the basis of whatever title he or a third person may have. This may turn out to be a right of possession only. Nevertheless such a contract is a contract of sale of goods. A common example of the use of s. 12(3) occurs where the sale is of goods taken in execution by the bailiffs to satisfy a judgment debt. Some of these goods, which are sold very cheaply, may not be owned by the debtor, as where he has them on hire purchase, although the bailiffs try to avoid this. If a finance company takes the goods away from the buyer he has no claim for breach of condition under s. 12 but the warranties of quiet possession in s. 12 apply (*see further* p. 246). Thus a purchaser has no claim unless the true owner repossesses the goods which he many not in the event do.

Delivery is the voluntary transfer of possession from one person to another, and whether the property in the goods passes on delivery is a question to be decided from the contract or, where the contract is silent, from the circumstances.

MEANING OF GOODS

Section 61 provides that goods includes all personal chattels but excludes all choses in action (e.g. cheques and share certificates) and money, although a coin which is a curio piece is goods for the purposes of a contract of sale (*Moss* v *Hancock* [1899] 2 QB 211). The term also includes *emblements*, i.e. crops to be severed before sale or under the contract of sale. Products of the soil are generally sold with a view to severance and though they may sometimes be of the nature of land for the purposes of the Law of Property (Miscellaneous Provisions) Act 1989 (*see* p. 66), they are usually goods within the meaning of the Act of 1979. The Act does not apply to the sale of an interest in the land itself. The sale of gravel *in situ* under land would not be covered by the Act. Nor would crops sold with the land on which they are growing because they are not in such a case to be 'severed before sale or under the contract of sale' as s. 61 requires.

Goods may be:

(a) *existing goods*, i.e. goods actually in existence when the contract is made, though they need not be specific and may yet have to be appropriated to the contract (s. 5(1));

(b) *future goods*, i.e. goods yet to be acquired or manufactured or grown by the seller (s. 5(1)) as in *Sainsbury* v *Street* [1972] 3 All ER 1127 where the seller agreed to sell to the buyers a crop of some 275 tons of barley to be grown by him on his farm;

(c) *specific goods*, i.e. goods identified and agreed upon at the time the contract of sale is made (s. 61(1)), e.g. the sale of a raincoat at a market stall;

(d) *unascertained goods*, as where A agrees to sell to B two hundred bags of flour from a stock of two thousand lying in A's warehouse. The main problem in examination terms arises in questions which are concerned with when ownership in such goods passes from seller to buyer. These problems will be considered later.

CONTRACTS OF SALE AND RELATED TRANSACTIONS

Students are sometimes asked to illustrate their knowledge of what goes to make a contract of sale of goods by making a comparison with business transactions which are broadly within the 'supply of goods' environment but to which the Sale of Goods Act does not apply. These are considered below.

Contracts for sale and contracts for work and materials

If the contract is for the sale of goods it is governed by the Sale of Goods Act 1979; a contract for work and materials is not. Hence the need to distinguish between the two. A contract for work and materials results in the transfer of goods but also involves the supply of skill and labour over and above what is required to produce the goods as an essential and significant part of the contract. Thus in *Cammell Laird & Co Ltd* v *Manganese Bronze & Brass Co Ltd* [1934] AC 402 the construction of two ship's propellers was held to be a contract of sale of goods; so, too, was a contract for the making of a fur coat from selected skins (*see Marcel (Furriers) Ltd* v *Tapper* [1953] 1 All ER 15).

Before 1983 contracts for work and materials were governed by common law only. The court would normally imply into those contract terms which were similar to those implied into contracts of sale by the sale of goods legislation, e.g. that the goods were fit for the purpose and of merchantable quality. Now the Supply of Goods and Services Act 1982 applies (*see* p. 334). However, as a matter of contrast between the two types of contract, some examples of work and materials must be given. In *Robinson* v *Graves* [1935] 1 KB 579 it was held that a contract to paint a portrait was a contract for work and materials and not a sale of goods, even though the property in a chattel, i.e. the portrait, was eventually to be transferred. In general terms, all forms of repair and maintenance contracts fall into the category of work and materials, e.g. repair of cars, the servicing of computers and X-ray and photocopying machines, roof repairs, painting and decorating, and the installation of double-glazing and air-conditioning and so on.

Contracts for sale and barter or exchange

Section 2(1) requires that the consideration in a sale of goods be money, and contracts of pure exchange are not within the Sale of Goods Act. Difficulties arose where a seller took goods in part-exchange, as where a car dealer took in part-exchange the car of the purchaser in reduction of the purchase price of another car. Certainly the contract was a sale of goods so long as money was a substantial part of the consideration, and even if it was not the court might regard the transaction as a sale if the parties appeared to have done so. Thus where the difference in price between the car which was 'traded in' and the one which was purchased is marginal, there would most probably be a sale since that is what the parties envisaged.

Since the 1982 Act was passed the problem of sale or barter is of no real practical importance. Whether the contract is a contract of sale or an exchange of goods for goods, or goods for money and goods, almost identical terms will be implied in the contract under the 1979 Act (if a sale) or under the 1982 Act (barter and exchange).

Sale and hire purchase

A sale of goods differs from a hire-purchase transaction because a hire-purchase contract gives the hirer a mere bailment of the goods, with an option to purchase them, an option which the hirer may or may not exercise after payment of the agreed instalments. There is a contract of sale when the hirer exercises his option to purchase, which he will normally do, since the purchase price is then nominal and the eventual sale of the goods is the object of the contract. However, because under a contract of hire-purchase a person does not *legally* commit himself to purchase the goods, there is no contract of sale.

A further distinction is that, while a contract of sale normally involves two parties only, a hire-purchase contract generally involves three. The owner of the goods selected by the hirer sells them to a finance company which in turn hires them to the hirer. The Sale of Goods Act does not apply to the hiring contract, but certain terms are implied into that contract by ss. 8–11 of the Supply of Goods (Implied Terms) Act 1973 (as substituted by the Consumer Credit Act 1974, Sch. 4, para. 35, which made some changes in terminology in the original provisions of the 1973 Act), and are available against the finance company.

The distinction between a contract of sale and hire-purchase is also important in the matter of title. If the contract is one of hire-purchase it does not come within the provisions of s. 25(1) of the Sale of Goods Act, under which a buyer in possession can give a good title to a purchaser if he sells the goods, because the hirer is not a person who has bought or agreed to buy the goods. He is hiring with an option to purchase and is under no obligation to buy. The hirer, therefore, cannot give a good title to a third party and, on the bankruptcy of the hirer, the owner of the goods can recover them.

Where the contract is one of sale, but payment is to be made by instalments, the contract may pass the property, in which case there is an unconditional contract of sale and the buyer, having ownership, can give a good title to a third party. On the bankruptcy of the buyer, his trustee takes the goods, and the seller must prove in the bankruptcy for the instalments.

If, although the goods have been delivered, the passing of the property is postponed until all instalments are paid, then there is a conditional contract of sale; such a contract is within s. 25(1) and the buyer can give a good title to a third party if the total purchase price exceeds £15,000. If the total purchase price is £15,000 or under, the contract is governed by the Consumer Credit Act 1974, and the conditions and warranties implied will be those under the Supply of Goods (Implied Terms) Act 1973 and not those under the Sale of Goods Act, and the buyer cannot give a good title to third parties, though there are exceptions in the case of motor cars (*see* p. 360). In both cases, however, the seller can claim the goods on the bankruptcy of the buyer. (Hire-purchase contracts are considered further on pp. 347–71.)

Sale and hire (or leasing)

Hire-purchase and hire have a lot in common. However, the distinction between them is that a contract of hire is only a contract of bailment which gives the hirer only the right to possess the goods. Hire-purchase is, as its name suggests, hire *plus* purchase. The hirer in hire-purchase has a right to possess plus an option to buy the goods when the instalments have been paid. Contracts of hiring were governed by the common law; now the Supply of Goods and Services Act 1982 applies. Examples of hiring agreements abound; office equipment, photocopying machines, type-writers and cars are commonly hired. More modern expressions include 'leasing', 'contract hire' and 'rental agreements', but whatever called they are all contracts of hire and the rights and obligations of the parties are in the 1982 Act (*see* p. 334).

Sale and agency

Brief mention should be made of certain problems arising in agency. If the person who is selling the goods is an agent there will be privity of contract between the buyer and the manufacturer or other supplier, e.g. wholesaler. If the seller is not an agent but, for example, a distributor who has purchased the goods himself, no action can be brought against the supplier in respect of the condition and quality of the goods (*Dunlop* v *Selfridge* (1915) at p. 35, but *see* now *Junior Books Ltd* v *Veitchi Co Ltd* (1982), p. 270, bearing in mind that this case has not received much support from the judiciary in recent times).

Problems may arise in relation to title. If the seller is an agent he cannot pass a title in the goods to a buyer unless the sale is within the agent's actual or apparent authority (*see* p. 497) or he has the goods on 'sale or return' terms. (*See further* p. 278.)

Thus a contract under which F (a finder) transfers goods to a purchaser is not a contract of sale to which the Act applies. F is not the owner, nor is he the agent of the owner (but *see* sales in market overt p. 293).

Sale and loans on security

If A, who is the owner of goods, borrows money by using the goods as security and gives a charge or mortgage over them but retains possession, the transaction resembles a sale in the sense that the lender has a right to take the goods if A does not repay the loan or interest. This is not, however, a sale, but in view of the fact that A retains the goods so that third parties might give him credit on the strength of his apparent absolute ownership of them, the transaction must be committed to writing as a bill of sale which must be registered under the Bills of Sale Acts 1878 and 1882. If the transaction is unregistered (which is often the case) the contract is void and the lender will not be able to seize the goods or even recover the agreed interest, although the actual loan itself is recoverable in quasi-contract as money had and received (*North Central Wagon Finance Co Ltd* v *Brailsford* [1962] 1 All ER 502).

THE CONTRACT OF SALE

We are now in a position to consider certain of the general principles of the law of contract as they apply to a sale of goods.

Capacity of the parties

Capacity to buy and sell is regulated by the general law concerning capacity to contract and to transfer and acquire property. The problems relating to capacity have already been dealt with in Chapter 3 on the law of contract (*see* p. 69) and no further comment is necessary, other than to refer to the capacity problems which may arise in business from dealing with minors and to a lesser extent these days to companies (*see* p. 74).

The price

Section 8 provides that the price may be:

(a) fixed by the contract; or
(b) left to be fixed in a manner provided by the contract, e.g. by a valuation or an arbitration; or
(c) determined by the course of dealing between the parties, e.g. previous transactions between them or any relevant custom of the trade or profession.

If the price is not fixed, there is a presumption that the buyer will pay a reasonable price. What is a reasonable price is a question of fact dependent upon the circumstances of each case. Thus a contract of sale of goods should not be regarded as *inchoate* simply because the parties have not agreed a price. (For inchoate agreements *see* p. 11.)

Section 9 provides that where the price is to be determined by the valuation of a third party, and no such valuation is made, then the contract is avoided, but:

(a) If the goods or part thereof have been delivered to the buyer and he has appropriated them to his use, the buyer must pay a reasonable price for them.
(b) If the valuation is prevented by *either party* to the contract, the non-defaulting party may sue for damages against the party in default.

It is difficult to see how the buyer would be able to prevent valuation, but presumably the Act is concerned to cover all possibilities. Section 9 applies only if the agreement names a valuer. Thus a sale of 'stock at valuation' is an agreement to sell at a reasonable price, and s. 8 will apply if the parties do not appoint a valuer or otherwise agree a price.

If the buyer pays part of the price when he makes the contract it may be a *deposit* or *a part payment*. If it is a deposit it will be forfeited if the buyer does not go on with the contract. A part-payment must be returned. Whether a payment is one or the other is a matter for the parties to decide in their contract. If they do not do so the court will have to discover as best it can what their intention was. In this connection the use of the word 'deposit' without more is a strong indication of a guarantee that the purchaser will complete and that the payment will be forfeit if he does not.

The consideration

It has already been mentioned that the consideration for a sale must consist wholly or in part of money; otherwise the transaction is an exchange or barter. Where goods are to be conveyed without consideration there is a gift, and any agreement to be enforceable must be made by deed, though actual delivery of the goods together with an intention to make a gift and not merely to lend will give the recipient or donee a good title.

Formalities of the contract

Under s. 4 contracts for the sale of goods can be made in writing (either with or without seal), or by word of mouth or partly in writing and partly by word of mouth, or may be implied from the conduct of the parties. By reason of s. 36 of the Companies Act 1985, registered companies need not now contract by a deed, except where an ordinary person would have to do so. For example, a company must use a deed to convey land. The Corporate Bodies Contract Act 1960 extends this privilege to all companies no matter how formed.

Nevertheless provisions in other statutes may affect a sale. For example, s. 24 of the Merchant Shipping Act 1894 provides that the sale of a ship or a share in a ship must be in writing. Furthermore, since s. 61 defines goods as including emblements, e.g. growing crops which are agreed to be severed before sale or under the contract of sale (which covers most cases), it may be that crops which are not to be severed are land under the Law of Property Act 1925, in which case the contract if made before severance may have to be made in writing under the Law of Property (Miscellaneous Provisions) Act 1989 (*see* p. 66). Singleton LJ seemed to think a memorandum in writing was required in such a case in *Saunders* v *Pilcher* [1949] 2 All ER 1097 where a person bought a cherry orchard 'inclusive of this year's fruit crop'. The crop was not severed before sale or under the contract of sale and Singleton was of the view that s. 61 had no application and that the contract including the fruit crop was a sale of land.

In addition certain formalities are prescribed for credit sale agreements covered by the Consumer Credit Act 1974 (*see* p. 350).

The provisions of the Bills of Sale Acts may also affect the position regarding formalities. It is necessary to distinguish two situations.

(a) *A straight sale – the seller retaining possession:*
   (i) If the sale is and remains oral the Acts do not apply and the buyer takes the risk (subject to an action for breach of contract or non-delivery) that the seller may dispose of the goods either voluntarily (by subsequent sale) or involuntarily (by, for example, execution of a judgment or on bankruptcy).
   (ii) If, as is usual, the buyer takes written evidence by means of a bill of sale this must be registered, though it need not be in any special form. If this is not done, the contract of sale is void in respect of involuntary dispositions, e.g. to a trustee in bankruptcy or a sheriff levying execution; but if the seller, while still in possession of the goods already sold, voluntarily transfers the property by way of sale to a third party, the latter may obtain a good title under s. 24 of the Sale of Goods Act or under s. 8 of the Factors Act 1889.

(b) *A sale operating as a security – the seller retaining possession:*
   (i) The Sale of Goods Act does not apply (*see* s. 62(4) of that Act).
   (ii) The Bills of Sale Act 1882 covers the transaction and unless there is a registered bill of sale made out in the form required by ss. 8–10 of the Act of 1882 the transaction is void altogether, even as between the parties, though money advanced on an unregistered bill may be recovered in quasi-contract (*see* p. 226) as money had and received (*North Central Wagon Finance Co Ltd* v *Brailsford* [1962] 1 All ER 502). Thus involuntary and voluntary dispositions by the seller are effective to give title.

The position where a seller of goods delivers them but provides in the contract that ownership is not to pass until the goods are paid for is considered at p. 280.

CONDITIONS AND WARRANTIES

In Chapters 5 and 6 on the law of contract we have discussed the problems relating to statements made in the course of negotiating an agreement, and we have seen that such statements may be:

(a) pre-contractual, i.e. representations; or
(b) contractual, i.e. terms of the contract which may be either conditions or warranties.

The importance of the distinction lies in the remedies which are available.

Conditions and warranties defined and distinguished

In the chapter on the law of contract we were concerned in the main with *express* statements made by the parties; here we are concerned with the conditions and warranties *implied* into contracts for the sale of goods by the Sale of Goods Act 1979, and with how those conditions and warranties are defined by the Act.

The Act does not define a condition, but a condition may be said to be a material term or provision which, while going to the root of the contract, falls short of non-performance. A condition is a contractual term of a major description.

A warranty is defined by s. 61 as an agreement with reference to goods which are the subject of a contract of sale, but collateral to the main purpose of the contract, the breach of which gives rise to a claim for damages, but not the right to reject the goods and treat the contract as repudiated. Although s. 61 uses the word 'collateral' which gives the impression that a warranty is a term outside the contract a warranty in the intention of s. 61 is a term inside the contract but of a minor description which does not go to the root of the contract.

The Act does not say how we are to distinguish between conditions and warranties, and, although the words used by the parties are relevant, a stipulation may nevertheless be a condition though called a warranty in the contract (s. 11(3)). When in doubt as to the nature of a stipulation, the court will look at the contract and the surrounding circumstances, and decide what the intentions of the parties were by looking at the effects of the breach, and whether those intentions can best be carried out by treating the statement as a condition or as a warranty. **This as we have seen is the concept of the intermediate or innominate term and the following case provides an illustration of its application.**

Cehave NV v Bremer Handelsgesellschaft mbH The Hansa Nord [1975] 3 All ER 739

The defendants sold citrus pulp pellets to the plaintiffs. A term of the contract was 'shipment to be made in good condition'. The goods were not delivered all at once but in consignments, and when a particular consignment arrived at Rotterdam the market price of the goods had fallen and it was found that 1,260 tons of the goods out of a total consignment of 3,293 tons was damaged. The plaintiffs rejected the whole cargo on the grounds that the shipment was not made in good condition. They then claimed the recovery of the price which amounted to £100,000. In the event, a middle man bought the goods at the price of £33,720 and resold them to the plaintiffs at the same price. The plaintiffs then used the pellets for making cattle food as was the original intention. The total result of the transaction, if it had been left that way, was that the plaintiffs had received goods which they had bought for £100,000 for the reduced price of £33,720. The Court of Appeal decided in favour of the sellers. The court *held* that the contractual term 'shipment to be made in good condition' was not a condition within the meaning of the Sale of Goods Act, but was an intermediate or innominate term. As Lord Denning MR said: 'If a small portion of the whole cargo was not in good condition and arrived a little unsound, it should be met by a price allowance. The buyers should not have the right to reject the whole cargo unless it was serious or substantial.'

Lord Denning also rejected the view that the goods were not of merchantable quality simply because they were not perfect in every way. He said that the definition now contained in s. 14(2) of the Sale of Goods Act 1979 was to be preferred because it was more flexible than some of the earlier judicial decisions on previous legislation. In fact the definition delegates to the court the task of deciding what is merchantable in the circumstances of each particular case.

Comment: This intermediate or innominate term approach was endorsed by the House of Lords in *Reardon Smith Line* v *Hansen-Tangen* [1976] 3 All ER 570.

IMPLIED TERMS AND NEGLIGENT MISSTATEMENT – THE RELATIONSHIP

With regard to the relationship of the Misrepresentation Act 1967 and the implied terms of the Sale of Goods Act 1979 the following matters should be noted.

(a) Claims based on negligent misrepresentation under s. 2(1) of the 1967 Act will usually be joined with claims for damages for breach of condition or warranty. This is especially likely where the action is based on a misdescription going to the *identity* of the goods under s. 13 of the 1979 Act (*see* p. 248).

(b) Under the 1967 Act the burden of disproving that the misrepresentation was negligent is on the representor, which is helpful to the plaintiff. Nevertheless the best remedy for a misdescription going to the *identity* of the goods is still one based on the Act of 1979 because liability under that Act is strict and cannot be avoided by the seller showing he was not negligent.

It should also be noted that in addition to the various remedies for loss arising out of false pre-contractual representations and breaches of contractual terms an action for negligence may lie in tort provided the false statement is made negligently and a special relationship of proximity exists between the parties (*Hedley Byrne & Co Ltd* v *Heller and Partners Ltd* (1963) – *see* p. 115). This action is probably of less importance in the context of contract since s. 2(1) of the Act of 1967 provides a statutory course of action in negligence specifically designed for the contractual situation.

However, the 1967 Act is available *only* in regard to negligent misrepresentation *by the other party to the contract*. Where the contract is induced by the negligent misstatement of an outsider *Hedley Byrne* and not the Misrepresentation Act 1967 must be used in order to get a remedy.

Thus a seller who makes a false statement about his goods may be liable at civil law in misrepresentation or for breach of an express or implied term. He may also be convicted of an offence under trade description legislation.

TERMS IMPLIED BY THE SALE OF GOODS ACT

Some contracts of sale are very detailed; the parties have dealt with all or most eventualities. Many contracts of sale are not so detailed. The only thing the parties have dealt with is the goods to be sold and the price to be paid. The provisions of the Sale of Goods Act are designed in large measure to fill in the gaps by implied terms and other rules, e.g. as to the passing of the property and damages. We must now consider the question of implied terms.

TIME

Where this has not been dealt with expressly the following rules apply.

Payment

The Act provides that, unless a different intention appears from the contract, stipulations as to the time of payment are not deemed to be of the essence of a contract of sale. Whether any other stipulation as to time is of the essence of the contract or not depends upon the terms of the contract (ss. 10(1) and(2)).

Thus failure to pay on time is a breach of warranty rather than a breach of condition. Consequently where under the contract payment is to be made before delivery of the goods but is not so made, the seller cannot repudiate the contract and resell the goods, but may sue the buyer for damages. However, where payment is delayed for an excessive time, the seller may treat the contract as abandoned and resell the goods. The seller can, of course, provide expressly for a right of resale in the absence of prompt payment, and this right is implied where the goods are perishable (s. 48(3)).

Delivery

The Act does not lay down any rules regarding the time of delivery of the goods, but the decided cases show that, where the time of delivery is fixed by the contract, failure to deliver or allow collection on time is a breach of condition and the buyer can reject the goods even though they are not damaged or in any way affected by the delay (*Bowes* v *Shand* (1877) – *see* p. 198). Where the goods are unaffected the buyer will normally only reject if external circumstances such as a fall in the market price lead him to do so. Nevertheless his right to reject has in the past remained. However, in view of the decision in *Cehave NV* v *Bremer Handelsgesellschaft mbH* (1975) (*see* p. 243) it may be that the courts are not so fully committed to the principle that any breach of condition by the seller entitles the buyer to take advantage of a fall in the market to reject the goods. Where the seller is bound to send the goods to the buyer but no time of delivery is fixed by the contract the seller is bound to deliver the goods within a reasonable time (s. 29(3)). Failure to deliver within a reasonable time may amount to breach of condition (*Borthwick (Thomas) (Glasgow) Ltd* v *Bunge & Co Ltd* [1969] 1 Lloyd's Rep 17). It is assumed that this rule applies also where the seller's duty is to have the goods ready for collection.

The time of delivery may be waived by the buyer even after the delivery date and such a waiver is binding even though the seller has given no consideration for it. The basis of this rule according to Denning LJ in *Rickards (Charles) Ltd* v *Oppenhaim* (1950) was equitable estoppel (*see further* p. 54).

Other rules relating to delivery will be considered when dealing with performance of the contract (*see* p. 303).

TITLE

The rules governing title are as follows.

Implied condition as to title

Section 12(1) provides that, unless the circumstances show a different intention, there is an implied condition on the part of the seller that in the case of a sale he has the right to sell the goods, and that in the case of an agreement to sell, he will have the right to sell the goods at the time when the property is to pass (*Rowland* v *Divall* (1923), p. 227).

The decision in *Rowland*, which has been applied in subsequent cases (*see Karflex Ltd* v *Poole* [1933] 2 KB 251), produces, as we have seen, an unfortunate result in that a person who buys goods to which the seller has no title is allowed to recover the whole of the purchase price even though he has had some use and enjoyment from the goods before he is dispossessed by the true owner. It is thus difficult to suggest that there has been total failure of consideration. The Law Reform Committee (*see* 1966 Cmnd 2958, para. 36) has recommended that, subject to further study of the law relating to restitution, an allowance in respect of use and enjoyment should be deducted from the purchase price and the balance returned to the plaintiff (*see also* p. 227). It should be noted that the 1979 Act does not deal with this matter.

Section 12(1) might be construed as meaning that the seller must have the power to give ownership of the goods to the buyer, but if the goods can only be sold by infringing a trade mark, the seller has no right to sell for the purposes of s. 12(1). **The following case illustrates this point.**

Niblett Ltd v Confectioners' Materials Co Ltd [1921] 3 KB 387

The defendants agreed to sell to the plaintiffs 3,000 cases of condensed milk to be shipped from New York to London. 1,000 cases bore labels with the word 'Nissly' on them. This came to the notice of the Nestlé Company and they suggested that this was an infringement of their registered trade mark. The plaintiffs admitted this and gave an undertaking not to sell the milk under the title of 'Nissly'. They tried to dispose of the goods in various ways but eventually discovered that the only way to deal with the goods was to take off the labels and sell the milk without mark or label, thus incurring loss. *Held* – by the Court of Appeal – that the sellers were in breach of the implied condition set out in s. 12(1) of the Sale of Goods Act. A person who can sell goods only by infringing a trade mark has no right to sell, even though he may be the owner of the goods. Atkin LJ also found the sellers to be in breach of the warranty under s. 12(2) because the buyer had not enjoyed quiet possession of the goods.

Implied warranties as to title

Section 12(2) provides that there is:

> An implied warranty that the goods are free, and will remain free until the time when the property is to pass, from any charge or encumbrance not disclosed or known to the buyer before the contract is made, and that the buyer will enjoy quiet possession of the goods except so far as it may be disturbed by the owner or other person entitled to the benefit of any charge or encumbrance so disclosed or known.

This does not apply where a limited interest is sold, but s. 12(4) and (5) do and contain similar provisions (*see below*).

It is not easy to see what rights this subsection gives over those in s. 12(1). The law does not recognize encumbrances over chattels unless the person trying to enforce them is in possession of the goods or in privity of contract with the person who is in possession (*Dunlop* v *Selfridge* (1915) – *see* p. 35). Thus if A uses his car as security for a loan from B then –

(a) if B takes the car into his possession the charge will be enforceable if necessary by a sale of the vehicle;

(b) the charge is equally enforceable against the car while it is still in A's possession, though if A sells it to C then B will be prevented by lack of privity of contract from enforcing any remedies against the vehicle once it is in the possession of C.

Thus if situation (a) above applied the subsection is unnecessary since A could not deliver the vehicle even if he sold it and would therefore be liable in damages for non-delivery to C. If situation (b) above applied then the encumbrances would not attach to the vehicle once C had taken possession. C would not, therefore, require a remedy.

However, the usefulness of s. 12(2) is illustrated by the decision of the Court of Appeal in *Microbeads AC* v *Vinhurst Road Markings Ltd* [1975] 1 All ER 529. In this case A sold road-marking machines to B. After the sale C obtained a patent on the machines so that their continued use by B was in breach of that patent and C was bringing an action against B in respect of this. In a claim by A against B for the purchase price, B wished to include in their defence breach of ss. 12(1) and (2). It was held by the Court of Appeal that they could include breach of s. 12(2) but not breach of s. 12(1). There had been no breach of s. 12(1) at the time of the sale so that A had not infringed that subsection but since B's quiet possession had been disturbed after sale, A was in breach of s. 12(2).

Sales under a limited title

Under s. 12(3), the sale of a limited interest is now possible. Where the parties intend only to transfer such a title as the seller may have, there is an implied warranty that all charges or encumbrances known to the seller and not known to the buyer have been disclosed to the buyer before the contract is made (s. 12(4)), and an implied warranty that the buyer's quiet possession will not be disturbed (s. 12(5)). There is an action by the buyer for breach of these warranties if, for example, he is dispossessed by the true owner. Furthermore, the seller is not able to contract out of this liability.

Sales under a limited title are common where the sale is of goods taken in execution by the bailiffs to satisfy a judgment debt.

SALE BY DESCRIPTION

Section 13(1) provides that, where there is a contract for the sale of goods by description, there is an implied condition that the goods shall correspond with the description.

(a) A sale is by description where the purchaser is buying on a mere description having never seen the goods. A classic example occurs in the case of mail-order transactions.

(b) A sale may still be by description even though the goods are seen or examined or even selected from the seller's stock by the purchaser, as in a sale over the counter, because most goods are described if only by the package in which they are contained. Therefore a sale in a self-service store would be covered by s. 13 though no words were spoken by the seller.

The following case provides an example of the rule that inspection or sight of the goods will not necessarily prevent the sale from being by description.

Beale v Taylor [1967] 3 All ER 253

The defendant advertised a car for sale as being a 1961 Triumph Herald 1200 and he believed this description to be correct. The plaintiff answered the advertisement and later visited the defendant to inspect the car. During his inspection he noticed, on the rear of the car, a metal disc with the figure 1200 on it. The plaintiff purchased the car, paying the agreed price. However, he later discovered that the car was made up of the rear of a 1961 Triumph Herald 1200 welded to the front of an earlier Triumph Herald 948. The welding was unsatisfactory and the car was unroadworthy. *Held* – by the Court of Appeal – that the plaintiff's claim for damages for breach of the condition implied in the contract by s. 13 of the Sale of Goods Act succeeded. The plaintiff had relied on the advertisement and on the metal disc on the rear and the sale was one by description even though the plaintiff had seen and inspected the vehicle.

Comment: It is however necessary for the buyer to show that it was the intention of the parties that the description should be relied upon by the buyer. In *Harlingdon Ltd* v *Hull Fine Art Ltd* [1990] 1 All ER 737 Hull were a firm of art dealers controlled by Mr Christopher Hull. They were asked to sell two oil paintings described as being by Münter, a German artist of the Impressionist School. Mr Hull had no knowledge of the German Impressionist School. He contacted Harlingdon who were art dealers specializing in that field. Mr Hull told them that the paintings were by Münter. Harlingdon sent an expert to examine the paintings and at this stage Mr Hull made it clear that he was not an expert in the field. Following the inspection Harlingdon bought one of the paintings which turned out to be a forgery. Harlingdon sued for breach of s. 13. It was *held* by the Court of Appeal that the claim failed. Harlingdon had not relied on the description of the painting. They bought it after a proper and expert examination. The 'description' had not therefore become an essential term or condition of the contract.

It should be noted that this matter was not raised in *Leaf* v *International Galleries* (1950) (see p. 93) because Mr Leaf did not claim a breach of s. 13. Presumably if he had done so he would have been required to show that it was the intention of the parties that he should rely on the description that the painting was by John Constable. This will normally be fairly easy to prove where the purchaser is an inexpert consumer. However, it was held in *Cavendish-Woodhouse* v *Manley* (1984) 82 LGR 376 that a seller could show that the sale was not by description by using such phrases as 'Sold as seen' or 'Bought as seen'. Such phrases do not, however, avoid the conditions of fitness and merchantable quality.

If s.13 applies it is enforced strictly, and every statement which forms part of that description is treated as a condition giving the buyer the right to reject the goods, even though the misdescription is of a minor nature. There is no such thing as a 'slight breach' of condition.

Buyers have been allowed to reject goods on seemingly trivial grounds, e.g. misdescriptions of how the goods are packed, and regardless of the fact that no damage has been suffered. **The following case illustrates this point.**

Moore & Co v Landauer & Co [1921] 2 KB 519

The plaintiffs entered into a contract to sell the defendants a certain quantity of Australian canned fruit, the goods to be packed in cases containing 30 tins each. The goods were to be shipped 'per S.S. Toromeo'. The ship was delayed by strikes at Melbourne and in South Africa, and was very late in arriving at London. When the goods were discharged about one half of the consignment was packed in cases containing 24 tins only, instead of 30, and the buyers refused to accept them. *Held* – Although the method of packing made no difference to the market value of the goods, the sale was by description under s. 13 of the Sale of Goods Act, and the description had not been complied with. Consequently the buyers were entitled to reject the whole consignment by virtue of the provisions of what is now s. 30(4) of the Sale of Goods Act (see *further* p. 305).

However, if the defect is a matter of quality and/or condition of the goods rather than an identifying description, s. 14 (*see below*) rather than s. 13 applies. Although the Sale of Goods Act applies in the main to sales by dealers, s. 13 applies even where the seller is not a dealer in the goods sold (*Varley* v *Whipp* [1900] 1 QB 513).

There can be no contracting out of s. 13 at all where a business sells to a consumer or the contract is between persons in a private capacity. In a non-consumer sale contracting out is allowed to the extent that it is 'fair or reasonable' (*see further* p. 155).

Where the sale is by sample as well as by description, s. 13(2) provides that the bulk must correspond with both the sample and the description. Thus in *Nichol* v *Godts* (1854) 10 Ex 191 a purchaser bought by sample 'foreign refined rape oil'. It was *held* that the goods must correspond, not only with the sample which they did, but must also be in fact 'foreign refined rape oil' and not a mixture of rape and hemp oil which was inferior.

Sale by description and misrepresentation distinguished

It should be noted that the description must be an identifying description to come under s. 13. Statements regarding the state of a car's tyres, e.g. 'they were fitted 5,000 miles ago', are concerned more with quality and/or condition of the goods and s. 13 probably does not apply, the claim being for misrepresentation. If s. 13 did apply, then every trivial statement about the goods would be a breach of condition and the law relating to misrepresentation would have no place – a rather unlikely situation.

Statements such as the one above do not identify the goods. Suppose I were to say to a student: 'The notes you require are in the boot of my car. Here are the keys. My car is the one which had new tyres fitted 5,000 miles ago.' How would the student find the car? Not easily: the statement does not identify the vehicle!

IMPLIED CONDITIONS AS TO FITNESS

Section 14(3) lays down the following conditions.

Where the seller sells goods in the course of a business and the buyer (or debtor in a credit sale), expressly, or by implication, makes known: (a) to the seller, or (b) to the dealer in a credit sale any particular purpose for which the goods are being bought, there is an implied condition that the goods supplied under the contract are reasonably fit for that purpose whether or not that is a purpose for which such goods are commonly supplied, except where the circumstances show that the buyer (or debtor) does not rely, or that it is unreasonable for him to rely, on the skill or judgment of that seller or dealer.

There is no need for the buyer to specify the particular purpose for which the goods are required when they have in the ordinary way only one purpose, e.g. a hot-water bottle. If ordinary goods in everyday use are required for a particular purpose this must be made known to the seller.

The following cases illustrate these rules.

Priest v Last [1903] 2 KB 148
The plaintiff, a draper who had no special knowledge of hot-water bottles, bought such a bottle from the defendant who was a chemist. It was in the ordinary course of the defendant's business to sell hot-water bottles and the plaintiff asked him whether the indiarubber bottle he was shown would stand boiling water. He was told that it would not, but that it would stand hot water. The plaintiff did not state the purpose for which the bottle was required. In the event the bottle was filled with hot water and used by the plaintiff's wife for bodily application to relieve cramp. On the fifth time of using, the bottle burst and the wife was severely scalded. Evidence showed that the bottle was not fit for use as a hot-water bottle. *Held* – The plaintiff was entitled to recover the expenses he had incurred in the treatment of his wife's injuries for the defendant's breach of s. 14(3) of the Sale of Goods Act. The circumstances showed that the plaintiff had relied on the defendant's skill and judgment, and although he had not mentioned the purpose for which he required the bottle, he had in fact used it for the usual and obvious purpose.

Comment: There was no question of the wife suing the chemist under Sale of Goods legislation because she was not a party to the contract. She could today have sued the manufacturer or the chemist in *negligence* (see *Donoghue v Stevenson* (1932), p. 267) if she could have proved negligence in either of them.

Griffiths v Peter Conway Ltd [1939] 1 All ER 685

The defendants, who were retail tailors, supplied the plaintiff with a Harris tweed coat which was made to order for her. The plaintiff wore the coat for a short time and then developed dermatitis. She brought this action for damages alleging that the defendants were in breach of s. 14(3) of the Sale of Goods Act because the coat was not fit for the purpose for which it was bought. Evidence showed that the plaintiff had an abnormally sensitive skin and that the coat would not have affected the skin of a normal person. *Held* – The plaintiff failed because s. 14(3) did not apply. The defendants did not know of the plaintiff's abnormality and could not be expected to assume that it existed.

Fitness for the purpose: meaning of reliance

Reliance on the seller's skill and judgment will be readily implied even to the extent of saying that, at least in sales to the general public as consumers, the buyer has gone to the seller because he relies on the seller having selected his stock with skill and judgment. The buyer must show that he has made known the purpose for which the goods are being bought. Reliance will then be presumed, unless it can be disproved, or if the seller can show that reliance was unreasonable.

The court has to decide what amounts to 'unreasonable reliance'. However, presumably the seller can disclaim responsibility. For example, suppose B goes into S's general stores and sees some tubes of glue. If he then asks whether the glue will stick metal to plastic and S says: 'I am not expert enough to say', then if B buys the glue and it does not stick metal to plastic it would surely be unreasonable for B to suggest that he relied on S's skill and judgment.

There will in general be no implication of reliance where the buyer knows that the seller deals in only one brand of goods, e.g. where a public house sells only one brand of beer.

The following cases provide illustrations of these rules.

Grant v Australian Knitting Mills Ltd [1936] AC 85

This was an appeal from the High Court of Australia to the Privy Council in England by a Dr Grant of Adelaide, South Australia. Dr Grant bought a pair of long woollen underpants from a retailer, the respondents being the manufacturers. The underpants contained an excess of sulphite which was a chemical used in their manufacture. This chemical should have been eliminated before the product was finished, but a quantity was left in the underpants purchased by Dr Grant. After wearing the pants for a day or two, a rash, which turned out to be dermatitis, appeared on the appellant's ankles and soon became generalized, compelling the appellant to spend many months in hospital. He sued the retailers and the manufacturers for damages. *Held* – (a) The retailers were in breach of the South Australian Sale of Goods Act 1895 (which is in the same terms as the English Act of 1979). They were liable under s. 14(3) because the article was not fit for the purpose. They were liable under s. 14(2) because the article was not of merchantable quality. (b) The manufacturers were liable in negligence, following *Donoghue* v *Stevenson* (see p. 267). This was a latent defect which could not have been discovered by a reasonable examination. It should also be noted that the appellant had a perfectly normal skin. (Compare *Griffiths* v *Peter Conway Ltd* (1939) at p. 252.)

Comment: (i) Section 13 (sale by description) also applied even though this was a sale of a specific object which was seen by the purchaser. On the issue of reliance Lord Wright said: '... the reliance will be in general inferred from the fact that a buyer goes to the shop in confidence that the tradesman has selected his stock with skill and judgment.'

(ii) This case provides an interesting contrast between the liability of the supplier who was liable although not negligent, Sale of Goods Act liability being *strict*, and the liability of the manufacturer where the plaintiff was put to the extra burden of proving the manufacturer negligent. (*See* now Consumer Protection Act 1987 at p. 272.)

Wren v Holt [1903] 1 KB 610

The plaintiff was a builder's labourer at Blackburn, and the defendant was the tenant of a beerhouse in the same town. The beerhouse was a tied house so that the defendant was obliged to sell beer brewed by a firm called Richard Holden Limited. The plaintiff was a regular customer and knew that the beerhouse was a tied house, and that only one type of beer was supplied. The plaintiff became ill and it was established that his illness was caused by arsenical poisoning due to the beer supplied to him. He now sued the tenant. *Held* – There was no claim under s. 14(3) because the plaintiff could not have relied on the defendant's skill and judgment in selecting his stock, because he was bound to supply Holden's beer. However, s. 14(2) applied, and since the beer was not of merchantable quality, the plaintiff was entitled to recover damages.

Fitness: application to non-manufactured goods

The rules relating to fitness for the purpose under s. 14(3) apply also to non-manufactured goods. **The following case illustrates this point.**

Frost v Aylesbury Dairy Co Ltd [1905] 1 KB 608

The defendants, whose business was the selling of milk, supplied milk to the plaintiff's household. The account book supplied to him contained several statements regarding the precautions taken by the defendants to keep their milk free from germs. This action was brought by the plaintiff for damage sustained by him on the death of his wife by typhoid fever contracted from the milk supplied by the defendants. *Held* – The plaintiff succeeded because the circumstances showed that he had relied on the defendant's skill and judgment to select and supply milk free from germs. He was, therefore, entitled to the benefit of s. 14(3) of the Sale of Goods Act because the milk was not fit for human consumption. It was not a defence that no skill or judgment would have enabled the sellers to find out the defect. This emphasizes that the liability of the supplier under the Sale of Goods Act is strict.

Fitness: second-hand goods

In deciding the matter of fitness for the purpose in the case of second-hand goods the buyer must expect that defects are likely to emerge sooner or later. However, if defects occur fairly quickly after sale this is strong evidence that the goods were not reasonably fit at the time of sale. **The following case shows this point.**

Crowther v Shannon Motor Company [1975] I All ER 139

The plaintiff, relying on the skill and judgment of the defendants, bought a second-hand car from them. After being driven for over 2,000 miles in the three weeks after the sale the engine seized and had to be replaced. In his evidence the previous owner said that the engine was not fit for use on the road when he sold it to the defendants and on that basis the Court of Appeal *held* that there was a breach of s. 14(3) at the time of resale. The fact that a car does not go for a reasonable time after sale is evidence that the car was not fit for the purpose at the time of sale.

Fitness and merchantable quality distinguished

Before proceeding to consider merchantable quality, we must distinguish the two heads of liability, i.e. fitness and merchantable quality. Under s. 14(2) an article is regarded as not merchantable because of a manufacturing defect so that a perfect article would have served the purpose, or in other words it is the right article but it is faulty. Under s. 14(3) an article is regarded as not fit for the purpose because of its design or construction. It may be perfect in terms of its manufacture but its construction or design does not allow it to fit the purpose and consequently no amount of adjustment or repair will ever make it right. In other words, it is a perfect article but the wrong article for the purpose.

The following case provides a useful illustration.

Baldry v Marshall [1925] I KB 260

The plaintiff was the owner of a Talbot racing car and was anxious to change it for a touring car because his wife refused to ride in the Talbot. The plaintiff wrote to the defendants asking for details of the Bugatti car for which they were agents. The plaintiff knew nothing of the Bugatti range, but asked for a car that would be comfortable and suitable for touring purposes. The defendants' manager said that a Bugatti would be suitable. The plaintiff later inspected a Bugatti chassis and agreed to buy it when a body had been put on it. When the car was delivered it was to all intents and purposes a racing car and not suitable for touring. The plaintiff returned the car, but he had paid £1,000 under the contract and now sued for its return on the grounds that the defendants were in breach of s. 14(3) of the Sale of Goods Act, the car not being fit for the purpose. *Held* – The plaintiff had relied on the skill and judgment of the defendants and it was in the course of their business to supply cars. Therefore, there was a breach of s. 14(3).

Comment: It will be appreciated that the Bugatti was superbly merchantable!

MERCHANTABLE QUALITY

By s. 14(2) *where the seller sells goods in the course of a business* there is an implied condition that the goods supplied under the contract are of merchantable quality, except that there is no such condition:

(a) as regards defects specifically drawn to the buyer's attention before the contract is made; or

(b) if the buyer examines the goods before the contract is made, as regards defects which that examination ought to reveal.

If the seller does not normally deal in goods of the type in question, there is no condition as to fitness (nor as to merchantability unless the sale is by sample which is dealt with below). The *only* condition in such a case is that the goods correspond with the description. This arises because s. 14(1) provides that except as provided by s. 14 and s. 15 (sale by sample), and subject to any other enactment, there is no implied condition or warranty about the quality or fitness for any particular purpose of goods supplied under a contract of sale. If, therefore, S (who is not a dealer) sells a car to B with no express terms as to quality and fitness, the court is prevented by s. 14 from implying conditions or warranties, even though S seems, from the circumstances, to have been warranting the car in good order.

The s. 14 provision regarding merchantable quality applies where the sale is by a dealer who does not ordinarily sell goods of precisely the same description. Thus if B ordered an 'X' brand motor bike from S who has not formerly sold that make, s. 14 applies if the motor bike is unfit or unmerchantable.

There is no need under s. 14(2) for the buyer to show that he relied on the seller's skill and judgment, and the seller is liable for latent defects even though he is not the manufacturer and is merely marketing the goods as a wholesaler or retailer. Such a seller can, however, obtain an indemnity from the manufacturer if the buyer successfully sues him for defects in the goods.

Sales through an agent

Section 14(5) is concerned with the problem of a private seller who sells through an agent. The subsection provides that the implied conditions of fitness and merchantability operate if the agent is selling in the ordinary course of business unless the principal is not acting in the course of business and the buyer is aware of this, or reasonable steps have been taken to bring it to his notice. Thus, for example, an auctioneer acting for a private seller could exclude these sections by making it clear that the principal was a private seller.

Examination of the goods

The buyer is not obliged to examine the goods but if he does do so he will lose the protection of s. 14(2) if he fails to notice obvious defects, at least in respect of such defects as where a new washing machine is examined and the buyer misses a rather obvious scratch on the front of the machine. The buyer can also lose his right to complain where the seller actually points out the defects.

The price paid

The interpretation of the word 'merchantable' has often been discussed in the courts. Section 14(6) provides: goods of any kind are of merchantable quality within the meaning of this Act if they are as fit for the purpose or purposes for which goods of that kind are commonly bought as it is reasonable to expect having regard to any description applied to them, the price (if relevant) and all the other relevant circumstances.

The price paid by the buyer is therefore a factor to be taken into account. Goods (provided they are not defective) are not unmerchantable simply because their resale price is slightly less than that which the buyer paid, though they may be if the difference in purchase and resale price is substantial.

The following case provides an example.

BS Brown & Son Ltd v Craiks Ltd [1970] 1 All ER 823

Brown and Son ordered a quantity of cloth from Craiks who were manufacturers. Brown's wanted it for making dresses but did not make this purpose known to Craiks who thought the cloth was wanted for industrial use. The price paid by Brown's was 36.25p per yard which was higher than the normal price for industrial cloth but not substantially so. The cloth was not suitable for making dresses and Brown's cancelled the contract and claimed damages. Both parties were left with substantial quantities of cloth but Craiks had managed to sell some of their stock for 30p per yard. Having failed in the lower court to establish a claim under s. 14(3) since they had not made the purpose known to Craiks, Brown's now sued for damages under s. 14(2). *Held* – by the House of Lords – that the claim failed. The cloth was still commercially saleable for industrial purposes though at a slightly lower price. It was not a necessary requirement of merchantability that there should be no difference between purchase and resale price. If the difference was substantial, however, it might indicate that the goods were not of merchantable quality. The difference in this case was not so material as to justify any such inference.

Comment: Even where the goods are not purchased for resale the purchase price may be relevant. Thus the sale of a car with a defective clutch would be a sale of unmerchantable goods but if the seller makes an allowance in the price to cover the defect it may not be (*Bartlett* v *Sydney Marcus Ltd* [1965] 2 All ER 753).

How were the goods described?

As regards the description applied to the goods, old cars or other mechanical items which are sold and described as scrap need not be merchantable. Furthermore, 'shop-soiled', 'fire-damaged', 'flood-salvage' and so on might imply non-merchantable lines. In addition, old items, such as antiques and curios would not presumably be required to be in perfect working order. However, as we have seen it was *held* in *Cavendish-Woodhouse* v *Manley* (1984) 82 LGR 376 that the phrase on an invoice 'bought as seen' merely confirms that the purchaser has seen the goods. It does not exclude any implied terms as to quality or fitness.

Duration of merchantable quality

As regards the time during which the goods must be merchantable: the law is not clear. So far as perishable goods are concerned, the decision in *Mash and Murrell* v *Joseph I. Emmanuel* [1961] 1 All ER 485 is relevant. In that case potatoes, though sound when loaded in Cyprus, were rotten by the time the ship arrived in Liverpool, though there was no undue delay. It was held by Diplock J that the sellers were liable under s. 14(2) because the goods should have been loaded in such a state that they could survive the normal journey and be in merchantable condition when they arrived. In addition, the seller is liable for defects inherent in the goods when they are sold and will not escape merely because the defects do not become apparent until a later time. Circumstances such as those seen in *Crowther* v *Shannon Motor Co* (1975) (at p. 254) provide an illustration of this situation.

Goods partially defective

Where part only of the goods are unmerchantable it seems to depend on how much of the consignment is defective. In *Jackson* v *Rotax Motor and Cycle Co Ltd* [1910] 2 KB 937 the plaintiffs supplied motor horns to the defendants and one consignment was rejected by the defendants who alleged they were unmerchantable. Half the goods were dented and scratched because of bad packing and the Court of Appeal *held* that the buyers were entitled to reject the consignment.

Merchantable quality: an unsatisfactory test

The test of merchantable quality in s. 14(6) is now regarded as somewhat unsatisfactory. A buyer of goods has no rights at all where there are a number of minor defects such as small scratches and dents in a new car. The car is not necessarily unmerchantable because of these defects, nor is it unfit for the purpose. The Law Commission in Working Paper 85 suggest a new test as follows: 'The goods should be of such quality as would in all the circumstances of the case be fully acceptable to a reasonable buyer who had full knowledge of their condition, quality and characteristics.'

However, recent cases show a more helpful interpretation even of existing law by the judiciary. In *Shine* v *General Guarantee Corporation* [1988] 1 All ER 911 the Court of Appeal held that a second-hand car was not of merchantable quality where the manufacturers' rust warranty had been terminated because, unknown to the buyer, the car had been involved in an accident and had been submerged in water. The plaintiff brought his action on learning this, though he had only minor problems with the car. Bush J said: 'Irrespective of its condition, it was a car which no member of the public knowing the facts would touch with a barge pole unless they could get it at a substantially reduced price to reflect the risk they were taking.' He went on to add that a car was not just a form of transport it was also an investment and those who bought cars must have in mind their eventual saleability and in the case of Mr Shine, and no doubt others, pride in what was a specialist car (a Fiat X19 Bertoni-bodied sports car) for the enthusiast.

Again, in *Rogers* v *Parish (Scarborough) Ltd* [1987] 2 All ER 232 the Court of Appeal decided that a new Range Rover was not of merchantable quality or fit for the purpose although it was capable of being driven and the defects repaired. Mustill LJ made clear that it was not enough to consider whether a car was roadworthy and driveable. There were other relevant factors. These were: 'The appropriate degree of comfort, ease of handling and reliability and, one may add, a pride in the vehicle's outward and interior appearance . . . The buyer was entitled to value for his money.' These cases do begin to extend the concept of merchantability more into line with what most consumers would think it should be.

FITNESS AND MERCHANTABILITY

Private sales

The rules as to fitness for purpose and merchantable quality do not apply to private sales of second-hand goods and there is still a fairly wide application of the maxim *caveat emptor* (let the buyer beware). In practice only manufacturers, wholesalers, retailers and dealers in new or second-hand goods will be caught by the implied conditions. The courts cannot imply conditions and warranties into private contracts similar to those implied by the Act into sales by dealers, because, as we have seen, s. 14(1) forbids it.

Extension to items supplied with goods

The implied terms relating to fitness and merchantable quality extend also to other items supplied under the contract of sale of goods, e.g. containers, foreign matter and instructions for use. **The following cases cover these areas.**

Geddling v Marsh [1920] 1 KB 668

The defendants were manufacturers of mineral waters and they supplied the same to the plaintiff who kept a small general store. The bottles were returnable when empty. One of the bottles was defective, and whilst the plaintiff was putting it back into a crate, it burst and injured her. *Held* – Even though the bottles were returnable, they were supplied under a contract of sale within s. 14 of the Sale of Goods Act. The fact that the bottles were only bailed to the plaintiff was immaterial. There was an implied warranty of fitness for the purpose for which they were supplied, and the defendant was liable in damages.

Comment: Bray J was careful to point out that his decision was an interpretation of s. 14 of the Sale of Goods Act only. It does not decide that the liability of a bailor is the same as that of a vendor.

Wilson v Rickett, Cockerell & Co Ltd [1954] 1 QB 598

The plaintiff, a housewife, ordered from the defendants, who were coal merchants, a ton of 'Coalite'. The Coalite was delivered and when part of it was put on a fire in an open grate, it exploded causing damage to the plaintiff's house. In this action the plaintiff claimed damages for breach of s. 14 of the Sale of Goods Act. The County Court judge found that the explosion was not due to the Coalite but to something else, possibly a piece of coal with explosive embedded in it, which had got mixed with the Coalite in transit and had not come from the manufacturers of the Coalite. Therefore, he held that s. 14(3) applied only to the Coalite and dismissed the action since the Coalite itself was fit for the purpose. The Court of Appeal, however, in allowing the appeal, pointed out that fuel of this kind is not sold by the lump but by the bag, and a bag containing explosive materials is, as a unit, not fit for burning. The explosive matter was 'goods supplied under the contract' for the purposes of s. 14 and clearly s. 14(2) applied, because the goods supplied were not of merchantable quality. Damages were awarded to the plaintiff. Regarding the applicability of what is now s. 14(3), the Court of Appeal did not think this applied since the sale was under a trade name, and the plaintiff had not relied on the defendants' skill and judgment in selecting a fuel.

Comment: The assumption of no reliance where goods are purchased under a trade name no longer applies under the 1979 Act.

Wormell v RHM Agriculture (East) Ltd [1986] 1 All ER 769

Mr Wormell, who was an experienced arable farmer, was unable by reason of cold, wet weather to spray his winter wheat crop to kill wild oats until much later than usual in the spring of 1983. He asked the defendants to recommend the best wild oat killer which could be used later than normal. The agricultural chemical manager recommended a particular herbicide and Mr Wormell bought £6,438 worth of it.

The instructions on the cans stated that it ought not to be applied beyond the recommended stage of crop growth. It was said that damage could occur to crops sprayed after that stage and the herbicide would give the best level of wild oat control at the latest stage of application consistent with the growth of the crop.

Mr Wormell felt that the need to kill the wild oats was so important that he would risk some damage to the crops by applying the herbicide quite late. From his understanding of the instructions the risk was not that the herbicide would not be effective on the wild oats, but if the spray was used after the recommended time then the crop might be damaged. The herbicide was applied but proved to be largely ineffective.

Mr Wormell claimed damages for breach of contract in respect of the sale of the herbicide. He alleged that it was not of merchantable quality contrary to s. 14(2) of the Sale of Goods Act, nor was it fit for the purpose for which it was supplied, namely to control weeds, and in particular, wild oats, contrary to s. 14(3) of the same Act.

RHM argued that since the herbicide would kill the wild oats, the fact that the instructions caused it to be applied at a time when it was not effective did not make the herbicide itself unmerchantable or unfit for the purpose.

Piers Ashworth QC sitting as a Deputy Judge of the High Court, said that one had to look at how Mr Wormell understood the instructions and how a reasonable user would understand them. Mr Wormell understood the instructions to mean that the herbicide would be effective if it was sprayed at any time, but if sprayed late there was a risk of crop damage. The judge concluded that a reasonable farmer would have understood the instructions in the same way. He thought that the instructions were consequently misleading.

For the purposes of the Sale of Goods Act 'goods' included the container and packaging for the goods and any instructions supplied with them. If the instructions were wrong or misleading the goods would not be of merchantable quality or fit for the purpose for which they were supplied under s. 14(2) and (3). This statement was approved in a 1987 appeal to the Court of Appeal though on the facts the court found the instructions adequate.

Comment: It may be that manufacturers look upon instructions for use of the product as merely an aspect of marketing. However, this case shows that there is a legal obligation to give adequate guidance as to how the product is to be used.

Injury to third party, purchaser's indemnity

It should be noted that if a retailer sells goods which are faulty and in breach of s. 14 he is obliged to indemnify the purchaser if the faulty goods injure a third party to whom the purchaser is found liable. However, no such indemnity is payable if the purchaser has continued to use the goods having become aware that they are faulty and dangerous. **The following case makes this point.**

Lambert v Lewis [1981] 1 All ER 1185

Mr Lewis owned a Land Rover and a trailer. His employee, Mr Larkin, was driving it when the trailer broke away. It collided with a car coming from the opposite direction. Mr Lambert, who was driving that car, was killed and so was his son. His wife and daughter, who were also passengers, survived and then sued Mr Lewis for damages in negligence. He joined the retailer who sold him the towing hitch which had become detached from the trailer and was basically the cause of the collision. The retailer was sued under s. 14 (goods not fit for the purpose nor of merchantable quality). The court found that the towing hitch was badly designed and a securing brass spindle and handle had come off it so that only dirt was keeping the towing pin in position. It had been like that for some months and Mr Lewis had coupled and uncoupled the trailer once or twice a week during that time and knew of the problem.

The plaintiffs succeeded in their action against Mr Lewis. He failed in his claim against the retailer. The House of Lords decided that when a person first buys goods he can rely on s. 14. However, once he discovers that they are defective but continues to use them and so causes injury, he is personally liable for the loss caused. He cannot claim an indemnity under s. 14 from the retailer. The chain of causation is broken by the buyer's continued use of the goods while knowing that they are faulty and may cause injury.

Comment: The above summary does not concern itself with the possible liability of the manufacturers in terms of the design problem. However, a point of interest arises in connection with it. The issue of the manufacturers' liability was taken by an action in negligence. The court refused to construe a collateral contract between Mr Lewis and the manufacturers although he bought the hitch on the strength of the manufacturers' advertising. (Compare *Carlill*, p. 2, where such a contract was rather exceptionally construed.)

Usage of trade

Section 14(4) provides that an implied warranty or condition as to quality or fitness for a particular purpose may be attached to a contract of sale by usage. Where the transaction is connected with a particular trade, the customs and usages of that trade give the context in which the parties made their contract and may give a guide as to their intentions. Thus in a sale of canary seed in accordance with the customs of the trade it was *held* that the buyer could not reject the seed delivered on the grounds that there were impurities in it. A custom of the trade prevented this but allowed instead a rebate on the price paid (*Peter Darlington Partners Ltd* v *Gosho Co Ltd* [1964] 1 Lloyd's Rep 149).

SALE BY SAMPLE

Section 15(1) states that a contract of sale is a contract of sale by sample where there is a term in the contract, express or implied, to that effect. The mere fact that the seller provides a sample for the buyer's inspection is not enough: to be such a sale there must be either an express provision in the contract to that effect, or there must be evidence that the parties intended the sale to be by sample.

There are three implied conditions in sale by sample.

(a) *The bulk must correspond with the sample in quality* (s. 15(2)(a)).
(b) *The buyer shall have a reasonable opportunity of comparing the bulk with the sample*

(s. 15(2)(b)). The buyer will not be deemed to have accepted the goods until he has had an opportunity to compare the bulk with the sample, and will be able, therefore, to reject the goods, even though they have been delivered, if the bulk does not correspond with the sample. He is not left with the remedy of damages for the breach of warranty (*see* s. 34, p. 307).

(c) *The goods shall be free from any defect, rendering them unmerchantable, which would not be apparent on reasonable examination of the sample* (s. 15(2)(c)).

The effect of s. 15(2)(c) is to exclude the implied condition of merchantability if the defect could have been discovered by reasonable examination of the sample whether or not there has in fact been any examination of the sample. This is presumably based upon the premise that the seller is entitled to assume that the buyer will examine the sample. The provision is in contrast with s. 14(2) where the implied condition of merchantability is not excluded unless an examination has actually taken place (*see* p. 255).

A reasonable examination for the purpose of a sale by sample is such an examination as is usually carried out in the trade concerned.

The following case shows how s. 15 applies.

Godley v Perry [1960] I All ER 36

The first defendant, Perry, was a newsagent who also sold toys, and in particular displayed plastic toy catapults in his window. The plaintiff, who was a boy aged six, bought one for 6d. While using it to fire a stone, the catapult broke, and the plaintiff was struck in the eye, either by a piece of the catapult or the stone, and as a result he lost his left eye. The chemist's report given in evidence was that the catapults were made from cheap material unsuitable for the purpose and likely to fracture, and that the moulding of the plastic was poor, the catapults containing internal voids. Perry had purchased the catapults from a wholesaler with whom he had dealt for some time, and this sale was by sample, the defendant's wife examining the sample catapult by pulling the elastic. The wholesaler's supplier was another wholesaler who had imported the catapults from Hong Kong. This sale was also by sample and the sample catapult was again tested by pulling the elastic. In this action the plaintiff alleged that the first defendant was in breach of the conditions implied by s. 14(2) and (3) of the Sale of Goods Act.

The first defendant brought in his supplier as third party, alleging against him a breach of the conditions implied by s. 15(2)(c), and the third party brought in his supplier as fourth party, alleging breach of s. 15(2)(c) against him. *Held* –

(a) The first defendant was in breach of s. 14(2) and (3) because:
 (i) the catapult was not reasonably fit for the purpose for which it was required. The plaintiff relied on the seller's skill or judgment, this being readily inferred where the customer was of tender years (s. 14(3));
 (ii) The catapult was not merchantable (s. 14(2)).
(b) The third and fourth parties were both in breach of s. 15(2)(c) because the catapult had a defect which rendered it unmerchantable, and this defect was not apparent on

reasonable examination of the sample. The test applied, i.e. the pulling of the elastic, was all that could be expected of a potential purchaser. The third and fourth parties had done business before, and the third party was entitled to regard without suspicion any sample shown to him and to rely on the fourth party's skill in selecting his goods.

LIABILITY OF SELLER WHERE GOODS ARE IN A DANGEROUS CONDITION

The Sale of Goods Act 1979 deals only with contractual rights and duties. However, a seller of goods may be liable in the tort of negligence to the buyer or third parties because the goods sold are dangerous and might cause injury. **The following case provides an illustration.**

Fisher v Harrods (1966) 110 SJ 133

The defendants bought a jewellery cleaner from a manufacturer without making inquiries as to its safety in use. It contained substances which were injurious to the eyes but no indication or warning of this was given either on the bottle or in any other way. A bottle of the cleaner sold by the defendants injured the plaintiff. The contents would not come out of the container. The plaintiff applied gentle pressure. The bung flew out and some of the contents damaged her eyes. She now claimed damages from the defendants and it was held that they had been negligent in the circumstances of the case by failing to make inquiries of the manufacturer, failing to have the cleaner analysed, and selling it without a warning. Damages of £1,995 were awarded.

Comment: The action against Harrods was particularly important to the plaintiff because the manufacturers of the cleaner had few assets and were not insured.

GRADED QUESTIONS

Essay mode

1. (a) What liability is imposed on the seller of goods as regards their merchantable quality and their fitness for the purpose of those goods?

   (b) To what extent, if any, is the seller able to exclude his liability in respect of such obligations?

   (The Institute of Company Accountants. Part 3: Law Relating to Business. November 1987)

2. (a) Explain the legal protection given in the Sale of Goods Ac, to a buyer with respect to the quality of the goods bought.

   (12 marks)

   (b) Henry bought some meat from Bernard, a butcher, but the meat, unknown to Bernard, was contaminated. Wilma, Henry's wife, cooked the meat but, after eating it, both Henry and Wilma became seriously ill. Advise Bernard as to his possible liability.

   (8 marks)

   (Total: 20 marks)

   (The Chartered Institute of Management Accountants. Stage 1: Business Law. November 1988)

3. P approached Q Garages Ltd and informed a car salesman that he wished to buy a second-hand car. One of the cars for sale at the garage was advertised as '1976 Model Volvo estate, one previous owner, excellent condition, good for thousands of trouble-free miles. Exceptional value at only £5,000'. P expressed an interest in the vehicle. Following a test drive, P purchased the vehicle.

   After four months, during which time the car covered 10,000 miles, the car broke down and required expensive engine repairs. In addition, P has recently discovered that the car is, in fact, a 1975 model.

   Advise P as to his rights, if any, under the Sale of Goods Act 1979.

   (20 marks)

   (The Chartered Institute of Certified Accountants. Paper 1.4(E): Law. December 1988)

Objective mode

Four alternative answers are given. Select ONE only. Circle the answer which you consider to be correct. Check your answers by referring back to the information given in the relevant chapter and against the answers in the back of the book.

1. Is an agreement by Rose in 1991 to buy, from Premier Garages Ltd, a 1992 factory-built BMW 323 in a certain colour with extras as specified by her (the car to be obtained from the manufacturers by Premier):

A A contract for the sale of future goods.
B A contract for the supply of work and materials.
C A contract for the sale of unascertained goods.
D A contract for the sale of goods by sample.

2. Jane enters into a hire-purchase agreement with Merchant Credit Ltd for the purchase of a second-hand Fiat Panda motor car for a deposit of £1,000 followed by 12 monthly instalments of £150 with an option to purchase on completion of these payments. Jane is not protected by the Sale of Goods Act 1979:

A Because the Act does not apply to second-hand goods.
B Because the Act does not apply to motor vehicle sales.
C Because the contract is not for sale of goods but for hire of goods and governed by a different statute.
D Because the whole price should be paid at once to be a sale of goods.

3. Carol wishes to buy a new carpet for her bedroom. She goes to Barry's showroom and sees a carpet of the colour and design she requires. The carpet is described as 'best quality Axminster' and costs £10.00 per square yard. Carol orders the carpet but on delivery discovers that it is not 'Axminster' but an inferior mixture of wool and nylon. What is the legal position?

A Carol must accept the carpet since she saw and inspected it. The maxim is *caveat emptor*.
B Carol may reject the carpet. Since she has made known the purpose for which the carpet was required it must be of merchantable quality.
C Carol must accept the carpet, since the condition that goods must correspond to the description cannot apply if the buyer has inspected and selected the goods in question.
D Carol may reject the carpet for breach of condition that the goods must correspond with the description.

4. Porter, a gentleman of means, advertised one of his private motor cars for sale at £1,000. Alice, an impecunious student, bought the car intending to use it to get to work. The car was a 1958 Sunbeam Alpine and was unreliable and temperamental. Alice sued for the return of the price paid.

A Porter is liable since the goods were not fit for the purpose required impliedly made known to him by Alice.
B Porter is not liable since there is no implied condition of fitness for use in a private sale.
C Porter is not liable since Alice should have known that as the price was low the conditions of merchantable quality or fitness for use would be excluded.
D Porter is liable. Since Alice was going to use the car for business the condition of merchantable quality will apply.

5. In a contract for the sale of goods there is an implied warranty under the Sale of Goods Act 1979 that:

   A The seller has the right to sell the goods.

   B In goods sold by description the goods correspond with the description.

   C In goods sold by sample the bulk corresponds with the sample.

   D The goods are free from any charge or encumbrance not known to the buyer.

6. In the law of contract the so-called 'postal rules' state that:

   A Both acceptance and revocation will take effect from the time the letter conveying the acceptance or revocation is properly posted.

   B Where any written offer is made acceptance is effective as soon as the letter of acceptance is posted.

   C Where the post has been signified as an acceptable means of communication the acceptance is effective as soon as the letter of acceptance is posted.

   D Where the post has been signified as an acceptable means of communication the acceptance is effective when the letter of acceptance is delivered.

Answers to questions set in objective mode appear on p. 551.

11 | The sale of goods II

The OBJECTIVES of this chapter are to consider *civil* claims against manufacturers of goods, the conversion of conditions into warranties for the purpose of remedies, the transfer of property in goods and the transfer of title in goods by non-owners.

In the last chapter we considered the liability of the seller of goods in the law of contract. We now turn to the liability of the manufacturer for defective goods, where, in the absence of a contract between the parties, liability is based on the common law of negligence and to some extent on statute law.

CLAIMS AGAINST THE MANUFACTURER IN NEGLIGENCE

Physical injuries

Where the goods are purchased from a retailer, no action can be brought under the Sale of Goods Act by the purchaser against the manufacturer. The doctrine of privity of contract applies (*see* p. 34) with the result that there is no contract between them into which the warranties and conditions set out in the Act can be implied. However, the purchaser may have an action in negligence against the manufacturer in respect of *physical* injuries caused by defects in the goods.

The following classic case provides the starting point.

Donoghue (or M'Alister) v Stevenson [1932] AC 562

A friend of the appellant, Mrs Donoghue, purchased a bottle of ginger beer from a Mr Francis Minchella, who ran the Wellmeadow cafe, on a warm August afternoon in Paisley and gave it to her. The respondents were the manufacturers of the ginger beer. The appellant consumed some of the ginger beer and her friend was replenishing the glass, when, according to the appellant, the decomposed remains of a snail came out of the bottle. The bottle was made of dark glass so that the snail could not be seen until most of the contents had been consumed. The appellant became ill and served a writ on the manufacturers claiming damages. The question before the House of Lords was whether the facts outlined above constituted a cause of action in negligence. The House of Lords *held* by a majority of three to two that they did. It was stated that a manufacturer of products, which are sold in such a form that they are likely to reach the ultimate consumer in the form in which they left the manufacturer with no possibility of intermediate examination, owes a duty to the consumer to take reasonable care to prevent injury. This rule has been broadened in subsequent cases so that the manufacturer is liable more often where defective chattels cause injury. The following important points also arise out of the case.

(a) It was in this case that the House of Lords formulated the test that the duty of care in negligence is based on the foresight of the reasonable man.
(b) Lord Macmillan's remark that the categories of negligence are never closed suggests that the tort of negligence is capable of further expansion though as yet there is difficulty in cases involving economic (money) loss as distinct from physical injury.
(c) The duty of care with regard to chattels as laid down in the case relates to chattels not dangerous in themselves. The duty of care in respect of chattels dangerous in themselves, e.g. explosives, is much higher.
(d) The appellant had no cause of action against the retailer in contract because her friend bought the bottle, so there was no privity of contract between the retailer and the appellant. Therefore terms relating to fitness for purpose and merchantable quality, implied into such contracts by the Sale of Goods Act, did not apply here.

Comment: A remedy under the Sale of Goods Act could have been given to the appellant if the reasoning of Tucker J in *Lockett* v *A & M Charles Ltd* [1938] 4 All ER 170 had been applied in *Donoghue*. In *Lockett* husband and wife went into a hotel for lunch. The wife ordered whitebait which was not fit for human consumption. She only ate a small amount of the whitebait and was then taken ill. In the subsequent action against the hotel Tucker J held that although the husband ordered the meal there was an assumption in these cases that each party would be, if necessary, personally liable for what he or she consumed. There was therefore a contract between the hotel and the wife into which Sale of Goods Act terms could be implied and she was awarded damages because the whitebait was not fit for the purpose or of merchantable quality. This approach is surprisingly modern in spite of the fact that the case was decided in 1938.

The rule arrived at in *Donoghue* v *Stevenson* has been widened since 1932, and now applies to defective chattels generally which cause injuries to purchasers (*see Grant* v *Australian Knitting Mills Ltd* (1936), p. 252). However, although the above case shows that the manufacturer has a duty to take care, evidence may show that he was not in breach of that duty because he took proper precautions.

In addition liability in negligence is not strict as it is under the Sale of Goods Act. The plaintiff must prove negligence in the process of manufacture. However, assistance is given by the plea of *res ipsa loquitur* (the thing speaks for itself). If this plea is accepted by the court the defendant must show he was not negligent or explain how the matter could have come about without his negligence. If he fails to do this the plaintiff wins the case. **The following case provides an illustration**.

Daniels v R White and Sons [1938] 4 All ER 258

The plaintiffs, who were husband and wife, sued the first defendants, who were manufacturers of mineral waters, in negligence. The plaintiffs had been injured because a bottle of the first defendants' lemonade, which they had purchased from a public house in Battersea, contained carbolic acid. The plaintiffs pleaded *res ipsa loquitur*. This plea was accepted by the court and the defendant was therefore required to produce evidence of a safe system and proper supervision. Evidence showed that the manufacturers took all possible care to see that no injurious matter got into the lemonade, and that the husband when he bought the lemonade from the public house asked for it by mentioning the manufacturers' name. It was *held* that the manufacturers were not liable in negligence because the duty was not to ensure that the goods were in perfect condition but only to take reasonable care to see that no injury was caused to the eventual consumer. This duty had been fulfilled. The second defendant, who was the landlady of the Battersea public house from which the goods were purchased, was held liable under s. 14(2) of the Sale of Goods Act, because the goods were not of merchantable quality.

Comment: (i) The court in this case does not seem to have taken the point that if the system was a good one then the alien matter must have got into the lemonade because of the negligence of an employee, and since an employer is liable for the negligence of his employees, White's ought to have been liable in this case. The decision has been much criticized and MacKenna J in *Hill v James Crowe (Cases)* [1978] 1 All ER 812 refused to follow it saying that a manufacturer can be vicariously liable for the negligence of his workman, notwithstanding the fact that he has a good system of work and adequate supervision.

(ii) A more successful case was *Steer v Durable Rubber Manufacturing Co Ltd, The Times*, 20 November 1958, where the plaintiff was a six-year-old girl. She was scalded when her hot-water bottle burst. The bottle was only three months old. She had no evidence to show exactly how the bottle was defective. However the Court of Appeal accepted a plea of *res ipsa loquitur* after it was established that a bottle of this kind would normally last for at least three years. The manufacturers could not show that they had not been negligent and were held liable.

In certain of the cases mentioned above the question of inspection of the goods was raised. It was an important fact in the decision in *Donoghue* v *Stevenson* (1932) that the bottle was made of dark glass, so that the snail could not be seen on external inspection of the bottle, and that normally no inspection of goods would take place until they reached the consumer. It is not thought that in the developing law of negligence a manufacturer can rely on an inspection revealing the defects in his product, except perhaps in a special case where it is known that an expert inspection normally takes place. If such an inspection does not take place, or fails to find the defect which it should have found, the manufacturer may regard this as a *novus actus intervениens* (a new act intervening) breaking the chain of causation between his negligence and the injury so that the plaintiff's claim will fail.

Economic loss

Product liability in negligence has, up to recent times, been confined to defective chattels which cause *physical* injury to purchasers as in *Donoghue* and *Grant*. **The law seemed to have taken a step forward in the following case by extending product liability in negligence to complaints relating to defects in goods which had caused economic loss rather than physical injury. This seems unlikely to develop at the present time for the reasons given in the comment to the case.**

Junior Books Ltd v Veitchi Co Ltd [1982] 3 All ER 201

Junior Books (J) owned a building. Veitchi (V) were flooring contractors working under a contract for the main contractor who was doing work on the building. There was no privity of contract between J and V. It was alleged by J that faulty work by V left J with an unserviceable building and high maintenance costs so that J's business became unprofitable. The House of Lords decided in favour of J on the basis that there was a duty of care. V were in breach of a duty owed to J to take reasonable care to avoid acts or omissions including laying an allegedly defective floor which they ought to have known would be likely to cause the owners economic loss, including loss of profits caused by the high cost of maintaining the allegedly defective floor, and in so far as J were required to mitigate the loss by replacing the floor itself, the cost of replacement was the appropriate measure of V's liability. The standard of care required is apparently the contractual duty and so long as the work is up to contract standard, then the defendant in a case such as this will not be in breach of his duty. Lord Fraser of Tullybelton said:

> Where a building is erected under a contract with a purchaser, then provided the building, or part of it, is not dangerous to persons or to other property and subject to the law against misrepresentation, I can see no reason why the builder should not be free to make with the purchaser whatever contractual arrangements about the quality of the product the purchaser wishes. However jerry-built the product, the purchaser would not be entitled to damages from the builder if it came up to the contractual standards.

Comment: The decision in this case has been doubted in a number of more recent decisions. In *Simaan General Contracting Co v Pilkington Glass* [1988] 1 All ER 791 the plaintiffs S Ltd were the main contractors to construct a building in Abu Dhabi for a sheikh. The erection of glass walling together with supplying the glass was subcontracted to an Italian company (Feal). Feal bought the glass from the defendants Pilkingtons (P Ltd). The glass units should have been a uniform shade of green but some were various shades of green and some were red. The sheikh did not pay S Ltd. They chose to sue P Ltd in tort rather than Feal in contract for their loss, i.e. the money which the sheikh was withholding. *Held* – by the Court of Appeal – that since there was no physical damage this was purely a claim for economic loss and P Ltd had no duty of care. S Ltd's claim failed. Feal would have been liable under the Supply of Goods and Services Act 1982 (see p. 333) but for some reason were not sued. Economic loss can be recovered in contract. Dillon LJ said of *Junior Books* that it had 'been the subject of so much analysis and discussion that it cannot now be regarded as a useful pointer to any development of the law. It is difficult to see that future citation from *Junior Books* can ever serve any useful purpose.'

Contributory negligence

Even though the plaintiff has managed to prove negligence in the manufacturer the latter may still be able to obtain a reduction in the damages or even defeat the claim by proving that the plaintiff was guilty of contributory negligence as where he contributed to the damage or was even entirely responsible for it by, for example, failing to observe operating instructions or using the product after knowledge that it was defective. The Law Reform (Contributory Negligence) Act 1945 applies. Under it the court may, for example, assess damages at £20,000 but decide that the plaintiff was 50 per cent to blame and reduce the damages to £10,000. In an extreme case the court may decide that the plaintiff was 100 per cent to blame so that he recovers nothing.

Third party proceedings

Strict liability under the Act of 1979 can, in effect, be imposed on a manufacturer by means of third (or fourth) party proceedings. Thus if the seller is sued by the buyer for breach of an implied condition under the Act, the seller may claim an indemnity from his own supplier which may be the manufacturer. If the retailer has purchased from a wholesaler the retailer may claim an indemnity from the wholesaler who may in turn claim an indemnity from the manufacturer who supplied the goods. In this way the manufacturer can be made to pay for defects affecting the quality or fitness of the goods. *Godley* v *Perry* (1960) provides an example of joinder of parties (*see* p. 262). In connection with third party proceedings it should be borne in mind that the retailer may be unable to make a successful claim because of a 'reasonable' exclusion clause in the contract between him and his previous suppliers. In addition, the retailer's claim will be ineffective if one or more of the previous suppliers is insolvent.

COLLATERAL CONTRACTS WITH THE MANUFACTURER

The manufacturer may also be liable for defects in quality or fitness under a collateral contract. Thus in *Shanklin Pier Ltd* v *Detel Products Ltd* [1951] 2 All ER 471 Shanklin entered into a contract with A to paint the Pier and asked A to use paint made by Detel, the suitability of which had been communicated to Shanklin by Detel's agent. The paint was not suitable and Shanklin recovered damages against Detel for breach of a contract which the court *held* was collateral to the main contract with A. This applies however, only where a specific and express undertaking has been given by the manufacturer to the seller and it is doubtful whether such a claim could be based on statements made in a manufacturer's public advertisements. There are no firm illustrations of this in English law, though *Carlill* v *Carbolic Smoke Ball Co* (1893) (*see* p. 2) could perhaps be developed. The court did not in fact go for the collateral contract solution in *Lambert* v *Lewis* (1981) (*see* p. 260). The action against the manufacturer in that case was framed in negligence.

The Law Commission has recognized the need to provide some general form of action against the manufacturer but has felt that this cannot be done by a simple amendment to the Sale of Goods Act 1979. The Commission therefore recommends that a wider study of the problem be made before embarking upon legislative measures (Exemption Clauses, First Report, para. 63).

MANUFACTURERS' GUARANTEES

A manufacturers' guarantee (or warranty, as it is sometimes called) normally amounts to a warranty to repair or replace during a specified time with the addition in the case of vehicles of a mileage limit. Such guarantees are presumably enforceable by the buyer as a collateral contract as in *Carlill* v *Carbolic Smoke Ball Co* (1893) (*see* p. 2).

They cannot affect the purchaser's right to sue upon the implied conditions and warranties set out in the Sale of Goods Act 1979 or at common law for negligence because under s. 5 of the Unfair Contract Terms Act 1977 a clause in a manufacturer's or distributor's guarantee cannot operate to exclude or restrict the manufacturer's or distributor's liability to the customer provided the goods are of a type ordinarily supplied for private use or consumption and prove defective whilst in consumer use, i.e. not used exclusively for the purposes of a business.

STATUTORY PRODUCT LIABILITY: CLAIMS AGAINST THE MANUFACTURER

Part I of the Consumer Protection Act 1987

This brings into law strict product liability so that the consumer will no longer have to prove negligence when claiming compensation for damage or injury caused by products which are defective or unsafe. Civil liability will arise if damage is caused by a defective product. The Act is by no means a 'cure-all' because the plaintiff will still have to prove that the product *caused* the injury – not always an easy matter.

Damage is described as death, personal injury, or loss of or damage to *private* property. Thus damage to business property is not included. Furthermore, damage to property cannot be recovered unless it exceeds £275. If it does then the whole amount is recoverable, including the first £275. This is to prevent trivial claims for damage to property.

In assessing whether the product is unsafe the court must have regard to any warnings as to its use in advertising and marketing in general, instructions for use, how long ago the goods were supplied, and whether the product was put to what might be described as a reasonable use.

The following may be liable under the Act: the manufacturer of the product; a person who puts his name on the product thus holding himself out to be the manufacturer, i.e. a supermarket 'own brand' which is made for it by another manufacturer; an importer and a supplier if that supplier will not respond to a request to identify the person who supplied the product to him.

It is a defence to show that: (a) the product was not supplied in the course of a business; (b) the defect did not exist when the product was supplied; (c) technical knowledge was such that the defect could not have been known (called the 'development risk defence'). Thus the manufacturers of the drug Thalidomide may well have had a defence under the Act. However, manufacturers pressed for the retention of the development risk defence so as not to inhibit the development of new products.

The Act provides that any attempt to exclude liability by a term of a contract or notice will be ineffective. An injured party has three years in which to commence an action after the injury and discovery of the producer. There is a time bar on claims in any event ten years from when the product was supplied.

The Act does not impose liability on the producer of game or agricultural produce provided it has not undergone an industrial process.

Part II of the Consumer Protection Act 1987

This repeals the Consumer Safety Act 1978 and the Consumer Safety (Amendment) Act 1986 and provides a better legal framework to give the public protection from unsafe goods. The main provisions are as follows:

(a) A person is guilty of an offence if he supplies any *consumer* goods which fail to comply with the general safety requirement. In general therefore the goods must be ordinarily intended for private use or consumption.
(b) The government may make safety regulations for the purpose of defining the general safety requirement set out in (a) above.
(c) The Department of Trade and Industry may serve upon a supplier a 'prohibition notice' prohibiting him from supplying goods which are

considered unsafe or a 'notice to warn' requiring him to publish a warning about the goods at his own expense.

(d) A suspension notice may also be served by enforcement authorities, e.g. trading standards officers of local authorities, prohibiting a supplier from supplying specified goods where the authority has reasonable grounds for suspecting that there has been a contravention of the general safety requirement, any safety regulations or any prohibition notice.

Part II is primarily enforced by criminal sanctions, with which examination syllabuses are not normally concerned. However, the duties laid down in Part II can assist a plaintiff in a civil claim which is why reference has been made to them. A plaintiff injured by goods which infringe the safety requirements of the Act will be able to bring a claim for damages in negligence on the basis that the manufacturer is in breach of his statutory duty under the Act. This will make the plaintiff's claim much easier since he or she will not have to show a duty of care at common law. In this respect the Act is available to those who have no contractual claim against the seller as where they have received the goods as a gift.

TREATING A BREACH OF CONDITION AS A BREACH OF WARRANTY

Section 11(2) provides that the buyer can waive a breach of condition altogether or may treat it as a breach of warranty. If he chooses to treat the breach of condition as a breach of warranty, then he may sue for damages but cannot reject the goods.

However, unless there is a contrary provision in the contract, a breach of a condition implied under the Sale of Goods Act *must* be treated as a breach of warranty *where the contract is not severable and the buyer has accepted the goods or part thereof* (s. 11(4)).

Problems of severability arise where the goods are delivered by instalments. Where the price is paid for the whole consignment and delivery is by instalments, the contract is probably not severable, and acceptance by the buyer of early instalments will prevent him from rejecting later instalments which are not in accordance with the contract.

However, if, under the terms of the contract, each instalment is to be paid for separately the contract is probably severable (s. 31(2)), and acceptance of earlier instalments will not prevent the buyer from rejecting later deliveries which are not in accordance with the contract.

A contract may, however, be regarded as severable in a number of other situations. Thus in *Longbottom & Co Ltd* v *Bass Walker & Co Ltd* [1922] WN 245 a contract for the sale of cloth was regarded as severable where delivery was by instalments but the price was paid as part of a monthly account and not separately for each delivery of cloth.

Section 11(4) does not come into force when the goods are merely delivered; there must be some act by the buyer indicating his acceptance of the goods. A buyer is deemed to have accepted the goods:

(a) when he informs the seller that he has accepted them; or
(b) where, after delivery, and provided he has had a reasonable opportunity to examine the goods to see if they comply with the contract, he acts in a manner inconsistent with the continued ownership of the seller, as where he uses or consumes the goods; or
(c) where, after the lapse of a reasonable time, he still retains the goods, without giving notice of rejection (ss. 34 and 35(1)).

A combination of s. 11(4) and s. 35(1) can produce injustice for the consumer. For example, it was *held* by Rougier J in *Bernstein* v *Pamsons Motors (Golders Green) Ltd* [1987] 2 All ER 220 that a purchaser of a new car could not repudiate the contract and return the car for breach of condition under s. 14 (fitness and merchantability) when the engine seized up at 142 miles. The judge said that because he had owned the car for three weeks he had had a reasonable time to try the car out under s. 35(1). He was only entitled to damages of £232 for general inconvenience. The judge said he must in law accept the car as repaired under his warranty. The case is unfortunate for the consumer who can lose his right to return seriously defective goods even before a latent defect has emerged. The problem is really the law's reliance on *time* as the yardstick for discovering defects. In the case of many consumer goods a period of *use* would be better.

Thus the right to return goods would appear to be lost quite rapidly after purchase – three weeks in the above case. Those who wish to return unsatisfactory goods must get back to the shop quickly and complain. It is a pity in a way that Mr Bernstein's appeal to the Court of Appeal was never heard because the appeal court might have taken a different view. When Pamsons heard he was going to appeal they settled by giving him all his money back! (*See Which?*, December 1987.)

RESCISSION OF A CONTRACT OF SALE

It is useful at this point to compare the rules set out in s. 11 of the Act of 1979 with the right to rescind a contract of sale for misrepresentation arising from a misstatement of fact. The rules relating to rescission are governed by separate principles (*see* p. 117). Since the Misrepresentation Act 1967, rescission of a contract of sale is barred only where there is affirmation, lapse of time, inability to make restitution or acquisition of rights by innocent third parties for value. It seems that a buyer's right to rescind for misrepresentation and his right to reject for breach of condition are now much the same in principle, since an act which amounts to acceptance under s. 35(1) of the 1979 Act will almost always amount to affirmation so as to bar rescission. There may, however, be exceptional cases where rescission is available when rejection is not. For example, under s. 35(1) if a buyer does not intimate his rejection of the goods within a reasonable time he is automatically deemed to have accepted them and cannot reject. In equity lapse of time is not in itself sufficient to prevent rescission unless it amounts to affirmation, or the person making the representation (i.e. the seller) is prejudiced. Thus if in spite of lapse of time there is no prejudice to the seller, equity may allow rescission although the right to reject has been lost under s. 35(1).

TRANSFER OF THE PROPERTY IN GOODS

The provisions of the Act regarding the transfer of the property in the goods are important because the parties to contracts of sale do not usually express their intentions as to the passing of the property. In addition the risk normally passes when the property passes and the seller can in general terms only sue for the *price* as distinct from *damages* if the property has passed.

The relevant statutory provisions are outlined in the following sections.

WHERE THE GOODS ARE SPECIFIC

General

We will consider six cases.

Section 17

Section 17 provides that, where there is a contract for a sale of specific or ascertained goods, the property in them is transferred to the buyer at such time as the parties intend it to be transferred and, for the purpose of ascertaining the intention of the parties, regard shall be had to the terms of the contract, the conduct of the parties, and the circumstances of the case. Thus, an obligation on one party to insure is an indication that he has the risk and, by inference, and in the absence of an express provision to the contrary, the property (*Allison* v *Bristol Marine Insurance Co Ltd* (1876) 1 App Cas 209).

Section 17 is the overriding one, i.e. the intentions of the parties must be taken into account first. The following rules apply only if no different intention appears.

Section 18, Rule 1

Section 18, Rule 1, provides that, where there is an unconditional contract for the sale of specific goods, in a deliverable state, the property in the goods passes to the buyer when the contract is made, and it is immaterial whether the time of payment or the time of delivery, or both, are postponed.

However, since s. 18 provides that the statutory rules do not apply if a contrary intention appears, it may be that *an agreement to the* postponement of payment or delivery would indicate that the parties do not want the property to pass. The mere fact that the buyer has not paid and the seller has not delivered does not prevent ownership passing.

Other factors may indicate that there is no intention to pass the property. Thus in *Ingram* v *Little* (1961) (*see* p. 90) it seems to have been assumed that no property was to pass until the method of payment, i.e. cash or cheque, had been agreed by the parties, and in *Lacis* v *Cashmarts* [1969] 2 QB 400 it was *held* that in a supermarket the property did not pass until the price was actually paid.

The following case is relevant to these rules.

Underwood Ltd *v* Burgh Castle Brick & Cement Syndicate [1922] I KB 343

The plaintiffs agreed to sell a condensing engine to the defendants. At the time the contract was made the engine was at the plaintiffs' premises in Millwall and was fixed to a bed of concrete by bolts. It was necessary to detach the engine before it could be delivered. The engine was damaged in the course of preparing it for dispatch, and when it was delivered the defendants refused to accept it. The plaintiffs argued that the property had passed when the contract was made, so that the defendants must accept their own goods. *Held* – The property had not passed to the defendants because the goods were not in a deliverable state when the contract was made. The engine was at that time a fixture and not in the true sense of the word a moveable chattel.

Comment: If the goods are identified and agreed upon and ready for delivery, the buyer becomes owner immediately the contract is made unless there is a contrary intention under s. 17. Thus in *Dennant* v *Skinner and Collom* [1948] 2 All ER 29, a van in a deliverable state was knocked down at auction to a purchaser. He paid by cheque and when he paid he signed a statement that the ownership was not to pass to him until the cheque had cleared. The court *held* that the ownership had passed to him on the fall of the hammer. The condition in the statement was made too late and after the purchaser became owner. Section 18, Rule I applied.

Section 18, Rule 2

In the case of specific goods not in a deliverable state, s. 18, Rule 2, provides that the property does not pass until the seller puts them into a deliverable state, and the buyer is notified thereof. For example, if a person buys a suit from a tailor's shop but the trousers need shortening, the property or ownership will not pass until the alterations are done and the buyer has been informed of this. It is assumed that 'notice' to the buyer means what it says and that if a letter of notification is posted to the buyer it is not effective on posting but only when it reaches him and would have been read in the ordinary course of business (*see Holwell Securities* v *Hughes* (1974), p. 17).

Section 18, Rule 3

In the case of conditional sales of specific goods, s. 18, Rule 3, provides that, where there is a contract for the sale of specific goods in a deliverable state, but the seller is bound to weigh, measure, test or do some other act or thing with reference to the goods for the purpose of ascertaining the price, the property does not pass until such act or thing is done, and the buyer has notice thereof. So if you buy a sack of potatoes for 12p per lb, the property will not pass until the seller has weighed the sack and told you how much it will cost. Rule 3 applies only to acts which must be done by the seller. Thus where X sold a consignment of cocoa to Y at an agreed price per 60lb, the arrangement being that Y would resell the cocoa and weigh it in order to ascertain the amount owed to X, it was *held* that the fact that Y had to weigh the cocoa did not make the contract conditional. The property passed to Y before the price was arrived at (*Nanka Bruce* v *Commonwealth Trust Ltd* [1926] AC 77).

Section 18, Rule 4

In the case of sales on approval, or on sale or return, or other similar terms, s. 18, Rule 4, provides as follows.

(a) The property passes to the buyer when he signifies his approval or acceptance to the seller, or does any other act adopting the transaction, such as pledging the goods with a third party (Rule 4(a)). **The following case illustrates this point**.

London Jewellers Ltd v Attenborough [1934] 2 KB 206

A fraudulent person named Waller told the plaintiffs that he could sell jewellery to a well-known actress and the plaintiffs gave him certain items of jewellery for that purpose. Waller signed a note in respect of each article and the note described the goods as being 'on appro' or on approval. Waller was also entitled to the difference between the selling price and the price marked on the note. Waller pledged the goods using women agents, and the defendants, who were pawnbrokers, received the goods bona fide. Waller was later arrested and charged with theft while a bailee, and the plaintiffs sued the defendants in detinue and conversion. *Held* – The defendants had a good title and were not liable. When Waller pledged the goods he signified that he adopted the transaction and had approved them. The property therefore passed to him at that moment and he was able to give the defendants a good title.

(b) If the buyer does not signify his approval or acceptance to the seller but *retains the goods without giving notice of rejection*, then the property passes on the expiration of the time, if any, fixed for the return of the goods, or on the expiration of a reasonable time (Rule 4(b)). What is a reasonable time is a question of fact. This part of the rule applies only if it is the buyer who retains the goods. Thus, if goods on sale or return are seized and retained by the buyer's unpaid creditors, the property will not pass under 4(b) (*Re Ferrier* [1944] Ch 295). **The following case provides an example of the application of Rule 4(b).**

Poole *v* Smith's Car Sales (Balham) Ltd [1962] 2 All ER 482
In August 1960, the plaintiff, a car dealer, supplied two second-hand cars to the defendants who were also car dealers. The cars were supplied on 'sale or return' terms whilst the plaintiff went on holiday, the agreement being that the defendants would return the cars if they were not sold in that time. One car was sold and paid for on 21 September 1960, but the other car, a 1956 Vauxhall Wyvern, had not been sold or returned by the end of October 1960. The plaintiff tried to get it returned by making telephone calls but finally he wrote a letter to the defendants, dated 7 November, in which he said that, if the car was not returned by 10 November 1960, it would be deemed sold to the defendants. The car was not returned until about 24 November and was then in a bad condition, having been used by the defendants' employees for their own purposes. The plaintiff rejected the car and sued for its price, i.e. £325, which was the sale or return value agreed in August 1960. *Held* – The contract was one of delivery 'on a sale or return' and therefore fell within s. 18, Rule 4. The property had passed to the defendants because it had not been returned within a reasonable amount of time and the court was particularly concerned with the depreciation of a 1956 car between September and October when the market was declining. The defendants must pay the contract price as agreed.

Where the goods are on approval and the seller has expressly provided in the contract that the property is not to pass until they are paid for, then Rule 4 will not operate because the express provision indicates a contrary intention. But if the buyer sells or disposes of the goods, a third party may still get a good title under the doctrine of estoppel, or under s. 2 of the Factors Act 1889. **The following case demonstrates this point**.

Weiner *v* Harris [1910] 1 KB 285
The plaintiff was a jeweller and he entrusted certain goods to a person called Fisher who was a traveller in the jewellery trade. The terms of the agreement were that Fisher had the goods on 'sale or return' and that they were to remain the property of the plaintiff until sold or paid for. The defendant was a moneylender and he advanced money to Fisher on the

security of the goods. The plaintiff now sued to recover the goods from the moneylender. *Held* – The defendant had a good title in spite of the terms of the contract between the plaintiff and Fisher. Fisher was a mercantile agent for the purposes of s. 1 of the Factors Act 1889, and therefore had power to pledge the goods under s. 2 of the Factors Act 1889 (*see further* p. 504).

Section 19

Section 19(1) provides that, where there is a contract for the sale of specific goods or where goods are subsequently appropriated to the contract, the seller may, by the terms of the appropriation or contract, reserve the right of disposal of the goods until certain conditions are fulfilled. In such a case, even if the goods are delivered to the buyer, or to a carrier or other bailee for the purpose of transmission to the buyer, the property in the goods does not pass until the conditions imposed by the seller are fulfilled.

The section does not safeguard the seller as much as might appear because the buyer, being a person who has bought or agreed to buy the goods, can give a good title to a third party under s. 25(1) of the Act.

Section 19(3) provides that where the seller of goods draws a bill of exchange (*see* p. 248) on the buyer for the price, and transmits the bill of exchange and bill of lading to the buyer together to secure acceptance or payment of the bill of exchange, the buyer is bound to return the bill of lading if he does not honour the bill of exchange, and if he wrongfully retains the bill of lading, the property in the goods does not pass to him.

Here again there is no complete safeguard for the seller. It is true that the passing of the property is conditional upon the bill of exchange being accepted and honoured, but a transfer of the bill of lading to a third party who takes bona fide and for value gives the third party a good title under s. 25(1) of the Sale of Goods Act, and prevents the seller from exercising his right of lien or stoppage *in transitu* (*see* p. 311) against the third party under s. 47(2) of the Sale of Goods Act and s. 10 of the Factors Act 1889.

Reservation of title by seller

It is now common for sellers of goods to try to protect themselves against the worst effects of a company receivership or liquidation by inserting retention clauses of one form or another into their contracts of sale. These are allowed by s. 19(1) of the Sale of Goods Act 1979 (*see above*). These clauses sometimes called 'Romalpa' clauses after the name of the case in which they first gained prominence in the UK, have as their purpose the retention of the seller's ownership in the goods until the buyer has paid for them, even though the buyer is given possession of the goods.

If the clause works and the purchasing company goes into receivership or liquidation because of insolvency, then the seller is able to recover the goods which the purchasing company still has and the proceeds of resale by the purchasing company. The seller will normally find such a procedure more advantageous than:

(a) proving in a liquidation for whatever he can get by way of dividend leaving his goods to be sold for the benefit of creditors generally, or

(b) in a receivership leaving his goods with the receiver who may in law continue the company's business without paying its existing debts, including that of the seller.

Retention clauses have been used on the Continent for much longer than they have in the UK. They are an understandable reaction by unsecured trade creditors to the increasing number of insolvencies in which a bank is found to hold a debenture giving a floating charge over the insolvent company's assets to secure an overdraft. The bank, being a secured creditor, takes the company's assets first, subject to certain preferential payments, through the medium of a receivership leaving trade creditors unprovided for. **There have been a number of legal decisions on the use of retention clauses. The following are among the most instructive**.

The Romalpa case (Aluminium Industrie Vaassen BV v Romalpa Aluminium [1976] 2 All ER 552)

This was the first case which alerted the legal and accountancy professions to the problems which retention clauses might cause in insolvency practice.

The facts of the case were that AIV sold aluminium foil to Romalpa, the contractual conditions of sale being:

(a) that the ownership of the material to be delivered by AIV would only be transferred to the purchaser when he had met all that was owing to AIV, no matter on what grounds;

(b) that Romalpa should store the foil separately;

(c) that if the foil was used to make new objects, those objects should be stored separately and be owned by AIV as *security* for payment;

(d) that Romalpa could sell the new objects but so long as they had not discharged their debt they should hand over to AIV if requested the claims they had against purchasers from Romalpa.

Romalpa got into financial difficulties and was in debt to its bankers in the sum of £200,000. The bank had a debenture secured over Romalpa's assets and appointed a receiver under that debenture. At the time of the receiver's appointment Romalpa owed AIV £122,000 and in order to recover some of that money at the expense of the bank AIV sought, under their conditions of sale, to recover from Romalpa foil valued in round terms at £50,000 and the cash proceeds of resold foil of some £35,000. The proceeds had been received from third-party purchasers from Romalpa after the receiver was appointed and he had kept the fund of £35,000 separate so that it was not mixed with Romalpa's other funds and was therefore identifiable.

The Court of Appeal *held* that the foil was recoverable and so were the proceeds of sale since there was a fiduciary relationship between AIV and Romalpa. This arose because ownership in the goods had not passed to Romalpa, so that Romalpa was a bailee of AIV's goods and AIV was the bailor. This relationship is fiduciary and allows the bailor to recover the goods from his bailee. In addition, the fiduciary duty stemming from the bailment includes the right to trace the proceeds of sale so long as the goods bailed have not been paid for. These rules derive from *Re Hallett's Estate* (1880) 13 Ch D 696.

Therefore Romalpa was accountable to AIV for the foil and the proceeds of its sale and AIV could trace the proceeds into the hands of the receiver.

As regards a claim by counsel for Romalpa that the retention clause created a charge which should have been registered under s. 396 of the Companies Act 1985, and that the retention clause was inoperative because there had been no such registration, the court decided that since ownership had not passed to Romalpa the charge was not over the property of Romalpa and so s. 396 did not apply, that section being confined to charges over the property of a company. In addition, the Romalpa clause included a contractual charge over mixed objects. The court did not give a decision as to the position in regard to this charge since there was no need in the case to use it. The claim was merely for foil remaining in the buyer's possession and for the proceeds of sale, and both of these items could be recovered on the basis of the bailor/bailee relationship.

The Borden case (Borden (UK) Ltd v Scottish Timber Products Ltd [1979] 3 All ER 961)

In this case Borden (B) supplied resin to Scottish Timber (S) which (S) used in making chipboard. B inserted the following retention clause in the contract under which the resin was supplied:

> Goods supplied by the company shall be at the purchaser's risk immediately on delivery to the purchaser or into custody on the purchaser's behalf (whichever is the sooner) and the purchaser should therefore be insured accordingly. Property and goods supplied hereunder will pass to the customer when: (a) the goods the subject of this contract, and (b) all other goods the subject of any other contract between the company and the customer which, at the time of payment of the full price of the goods sold under this contract, have been delivered to the customer but not paid for in full, have been paid for in full.

S went into receivership and B sought to trace their resin into chipboard made from the resin and also to trace the proceeds of sale of chipboard made with the resin.

The Court of Appeal decided that S was not a bailee in spite of the clause. Bailment implied the right to redelivery of the resin and B must have known that there would be no true bailment because resin was supplied only in sufficient quantities for two days' production because that is all the resin which S had room to store. B must therefore have been taken to know that the resin would be mixed with goods belonging to S almost immediately. The resin had ceased to exist except as chipboard over which there was *no contractual charge*. Thus there was no fiduciary relationship; tracing was not available. If the clause had created a contractual charge over the board it would apparently, have been registerable, being created by S at least in part over its own property. The decision in *Romalpa* was not overruled but distinguished.

Comment: The *Borden* case, and a rather large number of subsequent cases, suggest that in the company situation retention clauses over mixed goods will not be effective unless they are registered under s. 396 of the Companies Act 1985 as a charge over the assets of the purchasing company.

(ii) Furthermore, where the goods are to be used in manufacture the court is reluctant to find that a bailment exists. In a bailment, as for example, where you leave a suitcase in a left luggage office, it is normally the intention that the goods should be returned to the owner in their existing state. A person who delivers goods to another knowing that they will be used in manufacture must give that other some sort of ownership of them. This prevents a bailment so that any goods in stock which have yet to be used in manufacture cannot be traced. There is no fiduciary relationship.

Reservation of title: an extension of rights

In the past retention clauses in contracts of sale have worked only in relation to monies owed in respect of the goods actually made the subject of a retention clause. However, the House of Lords decided in an appeal from the Scottish Court of Session in which English law would also apply in the same way that a retention of title provision can cover not only the price of the very goods which are the subject of a particular contract of sale containing a retention clause, but also to debts due to the seller under other contracts.

Armour and Carron Co Ltd *v* Thyssen Edelstahlwerke AG, *The Times*, 25 October 1990

Thyssen were the owners of steel strip. They transferred possession in it to Carron under what was undoubtedly a contract of sale. Carron agreed that it should receive possession of the steel strip on delivery but should not acquire the property (ownership) until *all* debts due to Thyssen had been paid. It was also agreed that debts due to companies in the Thyssen group were deemed to be such debts. Armour & Co were the receivers of the assets of Carron which had not paid the £71,769 purchase price of the steel strip.

When the matter came before the Second Division of the Inner House of the Court of Session the argument put forward by the receivers of Carron that the clause was really an attempt to create a security over moveable property was accepted. However, this was rejected by the House of Lords on the grounds that it was not possible to create a security over goods which you did not own.

The judgment of the House of Lords was based upon an application of ss. 17 and 19 of the Sale of Goods Act 1979. Here, said the House of Lords, Thyssen, by the terms of the contract of sale, had in effect reserved the right of disposal of the steel strip until fulfilment of the conditions that *all* debts due to them by Carron had been paid. By reason of the 1979 Act that had the effect that the property in the goods did not pass to Carron until that condition had been fulfilled.

The same was true where the provision covered not only the price of the very goods which were the subject of a particular contract of sale, but also debts due to the seller under other contracts.

Therefore, the steel strip belonged to Thyssen and not to the receivers on behalf of Carron.

Comment: Presumably, also, since the goods were not the property of the company, the retention clause was not in the nature of a registerable charge over the company's property because the property was not that of the company. If, however, the goods are mixed with those of the company, as in *Borden (UK) Ltd v Scottish Timber Products Ltd* [1979] 3 All ER 961 (seller's resin mixed with the company's goods to make chipboard), then the retention clause would have been in the nature of a floating charge over part, at least, of the company's property and void in insolvency proceedings unless registered. This decision would seem to make no change in the position in *Borden.*

However, where the goods are identifiable in stock at the time of the insolvency proceedings, the seller can recover them, not only if the price of the goods themselves is not paid, *but also if other debts due to the seller have not been met.*

Reservation of title: appointment of an administrator

In addition, once a petition has been presented to the court for the appointment of an administrator to the purchasing company, the owner of goods delivered under a retention clause cannot take steps to recover them. He can against a receiver or liquidator, and indeed if a receiver or liquidator sells goods subject to a valid retention clause he is personally liable in damages to the owner for conversion of the goods (*Schott Sohne v Radford* [1987] CLY para. 3585). The administration procedure which is contained in the Insolvency Act 1986 is designed and intended to promote the survival of companies as a going concern and to secure the preservation of jobs. An administrator is appointed by the court on the petition of the company or on the petition of the directors or on the petition of any creditor. The debt need not be of any minimum value and unsecured creditors can petition. This is a major contrast with the appointment of a receiver, now called an administrative receiver, who can only be appointed by secured creditors. The Insolvency Act 1986 gives an administrator full powers to manage the company, hopefully to the point at which he can make it viable again and vacate office in favour of a permanent management.

WHERE THE GOODS ARE UNASCERTAINED

Section 16 provides that, where there is a contract for the sale of unascertained goods, no property in the goods is transferred to the buyer unless and until the goods are ascertained. This is a common-sense rule because until the goods have been identified it is not possible to say in which goods the property is passing. Where an unidentified part of a bulk is sold there is no appropriation until there is severance of the goods sold from the rest. **The following case provides an illustration**.

Laurie and Morewood v Dudin & Sons [1926] I KB 223

On 2 February 1925, Messrs Alcock and Sons sold to John Wilkes & Sons 200 quarters of maize from 618 quarters belonging to Alcock and Sons and lying in the defendants' warehouse. Wilkes & Sons were given a delivery note which they sent to the defendants who were therefore on notice of the sale. On 18 February, Wilkes & Sons sold the 200 quarters of maize to the plaintiffs and gave them a delivery note which the plaintiffs sent to the defendants on 19 February. On both occasions when they received delivery notes the defendants merely made entries in their books and no attempt was made to appropriate the goods to the contract. Wilkes & Sons failed to pay Alcock and Sons for the maize and Alcock and Sons instructed the defendants to withhold delivery. The plaintiffs now sued the defendants in detinue, claiming that the property in the maize had passed to them. *Held* – The plaintiffs' action failed. The maize did not belong to them because there had been no appropriation of the goods and therefore the property in the maize had not passed either to Wilkes & Sons or to the plaintiffs.

There are many contracts for the sale of unascertained goods where the parties do not deal in their contract with the passing of the property. Where this is so s. 18, Rule 5, applies. Rule 5(1) provides that where there is a contract for the sale of unascertained or future goods by description, and goods of that description and in a deliverable state are unconditionally appropriated to the contract either by the seller with the assent of the buyer, or by the buyer with the assent of the seller, the property in the goods thereupon passes to the buyer.

The relationship between s. 16 and s. 18, Rule 5(1), is a difficult one. It seems that the court may take the view that the property has passed where part of a larger quantity is sold leaving what is left belonging to the buyer, even though there is no unconditional appropriation of that balance within the terms of s. 18, Rule 5(1), if the court thinks that it was the intention of the parties that ascertainment should also be appropriation. **The following case and comment makes this point**.

Wait and James v Midland Bank (1926) 31 Com Cas 172

The sellers sold 1,250 quarters of wheat on credit from a larger cargo lying in a warehouse. The buyers were given delivery orders which were acceptable to the warehouseman for purposes of delivery when required. The buyers did not ask for delivery but pledged the delivery orders to a bank as security. At this time no severance of the buyers' wheat had taken place. Later the sellers sold and delivered the remainder of the wheat leaving the buyers' share of the cargo in the warehouse. It was *held* by Roche J – that the second sale had the effect of passing the property in the remaining wheat to the first buyers and the bank's security was good against the 1,250 quarters left.

Comment: (i) Roche J appears to have assumed that ascertainment was enough to pass the property. There had been no unconditional appropriation as required by s. 18, Rule 5.

(ii) This case was applied in *Karlshamns Oljefabriker* v *Eastport Navigation* [1982] I All ER 208. The buyer purchased 6,000 tons of copra under four contracts, 22,000 tons of copra was loaded on to the vessel *Elafi* which belonged to the defendants. It was to be shipped from the Philippines to Sweden. 16,000 tons were off-loaded at Hamburg and Rotterdam. The remaining 6,000 tons went on to Sweden. On arrival in Sweden it was discovered that the copra had been damaged by water. The *Elafi* was allegedly not seaworthy. The buyers said the goods were not theirs because the property had not passed. It was *held* in the High Court that it had. Mr Justice Mustill in applying the *Wait* case, referred to the judgment of Roche J and noted that it omitted any mention of s. 18, Rule 5. He then went on to say:

> In my judgment, this objection adds nothing to the argument in relation to ascertainment. It is true that in some cases the ascertainment of goods may not be the same as the unconditional appropriation of them, although the distinction would usually be difficult, if not impossible to draw. But here I cannot see any difference . . . Before leaving the question of appropriation I should draw attention to one other factor, namely that the want of an unconditional appropriation is not an absolute bar to the passing of the property but merely one of the factors to be taken into account when ascertaining the presumed intentions of the parties.

Assent to appropriation may be express or implied and be given before or after appropriation is made. Under s. 20(1) risk passes with the property. The person who has the risk is not necessarily in possession of the goods. **This is illustrated by the following case**.

Pignataro v Gilroy & Son [1919] I KB 459

By a contract made on 12 February 1918, the defendants sold to the plaintiff 140 bags of rice, the plaintiff to take delivery within 14 days. The rice was unascertained when the contract was made. On 27 February, the plaintiff sent a cheque for the rice and asked for a delivery order. On 28 February the defendants sent a delivery order for 125 bags which were lying at a place called Chambers' Wharf. A letter accompanying the delivery order said that the remaining 15 bags were at the defendants' place of business at 50 Long Acre, and requested the plaintiff to collect them there. The plaintiff did not send for the 15 bags until 25 March when it was found that they had been stolen without negligence on the part of the defendants. *Held* – the goods were at the plaintiff's risk. He had not dissented from the appropriation made by the defendants, and his assent to it must therefore be implied.

The necessity for the buyer's assent to appropriation gives rise to difficulties where a consumer orders goods by post. Where under a commercial contract the seller is required to ship the goods to the buyer the shipping is regarded as an unconditional appropriation and the assent of the buyer is *assumed* (*James* v *Commonwealth* (1939) 62 CLR 339). This rule seems inappropriate in the case of consumer sales by post. Though the law is not clear it is suggested that the posting of consumer goods should not pass the property otherwise the goods are, unknown to the buyer, at his risk during transit. There is no need to assume the consumer's consent to appropriation since in that sort of case he has agreed merely to dispatch of the goods and not to a particular appropriation.

An example of an unconditional appropriation, i.e. delivery to a carrier, is given in s. 18, Rule 5(2), which provides that where, in pursuance of the contract, the seller delivers goods to the buyer or to a carrier or other bailee (whether named by the buyer or not) for the purpose of transmission to the buyer, and does not reserve the right of disposal, he is deemed to have unconditionally appropriated the goods to the contract. However, delivery to a carrier does not pass the property if identical goods destined for different owners are mixed nor if the seller is bound to weigh, measure or test the goods in order to ascertain the price.

The following two cases provide illustrations of these rules.

Healey v Howlett & Sons [1917] 1 KB 337

Howlett & Sons were fish dealers in Ireland and they supplied fish to English customers. They had an agent at Holyhead, all fish being sent to the agent who selected parcels of fish for dispatch to customers in England. The appellant was a fish salesman in London and he ordered 20 boxes of mackerel from the respondents. The respondents dispatched 122 boxes of mackerel to their agent in Holyhead to fulfil the appellant's order and others. The agent selected 20 boxes for dispatch to the appellant, but because of delays in getting the fish to Holyhead, the fish was found to be bad on arrival in London. The delay in getting the fish to Holyhead was not the respondents' fault. The appellant refused to pay the respondents and the respondents sued for the full price on the ground that the dispatch of 122 boxes of fish to their agent was sufficient appropriation to pass the property to Healey in respect of his 20 boxes. Howlett succeeded at first instance and Healey now appealed from that decision. *Held* – There was no appropriation until the agent at Holyhead earmarked the 20 boxes for the appellant. The fish had deteriorated before arrival at Holyhead and was at the respondents' risk under s. 16 when it did deteriorate. The appellant was therefore not liable to pay for the fish.

Comment: A puts 100 boxes of fish on a train from Holyhead to London. No appropriation is made but 25 boxes are for B at Colwyn Bay, 25 for C at Crewe, 25 for D at Rugby, and 25 for E at London. Appropriation is made at each station. The goods are damaged in an accident at Watford. Do the goods belong to E? *Wait* and *Karlshamns* (see *above*) would suggest that they might.

National Coal Board v Gamble [1958] 3 All ER 203

The Coal Board supplied coal to a buyer at a colliery by loading from a hopper into the buyer's lorry. The lorry was then driven to a weighbridge so that the weight of the coal could be ascertained and a weight-ticket, as required by statute, issued. The court *held* that the property did not pass until the coal had been weighed and the ticket given to and accepted by the buyer. The court was also of opinion that under the system in operation at the colliery any coal in excess of the buyer's requirement could have been unloaded before the weight-ticket was issued and accepted. It would seem, therefore, that the court was assuming that although appropriation took place when the coal was loaded on to the lorry, it was not unconditional until it was weighed and the weight-ticket accepted by the buyer.

TRANSFER OF PROPERTY AND RISK

The question of the transfer of property in goods is important, because risk generally passes with the property. The maxim is *res perit domino* (a thing perishes to the disadvantage of its owner).

Section 20 provides that, unless otherwise agreed, the goods remain at the seller's risk until the property therein is transferred to the buyer, but when the property in them is transferred to the buyer, the goods are at the buyer's risk whether delivery has been made or not, i.e. the rule applies, irrespective of who had possession of the goods at the time the property passed (*see Pignataro v Gilroy & Son* (1919) *above*). It seems that there may sometimes be a transfer of risk without transfer of the property and a transfer of the property without risk.

The following cases provide an illustration of this.

Sterns Ltd v Vickers Ltd [1923] I KB 78

On 3 January 1920, the Admiralty sold to Vickers Ltd 120,000 gallons of white spirit out of a larger quantity of 200,000 gallons then lying at Thames Haven in Tank No. 78. The tank belonged to a storage company called London and Thames Haven Oil Wharves Company. Vickers Ltd sold the spirit to Sterns Ltd, who did not take delivery for some months. When they did take delivery, the specific gravity of the spirit had changed by deterioration over time. Sterns Ltd claimed damages for breach of warranty against the sellers. *Held* – The spirit was at the plaintiffs' risk from the time of sale and the defendants were not liable for breach of warranty.

Comment: This seems to be a wholly exceptional case. The property had clearly not passed to Sterns because there had been no appropriation.

Head v Tattersall (1870) LR 7 Ex 7

Tattersall sold a horse to Head warranting that it had hunted with the Bicester Hounds, and giving Head the right to return the horse by a certain date if it did not comply with the warranty. Head discovered that the horse had not hunted with the Bicester Hounds and returned it to Tattersall within the time stipulated. However, whilst the horse was in Head's possession, it was injured though without negligence on his part. *Held* – in the circumstances it was possible to take the view that the property had passed but not the risk, and Tattersall was obliged to accept the injured horse.

Comment: The general rule is that where goods are delivered on approval or on sale or return the property in them remains with the seller until the buyer adopts the transaction. However, this case shows that it is possible to enter into a transaction which has a similar purpose but under which the property passes immediately to the buyer, but not the risk.

The legal principle would seem to be that the risk remains with the seller where, under the contract, the buyer has a right of rejection.

Of course, the goods may be despatched at the seller's risk, in which case s. 33 provides that, where the seller of goods agrees to deliver them at his own risk at a place other than that where they are then sold, the buyer must, nevertheless, unless otherwise agreed, take any risk of deterioration in the goods necessarily incident to the course of transit.

In connection with this it is necessary to note two further provisions of s. 20:

(a) Where delivery has been delayed through the fault of either buyer or seller, the goods are at the risk of the party at fault as regards any loss which might not have occurred but for such fault. **The following case demonstrates this**.

Demby, Hamilton & Co Ltd v Barden [1949] 1 All ER 435

The plaintiffs were sellers of apple juice, and on 8 November 1945 they entered into a contract with the defendants who were wine merchants. Under the contract the plaintiffs were to supply and the defendants were to buy 30 tons of apple juice to be delivered by lorry in weekly instalments, the contract to be completed by the end of February 1946. The plaintiffs crushed a quantity of apples and put the juice into casks, but the property did not pass at that stage since the casks were not specifically appropriated to the contract. 20½ tons of apple juice were delivered and at that stage the buyers said that they could not take the other instalments until further notice. The last delivery was made on 4 April 1946. The plaintiffs repeatedly asked for delivery instructions, and on 7 November 1946 they informed the defendants that the contents of the remaining casks had gone putrid and had been thrown away. The plaintiffs now sued for the price of the goods sold and delivered, and for damages in respect of the apple juice which had been thrown away. *Held* – under the proviso to s. 20 the goods were at the buyer's risk because he was responsible for the delay. If the sellers could have sold the remainder of the apple juice elsewhere, the loss might have fallen on them, but their contract with the defendants obliged the plaintiffs to hold the goods available for delivery as and when required by the defendants. The plaintiffs' action for the price of the goods sold and for damages succeeded.

(b) Nothing in s. 20 affects the duties and liabilities of either seller or buyer as a bailee of the goods of the other party (s. 20(3)). A seller must still take proper care of the goods even though the buyer is late in taking delivery of them. Thus the risk which passes with the property does not include damage due to the other party's negligence.

TRANSFER OF TITLE BY NON-OWNERS

General

The sections in the Sale of Goods Act which will be discussed here are concerned with the circumstances in which a person who is not the owner of goods can give a good title to those goods to a third party.

The general rule of common law is expressed in the maxim *nemo dat quod non habet* (no one can give what he has not got). It follows that, if the seller's title is defective, so is the buyer's. This rule of the common law is confirmed by s. 21(1) which provides that, subject to certain other sections of the Act, where goods are sold by a person who is not the owner thereof, and who does not sell them under the authority or with the consent of the owner, the buyer acquires no better title to the goods than the seller had, unless the owner of the goods is by his conduct precluded from denying the seller's authority to sell.

There are, however, the following main exceptions to the rule.

Estoppel

Where the owner of goods, by his words or conduct, represents to the buyer that the seller is the true owner, the owner is precluded from denying the title of the buyer. The doctrine of estoppel is preserved in the final words of s. 21(1) of the Act, i.e. 'unless the owner of the goods is by his conduct precluded from denying the seller's authority to sell'. **The following case provides an example**.

Henderson & Co v Williams [1985] 1 QB 521

The plaintiffs were sugar merchants at Hull. The defendant was a warehouseman at Hull and Goole. On 3 June 1894, a fraudulent person named Fletcher, posing as the agent of Robinson, negotiated a purchase of sugar from Messrs Grey & Co, who were Liverpool merchants. The sugar was lying in the defendant's warehouse at Goole, and Messrs Grey & Co sent a telegram and later a letter advising the defendant that the sugar was to be held to the order of Fletcher, and the defendant entered the order in his books. Robinson was a reputable dealer and a customer of Messrs Grey & Co, and of course Fletcher had no right to act on Robinson's behalf. Fletcher sold the goods to the plaintiffs who, before paying the price, got a statement from the defendant that the goods were held to the order of Fletcher. The defendant later discovered Fletcher's fraud and refused to release the sugar to the plaintiffs who now sued in conversion. *Held* – The defendant was estopped from denying Fletcher's title and was liable in damages based on the market price of the goods at the date of refusal to deliver. Further the true owners, Messrs Grey & Co, could not set up their title to the sugar against that of the plaintiffs, since they had allowed Fletcher to hold himself out as the true owner.

Estoppel does not arise merely because the owner of goods allows another to have possession of them (*Mercantile Bank of India Ltd* v *Central Bank of India Ltd* [1938] AC 287) and attempts have been made to set up a doctrine of estoppel by negligence, the third party alleging that it is the negligence of the true owner which has given the non-owner the apparent authority to sell. However, in order to establish negligence, it is necessary to show the existence of a duty of care in the owner, and such a duty, which is a matter of law, does not seem to exist where the owner has even by negligence lost his property or facilitated its theft or other form of fraudulent disposition. (*See*, for example, *Cundy* v *Lindsay* (1878) (*see* p. 89) and *Ingram* v *Little* (1961) (*see* p. 90).)

However, where the owner is face to face with the person who defrauds him when the contract is made, it would seem that an element of negligence in the owner will prevent him from recovering the property from a third party (*see Lewis* v *Averay* (1971), p. 90).

So if X loses his watch and Y finds it and sells it to Z then X can still claim his property; and it does not matter that X's negligence enabled Y to sell the watch to Z. In order for s. 21(1) to apply to estop the true owner from denying the authority of the seller to sell there must be a representation by statement or conduct by the true owner that the seller was entitled to sell the goods. **The following case illustrates this point**.

Eastern Distributors Ltd v Goldring [1957] 2 QB 600

A person named Murphy was the owner of a Bedford van and wished to buy a Chrysler car from Coker who was a car dealer. Murphy could not find the money to pay the hire-purchase deposit on the Chrysler. Coker suggested that Murphy authorize him to sell the van to a finance company and get an agreement from the finance company under which they agreed to sell the van to Murphy on hire-purchase terms and then Murphy could apply the proceeds of the sale of his van in putting down deposits on the van and the Chrysler.

Murphy gave Coker authority, but limited it to selling the van and arranging the hire-purchase of the van and the Chrysler. Under the authority given to him Coker was bound to effect *both* transactions and not one only. Murphy then signed the necessary documents leaving Coker to fill them in. In the proposal form for the hire-purchase of the van Coker described himself as owner of the vehicle and without authority from Murphy sold the van to the plaintiffs, who were the finance company, as if it was his own. The plaintiffs then hired it out to Murphy and sent him a copy of the agreement. The hire-purchase of the Chrysler was not carried out and later Coker told Murphy that the whole deal had fallen through, and was cancelled. Murphy then sold the van which he believed to be his own to Goldring, who bought in good faith and without knowledge of Murphy's previous dealings. Murphy made no payments under the hire-purchase agreement, and the plaintiffs terminated it and claimed the van or its value from the defendant. *Held* – by the Court of Appeal –

(a) Coker had no actual authority to sell the van separately to the plaintiffs but only as part of a double transaction. However, Murphy, by providing Coker with documents which enabled him to represent himself to the plaintiffs as entitled to the van, had clothed Coker with apparent authority to sell and was prevented by s. 21(1) of the Sale of Goods Act from denying that authority. The plaintiffs had obtained a good title and Murphy had no title to give Goldring.

(b) Section 25(1) of the Sale of Goods Act did not make the sale to Goldring valid, because Murphy was, after the hire-purchase agreement, not in possession as a seller but as a bailee by virtue of the agreement.

Comment: (i) If Goldring was a private purchaser he would now obtain a good title under the

Hire-Purchase Act 1964, Part III, as substituted by s. 192 and Sch. 4, para. 22 of the Consumer Credit Act 1974.

(ii) Section 21(1) does not apply to an agreement to sell. In *Shaw* v *Commissioner of Police of the Metropolis* [1987] 3 All ER 405 A advertised his car for sale. B said he was interested in buying it. A let B have possession and signed a letter certifying that he had sold the car to B. A also signed the transfer slip attached to the car registration document to the same effect. B agreed to sell the car to C, the property to pass when B had been paid. B left the car with C and was not paid. B was not seen again. A claimed the car from C. The Court of Appeal said A was entitled to it. Lloyd LJ did not doubt that the signing of the letter and the transfer slip by A was 'the clearest possible representation intended to be relied on by the ultimate purchaser that the claimant had transferred the ownership to B'. Therefore, if C had *bought* the car he would have acquired a good title under s. 21, but it was accepted that the property in the car was not to pass until B was paid which he never was. Therefore, C had only 'agreed to buy'. Since s. 21 applied 'where goods are sold', the Court of Appeal decided that the section could not apply to an agreement to sell and therefore A was still entitled to his car.

(iii) Section 25 of the 1979 Act did not apply because B had not apparently 'bought or agreed to buy' on the evidence but had merely taken possession. Section 2 of the Factors Act 1889 did not help either because there was no evidence that B was a mercantile agent (see *further* p. 504).

Sales by factors and sales by other agents under apparent or usual authority

Section 21(2) provides that nothing in the Sale of Goods Act shall affect the provisions of the Factors Act 1889 or any enactment enabling the apparent owner of goods to dispose of them as if he were the true owner thereof. The Sale of Goods Act thus preserves the power of disposition in such cases. (*See further* p. 504.)

Section 62(2) provides that the rules relating to the law of principal and agent are to be preserved, and so a sale by an agent without actual authority will give the purchaser a good title if the sale is within the agent's apparent authority or usual authority. (*See further* pp. 497–8.)

Special powers of sale

Section 21(2)(b) provides that nothing in the Act shall affect the validity of any contract of sale under any special common law or statutory power of sale, or under the order of a court of competent jurisdiction. Thus a pawnbroker has the right to sell goods which have been pledged with him if the loan is not repaid. The person who buys from the pawnbroker will get a good title to the goods.

A *sheriff* has power by statute to sell goods taken by the bailiffs from the premises of a person who has not paid a judgment debt, and under s. 1 of the Innkeepers Act 1878, an *innkeeper's lien* over the goods of his guests for his charges may be converted into a power of sale. A sale giving a good title by a *bailee* who has carried out work on goods, e.g. a watch repairer, is possible under the provisions of the Torts (Interference with Goods) Act 1977, s. 12.

The Rules of the Supreme Court give the court a jurisdiction to order the sale of goods which for any just and sufficient reason it may be desirable to have sold at once, as where they are perishable goods. The purchaser of the goods sold will obtain a good title in spite of the owner's lack of consent.

Market overt

Section 22(1) provides that where goods are sold in *market overt*, according to the usage of the market, the buyer acquires a good title to the goods, provided he buys them in good faith and without notice of any defect or want of title on the part of the seller. The sale of horses is not covered by this section and is not within the rules of market overt. Apart from this the Act preserves the ancient rule relating to sales in open market, and applies to markets throughout England so long as the market is open, public and legally constituted either by grant of charter, long-standing custom or statute, provided the goods are usually sold in the market. There are no markets overt in Wales or Scotland. The person who wishes so to protect his title must prove that the place in which the sale took place was market overt. Every shop within the City of London is market overt in respect of goods usually sold in that shop. Thus a sale of a watch by a confectioner would not be a sale in market overt, even though the shop was within the market.

Market overt is held every day except Sunday and Bank Holidays in London, but elsewhere only on recognized market days. The rule does not apply to sales between traders in the same market; nor does it apply to dispositions other than sales, so that a pledge would not be covered by the rule.

To obtain the protection of market overt, the sale must commence and finish in open market in full view of the public between sunrise and sunset, and be according to the usage of the particular market and the buyer must act in good faith and give value. A sale in the back room of a shop to which the public can only gain access by invitation is not a sale in market overt.

The following cases provide illustrations of the operation of the above rules.

Reid v Commr of Police of the Metropolis [1973] 2 All ER 97

In December 1969 a pair of Adam candelabra were stolen from the plaintiff's home in Chelsea. In February 1970 between 7 a.m. and 8.15 a.m., a Mr Cocks bought them at a stall in a statutory market in Southwark, the permitted hour for the opening of which was 7 a.m. When the goods were purchased the sun had not risen and it was still only half light. The plaintiff discovered the whereabouts of the goods and informed the police who took them into custody. The plaintiff claimed their return and the Court of Appeal decided that in order to establish that a sale of goods had taken place in market overt so as to convey a good title to the goods even against the true owner, it must be shown that the goods were sold between sunrise and sunset. Seeing that this sale was made before sunrise, Mr Cocks did not get a good title. The plaintiff, the true owner, was entitled to have the pair of Adam candelabra returned to him.

Comment: Usage of the market is illustrated by *Bishopsgate Motor Finance Corporation* v *Transport Brakes Ltd* [1949] 1 All ER 37. In that case a person who had a car on hire purchase put it up for sale at an auction in Maidstone market. It was not sold at auction but by a private agreement later. Maidstone market was established in 1747 by Royal Charter and was therefore a market overt. The innocent buyer could not get a good title unless the sale was according to the usage of the market. It was *held* that it was because it was customary in the Maidstone market for goods not sold at auction to be sold privately in the market after the auction.

Clayton v Le Roy [1911] 2 KB 1031

In 1902 Mrs Clayton, the plaintiff's wife, bought a gold watch from the defendant for £100 and gave it to her husband. In 1908 the watch was stolen from Major Clayton whilst he was on the Riviera and shortly afterwards the watch was pawned with a firm of pawnbrokers. In 1909 the watch was sold as an unredeemed pledge by public auction at the auctioneer's auction rooms, No. 38, Gracechurch Street in the City of London. The watch was bought at the auction by a bona fide purchaser for £26 and eventually came into the hands of a Mr Bennett who bought it for £44. In May 1910, Mr Bennett brought the watch to the defendant for examination in order to find out if it was a genuine gold watch. Mrs Clayton had told the defendant that the watch had been stolen and the defendant recognized it, and wrote to Bennett telling him that the watch was stolen and asking him how much he wanted for it. Bennett said he would let the true owner have it back, the price being what Bennett gave for it. The defendant then wrote to Mrs Clayton telling her that he had found the stolen watch and of Bennett's proposals. The Claytons instructed their solicitor to act and he went to the defendant's shop and demanded the return of the watch. The defendant refused to give it up and this action was commenced. It was *held* by Scrutton J, after inspecting the auctioneer's sale rooms, that the defence of sale in market overt failed. The city auction rooms were not a shop, and because passers-by could not see the sale taking place, the sale was not open in the sense required by the custom. The ground floor windows of the premises were ordinary office windows, and nothing could be seen from the street of what took place on the ground floor. The first floor also had office windows only and, although the sales of jewellery were advertised, a passer-by could not see them actually taking place. Because of this decision on the defence of market overt, the purchaser at the auction did not get a good title, the goods being stolen, and Bennett had derived his title from the original purchaser. The plaintiff was therefore entitled to the watch and had no need to pay Bennett anything.

Comment: Sales by a member of the public to a trader in the market will not normally be sales in market overt because the member of the public will not have displayed the goods for sale (*Ardath Tobacco* v *Ocker* (1930) 47 TLR 177).

A purchaser in market overt obtains a good title against the whole world, even though the seller had no title, except:

   (a) where the purchaser is on actual notice that the seller has no title; or
   (b) where the goods belong to the Crown.

In former times the title of a purchaser in market overt could be defeated if the person responsible for dispossessing the true owner was later convicted of false pretences or larceny. The Theft Act 1968, s. 33(3), repeals this rule and there is no longer any question of a title acquired in market overt revesting in the true owner. Under s. 28 of the Theft Act a criminal court can give a restitution order to a person who has been deprived of his property by theft but such an order does not lie against a bona fide purchaser of the goods. However, an action in conversion may be brought against the seller by the true owner because market overt does not protect the seller but only the buyer (*Peer* v *Humphrey* (1835) 2 Ad & El 495).

Sale under a voidable title

Section 23 provides that, when the seller of goods has a voidable title, but his title has not been avoided at the time of the sale, the buyer acquires a good title to the goods, provided he buys them in good faith and without notice of the seller's defect of title. Thus, if B obtains goods from S by giving S a cheque which he knows will not be met, and B sells the goods to T, who takes them bona fide and for value, T obtains a good title, provided S has not avoided the contract with B before B sells to T. The section only applies to sales, but pledges are subject to the same rule by virtue of the common law. Where the fraud is such as to render the original contract of sale void for mistake, the fraudulent buyer cannot give a good title to a third party (*see Cundy* v *Lindsay* (1878), p. 89).

If the original owner of the goods sold in circumstances of fraud or misrepresentation wishes to avoid the contract he should inform the buyer who misled him. If he cannot find him the contract is avoided when the original owner has done everything he can in the circumstances to avoid the contract. **This is illustrated in the following case.**

Car & Universal Finance Co Ltd v Caldwell [1964] 2 All ER 547

On 12 January 1960, Mr Caldwell sold a motor car to a firm called Dunn's Transport, receiving a cheque signed 'for and on behalf of Dunn's Transport, W. Foster, F. Norris'. Caldwell presented the cheque to the bank but it was dishonoured, and so he went to see the police and asked them to recover the car. He also saw officials of the Automobile Association and asked them to trace the car by their patrols. The car was found on 20 January 1960, in the possession of a director of a firm of car dealers called Motobella & Co Ltd. The company claimed to have bought it on 15 January from Norris and to have a good title, though the director concerned was on notice of the defect in Norris's title. On 29 January, the defendant's solicitors demanded the car from Motobella and at the same time Norris was arrested and pleaded guilty to obtaining the car by false pretences. The defendant sued Motobella & Co Ltd for the return of the car and obtained judgment, but when he tried to repossess the car, a finance house, Car & Universal Finance Co Ltd, claimed that it belonged to them. It appeared that Motobella had transferred the ownership to a finance house called G & C Finance on 15 January 1960, and they had transferred it to the plaintiffs on 3 August 1960, the latter company taking the vehicle in good faith. In thi. action the plaintiffs claimed the car. It was *held* – that Caldwell was entitled to it because amongst other things, he had avoided the contract of sale to Norris when he asked the police to get the car back for him so that later sales of the car to Motobella and to G & C Finance did not pass the property.

Comment: (i) Although this case decides that a contract of sale induced by fraud can be rescinded without actually communicating with the fraudulent person, the third party will in many cases keep the property by relying on s. 25(1) of the Sale of Goods Act 1979. This happened in *Newtons of Wembley Ltd* v *Williams* [1964] 3 All ER 532. In that case the seller had rescinded a contract under which the buyer obtained goods by fraud but it was *held* that as the buyer had bought the goods and was in possession with the seller's consent, he could still pass a good title under what is now s. 25(1) of the Sale of Goods Act 1979 to a third party buyer who acted in good faith. The *Car & Universal Finance* case was distinguished on the grounds that there the person who bought from the seller with a voidable title had notice of the defect in his title and so could not be protected by s. 25(1).

(ii) The distinction is really between a *direct* and an *indirect* sale. In *Caldwell* the fraudsman did not sell direct to the purchaser. The first sale was to Motobella which had notice of the defect in title and so s. 25(1) did not apply, said the court, to give a good title to the finance house. In the *Newtons* case the sale was direct by the fraudsman to the innocent third party and the latter got a good title under s. 25(1). The distinction between a direct and an indirect sale is somewhat illogical and the Law Commission recommended in its 12th Report, Cmnd 2958 1966, that until the person deceived actually got in touch with the fraudsman all sales direct or indirect should give a good title to innocent purchasers.

Sale by a seller in possession of the goods after sale

Section 24, which is similar to s. 8 of the Factors Act 1889, provides that, where a person, having sold goods, continues in possession of the goods, or of the documents of title to the goods, the delivery or transfer by that person or by a mercantile agent acting for him, of the goods or documents of title under any sale, pledge, or other disposition thereof, to any person receiving the same in good faith and without notice of the previous sale, shall have the same effect as if the person making the delivery or transfer were expressly authorized by the owner of the goods to make the same.

The section applies where the property in the goods has passed but the seller still retains possession. If the property in the goods has not passed, the seller gives a good title by virtue of his ownership and not by virtue of the section.

There are a number of decisions which suggest that it is not enough to prove that the seller was still in possession but that the third party must show that the seller was in possession as a seller and that he had not changed his legal position by some subsequent transaction, e.g. as where he had become a bailee under a hire purchase agreement (*see*, for example, *Eastern Distributors* v *Goldring* (1957), p. 291). These decisions were put in doubt by the ruling of the Privy Council in *Pacific Motor*

Auctions v *Motor Credits Ltd* [1965] 2 All ER 105. In that case dealers sold cars to the plaintiffs but remained in possession of them for display purposes. They were authorized to sell as agents for the plaintiffs. This authority was later revoked by the plaintiffs but the dealers sold to the defendants who were bona fide purchasers. It was *held* that the defendants had obtained a good title by reason of the provision in the New South Wales Sale of Goods Act which was identical to s. 24 of the 1979 Act. The Privy Council decided that the words 'continues . . . in possession' in s. 24 must be regarded as referring to the continuity of physical possession regardless of any private transaction between seller and buyer which might alter the legal title under which possession was held. This decision was followed later by the Court of Appeal in *Worcester Works Finance Ltd* v *Cooden Engineering Co Ltd* [1971] 3 All ER 708 and it would seem that there is now no need to show that the seller was in possession as a seller.

The section only protects the title of third parties, and the original buyer can sue the seller either in conversion, or for breach of contract when he fails to deliver the goods, or may protect himself by means of a Bill of Sale.

Sale by a buyer in possession

Section 25(1) of the Sale of Goods Act, which is similar to s. 9 of the Factors Act 1889, provides that, where a person, having bought or agreed to buy goods, obtains, with the consent of the seller, possession of the goods or the documents of title thereto, the delivery or transfer by that person, or by a mercantile agent acting for him, of the goods or documents of title, under any sale, pledge, or other disposition thereof, to any person receiving the same in good faith and without notice of any lien or other right of the original seller in respect of the goods, shall have the same effect as if the person making the delivery or transfer were a mercantile agent in possession of the goods or documents of title with the consent of the owner.

The section applies where the buyer has possession, but the property has not passed to him. If the buyer has the property in the goods, he can give a good title without the aid of the section.

The section does not apply to persons in possession under hire-purchase contracts, because a person who is hiring the goods is not a person who has agreed to buy them. A hire-purchase contract is a contract of bailment only, with an option to purchase. However, Part III of the Hire-Purchase Act 1964 (as substituted by s. 192 and Sch. 4. para. 22 of the Consumer Credit Act 1974) protects a bona fide private (not a trade) purchaser of a motor vehicle who has bought it from a person in possession under a hire-purchase or conditional sale agreement (*see* p. 360).

A person who has goods *on approval* cannot pass a good title under this section because he has not bought or agreed to buy the goods; he has a mere option. However, he may pass a good title by virtue of his ownership if, by selling the goods, he indicates his approval (*see London Jewellers Ltd* v *Attenborough* (1934), p. 278).

It appears that the 'consent' of the seller may be sufficient to protect the title of a purchaser from the original buyer even if the latter obtained the goods by criminal fraud, as where he paid for them by a cheque which he knew would not be met (*Du Jardin* v *Beadman Bros* [1952] 2 All ER 160. Furthermore the fact that the seller withdraws his consent after he has given the buyer possession does not prevent s. 9 of the Factors Act 1889 operating to protect the title of a purchaser from the buyer, since s. 2(2) of the 1889 Act specifically provides for this situation.

It should be noted that where the buyer has possession of the documents of title but not of the goods complications can arise in respect to the seller's lien and right of stopping the goods in transit (*see* pp. 309–11).

It was thought that s. 9 could also operate to validate the title of a purchaser from a thief because the purchaser could be regarded as in possession with the consent of the seller (i.e. the thief). This unfortunate result could be avoided if the court decided, as a matter of interpretation, that 'seller' meant 'owner' in this situation. This was the view taken by the trial judge in *National Employers Mutual General Insurance Association* v *Jones* [1987] 3 All ER 385. Thieves stole a car. They sold it to A. He sold it to B who sold it to C (a dealer). C then sold it to D (another dealer), and D sold it to Jones. In all of the transactions the buyers were unaware of the theft. The question before the court was whether Jones had a good title under s. 25(1) of the Sale of Goods Act 1979 and s. 9 of the Factors Act 1889. The trial judge found that Jones had no title, so did the Court of Appeal but for different reasons. May LJ said that if a person who 'buys' a car from a thief, then himself 'sells' it, he is not a 'seller' and indeed, the contract between him and his purchaser is not a 'contract of sale'. In other words, May LJ was really suggesting that the sale by a thief to an innocent purchaser is not a contract of sale at all. That being the case, the Sale of Goods Act could not apply to it, nor did s. 9 of the Factors Act. A person who 'buys' goods from a thief is not 'a person having bought or agreed to buy goods'. A contract of sale pre-supposes that the seller has or will obtain a good title. This is not true of a thief who is not a seller under relevant law (*see* s. 2(1), Sale of Goods Act 1979: 'A contract of sale of goods is a contract by which the seller transfers or agrees to transfer the property in the goods to the buyer . . .'). The House of Lords affirmed the decision (*see* [1988] 2 All ER 425).

Hire-purchase: motor vehicles

As we have seen, Part III of the Hire Purchase Act 1964 protects the title of a bona fide private purchaser of a motor vehicle from a seller in possession under a hire-purchase agreement (*see* p. 360).

GRADED QUESTIONS

Essay mode

1. Explain, giving illustrations, the rules of the Sale of Goods Act 1979 which concern the passing of property in unascertained goods. In what circumstances will these rules be of practical importance in commercial transactions?

   (The Institute of Chartered Secretaries and Administrators. English Business Law. June 1988)

2. (a) Albert contracts with Zebedee to buy a milling machine which Zebedee has hitherto used in his farmyard business. The machine weighs 20 tons and is embedded in a concrete floor. The contract provides that Zebedee must detach the machine from the floor, dismantle it, deliver it and re-erect it in Albert's mill. Albert pays a deposit of £3,000 out of a total price of £12,000. On the night after the contract is signed the premises of Zebedee are struck by lightning and the milling machine is totally destroyed. Advise Albert.

   (b) Explain the importance and use of Romalpa clauses in modern contracts giving illustrations from decided cases.

   (The Institute of Legal Executives. Part II: Commercial Law. June 1990)

3. Brenda visits Sparks, an electrical appliance retailer, to buy a food processor. She sees on display a 'Keninex' model. The accompanying sales literature, which Brenda glances at, proclaims: 'If you can eat it Keninex can beat it' and 'Keninex means simplicity – even a child can use it'. Sparks uses the display model to give a demonstration, using it to shred and mix vegetables. Brenda is extremely impressed and buys a Keninex, which Sparks takes from his storeroom and hands over in a sealed cardboard box. Sparks explains that the processor has a 12 month guarantee, details of which are inside the box.

   On unpacking the box at home Brenda discovers that there is no plug fitted. There was a plug on the display model. Fortunately she has a spare plug and uses that. She then is so keen to use the processor that she omits to read either the guarantee or the instructions, which are in leaflets inside the box. The guarantee requires her to fill in a card and post it to Keninex Ltd. The instructions explain that the body of the processor is held on to the base by two spring-loaded screws, which are tightened down for packing, but which must be loosened before use to prevent vibration. Sparks did not mention this.

   Brenda first uses the processor to beat up some eggs. Due to the excessive vibration it slides off the table and falls on the floor. This chips the plastic body, which in any event appears very thin and flimsy, but the machine remains operative. Having checked the instructions and loosened the screws. Brenda then attempts to use the shredding part of the processor to shell some walnuts. This causes the metal blades in the shredder to disintegrate. Fortunately no injury or other damage is caused.

Discuss the legal factors involved in considering any claims Brenda might have against either Sparks or Keninex Ltd.

(Staffordshire Polytechnic. LLB(Hons) Consumer Law. May 1990)

Objective mode

Four alternative answers are given. Select ONE only. Circle the answer which you consider to be correct. Check your answers by referring back to the information given in the relevant chapter and against the answers at the back of the book.

1. C. Gram are manufacturers of patent medicines and produce a cough mixture called Kicka Cough Linctus. Casper, an opera singer, had caught a severe cold and was concerned to recover from the associated cough before his next engagement that evening. His wife Marbella had recently bought a bottle of Kicka Cough from Brian a chemist but it remained unopened since she had recovered. The linctus should have contained 2 per cent alcohol but because of a temporary defect in the bottling plant at C. Gram some bottles contained 75 per cent alcohol. Some of these bottles had been supplied to retailers including Brian. An hour before going on stage Casper drank recommended doses of the linctus and became drunk. He staggered all over the stage, forgot his lines and sang obscene rugby songs. He lost the remainder of the engagement and wishes to bring a claim but is not sure who to sue. He thinks C. Gram would have more money to pay damages than Brian.
   The legal position is that:

   A Casper can only claim against Brian.
   B Casper can only claim against C. Gram.
   C Casper can claim against either C. Gram or Brian.
   D Casper has no claim since he did not purchase the linctus.

2. Rambo orders a new Cavalier GTS from Red Garages Ltd for delivery in one month, specifying various extras. His car arrives at Red Garages and before its pre-delivery checks is stolen and taken for a joy ride by Richard and Edwin, local juvenile delinquents, and is damaged.

   A Rambo must accept the loss since property in specific goods passes when the contract is made, and risk passes with the property.
   B Red Garages must make good the damage since the property in the car remained with them until they had put the goods in a deliverable state.
   C It is up to Red Garages to sue Edwin and Richard and recover the loss from them.
   D Red Garages will be liable to Rambo as negligent bailees of his motor car. They should have taken proper care of it.

3. When there is a contract for the sale of specific goods and the seller is bound to do something to the goods for the purpose of putting them into a deliverable state, the property does not pass.

A Until such thing is done.

B Until such thing is done and the buyer assents to it being done.

C Until such thing is done and the buyer has notice that it has been done.

D Until such thing is done and the buyer has had an opportunity to see that it has been done.

4. Dilwyn agrees to purchase a quantity of Beaujolais Noveau from Monsieur Scopes, a dealer in Burgundy. Monsieur Scopes agrees to deliver at his own risk to Dilwyn's warehouse in Liverpool, the journey to take one month. In that time the Beaujolais is no longer as 'nouveau' as it should be and Dilwyn reckons its price has gone down 50p per bottle. Is Scopes responsible for this deterioration?

A Yes, because the goods were at the seller's risk during transit.

B No, because the buyer must take any risk of deterioration in the goods necessarily incidental to the course of transit.

C Yes, because the risk and property were not to pass until delivery.

D No, because being specific goods in deliverable state the property and risk passed when the contract was made.

5. John agreed to buy Geoffrey's vintage 3-litre Lagonda motor car for £15,000. Unknown to John and Geoffrey a fire in David's garage, where the car was stored, the day before the contract had been made had destroyed the car. What is the legal position?

A John must pay the contract price since the risk of loss passes to the buyer when the contract is made.

B John must pay but can sue David for negligence as a bailee.

C John need not pay for the goods as the contract is void since the goods had perished when the agreement was made.

D John need not pay for the goods as the contract is voidable since the goods had perished when the agreement was made.

6. Which of the following is a prerequisite for the successful operation of a reservation of title clause in a contract of sale of goods?

A The buyer must be insolvent when the clause is enforced.

B The goods must be identifiable.

C The rights of third parties must not be prejudiced.

D The buyer must be solvent when the contract is made.

Answers to questions set in objective mode appear on p. 551.

12 | The sale of goods III

The OBJECTIVES of this chapter are to consider the principles of law which are relevant in a contract of sale of goods in terms of the performance of the contract, and the remedies of seller and buyer. The chapter concludes with a consideration of auction and export and import sales.

PERFORMANCE OF THE CONTRACT GENERALLY

A contract of sale of goods is, like any other contract, discharged or brought to an end by proper performance of it by the parties. The relevant rules are set out below.

DELIVERY

Section 61(1) defines delivery as the voluntary transfer of possession from one person to another. There are various forms of delivery as follows.

(a) by physical transfer as where the goods are handed to the buyer with the intention of transferring possession;
(b) by delivery of the means of control as where the key of a warehouse or store is handed to the buyer;
(c) by attornment as where the goods are in the possession of a third party, e.g. a warehouseman, who acknowledges to the buyer that he holds the goods on his behalf (s. 29(4));

(d) by delivery of documents of title as where a bill of lading representing the goods is delivered (s. 29(4)). A vehicle registration document is not a document of title for this purpose;

(e) by constructive delivery as where the buyer already has possession of the goods as a bailee. Thus in a hire-purchase contract the character of possession changes when the instalments have been paid and the hirer becomes owner by constructive delivery. This form of delivery also applies where a seller agrees to hold the goods as a bailee or agent of the buyer.

Place of delivery

Section 27 provides that it is the duty of the seller to deliver the goods, and of the buyer to accept and pay for them, in accordance with the terms of sale. The seller's duty to deliver does not mean he must necessarily take or send them to the buyer.

Section 29(1) provides that whether it is for the buyer to take possession of the goods or for the seller to send them to the buyer is a question depending in each case on the contract, express or implied, between the parties.

The place of delivery, in the absence of express agreement to the contrary, is the place of business of the seller or, if he has no place of business, his residence (s. 29(2)). If the contract is for the sale of specific goods which to the knowledge of the parties when the contract is made are in some other place, then that place is the place of delivery (s. 29(2)). Thus, in the absence of a contrary intention, the buyer is under a duty to collect the goods.

Where the seller is, under a special contract, bound to deliver the goods, he discharges the duty by delivering them to a person who, being at the buyer's premises, appears respectable and likely to be authorized to take delivery, even if in the event he is not.

The following case provides an illustration.

Galbraith & Grant Ltd v Block [1922] 2 KB 155

The plaintiffs were wine merchants and they sued the defendants for £16 2s 11d being the price of a case of champagne delivered to the defendant who was a licensed victualler. The defendant admitted the contract but said that champagne had never been delivered to him. Evidence showed that the defendant asked the plaintiffs to deliver the goods and they employed a carrier who delivered them to the defendant's premises and obtained a receipt signed in the defendant's name by a person on the defendant's premises who seemed to the carrier to have authority to receive them. In fact the person to whom the goods were delivered had no authority to receive them and did not hand them over to the defendant. It was *held* that, where a vendor had been told to deliver goods at the buyer's premises, he fulfils his obligation if he delivers them to those premises and without negligence gives them over to a person apparently having authority to receive them. The trial judge had not taken sufficient evidence on the care taken by the carriers so that it was not possible to say whether they were negligent or not, and the case was sent back for a new trial on this point.

Delivery of goods to the wrong address may amount to conversion by the carrier, thus providing the owner with a remedy in tort against him if the goods are not recovered.

Payment and delivery are concurrent conditions

Section 28 provides that, unless otherwise agreed, e.g. where the seller gives credit to the buyer, delivery and payment of the price are concurrent conditions. The seller must be ready and willing to give possession of the goods to the buyer in exchange for the price, and the buyer must be ready and willing to pay the price in exchange for possession of the goods.

Thus, if the buyer is suing the seller for non-delivery, he need not give evidence that he has paid, but merely that he was ready and willing to pay. In an action for non-acceptance of the goods, the seller need not prove that he has tendered delivery, but merely that he was ready and willing to deliver.

Other rules as to delivery

Where under the contract of sale the seller is bound to send the goods to the buyer, but no time for sending them is fixed, the seller is bound to send them within a reasonable time (s. 29(3)) and at a reasonable hour (s. 29(5)). What is reasonable in both cases is a matter of fact.

Quantity of goods delivered

Where the seller delivers to the buyer a quantity of goods less than he contracted to sell, the buyer may reject them, but if he accepts them, he must pay for them at the contract rate (s. 30(1)).

Where the seller delivers to the buyer a quantity of goods larger than he contracted to sell, the buyer may accept the goods included in the contract and reject the rest, or he may reject the whole. If the buyer accepts the whole of the goods so delivered, he must pay for them at the contract rate (s. 30(3)).

If the goods delivered are mixed with goods of a different description not included in the contract, the buyer may accept the goods which are in accordance with the contract and reject the rest, or he may reject the whole (s. 30(4)). (*See Moore & Co v Landauer & Co* (1921), p. 250.)

The above provisions are subject to any usage of trade, special agreement, or course of dealing between the parties (s. 30(5)), and the buyer's right to reject may not exist if the differences are microscopic (*de minimis non curat lex* – the law does not concern itself with trifles). Thus, in *Shipton Anderson & Co Ltd v Weil Bros* [1912] 1 KB 574 the sellers were to deliver 4,950 tons of wheat and in fact delivered 4,950 tons and 55lb. The court *held* that the buyers were not entitled to reject the whole consignment, which they in fact did, since the excess of 55lb was so trifling. The sellers were awarded damages for breach of contract by the buyers.

Delivery by instalments

Unless otherwise agreed, the buyer of goods is not bound to accept delivery by instalments (s. 31(1)). Thus the seller cannot excuse short delivery by undertaking to deliver the balance in due course. Where there is a contract of sale of goods to be delivered by stated instalments, which are to be separately paid for, and the seller makes defective deliveries in respect of one or more instalments, or the buyer neglects or refuses to take delivery of or pay for one or more instalments, it is a question in each case depending on the terms of the contract and the circumstances of the case, whether the breach of contract is a repudiation of the whole contract, or whether it is a severable breach giving rise to a claim for compensation but not a right to treat the whole contract as repudiated (s. 31(2)).

The main tests to be considered in applying s. 31(2) are:

(a) the ratio quantitatively which the breach bears to the contract as a whole; and
(b) the degree of probability or improbability that such a breach will be repeated.

The following case and comment provides an illustration.

Maple Flock Co Ltd v Universal Furniture Products (Wembley) Ltd
[1934] 1 KB 148

The plaintiffs agreed to sell to the defendants 100 tons of black linsey flock at £15 2s 6d per ton to be delivered three loads a week, 1½ tons per load, as required. The plaintiffs guaranteed that the flock should not contain more than 30 parts of chlorine to 100,000 parts of flock. The sixteenth delivery contained 250 parts of chlorine to 100,000 parts of flock. The buyers repudiated the contract and refused to take further deliveries. The sellers sued for breach of contract. Evidence showed that the first 15 deliveries were as per contract, and the plaintiffs' plant and equipment was good so that there was little chance of subsequent deliveries being affected. Held – The matter was covered by s. 31(2) of the Sale of Goods Act and the main tests to be applied in cases falling under that section were: (a) the ratio quantitatively which the breach bears to the contract as a whole, and (b) the degree of probability or improbability that such a breach will be repeated.

In this case a delivery of 1½ tons was defective out of a contract to supply 100 tons and there was little chance of the breach being repeated. The buyers were not, therefore, entitled to repudiate the contract and were liable for breach. They could have recovered damages in respect of the defects in the sixteenth delivery but did not claim any because the delivery had been used in the manufacture of bedding and furniture before the sample was tested and found defective.

Comment: (i) In Munro (Robert A) & Co Ltd v Meyer [1930] 2 KB 312 where the contract was for the sale of 1,500 tons of bone meal and 611 tons were found to be defective, it was held that the buyers were entitled to repudiate the contract.

(ii) In *Regent OHG Aisenstadt und Barig* v *Francesco of Jermyn Street Ltd* [1981] 3 All ER 327 the plaintiffs were delivering suits to the defendants by instalments. In one consignment there was one suit short. The defendants, who wished to cancel the arrangement, repudiated the contract under s. 30(1). Mustill J found that the contract was divisible and s. 31 applied. The defendants were liable in damages for non-acceptance of the instalment and repudiation of the contract.

Delivery to a carrier

Where the seller is authorized or required to send the goods to the buyer, delivery by the seller to a carrier is, in the absence of any evidence to the contrary, deemed delivery to the buyer (s. 32(1)). In the absence of a contrary agreement the seller is required to make a contract with a carrier which is reasonable in terms of the goods to be carried. If he does not and the goods are lost or damaged the buyer may refuse to regard delivery to the carrier as delivery to himself and may sue the seller for damages (s. 32(2)). Where the carriage involves a sea voyage where it is usual to insure, the seller must make it possible for the buyer to insure otherwise the goods are at the seller's risk during sea transit (s. 32(3)).

Where the seller of goods agrees to deliver them at his own risk at a place other than that where they are when sold, the buyer must, unless otherwise agreed, take the risk of accidental destruction or deterioration, but not the risk of damage caused by the fault of the seller (s. 33). Where the goods are perishable, they are not considered merchantable unless they are sent off by the seller in time to reach their destination in saleable condition (*see Mash & Murrell Ltd* v *Joseph I Emmanuel Ltd* (1961) p. 257).

THE BUYER'S RIGHT TO EXAMINE THE GOODS

A buyer who has not previously examined the goods is not regarded as having accepted goods delivered to him unless and until he has had a reasonable opportunity of examining them for the purpose of ascertaining whether they are in conformity with the contract (s. 34(1)). Unless otherwise agreed, when the seller tenders delivery of goods to the buyer, he is bound, on request, to give the buyer, a reasonable opportunity of examining the goods to see whether they are in conformity with the contract (s. 34(2)). The seller may attempt to introduce a waiver of the right to inspection. When goods are delivered to a person's home he may be asked to sign a document saying 'received this item in good condition'. If this is so, the buyer may have waived his rights. It is better to sign 'not examined'.

ACCEPTANCE OF THE GOODS

The buyer is deemed to have accepted the goods:

(a) when he intimates to the seller that he has accepted them; or

(b) when the goods have been delivered to him and he does any act in relation to them which is inconsistent with the ownership of the seller; or

(c) when after the lapse of a reasonable time, he retains the goods without intimating to the seller that he has rejected them (s. 35(1)).

Section 35(1) provides that s. 34 is always to prevail over s. 35 so that a buyer is not prevented from rejecting goods until he has examined them or at least has had a reasonable opportunity of examining them. It should be noted, however, that delay in rejection will still defeat a claim for repudiation for breach of condition, but not a claim for damages for breach of warranty (see Bernstein v Pamsons Motors (Golders Green) Ltd (1987) at p. 275).

The effect of this provision is, therefore, that persons who buy goods such as refrigerators, washing machines and radios will be able to examine and test them in their own homes. If the goods are faulty they will be able to repudiate the contract and return the goods demanding a refund of the purchase price. However, the goods must be returned within a reasonable time (a month would appear to be the maximum time), otherwise the buyer's only remedy will be an action for damages (see Bernstein v Pamsons Motors (Golders Green) Ltd (1987) at p. 275).

However, much depends upon the circumstances of the case, for example, many stores provide fitting rooms for garments and failure to use these may prevent a claim that a garment is not acceptable because it does not fit.

Where the buyer has the right to refuse to accept the goods and does so refuse he is not bound to return them but only to notify the seller of the refusal (s. 36). If the seller is able to deliver the goods and requests the buyer to take delivery the buyer must do so within a reasonable time. If he does not do so he is liable to the seller for any resulting loss and also for a reasonable charge for the care and custody of the goods. If the buyer's refusal amounts only to a request to postpone delivery for a short time, the seller is still bound to deliver. If, however, the refusal is absolute or involves a long postponement it may amount to a repudiation of the contract which discharges the seller from liability to deliver and gives him a right of action in damages against the buyer (s. 37(2)).

REMEDIES OF THE SELLER

We are now in a position to look at the remedies of the seller. These consist of remedies against the goods sold and personal remedies against the buyer.

Real remedies against the goods: generally

The unpaid seller, in addition to his personal remedies, e.g. an action for damages, has under Part V of the Act, certain real remedies against the goods.

Section 39(1) provides that, even if the property in the goods has passed to the buyer, the unpaid seller of goods, as such, has by implication of law:

(a) a lien on the goods or the right to retain them for the price while he is still in possession of them;
(b) in the case of the insolvency of the buyer, a right of stopping the goods *in transitu* (in transit) ofter he has parted with possession of them;
(c) a right of resale as limited by the Act.

Section 39(2) provides that, where the property in goods has not passed to the buyer, the unpaid seller has, in addition to his other remedies, a right of withholding delivery similar to and co-extensive with his rights of lien and stoppage *in transitu* where the property has passed to the buyer.

The rights set out in s. 39(1) may only be exercised by an unpaid seller, and s. 38(1) provides that a seller of goods is deemed to be an unpaid seller:

(a) when the whole of the price has not been paid or tendered;
(b) when a bill of exchange or other negotiable instrument has been received as conditional payment, and the condition on which it was received has not been fulfilled by reason of the dishonour of the instrument or otherwise.

The term seller includes in certain circumstances the agent of the seller (s. 38(2)). Thus where the goods are sold through an agent who has either paid the price to his principal, or has made himself liable to pay the price under the terms of his contract of agency, the agent can exercise any of the rights of the unpaid seller.

Lien

A lien is generally speaking the right of a creditor in possession of the goods of his debtor to retain possession of them until the price has been paid or tendered, or his debt has been secured or satisfied. *A lien does not normally carry with it a power of sale*, though the unpaid seller of goods has a statutory power, and will generally exercise his lien as a preliminary to resale.

The lien conferred by the Act is a particular lien, though a general lien may be conferred by an express contractual provision. Under a particular lien the unpaid seller can retain only the goods which are not paid for, and not other goods belonging to the buyer. However, where delivery is being made by instalments and an unpaid seller has made part delivery of the goods, he may exercise his lien on the remainder, unless such part delivery can, in the circumstances, be construed as a waiver of the right of lien by the seller (s. 42).

Where the goods have been sold without any stipulation as to credit, the unpaid seller who is in possession of them is entitled to retain possession until payment or tender of the price (s. 41(1)(a)). A lien can also be claimed, even though credit has been given:

(a) where the goods have been sold on credit but the term of credit has expired (s. 41(1)(b)). This presupposes that although credit was given the buyer did not take delivery of the goods. If he had done so no lien could be exercised because the seller would not have the goods; and

(b) where the buyer becomes insolvent (s. 41(1)(c)).

A person is deemed to be insolvent within the meaning of the Act if he has either ceased to pay his debts in the ordinary course of business, or cannot pay his debts as they become due (s. 61(4)).

The effect of the insolvency provision is that the seller cannot be compelled to deliver the goods to an insolvent person and to prove for a dividend in the bankruptcy. However, a trustee in bankruptcy can have the goods if he tenders the whole price.

The seller's lien is a possessory lien. The seller must be in possession of the goods, but he need not be in possession as a seller and may exercise his right of lien even if he is in possession of the goods as agent or bailee for the buyer (s. 41(2)). The seller's lien is for the price of the goods, and cannot be exercised in respect of other costs, e.g. storage charges and the like (*Soames* v *British Empire Shipping Co* (1860) 8 HL Cas 338).

Loss of lien

The right of lien is lost:

(a) if the price is paid or tendered;

(b) if the right of lien has been waived by the seller;

(c) if the buyer or his agent lawfully obtains possession of the goods;

(d) if the unpaid seller delivers the goods to a carrier or bailee for the purpose of transmission to the buyer, without reserving the right of disposal of the goods. A right of *stoppage in transitu* may arise here, but only if the buyer is insolvent.

A *waiver* may be an express waiver under the contract between the parties, or may be implied from the conduct of the seller. For example, suppose B buys furniture on credit from S, and after the sale has taken place, S then asks B to lend him the furniture for a week until he can get more furniture to display in his shop. Here the conduct of S would imply that, although the property was B's, he held the furniture on a new contract of loan, and that his right of lien on the contract of sale was waived.

The exercise of a lien by the seller does not rescind the contract (s. 48(1)) and the right of lien is not lost when the seller obtains a judgment from the court for the price of the goods (s. 43(2)).

Stoppage *in transitu*

When the buyer of goods becomes insolvent, the unpaid seller who is not in possession of the goods has the right of stopping them *in transitu*, i.e. he may resume possession of the goods as long as they are in course of transit, and may retain them until payment or tender of the price (s. 44).

The remedy is only available when the buyer is insolvent and, if exercised, means that the seller need not allow the goods to form part of an insolvent estate, leaving himself with a mere right to prove for a dividend for the price. Nevertheless, the exercise of stoppage *in transitu* does not rescind the contract of sale, nor does it vest the property in the goods in the unpaid seller (*Booth SS Co Ltd* v *Cargo Fleet Iron Co Ltd* [1916] 2 KB 570). Thus if the buyer's trustee in bankruptcy tenders the price, the seller must deliver the goods or be liable for breach of contract. Three conditions must be satisfied before the right can be exercised: (a) the seller must be unpaid; (b) the buyer must be insolvent; and (c) the goods must still be in transit.

Section 45(1) provides that goods are deemed to be in course of transit from the time when they are delivered to a carrier by land or water, or other bailee for the purpose of transmission to the buyer, until the buyer, or his agent in that behalf, takes delivery of them from such carrier or other bailee.

We have seen that delivery to a carrier is prima facie deemed to be a constructive delivery of the goods to the buyer, and where the carrier is the agent of the buyer this constitutes actual delivery and there can be no stoppage *in transitu*. Where, however, the carrier is an independent contractor, the remedy is available until the goods are actually delivered to the buyer.

If the buyer or his agent obtains delivery of the goods before their arrival at the appointed destination, the transit is at an end (s. 45(2)). If, after the arrival of the goods at the appointed destination, the carrier or other bailee acknowledges to the buyer, or his agent, that he holds the goods on his behalf and continues in possession of them as bailee for the buyer or his agent, the transit is at an end, and it is immaterial that a further destination for the goods may have been indicated by the buyer (s. 45(3)).

The following case provides an illustration.

Kendall v Marshall, Stevens & Co (1883) 11 QBD 356

This was an action to recover damages for conversion of 55 bales of waste cotton. The plaintiff was the liquidator of a person called Leoffer, trading as Higginbottom & Co. The defendants were shipping agents and carriers, and the second defendants were Peter Ward & Son of Bolton, who sold the bales of cotton. It appeared that on 9 November 1880, Ward & Son sold the cotton to Leoffer and on 12 November Leoffer asked the vendors to send the goods to Marshall, Stevens & Co at Garston. He also informed Marshall, Stevens & Co that they were to ship the goods as soon as possible to Durend & Co at Rouen, France. The actual transit of the goods was therefore from Bolton to Rouen. On 13 November, the goods were sent by the vendors to Marshall, Stevens & Co and they arrived at Garston on

15 November. The railway company's advice note which accompanied the goods gave Marshall, Stevens & Co notice that unless the goods were collected by a certain time, the company would hold them as warehousemen at owner's risk and not as common carriers. On 18 November, Leoffer filed a petition for the liquidation of his estate, and on 22 November, Ward & Son telegraphed Marshall, Stevens & Co to stop the goods. This was done and they were returned to Bolton on 24 November. The liquidator sued in conversion to recover the value of the goods for the benefit of the estate. *Held* – The right to stop the goods expired when they arrived at Garston and when the railway company's notice had expired, which it had in this case. Once the railway company held the goods as warehousemen the goods were in the constructive possession of the buyer, Leoffer, and the defendants were liable in conversion.

If, however, the goods are rejected by the buyer, and the carrier or other bailee continues in possession of them, the transit is not deemed to be at an end, even if the seller has refused to take them back (s. 45(4)). When goods are delivered to a ship chartered by the buyer, it is a question depending on the circumstances of the particular case, whether they are in the possession of the master as a carrier, or as an agent of the buyer (s. 45(5)). The ship's master will not normally be the agent of the buyer where the goods are shipped under a charter for one voyage. The master will be the buyer's agent where the ship belongs to the buyer, and may well be where the ship is chartered by the buyer for several voyages, as under a time charter.

Where the carrier or other bailee wrongfully refuses to deliver the goods to the buyer or his agent, the transit is deemed to be at an end (s. 45(6)).

Where part delivery of the goods has been made to the buyer or his agent, the remainder of the goods may be stopped in transit, unless such part delivery has been made under such circumstances as to show an agreement to give up possession of the whole of the goods (s. 45(7)).

The unpaid seller's right of lien or stoppage *in transitu* is not affected by any sale or other disposition of the goods which the buyer may have made unless the seller has agreed to it. However, where documents of title, e.g. bills of lading with respect to the goods, have been lawfully transferred to the buyer, and he has transferred them to a third party who takes them in good faith and for value by way of sale, the seller's right of lien or stoppage *in transitu* is defeated (s. 47).

Where the transfer of the document of title is not by way of sale but is, for example, by way of a security for a loan, the seller can still exercise his lien or right of stoppage *in transitu* but subject to the rights of the lender.

The following case provides an illustration.

Leask v Scott Bros (1887) 2 QBD 376

Green & Co, who were merchants, were indebted to the plaintiff, who was a broker, and asked him for a further advance of £2,000. The plaintiff agreed to make the further advance but wanted some security. Green & Co gave him a bill of lading which they had received from the defendants for goods shipped to Green & Co. Two days later Green & Co became insolvent and the defendants stopped the goods in transit. The jury found that the plaintiff took the bill of lading honestly and fairly and that he gave valuable consideration on the understanding that he was being given a security. *Held* – The plaintiff was entitled to the goods as against the defendants up to the amount of the advance.

Comment: If the goods which the seller stops or exercises a lien on are worth £3,000 and the lender has lent £2,000, the lender is entitled to £2,000 of the proceeds of sale of the goods and the seller is entitled to £1,000 of the proceeds in preference to the general creditors of the buyer. The seller will have to prove in the bankruptcy of the buyer for the balance.

Exercise of the right

The unpaid seller may exercise his right of stoppage *in transitu* either by taking actual possession of the goods, or by giving notice of his claim to the carrier or other bailee in whose possession the goods are. Such notice may be given either to the person in actual possession of the goods or to his principal. In the latter case the notice, to be effectual, must be given at such time and under such circumstances that the principal, by the exercise of reasonable diligence, may communicate it to his servant or agent in time to prevent delivery to the buyer (ss. 46(1),(2) and (3)).

When notice of stoppage *in transitu* is given by the seller to the carrier, or other bailee in possession of the goods, he must redeliver the goods to or according to the direction of the seller. The expenses of such redelivery must be borne by the seller (s. 46(4)). If the carrier delivers the goods after notice to the contrary, the unpaid seller has his remedy, for what it is worth, against the buyer who will by definition be insolvent, *or* may sue the carrier in tort for conversion.

The carrier can refuse to redeliver if his charges have not been paid, and his lien overrides the seller's right of stoppage *in transitu*. However, unless a general lien is conferred by the contract, a carrier's lien is normally a particular lien so that he can only refuse to redeliver the actual goods in respect of which charges are outstanding, and not other goods dispatched by the seller.

The right of resale

The unpaid seller of goods has a right to resell, without being in breach of contract, in the following circumstances.

(a) Where the buyer repudiates the contract either expressly or by conduct, the seller can resell the goods, retain any profit made, returning to the buyer any part payments.

(b) Where the contract of sale expressly provides for resale in case the buyer should make default, and the seller resells the goods on default, the original contract of sale is rescinded, but without prejudice to any claim the seller may have for damages (s. 48(4)).

(c) Where the goods are of a perishable nature, or where the unpaid seller gives notice to the buyer of his intention to resell, and the buyer does not within a reasonable time pay or tender the price, the unpaid seller may resell the goods and recover from the original buyer damages for any loss occasioned by the breach of contract (s. 48(3)). The contract of sale is not rescinded by the seller's mere exercise of his right of lien or stoppage *in transitu*, but it is when the unpaid seller resells the goods or part of them, either under s. 48(4), where the contract expressly provides for resale, or under s. 48(3), which gives a right of resale even where there is no express provision in the contract.

In either event resale, whether of the whole or part of the goods, rescinds the contract and the property reverts to the seller, who has then no action for the price against the buyer. Thus if the unpaid seller resells at a profit he does not have to account to the original buyer for it. If the original buyer has made a payment for the goods the seller can keep this if it is a *deposit* to be forfeited if the contract does not proceed. If it is regarded as a *part payment* it must be returned to the original buyer. Which of these it is will be dealt with either by the contract or by the court in case of dispute.

If the seller sells at a loss he has an action for *damages* from which must be deducted any payment received from the buyer.

The following case illustrates the application of the law.

R V Ward Ltd v Bignall [1967] 2 All ER 449

The defendant bought a Ford Zodiac and a Vanguard from the plaintiffs for a total price of £850, paying a deposit of £25 and leaving both cars with the plaintiffs until payment of the balance. The defendant refused to pay the balance, alleging that he had been misled as to the date of manufacture of the Vanguard, although he did offer to take the Zodiac but his offer was refused. Eventually the plaintiffs resold the Vanguard for £350 and brought an action against the defendant, claiming £497 10s, being the balance of the total purchase price less £350 with the addition of £22 10s for expenses incurred in advertising in order to resell the cars. *Held* – by the Court of Appeal – that when an unpaid seller exercised his right to resell the whole or part of the goods under s. 48(3) of the Sale of Goods Act, he could no longer perform his contract which must therefore be regarded as rescinded. Accordingly the plaintiffs' proper claim was for damages for non-acceptance. Sellers LJ said:

... the plaintiffs cannot recover the price of the Zodiac, which is in the circumstances their property. They can, however, recover any loss which they have sustained by the buyer's default. The parties have sensibly agreed that the value of the Zodiac in May 1965 was £450. The total contract price was £850, against which the plaintiffs have received £25 in cash and £350 in respect of the Vanguard, and have to give credit for £450 for the Zodiac. To the loss of £25 must be added the sum for advertising, which was admittedly reasonably incurred – £22 10s 0d. The plaintiffs' loss was, therefore, £47 10s 0d.

I would allow the appeal and enter judgment for £47 10s 0d in favour of the plaintiffs ...

Power of seller to give a second buyer a title

A seller has power to give a title, whether he has the right to sell or not, in the following circumstances:

(a) where, although the goods are sold, the property is still in the seller;

(b) under s. 24 of the Sale of Goods Act 1979, or s. 8 of the Factors Act 1889, if he is in possession;

(c) under s. 48(2) of the Sale of Goods Act, 1979, which provides that where an unpaid seller who has exercised his right of lien or stoppage *in transitu* resells the goods, the buyer acquires a good title thereto as against the original buyer.

Unless the seller resells in accordance with the rules laid down in ss. 48(3) and 48(4) he will usually be liable in breach of contract to the original buyer, though in most cases the second buyer will obtain a good title to the goods.

PERSONAL REMEDIES OF THE SELLER

In addition to the real remedies discussed above, the seller has a personal action against the buyer either:

(a) for the price under s. 49(1); or

(b) for damages for non-acceptance under s. 50(1).

The passing of the property and the conduct of the buyer will determine the sort of action which the seller will bring, and the property may, of course, have passed before delivery.

   If the property has passed and the buyer has accepted the goods, the seller has an action for the price. If the property has not passed and the buyer will not accept the goods, the seller has an action for damages. Finally, if the property has passed and the buyer will not accept the goods, the seller has an action either for the price or for damages. If the seller sues for the price he may also include a claim for losses or expenses, e.g. in storing the goods because the buyer would not take them (s. 37(1)). If the seller sues for damages, such losses will be taken into account. Where the price is due in foreign currency, it is now possible for an English court to give judgment for the debt in the foreign currency itself (*Miliangos* v *George Frank Textiles Ltd* [1975] 3 All ER 801). A plaintiff may also claim in a foreign currency for damages for breach of contract (*The Folias* [1979] 1 All ER 421) and in tort, e.g. for conversion of goods (*The Despina* [1979] 1 All ER 421). *The Miliangos* rule does not apply to the claims of creditors in the winding up of a company. Here the claim in foreign currency must be converted into sterling at the date of the winding up (*see Re Lines Bros Ltd* [1982] 2 All ER 183). This is to prevent the introduction of further complications in the administration of the assets of a company on winding up.

Section 49(2) provides that where, under a contract of sale, the price is payable on a certain day irrespective of delivery, and the buyer wrongfully neglects or refuses to pay such price, the seller may maintain an action for the price, although the property in the goods has not passed, and the goods have not been appropriated to the contract.

MEASUREMENT OF DAMAGES

The concept of available market

In an action for damages the main problem is that of assessment. Section 50(2) provides that the measure of damages is the estimated loss directly and naturally resulting, in the ordinary course of events, from the buyer's breach of contract.

Section 50(3) further expands the concept by providing that, where there is an available market for the goods in question, the measure of damages is prima facie to be ascertained by the difference between the contract price and the market or current price at the time or times when the goods ought to have been accepted, or, if no time was fixed for acceptance, then at the time of refusal to accept.

An available market exists where on the facts of the case the seller is in a position where the goods can be readily disposed of to a number of buyers, *all of whom want the identical article which is for sale*, e.g. as in the case of a new motor car. Given an available market then if the supply exceeds the demand the seller is entitled to the loss of profit on sale to a defaulting buyer.

If, however, the demand for the goods exceeds the supply so that the seller can readily sell every item he can obtain from the manufacturers, he is not entitled to loss of profit on the first sale where he has made the same profit on a substituted sale following the first buyer's default.

Section 50(3) does not apply where there is no available market, as is the case with second-hand cars, and damages must be assessed on general principles, i.e. what is the estimated loss directly and naturally resulting in the ordinary course of events from the buyer's breach of contract?

The following three cases clarify the application of these rules.

Thompson (WL) Ltd v Robinson (Gunmakers) Ltd [1955] 1 All ER 154

On 4 March 1954, the defendants agreed in writing with the plaintiffs who were motor car dealers to purchase from them a Standard Vanguard car. On 5 March 1954, the defendants said they were not prepared to take delivery. The plaintiffs returned the car to their suppliers who did not ask for any compensation. The plaintiffs now sued for damages for breach of contract. The selling price of a Standard Vanguard was fixed by the manufacturers and the plaintiffs' profit would have been £61 1s 9d. When the agreement was made there was not sufficient demand for Vanguards in the locality as would absorb all such cars available for sale in the area, but evidence did not show that there was no available market in the widest sense, i.e. in the sense of the country as a whole. *Held* – the plaintiffs were entitled to compensation for loss of their bargain, i.e. the profit they would have made being £61 1s 9d because they had sold one car less than they would have sold. Even if the 'available market' concept as used in s. 50(3) of the Sale of Goods Act meant taking in the whole of the country, it would not be just to apply s. 50(3) in this case. It is after all possible to translate 'available' as meaning 'at hand'. Therefore s. 50(3) was no defence to the plaintiffs' claim. Section 50(3) need not be applied if the court thinks it would be unjust in the circumstances.

Comment: The evidence in this case that the car could not be sold and *would never be sold by the plaintiffs* was compelling since they had returned it to the suppliers. In the *Charter* case (*below*) the plaintiffs had actually sold the car which the defendant had refused to buy to someone else.

Charter v Sullivan [1957] 1 All ER 809

The plaintiffs who were motor dealers agreed to sell a Hillman Minx car to the defendant for £773 17s 0d which was the retail price fixed by the manufacturer. The defendant refused to complete the purchase and the plaintiffs resold the car a few days later to another purchaser at the same price. The plaintiffs sued for breach of contract, the measure of damages claimed being £97 15s 0d, the profit the plaintiffs would have made on the sale to the defendant if it had gone through. Evidence showed that the plaintiffs could have sold the second purchaser another Hillman Minx which would have been ordered from the manufacturers' stock had the defendant taken the first Hillman Minx as agreed. The plaintiffs' sales manager said in his evidence, 'We can sell all the Hillman Minx cars we can get.' This evidence was accepted by the trial judge. The plaintiffs were really suggesting that, but for the defendant's refusal to complete, they would have sold two cars and not one and in so doing would have made two lots of profit. *Held* – Section 50(3) of the Sale of Goods Act did not apply here because the language of the subsection postulates that in the case to which it applies there will or may be a difference between the contract price and the market or current price which cannot be the case where the goods are, as here, saleable only at a fixed retail price. Having discarded s. 50(3), the Court of Appeal applied s. 50(2) which provides that damages should be the loss directly and naturally resulting in the ordinary course of events from the buyer's breach of contract. This was in the view of the court nominal damages of £2 only, because, as the plaintiffs' sales manager said, the plaintiffs could always find a purchaser for every Hillman Minx car they could get from the manufacturers and so the plaintiffs must have sold the same number of cars and made the same number of fixed profits as they would have sold and made if the defendant had duly carried out his promise.

Lazenby Garages v Wright [1976] 2 All ER 770

The plaintiffs were dealers in new and second-hand cars. They bought a secondhand BMW for £1,325. The defendant agreed in writing to buy it for £1,670 but before taking delivery he changed his mind and refused to purchase the car. Six weeks later the plaintiffs sold the same car for £1,770 to someone else but claimed damages from the defendant in the sum of £345, being the loss of profit on the agreed sale to him. The defendant contended that the plaintiffs had suffered no loss. The judge found that there was no 'available market' within s. 50(3) of the Sale of Goods Act, but applying s. 50(2) awarded the plaintiffs £172.50 on the basis that they would have had a 50/50 chance of selling an additional car had they sold the BMW to the defendant. On appeal it was *held* – by the Court of Appeal – allowing the appeal, that a second-hand car was a unique article, unlike new cars which are much the same and sell at fixed retail prices. Since the plaintiffs had sold the car at a higher price they had suffered no loss on the transaction and their action failed.

Comment: Since each second-hand car is unique, no two being in the same condition, there is no available market for them. There is no group of people interested in buying the same second-hand car. No group of people would be looking for, for example, a Ford Escort which had done 20,000 miles having two good and two worn tyres. In these circumstances the seller has to find a specific market.

Sales in an available market

Where there is an available market and the seller has sold the goods at the market price, then:

(a) if that price is less than the contract price, the seller can recover the balance by way of damages;

(b) if the market price is the same as or even higher than the contract price, the seller will only be entitled to nominal damages;

(c) if the seller sells for less than the market price, then he cannot recover the difference between the contract price and the resale price. It is the seller's duty to mitigate or reduce the loss and not to aggravate it;

(d) even if the seller keeps the goods after the buyer's breach of contract, and then later sells them for more than the market price was at the date of the breach, the seller can still recover the difference between the contract price and market price at the date of the breach, if the market price was then lower than the contract price.

Thus in *R Pagnan & Fratelli* v *Corbisa Industrial Agropacuaria* [1970] 1 All ER 165 Salmond LJ said ' . . . The innocent party is not bound to go on the market and buy or sell at the date of the breach. Nor is he bound to gamble on the market changing in his favour. He may wait if he chooses: and if the market turns against him this cannot increase the liability of the party in default; similarly, if the market turns in his favour, the liability of the party in default is not diminished.'

Suppose the contract price was £100 and the market price at the time of the breach was £80, then the seller is entitled to £20 damages. However:

(a) if he sells on the day of the breach for £60, the damages will still only be £20;

(b) if, hoping the market will improve, he delays the sale, he will still have the right to £20 damages and can retain the proceeds of the subsequent sale.

Anticipatory breach

Where there is an anticipatory breach of contract, e.g. where the goods are to be delivered in May but the buyer tells the seller in February that he will not accept, then if the seller refuses to accept the breach but sues upon the actual breach date damages are assessed on the market price at the date when the goods were to be delivered and accepted, i.e. the May market price. Where the seller accepts an anticipatory breach and sues upon it immediately, the date for delivery having not yet arrived when the case is tried, the court will have to estimate the market price at the date of delivery as best it can.

As regards the matter of *mitigation*, where there is an anticipatory breach and the market is falling, there are two possible situations.

(a) If the seller does not accept the repudiation, he need not resell the goods at once but is entitled to wait until the delivery date. If the buyer refuses to take delivery, the seller may resell and may recover from the original buyer as damages the difference between contract and market price at that date. It should be noted that the seller cannot be required to accept an anticipatory breach (*see White and Carter (Councils) Ltd* v *McGregor* (1961) at p. 209).

(b) If the seller accepts the repudiation, he must do all that he reasonably can to decrease the damages when the market is falling. If he delays in selling the goods, he will only be able to recover as damages the difference between contract and market price at the date of repudiation.

However, he has only to act reasonably and need not get the highest price possible. Thus in *Gebrüder Metelman GmbH & Co KG* v *NBR (London) Ltd* [1984] 1 Lloyd's Rep 614 the sellers, having accepted the buyers' repudiation, sold sugar immediately to a terminal market which stored sugar for future sales, rather like a marketing board. A higher price could have been obtained by shopping around the physical market. Nevertheless, the court held that the sellers had acted reasonably and their damages against the buyers could not be reduced by the higher price obtainable on the physical market.

Goods with no market

Where there is no market for the goods, as where the goods were made or procured specially for the purposes of the contract and cannot be sold to another buyer (e.g. because they are highly specialized goods), then there are two possible situations.

(a) Where the seller has actually made or procured the goods, he can claim the whole contract price, that is to say the cost to him of procuring or making the goods plus his profit.

(b) Where the seller has not made or procured the goods, he can claim his profit only.

REMEDIES OF THE BUYER

A number of remedies are available to the buyer where the seller is in breach of the contract. They are rejection of the goods, a claim for damages and an action for specific performance.

Rejection of the goods

The buyer may repudiate the contract and reject the goods where the seller is in breach of a condition. The effect of this is that the buyer may refuse to pay the price, or recover it if paid, or sue for damages, basing the latter claim on the seller's failure to deliver goods in accordance with the contract.

If the buyer rejects the goods, the property revests in the seller, and the buyer has no lien on the goods for the return of money paid by him under the contract. Section 36 provides that, unless otherwise agreed, where goods are delivered to the buyer, and he refuses to accept them, having the right to do so, he is not bound to return them to the seller, but it is sufficient if he intimates to the seller that he refuses to accept them.

Obviously the right to reject the goods will be lost where the property in them has passed to the buyer, and they have been accepted by him following a reasonable opportunity to examine them. A breach of condition will have to be treated as a breach of warranty and repudiation will not be possible (*see further* p. 274).

It is perhaps unfortunate that the law gives no right to a replacement of the goods but only to receive one's money back.

Damages

For non-delivery

Where the seller wrongfully neglects or refuses to deliver the goods to the buyer, the buyer may maintain an action against the seller for damages for non-delivery (s. 51(1)). The measure of damages is the estimated loss directly and naturally resulting, in the ordinary course of events, from the seller's breach of contract (s. 51(2)).

The buyer will, therefore, recover the difference (if any) between the market price and the contract price (s. 51(3)), and if he can buy similar goods cheaper in the market, the damages will be nominal. Where there is an anticipatory breach by the seller, the market price for the purpose of damages is that ruling when delivery ought to have been made, though if the buyer accepts the breach, he must buy quickly if the market price is rising for he has a duty to mitigate loss.

In addition where a buyer has lawfully rejected goods under a contract and makes a new agreement with the seller for the sale and purchase of the same goods at a reduced price, then although the buyer can sue under the original contract, the principle of mitigation of damages allows the court to take account of any profit made by the buyer on the subsequent contract provided that the subsequent contract is a part of a continuous dealing between the parties.

If, therefore, S delivers 100 tonnes of wheat at £30 per tonne to B, and B lawfully rejects the wheat because it is not up to standard, then according to s. 51(3), B has an action for damages based on the difference between the contract price and the market price. If we suppose that the market price was £32 per tonne B should recover damages of £200. If, however, at a later date B agrees to accept the same wheat at £28 per tonne he has no loss which is claimable, s. 51(3) being a mere guide to the assessment of damages which does not preclude other methods of assessment in appropriate cases (*R Pagnan & Fratelli v Corbisa Industrial Agropacuaria* [1970] 1 All ER 165).

Profit or loss on resale contracts made by the buyer is generally ignored in assessing damages for non-delivery (but *see Heron II* (1967) at p. 221). Thus in *Williams* v *Agius* [1914] AC 510 W agreed to buy from A a cargo of coal at a price of 16s 3d per ton. Later he agreed with X, a sub-purchaser, to sell him a similar cargo at 19s per ton. A failed to deliver the coal and W's damages were assessed to the buyer's benefit at the difference between the contract price of 16s 3d and the market price on the date when the delivery should have been made, which in this case was 23s 6d.

However, in *R H Hall Ltd* v *W H Pim & Co Ltd* [1928] All ER Rep 763 the House of Lords laid down exceptions to the rule that losses of profit on resale would be ignored. In general terms, a subsale will be taken into account where the first contract contemplates the creation of subsales so that the seller knows from the beginning that in the event of non-delivery the buyer could suffer loss in connection with such sales. In addition, the subcontract must be for the sale of *the same* goods as are to be supplied under the first contract and the subcontract must be created before the delivery date under the first contract and must not be an extravagant or unusual bargain. In *Hall v Pim* the buyers agreed to buy a cargo of wheat at 51s 9d per quarter and the contract clearly referred to the fact that goods might be resold. Later the buyers made a subsale of the same cargo at 56s 9d per quarter. When the seller refused to deliver the cargo the market price was 53s 9d per quarter and the buyers were awarded damages assessed at 5s per quarter and also damages which the buyers had to pay to their sub-buyer because they could not deliver.

The following cases illustrate the position where a subsale is not of the same goods and also that notice of subsales may be constructive as well as actual.

Slater *v* Hoyle and Smith Ltd [1920] 2 KB 11

The plaintiffs, who were manufactuers of cotton cloth, sued for damages for the refusal of the defendants to accept 1,375 pieces of unbleached cotton cloth, being the balance of 3,000 pieces which the defendants agreed to purchase from the plaintiffs. The defence was that the 1,625 pieces delivered and paid for were unmerchantable, and the defendants counter-claimed for damages in respect of this. The defendants had contracted to sell *bleached* cloth to other persons, and had bleached and sold 691 pieces of the cloth bought from the plaintiffs for this purpose. The plaintiffs took the view that the defendants should not recover on their counter-claim damages for 1,625 pieces of cloth as unmerchantable but 1,625 less the 691 pieces actually sold. *Held* – The subcontract should not be taken into account and the defendants should recover on their counter-claim for the reduced value of the 1,625 pieces of cloth delivered to them. The subcontracts were not known to the plaintiffs, and a subsale cannot be relied upon in mitigation of damages unless the subsale is of the identical article bought. Here what was bought was unbleached cloth and what was sold was bleached.

Pinnock Brothers v Lewis and Peat Ltd [1923] 1 KB 690

The plaintiffs bought from the defendants some East African copra cake which, to the defendants' knowledge, was to be used for feeding cattle. The cake was adulterated with castor oil and was poisonous. The plaintiffs resold the cake to other dealers, who in turn sold it to farmers, who used it for feeding cattle. Cattle fed on the cake died, and claims were made by the various buyers against their sellers, the whole liability resting eventually on the plaintiffs. In this action the plaintiffs sued for the damages and costs which they had been required to pay. Two major defences were raised, the first being an exemption clause saying that the goods were not warranted free from defects, and the other that the damage was too remote. The court dismissed the exemption clause and *held* that, when a substance is quite different from that contracted for it cannot merely be defective. Further the damage was not too remote, since it was in the implied contemplation of the defendants that the cake would at some time be fed to cattle.

For breach of condition or warranty

Where there is a breach of warranty by the seller or where the buyer elects, or is compelled, to treat any breach of condition on the part of the seller as a breach of warranty, the buyer is not by reason only of such breach of warranty entitled to reject the goods. However, he may:

(a) set up against the seller the breach of warranty in diminution or extinction of the price; or

(b) maintain an action against the seller for damages for the breach of warranty (s. 53(1)).

When there is late delivery, damages will be assessed on the basis of the actual loss resulting from the breach. Thus, if X should have delivered goods to Y on 1 January when the market price was £3.50 a tonne, and in fact delivers them on 1 February when the market price is £2.50 a tonne, the measure of damages would appear to be

£1 a tonne. But if Y in fact resells the goods at £3.25 a tonne, the damages will only be the difference between £3.25 and £3.50, i.e. 25p a tonne.

In the case of breach of warranty of quality the loss resulting is prima facie the difference between the value of the goods at the time of delivery to the buyer, and the value they would have had if they had answered to the warranty (s. 53(3)).

Losses incurred or damages paid by the buyer on subcontracts are, as we have seen, generally ignored in actions for breach of condition or warranty, as they are in actions for non- (or late) delivery unless the buyer can show either:

(a) that the seller had actual notice of the subcontracts; or
(b) that from the circumstances the seller had constructive notice of the sub-contracts.

For wrongful interference

Where the property in the goods has passed to the buyer he may bring an action for wrongful interference with goods. The action may be to recover possession or for damages.

Specific performance

Under s. 52(1) in any action for breach of contract to deliver specific or ascertained goods the court may, if it thinks fit, on the plaintiffs application by its judgment or decree direct that the contract shall be performed specifically, without giving the defendant the option of retaining the goods on payment of damages.

It will be appreciated that the remedy of specific performance is discretionary and will only be granted where damages would be insufficient. Thus in *Behnke v Bede Shipping Co* [1927] 1 KB 649 a shipowner agreed to buy a ship called *The City* which he required immediately and which satisfied all relevant shipping regulations in terms of equipment. There was only one other ship available. An order for specific performance was made since damages would not have been an adequate remedy in this case.

The court will not normally grant specific performance of a contract for the sale of unidentified goods, but its power to grant an injunction may have much the same effect. **The following case illustrates this point.**

Sky Petroleum v VIP Petroleum [1974] 1 All ER 954

In March 1970 the plaintiffs agreed to buy from the defendants all the petrol they required at their filling stations. The agreement was for 10 years. In December 1973, when the petrol crisis was at its height, the defendants said they would terminate the agreement on the grounds that the plaintiffs were in breach of contract, having exceeded the credit provisions. This would have meant that the plaintiffs would lose their only source of petrol supplies and they applied for an injunction to restrain the defendants from withholding the supply. It was *held* – by Goulding J – that the injunction would be granted, even though in this case it had the same effect as specific performance.

AUCTION SALES

Where goods are put up for sale by auction in lots, each lot is prima facie deemed to be the subject of a separate contract of sale (s. 57(1)). A sale by auction is complete when the auctioneer announces its completion by the fall of the hammer, or in other customary manner. Until such announcement is made, any bidder may retract his bid (s. 57(2)).

It seems also that, at an auction, each bid lapses when a new one is made. So, if X bids £10 for certain goods, and then Y bids £12, X's bid of £10 lapses. If Y withdraws his bid before the auctioneer has accepted it, the auctioneer cannot return to X's bid and accept that; X must be prepared to bid again.

A sale by auction may be notified to be subject to a reserve or upset price, and a right to bid may also be expressly reserved by or on behalf of the seller (s. 57(3)). Where a right to bid is expressly reserved, but not otherwise, the seller, or any person on his behalf may bid at the auction (s. 57(4)).

Seller's right to bid

If in a sale by auction the seller does not specifically reserve the right to bid, it is not lawful for the seller to bid himself or to employ any person to do so, or for the auctioneer knowingly to take any bid from the seller or any such person. Any sale contravening this rule may be treated as fraudulent by the buyer (s. 57(5)).

If there is no express statement as to the seller's right to bid, but he does bid, the buyer may repudiate the contract or sue for damages where he has paid a greater price than he would have had to pay because the seller has been bidding against him.

The seller is not allowed to bid merely because the sale is advertised to be without a reserve price. There must be some express notification of the seller's right to bid. Where the sale is subject to reserve price, and the seller bids without notification, the buyer may repudiate the contract or sue for damages, though, if the reserve was not reached, the would-be buyer will not have suffered loss, since he would not have obtained the *goods* even if the seller had not made bids.

Significance of reserve price

Where a sale is expressly notified to be subject to a reserve price the auctioneer has no power to sell below that reserve price. In addition the auctioneer cannot be made liable for breach of warranty if he will not sell below the reserve, nor is the owner liable for breach of contract since the auctioneer has no apparent authority to sell except at or above the reserve price. **The following case provides an illustration.**

McManus v Fortescue [1907] 2 KB 1

The defendants were auctioneers and offered for sale certain property on the terms of a printed catalogue and conditions of sale. Condition No. 2 was as follows:

> Each lot will be offered subject to a reserve price, and the vendors reserve the right of bidding up to such reserve price. The highest bidder for each lot shall be the purchaser. If any dispute arises concerning a bidding, the lot in question shall be put up again and re-sold, or the auctioneer may determine the dispute.

The lot in question was a corrugated iron building for which the plaintiff made a bid of £85. This was the highest bid and the auctioneer knocked the lot down to the plaintiff. Before the memorandum of sale was made and signed by the auctioneer, he opened a sealed envelope containing the reserve price and discovered that it was £200. The auctioneer then withdrew the lot and would not sign the memorandum of sale or accept the plaintiff's deposit. The plaintiff now sued the auctioneer for breach of his duty to sign the memorandum of sale. *Held* – When the hammer falls on a bid at an auction sale of property subject to a reserve, the auctioneer agrees on behalf of the vendor to sell at the amount of the last bid *provided* that such bid is equal to the reserve that has been made. The plaintiff's action failed.

Where there is no express statement as to a reserve price, the auctioneer is still entitled to refuse to accept any bid. The bid is an offer which the auctioneer is not forced to accept.

Where an auction is expressly advertised to be without reserve, it is clear that there is no sale of the goods if the auctioneer refuses to accept a bid (s. 57(2)). It is, however, possible that the auctioneer may be personally liable for breach of warranty of authority on the ground that he has contracted to sell to the highest bidder (*Warlow* v *Harrison* (1859) E & E 309).

The Auctions (Bidding Agreements) Act 1927, as amended by the Auctions (Bidding Agreements) Act 1969, provides for certain criminal penalties designed to prevent illegal auction rings which involve the giving of consideration to a person to abstain from bidding. Of interest as regards the civil law is s. 3 of the 1969 Act which provides that a sale at auction to any one party to an agreement with a dealer not to bid for the goods may avoid the contract. If the goods have been resold and cannot be handed back to the seller all the parties to the ring are liable to the seller to make good the loss he has suffered by selling at a lower price as a result of the activities of the ring.

EXPORT AND IMPORT SALES

Certain special clauses have been used over the years in sales where delivery has involved carriage by sea. These clauses have given rise to certain main types of contract, the major terms of which have become largely standardized, though there are variations as regards detailed provisions. These contracts and their major terms are dealt with briefly below.

FOB contracts

Under such a contract the seller must put the goods *free on board* a ship for despatch to the buyer. The buyer is generally responsible for selecting the port of shipment and the date of shipment of the goods. Where the contract provides for a range of ports from which the goods are to be shipped then it is the buyer's right and duty to select one of them and to give the seller sufficient notice of his selection (*David T Boyd & Co Ltd* v *Louis Louca* [1973] 1 Lloyd's Rep 209). The seller pays all charges incurred prior to the goods being put on board, but the buyer is liable to pay the freight or insurance. Once the goods are over the ship's rail, they are normally at the buyer's risk.

It is a matter for the buyer to insure the goods and his risk if they are lost, damaged, delayed or uninsured *en route* (*Frebold* v *Circle Products Ltd* [1970] 1 Lloyd's Rep 499). The seller may under a particular contract be responsible for shipping the goods and where this is so it is important to know whether the seller ships on his own account as principal or as an agent for the buyer. If he ships as principal the property in the goods will not normally pass on shipment, though it will usually do so if he ships as agent (*President of India* v *Metcalfe Shipping Co* [1969] 3 All ER 1549).

Section 32(3) provides that, unless otherwise agreed, where the goods are sent by the seller to the buyer by a route involving sea transit, under circumstances in which it is usual to insure, the seller must give such notice to the buyer as may enable him to insure them during their sea transit, and, if the seller fails to do so, the goods shall be deemed to be at his risk during such sea transit. Thus delivery to the carrier will not necessarily pass the risk in FOB contracts.

Nowadays the seller often makes the contract of carriage. It must be reasonable in terms of the nature of the goods and other circumstances. If not and the goods are lost or damaged in the course of transit, the buyer may decline to treat the delivery to the carrier as a delivery to himself or may hold the seller responsible in damages (s. 32(2)).

CIF contracts

Generally

A CIF contract is one by which the seller agrees to sell goods at a price which includes the *cost* of the goods, the *insurance* premium required to insure the goods, and the *freight* (or cost) of transporting them to their destination.

Duties of the seller

(a) To ship goods of the description contained in the contract under a contract of affreightment which will ensure the delivery of the goods at the destination contemplated in the contract. Undertakings in the contract as to time and place of shipment are nearly always treated as conditions. Thus the buyer may reject the goods if they are shipped too late or too soon (*see Bowes* v *Shand* (1877) at p. 198).

(b) To arrange for insurance which will be available to the buyer.

(c) To make out an invoice for the goods.

(d) To tender the documents to the buyer in exchange for the price, so that the buyer will know the amount of the freight he must pay as part of the price, and so that he can obtain delivery of the goods if they arrive, or recover for their loss if they are lost on the voyage.

Refusal of buyer to accept goods

In a CIF contract the buyer or his agent may repudiate the contract:

(a) by refusing to accept the documents if they do not conform with the contract; and

(b) by rejecting the goods on delivery if following inspection they do not comply with the contract.

Passing of the risk

The risk passes in a CIF contract when the goods are shipped and the buyer will still have to pay for the goods if they are lost on the voyage, though he will have the insurance cover. The property in the goods does not pass until the seller transfers the documents to the buyer and the latter has paid for them (*Mirabita* v *Imperial Ottoman Bank* (1878) 3 Ex D 164). If the goods have been shipped, but the documents have not been transferred, there is a conditional appropriation of the goods to the contract which will not become unconditional until the buyer takes up the documents and pays for them. It will be seen, therefore, that a CIF contract is in essence a 'sale of documents', the delivery of which transfers the property and the possession of the goods to the transferee. However, a CIF contract is regarded as a sale of goods because it contemplates the transfer of goods in due course, and for this reason the Act of 1979 applies.

Where S sells goods to B under an export contract and the ownership (or property) has not passed because B has not paid S (*see* the *Mirabita* case *above*), then if in transit the goods are lost or damaged by, say, the carrier's negligence B can claim on the insurance policy but cannot sue the carrier for any economic loss which may have arisen because the goods were not available to him. This was decided by the House of Lords in *Leigh & Sillavan Ltd* v *Aliakmon Shipping Co* [1986] 2 All ER 145 where Lord Brandon said: '... there is a long line of authority for a principle of law that, in order to enable a person to claim in negligence for loss caused to him by reason of loss of or damage to property, he must have had either the legal ownership of or a possessory title to the property concerned at the time when the loss or damage occurred and it is not enough for him to have only contractual rights in relation to such property which have been adversely affected by the loss of or damage to it.'

FAS contracts

In a *free alongside ship* contract the seller is required to deliver the goods to the buyer at a named port of discharge and place them alongside the ship which is to carry them. If the ship cannot enter port the seller must pay for barges or lighters to take the goods alongside the ship. The buyer must concern himself with loading. If the seller does not make delivery, the buyer cannot be made to pay the price, or, if the price has been paid, it can be recovered on the basis of total failure of consideration. The property and the risk in the goods pass when the goods are delivered alongside the ship, and the seller is under no obligation to insure them: if he does so it is entirely for his own benefit.

FOR contracts

The seller is responsible under an FOR (*free on rail*) contract for all charges incurred in delivering the goods to an appropriate rail depot for transportation to the buyer.

FOT contracts

The seller is responsible under an FOT (*free on truck*) contract for all charges incurred in delivering the goods to a carrier by road and for the loading of these on to the lorry or truck which is to transport them.

Ex-works or ex-store contracts

Here it is the duty of the buyer to take delivery of the goods at the works or store of the seller as the case may be. The property and risk usually pass when the buyer takes delivery. These sales are almost always of unascertained goods, the appropriation taking place when the goods are selected or handed over at the works or store. They are perhaps not ideally categorized as export sales because they consist of the mere collection of goods by the buyer who may then deal with them as he wishes. There need not in fact be any export involving carriage by sea.

GRADED QUESTIONS

Essay mode

1. (a) In what circumstances does a seller acquire a lien over goods he has sold?

   (b) Michael sold a consignment of diamonds in London to Simon for £10,000. Simon paid £4,000 when the sale was made and agreed to pay the balance of the price on delivery of the stones to his premises in Manchester. Michael instructed Transit Security Services Ltd to deliver the stones to Simon and to collect the balance of the purchase money. On arrival in Manchester, Transit Security Services Ltd were informed that Simon was insolvent and notified Michael. Michael ordered Transit Security Services Ltd to withhold delivery. Simon claims that he is not insolvent and threatens to sue Michael and Transit Security Services Ltd.
   Advise Michael and Transit Security Services Ltd.

   (The Institute of Company Accountants. Part: Law Relating to Business. May 1989)

2. How are damages assessed for breach of a contract for the sale of goods?

   (Staffordshire Polytechnic. BA(Hons) Business Studies: Business Law. June 1990)

3. In what circumstances may a seller of goods resell them to a second buyer, without rendering himself liable to the person who originally agreed to buy those goods.

   (10 marks)

AND:

Smith, a wholesaler, takes an order on 1st August for the sale of 1,000 boxes of Christmas crackers to Brown, a market trader, at a price of £2,500. Brown agrees to collect the boxes from Smith's warehouse by October 1st. On 15th September Brown telephones Smith to tell him he will have to cancel the order because he is shortly giving up his market stall due to lack of trade. By this time the market value of the crackers has fallen to £2,250, and by October 1st it will be approximately £2,000. It is likely that there will be a continued decline in the value as Christmas approaches, because suppliers reduce prices to clear stock.

The boxes are still stacked in Smith's warehouse, and no money has yet been paid.

Consider what Smith can claim by way of a remedy, raising any additional factors beyond those stated which might affect the position.

(15 marks)

(Staffordshire Polytechnic. BA(Hons) Business Studies: Commercial Law. May 1990)

Objective mode

Four alternative answers are given. Select ONE only. Circle the answer which you consider to be correct. Check your answers by referring back to the information given in the relevant chapter and against the answers at the back of the book.

1. Alf, a car dealer, sold a second-hand car to Bob for £600, which was the agreed market price. Bob left a part-payment of £20, promising to return later in the day and pick it up. Before taking the car away, Bob had another look at it and said he thought it was older than Alf alleged, and refused to accept it. Alf wrote to Bob, giving him one week to pay for the car and take delivery, otherwise he would sell it. Bob did not pay, and Alf sold the vehicle to Charlie for £550 after advertising it again at a cost of £20. Bob has told Alf he can keep the £20 part-payment. Alf is not satisfied.

   If Alf brought the matter before a court, which of the following amounts would be received by way of damages against Bob?

   A £50.
   B £70.
   C Nothing.
   D £20.

2. An unpaid seller has a lien on the goods until payment of the whole of the price. This lien is:

   A Equitable.
   B Possessory.
   C Discretionary.
   D Constructive.

3. The right of stoppage *in transitu* can be exercised by an unpaid seller only if:

   A The goods have been sold without stipulation as to credit.
   B The buyer is insolvent.
   C The term of credit has expired.
   D None of the goods have been delivered.

4. Where there is a contract for the sale of unascertained or future goods by description the property in the goods passes to the buyer when goods of that description are unconditionally appropriated to the contract:

   A Either by the buyer with notice to the seller or by the seller with notice to the buyer.
   B Either by the buyer with the assent of the seller or by the seller with the assent of the buyer.
   C Either by the buyer or the seller with an opportunity for examination of the goods by the other party.
   D By delivery to a carrier by the seller.

5. Polly agrees to buy William's vintage Bentley after inspecting and approving it at William's address in Brighton Polly asks William to arrange for Vintage Traction Ltd to deliver it to Polly's address in North Wales on a trailer, which he does. Vintage Traction Ltd present Polly with a bill for £200 which she pays but then presents to William on the basis that 'delivery is the responsibility of the seller'. What is the legal position?

   A William must pay for the delivery costs since it is the duty of the seller to deliver the goods.
   B Polly must pay for the delivery costs since the place of delivery is the seller's place of business or residence.
   C William must pay for delivery since the place of delivery is the buyer's place of business or residence.
   D William must pay for delivery since this is a case where delivery should have been agreed and William arranged the transport and should pay for it.

6. Fergus, a hotel proprietor, decides to sell the hotel's deep-freeze and advertises it. Robert, a boarding house proprietor, inspects the deep-freeze and makes an offer of £100 bearing in mind its general condition. Fergus agrees but excludes 'any liability for non-merchantability'. The freezer does not like the move and refuses to work.

   A Robert can claim back the £100 since this is a consumer purchase in which it is not possible to exclude the condition of merchantable quality.
   B Since Robert required the freezer for his own business then this would not be a consumer sale and the exclusion clause would be valid provided it was reasonable.
   C Robert cannot claim back the £100 since the price was so low it is not reasonable for the condition of merchantable quality to be applied. *Caveat emptor.*
   D Robert can claim back the £100 since an exclusion clause cannot excuse total non-performance of the contract.

7. The Sale of Goods Act s. 20 states that the risk in goods passes at the same time as the property. Which of the following is an exception to this?

   A Under a free on board (FOB) contract.
   B Under a cost insurance and freight (CIF) contract.
   C Under an 'ex-ship' contract.
   D When goods are sent on approval or on sale or return.

Answers to questions set in objective mode appear on p. 551.

13 | Contracts for the supply of goods and services

The OBJECTIVES of this chapter are to consider the law relating to contracts for work and materials, e.g. car repairs, and for the supply of services and the implied terms therein.

SUPPLY OF GOODS OTHER THAN BY SALE

As regards the rights of those who purchase goods, we have seen that the Sale of Goods Act 1979 applies and that ss. 12–15 of that Act imply terms to which a buyer may resort if the goods are faulty, defective or unsuitable. Conditional sales and credit sales come within the 1979 Act. Those who take goods on hire-purchase are similarly protected by ss. 8–11 of the Supply of Goods (Implied Terms) Act 1973.

As regards contracts for work and materials, the supply of goods (or the materials used) is governed by Part I of the Supply of Goods and Services Act 1982. The services supplied (or the work element) are governed by Part II of the 1982 Act.

Contracts of exchange or barter, hire, rental or leasing are governed by Part I of the 1982 Act, while contracts for services only, e.g. a contract to carry goods or advice from an accountant or solicitor, are governed by Part II of the 1982 Act. The relevant provisions of the Act are dealt with in detail below. Section references are to the 1982 Act unless otherwise indicated.

CONTRACTS FOR THE TRANSFER OF PROPERTY IN GOODS

The contracts concerned are dealt with in s. 1(1) which provides that a contract for the transfer of goods means a contract under which one person transfers, or agrees to transfer to another, the property in goods, unless the transfer takes place under an excluded contract. These excluded contracts are set out in s. 1(2). They are contracts for the sale of goods, hire-purchase contracts, and those where the property in goods is transferred on a redemption of trading stamps. (These are governed by the Trading Stamps Act 1964.) Transfer of property rights in goods by way of mortgage, pledge, charge or other security are excluded, as are gifts.

There must be a contract between the parties. If not, the statutory implied terms cannot be relied upon if the goods supplied prove to be defective. Thus a chemist supplying harmful drugs under a National Health Service prescription will not come within the Act. This is because the patient does not provide consideration. The chemist collects the prescription charge for the government and not for himself. The payment to the chemist does not come from the patient unless it is a private prescription where the patient has paid the full amount. Otherwise an action against the chemist would have to be framed in the tort of negligence.

As regards promotional free gifts, e.g. the giving away of a radio to a purchaser of a television set, the free gift may not be within the 1982 Act. The matter is not free from doubt, but s. 1(2)(d) excludes contracts for the supply of goods which are enforceable only because they are made by deed which would seem to exclude other gifts. Furthermore, the Law Commission Report (No. 95 published in 1979) on which the Act is based concludes that gifts are outside the scope of the Act.

CONTRACTS FOR WORK AND MATERIALS

Reference has already been made to the distinction between these contracts and contracts of sale of goods and some examples have been given (*see* p. 237). It is impossible to provide a complete list of contracts for work and materials but they fall under three broad heads as follows.

(a) *Maintenance contracts.* Here the organization doing the maintenance supplies the labour and spare parts as required. An example would be a maintenance contract for lifts.
(b) *Building and construction contracts.* Here the builder supplies labour and materials. An example would be the alteration of an office or workshop involving the insertion of new windows and extending the central heating system.
(c) *Installation and improvement contracts.* Here the contractor does not have to build or construct anything but, for example, fits equipment into an existing building or applies paint to it. Examples are the fitting of an air-conditioning system, or painting and decorating an office or workshop.

THE TERMS IMPLIED

Title

Section 2 implies terms about title. Under s. 2(1) there is an implied condition that the supplier has a right to transfer the property in the goods to the customer. Under s. 2(2) two warranties are implied:

(a) that the goods are free from any charge or encumbrance which has not been disclosed to the customer; and

(b) that the customer will enjoy quiet possession except when disturbed by the owner or other person whose charge or encumbrance has been disclosed.

The customer would have an action here if he suffered loss as a result of the true owner reclaiming or suing in conversion where the materials fitted had been stolen. Sections 2(3), (4) and (5) are concerned with sales under a limited title. If under the contract the supplier is to give only such title as he may possess, s. 2(1) does not apply but warranties are implied that the supplier will disclose all charges and encumbrances which he knows about and that the customer's quiet possession of the goods will not be disturbed by, for example, the supplier or the holder of an undisclosed charge or encumbrance.

Cases involving bad title have occurred not infrequently in the sale of goods but the problem seems to have arisen only rarely in contracts for work and materials.

Description

Under s. 3 there is an implied condition that where a seller transfers property in goods by description, the goods will correspond with the description. If the goods are supplied by reference to a sample as well as a description they must correspond with the sample as well as the description. Section 3 applies even where the customer selects the goods.

Section 3 will operate, for example, where a person is having his house or business premises extended and agrees with the contractor a detailed specification which describes the materials to be installed. It will not operate in some types of maintenance contract where the materials to be replaced are unknown until the maintenance is carried out. The materials fitted in the course of such a contract will not be described *before* the contract is made but probably only in an invoice *after* it has been made, which is too late to apply s. 3. It should be noted that ss. 2 and 3 apply to supplies in the course of a business *and* to a supply by person other than in the course of a business, e.g. a milkman 'moonlighting' by doing the odd decorating job, provided there is a contract. They would not apply to a mere friendly transaction without consideration.

Quality and fitness

The first implied term in this area is in s. 4 and it relates to *merchantable quality* (s. 4(2)). Merchantability is defined in s. 4(9) which states that the goods must be as fit for the purpose for which they are commonly supplied as it is reasonable to expect, having regard to their description, price and other relevant circumstances. This condition of merchantable quality does not apply to defects:

(a) drawn to the customer's attention before the contract is made; or
(b) which any prior examination the customer *has actually made* ought to have revealed.

Thus if the materials used are dangerous, unsafe, defective or faulty, and will not work properly under normal conditions, the supplier is in breach of s. 4(2).

However, if the materials are described as 'seconds' or 'fire-damaged' the customer cannot complain if the materials are of lower quality than goods not so described.

As regards defects which ought to have been revealed where the customer has examined the goods, it is not likely that materials used in a contract for work and materials will be identified before the contract or that the customer will examine them. If they are examined the customer should ensure that it is done properly so that obvious defects are seen and the goods rejected.

The second implied term in s. 4 relates to *fitness for the purpose* (s. 4(5)). Where a customer makes known, either expressly or by implication, to the supplier any particular purpose for which the goods are being acquired, there is an implied condition that the goods are reasonably fit for the purpose. This condition does not apply where the customer does not rely on, or it is not reasonable for him to rely on, the skill or judgment of the supplier.

If, for example, a factory process requires a lot of water supplied under high pressure, e.g. to clean special equipment, and the factory owners ask for the installation of a system of pressure hoses and a pump, revealing to the contractor precisely what the requirements are, then the contractor will be in breach of s. 4(5) if the pressure is inadequate. This will be so even though the pressure hoses and pump are perfectly merchantable and would have been quite adequate for use in a different type of installation.

Of course, the way out of the fitness problem for the supplier is for him to make it clear to the customer that he has no idea whether the equipment will be suitable for the customer's special requirements. In such a case he will not be liable, though he may put some customers off by his unhelpful attitude.

Sample

If under the contract there is a transfer of the property in goods by reference to a sample, then under s. 5 there is an implied condition that

(a) the bulk will correspond with the sample in quality;

(b) the customer will have a reasonable opportunity of comparing the bulk with the sample; and

(c) there will not be any defect making the goods unmerchantable which would not have been apparent on a reasonable examination of the sample.

Except as provided by ss. 4 and 5, no conditions or warranties as to quality or fitness are to be implied into contracts for the transfer of goods. Sections 4 and 5 apply only to a supply of goods in the course of a business, and not to a supply by our friend the moonlighting decorator.

REMEDIES

In so far as the implied terms are conditions and are broken by the supplier, then the customer can treat the contract as repudiated. The customer is discharged from his obligation to pay the agreed price and may recover damages. The breach of implied warranties gives the customer only the right to sue for damages.

EXCHANGE AND BARTER

The most likely transactions to emerge here are the exchange of goods for vouchers and coupons as part of promotional schemes. Part I of the 1982 Act applies and the retailer who supplies the goods under a contract to the customer is the one who is liable if they are in breach of, for example, the implied terms of fitness and/or merchantable quality. The manufacturer will be liable to the retailer, of course.

An exchange transaction in which goods are simply exchanged is not a sale but is covered by the 1982 Act. Where part of the consideration is money, as in a part-exchange of an old car for a new one with a cash difference, the contract is presumably a sale of goods because money is at least part of the consideration. It does not really matter now whether it is a sale or a supply, because the implied terms are almost identical.

Often where there has been a sale of faulty goods the seller exchanges them for other goods of the same type, although he is under no legal duty to do so unless a particular contract expressly provides. What happens if the other goods are faulty? The substitute goods must comply with the implied terms as to title, description, quality and fitness, and there is no longer any point in going into legal niceties as to whether the exchange is a sale or supply.

The terms implied

The implied terms in exchange or barter are the same as those implied in a contract for work and materials, i.e. s. 2 (title), s. 3 (description), s. 4(2) (merchantable quality), s. 4(5) (fitness) and s. 5 (sample).

CONTRACTS FOR THE HIRE OF GOODS

The main areas of hiring (or renting or leasing) are as follows:

(a) *office equipment*, e.g. office furniture and a variety of machines, including telephones;
(b) *building and construction plant and equipment*, e.g. cranes and JCBs;
(c) *consumer hiring*, e.g. cars, television and video.

Under s. 6(1) a contract for the hire of goods means a contract under which one person bails, or agrees to bail, goods to another by way of hire. There must be a contract, so that when the next-door neighbour makes a free loan of his lawnmower the Act does not apply. Also excluded are hire-purchase agreements. A contract is a contract of hire whether or not services are also provided. This would be the case where a supplier rented a television to a customer and also undertook to service it.

THE TERMS IMPLIED

Title

Section 7 deals with title. It reflects s. 2 except that being a contract of hire there is provision only for the transfer of possession and not ownership. There is an *implied condition* on the part of the supplier that he has the right to transfer possession of the goods to the customer by hiring for the appropriate period. There is also a *warranty* that the customer will enjoy quiet possession of the goods except where it is disturbed by the owner or other person entitled to the benefit of any charge or encumbrance disclosed to the customer before the contract was made.

If, for example, the undisclosed true owner retakes possession so that the supplier is in breach of s. 7, then the customer will have an action for damages. These will reflect the value he had had under the contract before the goods were taken from him. Thus if C pays S £120 for the year's rent of a television but the undisclosed true owner takes it back after, say, two months, the damages would, on the face of it, be £100.

Neither of the terms in s. 7 prevent the supplier from taking the goods back himself provided the contract allows this, as where it provides *expressly* for the repossession of the goods on failure to pay the rental or the court is prepared to *imply* that it does.

Description

Section 8 is the equivalent of s. 3. Where the supplier hires or agrees to hire the goods by description there is an implied condition that the goods will correspond with the description. If the goods are hired by reference to a sample as well as by description, they must correspond with the description as well as the sample. Section 8 applies even where the customer selects the goods. If the goods do not match the description the customer will be able to reject them and recover damages for any loss.

Quality and fitness

Section 9 enacts the same provisions for hiring contracts as s. 4 does for contracts of work and materials and exchange and barter. Except as provided by ss. 9 and 10 (hire by sample), there are no implied terms regarding quality or fitness for any purpose of goods hired.

There are two terms in s. 9 as follows.

(a) *An implied condition that the goods hired are of merchantable quality.* There is no such condition where a particular defect has been drawn to the customer's attention before the contract was made or to defects which he should have noticed *if he actually examined* the goods.

(b) *An implied condition that the goods hired are reasonably fit for any purpose to which the customer is going to put them.* The purpose must have been made known to the supplier, expressly or by implication. The condition does not apply if the customer does not rely on the skill of the seller or if it is unreasonable for him to have done so.

Once again, where goods are to be hired for a special purpose, the supplier should make it clear that the customer must not rely on him if he wishes to avoid the implied condition of fitness. This has rather special application to those who supply DIY equipment on hire. A supplier in this area should certainly not overestimate the capacity of, for example, power tools, in order to get business. If he does he certainly faces s. 9 liability.

Where the goods are leased by a finance house, it is responsible for breach of the implied terms in the hiring contract. It is in effect the supplier. This is also true of hire-purchase where the implied terms of the Supply of Goods (Implied Terms) Act 1973 apply against the finance company.

As regards fitness for the purpose, it is enough to involve the finance company in liability if the customer has told the distributor of the purpose. Generally, of course, the finance house will have an indemnity against the distributor under which it may recover any damages it has to pay, so it will all get back to the distributor in the end.

The above conditions relate to the state of the goods at the beginning of the hiring and for a reasonable time thereafter. It does not impose upon the supplier a duty to maintain and repair. This must be provided for separately in the contract.

Thus in *UCB Leasing Ltd* v *Holtom* (1987) 137 NLJ 614 the Court of Appeal decided that where a car was the subject of a long leasing agreement, the owner was not under an obligation to provide a vehicle which was fit for the purpose during the whole period of the leasing. Instead, rather like a sale of goods, the obligation is to provide a vehicle which is fit at the outset of the agreement. If it is not, the hirer must rescind quickly if he wishes to return the car. If he does not do so he cannot return the vehicle but is entitled to damages only.

Sample

Section 10 applies and is in line with s. 5 (above). Section 10 states that in a hiring by sample there is an implied condition that the bulk will correspond with the sample in quality; that the customer will have a reasonable opportunity to compare the bulk with the sample; and that there will be no defects in the goods supplied rendering them unmerchantable which would not have been apparent on a reasonable examination of the sample.

As with ss. 4 and 5 (above) the terms of ss. 9 and 10 are implied only into contracts for hiring entered into in the course of a business. Thus if there is a hiring for value with a private owner, or a mere friendly lending without consideration, s. 9 of the Act would not apply. Incorrect and express statements by a private owner would be actionable in the common law of contract provided that there was consideration. In a friendly lending there could be an action for negligent misstatements made by the owner about the goods if they cause damage (*see Hedley Byrne* v *Heller & Partners* (1963), p. 115).

EXCLUSION CLAUSES

Section 11 of the 1982 Act applies the provisions of the Unfair Contract Terms Act 1977 to exclusion clauses in work and materials barter and exchange, and hiring contracts. The effect of this is set out below.

(a) *Consumer transactions.* In a contract covered by Part I of the Act, the rights given by the implied terms under ss. 3–5 and ss. 8–10 of the 1982 Act cannot be excluded or restricted. We have already described the circumstances in which a person deals as a consumer (*see* p. 154).

(b) *Business contracts.* In these circumstances the supplier can only rely on an exclusion clause if it is reasonable. However, the obligations relating to title in

s. 2 of the 1982 Act cannot be excluded in a business dealing relating to work and materials and barter and exchange any more than they can in a consumer dealing (*see* s. 7, Unfair Contract Terms Act 1977, as amended by s. 17(2) of the 1982 Act).

However, the term in s. 7 relating to the right of possession in the case of a hiring can be excluded in a consumer or business contract if reasonable.

THE SUPPLY OF SERVICES

The main areas of complaint in regard to services have been the *poor quality of service*, e.g. the careless servicing of cars; *slowness in completing work*, where complaints have ranged over a wide area from, for example, building contractors to solicitors; *the cost of the work*, i.e. overcharging. Part II of the Act is concerned to deal with these matters.

The contracts covered

Under s. 12(1) a contract for the supply of a service means a contract under which a person agrees to carry out a service. A contract of service (i.e. an employment contract) or apprenticeship is not included, but apart from this no attempt is made to define the word 'service'. However, the services provided by the professions, e.g. accountants, architects, solicitors, and surveyors, are included.

Section 12(4) gives the Secretary of State for Trade and Industry power to exempt certain services from the provisions of Part II. Of importance here is the Supply of Services (Exclusion of Implied Terms) Order 1982 (SI 1982/1771) which retains the common-law liability in negligence of lawyers by exempting barristers and solicitors when acting as advocates before various courts and tribunals. It also exempts services rendered by a director to his company, thus retaining existing common-law liability in this area, too. This is largely because more time is needed to consult the relevant interests and decide what sort of liability there should be in the areas referred to.

Part II applies *only to contracts*. If there is no contract there cannot be implied terms. This will exclude work done free as a friendly gesture by a friend or neighbour. If, however, injury is caused to a person who is not in a contractual relationship with a supplier as a result of the negligence of the supplier, there may be an action in the tort of negligence at common law (*see* p. 267).

Duty of care and skill

This duty applies to contracts which are purely for service, e.g. advice from an accountant or solicitor, and also to the service element of a contract for work and materials. Section 13 provides that where the supplier of a service is acting in the course of a business there is an implied term that the supplier will carry out that service with reasonable skill and care. This means that the service must be performed with the care and skill of a reasonably competent member of the supplier's trade or profession. In other words, the test is objective, not subjective. Thus an incompetent supplier may be liable even though he has done his best. A private supplier of a service, e.g. a moonlighter, will not have this duty.

There is no reference to conditions and warranties in regard to this implied term. Generally, therefore, the action for breach of the term will be damages. In a serious case repudiation of the contract may be possible. This is rather like the intermediate term concept discussed at p. 141.

Cases such as *Woodman* v *Photo Trade Processing Ltd* and *Waldron-Kelly* v *British Railways Board*, which were brought on the basis of the common-law tort of negligence, would now be brought under the 1982 Act (*see further* p. 160).

Time for performance

Section 14 provides that a supplier who acts in the course of a business will carry out the service within a reasonable time. This term is only implied where the time for performance is not fixed by the contract, but left to be fixed in a manner agreed by the contract, or determined by the dealings of the parties. Section 14 states that what is a reasonable time is a question of fact. A plaintiff can claim damages for unreasonable delay. Of course, if a time for performance is fixed by the contract, it must be performed at that time and the question of reasonableness does not arise. Time is of the essence in commercial contracts unless the parties expressly provide otherwise or there is a waiver (*see further* p. 197).

The charges made for the service

Under s. 15 the customer's obligation is to pay 'a reasonable charge' which is again a matter of fact. This matter is not implied where the charge for the service is determined by the contract, left to be determined in a manner agreed by the contract, or determined by the dealings of the parties. The section in essence enacts the common-law rule of *quantum meruit* (*see* p. 226); it protects both the supplier and the customer, and applies to a supply in the course of a business and to a supply by a moonlighter.

EXCLUSION CLAUSES

Section 16 of the 1982 Act applies the provisions of the Unfair Contract Terms Act

1977 to exclusion clauses in regard to services. Section 2 of the 1977 Act is, as we have seen, concerned with liability for negligence. There can be no exclusion of liability if death or personal injury is caused. In other cases an exclusion clause may apply if reasonable.

Section 3 of the 1977 Act is concerned with liability for breach of contract. Broadly speaking, as we have seen, there can be no exclusion of liability for breach of contract, or a different performance or non-performance, unless reasonable. The terms implied by the 1982 Act cannot be excluded in a consumer transaction. They can in a non-consumer deal if reasonable. The criteria relating to bargaining power and so on apply only to the exclusion of implied terms in a non-consumer transaction relating to goods, but they will no doubt be applied by analogy to contracts under the 1982 Act.

GRADED QUESTIONS

Essay mode

1. (a) Explain, with illustrations, the distinction between a contract for the sale of goods and a contract for work and materials.
   (b) De Luxe Kitchens has published the following advertisement in the national press: 'Free Double Oven worth £500 when you buy a Luxury Fitted Kitchen from us'. Alec responds to the advertisement and has a fitted kitchen supplied and installed by De Luxe Kitchens. The installation is quite satisfactory but the oven is defective and does not work. Alec seeks your advice.
   Advise Alec as to his remedies, if any, in relation to the oven.
   (Institute of Chartered Secretaries and Administrators. English Business Law. June 1989)

2. (a) In what circumstances, if any, may the purchaser of goods acquire a valid title from the vendor where the vendor is not the owner of the goods?

   (10 marks)

   (b) S owns a personal computer which he uses for word processing. Following a malfunction S took the machine to T Ltd, a firm in business selling and repairing personal computers. T Ltd told S that the repair would be a straightforward matter, but it took them over five months to repair the machine and return it to S. When the machine was returned its plastic cover was badly scratched and damaged in several places. An invoice was sent with the machine saying 'Parts – £3.00; two hours labour – £80.00'. S is extremely annoyed at what he considers to be the gross delay in repairing the machine, the damage to its cover and at what he thinks is an exorbitant charge for the repair.

Advise S as to his rights, if any, under the Supply of Goods and Services Act 1982.

(10 marks)

(20 marks)

(The Chartered Institute of Certified Accountants. Paper 1.4: Law. December 1989)

3. Simon agrees to sell goods to Brian, delivery to be made by three instalments. The first instalment has been delivered and the second instalment has just been despatched when Simon hears that Brian is in financial difficulty. The third instalment is in Simon's warehouse awaiting despatch.

(a) What action may Simon take to safeguard his position?

(14 marks)

(b) Explain how a reservation of title clause might give Simon better protection in this situation.

(6 marks)

(Total: 20 marks)

(The Chartered Institute of Management Accountants. Business Law. May 1990)

Objective mode

Four alternative answers are given. Select ONE only. Circle the answer which you consider to be correct. Check your answers by referring back to the information given in the relevant chapter and against the answers at the back of the book.

1. Mrs Smith wanted a new fitted kitchen. She eventually agreed with a company called Boxo Ltd to carry out the work. The materials and labour were supplied by Boxo Ltd but Mrs Smith did ask them to fit a 'Whoosh' extractor fan. After being used normally for two months the motor stopped and could not be put right. Mrs Smith could not contact the company which made the fan because it had been wound up. She therefore contacted Boxo Ltd saying that it was their responsibility. Boxo's representative said: 'Oh, no it's not. You told us to get a "Whoosh". Actually, if you had left it to us we would have fitted a "Zoom".'

Advise Mrs Smith.

   A Mrs Smith has no claim since she did not rely on the skill and judgment of Boxo Ltd.

   B Mrs Smith can claim against Boxo Ltd because they should have advised that a 'Zoom' be fitted.

   C Mrs Smith has no claim because the fan ran for two months and she has affirmed the contract.

   D Mrs Smith may only claim against the company which made the fan.

2. Mrs Mopp's electric pop-up toaster would not toast because she could not push the handle down fully. She took it to a small electrical shop owned by Fred Sparks for repair. Fred said: 'Leave it with me. I'll fix it. Call back in a couple of hours.'

Mrs Mopp returned some two hours later and Fred said: 'It's fine now, that'll be £10.' Mrs Mopp was a bit shocked and asked what was wrong with the toaster. Fred said: 'Not much; we had to bend the handle straight and oil it, that's all.' Mrs Mopp said: 'But surely you cannot charge me £10 for that.' 'Sorry, Madam,' said Fred, 'It's our minimum charge; labour costs, you know.'

Advise Mrs Mopp.

   A Mrs Mopp is obliged by statute to pay £10.
   B Mrs Mopp is obliged by statute to pay only a reasonable charge.
   C Mrs Mopp is obliged to pay £10 because she did not agree a fee for the work.
   D Mrs Mopp is obliged by the common law to pay £10.

3. James has offered to sell his Teenage Mutant Ninja Turtle collection to Eddie and has promised to keep the offer open until Thursday. On Tuesday he decides he wants to withdraw the offer and posts a letter of revocation that day. On Wednesday, Eddie posts his letter of acceptance. Both letters reach their destination on Thursday.

Can Eddie sue James?

   A Yes, James promised to keep the offer open until Thursday. As Eddie accepted by that day his acceptance is valid.
   B No, James posted his letter of revocation before Eddie posted his letter of acceptance therefore James' letter takes precedence.
   C Yes, as he had not received notice of revocation Eddie's acceptance is binding once the letter has been posted.
   D No. Acceptance must reach the offerer before revocation takes place.

4. Alan promises Dave £1,000 if he completes a 20km run. Dave faints 500m from the finishing line. Can Dave claim the £1,000?

   A Dave can sue Alan for the whole sum under the doctrine of substantial performance.
   B Dave can sue Alan for part of the sum as a *quantum meruit*.
   C Dave cannot sue Alan as Dave's completion of the run was a condition for recovery under the contract.
   D Dave cannot sue Alan as his failure to complete the run will be regarded as self-induced frustration.

5. Tom and Dick enter into face to face negotiations. Dick has made out that he is a wealthy film star and therefore thoroughly creditworthy. Dick is neither of these things. If Tom makes Dick an offer and Dick accepts, the contract is:

   A Void, as Tom has made a mistake as to Dick's attributes.
   B Voidable, as Dick has fraudulently misrepresented the true facts
   C Void, as Tom has made a mistake as to Dick's identity.
   D Void, as there has been a mutual mistake as to purpose.

6. In which of the following situations would there not be a termination of an offer?

    A Where there is a revocation directly communicated by the offeror prior to receipt of acceptance.

    B Where there is acceptance subject to conditions laid down by the offeree.

    C Where a specific time period for acceptance expires just prior to the acceptance.

    D Where the offeror dies and the contract is not for personal services.

Answers to questions set in objective mode appear on p. 551.

14 | Supply of goods on credit

The OBJECTIVES of this chapter are to set out the principles and rules laid down by statute – in the main by the Consumer Credit Act 1974 – in terms of the liability of the parties to a hire-purchase agreement, the formalities, the duties of creditor and debtor, and their remedies if there is default. The chapter concludes with the provisions of the Hire Purchase Act 1964 relating to motor vehicle hire-purchase and some of the more important business aspects of the Consumer Credit Act, e.g. credit cards.

HIRE-PURCHASE GENERALLY

A *hire-purchase contract* takes the form of a bailment under which the goods are hired. This contract of bailment is accompanied by an option to purchase the goods, subject to the conditions of the agreement being complied with. The law is derived from two sources as follows:

(a) the common law, where the total credit exceeds £15,000 or the hirer is a corporation; and

(b) the Consumer Credit Act 1974 which applies where the total credit does not exceed £15,000 and the hirer is not a corporation. This is known as a *regulated agreement*.

Under s. 189(1) of the 1974 Act the operation of the above rules is to be calculated by reference to the balance of the price which is financed and not to the total price of the goods. If the cash price of the goods is £17,000 and the hirer (being an individual) pays a deposit of £4,000, the agreement is a consumer credit agreement within the Act. The balance financed, i.e. £13,000, does not exceed £15,000.

Under s. 17 of the 1974 Act 'small agreements', i.e. those where the amount of credit does not exceed £50, are not in principle excluded from the Act but some provisions of Part V of the Act, e.g. the 'cooling off' period (*see* p. 359), do not apply to small agreements.

Throughout this chapter section references are to the 1974 Act unless otherwise indicated. The whole of the Consumer Credit Act 1974 was brought into force by SI 1983/1551, with the exception of ss. 123–125. These sections, which prevent a creditor from taking bills of exchange and promissory notes in discharge of sums payable by a debtor or hirer under a regulated agreement, were brought into force by SI 1984/436. Cheques can be taken but can only be paid into a bank and not endorsed over to another. The object of this is that holders in due course cannot arise. They would be entitled to payment of the instrument from the debtor or hirer, even though the contract between the debtor or hirer and the dealer was affected, e.g. by fraud as to the quality of the goods hired. A holder in due course can overcome defects of this kind (*see further* p. 460).

THE LIABILITY OF THE PARTIES

Before reading the following material revise again the distinction between a hire-purchase contract and a conditional sale agreement set out in p. 239.

Hire-purchase and conditional sale agreements

Financial institutions conducting business in these areas are liable under the contract in their own right and not jointly and severally with the supplier, under ss. 8–11 of the Supply of Goods (Implied Terms) Act 1973. Thus the conditions and warranties as to title, description, merchantable quality, fitness and sample apply. They have an indemnity against the supplier under the Sale of Goods Act 1979 if they are sued by the debtor because there is a contract of sale between them and the supplier.

In addition, they are liable under s. 56(4) of the 1974 Act for misrepresentation and breach of terms by the supplier arising from the negotiations leading to the hire-purchase or conditional sale agreement. For this purpose the supplier is the agent of the financial institution. The action is brought directly against the finance house under s. 56(4). There is no need to construe a collateral contract as in *Andrews* v *Hopkinson* (1957) (*see below*). This liability cannot be excluded (s. 56(3)) but the finance house has an indemnity against the supplier.

The agreement must be a regulated agreement. That is, an agreement in which the credit is not more than £15,000 or the hirer is a corporation (SI 1983/1878).

Retailer and hirer

There is no contract between the supplier and the debtor under a hire-purchase transaction financed by a finance house. If there is anything wrong with the goods there is no straightforward contractual claim against the retailer. (This was decided in *Drury* v *Victor Buckland Ltd* [1941] 1 All ER 269. The law on this matter has not been changed by the 1974 Act.

The supplier may, of course, become liable to indemnify the finance company if the latter has been held liable for what are, in effect, the supplier's breaches (*Porter* v *General Guarantee Corporation* [1982] RTR 384).

However, a debtor may have an action against the retailer or supplier in *negligence* where the goods are in a dangerous condition or by establishing a separate contract with the supplier, the consideration for which is the debtor's agreement to enter into a hire-purchase contract with the finance company.

Thus in *Andrews* v *Hopkinson* [1956] 3 All ER 422 a dealer, during the sale of a car, told the customer: 'It's a good little bus, I would stake my life on it.' Following this remark the customer made a hire-purchase contract with a finance company. However, soon after taking delivery of the car he had an accident in it because of its defective steering mechanism. The court *held* that the dealer was liable in damages to the customer on two grounds – (a) there was a contract between the dealer and the customer. This consisted of the dealer promising that the car was a 'good little bus' in return for the customer agreeing to apply to a finance company to acquire the car on hire-purchase terms. The dealer was therefore liable for breach of his warranty as to the car's condition; (b) the defect in the steering mechanism was due to lack of inspection and proper servicing by the dealer who was therefore liable, regardless of contract, to anyone foreseeably injured by his negligence under the neighbour principle in *Donoghue* v *Stevenson* (1932) (*see* p. 267).

As we have seen, the action against the finance company is based on s. 56. There is no need to construe a collateral contract. However, it is necessary to construe such a contract for a claim against the supplier.

Finance company and retailer

The relationship is basically that of buyer and seller. However, under ss. 56(2) and 69(1) of the 1974 Act the retailer is also made an agent of the finance company for two purposes, i.e. as regards the making of representations about the goods whether these are terms of the contract or not, and also in regard to receiving notices of cancellation under the 'cooling-off' provisions of the 1974 Act (*see further* p. 359). The above sections apply only where the agreement is a regulated agreement and is protected by the 1974 Act but where they are applicable they cannot be excluded by the agreement (s. 173). Finally under s. 75(2) the finance company has a statutory right to an indemnity from the dealer where the finance company has been made liable for a breach of the hire-purchase agreement which is a result of the dealer's acts.

Finance company and guarantor

The supplier may give a guarantee of payment by the debtor to the finance company.

This is, of course, to protect the finance company, but in order to protect the supplier it is usual to ask the debtor to obtain his own guarantor. The contract of guarantee usually allows the finance company, for example, to extend the period of credit without discharging the guarantor. Such a discharge would occur if there was no special provision in the contract. If the debtor terminates the agreement, e.g. under s. 99 (*see* p. 359), then if he discharges his liability (*see* p. 359) the guarantor is also discharged. Section 113 makes it clear that the guarantor can in no situation be liable to a greater extent than the debtor is. Section 113 is designed to prevent evasion of the Act by the use of a security.

A guarantor who pays the finance company because the debtor does not do so stands in the finance company's place and may use its remedies against the debtor. The better view is that this includes the right to seize the goods.

There are a number of provisions in the 1974 Act which relate to guarantors. These are as follows:

(a) a guarantor, along with the debtor, is not liable if an agreement controlled by the Act does not comply with the statutory formalities (*see below*).

(b) a guarantor is entitled to a copy of the contract of guarantee and to the agreement together with a statement of account (ss. 107–9);

(c) a guarantor and the debtor are discharged from liability if the owner seizes the goods without a court order when a third of the price has been paid (ss. 91 and 113);

(d) the statutory provisions relating to guarantees apply also to contracts of indemnity (ss. 189(1)).

There is one situation where s. 113 allows a security to be enforced, even though the regulated agreement itself is not enforceable. This occurs where the security is an indemnity or guarantee and the only reason that the regulated agreement cannot be enforced is that the debtor or hirer is not of full age or capacity. The reason for this is that tradesmen will often not give credit to a person under 18 unless an indemnity or guarantee is given by an adult. The exception referred to above means that the indemnity or guarantee will not be valueless if the minor debtor or hirer defaults. The exception is contained in s. 113(7) (as amended by s. 4 of the Minors' Contracts Act 1987). (For the general law on the subject of guarantees and indemnities of a minor's liability *see* p. 73.)

FORMALITIES

The Act gives certain formalities for regulated agreements, i.e. agreements under which a person is given credit not exceeding £15,000.

Under s. 55 the pre-contractual requirements are left to be made by regulation. SI 1983/1553 (as amended by SI 1988/2047) applies and, for example, the debtor must be told in writing what the cash price of the goods is, as was the case under hire-purchase legislation.

Regulations set out in SI 1983/1553 also provide in the main for the form and contents of regulated agreements and cover the following:

(a) the names of the parties to the agreement and their addresses;
(b) the amounts of all payments due under the agreement and when and to whom they are payable;
(c) the total charge for the credit, i.e. the cost to the debtor of having the credit;
(d) the true annual rate of the total charge for credit, expressed as a percentage rate per annum;
(e) the debtor's right to pay off his debt earlier than agreed.

Furthermore, the agreement and every copy of it must:

(f) contain all the terms of the agreement, and
(g) contain details of the debtor's rights to cancel the agreement (*see* p. 359).

As regards the signing of the agreement, this must, under s. 61(1), be by the debtor *personally* who consequently cannot sign through an agent. The creditor may sign personally or through an agent.

The debtor must not be given blank forms to sign, the details in them being filled in at a later date by the creditor or supplier.

Section 61 provides that a regulated agreement is not properly executed unless it is in such a state that all its terms are readily legible when it is sent or given to the debtor or hirer for signature.

If the requirements relating to form are not complied with the creditor is unable to enforce the agreement unless the court so orders (s. 65). If it does not so order the creditor cannot repossess the goods, even where the debtor has stopped payment of instalments.

It was *held* in *Lombard Tricity Finance Ltd* v *Paton* [1988] New Law Journal Practitioner 332 that it is lawful for a consumer credit agreement to contain a provision that the lender may vary the rate of interest at his absolute discretion subject to proper notice to the borrower.

THE PARTIES AND THEIR DUTIES

The duties of the parties to a hire-purchase agreement must now be dealt with.

Duties of owner

Sections 8–11 of the Supply of Goods (Implied Terms) Act 1973 (as substituted by Sch. 4, Part 1, para. 35 of the Consumer Credit Act 1974) lay upon the owner duties identical to those of a seller of goods. The implied conditions and warranties are the same and exclusion clauses are, under the Unfair Contract Terms Act, forbidden in consumer sales, though allowed if reasonable in non-consumer sales. All of this applies in all the credit agreements under consideration with no financial limit and is applicable also even if a corporation is a party to the contract.

Duties of debtor

These depend upon the agreement and regulations made under the 1974 Act. However, it can be said that:

(a) The debtor must pay the instalments while the agreement is in force.
(b) If the debtor terminates the agreement then if it is covered by the 1974 Act he is liable to pay:
   (i) instalments in arrear;
   (ii) an additional sum to make up the total payments to 50 per cent of the total price (unless they already reach or exceed that figure). Thus, if the total price is £520 and the debtor terminates after he has paid £180 and owes £20 in unpaid instalments, he must pay the £20 and a further £60 so as to bring his total payments up to one-half of the total price. But if he has paid, or becomes liable to pay, more than one-half of the total price before the termination, he cannot recover or be relieved from the excess. By s. 100(3) the court may make an order for the payment of a sum less than one-half of the total price where it is satisfied that a sum less than half would equal the loss sustained by the creditor. Thus the one-half minimum payment is in practice the maximum amount recoverable by the creditor;
   (iii) damages if he has not taken reasonable care of the goods.
(c) The debtor must take reasonable care of the goods and, e.g. in the case of cars, take out a comprehensive insurance policy for the full value.

Finally, the agreement will usually contain prohibitions on the debtor under which he cannot move the goods from the place where they are normally kept or garage a car in other than its usual place. There are also commonly provisions preventing resale, pledge and parting with the possession of the goods. Regulations made under the Act control any additional prohibitions which can be inserted into agreements.

Under s. 80(1) the debtor has a duty to inform the owner, if requested, where the goods are kept and breach of this requirement is a criminal offence triable summarily before magistrates.

Section 86 contains provisions designed to prevent or inhibit the creditor or owner under a regulated agreement from, e.g. terminating the agreement or accelerating payment by reason only of the death of the debtor.

REMEDIES OF THE CREDITOR

These will depend upon whether the agreement is regulated by the 1974 Act, or not.

Agreements which are not regulated

Here we must consider claims for instalments and general damages and seizure of the goods.

Claims for instalments and general damages

The agreement may provide that where the debtor has accepted delivery of the goods failure to pay an instalment when due renders the whole amount due and payable immediately. A provision of this kind may be valid in a non-regulated agreement unless it is an extortionate bargain for the purposes of the 1974 Act (*see* p. 357) or a penalty (*see* p. 218).

Claims for instalments – contractual rights to terminate the contract

If a debtor exercises a contractual right to terminate the contract, the money, if any, which the contract requires him to pay in that event is not damages and is not therefore subject to the penalties rule. If however the debtor terminates his contract by breach any sum mentioned as payable on termination of the contract is then of the nature of liquidated damages and the penalty rules apply. **The following case provides an illustration**.

Bridge v Campbell Discount Co Ltd [1962] 1 All ER 385

A contract of hire-purchase of a Bedford Dormobile required the debtor to pay on termination: (a) arrears of payments due before termination; plus (b) an amount which together with payments made and due before termination amounted to two-thirds of the hire-purchase price. This was in addition to the fact that the creditor was entitled to the return of goods. After paying the deposit and one instalment the hirer wrote to the owners saying: 'Owing to unforeseen personal circumstances I shall be unable to pay any more payments on the Bedford.' The owner repossessed the vehicle and sued for £206 3s 4d under the clause. The Court of Appeal held that the hirer was exercising his option to determine the contract, the 'fee' for which was £206 3s 4d under the clause. Since this sum was never intended as damages it was not subject to the rules regarding penalties. The House of Lords reversed this decision, *holding* that from the general tone of the letter the hirer was in breach of the contract and was not exercising his option. On this view the sum of £206 3s 4d could be regarded as liquidated damages and was subject to the rules regarding penalties. Accordingly the sum was irrecoverable because it was in the nature of a penalty. The £206 3s 4d was not a genuine pre-estimate of the owner's loss, because if one included the value of the returned goods the clause would in nearly all cases give the creditor more than 100 per cent of the purchase price.

Claims for instalments – where creditor sues for damages

The amount recoverable will depend upon the following.

(a) Where the debtor is in serious breach which amounts to repudiation of the contract, as, for example, when a debtor has repeatedly refused to pay instalments. The creditor may accept this as repudiation of the contract and sue for general damages. This will be, according to the decision in *Yeoman Credit* v *Waragowski* [1961] 3 All ER 145, the total hire-purchase price, subject to the following deductions:
    (i)   the value of the goods if and when repossessed;
    (ii) payments already made;
    (iii) arrears of instalments due before termination which the court will award separately to the finance company.
    The *Waragowski* formula will in most cases mean that the finance company recovers virtually the whole of the hire-purchase price.

(b) Where the debtor's breach is not sufficiently serious to be regarded as a repudiation but the creditor exercises his right to terminate the contract, as where there has been an occasional failure to pay instalments by the debtor, then the measure of damages is as follows:
    (i) the instalments in arrears at the date of the commencement of the action, or if the goods have been repossessed, to the date of repossession (*Financings Ltd* v *Baldock* [1963] 1 All ER 443), *plus*
    (ii) damages for failure to keep the goods in proper repair if, as is commonly the case, the agreement contains a provision to that effect (*Brady* v *St Margaret's Trust Ltd* [1963] 2 All ER 275.

If the debtor refuses to accept delivery of the goods the creditor may sue for damages for non-acceptance which appears to be his only remedy, whatever a particular contract may provide (*National Cash Register Co Ltd* v *Stanley* [1921] 3 KB 292).

The amount of the damages will depend upon the market situation as follows:

(a) if the supply of goods is greater than, or matches demand, the loss is:
    (i) the total amount which would have been paid under the contract if it had run its full term; *less*
    (ii) deductions, e.g. in regard to depreciation of the goods which will not arise if they were not accepted;

(b) if demand exceeds supply the creditor may be regarded, as in the case of a sale, as having no loss (*see Charter* v *Sullivan* (1957) at p. 317), or at most as having lost rental, less deductions, e.g. for lack of depreciation, between the time of repudiation and the finding of a new debtor.

Seizure of goods

Under hire-purchase agreements this normally occurs on breach by the debtor, e.g. failure to pay instalments, or on the death of the debtor, or where another creditor is taking the debtor's goods to pay a judgment debt (execution).

In an unregulated agreement it is a matter for the contract itself to decide what the rights of seizure are. If the contract so provides a creditor can, so far as the common law is concerned, seize goods even though, say, nine-tenths of the purchase price has been paid. However, relief may be obtainable under those provisions of the 1974 Act which relate to extortionate bargains (*see* p. 357).

Regulated agreements

As regards claims for instalments or damages, s. 129 of the 1974 Act gives the court power to make a 'time order' under which the debtor is given more time to pay.

As regards awards of money, s. 129 gives the court absolute discretion in the matter, whether the debtor has repudiated the agreement or not and whether the goods have been delivered or not. In short, however he may frame his action, the creditor is at the mercy of the court.

As regards seizure of the goods, where a debtor is not a company and the credit does not exceed £15,000 (i.e. where the agreement is regulated) the right to retake the goods is much modified by the 1974 Act. The restrictions are as follows.

(a) Under s. 87 the creditor is unable to terminate the agreement or recover possession of the goods, or exercise any other remedy except possibly sue for instalments due, unless he has served a *default notice* on the debtor giving the debtor at least seven days in which to remedy any breach of the agreement. This gives the debtor fair warning that action may be taken against him.

(b) Under s. 90 if one-third of the total price has been paid by the debtor the creditor has no right to take possession of the goods without a court order unless the debtor has terminated the agreement himself. Should a creditor retake the goods in defiance of this section, s. 91 states that the debtor is released from all liability under the agreement and may recover from the creditor all sums paid by him under the agreement. The 1974 Act seems to confirm that there is no breach of these provisions if the hirer abandons the goods, as where he leaves a damaged car at a garage and disappears, so that they are no longer in his possession.

(c) Under s. 92 the creditor has no right without a court order to enter the debtor's premises to retake possession of any goods let to him under a hire-purchase agreement. This section applies whether or not one-third of the price has been paid, but again, the debtor may consent to the creditor's entry for the purpose of retaking the goods.

If the creditor brings an action to recover possession of the goods, the court has wide discretionary powers under ss. 129–136 to make reasonable orders regardless of the terms of the contract. The court may, for example, make an order for delivery but postpone its coming into force so that the debtor may have an opportunity to pay the balance due in such a way as the court thinks fit in terms of the number of instalments and their amount and the times on which they shall be payable. This is the most usual order for the court to make and in practical terms it means that the hirer will obtain additional time to pay and that the instalments will be reduced in amount, based on his ability to pay.

MINIMUM PAYMENTS AND FORFEITURE CLAUSES

Some agreements may contain express provisions relating to forfeiture of payments made and additional minimum payments by the debtor if the contract is terminated, either voluntarily by the debtor himself, or by the creditor seizing the goods for non-payment of the rental. For example, a particular contract may provide:

(a) that all payments made up to the termination of the contract are to be forfeited (a forfeiture clause); and

(b) that the debtor is to bring his total payments up to a certain percentage (generally ranging between 50 per cent and 75 per cent) of the full price if his payments do not reach that figure (a minimum payments clause).

Forfeiture of payments can produce an inequitable result, as where a contract involving the credit purchase of a car priced at £6,000 is terminated when the hirer has paid £5,500. Even so forfeiture clauses are permissible, except as regulated by statute, and no form of relief, either in law or equity, is available.

A minimum payments clause may, however, be avoided if it is not regarded by the court as a genuine pre-estimate of loss but in the nature of a penalty (*see* p. 218). Avoidance on this ground applies, however, only to a situation in which the debtor has broken the contract as where he is refusing to make the agreed payments. If the debtor voluntarily returns the goods he may be regarded as exercising a right to terminate given by the contract, the 'fee' for this 'privilege' being the minimum payment provided in the contract. The courts are, however, inclined to regard voluntary termination by the debtor as, in effect, a breach of contract except where the debtor was obviously fully aware of his rights and appears to have been exercising them (*see Bridge* v *Campbell Discount Co Ltd* (1962) at p. 353).

The above provisions are now of less practical importance. The Consumer Credit Act has two sets of rules relating to the enforcement of clauses of this kind, the first being general and applying to all credit agreements, and the second being applicable to regulated agreements only.

General provisions

Wide powers are given to the court under ss. 137–140 to re-open credit agreements so as to do justice between the parties. The power is not confined to regulated consumer credit agreements as 'credit agreements' means any agreement between a debtor and a creditor and there are no maximum financial limits or other exemptions.

The power is available if the credit bargain is extortionate, i.e. the payments are grossly exorbitant, or it otherwise grossly contravenes ordinary principles of fair dealing (s. 138). The section gives a number of factors to be taken into account, including prevailing interest rates, the debtor's age, experience, business capacity, state of health and financial pressure upon him, and the degree of risk accepted by the creditor, his relationship to the debtor and whether an inflated cash price was quoted for goods or services.

If the court finds that the agreement is extortionate it may re-open the transaction and has sweeping powers to adjust the rights and duties of the parties under s. 139(2). In particular, the court may set aside or reduce any obligation which has been imposed on the debtor or may require the creditor to repay any sums which the debtor has already paid.

The number of cases brought before the courts have been few and it is therefore interesting to note the case of *Barcabe Ltd* v *Edwards* (1983) 133 NLJ 713. Here, the borrower, a low-paid working man with four children and little business capacity, answered the lender's advertisement in a newspaper. The lender's credit reference check showed no money judgments against him. He took an unsecured loan of £400 at a flat rate of interest of 100 per cent per annum (APR 319%). Judge Gosling, of the Birmingham County Court, reduced the flat rate of interest to 40 per cent per annum (APR 92%). There was evidence that the money could have been obtained elsewhere at about half this rate. The Office of Fair Trading is of the opinion that the reason there are so few cases is that borrowers may be too scared to come before the courts. However, this case illustrates that the law can be of assistance if only borrowers will invoke it. Nevertheless, the rate which the court substituted is still very high. In *Ketley* v *Scott* [1981] ICR 241 a bridging loan of £20,500 made to enable the defendant to complete immediately on a house purchase at an APR of 57.35 per cent was *held* by Foster J not extortionate due to the speed at which the loan was made, the risk involved and the deceit of the defendant who failed to disclose particulars of another legal charge over the property.

These provisions will also cover minimum payments and forfeiture clauses. It is difficult to say how the courts will operate such wide powers but it is to be expected that the courts will generally regard a minimum payments or forfeiture agreement as extortionate if it contains provisions which would give the creditor significantly more than the repayment of his capital together with interest at the agreed rate on the assumption that the rate of interest itself is not extortionate. Thus minimum payments and forfeiture clauses will normally be unenforceable unless they provide solely for sufficient payments to make good any loss to the creditor caused by the debtor's breach or other act.

Regulated agreements – additional provisions

So far as regulated agreements are concerned, the 1974 Act provides additional safeguards against minimum payments and forfeiture clauses. As regards forfeiture clauses, the debtor's protection lies in provisions under which the creditor cannot retake possession of the goods without a court order when one-third of the price has been paid. If the court does allow a creditor to retake the goods, it will give the debtor every chance to pay the balance and avoid forfeiture. If the debtor has not paid one-third of the price the Act does not prevent the creditor from retaking the goods but he must first serve a notice of default and cannot enter the debtor's premises to recover the goods. In this situation there is nothing to prevent forfeiture of the amounts paid by the debtor other than the provisions relating to extortionate agreements. These are not likely to apply since the amounts paid by the debtor, i.e. less than one-third of the price, will not normally be sufficient to cover the drop in the value of the goods, unless they were second-hand.

In connection with minimum payments clauses, s. 99 entitles the debtor to terminate the agreement at any time before the final payment falls due and then the Act provides for its own minimum payments clause. The debtor in this situation is liable to pay enough to bring his total payments up to one-half of the total price, but if the creditor's loss is less than that, then his actual loss is the maximum of the debtor's liability.

REMEDIES OF THE DEBTOR

To reject the goods

The debtor may reject the goods for breach of condition by the creditor. The conditions are those set out in the Supply of Goods (Implied Terms) Act 1973 (as substituted by the Consumer Credit Act).

As regards the right to reject, the provisions of s. 11(4) and ss. 34 and 35 of the Sale of Goods Act 1979, which deal with acceptance and the right of examination of the goods, do not apply to hire-purchase contracts and the courts have to decide the question of the debtor's right to repudiate on the general principles of the law of contract. If, for example, the debtor has affirmed the contract the right to repudiate will have been lost. It should, however, be noted that the right to repudiate is not necessarily lost simply because there has been considerable use of the goods.

Thus in *Farnworth Finance Facilities* v *Attryde* [1970] 2 All ER 774 Mr Attryde bought a motor cycle on hire-purchase. The machine had many faults and although Mr Attryde always complained about them he did drive the machine for some 4,000 miles before deciding to repudiate the contract. He was then sued by the finance company. It was *held* by the Court of Appeal that Mr Attryde had not affirmed the contract by using the machine. He had always complained about the defects and had indicated that he would only finally accept the machine if they were remedied. Mr Attryde repudiated after payment of four monthly instalments. Lord Denning seems to have taken the view that the rules about loss of the right to repudiate were different here because, unlike a sale, the property had not passed. The machine did not belong to the defendant but was at the stage of repudiation only hired.

Damages

The debtor is not likely to claim damages. If the goods are defective he will normally stop paying the instalments and wait for the creditor to sue him. Consequently there is little authority on the law relating to damages in this area. However, if an action was brought by the debtor for damages, the position would appear to be as follows.

(a) If the debtor keeps the goods and has them repaired, the cost of repairing the goods is the appropriate measure of damages, together with damages for loss of use while they are being put right (*Charterhouse Credit Co* v *Tolley* [1963] 2 All ER 432).

(b) If the debtor elects to treat the contract as repudiated and rejects the goods there is some doubt as to the measure of damages which he is entitled to recover. However, it would seem that he can claim the return of all monies paid by him at the time of the termination of the agreement, plus any sum actually spent on repairing the goods bailed to him, less a deduction for the use of the goods during the period they have been in his possession (*Charterhouse Credit Co* v *Tolley* [1963] 2 All ER 432).

To terminate the contract

Under s. 99 in a regulated credit agreement the debtor can terminate the agreement at any time before the final payment falls due merely by giving notice to the creditor. The debtor is not obliged to return the goods to the creditor but must make them available when the creditor calls to collect them. The same rules apply to a conditional sale agreement in which the price is payable by instalments. The buyer can determine the agreement even after the property has passed to him, but not if he has sold the goods to a third party.

Cooling-off

The 1974 Act in ss. 67–74 substantially reproduces the cooling-off provisions of the old Hire-Purchase Act. Under these provisions the debtor can cancel the agreement *not later than five days after service on him of a second copy of the agreement as required by s. 63*, if the agreement has not been signed at the premises of the creditor, or the supplier or some associated party. Thus the exact cooling-off period depends upon how much time elapses between the debtor signing the agreement and his receipt of the second copy. Certainly it will be in most cases more than five days.

The cooling-off period is designed to prevent high-pressure salesmanship being carried out on the debtor's doorstep or in his home and not to affect transactions in shops. The provisions do not apply where the transaction takes place on 'appropriate trade premises'. This means premises at which goods of the description to which the contract relates or goods of a similar description are normally offered or exposed for sale in the course of the business carried on at those premises.

In order to exercise the right to cancel the agreement the debtor can give 'notice of cancellation' to the creditor or his agent (which includes the supplier of the goods). The notice need not be in any particular form so long as the intention to cancel is clearly indicated. It may be sent by post and to assist service by this method the agreement must give the name and address of the person to whom the notice may be sent.

When the notice is served it operates to cancel the agreement as to the provision of credit and also any 'linked transaction', e.g. an agreement to maintain the goods which was entered into at the same time as the hire-purchase agreement.

Once the notice has been served the debtor must take reasonable care of the goods (if they have been delivered to him) for 21 days. He is not under a duty to return the goods but must allow the creditor to collect them, though he may insist on being repaid anything he has paid under the agreement before he allows the owner to retake the goods. Where the debtor has traded in goods in part-exchange to the supplier, these must be returned to him or an amount equal to the part-exchange allowance repaid to him.

It should be noted that under the Consumer Credit Act the cooling-off provisions are no longer restricted to hire-purchase agreements but extend to a wider variety of consumer transactions. Thus a loan of an amount not exceeding £15,000 will be subject to cancellation under the cooling-off provisions if the agreement is signed at the debtor's own house. In the event of cancellation the money must be repaid.

Early payment

The Consumer Credit Act, ss. 94 and 95, provide that the debtor may pay off the whole amount due under a hire-purchase, or other credit agreement, at any time. Regulations made under the Act give the debtor a right to a rebate on the credit charges where he has paid early.

PROVISIONS RELATING TO MOTOR VEHICLES

Formerly, if the hirer of a motor vehicle sold the vehicle whilst it was bailed to him under a hire-purchase or conditional sale agreement, the purchaser did not get a good title and the true owner of the vehicle, usually a finance company, could recover the vehicle from the purchaser or sue him in conversion. This was so even though the hirer had all the appearances of ownership, including the registration document. Part III of the Hire Purchase Act 1964, i.e. ss. 27–29 (as substituted but not repealed by s. 192 and Sch. 4, para. 22, of the Consumer Credit Act 1974), is all that remains of the 1964 Act. It is designed to protect bona fide purchasers for value of motor vehicles where the seller is a mere bailee under a hire-purchase or conditional sale agreement and where he disposes of the vehicle before the property is vested in him. The provisions do not apply unless the vehicle has been let under a hire-purchase agreement or there is an agreement to sell under a conditional sale agreement. Thus they do not apply to an ordinary hiring, nor to situations such as those in *Central Newbury Car Auctions Ltd* v *Unity Finance Ltd* [1956] 3 All ER 905 where a dealer allowed a fraudulent person to take possession of a vehicle after he had signed hire-purchase forms which were then rejected by the finance company. It was *held* that a purchaser from the fraudulent person was not protected because the vehicle was not let under a hire-purchase agreement.

Private purchasers

A private purchaser is a purchaser who at the time of the disposition is not a motor vehicle dealer or a person engaged in financing motor vehicle deals.

Where the disposition is to a private purchaser who takes the vehicle in good faith and without notice of the hire-purchase or conditional sale agreement, that disposition shall have effect as if the title of the owner or seller of the vehicle had been vested in the hirer or buyer immediately before that disposition. Thus a private purchaser gets a good title and the owner or seller must pursue his remedies against the hirer or buyer.

The following case provides an illustration.

Barker v Bell (Ness, third party) [1971] 2 All ER 867

A man called Hudson had a Morris Mini on hire-purchase from Auto Finances (Hallamshire) Ltd. He sold it to Mr Ness, who was not a dealer in cars, after telling him that the car had formerly been on hire-purchase but that the last instalment had been paid. Hudson produced a receipt for £6 across which was written 'Final Payment'. This receipt was in fact from Bowmakers Ltd and had no connection with the hire arrangements with Auto Finances, though Mr Ness had no way of knowing this. Mr Ness resold the vehicle and eventually the car was purchased by a dealer, Mr Barker. The vehicle was repossessed by Auto Finances from Mr Barker who then sued the dealer from whom he bought the car, Mr Bell. Mr Bell brought in Mr Ness as third party. It was *held* by the court of Appeal – that Mr Ness had obtained a good title from Hudson and that in consequence Barker and Bell had good titles even though they were dealers. Mr Ness was a bona fide purchaser without notice of a hire-purchase agreement as required by s. 27(2) of the Hire-Purchase Act 1964. 'Notice' meant notice of a relevant existing agreement. A hire-purchase agreement which had supposedly been paid off was irrelevant for this purpose.

Comment: The case also illustrates that once a private purchaser gets a good title subsequent purchasers – even dealers – also get one. Therefore Mr Barker need not have given up the car to Auto Finances. Since Mr Barker got a good title – as indeed did Mr Bell – there was no claim against Mr Ness for breach of condition as to title, and presumably no claim against Mr Bell either, though the appeal to the Court of Appeal was by Mr Ness and concerned only his position.

Trade or finance purchasers

Where the disposition is made to a trade or finance purchaser, i.e. a person who deals in motor vehicles or finances such transactions, then the trade or finance purchaser does not get a good title.

In this connection it should be noted that a person who carries on a part-time business of buying and selling motor cars is a 'trade or finance purchaser' under the Hire-Purchase Act 1964 and is not within the protection given to a 'private purchaser' by that Act, even where he acquires a vehicle in his private capacity for personal use. **The following case shows this point.**

Stevenson v Beverley Bentinck [1976] 2 All ER 606

The plaintiff was a tool inspector who dealt in motor cars in his spare time. He bought a Jaguar for his own use without enquiring as to whether or not it was subject to any hire-purchase agreement. The car was subject to a hire-purchase agreement between the defendants and the seller. The latter having defaulted on his monthly instalments, the defendant repossessed the car. The plaintiff claimed the return of the car or damages for conversion. It was *held* – by the Court of Appeal – that the plaintiff was not protected because his part-time business brought him within the definition of 'trade or finance purchaser' and judgment was given for the defendants.

However, if a private purchaser buys the vehicle from a trade or finance purchaser, either by paying cash for it as a result of paying up all the instalments under a hire-purchase or conditional sale agreement, then the trade or finance purchaser is deemed to have had a good title in order that the private purchaser shall obtain one.

Factors

The provisions of the Act operate without prejudice to the provisions of the Factors Act or of any other Act enabling the apparent owner of goods to dispose of them as if he were the true owner. Thus a person may still claim a title because the person from whom he bought the goods was a factor. However, the provisions of the 1964 Act are wider than those of the Factors Act in that they protect a purchaser even though the goods have not been *delivered* to him, in the sense that he has bought the vehicle but not taken delivery. Under the Factors Act delivery is an essential part of the protection of title.

Liabilities after unlawful disposal

The liability of the hirer (or debtor) who has unlawfully disposed of the vehicle is not affected by the 1964 Act. Thus he may still be guilty of theft at criminal law and liable in conversion at civil law, provided that the creditor has served a default notice under ss. 87–89 of the Consumer Credit Act 1974 on the debtor so that the creditor has a right to immediate possession. Where the sale is by auction the auctioneer may similarly be liable in conversion (*Union Transport Finance* v *British Car Auctions* [1978] 2 All ER 385). The liability of any trade or finance purchaser to whom the hirer disposes of the vehicle is also unchanged, and such a person could be sued in conversion. The first private purchaser is not liable in conversion and as we have seen subsequent purchasers from him are not liable even though they be trade or finance purchasers (*see Barker* v *Bell* (1971) *above*).

Presumptions of the Act

In order to assist a purchaser to establish his title in any action, the 1974 Act provides that certain presumptions shall be made which will apply unless evidence is brought to the contrary.

(a) If the purchaser who seeks to establish his title can show that the vehicle he has acquired was let to someone under a hire-purchase or conditional sale agreement and that a private purchaser acquired the vehicle in good faith and without notice of the letting agreement, it is presumed that the hirer or buyer made the original disposition and that the Act applies to perfect the purchaser's title.

(b) If it is proved that the hirer or buyer did not in fact make the disposition, but that a purchaser from him did so, then it is presumed that the said purchaser was a private purchaser in good faith and without notice so that the present purchaser's title is again perfected by the Act.

(c) If it is proved that the purchaser from the hirer or buyer was not a private purchaser but a trade or finance purchaser, then it is presumed that the purchaser from the trade or finance purchaser was a private purchaser in good faith and without notice and that the present purchaser's title is again perfected under the Act.

A disposition for the above purposes includes any sale or contract of sale, including a conditional sale agreement., any letting under a hire-purchase agreement, or the transfer of the property to the hirer on payment of agreed instalments.

CREDIT CARDS AND ASPECTS OF CONSUMER CREDIT

The 1974 Act does not refer to credit cards as such but refers instead to credit tokens. These are defined so as to cover both a store credit card issued by a retailer to the holder of an 'option' or 'budget' account facility, and also bank credit cards, such as Barclaycard or Access. A 'credit token agreement' is defined by the Act as 'a regulated agreement for the provision of credit in connection with a credit token'.

The definition excludes American Express and Diners Club cards because they require accounts to be settled in full monthly. Both cards are credit tokens but the agreement covering the use of them is not a credit token agreement. Both American Express and Diners Club are subject to the prohibition on sending unsolicited credit tokens discussed below, but they are not otherwise governed by the Act.

Cheque guarantee cards are not credit tokens within the Act because they cannot be used by the debtor to obtain cash or services or goods on credit.

Prohibition of unsolicited credit tokens

Section 51(1) of the 1974 Act states: 'It is an offence to give a person a credit token if he has not asked for it'. A credit token is defined in s. 14(1) of the Act as follows: 'A credit token is a card, voucher, coupon, stamp, form, booklet or other document or thing given to an individual by a person carrying on a consumer credit business, who *undertakes* – (a) that on the production of it (whether or not some other action is also required) he will supply cash, goods and services . . . on credit'. It is thus an offence to send a credit token to any person without a request in a document signed by him.

The following case provides an example.

Elliott v Director General of Fair Trading [1980] 1 WLR 977

In an attempt to boost their sales, Elliott & Sons, shoe retailers, mailed to selected members of the public an envelope containing advertising literature relating to the Elliott Credit Account Card and a card which had the appearance of a bank credit card. The front of the card said: 'Elliott Shoe Account', and on the back there was a box for the holder's signature and the words: 'This credit card is valid for immediate use. The sole requirement is your signature and means of identification. Credit is immediately available if you have a bank account.' The Director General of Fair Trading instituted proceedings against the company alleging that the cards were sent contrary to s. 51(1) of the 1974 Act. The central issue in the case was whether the cards were credit tokens within the meaning of the Act. In the magistrates' court the company was found guilty of a contravention of s. 51(1) and appealed to the Divisional Court. In the Divisional Court counsel for the company argued that the word 'undertakes' in s. 14(1) implied that there was a need for a contractual agreement, i.e. making an offer capable of being accepted so as to impose upon the trader a legally binding obligation to supply to the consumer goods on offer. Taking this one step further counsel argued that since the production of the card did not entitle the customer to a supply of goods on credit, but only to apply for a credit card when he signed an agreement, the card was not a credit card; the card was not valid for immediate use, the sole requirement was not a signature, and credit was not immediately available since, in order to get credit, a customer would have to fill in a direct debiting mandate to his bank.

However, the Divisional Court did not accept these arguments. There was no need, they said, for a contractual agreement to exist. One looked at the card and asked, whether on its face or its back, the company undertook on the production of it that cash or goods would be supplied. The fact that none of the statements on the card were true did not prevent it being a credit token within the Act. The court found that the card in this case did fall within the meaning of s. 51(1) and that the company was guilty of a contravention of that subsection.

Section 66 of the 1974 Act deals with the situation in which a credit token, e.g. a credit card, is intercepted before it reaches the person for whom it was intended and is used to obtain credit. The section, which applies whether the token was unsolicited or requested, provides that the person for whom it was intended shall not be liable for its wrongful use unless he has accepted it. He accepts it, not when it reaches him, but when he signs a receipt for it or uses it.

Section 84 of the 1974 Act deals with a situation in which there is unauthorized use of a token after the debtor has accepted it. The debtor may be made liable for the unauthorized use but his liability cannot exceed £50 (or the limit of credit if lower) in regard to the *whole* of the period he is not in possession. The section does not apply to misuse by a user who obtained possession with the debtor's consent.

The section further provides that the debtor is not liable for any misuse after he has given notice to the creditor, e.g. Barclaycard. Notice may be oral, e.g. by telephone, but the agreement may provide for confirmation in writing. At least seven days must be allowed. If no confirmation is received in those circumstances the oral notice is invalid and the debtor becomes liable for all misuse. A debtor cannot be made liable for misuse unless the name, address and telephone number of the person to whom notice of loss or theft is to be given is shown clearly and legibly in the agreement. The creditor is required under s. 171 to prove that any misuse occurred before notice was given.

Liability for defective goods

Section 75 of the 1974 Act gives the debtor rights against a creditor where the purchase of goods or services is financed, either by a loan arranged through the supplier or by the use of a credit card, and there has been a misrepresentation or breach of contract by the supplier. Where a consumer has a claim against a creditor under s. 75 the creditor has a claim to be indemnified by the supplier for any resulting loss. It should be noted that an action under s. 75 is only available where the credit card agreement is a 'regulated agreement' (*see above*), so that while those issuing bank credit cards are liable for the defaults of their franchise holders, cards such as American Express or Diners Club are not.

In addition, the section only applies if the cash price of the item is between £100 and £30,000. Liability does not arise if the goods are purchased with a bank overdraft or with a cash advance under a credit card.

Other important aspects of the 1974 Act

Licensing

Those who grant credit, or arrange credit, or who offer goods to consumers on hire *as a business*, must have a licence from the Office of Fair Trading or be covered by a group licence (ss. 21 and 146). For example, the Law Society has a group licence covering solicitors with a practising certificate. Licences are granted for periods of ten years but can be withdrawn at any time (ss. 31 and 32). Details of licence applications are kept in a public register maintained by the Director of Fair Trading (s. 35). Under s. 39 unlicensed trading is a criminal offence. In addition, agreements made with unlicensed traders will be unenforceable against the debtor or hirer unless the Director of Fair Trading has made a validating order.

The above provisions do not apply to private lenders (*Wills* v *Wood* (1984) 128 SJ 222), e.g. a father who lends his son money to buy a house does not need a licence. The lending etc. must be as part of a business but business includes a profession or trade (s. 189(1)).

Further, s. 189(2) provides that a person is not to be treated as carrying on a particular type of business merely because he *occasionally* enters into transactions belonging to a business of that type.

Canvassing

Under ss. 48 and 49 it is an offence to canvass debtor–creditor agreements other than on trade premises. Thus traders are restricted from offering credit in a person's home. However, if a previous request has come from the potential debtor, which must be in writing and signed, no offence is committed. Convictions under these sections have, in the main, been for canvassing in response to an oral request.

Fees of credit brokers

A consumer may go through a credit broker for an introduction to a person who will give him credit. This is very often the trader who supplies the goods or services to the consumer. Under s. 155 the credit broker may only make a small token charge (such as regulations may from time to time provide) for his services if no credit agreement is made by the consumer within six months of the introduction.

Credit reference agencies

Before a supplier of goods or services gives credit he may consult a credit reference agency. This is an organization which collects information relating to the financial standing of people, e.g. how quickly they pay their debts. The trader can obtain the facts on a particular person's file. Section 158 gives a consumer the right to know what information is held by the agency in regard to him and ask that it be corrected if it is wrong.

The Act also helps the consumer to find the agency. There are national credit agencies and also local ones. If the consumer knows the name of the agency he can write at any time asking for a copy of any file relating to him. He does not have to be seeking credit at the time. A small fee (as regulations may from time to time provide) is payable (s. 158). If a trader is asked for credit the consumer has a right under s. 157 to be given the name and address of any agency which the trader intends to contact. The consumer's request must be in writing and made within 28 days after the consumer last dealt with the trader on the matter. The trader has seven working days to supply the information.

A consumer who thinks an entry on the file of a credit agency is wrong and may prejudice him may, under s. 159, require the agency to remove or correct it. The agency then has 28 days to say whether or not it has done this. If it has not the consumer can require the agency to put on his file a notice of correction of not more than 200 words which the consumer has drawn up. If the agency will not do this, then either the consumer or the agency may apply to the Director of Fair Trading who may make such an order as he thinks fit. Failure to obey the Director's order is a criminal offence.

There have been few convictions under this head, but they have occurred in the case of an agency which refused to disclose a file and in the case of a trader who refused to say which agency he was consulting.

Advertising

Section 56 of the 1974 Act forbids advertisements for credit or hire which are misleading. Regulations made under the Act set out the form which advertisements must take. Under the Consumer Credit (Advertisement) Regulations 1989 (SI 1989/ 1125) there are three kinds of advertisements about credit as follows.

Simple advertisements

Simple advertisements are those designed just to state that the individual is in the credit business. They include boards at sports events and give-away items such as pens and matches. For this reason, simple advertisements are only allowed to have a very limited amount of information.

(a) Simple advertisements *may* include:
    (i)   the advertiser's name, which must be the name shown on the consumer credit licence;
    (ii)   the address;
    (iii)   the telephone number;
    (iv)   a logo of the advertiser's, of his associate and of his trade association;
    (v)   occupation, e.g. credit broker or finance company.

(b) Other information may be included but *not*:
  (i)   Any suggestion that the advertiser or anyone else is willing to provide loans.
  (ii) Any reference to a cash price of anything.
  (iii) Any interest rate.

If any of these are included, the advertisement must comply with the detailed provisions that apply to intermediate or full credit advertisements.

Intermediate advertisements

These advertisements allow some choice of what can be included. Some items are compulsory, some may be included and some are forbidden. Intermediate advertisements must offer to provide written quotations so that clients know how to get all the information they need.

(a) Intermediate advertisements *must* include:
  (i)   name;
  (ii) address;
  (iii) telephone number (except for an advertisement permanently on trade premises, or in an advertisement including a credit broker's or dealer's name and address).
(b) They *must* include all the following items if they apply to the credit facility being advertised:
  (i)   a statement that the loan may be secured on land plus this warning in capital letters – YOUR HOME IS AT RISK IF YOU DO NOT KEEP UP REPAYMENTS ON A MORTGAGE OR OTHER LOAN SECURED ON IT;
  (ii)   if it is a foreign currency mortgage this warning in capital letters – THE STERLING EQUIVALENT OF YOUR LIABILITY UNDER A FOREIGN CURRENCY MORTGAGE MAY BE INCREASED BY EXCHANGE RATE MOVEMENTS;
  (iii) mention of any other security requirement;
  (iv)   mention of any insurance requirement;
  (v)   mention of any deposit requirement;
  (vi)   a statement so that a debtor can calculate the amount of any credit brokerage fee;
  (vii) a statement that written quotations are available on request;
  (viii) cash price of any goods or services featured and the APR plus a statement, if applicable, that the APR can vary;
  (ix)   if the APR is not given, a statement that the total amount payable is no greater than the cash price.
(c) They *may* include the following:
  (i)   details of any security requirements not affecting the borrower's home;
  (ii) the types of credit facility and periods of availability;

    (iii)   any restrictions of credit availability;

    (iv)   a description of any different treatment between cash and credit buyers;

    (v)   the amount, maximum or minimum, of credit available;

    (vi)   details of any advance payments needed but only if the APR is given;

    (vii) the APR plus, if appropriate, a statement that it can vary;

    (viii) any rate of interest, but only if the APR is also quoted;

    (ix)   name, address and telephone number of the creditor.

(d) They must *not* quote the total amount payable. If the advertisement includes any attempt to give a quotation of the cost, it has to comply with the rules governing full credit advertisements.

Full advertisements

Full credit advertisements give detailed information about the facilities offered. Much of the information is compulsory and extra information is allowed.

(a) A full advertisement *must* include:

    (i)   name;

    (ii)   address (except for an advertisement permanently on trade premises, or in an advertisement including a credit broker's or dealer's name and address);

(b) It *must* include all the following items if they apply to the credit facility being advertised:

    (i)   a statement that the loan may be secured on land plus this warning in capital letters – YOUR HOME IS AT RISK IF YOU DO NOT KEEP UP REPAYMENTS ON A MORTGAGE OR OTHER LOAN SECURED ON IT;

    (ii)   if it is a foreign currency mortgage this warning in capital letters – THE STERLING EQUIVALENT OF YOUR LIABILITY UNDER A FOREIGN CURRENCY MORTGAGE MAY BE INCREASED BY EXCHANGE RATE MOVEMENTS;

    (iii)   details of any other security requirement;

    (iv)   mention of any insurance requirement;

    (v)   mention of any deposit requirement;

    (vi)   a statement so that a debtor can calculate the amount of any credit brokerage fee;

    (vii) a statement that written quotations are available on request;

    (viii) cash price of any goods or services featured and the APR plus a statement, if applicable, that the APR can vary;

    (ix)   any restrictions of credit availability;*

    (x)   a description of any different treatment between cash and credit buyers;*

    (xi)   if the APR is not given, a statement that the total amount payable is no greater than the cash price;*

(xii)   for cash loans, or where any interest is charged, the APR plus, if applicable, a statement that it can vary;*

(xiii)   the frequency, number and amount of any advance payments;*

(xiv)   the frequency, number and amount of loan repayments, plus if MIRAS (mortgage interest relief at source) applies, whether the figures are before or after tax relief;*

(xv)   the total amount payable under the loan agreement including the credit itself and any advance payments;*

(xvi)   details of any other charges payable.*

*Extra items that must be included in a full advertisement compared with an intermediate advertisement.

Annual percentage rate (APR)

APR includes the interest on the loan itself *plus* any charges which have had to be paid as a condition of getting the loan, e.g. maintenance charges for a TV set on hire-purchase. The reason why APR is necessary is to make it possible to compare the cost of one type of credit with another. The concept removes problems of comparison which arise from, for example, different periods of payment and different levels of deposit. Credit traders must calculate APR according to standard formulae which are laid down in regulations made under the 1974 Act. It should be noted that simply because APR is expressed as a percentage, it should not be confused with rates of interest. For example, APR 30 per cent does not mean that the consumer will be paying a flat rate of 30 per cent, i.e. £30 on £100 over 12 months.

Calculating APR

In, say, a purchase of goods, the total charge for credit is divided by the price of the goods, and the resulting figure is looked up on the Consumer Credit Tables. This gives the APR. Thus in the purchase of a music centre for a cash price of £374 the calculation would be as follows:

(a) *Hire purchase from Barchester Stores*: Repayment by 24 monthly instalments of £21.39.

(b) *Borrowing from the Barchester Bank*: Loan of £375 repayment by 24 monthly instalments of £19.17

APR for hire purchase: Cost of credit =   24 × £21.39 = £513.36

                                       Less Cash price   £375.00

                                       Cost of credit   £138.36

$$APR = \frac{\text{Cost of credit}}{\text{Cash price}} \quad \frac{£138.36}{£375.00} = 0.3690$$

0.3690 in the Consumer Credit Tables gives an APR of 37.3%

APR for bank loan:

Cost of credit = 24 × £19.17 = £460.08

Less Value of loan £375.00

Cost of credit £85.08

$$APR = \frac{\text{Cost of credit}}{\text{Loan}} \quad \frac{£85.08}{£375.00} = 0.2269$$

0.2269 in the Consumer Credit Tables gives an APR of 22.4%

Clearly, the bank loan is the better bet. This is obvious enough from the instalments but the *precise* measure of the difference is given by the APR. APR is of greater assistance in comparing, e.g. different repayment periods and different sizes of loan, and cash prices. Suppose we are trying to compare the following credit with the two above.

A loan of £500 from a finance house repayable at £34.10 per month over 18 months.

Cost of credit = 18 × £34.10 = £613.80

Less Value of loan £500.00

Cost of credit £113.80

$$APR = \frac{\text{Cost of credit}}{\text{Loan}} \quad \frac{£113.80}{£500.00} = 0.2276$$

0.2276 in the Consumer Credit Tables gives an APR of 30.7%.

Thus the loan from the bank is the best, the loan from the finance house is second, and the hire purchase from Barchester Stores is the worst.

Quotations

Under s. 52 those offering credit must give a quotation if the consumer asks for one. The quotation need not be given if the terms of credit are set out in full, e.g. in an advertisement. A quotation can be requested by telephone, or in writing, or of course, in person at the trader's shop or office. A request by telephone need not be answered unless the trader has put out an advertisement inviting the consumer to telephone for further details.

GRADED QUESTIONS

Essay mode

1. Discuss any *two* of the following provisions of the Consumer Credit Act 1974.
   (a) Section 75 of the Act which imposes liability on 'connected lenders';
   (b) Part III of the Act which is concerned with the licensing of persons involved in the provision of credit;
   (c) Sections 67–73 of the Act under which consumer credit agreements may be cancelled by the customer in certain circumstances.
   (The Institute of Chartered Secretaries and Administrators. English Business Law. December 1988)

2. (a) How does a hire-purchase contract differ from:
       (i) a credit sale contract, and
       (ii) a conditional sale contract?
   (b) Henry buys a second-hand car from Ian after reading Ian's advertisement in the local newspaper. Henry pays Ian in cash the £2,500 agreed price and takes delivery of the car. A week later Henry is visited by a representative of the Automobile Finance Company who informs him that the car is the subject of a hire-purchase agreement with Ian who has not paid all the instalments. Henry refuses to surrender the car.
   Discuss the legal position.
   (The Institute of Company Accountants. Part 3: Law Relating to Business. November 1989)

3. *Either:*
   (a) The Consumer Credit Act 1974 contains provisions which attempt to protect consumers from being induced by misleading or incomplete information, or by pressure sales techniques, into committing themselves to a credit agreement from which they will then be unable to escape without substantial loss.
   Outline these provisions and comment on their effectiveness.
   Or:
   (b) Four months ago Ben entered into a hire-purchase agreement for a dining-room suite, total hire-purchase price £900. The deposit was £300 with 24 monthly instalments of £25. He has paid four of these instalments, but has now lost his job, so will have great difficulty in keeping up the payments. He is considering the idea of selling the suite for cash and hoping that with this money and the hope of getting another job he will be able to pay off the debt. Unfortunately the table has been badly scratched, so the value of the suite has diminished considerably.
   Advise Ben of his legal position and suggest possible courses of action.
   (Staffordshire Polytechnic. LLB (Hons): Consumer Law. May 1990)

Objective mode

Four alternative answers are given. Select ONE only. Circle the answer which you consider to be correct. Check your answers by referring back to the information given in the relevant chapter and against the answers at the back of the book.

With reference to the following information answer questions 1 to 3.

Snooks had a 1987 Austin Mini on hire-purchase from Motor Finance Ltd. In January, when returning from a party, he scraped the vehicle on the wall of a hump-backed bridge causing considerable damage to the near-side wing and door.

The following day when Snooks was surveying the damage outside his lodgings he was approached by Sharp, a student, who said it would 'cost a bomb' to repair the car and that he would take it off Snooks' hands for £50. Snooks agreed to sell and Sharp asked him whether the car was on hire-purchase: Snooks said it wasn't.

To prove the point Snooks went to his room and produced a receipt from Vehicle Finance Ltd for £6 dated some three months earlier. Across the receipt was written 'Final Payment'. This receipt related to an earlier hire-purchase transaction in respect of another vehicle which Snooks had owned.

Later the same day Sharp gave Snooks £50 for the car and was given a receipt in the following terms:

'I, Snooks, hereby confirm the said vehicle, Austin Mini E113 PJC, is not covered by any HP agreement whatsoever, and I accept the sum of £50 from Mr Sharp in absolute payment for the above-named vehicle.'

Sharp repaired the car and in February sold it to a dealer, Pedlar, who later in the month sold it to another dealer, Hawker.

On 1 March, while the vehicle was in Hawker's possession, an agent of Motor Finance Ltd saw it and on 4 March the company sent men to claim it from Hawker. They brought with them a letter from the company in the following terms:

'You have purported to acquire the above vehicle which is the property of this company under a rental agreement with one J. Snooks of Barchester. The bearer of this letter has instructions to collect our property forthwith, and legal proceedings will be taken against any person attempting to prevent him from carrying out these instructions.'

Hawker let the men take the car and intends to sue Pedlar for damages. Pedlar has said that he will bring Sharp into the action and claim damages from him. Snooks has left his lodgings and cannot be found. Examination of the legal position is required.

1. One of the following is relevant to the success or otherwise of the claims by Hawker against Pedlar and Pedlar against Sharp. Select:

    A   Sale of Goods Act 1979.
    B   Misrepresentation.
    C   Hire Purchase Act 1964.
    D   Mercantile Law Amendment Act 1856.

2. Only one of the following remedies or actions is available to compensate Motor Finance Ltd. Select:

    A   To repossess the vehicle from Hawker.
    B   To sue Pedlar.
    C   To sue Sharp.
    D   To sue Snooks.

3. Which one of the following is the owner of the vehicle?

    A   Pedlar.
    B   Hawker.
    C   Sharp.
    D   Motor Finance Ltd.

4. The Consumer Credit Act 1974 applies to all contracts as defined by it if the debtor is not a corporation and if the total credit does not exceed:

    A   £2,000.
    B   £300.
    C   £500.
    D   £15,000.

5. Protected goods are goods hired out under a regulated agreement under which at least one of the following fractions of the price has been paid or tendered and which has not been terminated by the debtor. Select:

    A   One third.
    B   One half.
    C   Two thirds.
    D   Three quarters.

6. Fred had a stereo on hire-purchase from Crafty Finance Ltd. The total credit was £240 and Fred agreed to pay £20 per month. Fred has terminated the agreement and returned the stereo. He had paid two instalments and terminated before the third was due. Unless the court decides otherwise or the agreement provides to the contrary Fred must pay Crafty Finance Ltd:

    A   Nothing.
    B   £80.
    C   £20.
    D   £200.

The answers to questions set in objective mode appear on p. 551.

15 | Employment I

The OBJECTIVES of this chapter are to explain how the relationship of employer and employee is established and the incidents of the contract of employment.

In this chapter we are concerned with employment law. This is based upon and deals with the relationship of employer and employee. Employment law is made up of common law and, more and more these days, of statute law passed by Parliament.

EMPLOYER AND EMPLOYEE

Generally

It is important to know how this relationship comes into being and to distinguish it from the relationship between a person who buys the services of someone who is self-employed (often called an independent contractor).

Usually it is not difficult to decide whether A is employed by B so that the relationship of employee and employer exists between them. If A is an employee he or she will have been *selected* by B; A will usually work *full-time* for B under a degree of *supervision* for a *wage or salary*.

Of course A may still be an employee even though working *part-time*. However, a part-timer will be unable to claim the protection of employment legislation, e.g. in regard to unfair dismissal, unless the working hours are at least 16 per week. After five years' employment this figure is reduced to eight hours.

Also, if A is an employee, B will deduct *income tax* from A's pay (if it exceeds A's allowances) under PAYE (pay as you earn) arrangements. B will also make *social security contributions* for A and will often provide a *pension scheme* which A can join. In addition, although a contract of employment (or service) need not be in writing, if

Smith and Keenan's Advanced Business Law

A is an employee, then B must, under the Employment Protection (Consolidation) Act 1978, give A within 13 weeks after the beginning of the employment *written particulars* of the major terms of the contract (*see further* p. 378).

The control test

In earlier times the above tests would not all have been available, particularly the deduction of income tax which, after some earlier experiments beginning in 1799, was finally brought in for good in 1842. Social security legislation and the modern deductions from pay, together with contributions from the employer, have only come in on the present scale since the Second World War.

In times past, therefore, a person, whether employed or self-employed, would simply receive money from the employer and it was less easy to distinguish one from the other.

There was, even so, a need to do so, because an employer was liable to pay damages to those injured by his employee if those injuries took place during the course of the employee's work. This is called an *employer's vicarious liability*.

A person was not vicariously liable for injury caused to others by a self-employed (or independent) contractor who was doing work for him. Obviously, then, it was necessary to find a test to decide whether A was, or was not, an employee of B.

The earliest test was called 'the control test'. Since it is not normally necessary to use this test today in order to decide whether A is the employee of B because we have much more evidence of the relationship now, why should we bother with it?

The answer is that it is sometimes necessary to decide whether B, who is truly employed by A, has been temporarily transferred to another person, C, so that C (the temporary employer) and not A (the general employer) is liable vicariously for the injuries caused to a person or persons by B.

The following case provides an illustration.

Mersey Docks and Harbour Board v Coggins & Griffiths (Liverpool) Ltd [1947] AC 1

The Board owned and hired out mobile cranes driven by skilled operators who were employees of the Board. Coggins & Griffiths, who were stevedores, hired one of the Board's cranes and an operator, Mr Newell, to unload a ship.

In the course of unloading the ship a person was injured because of Mr Newell's negligence and the court had to decide whether the Board or Coggins & Griffiths were vicariously liable along with Mr Newell for the latter's negligence. The matter was one of control because the Board was quite clearly the general employer. Actually, the answers given by Mr Newell to questions put to him by counsel in court were highly important. At one point he said: 'I take no orders from anybody'. Since he was not truly employed by Coggins & Griffiths *and* since he did not, so he said, take orders from them, there was no way in which he could be regarded as under their control. Therefore, his true employers, the Board, were vicariously liable for Mr Newell's negligence.

Comment: It is *presumed* in these cases that the general employer continues to be liable and it is up to him to satisfy the court that control has passed to a temporary employer. This is a very difficult thing to do and the temporary employer will not be liable very often, though it is a possibility.

The organization test

Later on a test called the 'organization or integration' test was brought in because the control test was not necessarily suitable for employees who were highly skilled.

There was a possibility that even though there was a lot of general evidence of employment, such as PAYE deductions from pay, an employer would not be vicariously liable for the acts of a highly skilled employee, such as a doctor, or, really, anyone qualified and experienced and acting in a professional field, if that employer could convince the court in his defence that he did not have the necessary control of the skilled person.

This has not been possible because of the organization test put forward by Lord Denning in *Stevenson, Jordan & Harrison Ltd* v *Macdonald & Evans Ltd* [1952] 1 TLR 101. He decided in that case, in effect, that an employee is a person who is integrated with others in the workplace or business, even though the employer does not have a detailed control of what he does.

Independent contractors – the self-employed

The main feature here is the absence of control or meaningful supervision which can be exercised by those who buy the services of an independent contractor by means of what is called a *contract for services*.

Particular cases examined

In the majority of cases there is no difficulty in deciding whether a person is employed or self-employed. For example, factory employees, office clerical staff, and agricultural workers are clearly employees. Garage proprietors, house-builders, and dry cleaners are contractors independent of the members of the public who use them.

A particularly compelling example comes from a comparison between a chauffeur and a person who owns and drives his own taxi. The chauffeur is an employee; the taxi-driver is an independent contractor. Suppose, then, that Fred is employed as my chauffeur: I would have enough control over him to ask him to drive more slowly in a built-up area. In the case of the taxi-driver, I would not have (or even feel I had) the necessary control to insist on a change of speed.

Contract of service or for services – why distinguish?

First of all, because of the existence of *vicarious liability*, an employer is liable, for example, for damage caused to another by his employee's negligent acts while that employee is acting in the course of his employment, that is, doing his job, but not otherwise.

Secondly, the *rights and remedies provided by employment legislation*, such as the Employment Protection (Consolidation) Act 1978, are available to an employee, but not to the self-employed. We shall be looking at these rights and remedies more closely later in this chapter.

THE CONTRACT OF EMPLOYMENT

Generally

The ordinary principles of the law of contract apply. So in a contract of employment there must be an offer and an acceptance, which is in effect, the agreement. There must also be an intention to create legal relations, consideration and capacity, together with proper consent by the parties, that is, no mistake, misrepresentation, duress or undue influence. In addition, the contract must not be illegal.

However, since we have already looked at these general principles of the law of contract, it is only necessary to highlight certain matters which are of importance in the context of employment law.

Written particulars

A contract of employment does not require any written formalities and can be made orally. However, certain written particulars of it are required to be given to the employee by the Employment Protection (Consolidation) Act 1978 (*see below*). These particulars must be given to the employee not later than 13 weeks after the employment started.

Contents – generally

The statement must contain the following information.

  (a) *The names of the employer and the employee.* A letter of engagement will usually be sent to the employee at his address. This will identify him and the letter-heading will identify the employer.
  (b) *The date when the employment began.* This is important if it becomes necessary to decide what period of notice is to be given. The 1978 Act provides for certain minimum periods of notice to be given by employers. For example, they must give one week's notice after four weeks' service, two weeks' after two years' service, and so on up to 12 weeks after 12 years' service (*see further* p. 193). The date when the job began obviously settles this point.

In addition, the length of the employment affects the period necessary to make certain claims. For example, redundancy claims require two years' continuous service *since the age of 18*. Unfair dismissal requires two years of continuous service, usually with a particular employer (but *see below*), regardless of the age at which the service began, unless the dismissal is automatically unfair, as where it was because the employee was (or proposed to become) a member of a trade union.

(c) *Whether the employment counts as a period of continuous employment with a previous employment, and the date of commencement of the previous employment where this is so.* This is important because the rights of an employee to complain of unfair dismissal or to claim a redundancy payment, depend upon whether that employee has served the necessary period of continuous employment. This may be with one employer, but if it is with more than one employer, it must be possible to regard the employments with the various employers as continuous. Situations of continuous employment, despite a change of employer, taken from the Employment Protection (Consolidation) Act 1978, are:

(i) *A transfer between associated employers.* For example, if A is employed by B Ltd and is transferred to work for C Ltd, and B Ltd and C Ltd are subsidiaries of X plc, then A's employment with B Ltd and C Ltd is regarded as continuous.

(ii) *A sale of the business in which the employee was employed to another person.* There are other provisions which now relate to this situation and protect employees from a break in continuous employment on a change of employer. The Transfer of Undertakings (Protection of Employment) Regulations 1981 apply. The main provisions of the Regulations in regard to the transfer of a business are that employees who are employed by the old employer 'immediately before' the transfer automatically become the employees of the new employer. The new employer takes over the employment protection liabilities of the old employer, but not, according to *Angus Jowett & Co v NUTWG* [1985] IRLR 326 liability to pay a protective award. A protective award is payable when an employer fails to consult with a recognized trade union when he is intending to make the workforce or some part of it redundant (*see further* p. 433). So, if A gives notice of future redundancy to his employees without proper consultation with their union, and they are still working for him when he sells the business to B, then A and not B is liable to pay the protective award.

There has been some difficulty with regard to the interpretation of the words 'immediately before'. Administrative receivers who took over insolvent companies on behalf of secured creditors such as banks used this when selling off the company. Purchasers would normally insist as a condition of buying the company that all employees be dismissed before the transfer. The administrative receiver concerned would therefore see that the employees were dismissed sometimes only one hour before the contract of purchase was signed. In cases brought by the employees for unfair dismissal or a redundancy payment the court had ruled that they were not transferred and must bring their claims against the insolvent transferor company with little prospect of success since the purchase money would normally be taken by secured creditors such as banks to pay off debts owed to them.

However, in *Litster* v *Forth Dry Dock and Engineering Co Ltd* [1989] 1 All ER 1134 the House of Lords held that an employee dismissed shortly before the transfer of business for a reason connected with the transfer, e.g. purchaser insistence, was to be regarded as being employed 'immediately before' the transfer so that employment protection liabilities were transferred to the purchaser. This is a fairer interpretation of the regulations but it will make it more difficult to sell off insolvent companies.

(iii) *A change in the partners where a person is employed by a partnership.* A partnership is not a separate person at law as a company is. Employees of a partnership are employed by the partners as people. So, if A works for a partnership of C and D, and D retires and is replaced by E, then A's employers have changed but his employment with C and D and C and E is regarded as continuous. Therefore, if C and E unfairly dismiss A he can make up his two years' continuous service to be able to claim by adding together his service with C and D and C and E in order to make a claim against C and E.

(iv) *A succession of contracts between the same parties are regarded as continuous.* So, if A works for B as a clerk and is then promoted to a manager under a new contract, the two contract periods can be added together to make a period of continuous employment.

Contents – terms of the employment

The written particulars then go on to set out the terms of the employment. The terms which must be given are:

(a) the scale or rate of pay and the method of calculating pay where the employee is paid by commission or bonus;

(b) when payment is made – that is weekly or monthly – and the day or date of payment;

(c) hours to be worked, e.g. 'The normal working hours are . . . '. Compulsory overtime, if any, should be recorded to avoid disputes with employees who may sometimes not want to work it;

(d) holiday entitlement and provisions relating to holiday pay if the employee leaves in a particular year without taking a holiday. If holiday entitlement is set out clearly it can help to avoid disputes regarding a requirement to work in what is a normal holiday period in the area or during the school holidays;

(e) sick pay and injury arrangements must be set out;

(f)   whether or not there is a pension scheme;

(g)   the length of notice which the employee must give and the length of notice the employee is entitled to receive. We have already said that there are minimum periods of notice required to end contracts of employment and full details of these appear on p. 193. The contract can, of course, provide for a longer period of notice but not a shorter one;

(h)   the job title, which is important in dealing with redundancy cases where to justify that a dismissal is because of redundancy and is not an unfair dismissal, the employer may show that there has been a reduction in 'work of a particular type'. The job title indicates what type of work the employee does. In equal pay claims, also, it may show that a man or woman is employed on 'like work'.

Contents – disciplinary rules and grievances

Disciplinary procedures deal, for example, with the number of warnings, oral or written, which will be given before suspension or dismissal.

Grievance procedures relate to complaints in regard to any aspect of the employment with which the employee is not satisfied. The employee should be told who to complain to and any right of appeal, as it were, beyond that to, say, a more senior manager. This procedure is to be available if the employee is not satisfied with the *disciplinary decision* or for some *other grievance*.

The written particulars need not actually contain the disciplinary and grievance procedures. They can be (and often are) in a separate booklet. If so, the written particulars should refer to that booklet and the employee must have a copy of it.

Section 9 of the Employment Act 1989 exempts employers with fewer than 20 employees on the date when the employment began from the requirement from s. 1 of the 1978 Act to provide employees with particulars of disciplinary procedures. However, the requirement to give employees the name of a person to whom they can make a grievance complaint continues to apply. If the organization grows beyond 19 employees new ones will have to have a statement of disciplinary procedures which will have to be set up if they do not exist. This will involve rights of appeal. Presumably if the organization did grow the original employees would be given the disciplinary procedures though there would be no legal requirement to do so.

Changes in the terms of the contract

If the terms of the contract are changed then, because of the provisions of the Employment Protection (Consolidation) Act 1978, the employee must be told *in writing* within one month of the change, either by a statement which is given to the employee to keep, or a reasonably obvious notice on, say, a well-sited notice board.

If the particulars which the employee received when he started the job referred to a document such as a handbook in which future changes in the terms of the employment were to be recorded, an employer, who includes the changes in that document within one month of the date when they were made need not give a written notice to each employee.

If the terms of the employment can be changed by a collective agreement with a trade union, the particulars should say so because if this is the case, the terms of the job can be changed *without* the employees' consent. The results of the employer's negotiations with the unions are incorporated into the contracts of the employees, and become binding as between employer and employee even though the agreement between the employer and the trade union is 'binding in honour only' (*Marley* v *Forward Trust Group Ltd* [1986]) IRLR 369).

In other cases, the terms of the employment cannot be changed unless the employee has agreed and if the employer introduces a variation in the contract as by, say, lowering pay, then the employer is in breach of the contract.

It was *held* in *Rigby* v *Ferodo Ltd* [1987] IRLR 516 that an employee can sue successfully for damages from his employer where he has suffered a cut in pay to which neither he nor his union have agreed.

Failure to comply with the obligation to give written particulars

The 1978 Act provides that if an employer fails to give written particulars at the start of the employment, or fails to notify changes in the terms of the contract, the employee can go to an industrial tribunal. If a statement is given but the employee thinks it is not complete, either the employee or the employer can go to an industrial tribunal to see which of them is right.

The tribunal may make a declaration that the employee has a right to a statement and also say what should be in it. The statement as approved by the tribunal is then assumed in law to have been given by the employer to the employee and forms the basis of the contract of employment. Failure to give written particulars does not make the contract of employment unenforceable by the parties.

Written particulars are a right of the employee not a mere entitlement. Therefore they must be given whether the employee asks for them or not (*Coales* v *John Wood (Solicitors)* [1986] IRLR 129).

Health and safety

The Health and Safety at Work Act 1974 states that an employer must prepare, and revise when necessary, a statement of his policy in regard to the health and safety at work of his employees. This must be contained in a separate document but it is often given out with the written particulars which are now being considered. Employers with fewer than five employees are not required to give this statement.

Sample statement of written particulars of terms of employment

Figure 15.1 provides a sample letter setting out terms of employment suitable for a shorthand-typist. The employee should be required to sign the employer's copy in the following way:

'I have received and read a copy of the above particulars which are correct in all respects.'
Signed Jane Doe
Date 9 March 1990

To:　Ms Jane Doe
　　　350 Elton Road
　　　Manchester M62 10AS

The following particulars are given to you pursuant to the Employment Protection (Consolidation) Act 1978

1.　The parties are as follows

　　Name and address of Employer:　　Michael Snooks Ltd
　　　　　　　　　　　　　　　　　　520 London Square
　　　　　　　　　　　　　　　　　　Manchester M42 14SA

　　Name and address of Employee:　　Jane Doe
　　　　　　　　　　　　　　　　　　350 Elton Road
　　　　　　　　　　　　　　　　　　Manchester M62 10AS

2.　The date when your employment began was 2 February 1990.
　　Your employment with John Bloggs Ltd from whom Michael Snooks Ltd purchased the business and which began on 3 February 1989 counts as part of your period of continuous employment with Michael Snooks Ltd. No employment with a previous employer counts as part of your period of continuous employment.
3.　The following are the particulars of the terms of your employment as at 9 March 1990.
　　(a)　You are employed at 520 London Square, Manchester M42 14SA as a shorthand-typist.
　　(b)　The rate of your remuneration is £185 per week.
　　(c)　Your remuneration is paid at weekly intervals.
　　(d)　Your normal working hours are from 9.30 a.m. to 5 p.m., Mondays to Fridays inclusive.
　　(e)　(i)　You are entitled to two weeks holiday with pay after one completed year of service and to four weeks holiday with pay every year after two completed years of service.
　　　　　　These holidays are to be taken at a time convenient to the employer between 1 May and 30 October in each year. If an employee's employment terminates before all holiday accrued due has been taken, the employee is entitled to payment in lieu thereof on leaving the said employment. You are also entitled to the customary holidays with pay, i.e. New Year's Day, Good Friday, Easter Monday, May Day, Spring Bank Holiday, Late Summer Bank Holiday, Christmas Day and Boxing Day.
　　　　(ii)　Regulations as to payment while absent during sickness or injury are available for inspection during normal working hours in the office of the Secretary/PA to the Personnel Manager.
　　　　(iii)　There is no pension scheme applicable to you.
　　(f)　The length of notice which you are obliged to give to end your contract of employment is one week and the length of notice you are entitled to receive unless your conduct is such that you may be summarily dismissed is as follows:
　　　　(i)　One week if your period of continuous employment is less than two years;
　　　　(ii)　One week's notice for each year of continuous employment if your period of continuous employment is two years or more but less than 12 years; and
　　　　(iii)　Twelve weeks if your period of continuous employment is twelve years or more.

NOTE
If you are not satisfied with any disciplinary decision relating to you or seek redress of any grievance relating to your employment you can apply in the first place to the person in charge of the typing pool. Details of the procedure available and to be followed in connection with your employment are posted in the staff room.

Date ninth day of March 1990.

　　　　　　　　　　　　Signed
　　　　　　　　　　　　Sarah Snooks
　　　　　　　　　　　　Company Secretary

Fig. 15.1　Sample statement of written particulars of terms of employment

Exemptions from the written particulars requirements

There are some situations under the 1978 Act where an employer does not have to give the written particulars. Those which may be found in the average business are as follows.

(a) An employee who leaves his job and comes back within six months on the same terms and conditions need not be given a statement when he comes back if he had one when he was first employed.
(b) Part-time workers who work less than 16 hours each week need not be given written particulars. However, when they have been employed for five years they must be given the written particulars unless they are then working less than eight hours a week.
(c) Employees with fully written contracts containing all the necessary terms need not be given also the written particulars.
(d) Written particulars need not be given to an employee whose job is wholly or mainly outside Great Britain.
(e) There is no need for written particulars where the employee is the husband or wife of the employer.
(f) It is not necessary to give an employee written particulars if he or she is employed for a specific job, e.g. to clear a backlog of office work, which is not expected to last more than 12 weeks. If it does last for more than 12 weeks the worker is entitled to written particulars.

RIGHTS AND DUTIES OF THE PARTIES TO THE CONTRACT

The duties of an employer and an employee come from common law and Acts of Parliament. They will be dealt with under the headings which follow.

DUTIES OF AN EMPLOYER

To provide remuneration

In business organizations the duty of the employer to pay his employees and the rate or amount of pay is decided as follows: (a) by the contract of employment; or (b) by the terms of what is called a collective agreement made between a trade union and the employer. The terms of this agreement, including the part on pay, are then assumed to be part of the individual contracts of employment of the members.

The pay which the worker is to get should nearly always be definite because it is included in the written particulars which we have just dealt with and also because the Employment Protection (Consolidation) Act 1978 requires itemised pay statements (*see further* p. 390).

If there is no provision for payment in the contract – which is highly unlikely – then if the worker sued for payment the court would fix a fair rate of pay for the job by taking evidence as to what rates of pay were usual in the type of work being done.

Unless the employment contract allows an employer to reduce an employee's pay during short-time working or the employee agrees to a reduction, the employer must continue to pay full wages during a period of enforced short-time working (*Miller* v *Hamworthy Engineering Ltd* [1986] IRLR 461).

However, it was decided by the House of Lords in *Miles* v *Wakefield Metropolitan District Council* [1987] 1 All ER 1089 that when an employee refuses to perform his contractual duties because he is taking industrial action, his employer can understandably lawfully withhold wages for the relevant period of time.

To give holidays and holiday pay

The rights and duties of the parties here depend upon what the contract of employment says or what the terms of a collective agreement with the union are. Again, there should be no doubt about holidays and holiday pay because the 1978 Act states that this information is to be given to the employee in the written particulars.

To provide sick pay

Entitlement to sick pay must be dealt with by the written particulars. An employer has *no general duty to provide sick pay from his own funds*. As we have already seen (p. 144) there is no implied term in a contract of service that an employee is entitled to sick pay (*Mears* v *Safecar Security* [1982] 2 All ER 865). There is a *statutory duty* under the 1978 Act to pay an employee who goes sick during the statutory period of notice and is not able to work out all or part of the notice.

Employers are required to provide what is called *statutory sick pay* on behalf of the government. The law is to be found in the main in the Social Security and Housing Benefit Act 1982, the Social Security Act 1985 and the Statutory Sick Pay Act 1991. It is not necessary in a book of this nature to go into detail in regard to the statutory sick pay scheme but the main principles are that when an employee falls sick he or she gets a weekly amount from the employer and not from the Department of Social Security. The employer partially recovers the amount paid as statutory sick pay by deducting 80 per cent of the gross amount of SSP from the total amount of employees' (primary) and employers' (secondary) Class I NI contributions due to the Collector of Taxes in respect of all employees for the tax month in which the SSP was paid, or from contributions due from subsequent months. Since 6 April 1985 employees have also been authorized to deduct from contributions a sum equivalent to the employers' NIC due on SSP. This was ended by the Statutory Sick Pay Act 1991.

SSP goes on for 28 weeks and since the vast majority of employees are not sick for anything like as long as this, employee sickness benefit is, in effect, now paid by the employer. It is not possible to avoid the statutory sick pay provisions and any clause in a contract of employment which sets out to do this is void.

To provide pay during suspension

(a) *On medical grounds.* Under the Employment Protection (Consolidation) Act 1978 an employee who has had at least four weeks' continuous service with his employer and who is suspended from work, for example, under the Health and Safety at Work Act 1974, normally on the advice of an Employment Medical Adviser, not because he is ill but because he might become ill if he continues at work, since he is currently engaged on an industrial process which involves a potential hazard to his health, is entitled to be paid his normal wages while he is suspended for up to 26 weeks. This could occur, for example, where there was a leak of radioactivity at the workplace.

An employee may complain to an industrial tribunal under the 1978 Act if his employer has not paid him what he is entitled to during a period of suspension and the tribunal may order the employer to pay the employee the money which he should have had.

(b) *On disciplinary grounds.* Suppose an employee takes a day off without permission, in order to go to a football match. His employer decides to suspend him for a further day without pay. Is this legal? Well, there is no implied right to suspend an employee for disciplinary reasons without pay. In practice, if the employer wants a power to suspend it must be made an express term of the contract which is agreed to by the employee and be in the written particulars of the job. If so, it will be justified and the employee will have to accept it.

Maternity provision

For ante-natal care

Under the Employment Protection (Consolidation) Act 1978, as amended by the Employment Act 1980, a pregnant employee who has, on the advice of her doctor or midwife or health visitor, made an appointment to get ante-natal care must have time off to keep it and she must also be paid. Except for the first appointment the employer can ask for proof of the appointment in the form, for example, of an appointment card. An employer who does not give the employee these rights can be taken to a tribunal by the employee but this must normally be during the three months following the employer's refusal. Compensation may be given to the employee, both where the employer has failed to give time off and also where he has given time off but has failed to pay the employee. In either case the compensation will be the amount of pay to which she would have been entitled if time off with pay had been given as the law requires. Part-time employees are entitled to this time off and it does not make any difference how many hours they work each week.

For statutory maternity pay

The Social Security Act 1986 made major alterations to the maternity payments scheme. Prior to the Act a woman who qualified received maternity pay from which was deducted the state maternity allowance. Maternity pay was then recouped by the employer from the Maternity Pay Fund.

(a) *As regards the amount and time for which it is paid,* under the Social Security Act of 1986 statutory maternity pay (SMP) is payable through the employer who recoups it from National Insurance contributions. To qualify the woman must have worked for her present employer for at least 26 weeks ending with the week immediately preceding the 14th week before the expected week of confinement, and her normal weekly wage must not be less than the lower limit for payment of national insurance contributions, currently £52. If so, she is entitled to a payment at the lowest rate of statutory maternity pay, currently £44.50 for 18 weeks. Women who have been with the employer for two years or more, if normally employed for 16 or more hours per week, or five years or more if normally employed for eight hours or more but less than 16 hours a week will receive SMP of nine tenths of earnings for the first six weeks of the maternity leave. The flat rate, currently £44.50 is paid for the rest of the period.

The period of 18 weeks can commence anywhere between the beginning of the 11th week before the expected week of confinement and the sixth week before the expected week of confinement and must end no later than 11 weeks after the expected week of confinement.

(b) *Non-payment – remedies.* If the employer does not make payments of SMP, to which the employee thinks she is entitled, she may under the Social Security Act 1986:

(i) Require the employer to supply her, within a reasonable time, with a written statement of his position in the matter. This will indicate why he feels that there is no entitlement, or a smaller entitlement.

(ii) If this does not resolve the dispute the employee, or the Department of Social Security, may refer the matter to an adjudication officer. An appeal from him lies to the Social Security Appeal Tribunal and from that tribunal to a Social Security Commissioner.

An employer who refuses to pay after a final decision has been made that he should commits a criminal offence.

If the employee cannot obtain payment from the employer, as where he is insolvent, she may apply to the Department of Employment for payment. If the Department of Employment makes the payment it may recover from the employer as by proving in the insolvency.

The right to return to work

The employee must comply with certain formalities in order that she may have the right to return to work. These are that she must be give her employer at least 21 days written notice before her absence begins:

(a) giving the reason why she will be absent and the expected week of confinement; and

(b) of her intention to return to work if this is what she is going to do.

The employer may require the employee to produce a medical certificate giving the expected date of confinement.

Although a woman gives notice of her intention to return to work she is not forced to do so. This leaves the employer in a state of some uncertainty. The 1978 Act, as amended by The Employment Act 1980, allows the employer to check what the situation is. The employer is allowed to make a request for information from the employee. The employer cannot do this until seven weeks have passed from the beginning of the week of confinement. The employer's request must be in writing and will ask the employee to confirm her intention to return. The request must also contain a warning to the employee of the consequences of failure to comply.

An employee intending to return must confirm the fact in writing within fourteen days of receiving the request or as soon as reasonably practicable, otherwise the right to return is lost. However, confirmation does not oblige the employee to return.

In order actually to get back to work, the woman must give written notice to the employer at least 21 days before the notified date of return, that date being not later than 29 weeks after the beginning of the week in which the birth occurred.

The return to work can be postponed by either the employer or the employee by up to four weeks from the date notified. The employer can postpone it for any reason so long as those reasons are notified to the employee. The employee can only postpone if she is ill and cannot work and has a medical certificate to that effect.

If there is, for example, industrial action, so that the woman cannot return on the date notified, then she may return when the interruption is over or as soon as is reasonably practicable afterwards.

If the employee carries out all the formalities for return to work but the employer refuses to allow her to return, she will be regarded as dismissed and the employer will have to show that this was not unfair dismissal (*see further* p. 424).

If, because of a reorganization in the firm during the woman's absence, her job is no longer available, the employer must offer her suitable alternative employment. If there is such employment and it is not offered to her she can claim unfair dismissal. If no such work is available she is redundant and can claim a redundancy payment. If she refuses to take suitable alternative work she will have no claim on the employer.

Small employers are specially protected because they cannot easily cope with a long absence by an employee. So, if there are not more than five employees counted together with those of an 'associated employer' (e.g. in a holding and subsidiary company situation you would have to count the employees in the holding company together with those of the subsidiary company in deciding whether the figure was five or less), at the time when the employee left, and it is not reasonably practicable for the employer to take the employee back or to offer alternative work, then the employer is not liable if he does not take the employee back.

It should also be noted that an employee who has been absent on maternity leave must be given, on return, any pay rises granted to her grade of employment during her absence and there must be no loss of seniority or pension rights.

To make payments during lay-off – guarantee payments

Lay-off

To avoid difficulty the right of the employer to lay off employees without pay because of lack of work should be made an express term of the contract of employment. However, even if the employer has given himself that right in the contract he must still comply with the provisions of the 1978 Act in the matter and cannot have clauses in the contract which are worse for the employee than the basic statutory rights which provide for guarantee payments.

Guarantee payments

The 1978 Act provides that employees with four weeks or more of continuous service are entitled to a guarantee payment up to a maximum sum, which is currently £13.65 per day, if they are not provided with work on a normal working day, e.g. because of a threatened power cut (*Miller* v *Harry Thornton (Lollies) Ltd* [1978] IRLR 430). This does not apply if the failure of the employer to provide work is because of industrial action or if the employee has been offered suitable alternative work but has refused it.

An employee can only receive a payment for five workless days during any period of three months. The effect of this is that in order to get payment for a day of lay-off the three months before that day of lay-off must be looked at to see whether the employee has already received the maximum five days guarantee pay. If the lay-off was, for example, on 20 June and the worker had been paid for lay-offs on 5 June, 27 May, 21 May, 4 April and 2 April, he would not be entitled to a payment but he would for a lay-off on 3 July.

An employee can go to a tribunal if the employer fails to pay all or part of a guarantee payment which the employee should have had. The tribunal can order the employer to pay it. The employee must apply to the tribunal within three months of the workless day or within such longer period as the tribunal thinks reasonable if it is satisfied that it was not reasonable or practicable for the employee to present the claim in three months.

To pay during statutory time off

The 1978 Act gives employees certain rights to time off work (*see also* p. 397). In *two* cases the employee is also entitled to be paid during the time off. These situations are dealt with here as part of the law relating to the right to be paid. They are as follows.

Time off for carrying out union duties

An employer must allow an employee, who is an official of an independent trade union (that is a union which is not dominated or controlled by the employer and is not liable to interference by the employer as some staff associations may be), which is recognized by the employer, to take time off during working hours to carry out the duties of a trade union official if those duties are concerned with industrial relations between the employer and his employees.

Time off must also be given for union officials to take training in aspects of industrial relations which are relevant to matters for which the union is recognized by the employer (s. 10, Employment Act 1989). Thus although trade union officials will be allowed paid time off for core union activities such as collective bargaining with management, they will not be allowed paid time off for, for example, courses to improve general education and training such as courses on the general issues raised by mergers and takeovers of companies and in particular the pension rights of employees. However, voluntary arrangements between employers and employees may well ensure that such courses continue in some organizations.

If there is a breach by the employer of this duty the employee may complain to a tribunal which may declare the employee's rights in its order, so that the employer may carry them out, and may also award money compensation.

Redundant employees

An employee who has been continuously employed by his employer for at least two years and who is given notice of dismissal because of redundancy has a right before the period of his notice expires to reasonable time off during working hours so that he can look for another job or make arrangements for training for future employment.

While absent the employee is entitled to be paid but not more than two-fifths of a week's pay in respect of the whole period of notice. If an employer is in breach of the above provisions, the employee can complain to a tribunal within three months but the tribunal's compensation is limited to two-fifths of a week's pay.

Itemized pay statements

Under the Employment Protection (Consolidation) Act 1978 an employer must give his employees an itemized pay statement. Before these provisions came into force an employer could simply state the amount of take-home pay with no details of how it had been arrived at.

Under the Act the employee must receive a statement at the time of or before receiving his pay, showing gross pay and take-home pay and the variable deductions, e.g income tax, which make up the difference between the two figures.

Details of how it is paid must also be given, e.g. is it contained in the pay packet or has it been credited to a bank account?

As regards fixed deductions, e.g. savings, these need not be itemized every pay day. If the employer gives the employee a separate statement setting out the fixed deductions he may simply show a lump sum representing these in the weekly/monthly pay statement. This fixed deduction statement must be updated in writing if it is changed and in any case it must be re-issued every 12 months.

If the employer does not comply with the pay statement requirements the employee can complain to a tribunal which will make a declaration of the law that a statement should have been given and as to what it should have included. The employer must comply with this declaration. In addition, the tribunal may order the employer to give back to the employee any deductions which were made from the employee's pay and which were not notified to him during the 13 weeks before the date of the application by the employee to the tribunal.

Method of payment and deductions from pay

Under the Wages Act 1986 employees no longer have a right to be paid in cash. The Truck Acts 1831–1940, which used to give this right, were repealed by the 1986 Act. Payment may still, of course, be made in cash, but an employer can if he wishes pay the employee, for example, by cheque or by crediting the employee's bank account. It should be noted, however, that if a worker was paid in cash before the 1986 Act came into force the method of payment may only be changed if the worker agrees to a variation of the contract of service.

Deductions from pay are unlawful unless they are (a) authorized by Act of Parliament, such as income tax and National Insurance deductions; or (b) contained in a written contract of employment. As regards (b) deductions from the wages of workers in the retail trade, e.g. petrol station cashiers, for stock and cash shortages are limited to ten per cent of the gross wages. These provisions are enforceable by the employee against the employer in industrial tribunals.

Equal pay

The Equal Pay Act 1970 (EPA), as amended by the Sex Discrimination Act 1975 (SDA) and the Equal Pay (Amendment) Regulations 1983, implies a term called an equality clause into contracts of service. This clause means that a man or a woman must be given contractual terms not less favourable than those given to an employee of the opposite sex when they are each employed: (a) *on like work*, in the same employment; (b) *on work rated as equivalent* in the same employment, e.g. by a job evaluation scheme; or (c) *on work which is in terms of demands made on the worker*, under such headings as effort, skill and decision making, *of equal value* to that of a worker in the same employment.

As regards the relationship between the EPA and the SDA, the EPA covers not only matters concerning wages and salaries, but also other terms in the contract of service, such as sick pay, holiday pay and unequal working hours. Other forms of sex discrimination in employment, such as discrimination in recruitment techniques, are covered by the SDA (*see further* p. 405).

Application of the Equal Pay Act

The Act applies to all forms of full and part-time work. There are no exemptions for small firms or in respect of people who have only recently taken up the employment, though the Act does not apply, for example, to those who do their work wholly outside Great Britain.

The Act applies to discrimination against men but in practice claims are normally made by women. We shall from now on consider the law on the basis of a claim by a woman.

The main provisions of the Equal Pay Act are as follows.

(a) *If a woman is engaged in the same or broadly similar work as a man* and both work for the same or an associated employer (*see below*) the woman is entitled to the same rate of pay and other terms of employment as the man.

The comparison can be made with a previous holder of the same job. In *Macarthys* v *Smith* [1980] ICR 672 the Employment Appeal Tribunal decided that Mrs Smith, a stockroom manageress, was entitled to pay which was equal to that of a previous manager of the stockroom, a Mr McCullough. However, the EAT did say that tribunals must be cautious in making such comparisons unless the interval between the two employments is reasonably short and there have not been changes in economic circumstances.

The term 'broadly similar work' means that although there may be some differences between the work of the man and the woman, these are not of sufficient practical importance to give rise to what the EPA calls a 'material difference'. **The following case is relevant here.**

Capper Pass v Lawton [1977] 2 All ER 11

A female cook who worked a 40-hour week preparing lunches for the directors of Capper was paid a lower rate than two male assistant chefs who worked a 45-hour week preparing some 350 meals a day in Capper's works canteen. The female cook claimed that by reason of the EPA (as amended) she should be paid at the same rate as the assistant chefs since she was employed on work of a broadly similar nature.

It was held by the EAT that if the work done by a female applicant was of a broadly similar nature to that done by a male colleague it should be regarded as being like work for the purposes of the EPA unless there were some practical differences of detail between the two types of job. In this case the EAT decided that the work done by the female cook was broadly similar to the work of the assistant chefs and that the differences of detail were not of practical importance in relation to the terms and conditions of employment. Therefore the female cook was entitled to be paid at the same rate as her male colleagues.

Comment: (i) An interesting contrast is provided by *Navy, Army and Airforce Institutes* v *Varley* [1977] 1 All ER 840. Miss Varley worked as a Grade E clerical worker in the accounts office of NAAFI in Nottingham. NAAFI conceded that her work was like that of a Grade E male clerical worker employed in NAAFI's London office. However, the Grade E workers in Nottingham worked a 37-hour week, while the male Grade E clerical workers in the London office worked a 36½-hour week. Miss Varley applied to an industrial tribunal under the EPA for a declaration that she was less favourably treated as regards hours worked than the male clerical workers in London and that her contract term as to hours should be altered so as to reduce it to 36½ hours a week. The industrial tribunal granted that declaration but NAAFI appealed to the EAT which held that the variation in hours was genuinely due to a material difference other than the difference of sex. It was due to a real difference in that the male employees worked in London where there was a custom to work shorter hours. Accordingly, NAAFI's appeal was allowed and Miss Varley was held not to be entitled to the declaration. The judge said that the variation between her contract and the men's contracts was due really to the fact that she worked in Nottingham and they worked in London.

(ii) Another common example of a sensible material difference occurs where, for example, employee A is a new entrant of, say, 21, and employee B is a long-serving employee of, say, 50, and there is a system of service increments, then it is reasonable to pay B more than A though both are employed on like work. Obviously, however, it is not enough to say that because at the present time men are on average paid more than women this is a material difference justifying paying a woman less in a particular job. This was decided in *Clay Cross (Quarry Services) Ltd* v *Fletcher* [1979] 1 All ER 474.

(iii) It was decided in *Rainey* v *Greater Glasgow Health Board* [1987] 1 All ER 65 that it is in order for an employer to pay more to a man if this is necessary to meet skill shortages. In this case a man was brought in from the private sector because of the shortage of prosthetists (persons who fit artificial limbs). He was paid more than a woman prosthetist who went into service with the public sector immediately after training. It would appear, also, that an employer may pay a man more for doing the same job where the man has greater experience. In other words, the employer can reward experience by giving a man higher pay (*McGregor* v *General Municipal Boilermakers and Allied Trades Union* [1987] ICR 505).

An employer may also pay a man more for doing the same job if the man works nights and the women do not (*Thomas* v *National Coal Board* [1987] IRLR 451).

(b) *If the job which one woman does has been given the same value as a man's job under a job evaluation scheme*, then the woman is entitled to the same rate of pay and other terms of employment as a man.

(c) *Equal value*. If the job which a woman does is in terms of the demands made upon her, for instance under such headings as effort, skill and decision-making, of equal value to that of a man in the same employment, then the woman is entitled to the same pay and other contractual terms as the man, as she is if her work has been graded as of higher value (*Murphy* v *Bord Telecom Eireann* [1988] IRLR 267). It might be thought that in such a case she should be paid more but at least the law can ensure equal pay for her.

A complaint may be made to a tribunal on the grounds of equal value even if the two jobs have been regarded as unequal in a job evaluation study. However, there must be reasonable grounds to show that the study was itself discriminatory on the grounds of sex. It was *held* in *Bromley* v *H & J Quick Ltd* [1987] IRLR 456 that the job evaluation need not be analytical but can be based on employees' expectations. This seemed a rather odd decision because circumstances over the years have lowered women's expectations in regard to pay in the first place, and if the study is based on expectations, the argument becomes somewhat circular. The decision was out of line with the experience of those working in the field of race and sex discrimination. The decision was reversed by the Court of Appeal in early 1988 (*see* [1988] IRLR 249). A non-analytical scheme would be unlikely to satisfy the requirements of European law according to the decision of the European Court of Justice in *Rummler* v *Dato-Druck GmbH* [1987] IRLR 32.

When a complaint about equal value is made, the tribunal can commission a report from an expert on the matter of value. The report of the expert goes to the tribunal and copies go to the parties. Although the report will obviously be extremely important in the decision which the tribunal makes, it is not in any way bound by it and can disregard it.

It was once thought that in claims for equal pay the tribunal must look not merely at pay, but also at fringe benefits. In *Hayward* v *Cammell Laird Shipbuilders Ltd* [1986] ICR 862, a qualified canteen cook, Miss Julie Hayward, who had convinced a tribunal that she was of equal value with male painters, joiners and thermal heating engineers and therefore entitled to equal pay, was told by the Employment Appeal Tribunal that she could not isolate the term about pay. The EAT asked the Tribunal to look at the case again. Although Miss Hayward's pay was not equal, her employers claimed that she had better sickness benefit than the men and also paid meal breaks and extra holidays which they did not have. So it might be possible to say that she was, looked at overall, treated as well. However, Julie Hayward won her appeal in the House of Lords. It was *held* that her claim to equal pay for work of equal value was justified even though she had better fringe benefits. Her employers were not entitled to compare her total package but should instead consider her basic pay. The decision should ensure that miscellaneous benefits are not seen as 'pay' and will not be used to keep wages down in future.

It is also interesting to note that in *Pickstone* v *Freemans plc* [1986] ICR 886 the Employment Appeal Tribunal decided that a woman could not bring a claim that her work was of equal value to that done by a man employed by the same firm in a different job because men were employed in the same job as her own on the same rates of pay and terms.

On the facts of the case this meant that the woman could not claim that her work as a warehouse packer was of equal value to that of a checker warehouse operative merely because she worked on the same terms with other male warehouse packers. The decision was eventually overruled by the House of Lords which decided that a woman is not debarred from making a claim for parity of pay with a male comparator in a different job merely because a man is doing the same job as herself for the same pay. The decision effectively kills off the device of employing a 'token man' with the women employees as a way of defeating equal pay claims.

Associated employers

Comparison of contracts of service for equality purposes is usually made with people who work at the same place. However, comparison can be made with people who work at different places so long as the employer is the same or is an associated employer. As regards an associated employer, this would be the case with a group of companies. Thus if H plc has two subsidiaries, A Ltd and B Ltd, workers in A Ltd could compare themselves with workers in B Ltd, and workers in B Ltd with those in A Ltd, and workers in A Ltd and B Ltd could compare themselves with workers in H plc. Workers in H plc could, of course, compare themselves with workers in A Ltd and B Ltd.

Reference to an industrial tribunal

A complaint of unequal treatment under the EPA may be made to a tribunal at any time while the person who wants to complain is still doing the job or within six months after it came to an end. There is no power to extend the time.

Where the claim is successful the employee will get the difference in pay between herself (or himself) and the comparator. Arrears of pay for up to two years before the date on which the tribunal received the application may be awarded.

Employer's duty to provide work

There is, in general, no duty at common law for an employer to provide work. If the employer still pays the agreed wages or salary the employee cannot regard the employer as in breach of contract. The employee has no right to sue for damages for wrongful dismissal but must accept his pay. The main authority for this is *Collier* v *Sunday Referee* [1940] 2 KB 647, where Mr Justice Asquith said: 'If I pay my cook her wages she cannot complain if I take all my meals out.'

There are some exceptions at common law. For example, a salesman who is paid by commission must be allowed to work in order to earn that commission and if he is not his employer is in breach of contract and can be sued for damages. This is also the case with actors and actresses because they need to keep a public image which requires occasional public performances.

Employee's property

An employer has in fact no duty to protect his employee's property. **The following case illustrates this**.

Deyong v Shenburn [1946] 1 All ER 226

The plaintiff entered into a contract of employment with the defendant under which the plaintiff was to act the dame in a pantomime for three weeks. Rehearsals took place at a theatre and on the second day the plaintiff had stolen from his dressing room his overcoat as well as two shawls and a pair of shoes forming part of his theatrical equipment. In the County Court the judge found that the defendant had been negligent in failing to provide a lock on the dressing room door and having no one at the stage door during the morning of the particular rehearsal day to prevent the entry of unauthorized persons. However, the County Court judge decided that the defendant was under no duty to protect the clothing. The plaintiff appealed to the Court of Appeal which also decided that the defendant was not liable. The Court of Appeal accepted that if there was an accident at work caused by the employer's negligence, then in an action for personal injury the employee could also include damage to his clothing if there had been any. In addition, if in such an accident the employee's clothes were, say, torn off his back but he suffered no personal injury, then it would seem, that he could be entitled to recover damages in respect of the loss of his clothes. However, outside of this an employer has no duty to protect the property of his employee.

Comment: This decision was also applied in the later case of *Edwards* v *West Herts Group Hospital Management Committee* [1957] 1 All ER 541 where the plaintiff, a resident house physician at the defendants' hospital, had some articles of clothing and personal effects stolen from his bedroom at the hostel where he was required to live. He brought an action for breach of an implied duty under his contract of employment to protect his property. His action was dismissed in the County Court and his appeal to the Court of Appeal was also dismissed on the basis that there was no such contractual duty in respect of property.

Employee's indemnity

An employer is bound to indemnify (that is, make good) any expenses, losses and liabilities incurred by an employee while carrying out his duties. **The following case illustrates this.**

Re Famatina Development Corporation Ltd [1914] 2 Ch 271

A company employed a consulting engineer to make a report on its activities. The written report contained matters which the managing director alleged were a libel upon him and he brought an action against the engineer in respect of this on the basis of the publication of the report to the directors of the company, all of whom had received a copy. The managing director's action failed but the engineer incurred costs in defending the claim, not all of which he could recover and he now sought to recover them from the company.

The Court of Appeal decided that the comments made in the report were within the scope of the engineer's employment. His terms of engagement required him to report fully and frankly and in the circumstances he was entitled to the indemnity.

Comment: There is no duty to indemnify an employee against liability for his own negligence. Thus, if by negligence an employee injures a third party in the course of employment and the third party sues the employee, the employer is not required to indemnify the employee and indeed, if the employer is sued as vicariously liable (see p. 376) he has a right to an indemnity against the employee. This was decided in *Lister* v *Romford Ice and Cold Storage Ltd* [1957] I All ER 125, though the action is unlikely to be brought because it upsets industrial relations.

Trade union membership and activities

Under the Employment Protection (Consolidation) Act 1978 employers have a duty not to take action against employees just because they are members of, or take part in at an appropriate time, the activities of a trade union which is independent of the employer. According to the decision in *Post Office* v *Union of Post Office Workers* [1974] 1 All ER 229 this includes activities on the employer's premises.

Under the provisions of s. 11 of the Employment Act 1988 dismissal for failing to join a trade union is always automatically unfair even if there is a closed shop situation within the industry concerned. This provision greatly weakens the maintenance by trade unions of closed shops.

If action is taken against employees they may complain to a tribunal which can award money compensation or make an order saying what the trade union rights of the employee are so that the employer can grant them in the future. If the employee has been dismissed then the unfair dismissal remedies apply (*see further* p. 417).

In addition ss. 1–3 of the Employment Act 1990 gives job seekers a new right not to be refused employment or the services of an employment agency on the grounds that they are or are not trade union members. The Act also protects people who will not agree to become or cease to be union members or to make payments in lieu of membership subscriptions. This means that it is no longer lawful to operate any form of closed shop. Any individual who believes that he or she has been unlawfully refused employment or the service of an employment agency because of union or non-union membership can complain to an industrial tribunal within three months of the refusal. If the case is made out the tribunal can award compensation up to the current maximum of £10,000.

The compensation will generally be paid by the employer or employment agency concerned but in cases where a trade union is joined as a party and the tribunal decides that the unlawful refusal resulted from pressure applied by the union it may order the union to pay some or all of the compensation.

The tribunal can also recommend that the prospective employer or employment agency should take action to remedy the adverse effect of their unlawful action on the complainant.

Time off work

Under the 1978 Act employees have a right to time off work in certain circumstances. Sometimes they are also entitled to pay as in the case of trade union officials and also redundant employees who are looking for work or wanting to arrange training for another job. These cases have already been looked at as part of the law relating to pay (*see* p. 389). However, there are two other cases in which employees are entitled to time off but the employer is not under a duty to pay wages or salary for it. These are as follows.

(a) *Trade union activities*. An employee who is a member of an independent trade union which the employer recognizes is entitled to reasonable time off for trade union activities. The Advisory, Conciliation and Arbitration Service (ACAS), a statutory body set up by the Employment Protection Act 1975 to promote, for example, the improvement of industrial relations, has published a Code of Practice 3 which gives guidance on the time off which an employer should allow.

(b) *Public duties*. Employers also have a duty to allow employees who hold certain public positions and offices reasonable time off to carry out the duties which go along with them. Details are given in the 1978 Act which covers such offices as magistrate, member of local authority, member of an industrial tribunal, and member of certain health, education, water and river authorities. There has recently been an extension to members of boards of visitors and visiting committees for prisons, remand centres and young offender institutions.

Complaints in regard to failure to give time off under (a) and (b) above may be taken to an industrial tribunal. In general the complaint must be made within three months of the date when the failure to give time off occurred. An industrial tribunal may make an order declaring the rights of the employee so that these can be observed by the employer and may also award money compensation to be paid by the employer where there is injury to the employee, e.g. hurt feelings.

Testimonials and references

There is no law which requires an employer to give a reference or testimonial to an employee or to answer questions or enquiries which a prospective employer may ask him. This was decided in *Carroll* v *Bird* (1800) 3 Esp. 201. However, if an employer does give a reference or testimonial, either orally or in writing, which is false, he commits a criminal offence under the Servants' Characters Act 1792. The employer may also be liable in civil law to pay damages to certain persons as follows.

(a) *To a subsequent employer*, who suffers loss because of a false statement *known* to the former employer to be untrue (*Foster* v *Charles* (1830) 7 Bing 105), or made *negligently* without reasonable grounds for believing the statement to be true, because there is a duty of care between an employer and a prospective employer (*Lawton* v *BOC Transhield Ltd* [1987] 2 All ER 608).

The Rehabilitation of Offenders Act 1974 is also relevant here. The provisions of the Act are an attempt to give effect to the principle that when a person convicted of crime has been successfully living it down and has avoided further crime, his efforts at rehabilitation should not be prejudiced by the unwarranted disclosure of the earlier conviction.

The Act therefore prevents any liability arising from failure by an employee to disclose what is called a spent conviction to a prospective employer. For example, the Act removes the need to disclose convictions *resulting in a fine* recorded more than five years before the date of the reference or testimonial. Sentences of imprisonment for life or of imprisonment for a term exceeding 30 months are not capable of rehabilitation. The rehabilitation period for a prison sentence exceeding six months but not exceeding 30 months is ten years, and for a term not exceeding six months it is seven years and, as we have seen, if the sentence was a fine, it is five years.

If an employer does refer to a spent conviction in a testimonial or reference the employee may sue him for *libel* in the case of a written testimonial or reference, or *slander* where the testimonial or reference is spoken. The defence of justification, i.e. that the statement that there was a conviction is true, will be a defence for the employer only if he can show that he acted without malice.

While discussing the 1974 Act it is worth noting that it makes provisions for questions by employers relating to a person's previous convictions to be treated as not applying to spent convictions.

The Act also provides that any failure to disclose a spent conviction shall not be a proper ground for dismissing or excluding a person from any office, profession, or occupation, or employment, or for prejudicing him in any way in any occupation or employment.

However, the Rehabilitation of Offenders Act 1974 (Exceptions) (Amendments) Order 1986, SI 1986/1249, allows those who employ persons who will have contact with those under 18 to ask, for example, questions designed to reveal even spent convictions, particularly any with a sexual connotation.

Certain employees are excluded from the 1974 Act and their convictions can be disclosed. Included in the exception are doctors, chartered and certified accountants, insurance company managers and building society officers (*see* s. 189, Financial Services Act 1986).

(b) *To the former employee*, for libel or slander if things have been stated in a testimonial or reference which damage the employee's reputation. However, the employer has the defence of qualified privilege, as it is called, so that he can speak his mind about the employee, and so in order to get damages the employee would have to prove that the employer made the statement out of malice, as where there was evidence that the employer had a history of unreasonable bad treatment of the employee.

A reference which negligently misrepresents the employee is actionable also by the employee, if he has suffered loss (*Lawton* v *BOC Transhield Ltd* [1987] 2 All ER 608). This could happen where, for example, a new employer set on an employee prior to receiving a reference and then when the reference was received it was inaccurate because of the previous employer's negligence so that the employee lost the new appointment.

Furthermore, any disclaimer in a reference must, so far as negligence is concerned, pass the test of reasonableness in s. 2(2) of the Unfair Contract Terms Act 1977.

An employee who maliciously defaces his own reference or testimonial commits a criminal offence under the Servants' Characters Act 1792.

(c) *What constitutes a satisfactory reference?* Suppose an employer offers a job to an applicant for employment 'subject to satisfactory references' which are then taken up. Who decides whether or not the references are satisfactory? In *Wishart* v *National Association of Citizens' Advice Bureaux, The Times*, 25 June 1990, the Court of Appeal dealt with this matter on which there had previously been no direct authority. It was, they said, a matter for the potential employer. So if potential employers' do not think references are satisfactory, they are not! Presumably, however, the employer must be reasonable and not regard a perfectly good reference as unsatisfactory merely to get out of a contract. Better in any case not to make an offer of any kind until the references are to hand.

Non-contractual duties of the employer

Before leaving the contractual duties of the employer, it should be noted that he has other duties in regard to the health, safety and welfare of his employees. These are based mainly on the common law of tort and statutes such as the Health and Safety at Work Act 1974 and the Factories Act 1961.

DUTIES OF AN EMPLOYEE

To use reasonable skill and care in the work

The *common law* provides that an employee who claims to have a particular skill or skills but shows himself to be incompetent may be dismissed without notice. His employer can also raise the matter of the incompetence of the employee if the employer is sued under *statute law*, i.e. the Employment Protection (Consolidation) Act 1978 for unfair dismissal (*see further* p. 417).

The common law also requires unskilled employees to take reasonable care in carrying out the job. However, they may be dismissed only if there is a serious breach of this implied term of the contract.

To carry out lawful and reasonable instructions

The law implies a term into a contract of employment which requires the employee to obey the lawful and reasonable instructions of his employer. However, an employee is not bound to carry out illegal acts. In *Gregory* v *Ford* [1951] 1 All ER 121 one of the decisions of the court was that an employee could not be required to drive a vehicle which was not insured so as to satisfy the law set out in what is now the Road Traffic Act 1972. If the employee does refuse he is not in breach of his contract.

The duty to give faithful service (or the duty of fidelity)

This is an implied term of a contract of employment. Certain activities of employees are regarded by the law as breaches of the duty to give faithful service. Thus, as we have seen, an employee who while employed copies the names and addresses of his employer's customers for use after leaving the employment can be prevented from using the information (*Robb* v *Green* (1895) – *see also* p. 173).

However, the implied term relating to fidelity does not apply once the contract of employment has come to an end. Therefore, a former employee cannot be prevented under this implied term from encouraging customers of his former employer to do business with him, though he can be prevented from using actual lists of customers which he made whilst still employed. If an employer (A) wants to stop an employee (B) from trying to win over his, A's, *customers*, then the contract of employment between A and B must contain an *express* clause in restraint of trade preventing this. Such a clause must, as we have seen, be reasonable in time and area (*see also* p. 169).

A former employee can, however, be prevented by the court from using his former employer's *trade secrets* or *confidential information* without a clause in the contract about restraint of trade.

Confidential information

It is an implied term of a contract of service that the employee must not disclose *trade secrets*, e.g. a special way of making glass as in *Forster & Sons Ltd* v *Suggett* (1918) (*see* p. 170), or *confidential information* acquired during employment. There is no need for an express clause in the contract.

However, the use by an employee of knowledge of trade secrets and information cannot be prevented if it is just part of the total job experience. An employee cannot be prevented from using what he could not help but learn from doing the job. **The following case shows this.**

Printers & Finishers v Holloway (No. 2) [1964] 3 All ER 731

The plaintiffs brought an action against Holloway, their former works manager, and others, including Vita-tex Ltd, into whose employment Holloway had subsequently entered. They claimed an injunction against Holloway and the other defendants based, as regards Holloway, on an alleged breach of an implied term in his contract of service with the plaintiffs that he should not disclose or make improper use of confidential information relating to the plaintiffs' trade secrets. Holloway's contract did not contain an express covenant relating to non-disclosure of trade secrets.

The plaintiffs were flock printers and had built up their own fund of 'know-how' in this field. The action against Vita-tex arose because Holloway had, on one occasion, taken a Mr

James, who was an employee of Vita-tex Ltd round the plaintiffs' factory. Mr James' visit took place in the evening and followed a chance meeting between himself and Holloway. However, the plant was working and James did see a number of processes. It also appeared that Holloway had, during his employment, made copies of certain of the plaintiffs' documentary material and had taken these copies away with him when he left their employment. The plaintiffs wanted an injunction to prevent the use or disclosure of the material contained in the copies of documents made by Holloway.

The court *held* that the plaintiffs were entitled to an injunction against Holloway so far as the documentary material was concerned, although there was no express term in his contract regarding non-disclosure of secrets.

However, the court would not grant an injunction restraining Holloway from putting at the disposal of Vita-tex Ltd his memory of particular features of the plaintiffs' plant and processes. He was under no express contract not to do so and the court would not extend its jurisdiction to restrain breaches of confidence. In this instance, Holloway's knowledge of the plaintiffs' trade secrets was not readily separable from his general knowledge of flock printing.

An injunction was granted restraining Vita-tex Ltd from making use of the information acquired by Mr James on his visit.

GRADED QUESTIONS

Essay mode

1. Although a contract of employment need not be in writing, s. 1 of the Employment Protection (Consolidation) Act 1978 does require that an employer provide his employee with written particulars of his contract of employment within thirteen weeks of its commencement.
What information do these written particulars provide?
   (*The Institute of Company Accountants. Part 3: Law Relating to Business. May 1989*)

2. (a) Under what circumstances, if any, does an employer who continues to pay wages also have a common law obligation to provide work for his employees?
   (10 marks)

   (b) What are the statutory rights of an employee who is laid off or put on short time because no work is available?
   (10 marks)
   (**Total: 20 marks**)
   (*The Chartered Institute of Management Accountants. Business Law. November 1988*)

3. Explain, with reference to decided cases, how the courts make the distinction between a contract of service (an employer–employee relationship) and a contract

for services (a principal–independent contractor relationship). Why is it important to make this distinction?

(North Staffordshire Polytechnic. BA Business Studies: Business Law)

Objective mode

Four alternative answers are given. Select ONE only. Circle the answer which you consider to be correct. Check your answers by referring back to the information given in the relevant chapter and against the answers at the back of the book.

1. Vicarious liability will render an employer liable for:

   A   Torts which he commits in the course of his business.
   B   Torts which his employees commit in the course of his business.
   C   Torts which his independent contractors commit in the course of his business.
   D   Torts which anyone commits in the course of his business.

2. An employee must be given particulars of his contract of service within one of the following periods. Select:

   A   10 weeks after the employment begins.
   B   13 weeks after the employment begins.
   C   12 weeks after the employment begins.
   D   11 weeks after the employment begins.

3. One of the following statements is correct. Select:

   A   An employer has a statutory duty to give holidays but not holiday pay.
   B   An employer has a statutory duty to give holidays and holiday pay.
   C   An employer is never bound to give holidays and holiday pay.
   D   An employer may be bound to give holidays and holiday pay.

4. As regards guarantee payments an employee can only receive pay for:

   A   Four workless days in any period of two months.
   B   Five workless days in any period of five months.
   C   Six workless days in any period of three months.
   D   Five workless days in any period of three months.

5. Small employers are not bound to reinstate formerly pregnant employees. A small employer is one who together with any associated employer has not more than the following number of employees:

   A   Four.
   B   Six.
   C   Five.
   D   Eight.

6. When deciding questions of equal pay for women the court must take into account:

A   Basic pay only.
B   Basic pay and fringe benefits.
C   The fact that a man is doing the same job for the same pay.
D   The findings of a job evaluation scheme properly conducted.

The answers to questions set in objective mode appear on p. 551.

16 | Employment II

The OBJECTIVES of this chapter are to explain the law which applies to discrimination when employees are recruited into a job together with discrimination at the workplace. The chapter concludes with the forms of dismissal and remedies.

DISCRIMINATION ON THE GROUNDS OF SEX, MARITAL STATUS OR RACE: GENERAL

The law relating to discrimination is to be found in the Sex Discrimination Acts 1975 and 1986, the Race Relations Act 1976 and the Employment Act 1989. Before looking at the detail of the relevant legislation we will consider some of the more general provisions of the Employment Act 1989.

Section 1 provides that any legislation dealing with employment and vocational training passed before the Sex Discrimination Act 1975 is overridden by the 1989 Act unless specifically continued in force by that Act. The 1989 Act identifies certain discriminatory provisions and either removes or preserves them (*see below*). However, because there could be some discriminatory provisions in existing legislation which have not been identified, s. 1 overrides them.

Section 2 supports s. 1 giving the Secretary of State power, by statutory instrument, to remove or amend any discriminatory legislation which may be discovered in the future. Section 1 overrides it unless and until it is discovered, and, for the avoidance of doubt, s. 2 and s. 6 allow the Secretary of State to repeal, or amend, or retain it, when it is discovered.

Section 3 amends s. 51 of the Sex Discrimination Act 1975 which exempts acts of discrimination required by statute before 1975. Section 51 was a blanket provision and s. 3 cuts it down so that it is still within the law to discriminate in regard to women if it is done to protect them in matters relating to pregnancy and maternity or to comply with those provisions of the Health and Safety at Work Act 1974 which relate to the protection of women.

The specific areas of protection are enacted by s. 4 and are set out in Sched. 1 to the 1989 Act. They include industrial processes which involve the use of lead and radiation. It is still within the law to discriminate against women workers in these areas because of the risk of foetal damage.

The provisions preventing women from returning to work in a factory within four weeks of childbirth are retained in force.

Section 7 repeals previous law so that women can now work in mines and quarries and clean machinery in factories. The prohibition on women lifting loads 'so heavy as to be likely to cause injury' remain but discrimination is removed by extending the prohibition to men.

Section 8 repeals previous law which had placed a variety of restrictions on the employment of young persons being persons who are over school leaving age. Thus the restriction to a 48-hour week and a nine-hour day is removed as are a number of provisions which formerly restricted starting times and latest finishing times, minimum meal breaks, rest breaks and holidays together with limits on weekend work shifts and night work most of which applied to young persons in factories, mines and shops. Most of the restrictions continue to apply to children under school leaving age. Restrictions on young persons working with dangerous machines, e.g. locomotives, are retained.

DISCRIMINATION ON GROUNDS OF SEX, MARITAL STATUS OR RACE IN RECRUITMENT AND SELECTION OF EMPLOYEES

The relevant provisions of the Sex Discrimination Act 1975 and 1986, the Race Relations Act 1976 and the Employment Act 1989 are set out below.

Offers of employment

It is unlawful for a person in relation to an employment by him at a place in England, Wales or Scotland to discriminate against men or women on grounds of sex, marital status, colour, race, nationality or ethnic or national origins:

(a) in the arrangements he makes for the purpose of deciding who should be offered the job; or

(b) in the terms on which the job is offered; or

(c) by refusing or deliberately omitting to offer the job.

'Arrangements' is a wide expression covering a range of recruitment techniques, e.g. asking an employment agency to send only white applicants, or male applicants. Discrimination by employment agencies themselves is also covered.

As regards the terms of the contract of employment, it is unlawful to discriminate against an employee on the grounds listed above in terms of the employment which is given to him or the terms of access to opportunities for promotion, transfer or training, or to any other benefit, facilities or services, or subjecting him to any other detriment. Thus it is unlawful to discriminate in regard to matters such as privileged loans and mortgages by banks and building societies and discounts on holidays given to employees of travel firms.

A person who takes on workers supplied by a third party rather than employing them himself is obliged by the Acts not to discriminate in the treatment of them or in the work they are allowed to do. This means that temporary staff supplied by an agency are covered by the anti-discrimination provisions.

The anti-discrimination provisions are also extended to partnerships as regards failure to offer a partnership, or the terms on which it is offered including benefits, facilities and services. The provision regarding race (but not sex discrimination) applies only to firms of six or more partners, although there is a power in the legislation to reduce this number. The provision as it stands will allow race (but not sex) discrimination in the majority of medical practices but not, for example, in the major accounting and law firms.

Exceptions

There are some circumstances in which it is lawful to discriminate and these will now be considered.

Genuine occupational qualification

So far as sex discrimination is concerned, an employer may confine a job to a man where male sex is a 'genuine occupational qualification' (GOQ) for a particular job. This could arise, for example, for reasons of physiology as in modelling male clothes, or authenticity in entertainment, as where a part calls for an actor and not an actress. Sometimes a man will be required for reasons of decency or privacy, such as an attendant in a men's lavatory. Sometimes, too, where the job involves work outside the United Kingdom in a country whose laws and customs would make it difficult for a woman to carry out the job, being a male may be a GOQ. As regards marital status, it may be reasonable to discriminate in favour of a man or a woman where the job is one of two held by a married couple, as where a woman is a housekeeper living in with her husband who is employed as a gardener.

There are, of course, a number of situations where female sex would be a GOQ for a certain type of job. **The following case illustrates this point**.

Sisley v Britannia Security Systems [1983] IRLR 404

The defendants employed women to work in a security control station. The plaintiff, a man, applied for a vacant job but was refused employment. It appeared that the women worked 12 hour shifts with rest periods and that beds were provided for their use during such breaks. The women undressed to their underwear during these rest breaks. The plaintiff complained that by advertising for women the defendants were contravening the Sex Discrimination Act 1975. The defendants pleaded genuine occupational qualification, i.e. that women were required because of the removal of uniform during rest periods was incidental to the employment. The Employment Appeal Tribunal accepted that defence. The defence of preservation of decency was, in the circumstances, a good one. It was reasonably incidental to the women's work that they should remove their clothing during rest periods.

However, s. 7(4) of the 1975 Act imposes a duty on employers to take reasonable steps to avoid relying on GOQ exceptions. **The following case and comment illustrates this point.**

Etam plc v Rowan [1989] IRLR 150

Steven Rowan applied for a vacancy as a sales assistant at Etam's shop in Glasgow which sold only womens' and girls' clothing. He was not considered for the post because of his sex and complained to an industrial tribunal.

Etam's said that he had not been discriminated against because being a woman was a genuine occupational qualification (GOQ) for the job within the meaning of s. 7(2)(b) of the Sex Discrimination Act 1975: it was likely to involve physical contact with women in a state of undress in circumstances where they might reasonably object to the presence of a man.

Mr Rowan's case was based on s. 7(4), which imposes a duty on employers to take reasonable steps to avoid relying on the GOQ exception. Section 7(4) in the context of this case provides that the GOQ exceptions do not apply if the employer already has female employees who are capable of carrying out the relevant parts of the job, whom it would be reasonable to employ on such duties and the number of suitable women employees are sufficient to meet the employer's likely requirements without giving rise to undue inconvenience.

The Industrial Tribunal found in favour of Mr Rowan and made a compensatory award of £500. The employers appealed to the Employment Appeal Tribunal. The EAT dismissed the appeal, on the basis that Mr Rowan would have been able quite adequately to carry out the bulk of the job of sales assistant. Such parts as he could not carry out, such as attendance on women in fitting rooms for the purpose of measuring or otherwise assisting them, could easily have been done by other sales assistants without causing any inconvenience or difficulty for the employer.

Comment: It is worth noting that in *Wylie v Dee & Co (Menswear) Ltd* [1978] IRLR 103, a woman was refused employment in a men's tailoring establishment in which the remainder of the staff were men because it was inappropriate for her to measure the inside legs of male customers. She complained to an industrial tribunal and succeeded on the basis that it could have been carried out by other male employees.

As regards race, it is lawful to discriminate where there is a GOQ for the job as, for example, in the employment of a West Indian social worker or probation officer to deal with problems relating to young West Indians. Other instances are dramatic performances or other entertainment, artists or photographic models and employment in places serving food or drink to be purchased and *consumed* on the premises by the public. Thus being Chinese is a GOQ for employment in a Chinese restaurant, but not necessarily in a 'takeaway'.

Other major exceptions

These are as follows.

(a) *Private households.* Race discrimination is not unlawful where the employment is in a private household. Sex and marital discrimination is now unlawful even in private households (Sex Discrimination Act 1986). However, the 1986 Act provides that sex discrimination may take place where the job is likely to involve the holder of it doing his work or living in a private house and needs to be held by a man because objection might reasonably be taken to allowing a woman the degree of physical or social contact with a person living in the house or acquiring the knowledge of intimate details of such a person's life. This gives, in effect, a new GOQ for a man.

(b) *Work outside Great Britain.* Discrimination legislation does not apply to work which is done wholly or mainly outside Great Britain. However, it does apply to work on a British ship, aircraft or hovercraft unless the work is wholly outside Great Britain. The Court of Appeal decided in *Haughton* v *Olau Line (UK) Ltd* [1986] 2 All ER 47 that an industrial tribunal had no jurisdiction to hear a claim for unlawful discrimination contrary to the Sex Discrimination Act 1975 where the case was brought by a woman who was employed by an English company on a German registered ship which operated mainly outside British territorial waters. Her employment was not 'at an establishment within Great Britain' as the 1975 Act requires.

(c) *Special cases.* The anti-discriminatory rules apply to Crown appointments but the provisions regarding sex discrimination do not apply to the armed forces. In general terms, service with the police is covered by anti-discrimination provisions, as is service in HM Prisons. Furthermore, the legal barriers to men becoming midwives have been removed.

Other special cases are set out in s. 5 of the Employment Act 1989 under which the appointment of head teachers in schools and colleges may be restricted to members of a religious order where such a restriction is contained in the trust deed or other relevant instrument. Furthermore, a university professorship may be restricted to a man if there is a statutory requirement that the holder of the post should also be a canon. In practice this will apply only to certain professorships of Divinity. Finally, academic appointments in university colleges may be restricted to women where this was required when the 1989 Act came into force. In practice the provision applies to two colleges at Oxford – Somerville and St Hilda's – and to two at Cambridge – Lucy Cavendish and Newnham. The Secretary of State has power to remove these exemptions by statutory instrument.

Types of discrimination

There are two forms of discrimination as follows.

(a) *Direct discrimination*, which occurs where an employer or prospective employer treats a person less favourably than another on grounds of sex, race, or marital status, as where an employer refuses, on grounds of sex or race, to grant a suitably qualified person an interview for a job. In addition, the segregation of workers once in employment on the grounds of sex or race is also unlawful direct discrimination.

Examples are provided by the following cases.

Coleman v Skyrail Oceanic Ltd, *The Times*, 28 July 1981

The plaintiff, Coleman, who was a female booking clerk for Skyrail, a travel agency, was dismissed after she married an employee of a rival agency. Skyrail feared that there might be leaks of information about charter flights and had assumed that her dismissal was not unreasonable since the husband was the breadwinner. The Employment Appeal Tribunal decided that the dismissal was reasonable on the basis that the husband was the breadwinner. However, there was an appeal to the Court of Appeal which decided that those provisions of the Sex Discrimination Act which dealt with direct discrimination and dismissal on grounds of sex had been infringed. The assumption that husbands were breadwinners and wives were not was based on sex and was discriminatory. The plaintiff's injury to her feelings was compensated by an award of £100 damages.

Comment: The plaintiff was also *held* to be unfairly dismissed having received no warning that she would be dismissed on marriage. The additional and discriminatory reason regarding the breadwinner cost the employer a further £100.

Johnson v Timber Tailors (Midlands) [1978] IRLR 146

When the plaintiff, a black Jamaican, applied for a job with the defendants as a wood machinist the defendants' works manager told him that he would be contacted in a couple of days to let him know whether or not he had been successful. Mr Johnson was not contacted and after a number of unsuccessful attempts to get in touch with the works manager, was told that the vacancy had been filled. Another advertisement for wood machinists appeared in the paper on the same night as Mr Johnson was told that the vacancy had been filled. Nevertheless, Mr Johnson applied again for the job and was told that the vacancy was filled. About a week later he applied again and was again told that the job had been filled although a further advertisement had appeared for the job on that day. An industrial tribunal decided that the evidence established that Mr Johnson had been discriminated against on the ground of race.

(b) *Indirect discrimination*, as where an employer has applied requirements or conditions to a job but the ability of some persons to comply because of sex, marital status or race is considerably smaller and cannot be justified.

Examples are provided by the following cases.

Price v The Civil Service Commission [1978] 1 All ER 1228

The Civil Service required candidates for the position of executive officer to be between 17½ and 28 years. Belinda Price complained that this age bar constituted indirect sex discrimination against women because women between those ages were more likely than men to be temporarily out of the labour market having children or caring for children at home. The Employment Appeal Tribunal decided that the age bar was indirect discrimination against women. The court *held* that the words 'can comply' in the legislation must not be construed narrowly. It could be said that any female applicant could comply with the condition in the sense that she was not obliged to marry or have children, or to look after them – indeed, she might find someone else to look after them or, as a last resort, put them into care. If the legislation was construed in that way it was no doubt right to say that any female applicant could comply with the condition. However, in the view of the court to construe the legislation in that way appeared to be wholly out of sympathy with the spirit and intention of the Act. A person should not be deemed to be able to do something merely because it was theoretically possible; it was necessary to decide whether it was possible for a person to do so in practice as distinct from theory.

Bohon-Mitchell v Council of Legal Education [1978] IRLR 525

The plaintiff, an overseas student, complained of discrimination in regard to a requirement of the defendants that a student would have to undergo a 21-month course, as opposed to a diploma of one year, to complete the academic stage of the bar where he did not have a UK or Irish Republic university degree. This rule was regarded by an industrial tribunal to be discriminatory because the proportion of persons not from the UK or Irish Republic who could comply was considerably smaller than persons from the UK or Irish Republic who could and the rule was not justifiable on other grounds. The plaintiff satisfied the tribunal that there had been indirect discrimination.

Comment: The other side of the coin is illustrated by *Panesar v Nestlé Co Ltd* [1980] IRLR 64 where an orthodox Sikh who naturally wore a beard which was required by his religion, applied for a job in the defendants' chocolate factory. He was refused employment because the defendants applied a strict rule under which no beards or excessively long hair were allowed on the grounds of hygiene. The plaintiff made a complaint of indirect discrimination but the defendants said that the rule was justified. The Court of Appeal decided that as the defendants had supported their rule with scientific evidence there was in fact no discrimination.

Remedies

Allegations of discrimination may be the subject of a complaint to an industrial tribunal which may, among other things, award monetary compensation.

In addition, the Equal Opportunities Commission, which is responsible for keeping under review the working of sex discrimination legislation, including equal pay, and the Commission for Racial Equality, which has a similar function in terms of racial discrimination, may carry out formal investigations into firms where discrimination is alleged and may issue non-discrimination notices requiring the employer to comply with the relevant legislation.

The employer may appeal to an industrial tribunal within six weeks of service of the notice. If there is no appeal, or the industrial tribunal confirms the notice, then the employer must comply with it, and if he does not the relevant Commission may ask the County Court for an injunction which, if granted, will make an employer who ignores it in contempt of court and he may be fined and/or imprisoned for that offence.

The Commissions are also required to enter non-discrimination notices which have become final in a Register. Copies of the Register are kept in Manchester (Equal Opportunities Commission) and in London (Commission for Racial Equality), and are available for inspection to any person on payment of a fee and copies may also be obtained.

Relationship between the Sex Discrimination Act and the Equal Pay Act

The two Acts do not overlap. Complaints of discrimination in regard to pay and other non-monetary matters governed by the contract of employment, such as hours of work, are dealt with under the Equal Pay Act and complaints of discrimination in regard, for example, to access to jobs, are dealt with under the Sex Discrimination Act. A complaint to an Industrial Tribunal need not be based from the beginning on one Act or the other. A tribunal is empowered to make a decision under whichever Act turns out to be relevant when all the facts are before it.

Discriminatory advertisements for employees

The sex discrimination and racial discrimination legislation make it unlawful to place advertisements for employees which are discriminatory unless they relate to a recognized exceptional case, as where, for example, there is a GOQ. Thus job descriptions such as a 'waiter', 'salesgirl', 'stewardess' or 'girl friday' have largely disappeared from our newspapers and one now finds the descriptions 'waiter/ waitress' or the expression 'male/female' as indicating that both sexes are eligible for employment. However, one still sees advertisements which are clearly intended to attract female applicants which, nevertheless, remain within the law, e.g. 'publishing director requires sophisticated PA/secretary with style and charm who can remain cool under pressure'.

Before legislation relating to discrimination came into force, advertisements in the UK were discriminatory mainly as regards sex, but obviously an advertisement which said 'Chinese only' would be unlawful unless there was a GOQ as, for example, there would be where the advertisement was for a waiter in a Chinese restaurant.

As regards sanctions, the placing of discriminatory advertisements may lead to the issue of a non-discrimination notice by the appropriate Commission which, if not complied with, may lead to proceedings being taken by the Commission in an industrial tribunal. If the industrial tribunal accepts the contention of discrimination and yet the advertiser does not comply but continues to advertise in a discriminatory way, the Commission may take proceedings in the County Court for, amongst other things, an injunction, and if this is not complied with the advertiser is in contempt of court and may be punished by a fine or imprisonment until he complies.

In addition, it is a criminal offence to place a discriminatory advertisement and those who do so may be tried by magistrates and are subject to a fine. The person who publishes the advertisement, e.g a newspaper proprietor, also commits a criminal offence. However, he may not know precisely that the advertisement is discriminatory. For example, without a knowledge of the advertiser's business, he cannot really know whether there is a GOQ or not. Accordingly, he is given a defence to any criminal charge if he can show that in publishing the advertisement:

(a) he relied on a statement by the person placing it to the effect that it was not unlawful and on the face of it might come within one of the exceptional cases; and

(b) it was reasonable for him to rely on that statement.

Discrimination once in employment

We have already considered the law relating to discrimination in formation of the contract, i.e. in recruitment and selection, and in terms of remuneration, i.e. equal pay. Discrimination on termination of the contract will be dealt with later when we look at discriminatory dismissal. Here we are concerned with discrimination in the treatment of employees during the course of the contract of employment.

Discrimination on the grounds of sex or race

Under the sex and race discrimination legislation it is unlawful to discriminate against a person on grounds of sex or race as regards opportunities for promotion, training or transfer to other positions, or in the provision of benefits, facilities, or services, or by dismissal, or by any other disadvantages, or detriment.

It was decided in *Porcelli* v *Strathclyde Regional Council* [1986] ICR 564 that sexual harassment which affects a woman's working conditions is contrary to ss. 1(1) and 6(2)(b) of the Sex Discrimination Act 1975, under the general heading of subjection to 'any other detriment'.

However, as we have seen, the law allows women to receive special treatment when they are pregnant and there is no discrimination where the sex or racial status of the employee is a genuine occupational qualification.

There are some exemptions in special cases, for example the armed forces are not covered.

There is also an exemption in respect of discriminatory training. An employer or a body responsible for training may provide training exclusively applicable to persons of a particular sex or racial group where the purpose is to enable them to take up work in situations where that sex or racial group is under-represented, but there may not be discrimination in terms of recruitment for such work. Section 8 of the Employment Act 1989 allows discrimination in favour of lone parents in connection with training. Trade unions may also take special action to attract members of particular sexual or racial groups into membership or to office in the union where there is under-representation.

As regards enforcement, if an unlawful act of discrimination, e.g. sexual harassment (*see above*), is committed by an employee the employer is held responsible for the act along with the employee unless the employer can show that he took all reasonable steps to prevent the employee from discriminating. If he can do this, only the employee is responsible.

Individual employees who believe that they have been discriminated against may make a complaint to an industrial tribunal within three months of the act complained of. It is then the duty of a conciliation officer to see whether the complaint can be settled without going to a tribunal. If, however, the tribunal hears the complaint, it may make an order declaring the rights of the employer and the employee in regard to the complaint, the intention being that both parties will abide by the order for the future.

The tribunal may also give the employee monetary compensation and may additionally recommend that the employer take, within a specified period, action appearing to the tribunal to be practicable for the purpose of obviating or reducing discrimination.

It is also of interest to note that rulings by industrial tribunals have strengthened the rights of those women who are dismissed when they become pregnant. It will be recalled that employment protection legislation requires that a woman should have been in the job for at least two years before the rules relating to dismissal because of pregnancy in employment protection legislation can be applied to her. However, industrial tribunals have held that even if a woman has not been employed for two years or more a remedy is available to her under the Sex Discrimination Act 1975. The 1975 Act is, however, weak in that the remedies under it are restricted to damages and an order to reduce the effect of discrimination in a particular organization. There is no power to order re-instatement as there is under employment protection legislation.

Finally, the Sex Discrimination Act 1986 deals with discrimination in retirement. Under the Act all companies with a compulsory retirement age will have to make sure that it is the same for men and women. This means that women will be able to work beyond the age of 60 provided that their male colleagues are also allowed to do so. Women who do not want to carry on working after 60 will still be free to resign. A woman over 60 who is made to retire earlier than her male colleagues will be entitled to claim unfair dismissal. This legal reform does not affect pensions payable under company schemes, nor the different ages at which men and women can receive the State retirement pension.

However, in the following case the European Court of Justice upheld the principle that occupational pension schemes should apply the same retirement benefits to men and women.

Barber v Guardian Royal Exchange Assurance Group, *The Times*, 18 May 1990

Douglas Barber was a member of the pension fund set up by the defendants, Guardian Royal Exchange (GRE). The fund applied a non-contributory 'contracted out' scheme approved under the Social Security Pensions Act 1975.

Under the GRE scheme the normal pensionable age was fixed for the category of employer to which Mr Barber belonged at 62 for men and 57 for women. The difference was the equivalent to that which existed under the State Social Security Scheme (65 for men and 60 for women).

There was a *GRE Guide to Severance Terms*. It formed part of Mr Barber's contract of service and provided that, in the event of redundancy, members of the pension fund were entitled to an immediate pension, subject to having attained the age of 55 (men) or 50 (women).

Mr Barber was made redundant on 31 December 1980. He was then aged 52. GRE paid him the cash benefits provided for in the severance terms, a statutory redundancy payment and an *ex gratia* payment. He was, of course, entitled to a deferred retirement pension from the date of his 62nd birthday.

A woman in the same position as Mr Barber would have received an immediate retirement pension as well as the statutory redundancy payment, the total value of which would have been greater than the amount paid to Mr Barber. Mr Barber commenced proceedings before an industrial tribunal because he took the view that he had been subjected to unlawful sexual discrimination. His claim was dismissed by the tribunal and eventually reached the Court of Appeal which decided to stay the proceedings and ask the European Court at Luxembourg to give a ruling on the following questions.

Firstly, were redundancy benefits, including pension benefits, 'pay' within Art. 119 of the Treaty of Rome which deals with equal pay? The European Court said that they did fall within Art. 119.

Second, did each element of a redundancy package have to be equal or was it enough if the total package was the same? The European Court said that the principle of equal pay must be applied to each item of a redundancy package. It was not enough that the value of the total package was the same.

Third, did Art. 119 have direct effect in the UK without the need for UK legislation implementing it? The answer given by the Court was that Art. 119 was of direct effect in national courts of member states of the EEC and no national legislation was required to implement it.

The judgment of the European Court was not to be fully retrospective and could not be relied on in order to claim entitlement to a pension except by those who had actually initiated legal proceedings before the judgment. The judgment, of course, does apply to those who institute proceedings after it.

Comment: The judgment of the European Court makes clear that pensions are 'pay' within the equal pay provisions of Art. 119. They must therefore be equal as between men and women. So it would seem that all pensions granted on or after 17 May 1990 (the date of the judgment), whether immediate or deferred, will have to be equal in terms of amount and payable at the same age where the same circumstances, such as length of service and salary, apply.

The European Court was, of course, looking at a contracted-out scheme, but the generally accepted view is that Art. 119 applies to and affects contracted-in schemes in the same way.

The Social Security Act 1989, which is the UK's response to a 1986 EC directive on equal treatment of men and women in occupational social service schemes, allows exceptions from equal treatment, the most relevant here being 'permitted age related differences'. The Act was not to come into force until 1 January 1993. By the *Barber* decision, the European Court has brought the principles of equality underlying the Act into force now and has almost certainly wiped out the exception referred to.

Employers should provide equal pensions now if they are to avoid successful claims against them in industrial tribunals. The easiest age at which to equalize will be 60 even though this may be more costly. A common age of 65 may reduce costs but could cause difficult industrial relations problems with female employees who had expected to retire at 60 – many of them may also have contractual rights to take a pension at the earlier age.

Discrimination against married persons

The anti-discriminatory provisions outlined in the previous section are applied also to discrimination against married persons. An employer must not treat a married person of either sex, on the ground of his or her marital status, less favourably than he treats or would treat an unmarried person of the same sex, e.g. there must not be a marriage bar attached to a particular employment, unless, of course, there is a GOQ.

Victimization in employment

Under the sex and racial discrimination legislation it is unlawful to treat a person less favourably than another because that person asserted rights under the equal pay or other anti-discriminatory legislation relating to sex or race or has helped another person to assert such rights or has given information to the Equal Opportunities Commission or the Commission for Racial Equality, or it is thought that he or she might do so.

TERMINATION OF THE CONTRACT OF EMPLOYMENT

Unfair dismissal: generally

Before a person can ask an industrial tribunal to consider a claim that another has unfairly dismissed him or her it is once again essential to establish that the relationship of employer and employee exists between them. In this connection the Employment Protection (Consolidation) Act 1978 provides that an employee is a person who works under a contract of service or apprenticeship, written or oral, express or implied.

An example of a case where a person failed in an unfair dismissal claim because he was unable to show that he was an employee is given below.

Massey v Crown Life Insurance Co [1978] 2 All ER 576

Mr Massey was employed by Crown Life as the manager of their Ilford branch from 1971 to 1973, the company paying him wages and deducting tax. In 1973, on the advice of his accountant, Mr Massey registered a business name of J.R. Massey and Associates and with that new name entered into an agreement with Crown Life under which he carried out the same duties as before but as a self-employed person. The Inland Revenue were content that he should change to be taxed under Schedule D as a self-employed person. His employment was terminated and he claimed to have been unfairly dismissed. The Court of Appeal decided that being self-employed he could not be unfairly dismissed.

In addition to showing that he is an employee the claimant must comply with an *age requirement*. The unfair dismissal provisions do not apply to the dismissal of an employee from any employment if the employee has on or before the effective date of termination attained the age which, in the undertaking in which he is employed, was the normal retiring age for an employee holding the position which he held, or for both men and women aged 65 (Sex Discrimination Act 1986).

However, such persons are not excluded where the dismissal is automatically unfair, e.g. for taking part in trade union activities (*see further* p. 423).

As regards the period of employment, the unfair dismissal provisions do not apply to the dismissal of an employee from any employment if the employee has not completed one year's continuous employment ending with the effective date of termination of employment unless the dismissal is automatically unfair. For those who started work on or after 1 October 1980 the total length of employment must exceed two years provided that during that period there were no more than 20 employees in the same firm, together with any associated employer. Again, this does not apply if the dismissal is automatically unfair and, clearly, companies within a group are associated employers. Those who started work on or after 1 June 1985 must also complete at least two years' service regardless of the size of the firm unless the dismissal is automatically unfair.

In addition, the 1978 Act states that no account should be taken of employment during any period when the hours of employment are normally less than 16 hours per week. After five years' employment the figure is reduced to eight hours. Again, the requirement of having worked 16 or eight hours, as the case may be, does not apply to dismissals which are automatically unfair.

As regards persons ordinarily employed outside Great Britain, the 1978 Act states that an employee has no protection against unfair dismissal if he is engaged in work wholly or mainly outside Great Britain. The following are also ineligible and cannot claim.

(a) Those on fixed contracts of two years or more if they have agreed in writing, either in the contract or during its duration, to forgo the right to compensation. If the contract was made on or after 1 October 1980 the period of the fixed term is reduced to one year.

(b) Any employee dismissed while taking unofficial strike or other industrial action is unable to complain of unfair dismissal (s. 9, Employment Act 1990).

(c) Women who are dismissed because of pregnancy if they have not been employed for two years prior to the 11th week before the expected week of confinement.

(d) Certain other categories are excluded by the 1978 Act, e.g. members of the armed forces and of the police.

It should also be noted that s. 16 of the Employment Act 1989 allows regulations to be made to test the strength of the case of each party before a full hearing proceeds. Pre-hearing reviews are introduced at which the chairman of the tribunal may sit alone without the two lay assessors. The chairman may, at his discretion and following an application by one of the parties, or of his own motion, require a deposit of up to £150 from the other party as a condition of proceeding further if it is considered that his or her case has no reasonable prospect of success, or that to pursue it would be frivolous, vexatious or otherwise unreasonable.

Industrial Tribunal Regulations also provide for pre-hearing assessments, and if a party to the proceedings before an industrial tribunal considers that an application, or a particular contention, is unlikely to succeed or be accepted he can ask for a pre-hearing assessment to be made. A tribunal can make such an assessment of its own volition. Following the pre-hearing assessment, at which the parties may submit written representations and put forward oral argument but not evidence, the tribunal may indicate its opinion that if the party who is unlikely to succeed carries on with the application or persists in the contention an order for costs may be made against him. The opinion is placed before the tribunal which conducts the full hearing if it takes place. No member of the tribunal which gave the opinion may be a member of the tribunal which takes the full hearing.

Dismissal – meaning of

An employee cannot claim unfair dismissal unless there has first been a dismissal recognized by law. We may consider the matter under the following headings.

Actual dismissal

This does not normally give rise to problems since most employees recognize the words of an actual dismissal, whether given orally or in writing.

A typical letter of dismissal appears below.

> Dear Mr Bloggs
>
> I am sorry that you do not have the necessary aptitude to deal with the work which we have allocated to you. I hope that you will be able to find other work elsewhere which is more in your line. As you will recall from your interview this morning, the company will not require your services after the 31st of this month.

Constructive dismissal

This occurs where it is the employee who leaves the job but is compelled to do so by the conduct of the employer. In general terms the employer's conduct must be a fundamental breach so that it can be regarded as a repudiation of the contract. Thus, if a male employer were to sexually assault his female secretary then this would be a fundamental breach entitling her to leave and sue for her loss on the basis of constructive dismissal.

Fixed term contracts

When a fixed term contract expires and is not renewed there is a dismissal. However, where a contract is for two years or more the employee may have waived his right to complain of unfair dismissal. If the contract is made on or after 1 October 1980 the period of the fixed term is reduced to one year.

Dismissal – grounds for

If an employer is going to escape liability for unfair dismissal he must show that he acted *reasonably* and, indeed, the 1978 Act requires the employer to give his reasons for dismissal to the employee in writing.

It should be remembered that the question whether a dismissal is fair or not is a matter of *fact* for the particular tribunal hearing the case and one cannot predict with absolute accuracy what a particular tribunal will do on the facts of a particular case. Basically, when all is said and done, the ultimate question for a tribunal is – 'was the dismissal fair and reasonable' in fact.

The Employment Act 1980 amended the Employment Protection (Consolidation) Act 1978 by including in the test of reasonableness required in determining whether a dismissal was fair, the 'size and administrative resources of the employer's undertaking'. This was included as a result of fear that the unfair dismissal laws were placing undue burdens on small firms and causing them not to engage new workers. The 1980 Act also removed the burden of proof from the employer in showing reasonableness so that there is now no 'presumption of guilt' on the employer and the tribunal is left to decide whether or not the employer acted reasonably.

Reasons justifying dismissal

These are as follows.

(a) *Lack of capability*. This would usually arise at the beginning of employment where it becomes clear at an early stage that the employee cannot do the job in terms of lack of skill or mental or physical health. It should be remembered that the longer a person is in employment the more difficult it is to establish lack of capability.

By way of illustration we can consider the case of *Alidair v Taylor* [1978] IRLR 82. The pilot of an aircraft had made a faulty landing which damaged the aircraft. There was a board of inquiry which found that the faulty landing was due to a lack of flying knowledge on the part of the pilot who was dismissed from his employment. It was decided that the employee had not been unfairly dismissed, the tribunal taking the view that where, as in this case, one failure to reach a high degree of skill could have serious consequences, an instant dismissal could be justified.

However, it was decided in *British Sulphur v Lawrie* [1987] IRB 338 that the dismissal of an employee who was alleged to be unwilling or incompetent to do a particular job could still be unfair if the employee was not provided with adequate training.

(b) *Conduct*. This is always a difficult matter to deal with and much will depend upon the circumstances of the case. However, incompetence and neglect are relevant, as are disobedience and misconduct, e.g. by assaulting fellow employees. Immorality and habitual drunkenness could also be brought under this heading and, so it seems, can dress where this can be shown to affect adversely the way in which the contract of service is performed. **The following case provides an illustration.**

Boychuk v HJ Symons (Holdings) Ltd [1977] IRLR 395

Miss B was employed by S Ltd as an accounts audit clerk but her duties involved contact with the public from time to time. Miss B insisted on wearing badges which proclaimed the fact that she was a lesbian and from May 1976 she wore one or other of the following: (a) a lesbian symbol consisting of two circles with crosses (indicating women) joined together; (b) badges with the legends 'Gays against fascism'; and 'Gay power'; (c) a badge with the legend

'Gay switchboard' with a telephone number on it and the words 'Information service for homosexual men and women'; (d) a badge with the word 'Dyke', indicating to the initiated that she was a lesbian.

These were eventually superseded by a white badge with the words 'Lesbians ignite' written in large letters on it. Nothing much had happened in regard to the wearing of the earlier badges but when she began wearing the 'Lesbians ignite' badge there were discussions about it between her and her employer. She was told that she must remove it – which she was not willing to do – and that if she did not she would be dismissed. She would not remove the badge and was dismissed on 16 August 1976 and then made a claim for compensation for unfair dismissal.

No complaint was made regarding the manner of her dismissal in terms, e.g. of proper warning. The straight question was whether her employers were entitled to dismiss her because she insisted on wearing the badge. An industrial tribunal had decided that in all the circumstances the dismissal was fair because it was within an employer's discretion to instruct an employee not to wear a particular badge or symbol which could cause offence to customers and fellow-employees. Miss B appealed to the Employment Appeal Tribunal which dismissed her appeal and said that her dismissal was fair. The court said that there was no question of Miss B having been dismissed because she was a lesbian or because of anything to do with her private life or private behaviour. Such a case would be entirely different and raise different questions. This was only a case where she had been dismissed because of her conduct at work. That, the court said, must be clearly understood.

Comment: (i) The decision does not mean that an employer by a foolish or unreasonable judgment of what could be expected to be offensive could impose some unreasonable restriction on an employee. However, the decision does mean that a reasonable employer, who is, after all, ultimately responsible for the interests of the business, is allowed to decide what, upon reflection or mature consideration, could be offensive to customers and fellow employees, and he need not wait to see whether the business would in fact be damaged before he takes steps in the matter.

(ii) In *Kowalski* v *The Berkeley Hotel* [1985] IRLR 40 the EAT decided that the dismissal of a pastrycook for fighting at work was fair though it was the first time he had done it.

(c) *Redundancy*. Genuine redundancy is a defence. Where a person is redundant his employer cannot be expected to continue the employment, although there are safeguards in the matter of *unfair selection for redundancy* (*see* p. 424).

(d) *Dismissals which are union-related*. An employee will be regarded as automatically unfairly dismissed if the principal reason for the dismissal was that he was, or proposed to become, a member of a trade union which was independent of the employer; that he had taken part or proposed to take part in the activities of such a union at an appropriate time, i.e. outside working hours or within working hours with the consent of the employer; that he was not a member of any trade union or of a particular one or had refused or proposed to refuse to become or remain a member. Under the relevant provisions of the Employment Act 1988 all closed shop dismissals are now automatically unfair.

The position in regard to job applicants under the Employment Act 1990 has already been considered (*see* p. 397).

(e) *Statutory restriction placed on employer or employee.* If, for example, the employer's business was found to be dangerous and was closed down under Act of Parliament or ministerial order, the employees would not be unfairly dismissed. Furthermore, a lorry driver who was banned from driving for 12 months could be dismissed fairly.

(f) *Some other substantial reasons.* An employer may on a wide variety of grounds which are not specified by legislation satisfy an industrial tribunal that a dismissal was fair and reasonable.

Crime and suspicion of crime may be brought under this heading, though if dismissal is based on suspicion of crime, the suspicion must be reasonable and in all cases the employee must be told that dismissal is contemplated and in the light of this information be allowed to give explanations and make representations against dismissal.

Where an employee has been charged with theft from the employer and is awaiting trial, the best course of action is to suspend rather than dismiss him, pending the verdict. Investigations which the employer must make, as part of establishing a fair dismissal, could be regarded as an interference with the course of justice. It is best, therefore, not to make them, but to suspend the employee. The case of *Wadley* v *Eager Electrical* [1986] IRLR 93 should be noted. In that case husband and wife worked for the same firm. The wife was convicted for stealing £2,000 from the company whilst employed as a shop assistant. The husband was a service engineer with the firm. Husband and wife were dismissed and it was held that the husband's dismissal was unfair. He was a good employee of 17 years' standing and no misconduct had been made out against him.

The matter of fair or unfair dismissal depends also upon the terms of the contract. If the difficulty is that a particular employee is refusing to do work which involves him, say, spending nights away from home, then his dismissal is likely to be regarded as fair if there is an *express term* in his contract requiring this. Of course, the nature of the job may require it, as in the case of a long-distance lorry driver where such a term would be implied, if not expressed.

Employees who are in breach of contract are likely to be regarded as fairly dismissed. However, this is not an invariable rule. Thus a long-distance lorry driver who refused to take on a particular trip because his wife was ill and he had to look after the children would be unfairly dismissed (if dismissal took place) even though he was, strictly speaking, in breach of his contract.

Grievance and disciplinary procedures

These are usually part of the contract. The employer must comply with them if he wishes to avoid liability. If a series of oral and written warnings is laid down, the procedure should be observed. However, reasonableness will always prevail.

No matter how good the employer's reason for dismissal may be there may still be a claim by the employee for unfair dismissal if the dismissal was 'unfair in all the circumstances'.

In *Whitbread & Co plc* v *Mills* [1988] IRLR 43 the President of the Employment Appeal Tribunal, Mr Justice Wood, gave guidance on the issue of whether an employer had acted reasonably as the law requires. In applying the guidance let us assume that the main reason for dismissal is the acceptable one of incompetence as in the case of a senior member of a publisher's staff who commissions books without proper market research so that they do not sell and the publisher is caused loss.

Having reached the conclusion that the incompetence is established the employer must according to Mr Justice Wood satisfy a tribunal on four other matters, otherwise the dismissal might still be unfair, though the employee's compensation might be reduced for contributory fault (*see below*). The four matters are:

(a) Can the employer satisfy a tribunal that he complied with the pre-dismissal procedures which a reasonable employer could and should have applied in the circumstances of the case? If the tribunal finds that the employer has not acted reasonably in this regard, at the date of dismissal, then according to the decision in *Polkey* v *A E Dayton Services Ltd* [1988] ICR 564 it is not open to the tribunal to say that the procedures do not matter since it is clear that the employee was incompetent. The unfairness of the dismissal could still give the employee a successful claim.

(b) Where there is a contractual appeal process the employer must have carried it out in its essentials. A minor departure may sometimes be ignored but a total or substantial failure entitles a tribunal to find that the dismissal was unfair. Even though no contractual appeal process exists it may nevertheless be reasonable, as was decided in *West Midland Co-operative Society Ltd* v *Tipton* [1986] ICR 192, for some sort of appeal to be arranged since this is encouraged by the Code of Practice issued by the Advisory, Conciliation and Arbitration Service.

(c) Where conduct is the main reason the employer must show, on a balance of probabilities, that at the time of the dismissal he believed the employee was guilty of misconduct and that in all the circumstances of the case it was reasonable for him to do so.

(d) During the disciplinary hearings and the appeal process the employer must have been fair to the employee. In particular the employee must have been heard and allowed to put his case properly or, if he was not at a certain stage of the procedures, this must have been corrected before dismissal.

Thus if an employee commits an armed robbery on his employer's premises he could, and would, be dismissed quite fairly without going through a warning procedure. There would be no need to tell him that if he robbed the premises again he was in danger of losing his job!

Employee's contributory fault

This can reduce the compensation payable to the employee by such percentage as the tribunal thinks fit. Suppose an employee is often late for work and one morning, his employer who can stand it no more, sacks him. The dismissal is likely to be unfair in view of the lack of warning but a tribunal would very probably reduce the worker's compensation to take account of the situation.

Principles of natural justice also apply; it is necessary to let the worker state his case before a decision to dismiss is taken. Furthermore, reasonable inquiry must be made to find the truth of the matter before reaching a decision. Failure to do this will tend to make the dismissal unfair.

Unacceptable reasons for dismissal

These are as follows.

(a) *Dismissal in connection with trade unions.* This has already been considered on p. 421.

(b) *Unfair selection for redundancy.* An employee dismissed for redundancy may complain that he has been unfairly dismissed if he is of the opinion that he has been unfairly selected for redundancy, as where the employer has selected him because he is a member of a trade union or takes part in trade union activities, or where the employer has disregarded redundancy selection arrangements based, for example, on 'last in, first out'. Ideally, all employers should have proper redundancy agreements on the lines set out in the Department of Employment booklet *Dealing with Redundancies.*

However, even though there is in existence an agreed redundancy procedure, the employer may defend himself by showing a 'special reason' for departing from that procedure, e.g. because the person selected for redundancy lacks the skill and versatility of a junior employee who is retained.

There is, since the decision of the Employment Appeal Tribunal in *Williams v Compair Maxam* [1982] ICR 156, an overall standard of fairness also in redundancy arrangements. The standards laid down in the case require the giving of maximum notice; consultation with unions, if any; the taking of the views of more than one person as to who should be dismissed; a requirement to follow any laid down procedure, i.e. last in, first out; and finally, an effort to find the employees concerned alternative employment within the organization. However, the EAT stated in *Meikle* v *McPhail (Charleston Arms)* (1983) (*see* p. 426) that these guidelines would be applied less rigidly to the smaller business.

(c) *Industrial action.* The position in this context has already been considered at p. 421.

(d) *Dismissal of pregnant employee.* A woman who is dismissed because she is pregnant will be treated as having been unfairly dismissed unless certain circumstances apply, for example that she is unable to do her job and cannot be offered, or has refused, suitable alternative work. Even in these cases where the dismissal would be regarded as fair, the woman is nevertheless entitled to maternity pay and may claim re-instatement after confinement.

Refusal to take a woman back after pregnancy is also unfair dismissal. If at the start of the absence due to pregnancy there are five employees or less (including those employed by an associated company) the employer may show that it is not reasonably practical to offer the worker her old job back or another one substantially similar in terms and there is no unfair dismissal. In larger firms than this, as we have seen above, the employee's rights can be curtailed only if the employer can show that it is not reasonably practical to give the old job back and that a suitable alternative has been offered and unreasonably refused. Failure by the employer to comply with the obligations placed on him by law can result in the employee obtaining an order that she can be taken back or, if this is refused or is not practical, an order for compensation on the grounds of unfair dismissal.

An employee who delays her return to work beyond the appropriate date may be dismissed and if she is the dismissal will not be unfair (*Dowouna* v *John Lewis Partnership plc* [1987] IRLR 310).

(e) *Pressure on employer to dismiss unfairly.* It is no defence for an employer to say that pressure was put upon him to dismiss an employee unfairly. So, if other workers put pressure on an employer to dismiss a non-union member so as, for example, to obtain a closed shop, the employer will have no defence to a claim for compensation for the dismissal if he gives in to that pressure. If an employer alleges that he was pressurized into dismissing an employee and that pressure was brought on him by a trade union or other person by the calling, organizing, procuring or financing of industrial action, including a strike, or by the threat of such things, and the reason for the pressure was that the employee was not a member of the trade union, then the employer can join the trade union or other person as a party to the proceedings if he is sued by the dismissed worker for unfair dismissal. If the tribunal awards compensation it can order that a person joined as a party to the proceedings should pay such amount of it as is just and equitable, and if necessary this can be a complete indemnity so that the employer will recover all the damages awarded against him from the union.

(f) *Transfer of business.* The Transfer of Undertakings (Protection of Employment) Regulations 1981 apply to transfers of businesses which take place on or after 1 May 1982. Under the Regulations if a business or part of it is transferred and an employee is dismissed because of this, the dismissal will be treated as automatically unfair. However, the person concerned is not entitled to the extra compensation given to other cases of automatically unfair dismissal (*see* p. 430).

If the old employer dismissed before transfer, or the new employer dismissed after the transfer, either will have a defence if he can prove that the dismissal was for 'economic, technical or organizational' reasons requiring a change in the workforce and that the dismissal was reasonable in all the circumstances of the case. **The following case is relevant**.

Meikle v McPhail (Charleston Arms) [1983] IRLR 351

After contracting to take over a public house and its employees, the new management decided that economies were essential and dismissed the barmaid. She complained to an industrial tribunal on the grounds of unfair dismissal. Her case was based upon the fact that the 1981 Regulations state that a dismissal is to be treated as unfair if the transfer of a business or a reason connected with it is the reason or principal reason for the dismissal. The pub's new management defended the claim under another provision in the 1981 Regulations which states that a dismissal following a transfer of business is not to be regarded as automatically unfair where there was, as in this case, an economic reason for making changes in the workforce. If there is such a reason, unfairness must be established on grounds other than the mere transfer of the business.

The Employment Appeal Tribunal decided that the reason for dismissal was an economic one under the Regulations and that the management had acted reasonably in the circumstances so that the barmaid's claim failed.

Comment: It should be noted that in *Gateway Hotels Ltd v Stewart* [1988] IRLR 287 the Employment Appeal Tribunal decided that on a transfer of business dismissal of employees of the business transferred prior to the transfer at the insistence of the purchaser of the business is not an 'economic' reason within the regulations so that the dismissals are unfair.

Unfair dismissal and frustration of contract

In cases appearing before industrial tribunals there is a certain interplay between the common law rules of frustration of contract (*see* p. 201) and the statutory provisions relating to unfair dismissal. At common law a contract of service is frustrated by incapacity, e.g. sickness, if that incapacity makes the contract substantially impossible of performance at a particularly vital time, or by a term of imprisonment. If a contract has been so frustrated then a complaint of unfair dismissal is not available because the contract has been discharged on other grounds, i.e. by frustration. Thus termination of a contract of service by frustration prevents a claim for unfair dismissal.

Remedies for unfair dismissal

These are as follows.

Conciliation

An industrial tribunal will not hear a complaint until a conciliation officer has had a chance to see whether he can help. A copy of the complaint made to the industrial tribunal is sent to the conciliation officer and if he is unable to settle the complaint, nothing said by the employer or employee during the process of conciliation will be admissible in evidence before the tribunal.

Other remedies

An employee who has been dismissed may:

(a) seek reinstatement or re-engagement; or
(b) claim compensation.

The power to order (a) above is discretionary and in practice rarely exercised. However, reinstatement means taken back by the employer on exactly the same terms and seniority as before; re-engagement is being taken back but on different terms.

Calculation of compensation

The compensation for unfair dismissal is in four parts as follows.

(a) *The basic award* (maximum: £5,160). This award is computed as a redundancy payment (*see* p. 431 before reading on) except there is no maximum age limit. Contributory fault of the employee is taken into account.

 Example: Fred, a 35-year old lorry driver employed for ten years earning £140 per week (take home £120) is unfairly dismissed. He did his best to get a comparable job but did not in fact obtain one until two weeks after the tribunal hearing. Fred had a history of lateness for work and his contributory fault is assessed at 25 per cent.

 Fred's basic award: Fred is in category 22 years of age but under 41 years of age for redundancy which allows one week's pay for every year of service:

10 × £140	£1,400	
Less: 25%	£350	
	£1,050	= basic award

If Fred's dismissal had been automatically unfair, e.g. for union membership, the minimum award would be £2,620. This may be reduced for contributory fault.

(b) *Compensatory award* (maximum: £10,000). This consists of:
  (i) estimated loss of wages, net of tax and other deductions to the date of the hearing less any money earned between date of dismissal and the hearing;
  (ii) estimated future losses;
  (iii) loss of any benefits such as pension rights and expenses;
  (iv) loss of statutory rights. It is rare to get an award under this heading but it can be given for loss of minimum notice entitlement. For example, Fred has been continuously employed for ten years. He was entitled to ten

weeks' notice which he did not get. He now has a new job but it will take him time to build up that entitlement again. A tribunal can award something for this. Once again contributory fault is taken into account.

Fred's compensatory award:

			£
The loss up to the hearing	10 × £140		1,400
Loss up to time of getting new job	2 × £140		280
			1,680
Less: 25%			420
		£	1,260
Loss of statutory rights: a nominal figure of		100	
Less: 25%		25	75
			£1,335

Fred's total award is therefore:

	£
Basic	1,050
Compensatory	1,335
	£2,385

If Fred has lost anything else, e.g. use of firm's van at weekends and/or pension rights, these would be added to the compensatory award subject to 25 per cent discount for contributory fault.

Additional award. This is available in addition to the above where an employer fails to comply with an order for reinstatement or re-engagement unless it was not practicable for him to do so.

(i)   If the original dismissal was unlawful under the Race Relations Act or Sex Discrimination Act, it is not less than 26 weeks' pay nor more than 52 weeks' pay with a maximum of £198 per week, and an overall maximum of £10,000.

(ii) In other cases (not where dismissal is automatically unfair – *see below*), it is not less than 13 weeks' pay nor more than 26 weeks' pay calculated as in (i) above.

(c) *A special award.* This is payable where the dismissal is automatically unfair and the employee has asked for reinstatement or re-engagement but the tribunal has refused to make such an order. It can make a special award instead. The compensation is a week's pay but without limit as to amount, multiplied by 104 weeks with a minimum amount of £13,180 and a maximum of £26,290. However, if a tribunal does make an order for reinstatement or re-engagement and the employer does not comply but cannot show that it was reasonably impracticable for him to do so, the compensation is increased to a week's pay (no limit) multiplied by 156 with a minimum of £19,735 and no maximum. In all cases a deduction will be made for contributory fault, if any, of the employee.

Any unemployment or supplementary benefits received by the employee are deducted from any award made by a tribunal. However, the employer must pay the amount(s) in question direct to the DSS.

(d) *Time limits*. A claim for compensation against an employer must reach the tribunal within three months of the date of termination of employment. The period in regard to dismissal in connection with a strike or other industrial action is six months. A worker can claim while working out his notice but no award can be made until employment ends.

A tribunal can hear a claim after three months if the employee can prove that:

(i) it was not reasonably practicable for him to claim within three months;

(ii) he did so as soon as he could in the circumstances.

DISCRIMINATORY DISMISSAL

In addition to legislation relating to unfair dismissal generally, the Sex Discrimination Act 1975 and the Race Relations Act 1976 deal with complaints to industrial tribunals for dismissal on the grounds of sex, marital status or race. The nature and scope of these provisions have already been considered and it is only necessary to add here that there are provisions in the Employment Protection (Consolidation) Act 1978 which prevent double compensation being paid, once under sex discrimination legislation or race discrimination legislation, and once under the general unfair dismissal provisions of the 1978 Act.

REDUNDANCY

The Employment Protection (Consolidation) Act 1978 gives an employee a right to compensation by way of a redundancy payment if he is dismissed because of a redundancy.

Meaning of redundancy

Under the 1978 Act redundancy is *presumed* to occur where the services of employees are dispensed with because the employer ceases, or intends to cease carrying on business, or to carry on business at the place where the employee was employed, or does not require so many employees to do work of a certain kind. Employees who have been laid off or kept on short time without pay for four consecutive weeks (or for six weeks in a period of 13 weeks) are entitled to end their employment and to seek a redundancy payment if there is no reasonable prospect that normal working will be resumed.

Eligibility

In general terms, all those employed under a contract of service as employees are entitled to redundancy pay, including a person employed by his/her spouse. Furthermore, a volunteer for redundancy is not debarred from claiming. However, certain persons are excluded by statute or circumstances. The main categories are listed below:

(a) a domestic servant in a private household who is a close relative of the employer. The definition of 'close relative' for this purpose is father, mother, grandfather, grandmother, stepfather, stepmother, son, daughter, grandson, granddaughter, stepson, stepdaughter, brother, sister, half-brother, or half-sister;

(b) an employee who has not completed at least two years of continuous service since reaching the age of 18;

(c) men and women who have reached retirement age. In this connection s. 16 of the Employment Act 1989 removes a previous discriminatory feature which was that men could receive statutory redundancy payments up to age 65 but women only up to age 60. This anomaly remained even though the Sex Discrimination Act 1986 removed the right of employers to set discriminatory retiring ages. Where there is a 'normal retiring age' for the job in question which is below 65 and is the same for men and women, i.e. non-discriminatory, the entitlement of both sexes is restricted to that age. In all other cases women's entitlement is extended to age 65 in line with that of men.

(d) part-time workers who normally work less than 16 hours per week. After five years' employment the figure is reduced to 8 hours;

(e) where in the case of a fixed term contract of two years or more the employee has agreed in writing in the contract or at any stage of the contract to forgo his right to claim redundancy payment;

(f) employees who normally work outside Great Britain under their contract;

(g) workers on strike can generally be dismissed by their employers without liability to make a redundancy payment. This applies even though the employer was short of work at the time of the strike so a redundancy situation did exist. Where the strike takes place after a redundancy notice has been given, the employee concerned may still get part or all of his redundancy pay by applying to a tribunal which has a power under the Employment

Protection (Consolidation) Act 1978 to make an award which is 'just and equitable', the amount being arrived at by the tribunal.

An employee who accepts an offer of suitable alternative employment with his employer is not entitled to a redundancy payment. Where a new offer is made, there is a trial period of four weeks following the making of the offer, during which the employer or the employee may end the contract while retaining all rights and liabilities under redundancy legislation. **An employee who unreasonably refuses an offer of alternative employment is not entitled to a redundancy payment, as illustrated in the following case.**

Fuller v Stephanie Bowman [1977] IRLR 7

F was employed as a secretary at SB's premises which were situated in Mayfair. These premises attracted a very high rent and rates so SB moved their offices to Soho. These premises were situated over a sex shop and F refused the offer of renewed employment at the same salary and she later brought a claim before an industrial tribunal for a redundancy payment. The tribunal decided that the question of unreasonableness was a matter of fact for the tribunal and F's refusal to work over the sex shop was unreasonable so that she was not entitled to a redundancy payment.

Comment: (i) It should be noted that in *North East Coast Ship Repairers* v *Secretary of State For Employment* [1978] IRLR 149 the Employment Appeal Tribunal decided that an apprentice who, having completed the period of his apprenticeship, finds that the firm cannot provide him with work, is not entitled to redundancy payment. This case has relevance for trainees and others completing contracts in order to obtain relevant practical experience.

As regards time limits, the employee must make a written claim to the employer or to an industrial tribunal within six months from the end of the employment. If the employee does not do this an industrial tribunal may extend the time for a further six months, making 12 months in all, but not longer, from the actual date of termination of the employment, provided that it can be shown that it is just and equitable having regard to the reasons put forward by the employee for late application and to all relevant circumstances.

(ii) In *Elliot* v *Richard Stump Ltd* [1987] IRLR 215 the EAT decided that a redundant employee who is offered alternative employment by an employer who refuses to accept a trial period is unfairly dismissed.

Amount of redundancy payment

Those aged 41 to 65 (60 women) receive one and a half weeks' pay (up to a maximum of £198 per week) for each year of service up to a maximum of 20 years. In other age groups the above provisions apply except that the week's pay changes, i.e. for those aged 22, but under 41, it is one week's pay, and for those 18, but under 22, it is a half week's pay.

For example, a man of 52 who is made redundant having been continuously employed for 18 years and earning £120 per week as gross salary at the time of his redundancy would be entitled to a redundancy payment as follows:

34 to 41 years = 7 years at one week's pay		= 7 weeks
41 to 52 years = 11 years at one and a half week's pay		= 16½ weeks
		23½ weeks

It follows, therefore, that the redundancy payment would be 23½ weeks × £120 = £2,820.

Employees over 64 (59 women) have their redundancy payment reduced pro–gressively so that for each complete month by which the age exceeds 64 (or 59) on the Saturday of the week on which the contract ends, the normal entitlement is reduced by one twelfth. Thus a man aged 64 years and three months would have three twelfths of the award deducted. The rule relating to the reduction in women's redundancy pay is not changed by the retirement provisions of the Sex Discrimination Act 1986. Complaints by employees in respect of the right to a redundancy payment or questions as to its amount, may, as we have seen, be made to an industrial tribunal which will make a declaration as to the employee's rights which form the basis on which payment can be recovered from the employer.

Rebates for employers

Section 13 of the Employment Act 1989 abolished the scheme under which employers with less than ten employees could claim a rebate from the government towards the cost of payment.

Procedure for handling redundancies

A good starting point is to ask for voluntary redundancies. If this does not provide enough persons then any agreed formula must be followed, e.g. last in, first out. Selection procedures may also be based on poor work performance or attendance record and there is no requirement in the employer to determine reasons for this (*Dooley* v *Leyland Vehicles Ltd* [1986] IRLR 36). If there is no agreed procedure the employer must decide after considering the pros and cons in each case. Everyone should, as far as possible, be allowed to express their views, e.g. through elected representatives, if any. An attempt to relocate a redundant worker should be considered. Failure to do so can result in a finding of unfair dismissal unless, of course, there was no chance of finding suitable alternative work.

Selecting, say, a white single girl, or a West Indian single man to go, rather than a married white man with two children and a mortgage might appear to be humane. However, unless the decision is made on the basis of competence, experience, reliability, and so on, the dismissal is likely to be unfair and also a breach of the Sex Discrimination Act 1975 and/or the Race Relations Act 1976.

Under the Employment Protection Act 1975 where an employer proposes to dismiss as redundant *any* employee where there is an independent trade union recognized by that employer in regard to the class of the employee concerned, the employer has a duty to consult with representatives of that union. This means there must be consultation even for one dismissal. However, where 100 or more workers are to be dismissed within 90 days or less, the employer must consult at least 90 days before the first dismissal takes place. If the proposal is to dismiss ten or more workers within 30 days at one establishment he must consult at least 30 days before the first dismissal.

Failure to do this gives the union(s) a right to go to a tribunal which, unless it finds that the employer could not reasonably consult because of circumstances, may make a declaration of non-compliance and possibly grant *protective awards*. These are awards of remuneration for a protected period for those employees dismissed without proper consultation. The maximum period where 100 or more workers are dismissed is 90 days; 10 or more, 30 days; less than 10, 28 days.

The employer must also inform the Department of Employment if dismissing 100 or more employees within 90 days or less, or 10 or more within 30 days or less. The DoE must be informed of this intention at least 90 days or 30 days respectively, before the first dismissal is to take place. There is no need to notify if it is proposed to make less than ten employees redundant. Failure to notify can mean a fine on conviction by the court. Notification to the DoE applies whether or not there is a recognized trade union.

General standards of fairness for redundancy were laid down by the Employment Appeal Tribunal in *Williams* v *Compair Maxam* [1982] ICR 156. These were the giving of maximum notice; consultation with unions, if any; the taking of the views of more than one person as to who should be dismissed; the requirement to follow any laid down procedure, e.g. last in, first out; and, finally, an effort to find the employees concerned alternative employment within the organization. It should be noted that in *Meikle* v *McPhail (Charleston Arms)* [1983] IRLR 351 the Employment Appeal Tribunal stated that these guidelines would be applied less rigidly to the smaller business.

As we have seen, when a worker is to be made redundant, the ACAS Code of Practice and the decision in *Williams* v *Compair Maxam* (1982) (*above*) both stress the importance of consultation.

However, as the result of the EAT's decision in *British Labour Pump Co* v *Byrne* [1979] IRLR 94 mere failure to consult on the employer's part was not in itself enough to make a dismissal for redundancy automatically unfair. Under the *British Labour Pump* principle a failure to consult was not to be regarded as unreasonable if consultation would have made no difference in the end, as where, for example, the company was insolvent and its state so grave that redundancy was probably inevitable anyway.

However, the House of Lords decided to overrule the *British Labour Pump* principle in *Polkey* v *A E Dayton Services Ltd* [1987] ICR 142. The House of Lords decided that where an employer failed to consult or warn an employee it was not right for an industrial tribunal to ask in considering whether the employee had been unfairly dismissed whether he would nevertheless have been dismissed even if he had been consulted or warned. The correct question was whether the employer's action in regarding his reason for dismissing the employee as sufficient had been reasonable or unreasonable *at the time of dismissal*. That the facts subsequently showed that redundancy had been inevitable was not the point.

While the *British Labour Pump* case reigned supreme, the consultation procedures of Codes of Practice and judicial decisions were much weakened. Subsequent events might justify a redundancy without consultation so that the employer could say that he would not have acted differently in the event even if there had been consultation with employees. The House of Lords in *Polkey* was clearly concerned to re-establish good industrial relations practice which involves consultation except, perhaps, where the employer's situation is so totally hopeless that there would be no point in consultation. However, in other cases consultation is not only a courtesy, it can sometimes produce solutions leading to the retention of employees.

Collective agreements on redundancy

The Secretary of State may, on the application of the employer and the unions involved, make an order modifying the requirements of redundancy pay legislation if he is satisfied that there is a collective agreement which makes satisfactory alternative arrangements for dealing with redundancy. The provisions of the agreement must be 'on the whole at least as favourable' as the statutory provisions, and must include, in particular, arrangements allowing an employee to go to an independent arbitration or to make a complaint to an industrial tribunal.

OTHER METHODS OF TERMINATION OF CONTRACT OF SERVICE

Having considered the termination of the contract by unfair or discriminatory dismissal or redundancy, we must now turn to other ways in which the contract of service may be brought to an end. These are set out below.

By notice

A contract of service can be brought to an end by either party giving notice to the other, although where the employer gives notice, even in accordance with the contract of service or under the statutory provisions of the Employment Protection (Consolidation) Act 1978, he may still face a claim for unfair dismissal or a redundancy payment.

The most important practical aspect is the length of notice to be given by the parties, in particular the employer. The 1978 Act contains statutory provisions in regard to *minimum* periods of notice and the only relevance of the express provisions of a particular contract of service on the matter is that a contract may provide for longer periods of notice than does the Act. Under the 1978 Act an employee is entitled to one week's notice after employment for one month or more; after two years' service the minimum entitlement is increased to two weeks, and for each year of service after that it is increased by one week up to a maximum of 12 weeks' notice after 12 years' service.

An employee, once he has been employed for one month or more, must give his employer one week's notice and the period of one week's notice applies for the duration of the contract so far as the employee is concerned, no matter how long he has served the employer. It should be noted that so far as oral notice is concerned it does not begin on the day it is given but on the following day. This means, for example, that in the case of oral notice, seven days' notice means seven days exclusive of the day on which the notice is given (*see West* v *Kneels Ltd* (1986) *below*). There appears to be no particular ruling on written notice and so it may be that one could give notice starting from the date of the letter if the letter was served on the employee (or employer) on that day. However, it would seem preferable to commence the notice from the day after service of the letter.

West v Kneels Ltd [1986] IRLR 430

Julie West claimed that her employers had dismissed her unfairly. An industrial tribunal decided that the claim failed because she had not been employed for the necessary qualifying period. This was true if the week's notice commenced on the day it was given. If it started the next day she would qualify. Mr Justice Popplewell decided that it accorded with good industrial practice that in the case of oral notice seven days' notice meant seven days exclusive of the day on which the notice was served. This meant that Julie West had in fact been employed for the necessary qualifying period.

Breach of the provisions relating to minimum periods of notice do not involve an employer in any penalty, but the rights conferred by the 1978 Act will be taken into account in assessing the employer's liability for breach of contract. Thus an employer who has dismissed his employee without due notice is generally liable for the wages due to the employee for the appropriate period of notice at the contract rate.

It should be noted that the 1978 Act provisions regarding minimum periods of notice do not affect the common law rights of an employer to dismiss an employee at once without notice for misconduct, e.g. disobedience, neglect, or drunkenness (*see* p. 420).

In practice a contract of service is often terminated by a payment instead of notice and this is allowed by the 1978 Act.

In these days when there is a great need for skilled personnel it is tempting for employees to break their contracts by leaving at short notice to go to other jobs. However, in *Evening Standard Co Ltd* v *Henderson* [1987] IRLR 64 the employer, Evening Standard, was granted an injunction to restrain an employee from working for a rival during his contractual notice period of 12 months as long as the employer agreed (which he did) to provide him with remuneration and other contractual benefits until the proper notice period would have run out, or, alternatively, let him stay at work until the proper notice period had expired.

By agreement

As in any other contract the parties to a contract of employment may end the contract by agreement. Thus if employer and employee agree to new terms and conditions on, for example, a promotion of the employee, the old agreement is discharged and a new one takes over.

An employee could agree to be 'bought off' by his employer under an agreement to discharge the existing contract of service. In this connection it should be noted that discharge of a contract of service by agreement is not a 'dismissal' for the purposes, for example, of an unfair dismissal claim, but should a claim for unfair dismissal be brought by an employee who has been 'bought off' the tribunal concerned will want to see evidence of a genuine and fair agreement by employer and employee and may allow a claim of unfair dismissal if the discharging agreement is one-sided and biased in favour of the employer.

By passage of time

In the case of a fixed term contract, as where an employee is engaged for, say, three years, the contract will terminate at the end of the three years though there may be provisions for notice within that period.

By frustration

A contract of service can, as we have already seen, be discharged by frustration which could be incapacity, such as illness. However, other events can bring about the discharge of a contract of service by frustration, e.g. a term of imprisonment.

Furthermore, death of either employer or employee will discharge the contract by frustration from the date of the death so that, for example, the personal representatives of the employer are not required to continue with the contract. However, the estate has a claim for wages or salary due at the date of death.

Under the 1978 Act claims for unfair dismissal arising before the employer's death survive and may be brought after the death of the employer against his estate. Furthermore, the death of a human employer is usually regarded as a 'dismissal' for redundancy purposes and the employee may make a claim against the employer's estate.

If the employee is re-engaged or the personal representatives renew his contract within eight weeks of the employer's death, the employee is not regarded as having been dismissed. Where an offer of renewal or re-engagement is refused on reasonable grounds by the employee, then he is entitled to a redundancy payment. If he unreasonably refuses to renew his contract or accept a suitable offer of re-engagement he is not entitled to such a payment.

Partnership dissolution

A person who is employed by a partnership which is dissolved is regarded as dismissed on dissolution of the firm. Under the 1978 Act this is regarded as having occurred because of redundancy.

The dismissal is also regarded as wrongful at common law and there may be a claim by the employee for damages but these will be nominal only if the partnership business continues and the continuing partners offer new employment on the old terms (*Brace* v *Calder* (1895) – *see* p. 222).

A partnership is dissolved whenever one partner dies or becomes bankrupt or leaves the firm for any reason.

Of course, if a firm or sole trader sells the business as a going concern, employees are transferred to the new employer automatically under the Transfer of Undertakings (Protection of Employment) Regulations 1981.

Appointment of an administrator – corporate rehabilitation

The object of administration orders is to allow a company to be put on a profitable basis if possible, or at least disposed of more profitably than would be the case if other forms of insolvency proceedings, such as liquidation, were used. On the appointment of an administrator the company's executive and other directors are not dismissed but their powers of management are exercisable only if the administrator consents. He also has power to dismiss and appoint directors.

Since an administrator is made an agent of the company by the court under the administration order, employees are not automatically dismissed. In addition, an administrator is not taken to have adopted a contract of employment by reason of anything done or omitted to be done within 14 days after his appointment. This provision, which is also applied to an administrative receiver (*see below*), is to correct a possible unfairness which existed under the previous law before the coming into force of the present insolvency provisions which are contained in the Insolvency Act 1986. In earlier times an administrator or administrative receiver would have been able to take the services of an employee of the company for some weeks and then say 'your contract is with the company: the company is insolvent and I do not intend to pay you'. Thus the employee might work for some time without any right to pay. Under the provisions of the Insolvency Act 1986 if an administrator or an administrative receiver allows an employee of the company to contribute his services and says nothing to him for more than 14 days about his contract of employment, then he is deemed to have adopted it and the employee must be paid before the insolvency practitioner is entitled to his fees and expenses.

If, of course, an administrator or administrative receiver dismisses an employee, that employee can make a claim for a redundancy payment.

Appointment of an administrative receiver

Where a company has borrowed money and given security for the loan by charging its assets under a debenture, the debenture holders may, if, for example, they are not paid interest on the loan, appoint a receiver and manager, now referred to as an administrative receiver. The most common appointment is by a bank in respect of an overdraft or loan facility to a company.

If the administrative receiver is appointed under the terms of the debenture he is under the Insolvency Act 1986 an agent of the company and where this is so employees of the company are not dismissed on his appointment and their employment is continuous for the purposes of employment legislation. Employees are, however, dismissed if the administrative receiver sells the undertaking or where continuance of the employees' contracts would be inconsistent with the appointment of a receiver as could be the case in regard to the contract of a managing director. However, even a managing director may not be regarded as dismissed where the receiver has a part-time appointment, as was the case in *Griffiths* v *Secretary of State for Social Services* [1973] 3 All ER 1184.

If the appointment is made by the court then the administrative receiver is not the agent of the company but an officer of the court and his appointment terminates the contracts of all employees and the continuity of their employment ceases and they have a claim for a redundancy payment. The receiver may, of course, continue the employment by offering what are in effect new contracts, but where this so there is a break in the continuity in the employment for the purposes of employment legislation. The employees are now employed by the administrative receiver and not by the company of which he is agent.

Company liquidation

The possibilities are as follows:

(a) *A compulsory winding up.* Here the court orders the winding up of the company, usually on the petition of a creditor because it cannot pay his debt. The making of a compulsory winding up order by the court may have the following effects according to the circumstances of the case:

(i) where the company's business ceases the winding up order will operate as a wrongful dismissal of employees;

(ii) where the liquidator continues the business he may be regarded as an agent of the company so that the employment continues or, alternatively, the court may regard the appointment of the liquidator as a giving of notice to the employee who then works out that notice under the liquidator. It is, however, the better view that employees may, if they so choose, regard themselves as dismissed because the company has ceased to employ them, the new contract being with the liquidator.

(b) *A voluntary winding up.* This commences on the resolution of the members and if the company's business ceases there is a dismissal of employees. If the company's business continues the position would appear to be as set out in (a)(ii) above.

Bankruptcy

The bankruptcy of a human employer, or indeed of the employee, does not automatically discharge the contract of service, though it will, if there is a term to that effect in the agreement. Thus, the employment can continue, though in practical terms it may be impossible to pay employees' wages, and in this case they will be discharged and be able to make a claim for redundancy payment and also in the bankruptcy for wages accrued due in regard to which they have a preferential claim in the bankruptcy.

A trustee in bankruptcy cannot insist that an employee should continue in service because the contract is one of a personal nature. The bankruptcy of an employee will not normally affect the contract of service unless there is a term to that effect in the contract. Company directors provide a special case since the articles of most companies provide for termination of the office on becoming bankrupt.

Wrongful and summary dismissal at common law

The claim at common law for wrongful dismissal is based on a general principle of the law of contract, i.e. wrongful repudiation of the contract of service by the employer.

The common law action has, of course, been largely taken over by the statutory provisions relating to unfair dismissal and a common law claim is only likely to be brought by an employee who has a fixed term contract at a high salary. Thus a company director who has a fixed term contract for, say, three years at a salary of £50,000 per annum might, if wrongfully dismissed, find it more profitable in terms of damages obtainable to sue at common law for breach of contract, though the employer may be able to resist the claim where the employee was guilty, for example, of misconduct, disobedience or immorality.

In other cases where the contract of service is not for a fixed term, there is no claim for damages at common law provided the employer gives proper notice or pays wages instead of notice, though in such a case the employee has at least potentially, a claim for unfair dismissal which he could pursue. Again, the employer may resist a claim for unfair dismissal on the basis of misconduct, disobedience or immorality, and we have already given some consideration to these matters in the context of statutory unfair dismissal.

RIGHTS AND REMEDIES ON DISMISSAL

These are as follows.

Written statement of reasons for dismissal

At common law an employer is not required to give his employee any reasons for dismissal. However, the Employment Protection (Consolidation) Act 1978 provides that where an employee is dismissed, with or without notice, or by failure to renew a contract for a fixed term, he must be provided by his employer on request, within 14 days of that request, with a written statement giving particulars of the reasons for his dismissal. This provision applies only to employees who have been continuously employed for a period of two years (Employment Act 1989, s.11). The written statement is admissible in evidence in any proceedings relating to the dismissal and if an employer refuses to give a written statement the employee may complain to an industrial tribunal. If the tribunal upholds the complaint it may make a declaration as to what it finds the employer's reasons were for dismissing the employee and must make an award of two weeks' pay without limit as to amount to the employee.

Employer's insolvency

If the employer is bankrupt or dies insolvent, or where the employer is a company and is in liquidation, the unpaid wages of an employee have priority as to payment but only to a maximum of £800 and limited to services rendered during the period of four months before the commencement of the insolvency. Any balance over £800 or four months ranks as an ordinary debt. Also preferential is accrued holiday remuneration payable to an employee on the termination of his employment before or because of the insolvency.

The 1978 Act adds to the above preferential debts by including in the list sums owed in respect of statutory guarantee payments, guaranteed payments during statutory time off, remuneration on suspension for medical grounds, or remuneration under a protective award given because of failure to consult properly on redundancy. Statutory sick pay under the Social Security and Housing Benefits Act of 1982 is also preferential.

It should also be noted that under the 1978 Act an employee may, in the case of his employer's insolvency, make a claim on the Redundancy Fund rather than relying on the preferential payments procedure set out above. If the employee is paid from the Redundancy Fund the Secretary of State for Employment may then claim in the employer's insolvency for the amount paid out of the Redundancy Fund and is a preferential creditor to the extent that the employee paid would have been.

The limits of the employee's claim on the Redundancy Fund are as follows.

(a) arrears of pay for a period not exceeding eight weeks with a maximum of £198 per week;

(b) holiday pay with a limit of six weeks and a financial limit of £198 per week;

(c) payments instead of notice at a rate not exceeding £198 per week;

(d) payments outstanding in regard to an award by an industrial tribunal of compensation for unfair dismissal;

(e) reimbursement of any fee or premium paid by an apprentice or articled clerk.

There is no qualifying period before an employee becomes eligible and virtually all people in employment are entitled.

It should also be noted that claims on the Redundancy Fund will not normally be admitted if the liquidator or trustee in bankruptcy can satisfy the Secretary of State by a statement that the preferential payments will be paid from funds available in the insolvency and without undue delay. Section 14 of the Employment Act 1989 now allows the Department at its option to make payments without a statement from an insolvency practitioner as to the amounts due where it has adequate records of its own as to what is due.

Damages for wrongful dismissal

These are covered by common law rules and will be looked at in the context of a fixed term contract which has been wrongfully repudiated by the employer before the term has expired. The damages will be the amount of money which the employee would have earned under the contract less the amount of money which he could reasonably have expected to earn elsewhere. Arrears of pay for work done prior to dismissal, if any, are also included.

A general principle of the common law which is that a plaintiff suing for breach of contract must mitigate his loss applies and reference should be made at this point to the case of *Brace* v *Calder* (1895) (*see* p. 222).

Damages for loss of benefits other than salary may be included, e.g. rent-free house, provided these were rights given in the contract of service. There is no claim for discretionary benefits which an employer may or may not give, such as discretionary bonuses.

It should be noted that since damages for wrongful dismissal normally involve an assessment of lost salary, a deduction for income tax must be made before the plaintiff receives his award (*Beach* v *Reed Corrugated Cases Ltd* [1956] 2 All ER 652).

Furthermore, sums which the employer would have had to deduct from salary for social security contributions and any unemployment benefit received by the employee will also go to reduce damages. Social security benefits received by the employee are not deducted from the damages since they are discretionary. In addition, sums which the employee has received by way of redundancy payments also go to reduce the damages (*Stocks* v *Magna Merchants Ltd* [1973] 2 All ER 329) and so it would seem on the basis of the above case do amounts received by the employee in respect of a claim for unfair dismissal. The deduction of these sums seems wrong in that they are rewards for past services rather than compensation for loss of a job.

The equitable remedy of specific performance and injunction

A decree of specific performance is, as we have seen, an order of the court and constitutes an express instruction to a party to a contract to perform the actual obligations which he undertook under its terms. If the person who is subject to the order fails to comply with it, he is in contempt of court and potentially liable to be fined or imprisoned until he complies with the order and thus purges his contempt. For all practical purposes the remedy is not given to enforce performance of a contract of service, largely because the court cannot supervise that its order is being carried out. A judge would have to attend the place of work on a regular basis to see that the parties were implementing the contract.

An injunction is, as we have seen, an order of the court whereby an individual is required to refrain from the further doing of the act complained of. Again, a person who is subject to such an order and fails to comply with it is in contempt of court and the consequences set out above follow from the contempt. An injunction may be used to prevent many wrongful acts, e.g. the torts of trespass and nuisance, but in the context of contract the remedy will be granted to enforce a negative stipulation in a contract in a situation where it would be unjust to confine the plaintiff to damages. In a proper case an injunction may be used as an indirect method of enforcing a contract for personal services, such as a contract of employment, but in that case a clear negative stipulation is required. Reference should be made to *Warner Brothers* v *Nelson* (1937) at p. 224 as an illustration of the application of the negative stipulation rule.

In this connection it should also be noted that the Trade Union and Labour Relations Act 1974 provides that no court shall by way of specific performance or an injunction compel an employee to do any work or attend any place for the doing of any work. Thus the Act is in line with the judicial approach to specific performance but to some extent out of line with the judicial approach to the granting of an injunction. Thus the availability of an injunction in cases involving contracts of service is subject to the provisions of the 1974 Act and although the matter has not been worked out by the courts, it would seem that on general principles the granting of an injunction in the context of a contract of employment is no longer possible since statute law prevails over decisions of the judiciary, but the matter is not beyond doubt.

Employee's breach of contract

An employer may sue his employees for damages for breach of the contract of service by the employee. Such claims are potentially available, for example, for damage to the employer's property, as where machinery is damaged by negligent operation, as was the case in *Baster* v *London and County Printing Works* [1899] 1 QB 901, or for refusal to work resulting in damage by lost production, as was the case in *National Coal Board* v *Galley* [1958] 1 All ER 91. Such claims are rare and impractical because of the fact that the employee will not, in most cases, be able to meet the claim, and also, perhaps more importantly, because they lead to industrial unrest. In these circumstances we do not pursue the matter further here.

GRADED QUESTIONS

Essay mode

1. When may an employee claim a redundancy payment?

   (The Institute of Company Accountants. Part 3: Law Relating to Business. November 1988)

2. P Ltd employs 500 employees. In 1987 it advertised for a marketing adviser, and Q was recruited. When Q was appointed it was agreed between him and P Ltd that Q would be responsible for the payment of his own income tax and national insurance contributions, that he could work the agreed hours of work each week whenever he chose, and that he could work for other employers as long as they were not competitors of P Ltd.

   During 1989 P Ltd became dissatisfied with Q's work and in March 1990 the decision was made to reduce the importance of Q's work and to reduce his remuneration accordingly. In April 1990 Q resigned from P Ltd and now wishes to seek compensation for unfair dismissal. P Ltd claim that Q was never employed under a contract of service but under a contract for services.

   Advise Q.

   (20 marks)

   (The Chartered Institute of Certified Accountants. Paper 1.4(E): Law. June 1990)

3. (a) Explain the extent to which the Unfair Contract Terms Act 1977 has restricted the use of exclusion clauses and limitation of liability clauses in contracts.

   (b) Wily & Co contract to supply printed circuits to Shadydeals Ltd. The circuits have been made to a detailed specification supplied by Shadydeals Ltd. On the back of the invoice, there is stated in print so tiny as to be almost illegible, a set of standard conditions including the following provision:

   'The company accepts no liability under the Sale of Goods Act 1979 or any other legislation in respect of the quality of the goods or their fitness for any purpose whatsoever.'

   The printed circuits turn out to be defective, and Shadydeals have raised an action for damages against Wily & Co, who have raised the defence that they are not liable by virtue of their exclusion clause.

   Advise Shadydeals of their chances of success in court.

   (Napier Polytechnic of Edinburgh. CNAA BA in Business Studies (Part Time). May 1990)

4. (a) Misconduct of the employee is a good defence against both actions for wrongful dismissal and claims for unfair dismissal. What is meant by misconduct in this context?

   (12 marks)

   (b) Mary and Jane, two shop assistants, are short of money and decide to borrow from the till. Mary leaves a note in the till and replaces the money the following morning, Jane neither leaves a note nor does she replace the money. If the employer later discovers what has happened, may he dismiss them?

(8 marks)

(Total: 20 marks)

(*The Chartered Institute of Management Accountants. Business Law. November 1989*)

Objective mode

1. An employer may practise sex and racial discrimination where sex or race is a _____. Complete.

2. Mrs Bloggs says: 'I want some part-time help with my housework but I shall tell the Jobcentre that I do not want a coloured person.'
   Mrs Bloggs is acting contrary to law.   TRUE/FALSE

3. Mr Bloggs is about to place an advertisement for a job in his restaurant. It says: 'Waiter required for upmarket restaurant in Barchester. Apply Box 30.'
   Mr Bloggs is quite within his legal rights to do this.   TRUE/FALSE

4. To claim unfair dismissal a person employed on or after 1 June 1985 must have been employed by the dismissing employer for at least *two/three* years unless the dismissal is _____ unfair.
   Delete and complete.

5. Joe has been sexually harassing his secretary, Jane. Jane resigned last week.
   Jane *can/cannot* claim unfair dismissal.

6. Correctly complete the following.
   Under the Employment Protection Act 1975 an employer is obliged to consult with the representatives of an independent trade union representing employees being made redundant. In particular, where _____ or more workers are to be dismissed within _____ days or less, the employer must consult at least _____ days before the first dismissal takes place. If the proposal is to dismiss _____ or more workers within _____ days at one establishment, he must consult at least _____ days before the first dis–missal.

7. Correctly complete the following.
   Under the Employment Protection (Consolidation) Act an employee is entitled to _____ notice after employment for _____ or more; after _____ service the minimum entitlement is increased to _____ and for each year of service after that is increased by _____ up to a maximum of _____ weeks' notice after _____ years' service.

8. Correctly complete the following.

   If the employer is bankrupt or dies insolvent, or where the employer is a company and is in liquidation, the unpaid wages of an employee have priority as to payment, but only to a maximum of _____ and limited to service rendered during the period of _____ before the commencement of the insolvency.

Answers to questions set in objective mode appear on p. 551.

17 | Negotiable instruments

The OBJECTIVES of this chapter are to consider the characteristics of negotiability and give a detailed definition of bills of exchange together with the legal environment of their use.

NEGOTIABILITY

Meaning of negotiability

Items of property are transferable physically from one person to another but ownership cannot pass unless a good title accompanies the physical transfer.

A good title will not pass if the person who owns the property did not consent in any way to its transfer. Thus, if B's car is stolen by T so that there is no consent of any kind by B to the transfer of the property and T sells the car to C then C does not get a good title, even though he takes in good faith and for value without knowledge of the theft. B can recover the car from C or sue T or C for damages under the tort of conversion. If, on the other hand, T obtains B's car by fraud as where he offers a cheque for the car and the cheque is not met, then if T subsequently sells the car to C, before B has rescinded the contract (*see* p. 295), C obtains a good title because B did consent to the transfer, though no doubt he afterwards regretted it.

Certain items of property referred to as negotiable instruments are capable of transfer with a good title even where the true owner does not consent in any way to the transfer. These items of property were created by the custom of merchants in years past but are now recognized by statute, i.e. the Bills of Exchange Act 1882 and the Cheques Act 1957.

Types of negotiable instruments

There are a number of different types of negotiable instruments. For example, bank notes, banker's drafts, dividend warrants and treasury bills are negotiable. However, we are concerned mainly with cheques and not so much with other bills of exchange or promissory notes which are only found in specialized areas of business. Cheques are to a large extent governed by the Bills of Exchange Act 1882, and all section references are, unless otherwise stated, to sections of that Act.

Negotiability following theft – a restricted concept

While it is true to say that the attribute of negotiability allows a person to obtain a good title to a negotiable instrument from a thief, the concept of negotiability after a theft is very restricted and applies in practice only to bearer bills. Before an instrument can be negotiated in such a way as to give the transferee a better title than the transferor it must be in a negotiable state. A bearer bill is in a negotiable state without endorsement. However, since most cheques are order cheques payable to (or to the order of) a particular person, they are not in a negotiable state unless they are endorsed. If, therefore, they are stolen, they can only be passed on without endorsement or by means of a forged endorsement and in both these instances the transferee will not get a good title even if he takes for value with no notice of defects in the title of the transferor.

For example, if T steals a bearer cheque from A and transfers it to B for value, B having no notice of the theft, then B's title will be good. If, however, the cheque was made payable to A, B's title will be incomplete because he will either take the cheque without an endorsement or as a result of T forging A's endorsement and in either event B's title will be affected adversely. A forged endorsement does not pass on the drawer's promise to pay 'to order' under s. 55 of the 1882 Act.

EXAMPLES OF USE OF BILLS AND CHEQUES

Bills of exchange

Bills of exchange are not frequently used now except in foreign trade. However, their two main uses are as follows.

(a) *A tripartite transaction with credit.* C. Jones Ltd in London has sold goods worth £1,000 to A. Ziegler in Amsterdam, payment to be in sterling. C. Jones Ltd owes £1,000 to C. Poutier in Paris. Jones draws a bill on Ziegler payable to Poutier.

£1,000   London 1 July 1991

     Three months after date pay to C. Poutier or order the sum of One Thousand Pounds, value received.

To A. Ziegler
Polskistraat, Amsterdam   C. Jones Ltd

     If Ziegler accepts, Poutier may keep the bill for three months and ask Ziegler to pay or he may discount it at a bank or endorse it over to pay a debt or, more likely, part of a debt which he owes to one of his creditors.

(b) *Solely to obtain credit.* A. Adams Ltd has sold goods to B. Brown Ltd. Adams Ltd wants prompt payment; Brown Ltd wants four months' credit. Adams draws a bill on Brown payable at four months which Brown accepts.

£300   London, 7 July 1991

     Four months after date pay to our order the sum of Three Hundred Pounds, value received.

To B. Brown Ltd
3 High Street, Barchester.   A. Adams Ltd

     Adams may discount the bill at a bank for a sum smaller than £300 depending upon the rate of interest because the bank will not get the money straightaway. This is taken into account in the price of the goods and the amount of the bill. The bank will wait four months and then obtain payment from Brown.

Cheques

A cheque is a bill of exchange, but the following differences should be noted:

(a) the drawee of a cheque is always a bank, and there is no need for a cheque to be accepted;
(b) a cheque is payable on demand (s. 73);
(c) there is no indication on the face of a cheque as to the date on which it is payable, but s. 10(1) of the Bills of Exchange Act 1882 says that a bill is payable on demand if no time is stated, and for this reason a cheque is payable on demand, unless post-dated. (The treatment of such cheques is further considered at p. 471.)

Barchester Bank Ltd, High Street Branch.   2 July 1991
Pay John Smith or order Two Hundred Pounds   £200.00
                                                             William Brown

In the example given above John Smith may cash the cheque at the Barchester Bank High Street Branch, since it is not crossed or pay it into his own bank for collection or endorse it over to someone else.

As we have seen, bills of exchange proper are used mainly in export transactions and as such have little relevance, except in that rather specialized field. In addition, many practitioners in the field of business will conclude their careers without ever having seen a promissory note, other than a bank note. For these reasons the rest of this chapter interprets legislation relating to negotiable instruments in terms of the cheque, referring to bills of exchange proper only where it is necessary in order to understand the law relating to cheques.

The usefulness of an action on a cheque

It should be borne in mind throughout this chapter that if a cheque is dishonoured then, unless it was a gift, e.g. a birthday present, the holder may at his option sue upon the cheque or upon the consideration, i.e. the underlying contract. Thus in a sale of goods, if the buyer gives the seller a cheque and that cheque is not met, the seller can sue either on the cheque or upon the contract of sale under which he is entitled to cash (legal tender).

It is advisable to sue upon the cheque (a) because it makes the debt certain – it is a promise to pay a sum certain in money; (b) the cheque provides good evidence of the promise to pay; and (c) the defendant to an action on a cheque may not normally set up a counter-claim. He must pay the cheque in full and bring a separate action if he has any complaint, e.g. about the quality of goods supplied in exchange for which he gave the cheque (*see Jade International Steel* v *Robert Nicholas (Steels)* (1978) at p. 460).

STATUTORY DEFINITION

A cheque is a bill of exchange drawn on a banker and payable on demand. As such it must comply with certain aspects of the definition of a bill of exchange. The definition given in the Bills of Exchange Act 1882, s. 3(1), is as follows.

> A bill of exchange is an unconditional order in writing, addressed by one person to another, signed by the person giving it, requiring the person to whom it is addressed to pay on demand or at a fixed or determinable future time a sum certain in money to or to the order of a specified person, or to bearer.

This definition must be analysed in some detail because any instrument which does not comply with the relevant aspects of it cannot be a cheque. If it is not, the concept of negotiability does not apply to it and certain protections given to bankers who pay out or collect instruments to or on behalf of persons who have no title would not apply.

Unconditional order

An order to pay is not a cheque if it is conditional on a certain event happening or a certain thing being done. Problems have arisen in the following areas.

Receipts on cheques

Some cheques contain a form of receipt together with a form of words indicating that it must be signed by the payee. If it appears that the instruction that the receipt must be signed is *directed to the banker*, the instrument is conditional and cannot be a cheque. If the instruction to sign the receipt is *addressed to the payee* and not the bank the cheque is an unconditional instrument.

However, bankers usually obtain an indemnity from customers having receipt forms on their cheques. This indemnity protects the bank if it incorrectly treats an instrument requiring a receipt as a cheque, although the bank should be protected by the Cheques Act 1957 (*see below*).

It should be noted that receipts on the backs of cheques are not common now because of s. 3 of the Cheques Act 1957, which provides that an unendorsed cheque which appears to have been paid by the banker on whom it is drawn is evidence of receipt by the payee of the sum payable by the cheque. In addition, where receipts are used they must, by reason of banking practice, carry a large 'R' on the face because bankers are not required to look for endorsements on cheques under the Cheques Act 1957. Furthermore, if an unconditional instrument was not regarded as a cheque a banker should still be protected by ss. 1, 4 and 5 of the Cheques Act 1957, since these sections protect a banker who collects an instrument which is not a cheque or pays an instrument which is not.

The following cases are relevant.

Bavins v London and South Western Bank Ltd [1900] 1 QB 270

In the course of this action, the Court of Appeal had to deal with an instrument in the form of a cheque given to the plaintiffs by the Great Northern Railway Co for work done. The instrument read as follows, 'The Great Northern Railway Company No. 1 Accountants drawing account London, 7 July 1898, the Union Bank of London Limited . . . Pay to J. Bavins Jnr and Sims the sum of Sixty-nine Pounds Seven Shillings, Provided the receipt form at the foot hereof is duly signed, stamped and dated £69 7s'. *Held* – that the instrument was not a cheque within the definition given by the Bills of Exchange Act 1882, because it was not an unconditional order. The bank was not to pay the instrument unless the receipt was signed.

Comment: In the above case the bank lost its protection because the instrument was not a cheque and had been collected by the bank for a person who had stolen it. The bank was liable in conversion to the true owner, Bavins.

Nathan v Ogdens Ltd (1906) 94 LT 126

In the course of this action the Court of Appeal was dealing with an instrument on the face of which were printed the words 'The receipt at the back hereof must be signed, which signature will be taken as an endorsement of the cheque.' *Held* – The order to pay was unconditional and therefore the cheque was valid. The words could be taken as addressed to the payee and not to the bank.

Special accounts

An order to pay out of a particular fund and that fund only is not unconditional. However, an unqualified order to pay coupled with an indication of a particular fund out of which the money is to come is unconditional (s. 3(3) of the 1882 Act). Thus a cheque is perfectly good although there is an indication on it that one particular account rather than another should be debited with the amount. Thus the cheque may, for example, be overstamped 'client account' or 'No. 2 account' but this will not render the cheque a conditional order provided it is clear that the payee is to be paid anyway, even if the particular account is not large enough.

Writing

The Act provides that 'writing' includes print (s. 2).

One person to another

The drawer and drawee are usually different persons, e.g. the customer (drawer) and a bank (drawee), but they may be the same person. The commonest example is a *banker's draft*. This is an order by the bank addressed to itself in favour, for example, of the vendor of property, the purchaser being the bank's customer whose account the bank has already debited. This kind of draft is, provided it is genuine and not forged, a safer method of payment from the vendor's point of view than a cheque signed only by the purchaser which may not be honoured. Under s. 5(2) such a draft is negotiable as a bill of exchange or promissory note.

Signature

A 'signature' is not defined in the Act but it would seem to permit a mechanically produced signature, and certainly a mark may be used if there is evidence that the person signing by mark habitually so signs. A bank will take an indemnity from a customer using cheques which bear a printed facsimile reproduction of an official signature.

Under s. 23(2) no person is liable as drawer, endorser or acceptor of a bill who has not signed it as such: provided that the signature of the name of a firm is equivalent to the signature by the person so signing of the names of all persons liable as partners in that firm. It is quite usual for a partner to sign on behalf of all the partners by writing the name of the partnership, e.g. 'Bloggs & Co'.

On demand

This is dealt with by s. 10(1) which provides, amongst other things, that a bill is payable on demand if no time for payment is stated. It has already been noted that a cheque contains no specific indication that it is payable on demand but is so payable by reason of this sub-section, unless post-dated.

Sum certain in money

This is dealt with by s. 9 and its main relevance in practice is where the words and figures on a cheque are different. In such a case the words prevail and are taken to be the sum payable. In practice, however, bankers usually return such cheques with the comment 'words and figures differ'.

To or to the order of a specified person

Sections 7 and 8 of the Act apply here and the main points arising are as follows.

(a) *Joint payees*. Payment may be to A and B (as joint payees) as where A and B are partners.

(b) *A cheque may be payable in the alternative to one of two or more payees*, e.g. 'Pay A or B'. This form is not usual in the UK, but in some jurisdictions, e.g. the USA, where married persons have had separate bank accounts for much longer than perhaps is the case in the UK, the alternative form is more common, e.g. a US public utility, such as a gas company, may in making a refund for an overpayment, send a cheque in the alternative form, payment being to the husband or wife. Either party can then pay that cheque into their own account as they decide.

(c) *Holders of offices*. A bill may also be payable to the holder of an office for the time being, e.g. 'The Treasurer of Barchester Football Club'.

(d) *Payments to wages or cash*. Instruments made out in a form 'pay wages' or 'pay cash' are not payable to a specified person and cannot be regarded as cheques. Such an instrument is not therefore negotiable but it is, under the Cheques Act 1957 a mandate to the bank concerned to pay unless countermanded. Thus, unless the instrument is countermanded by the drawer the bank may properly pay out on it and debit the drawer's account. **The following case illustrates this point**.

Orbit Mining and Trading Co Ltd v Westminster Bank [1962] 3 All ER 565
The plaintiff company had an account with the Midland Bank, and the cheques drawn on this account had to be signed by two directors. One of these directors, A, was often abroad and had been in the habit of signing cheque forms in blank before going abroad, assuming that the other director authorized to sign, B, would use the cheques only for trading purposes.

B added his signature to three cheque forms and inserted the word 'cash' between the printed words 'Pay' and 'or order' and passed cheques for collection to the Westminster Bank Ltd, where he had a private account. The Westminster Bank collected the sums due on the cheques and B used the money for his private purposes. The Westminster Bank did not know that B was connected with the plaintiff company and his signature on the cheques was, in any case, illegible. Each cheque form was crossed generally and was stamped 'for and on behalf of' the company' under which appeared the signatures of A and B. *Held* – The three instruments in this case were not cheques, but were documents issued by a customer of a banker intended to enable a person to obtain payment from the banker within s. 4(2) of the Cheques Act 1957, and since the bank had acted without negligence it was entitled to the protection of the Act in respect of the collection of an instrument to which the customer had no title.

Comment: This case decides that there is no duty upon a bank to keep itself continually up to date as to the identity of a customer's employers. In addition, the case is somewhat unusual in that the normal use of 'pay cash or order' instruments is to obtain cash over the counter and usually only when presented by the drawer or his known agent. They are rarely, if ever, paid into an account for collection. Nevertheless the court seems to have regarded the bankers as not being negligent in dealing with such a cheque in the way that they did.

'Or order' assumed

By s. 8 such directions on a bill as 'Pay C' or 'Pay C or order' all have the same meaning and amount to a direction to pay C or the person to whom the instrument is subsequently transferred. Therefore merely crossing out the words 'or order' does not render a cheque not transferable or not-negotiable.

Instruments marked 'not transferable'

By s. 8 these are valid as between the parties only. The same is true of an instrument which is drawn in favour of 'C only'. If such a cheque is endorsed by C to D then D cannot sue upon it. However, D will normally have an action on the underlying contract, e.g. a sale of goods, which gave rise to the transfer of the cheque.

Instruments marked 'not negotiable'

Where this appears on a cheque the result is that the *cheque is transferable* but subject to equities, i.e. to defects in title of previous holders. Thus a person who takes a cheque crossed 'not negotiable' does not acquire and cannot give a better title to it than that of the person from whom he received it.

'To bearer'

By the provisions of s. 8(3) a bearer cheque is a cheque payable to bearer or one on which the only or last endorsement is in blank. The following points should be noted.

(a) *Bearer cheques generally.* These do not require endorsement and are transferred by delivery. Bearer cheques can be converted into order cheques by an appropriate endorsement, e.g. 'Pay C or order', and converted back to bearer cheques again by an appropriate endorsement, e.g. the signature of the endorsee without more.

(b) *Non-existing payees.* Section 7(3) provides that where the payee is a non-existing person the cheque is to be treated as payable to bearer. Thus forged or unauthorized endorsements are irrelevant and a good title can pass under a forged or unauthorized endorsement to a bona fide third party who takes the instrument for value. The judicial interpretation of this section is as follows:

(i) The payee is *existing* when the drawer knows of him and intends that he should receive payment.

(ii) The payee is *non-existing* when the drawer does not know of him though a person with that name may exist.

The basis of the above provision is that the drawer is negligent when he signs a cheque in the non-existing payee situation, and a bona fide third party for value is protected against that negligence because the Act converts the cheque into a bearer bill to which a good title can pass, forged or unauthorized endorsements being irrelevant.

The following cases are relevant.

Vinden v Hughes [1905] 1 KB 795

A clerk persuaded the plaintiff, his employer, to draw cheques in favour of his actual customers by saying the employer owed money to them which he did not. The clerk then forged the customers' endorsements and negotiated the cheques to an innocent third party, who obtained payment from the firm's bankers. *Held* – These were existing payees and therefore order cheques and the defendants had no title because of the forged endorsements of the clerk.

Clutton v Attenborough & Son [1879] AC 90

A clerk persuaded his employers, Cluttons, who were land agents, to draw cheques in favour of a person called Brett by telling them that Brett had done work for the firm. The employers had never heard of Brett. The clerk then forged the endorsements and transferred the cheques to Attenboroughs who obtained payment on them. Cluttons sued Attenboroughs for the money they had received and it was *held* that since Brett was a non-existent payee the cheques were bearer cheques and Attenboroughs had received a good title to them and were not obliged to compensate Cluttons.

NEGOTIATION

Negotiation takes place where there is a transfer of a cheque from A to B in such a way as to make B the holder (s. 31).

In the case of a bearer cheque this is achieved by simple delivery and in the case of an order cheque by means of endorsement plus delivery. Thus the holder of a bearer cheque is the person in possession of it, even a thief, while the holder of an order cheque must be in possession of it either as payee or endorsee.

Restrictive endorsements

A restrictive endorsement makes the endorsee a holder, but for certain limited or restricted purposes only.

There are two types of restrictive endorsements as follows.

(a) Where further negotiation is prohibited, i.e. 'pay D only'. Cheques are seldom endorsed like this.
(b) Where negotiation is permitted but with mere authority to deal as directed, e.g. 'pay D for the account of Y' or 'Pay D or order for collection'. Examples of the use of the above restrictive endorsements are as follows.

    (i) X, the payee of a cheque, owes a debt to an overseas supplier, B, and wants to endorse the cheque to B's agent, A, who is in England but wishes to make it clear that A is not the beneficial owner of the cheque. X can endorse 'Pay A for the account of B'. A can now obtain payment but must then account to B, though A cannot transfer the bill.

    (ii) Suppose X is the payee of a cheque drawn on a German bank and wishes A, his German agent, to collect payment for him. X can endorse 'Pay A for collection' or 'Pay A or order for collection'. A can obtain payment but must then account to X who authorized him to collect. Where the words 'or order' are used, A can transfer the cheque to another person but such person cannot obtain a better title than A because A's ownership is restricted and these restrictions pass with the cheque. It is therefore unlikely that a cheque so endorsed would ever be taken, say, for goods supplied. The use of the words 'or order' might, however, be useful where A was known to have sub-agents and make collection through them. In these circumstances A may be given the power to endorse over to a particular sub-agent for collection.

Holder of a bill

It should be noted that a holder of a bill is *not necessarily the person who is legally entitled to it*. Thus a thief who steals a bearer cheque is a person in possession and therefore a holder, though obviously he has no title to the cheque and cannot sue upon it.

However, if he delivers it to D who takes in good faith and for value, then D will get a good title (s. 38(3)(a)). But if D knows of the theft and is not in good faith or does not give value or both, then his title is no better than the thief's.

This arises because where there is a 'defect' on the cheque as where, for example, it has been stolen or obtained by fraud or undue influence, then no one can sue upon it and obtain its face value unless he has taken it in good faith for value and without knowledge of previous defects (*see further* p. 460).

Holder for value: consideration

Section 27 deals with the matter of consideration sufficient to support a bill as follows.

(a) Section 27(1)(a) provides that any consideration sufficient to support a simple contract will support a bill of exchange. **The following case illustrates this point.**

Pollway Ltd v Abdullah [1974] 2 All ER 381

D contracted at an auction to purchase land from V. P, the auctioneer acting for V in the sale, signed the memorandum of the contract and, as agent for V, accepted D's cheque in payment of the ten per cent deposit. The payee named in the cheque was P. D wrongfully stopped the cheque and refused to pay the deposit, whereupon V exercised his right to treat the contract as repudiated. Was P a holder for value and able to enforce the cheque against D?

It was *held* by the Court of Appeal that P was the holder of the cheque within the Bills of Exchange Act 1882, s. 2. The consideration for the cheque was sufficient to support a simple contract. It was either (a) P's warranty of his authority to sign the memorandum on V's behalf and to receive the cheque, or (b) P's acceptance of a cheque in place of legal tender. Valuable consideration within the Bills of Exchange Act 1882, s. 27(1) having been given. P could enforce payment against D.

Comment: (i) In this case the vendors had not supplied consideration to the defendant because they had not gone on with the sale. The defendant had forfeited his deposit and the plaintiffs were the only ones who might have been in a position to claim consideration sufficient to enforce the cheque, which, in the event, the court *held* they had done. The cheque was, of course, also in the plaintiffs' name but if they had endorsed it over to the vendors this would not have enabled the vendors to sue because, as we have seen, they had not supplied consideration to the defendant.

(ii) The decision was vital to auction practice. Roskill J said that if the purchaser had not been liable to the auctioneer, no auctioneer could safely accept cheques at an auction.

(b) Section 27(1)(b) provides that a form of *past consideration*, i.e. an antecedent debt or liability, is enough. This is essential, particularly in the case of cheques, many of which are based on this form of past consideration. Thus if S sells goods to B a debt comes into being when the contract is made and S is entitled to be paid in legal tender (*see* p. 199), so that when B decides to pay S by cheque the cheque is based on a previous or antecedent debt or liability and is for past consideration. However, if in *Re McArdle* (1951) (*see* p. 33), Mrs McArdle had received a cheque from the estate she would not have succeeded in an action on the cheque because there was no antecedent debt or liability. In other words, there was no valid underlying contract at all.

(c) Section 27(2) provides that *consideration need not have moved from the holder* so that the doctrine of privity of contract does not apply. Therefore, if P signs a cheque in favour of Q for the price of goods sold by Q to P and Q endorses the cheque to R as a gift, R may not sue Q on the cheque, but he may sue P, since R is a holder for value to that extent under s. 27(2). As between immediate parties absence of consideration prevents an action on the bill.

Consideration must exist, but it is not essential that consideration has passed from one party to a cheque to another party on the *same* cheque. (*See* Diamond v Graham (1968) *below*.) But it must if the holder relies on past consideration (See *Oliver* v *Davis* (1949) below).

Diamond v Graham [1968] 2 All ER 909

A Mr Herman was anxious to borrow the sum of £1,650 for immediate commitments and he asked a Mr Diamond whether he would lend him that sum. Diamond agreed provided Herman could repay by the following Monday the sum of £1,665. Herman said that he would have a cheque from a Mr Graham by that time which he would ask to be made payable to Diamond. Diamond then drew a cheque for £1,650 in favour of Herman. Herman could not get a cheque from Graham on the following Monday because he was not available on that day. However, Herman presented the cheque for payment but Diamond countermanded payment and told the bank manager not to pay it until authorized by Diamond. Some days later Herman obtained a cheque from Graham in favour of Diamond. Graham asked who was providing Herman with temporary relief and was told it was the plaintiff. Mr Herman gave the cheque to Diamond who paid it into his bank and authorized payment of his cheque to Herman. However, the cheque drawn by Graham was dishonoured, Herman had also drawn a cheque in favour of Graham and this also was dishonoured, Diamond's cheque being the only one paid. Diamond now sued Graham on his unpaid cheque. The defendant argued that the plaintiff was not a holder for value within s. 27(2) of the Bills of Exchange Act 1882, because no value had passed between him and Graham. It was held by Danckwerts LJ that there was nothing in s. 27(2) which required value to be given by the holder of a cheque to the drawer so long as value had been given by someone. Here value had been given by Diamond when he released his cheque to Herman.

Thus, Diamond was a holder for value of the cheque and was entitled to judgment and the appeal must be dismissed. Diplock and Sachs LJJ also dismissed the appeal.

Comment: The plaintiff in this case gave consideration after the defendant's cheque was issued, i.e. he released his cheque to Herman.

Oliver v Davis and Another [1949] 2 All ER 353

On 18 July 1947, the plaintiff lent £350 to William Davis and received from him a cheque for

£400, post-dated to 8 August 1947. This was presented on 19 August 1947, and Davis was not able to meet it. Davis persuaded a Miss Marjorie Woodcock (he was 'engaged' to her sister although he was married) to draw a cheque for £400 in favour of the plaintiff, and an envelope containing this cheque, but without any covering letter, was left at the plaintiff's house.

The plaintiff was away at the time and returned on 22 August when he received Miss Woodcock's cheque but did not know who had sent it. Miss Woodcock, however, had discovered that Davis was a rogue and she informed the plaintiff within an hour or two of his receiving the cheque why she had sent it and also that she had stopped payment of it. On 23 August, the plaintiff presented Davis's cheque which was dishonoured and later presented Miss Woodcock's cheque which was returned marked 'Stopped by order of the drawer'. In an action by the plaintiff against Miss Woodcock, suing her on the cheque, the plaintiff relied amongst other things on s. 27(1)(b) of the Bills of Exchange Act 1882. Miss Woodcock contended that there was no consideration for the cheque. *Held* – An antecedent debt or liability within the meaning of s. 27(1)(b) was a debt or liability due from the maker or negotiator of the instrument and not from a third party. The plaintiff, therefore, could not rely on s. 27(1)(b) but must show consideration sufficient to satisfy a simple contract under s. 27(1)(a). This he could not do because he had not given her any promise, express or implied, to forbear in respect of any remedy he might have against Davis, nor had he changed his position for the worse in regard to his claim on Davis's cheque. There was no evidence of any consideration and the plaintiff's action failed.

Comment: In this case the plaintiff did nothing after Miss Woodcock's cheque was issued which could be regarded as amounting to consideration to Davis or Miss Woodcock. If, for example, he had said after receiving Miss Woodcock's cheque that he would not sue Davis, he might have provided consideration sufficient to enable him to enforce Miss Woodcock's cheque since forbearance to sue can amount to consideration.

Holder in due course

If there is no 'defect' on a cheque the holder can claim its full face value merely by being a holder for value within s. 27.

If there is a 'defect' on a cheque it is not enough to be a holder for value, and in order to claim its full face value the holder must show that he is either:

(a) a holder in due course under s. 29(1); or
(b) a person who has taken the bill through a holder in due course under s. 29(3).

Thus, if a cheque drawn in favour of C has been negotiated by C to D as a result of fraud or misrepresentation or duress or undue influence on D's part or for an illegal consideration, there is a 'defect' on the bill. Let us then suppose that D negotiates it for value to E. E will undoubtedly be a holder for value, but because there is a 'defect' on the cheque E can only take it free from the defect in the title of D and successfully sue on it if he is a holder in due course, which means amongst other things that he took it without notice of any defect in the title of D.

If it is established that E is a holder in due course then the defect is said to be 'cured' and E can sue the various parties to the cheque for its full face value. Further, if E subsequently negotiated the cheque to F, then even though F himself may not be a holder in due course because, say, he gave no value and/or had notice of the defect in the title of D, then provided F was not a party to any fraud or illegality affecting the cheque, he has all the rights of a holder in due course as regards the drawer and all endorsers prior to the holder in due course from whom he took the cheque (s. 29(3)). A person taking from F will not be a holder in due course unless he can satisfy the definition in s. 29(1) himself.

Section 29(3) is the most cogent illustration of the favoured position which the holder in due course occupies. If the subsection did not exist the holder in due course might be prejudiced, for in order to dispose of a cheque with a defect upon it, he would have to find a transferee who knew nothing of the irregularity. The subsection makes this unnecessary.

A modern example of the use of s. 29(3) is to be seen in the following case.

Jade International Steel v Robert Nicholas (Steels) [1978] 3 All ER 104

Jade sold steel to Nicholas and drew a bill of exchange on Nicholas payable after 120 days. Nicholas accepted the bill and returned it to Jade. Jade discounted it with their bankers who became holders in due course. The bank presented the bill to Nicholas who dishonoured it because they said the steel supplied by Jade was substandard. The bank then debited Jade's account and passed the bill to Jade. Jade were not holders in due course when they received the bill from the bank because they took the bill after dishonour and with notice of same, but they were holders in due course under s. 29(3) of the Bills of Exchange Act 1882 because they took from a holder in due course, i.e. the bank, and so judgment was given for Jade on the bill and the counter-claim by Nicholas could not be admitted against Jade in this action because Jade were holders in due course who had overcome defects on the bill. Nicholas would have to pursue a separate action for a reduction of price in a subsequent claim.

Comment: It will be noted that here the defect was substandard goods and not fraud or illegality.

Holder in due course: definition

Section 29(1) provides that a holder in due course is a holder who has taken a cheque, complete and regular on the face of it, under the following conditions; namely:

> that he became the holder of it before it was overdue and without notice that it had been previously dishonoured if such was the fact; that he took the cheque in good faith and for value; and that at the time that the cheque was negotiated to him he had no notice of any defect in the title of the person who negotiated it to him.

This important definition is analysed as follows.

(a) *Complete and regular on the face of it.* If someone takes a cheque which is lacking or defective in any material particular, e.g. as where the amount or the payee's name is omitted or appears to have been materially altered, or the endorsement and the payee's name do not match, he cannot be a holder in due course.

(b) *Before it was overdue*. A bill payable on demand is deemed to be overdue when it appears on the face of it to have been in circulation for an unreasonable length of time. What is an unreasonable length of time for this purpose is a question of fact (s. 36(3)). In the case of a cheque and in the absence of special circumstances, 10 days or so would normally be held to be the limit (Paget's *Law of Banking*).

If a cheque is overdue it is still valid and can be transferred but the transferee obtains no better title than the transferor since no one can be a holder in due course after a bill is overdue.

The rules relating to overdue cheques should be distinguished from those which relate to out-of-date cheques which a bank will not pay.

(c) *Without notice that it had previously been dishonoured if such was the fact*. If a cheque is dishonoured by non-payment a subsequent holder can only be a holder in due course if he had no notice of the dishonour. Subsequent holders with notice of dishonour take the bill subject to defects in title at the time of dishonour (s. 36(5)).

It would be difficult for an endorsee to suggest that he had taken a dishonoured cheque without notice. Cheques are dishonoured for two main reasons as follows:

(i) that the drawer has no funds in the sense of cash in his account or an agreed overdraft; or

(ii) that the drawer has stopped payment.

In each case the bank will return the cheque to the holder marked 'refer to drawer'. If the cheque was then put back into circulation by the holder and endorsed over to another person, the endorsee could hardly claim that he had no notice of dishonour and therefore would not be a holder in due course.

(d) *For value*. A holder in due course must give value *himself*, but as we have seen past consideration in the form of an antecedent debt or liability is enough.

(e) *In good faith and without notice of any defect in the title of the person who negotiated it*. Notice means actual knowledge or wilful disregard of the means of knowledge.

The original payee of an order cheque cannot be a holder in due course because the cheque is *issued* to him and not *negotiated* to him, and the concept of holder in due course arises only when the cheque is negotiated by the payee to the first endorsee who may be a holder in due course.

Thus if the fraud of X causes A to draw a cheque in favour of C, A has a good defence to a claim by C, though C is innocent of X's fraud. A would not, however, have a good defence to a claim on the cheque made by any subsequent holder of it provided he had no knowledge of the fraud and was in all other respects a holder in due course.

The following cases illustrate the relevant rules.

Arab Bank Ltd v Ross [1952] I All ER 709

The plaintiffs claimed to be holders in due course of two promissory notes made by Ross and payable to 'Fathi and Faysal Nabulsy Company', a firm of which the two men named were the only partners. Ross alleged that he had been induced to make the notes by the fraud of the payees, and attempted unsuccessfully to show that the plaintiffs had knowledge of this fraud and had not taken the notes in good faith. The plaintiffs claimed to be holders in due course, but the point was taken that the endorsement on the notes was simply 'Fathi and Faysal Nabulsy' with the omission of the word 'Company'. Held – by the Court of Appeal – that an endorsement could be valid to pass the property without being regular on the face of it. Regularity is different from validity. The Arab Bank were not holders in due course, because the endorsement was not regular, but were holders for value. Although the endorsers were in fact the only two partners, the word Company did not imply this, and therefore the endorsement was not manifestly regular by reference only to the instrument. The circumstances under which an endorsement gives rise to doubt is a practical matter and is best answered by the practice of bankers. This practice insists that the endorsement shall correspond exactly with the payee as named.

Sheffield (Earl) v London Joint Stock Bank (1888) 13 App Cas 333

A moneylender advanced money to clients on the security of negotiable instruments. The moneylender deposited these instruments with the defendant bank as security for the loan of a higher amount than he himself had advanced to his clients. The bank knew the nature of the moneylender's business and that he was in the habit of lending money on such securities. The moneylender became bankrupt. The House of Lords held that the bank was not a holder in due course of the instruments because it had knowledge of facts which were calculated to be had on inquiry as to the moneylender's authority to deal with the instruments. In the result the bank had no better title to the instruments than the moneylender, and upon payment to the bank by the moneylender's clients of the money he had lent them the bank had to give up the instruments.

Jones (R E) Ltd v Waring & Gillow [1926] AC 670

A fraudulent person named Bodenham was indebted to Waring & Gillow in the sum of £5,000 which he could not pay. He went to the plaintiffs and said that he was an agent for International Motors' new car the Roma, but they would have to take 500 cars and pay a deposit of £5,000. The plaintiffs were interested in the deal but did not wish to pay Bodenham or International Motors because they did not know these parties. Bodenham then said that Waring & Gillow were the real backers and asked the plaintiffs to make out a cheque for £5,000 to them, which the plaintiffs did. Waring & Gillow received payment of the cheque and when the fraud was discovered the plaintiffs sought to recover their money from Waring & Gillow. The House of Lords held that the plaintiffs succeeded because the money was paid under a mistake of fact and that the original payee of a bill of exchange is not a holder in due course.

The effect of a forged or unauthorized endorsement

By s. 24 a *forged endorsement* is wholly inoperative and no title passes even to a person who would in other circumstances be a holder in due course. However, there may be rights against those taking after the forgery by reason of s. 55(2).

Suppose a cheque is drawn by X in favour of C and endorsed by C to D. It is then stolen from D by a thief who forges D's endorsement and negotiates the cheque to E who endorses it to F, who endorses it to G. G has no knowledge of the forgery and in all respects complies with the definition of a holder in due course in s. 29. G has no title to the cheque because it rests on a forgery. He cannot, therefore, sue D or C, but he has rights against E or F by virtue of s. 55(2). When E endorsed the cheque to F he impliedly guaranteed that it was a valid cheque and that the signatures of the drawer and previous endorsers were valid signatures; F made a guarantee to the same effect when he endorsed the cheque to G. In the result, because one of the earlier endorsements (D's) was forged, E is liable for the amount of the cheque to G or if G chooses to claim it from F, E is then liable to indemnify F. A forged endorsement does not pass on the guarantees.

If X stops the cheque then he must give D another cheque or settle with him otherwise X is unjustly enriched. He has had goods and has not paid. G and F may sue E and get payment. E must sue the thief on the underlying contract.

If the cheque is not stopped and G obtains payment then there is no need for G to sue F or E. D has sold goods to C and has not been paid, but the risk of the loss of the cheque is his. X has received goods from C but has paid and is not unjustly enriched, so that the only claim is by D against the thief for conversion of the cheque.

The only proviso to the above rule is if the party against whom it is sought to enforce payment of the bill is precluded (i.e. estopped) from setting up the forgery or lack of authority (see *Greenwood* v *Martins Bank* (1933) at p. 475).

The position is the same where the *endorsement is unauthorized* as where an agent endorses a cheque made payable to his principal for and on behalf of that principal although he has no authority to do so.

It should be noted, however, that an unauthorized signature may be ratified. Thus, if a cheque is made payable to a company and a clerk in the company's employ without authority endorses the cheque on behalf of the company to a creditor of the company, and, where, say, the company disputes the debt or the debt is not yet due, then the creditor has no title to the cheque, but the company can ratify the unauthorized endorsement and the creditor (the endorsee) could then sue the company on the cheque. If the clerk had endorsed the cheque over to his private creditors to clear his own debts, the company would not normally wish to ratify his acts but could not do so in any case because the law does not allow ratification of a forgery or fraud.

Negotiation of a bearer cheque

Since a bearer cheque can be transferred without endorsement, the person who transfers it does not give the 'guarantees' of an endorser under s. 55(2) in regard to the validity of the cheque. Instead s. 58 of the Act applies to the transferor of a bearer cheque who is called a transferor by delivery and under s. 58 warrants to his immediate transferee being a holder for value, *and him alone*:

(a) that the cheque is valid,
(b) that he has the right to transfer it, and
(c) that he is not aware at the time of the transfer that it has become valueless, e.g. as where payment has been stopped.

Thus if a bearer cheque apparently drawn by A is negotiated to B who negotiates it to C, who negotiates it to D, then if A's signature is forged D cannot sue A on it, nor can he sue B or C on the cheque. He can only sue C for breach of warranty. C has an action against B and could join him as defendant in any action which D brought against him.

Order cheques transferred without endorsement

If an order cheque is transferred without endorsement the transferee for value is merely an equitable assignee (s. 31(4)). Thus, if D transfers an order cheque without endorsement to E, E would have to join D in any action on the cheque and could not sue in his own name. Under s. 39 of the Supreme Court Act 1981, D could be required to endorse by the court and if he will not do so the court can appoint someone else to do it in his stead. Often the court order directs that the transferee, E, may sign the endorsement.

Delivery

Section 21(1) provides that every contract on a cheque, whether it be the drawer's or an endorser's, is incomplete and revocable until delivery of the instrument. Thus, where an endorsement or other signature is required the mere fact that a signature is placed upon the instrument is not enough; there must also be delivery, which would not be the case where an order instrument was stolen after endorsement. The endorser must deliver it. However, there are certain presumptions of delivery as follows:

(a) Under s. 21(2) valid delivery by all prior parties is *conclusively* presumed in favour of a holder in due course but not if the bill is inchoate (or incomplete) (*see below*).
(b) Under s. 21(3) valid delivery is presumed *until the contrary is proved* in the case of other holders.

Thus presumption of valid delivery cannot be disproved against a holder in due course but it may be as regards other holders.

Inchoate cheques

These are cheques lacking in some material particular(s) such as the names of the parties other than the drawer and the amount of the cheque. Problems arise from completion of the cheque in excess of authority given by the drawer. Section 20 applies and requires 'delivery by the signer in order that it may be converted into a bill'. The law does not presume delivery under s. 21 because two elements are required:

(a) delivery, and
(b) the intention in the signer that the order be converted into a bill.

Thus, if A signs a cheque form and does not complete it and it is stolen from his desk and filled in, A is under no liability to anyone on his signature, not even to a holder in due course, because he did not deliver it *in order that it might be converted into a bill*.

However, if A signs a blank cheque and gives it to his gardener to buy a lawn mower and the gardener fills it in and pays a private debt, then A would be liable to a holder in due course because he did deliver it with the intention that it should be converted into a bill. The gardener's lack of authority is a 'defect' so far as a holder for value is concerned and A would not be liable to him.

It has already been noted that a payee cannot be a holder in due course (*see Jones v Waring & Gillow* (1926) at p. 462) so that the private creditor of the gardener would not be able to sue A because, being the payee, he would only be a holder for a value. However, an endorsee from the private creditor could sue A if the cheque had been passed on in that way. However, an original payee may rely on the doctrine of estoppel. Thus in *Lloyds Bank* v *Cooke* [1907] 1 KB 794, Cooke signed his name on a blank promissory note and gave it to another person with authority to complete it for £250 payable to the plaintiffs as security for an advance made by them. The other person completed it for £1,000 and took the balance for himself. It was *held* that although the bank were payees and not holders in due course, Cooke was liable to them by estoppel. He had held out the other party as having authority.

DUTIES OF A HOLDER

Cheques must be presented within a reasonable time:

(a) of *issue* in order to make the *drawer* liable;
(b) of *endorsement* to make the *endorser* liable (s. 45(2)).

Bankers usually return a cheque marked 'out of date' or 'stale' if it bears a date more than six months prior to presentation.

Notice of dishonour

Where a cheque is dishonoured by non-payment, the holder must give notice to prior endorsers (but not the drawer) otherwise they will be discharged. However, it is likely that if the holder only gives notice to his immediate endorser that endorser will give notice to prior parties and it will be passed back in this way.

Furthermore, it should be noted that under s. 49(3) 'notice of dishonour operates for the benefit of all subsequent holders and all prior endorsers who have a right of recourse against the party to whom notice was given'. Thus, let us assume that on a cheque B is the drawer and C is the payee. Let us now assume that C has negotiated the cheque to D, D to E, and E to F. Suppose that F is the holder at the time of dishonour and that he gives notice to E and to C but not to D. The result would be that F could claim on E and C because he gave notice. E could claim on C by reason of s. 49(3), being a prior endorser who had a right of recourse against C. Finally, endorsers subsequent to F can also claim on E and C by reason of F's notice to them being subsequent holders. Furthermore, D can sue C because he is a prior endorser who has a right of recourse against C.

Form

Notice may be given in writing or orally and the return of a dishonoured cheque to an endorser is deemed sufficient notice.

Time for giving notice

Notice may be given as soon as the cheque is dishonoured (but not before) or within a reasonable time thereafter. As regards what is reasonable time, s. 49(12) provides that notice will not have been deemed given within a reasonable time unless:

(a) where the parties live in the *same place* notice must have been given or sent off so that it arrives on the day after the dishonour of the cheque;

(b) where the parties live in *different places* notice was sent off on the day after the dishonour or if there is no post on that day then by the next post thereafter.

There is no definition of the word 'place' in the Act but it is suggested by Chalmers on *Bills of Exchange* that it means postal district.

It should be noted that the endorsers receiving notice have the same time in which to pass it on to other endorsers whose names appear on the cheque. If the notice of dishonour is properly addressed and posted it is deemed to have been given although it miscarried in the post and arrived late (s. 49(15)).

The following case deals with notice of dishonour.

Eaglehill Ltd v J Needham (Builders) Ltd [1972] 3 All ER 895

The plaintiffs were holders for value of a bill of exchange for £7,660 drawn by the defendants and accepted by Fir View Furniture Co payable at a certain bank. The bill became due and payable on 31 December 1970 but prior to that date Fir View Furniture Co went into liquidation. By mistake the plaintiffs posted their notice of dishonour dated 1 January 1971 on 30 December 1970 and it arrived at Fir View Furniture Co's office on 31 December. The Court of Appeal *held* that the notice was not subsequent to the dishonour within the Bills of Exchange Act 1882 and was therefore invalid. On appeal by the plaintiffs it was *held* – by the House of Lords allowing the appeal – that a notice of dishonour was given when it was received, i.e. when it was opened in the ordinary course of business, or would have been if the ordinary course of business had been followed. Provided that notice is received after dishonour it is valid regardless of when it is sent off. The notice was valid and the plaintiffs' action succeeded.

Excuses for non-notice and delay

The relevant rules are as follows:

(a) *Delay*. This is excused by circumstances beyond the control of the person giving notice so long as the delay was not caused by his misconduct or negligence. Thus the existence of a postal strike or civil disturbance could provide circumstances beyond the control of the sender excusing him for delay. When the reason for delay is over notice must be given with reasonable diligence (s. 50(1)).

(b) *Non-notice – endorser*. If after the exercise of due diligence the holder cannot give notice then notice is excused. Once again this assumes the situation of a civil disturbance or postal strike. In addition notice may be waived either expressly *where* the particular party to whom notice is being given has said that he does not require it, or has in the past waived notice, thus setting up a course of dealing (s. 50(2)(a) and (b)).

(c) *Non-notice – drawer*. Notice to the drawer of a cheque need not be given because dishonour normally results from his lack of funds or countermand and the 1882 Act excuses notice being given if dishonour is for these reasons (s. 50(2)(c)).

DISCHARGE OF A CHEQUE

A cheque or one or more of the parties thereto may be discharged as follows.

Payment

In most cases a cheque is discharged when it is paid by a bank on which it is drawn to a holder who is entitled to the cheque.

Where payment is made to a thief the bank will be protected (*see* p. 484) if it acts in good faith without negligence and in the ordinary course of business. The drawer or endorser will not be liable provided the cheque reached the party from whom it was stolen.

Cancellation

Cancellation takes place where a holder crosses out the signature of a party and writes 'cancelled' on the cheque or burns it. The cancellation must be apparent, intentional, and not by mistake or by an agent without authority (s. 63(1)). Any party may be discharged by cancellation. If an endorser's signature is cancelled, subsequent endorsers are also discharged (s. 63(2)).

An unintentional or mistaken cancellation or one made without authority is inoperative, but if it is apparent on the bill then the burden of proving that the cancellation was unintentional, mistaken or without authority is on the party who alleges that it was so made (s. 63(3)).

Material alteration

The results of this depend upon whether the alteration is apparent or not, as follows.

(a) *Apparent alteration.* If the material alteration is apparent then the cheque may be totally avoided except against the person who made the alteration and subsequent endorsers (s. 64)). For example, suppose that A draws a cheque for £100 in favour of C and C endorses it to D who alters it to £1,000 before endorsing it to E, who in turn endorses it to F. If the alteration is apparent the cheque is avoided except as against D and E. Only these two can be sued for £1,000 by F.

Such a cheque would not be paid by a bank but actions between the parties to the cheque would be affected by the above rules.

(b) *Non-apparent alteration.* If the alteration cannot be ascertained by reasonable scrutiny all the parties can retain some liability, at least to a holder in due course. C and A would be liable up to £100 to F or to E if F had sued E for £1,000. Such a cheque would be paid by the bank and the bank would normally be able to debit the customer's account, since such an alteration could only arise from the customer's negligence in drawing the cheque (*see further* p. 474).

The following alterations to a cheque are regarded as material:

(i) to the date;

(ii) to the sum payable.

Limitation Act 1980

Actions on a cheque are barred after six years from the time when the action accrued.

As regards the accrual of an action, this is six years from dishonour as regards the drawer and notice of dishonour as regards endorsers.

CAPACITY

The general law of contract applies and capacity to incur liability as a party to a cheque is co-extensive with a capacity to contract (s. 22).

If a limited company, therefore, acts *ultra vires* in drawing a particular cheque, it is not bound, but a company incorporated for the purposes of trade does have implied authority to make itself liable as a party to a cheque because such a power is clearly incidental to the performance of its objects.

A minor will never be liable on a cheque even though he might have been liable on the transaction giving rise to it. Thus a minor cannot be made liable on a cheque drawn by him in payment for necessaries. However, the seller could sue the minor in quasi-contract for a reasonable price.

If a cheque is drawn or endorsed by a minor or by a corporation having no capacity to incur liability on the cheque, the drawing or the endorsement is effective for all purposes except to make the minor or corporation liable.

In consequence the holder can proceed against any other party. Suppose, for example, a cheque is drawn by A on his bank in favour of C who is a minor. C endorses the cheque to D in return for goods sold by D to C. A stops payment of the cheque. D has no right to sue C but C's endorsement was effective to transfer the title in the cheque to D so D has a right of action on the cheque against A. If a minor draws a cheque his bank has the same right to debit his account on paying the holder as if the drawer were an adult.

GRADED QUESTIONS

Essay mode

1. In relation to a bill of exchange, explain:
   (a) the meaning of the expression 'holder in due course'; and
   (b) the various ways in which a bill may be indorsed.
   (The Institute of Chartered Secretaries and Administrators. English Business Law. December 1989.)

2. (a) What is a bill of exchange?
   (b) Giving your reasons, state whether documents containing the following wording are valid bills of exchange (assuming that in each case they comply with all other statutory requirements).
   (i) 'Pay on demand £25,000 to either Arnold Baines or Cedric Davies and debit the company's No. 2 Account.'
   (ii) 'I hereby authorize you to pay on my account to the order of Ernest Frank £8,000.'

(iii) 'At 60 days after acceptance pay George Harvey £5,500.'
(The Institute of Company Accountants. Law Relating to Business. May 1990)

3. (a) Define a holder in due course.
   (b) Which, if any, of the following rank as a holder in due course:
       (i)   the payee of an order cheque?
       (ii) a person who has received an order cheque bearing a valid endorsement as a birthday present?
   (c) When is it important for a holder of a cheque to prove that he is a holder in due course? *(Author's question)*

Objective mode

1. (a) A holder for value must always have given value himself for the cheque.
                                                                      True/False

   (b) Where value has at any time been given for a cheque the holder of it is deemed to be a holder for value as regards all parties to the bill who became parties before value was given.   True/False

2. What is a holder who takes a cheque free from any defects in the title of previous holders known as? _____

3. X draws a cheque payable to Z. S steals the cheque from X, forges Z's endorsement and negotiates the cheque to T.
   T has no title to the cheque and it still belongs to Z.   True/False

4. X gives Y a blank cheque so that Y can purchase for X a lawnmower up to, but not in excess of £40 in value. Y fills in the cheque for £50 and inserts his own name. He then negotiates it to Z, a holder in due course:

   (a) Z can sue X for £50.   True/False
   (b) Z can sue X for only £40.   True/False
   (c) Z cannot recover any money from X.   True/False

5. William Brown is in business as 'William Brown & Co' and he endorses a cheque made out in favour of the business by signing 'Brown'. He then delivers the cheque to Green. Brown's title is defective but Green claims a good title as a holder in due course. He cannot be a holder in due course.   True/False

Answers to questions set in objective mode appear on p. 551.

18 | Banker and customer

The OBJECTIVES of this chapter are to deal with the legal ramifications of the banking operation. A study of negotiable instruments invariably requires some knowledge of banking law. Banks deal with millions of cheques each year and the ramifications of that operation must be studied, at least in outline, by those involved in business.

CHEQUES AND RELATIONSHIP OF BANKER AND CUSTOMER

Definition

Section 73 of the 1882 Act defines a cheque as 'a bill of exchange drawn on a banker payable on demand'.

Thus a post-dated cheque, i.e. a cheque dated later than the date of its issue, is not in the strict sense a cheque at all but operates as a bill of exchange. However, under s. 13(2) the cheque is not invalid merely because it is post-dated. However, if the banker pays before the date given on the cheque he cannot debit the drawer's account until the date arrives and not then if the drawer has countermanded payment.

In practice even though a banker may pay a post-dated cheque in law, if a post-dated cheque is presented for payment it will be returned 'post-dated'. The banker will not pay it or hold it until the due date or hold funds for it and he is under no duty to do so.

Differences between cheques and other bills

The provisions of the 1882 Act applicable to bills of exchange payable on demand apply to cheques. However, there are certain important differences between cheques and other bills. These are as follows.

(a) The drawee of a cheque is always a banker and therefore a cheque is never accepted.

(b) The holder of a cheque has no rights against the banker himself if the cheque is not paid. Instead he must pursue his remedies against the drawer or any endorser.

(c) Notice of dishonour is not required in order to render the drawer of a cheque liable on it. This is because non-payment usually results from the fact that the drawer has no funds or has countermanded the cheque and s. 50(2)(c) excuses notice of dishonour being given in those cases. However, notice to an endorser is necessary to make him liable.

(d) Crossings are instructions to a banker and do not apply to bills of exchange, though they are of course used on cheques A 'not negotiable' crossing affects endorsees and is not addressed to the banker.

(e) Considerable protection is given to a banker in respect of payment out on a forged or unauthorized endorsement. Such protection is not given to the acceptor of a bill who is liable if he pays out on forged or unauthorized endorsements (*see further* p. 484).

Mutual duties of banker and customer

The relationship is basically that of debtor and creditor and demand for repayment is necessary before there is an enforceable debt. However, time under the Limitation Act 1980 does not begin to run against a customer until he has made the demand for repayment and it has been rejected. Thus, if A deposited £500 with his bank in a current account in 1980 and up to the present has not written any cheques on that account, the banker is not excused from paying the money on the grounds that the deposit was made more than six years ago. However, if a cheque is drawn on the account and the banker refuses to pay it, then the customer must take action against the bank within six years, otherwise the debt will be statute barred. The relationship of banker and customer is not that of principal and agent, so that the banker can do what he likes with the customer's money, subject to his willingness to repay a like sum.

However, the relationship goes in some respects beyond the ordinary creditor–debtor situation as follows.

The banker must obey his customer's mandate

Thus, a bank has no right to debit a customer's account for the amount of a cheque on which the customer's signature has been forged because the bank has then no mandate from the customer to pay. However, the customer may be estopped in some cases from denying the validity of his signature and in these circumstances the bank may debit his account (*see Greenwood* v *Martins Bank Ltd* [1933] AC 51 where G knew his wife was forging his signature but said nothing).

Generally, *knowledge* by the customer of the forgery is required if an estoppel is to be successfully raised by the bank. In the USA an estoppel can be raised where the customer fails to examine and draw inferences from his bank statements on which the forged cheques are recorded. However, McNeill J refused to bring UK law into line on this in *Wealden Woodlands (Kent) Ltd* v *National Westminster Bank Ltd, The Times*, 12 March 1983. In that case cheques drawn on the plaintiffs' account required the signature of two directors. One director got money from the company's account by forging the signature of another director. The court *held* that the plaintiffs were not estopped from making a claim against the bank even though they might have discovered the fraud by diligent examination of the company's bank statements. They had not discovered the fraud in this way and the court *held* they could not be regarded as negligent because they had not done so.

The case of *Tai Hing Cotton Mill Ltd* v *Liu Chong Hing Bank Ltd* [1985] 2 All ER 947 is also of interest. In that case an accounts clerk employed by a company which was a customer of three banks forged the signature of the company's managing director on some 300 cheques to the value of 5.5m Hong Kong dollars. He presented the cheques as appropriate to the three banks and they debited the company's current account with the amounts. The clerk's fraudulent activities lasted five years and were only discovered when a newly-appointed accountant began reconciling bank statements with the company's books.

The company sued the banks, claiming that the money was wrongly debited to the company's current account. The case eventually came to the Privy Council which decided that the company succeeded; the bank had no right to debit the cheques.

A customer of a bank owes a well-known duty of care to the bank not to draw cheques in such a way as to assist fraud (*see London Joint Stock Bank Ltd* v *Macmillan & Arthur* (1918) *below*), and a duty to tell the bank of any forgery of cheques if and when he becomes aware of it (*see Greenwood* v *Martins Bank Ltd* (1933) *above*). There is no wider duty.

A customer has apparently no duty to take reasonable care in the running of his business to prevent forged cheques being presented for payment and is not under a duty to check bank statements in order to see whether there are any unauthorized debit entries. It will be recalled that if a bank pays out on cheques which are forged it acts outside its mandate and cannot debit the customer's account. As Lord Scarman said in the *Tai Hing* case: 'This is a risk of the service which it is their business to offer.'

It should also be noted that if a bank pays a cheque on which the signature of its customer as drawer has been forged the bank can sue the person to whom payment was made for restitution of the amount paid out for the money with which payment was made was the property of the bank. A paying bank merely by paying a cheque on which its customer's signature has been forged does not thereby represent that the signature is genuine so as to estop itself from recovering the money paid to the recipient in quasi-contract (*National Westminster Bank Ltd* v *Barclays Bank International Ltd* [1974] 3 All ER 834).

Furthermore, the bank has no right to debit a customer's account where the mandate requires two signatures and only one signature in fact has been used.

It should also be noted that if the bank's failure to pay in accordance with its customer's mandate is caused by the customer's negligence, the bank is entitled to debit the customer's account with the cheque.

The following cases illustrate the rules set out above.

Ligget (Liverpool) Ltd *v* Barclays Bank [1928] I KB 48

In this case a bank which had been mandated by a company to pay cheques when drawn by two directors, paid a cheque drawn by one director only. It was *held* that the bank had exceeded its mandate and was entitled to debit the company's account only because the cheque was issued to pay a genuine debt of the company and so in equity the bank was entitled to be subrogated, i.e. stand in the shoes of the creditor whose debt had been discharged.

London Joint Stock Bank Ltd *v* Macmillan and Arthur [1918] AC 777

Macmillan and Arthur were customers of the bank and entrusted their clerk with the duty of filling in cheques for signature. The clerk presented a cheque to a partner for signature, drawn in favour of the firm or bearer, and made out for £2 0s 0d in figures but with no sum written in words. The clerk then easily altered the figures to £120 0s 0d and wrote 'one hundred and twenty pounds' in words, presenting the cheque to the bank and obtaining £120 in cash. The firm contended that the bank could only debit them with £2; the bank alleged negligence on the part of the firm. *Held* – by the House of Lords – that the relationship of banker and customer imposes a special duty of care on the customer in drawing cheques. A cheque is a mandate to the banker to pay according to the tenor. The customer must exercise reasonable care to prevent the banker being misled. If he draws a cheque in a manner which facilitates fraud, he is guilty of a breach of duty between himself and the banker, and he will be responsible to the banker for any loss sustained by the banker as a natural and direct consequence of this breach of duty. If the cheque is drawn in such a way as to facilitate or almost to invite an increase in the amount by forgery if the cheque should get into the hands of a dishonest person, forgery is not a remote but a very natural consequence of such negligence. The bank could, therefore, debit Macmillan and Arthur with the full £120 0s 0d.

Slingsby *v* District Bank [1931] 2 KB 588

The executors of an estate drew a cheque payable to John Prust & Co but left a space between the payee's name and the printed words 'or order'. A fraudulent solicitor named Cumberbirch wrote 'per Cumberbirch and Potts' after the payee's name. He then endorsed the cheque and received payment. *Held* – There was no negligence on the part of the executors; it was not a usual precaution to draw lines before or after the name of the payee and the executors were entitled to recover the amount of the cheque from the bank.

Comment: If the precaution of filling in the gap after the payee's name is more usual now than in 1931, then a present-day court may not follow *Slingsby* because the question of what is usual is purely one of evidence.

As regards joint accounts in, *Brewer* v *Westminster Bank* [1952] 2 All ER 650 McNair J decided that in the case of a joint account, the bank's duties were owed to the account holders *jointly* and not *severally*. The result of this decision was that where one account holder forged the other's signature on cheques drawn on the account and then added his own signature, the innocent account holder had no action against the bank.

However, in *Jackson* v *White and Midland Bank Ltd* [1967] 2 Lloyd's Rep 68 where one joint account holder forged the signature of the other, Park J declined to follow *Brewer*'s case *holding* that where there was a joint account with, say, A and B, the bank in effect agreed with A and B *jointly* that it would honour cheques signed by them both and with A *separately* that it would not honour cheques unless signed by him, and with B *separately* that it would not honour cheques unless signed by him. Thus where the bank honours a cheque on which B has forged A's signature, A should be able to sue the bank because it is in breach of the separate agreement with him. The reasoning in *Jackson*'s case seems to be more satisfactory and makes better commercial sense.

It was applied in *Catlin* v *Cyprus Finance Corporation (London) Ltd* [1983] 1 All ER 809. Mr and Mrs Catlin had a joint deposit account with the defendants. Withdrawals required the written instructions of them both. They separated in 1972. At that time there was £21,642 in the account. In 1975 the bank let Mr Catlin take various sums from the account on his signature alone. Mrs Catlin eventually discovered this. The account then stood at £897. Mrs Catlin claimed against the bank for the money withdrawn on the grounds that they had failed to observe the mandate. Mr Catlin was not joined in the action, either as co-plaintiff or co-defendant. Could Mrs Catlin succeed on her own? Bingham J preferred the type of reasoning in *Jackson*. Therefore Mrs Catlin succeeded in her claim. The judge said, among other things: 'The duty could, in theory, have been owed jointly, but in my mind, to make sense has to be owed severally. The only possible purpose of requiring two signatures is to obviate the possibility of independent action by one account holder to the detriment of the other. A duty on the bank which could only be performed jointly with Mr Catlin would be worthless to Mrs Catlin in practical terms and would deprive her of any remedy.' Thus joint account holders also have separate actions against the bank.

Where there is a joint account between husband and wife and under the mandate either party can sign cheques, the bank may, if it is put on notice that the parties have separated or are about to separate, insist that both signatures appear on cheques. This would prevent either party emptying the account without the agreement of the other. The bank's power to do this seems dubious in law in view of the 'one signature' mandate.

A banker must honour his customer's cheques

A bank is bound to honour its customer's cheques to the extent that the customer is in credit or to the extent of any agreed overdraft.

If a cheque is 'referred to drawer' although the customer is in funds or has an agreed overdraft the matter is treated as follows.

(a) If the customer is in business or practice as a professional it is assumed that his creditworthiness has been affected and damages will be awarded without proof of actual loss. Thus in *Davidson* v *Barclays Bank Ltd* [1940] 1 All ER 316 the plaintiff, who was a bookmaker, drew a cheque for £2.78 and the bank erroneously returned it to the payee marked 'not sufficient' on its face. It was held that the plaintiff was entitled to substantial damages of £250 for libel.

(b) Where the customer is not in trade or practising a profession damage to credit is not assumed and nominal damages will be awarded unless a particular loss is proved as where, for example, the customer can show that a particular creditor has refused to do business with him again. Thus in *Gibbons* v *Westminster Bank Ltd* [1939] 3 All ER 577 the plaintiff, who was not in trade, paid into her bank account a sum of money which, because of the bank's error, was credited to another customer's account. The plaintiff then issued a cheque to pay her rent and this cheque was dishonoured by the bank because there were insufficient funds to meet it. The plaintiff brought a claim for libel but it was *held* that she was entitled to nominal damages only; she was not in trade and was not able to prove any special damage.

Again, in *Rae* v *Yorkshire Bank plc* [1988] FLR 1 where a bank, in breach of a contract to extend the overdraft facility of a customer who was not in trade, dishonoured his cheques, a customer was only entitled, said the Court of Appeal, to nominal damages unless he could prove special damage arising from the breach, which he could not. He was not entitled on an action for breach of such a contract to recover general damages for any mental or physical distress caused by having the cheques dishonoured. Parker LJ thought that the figure of damages awarded in the court below, i.e. £20, was too high a figure for nominal damages for the three breaches that had in fact occurred, but since it had not been challenged by the bank, he allowed it.

The bank's duty to honour cheques ceases on the customer countermanding payment. In this connection it should be noted that notice to the bank must be actual, not constructive. It should also be noted that for the purposes of countermand of payment the branches of a bank are treated as separate parties. Thus a countermand must be sent to the branch on which the cheque is drawn.

A bank which overlooks its customer's instructions to stop payment of a cheque and consequently pays the cheque when it has been presented, can recover the money from the payee because it has been paid under a mistake of fact (*see Barclays Bank* v *W J Simms Son and Cooke (Southern)* [1979] 3 All ER 522).

The following cases are illustrative of the above rules.

Curtice v London City & Midland Bank Ltd [1908] 1 KB 293

The plaintiff drew a cheque for £63 in favour of a Mr Jones to pay for some horses. When the horses were not delivered he stopped the cheque by a telegram to the bank which was delivered into the bank's letter box at 6.15 p.m. The telegram was not noticed on the next day and the bank paid the cheque, only to find on the following day both the telegram which had been overlooked and a written confirmation of countermand which had been posted. The plaintiff was notified that the countermand was received too late to be effective, and he retorted by drawing a cheque on the bank for the whole of his funds, including the £63, which the bank naturally enough dishonoured. The plaintiff brought an action for money had and received. The County Court gave judgment for the plaintiff; the Divisional Court dismissed the bank's appeal; but it was *held* by the Court of Appeal that there had been no effective countermand of payment and the bank was not liable for money had and received. The bank might have been held liable in negligence, but the damages would not then have been the same. Cozens-Hardy MR said: 'There is no such thing as a constructive countermand in a commercial transaction of this kind.'

Comment: (i) Although damages would have been available in negligence, they would have been based upon the loss which the bank's negligence had caused and this would not necessarily have amounted to the full sum in the plaintiff's account. The court would have had to investigate what the real value of the horses was set against the amount which Mr Curtice was eventually made to pay for them by reason of the bank's negligence.

(ii) In practice a bank will normally act upon a customer's instructions in order to countermand an instrument but require written confirmation immediately. There can be no stopping of a cheque accepted against a cheque guarantee card. Where a customer has lost his cheque book and tells the bank, they will put a stop on the remaining cheques. If a bank pays a stopped cheque it is liable to the customer and cannot recover from the payee, but it seems where the cheque has been used to pay for goods the bank can claim the goods.

Burnett v Westminster Bank [1965] 3 All ER 81

B had for some years accounts at both the Borough and the Bromley branches of the Bank and eventually, because the Borough branch had introduced computer accounting, his cheque book on that branch for the first time included a notice that 'the cheques in this book will be applied to the account for which they have been prepared'. B drew a Borough branch cheque for £2,300 but altered the branch in ink to Bromley and later instructed Bromley branch to stop payment; but the cheque, as the computer could not read the ink of the alteration, was sent to Borough branch where no action was taken on the alteration and the cheque was paid because no 'stop' had been received at that branch. It was *held* that although in the ordinary course of events a countermand must be sent to the branch on which the cheque was drawn, B could recover the £2,300 from the bank in this case. The cheque book cover fell within a class of documents which recipients would normally assume did not contain conditions varying existing contractual arrangements between themselves and their bank and as the plaintiff had long had accounts with the bank he was not bound by the notice on the cheque book cover as to the restricted use of the cheque forms for only one account.

Comment: It is not certain how this decision would be applied if the same circumstances occurred today. For one thing, the court said that if B had been a new customer it might have been reasonable to expect him to read the instruction in the cheque book. In addition, of course, customers of banks are normally aware these days that sorting is done by computer and might therefore be deemed to know that an ink alteration would not be read by the computer.

The bank's duty to honour cheques ceases also on receiving notice of the customer's death, i.e. probate of a will or letters of administration. This is because the death of a customer revokes his mandate to the bank and where this happens the payee of the cheque must settle the matter with the deceased customer's personal representatives. Cheques are returned stamped 'deceased'. However, death does not revoke the mandate of a living person who is party to a joint account with the deceased.

The duty of a bank to honour cheques also ceases on receiving notice of the customer's mental incapacity, usually notice of the appointment of a receiver. This again revokes the mandate and the payee of the cheque must deal with the drawer's representatives. These representatives are normally appointed by the court on application and may be, for example, a relative, or a solicitor who has been put in charge of the estate, or in some cases there may be a committee of several persons concerned to deal with the estate.

Other situations in which a banker's duty to honour his customer's cheques ceases are as follows.

(a) *If the customer is a company and the banker has notice that it has commenced winding up.* Winding up commences in the case of a compulsory liquidation on presentation of a petition and in the case of a voluntary liquidation on the passing of a resolution for voluntary winding up.

(b) *The service of a garnishee order.* Such an order can be used where, for example, A owes B £200 and will not pay but B knows that A has an account with the Barchester Bank in which he has £500. B may ask the court for a garnishee order *nisi* freezing A's account with the bank in the hope that this inconvenience will cause A to pay. If not B may ask the court for an order absolute and if he obtains it the bank will be required to pay B £200 plus his costs out of A's account.

Service of an order *nisi* with no sum mentioned prevents any use of the account until the order is discharged, even though there is more money in the account than the order requires. However, if a sum is mentioned and the account is more than that sum then it can be operated by the customer as to the balance.

A garnishee order issues only on a judgment debt. The order *nisi* is addressed to the customer against whom a judgment has been obtained asking if there is any good reason why the judgment debt has not been paid. A copy of this order is sent to the bank. An order absolute will be made if the customer cannot show good cause as to why he has not paid and then, as we have seen, the bank is ordered to pay the plaintiff.

(c) *After the making of a bankruptcy order against the customer.*

(d) *Where the bank knows, or ought to know, that the cheque is a misapplication of funds.* For example, the use of a company's money to buy its own shares would be a misapplication of the funds in its account since it is forbidden, subject to certain exceptions, by Part V, Chapter IV of the Companies Act 1985. If the bank was therefore aware or put on inquiry that the company's money was being used for this purpose it would be liable for honouring cheques in those circumstances. Thus a takeover bidder may obtain a bridging loan from the bank in order to purchase a controlling interest in the shares of a company and then use the company's funds by means of a cheque immediately to repay the loan. In such circumstances the bank should not honour the company's cheque. If it does it can be required to reimburse the company (*Karak Rubber Co v Burden* [1971] 3 All ER 1118).

The same rule applies to money paid by the bank in breach of trust. These cases make life difficult for bankers, particularly where the money of companies is misapplied in breach of trust by the directors, the relevant cheque(s) having been drawn within the mandate on which the account is operated. An example of payment in breach of trust is to be found in *International Sales & Agencies* v *Marcus* [1982] 3 All ER 551. In that case money was owed to a moneylender by a Mr Fancy who died intestate. One of the directors of a company in which Mr Fancy was a substantial shareholder had promised the moneylender that he would do all he could to see that the debts were paid. In fact the director concerned paid the debts from money standing to the credit of the accounts of the company. This was, of course, a breach of trust. The debt was not an obligation of the company. In an action brought on behalf of the company it succeeded in recovering the money paid by the bank.

Banker's duty to observe secrecy

A bank must not disclose the financial affairs of a customer. This is based on an implied term in the contract between the banker and his customer (*see Tournier* v *National Provincial and Union Bank of England* (1924) *below*) and continues even after the account is closed.

However, Bankes LJ said in *Tournier*'s case that there were four exceptions as follows.

(a) *Where disclosure is required by law.* Thus, under s. 7 of the Banker's Books Evidence Act 1879 the court may by order authorize a party to an action to inspect and copy entries in a banker's books although the power is exercised with caution. Section 9 of the 1879 Act provides that 'expressions in this Act relating to "bankers" books include ledgers, day books, cash books, account books, and all other books used in the ordinary business of the bank.' Under

Sch. 6 of the Banking Act 1979 'books' include microfilm records.

Letters contained in a bank correspondence file are not within the terms of s. 9 and are inadmissible in evidence. Thus in *R v Dadson* (1983) 77 Cr App R 91, a main plank of the prosecution's case against the accused who was allegedly guilty of dishonestly borrowing by way of overdraft by *knowingly* drawing cheques in excess of his bank balance, were two letters written to him by the bank giving information about the state of his account. The defendant was convicted of the offence but his appeal was allowed by the Court of Appeal on the basis that the letters had been exhibited in the court at the trial but should not have been admitted in evidence.

Furthermore, under the Taxes Management Act 1970, s. 17, a bank must report to the Revenue authorities any case where interest of £25 or more is paid per year. In practice, only accounts showing more than £500 per annum interest or more are sent automatically, though the Revenue may request a statement to be made in respect of interest in excess of £25 per annum or more.

In addition to the above, there is power to require disclosure of a bank account under the Companies Act 1985 on a prosecution of a company's officers or on an inspection by the Department of Trade or in a winding up. In addition, the Taxes Management Act 1970, s. 20, as extended by Sch. 6 of the Finance Act 1976, allows the Inspector of Taxes to call for documents of a taxpayer if relevant to tax liability. This could include the taxpayer's bank account.

(b) *Where there is a public duty to disclose* as where a banker can see that a customer is trading with the enemy in time of war, or more importantly where information is given to the police to protect the public against crime. Such information is not, however, given in evidence unless the bank is ordered to give it under the 1879 Act.

(c) *Where disclosure is required in the interest of the bank*, as where the bank is suing to recover an overdraft, since the amount of the overdraft is stated on the face of the writ, or where the bank is claiming against a person who has guaranteed an overdraft.

(d) *Where the customer gives permission*. Permission may be given *expressly* as when a customer gives the banker's name as reference. An additional example of this is where a corporate customer of the bank gives the bank permission to disclose the state of its account to the company's auditors. Permission may also be regarded as having been given by implication from conduct.

Disclosure without authority is an open question: there are those who believe that the state of an account can be disclosed on the basis of the implied consent of the customer when he joins the bank. However, the Younger Committee, which reported on new laws of privacy which have not yet received legislation, said that banks should tell customers of a reference system in use and get a standing consent or ask them every time the reference system was used.

The following cases provide illustrations of the above rules.

Tournier v National Provincial and Union Bank of England [1924] 1 KB 461

Tournier banked with the defendants and, being overdrawn by £9 6s 8d, signed an agreement to pay this off at the rate of £1 a week, disclosing the name and address of his employer, Kenyon & Co, with whom he had a three months' contract as a traveller. The agreement to repay was not observed and the bank also discovered, through another banker, that Tournier had endorsed a cheque for £45 over to a bookmaker. The manager of the bank thereupon telephoned Kenyon & Co to find out Tournier's private address and told them that Tournier was betting heavily. Kenyon & Co, as a result of this conversation, refused to renew Tournier's contract of employment. Tournier sued the bank for slander and for breach of an implied contract not to disclose the state of his account or his transactions. Judgment was entered for the defendants but the Court of Appeal allowed Tournier's appeal and ordered a new trial. Bankes LJ laid down four qualifications to the duty of non-disclosure: (a) where the disclosure is under compulsion of law; (b) where there is a duty to the public to disclose; (c) where the interests of the bank require disclosure; (d) where the disclosure is made by the express or implied consent of the customer. Atkin LJ said 'I do not desire to express a final opinion on the practice of bankers to give one another information as to the affairs of their respective customers, except to say it appears to me that if it is justified it must be upon the basis of an implied consent of the customer'.

Sunderland v Barclays Bank Ltd, The Times, 25 November 1938

Mrs Sunderland had drawn a cheque in favour of her dressmaker on an account containing insufficient funds. The cheque was returned because the bank knew she indulged in gambling and thought it unwise to grant her an overdraft. Mrs Sunderland complained to her husband and the manager of the bank informed him, over the telephone, of the wife's transactions with bookmakers. Mrs Sunderland regarded this as a breach of the bank's duty of secrecy, but in fact the husband's telephone conversation was a continuation of one of her own in which she requested the bank to give an explanation to the husband concerning the return of the cheque. The bank pleaded implied authority to disclose. Du Parcq LJ gave judgment for the defendants and affirmed the criteria relating to disclosure laid down in *Tournier* v *National Provincial and Union Bank of England* (1924) (see *above*). However, each case must depend on its own facts. The relationship of husband and wife was a special one.

The demand by Dr Sunderland for an explanation required an account of why the bank had done what it had done. It might be said that the disclosure was with the implied consent of the customer and the interests of the bank required disclosure. Since the husband had taken over conduct of the matter, the manager was justified in thinking that the wife did not object to the offer of an explanation. If judgment had been for the plaintiff, the damages were assessed at £2 – nominal damages.

Banker's duty to collect cheques paid in by a customer

A bank is under a duty to collect for its customer's account cheques paid in by the customer. The bank then acts as a collecting bank and has certain protections if its customer has a defective title to the cheque.

Fiduciary relationship of banker and customer

There is a special relationship between a banker and his customer which can give rise to a contract to give a security between the bank and the customer being set aside for undue influence (*see Lloyds Bank* v *Bundy* (1974), p. 128). The best way for a bank to avoid this situation is to recommend that the customer take independent legal advice.

CROSSED CHEQUES (ss. 76–82, BILLS OF EXCHANGE ACT 1882)

Where a cheque bears across its face an addition of the words 'and Co' or any abbreviation thereof between two parallel transverse lines, or simply two parallel transverse lines, in either case with or without the words 'not negotiable', the cheque is said to be crossed generally. Such a cheque will only be paid by the bank on which it is drawn through another bank, and not over the counter. It is therefore a hindrance for someone who obtains the cheque wrongly because he could only obtain payment through a bank and the loss may be discovered meanwhile and the cheque stopped. In addition, collection through a bank may help trace a thief.

If the cheque bears across its face the addition of the name of a banker it will only be paid by the paying bank to the bank which is so named. The cheque is then said to be specially crossed whether there are transverse parallel lines on the cheque as well or not. If the drawer does not know where the payee banks he can only write '& Co'. In early banking days the words '& Co' were essential to ensure collection through a bank. They are absolutely unnecessary today.

If the words 'Not negotiable' appear on or near the crossing of a cheque no one can claim to have a better title than the previous holder, i.e. no one can claim to be a holder in due course taking the cheque free from defects (if any). A person may satisfy the definition of a holder in due course but because of the 'Not negotiable' crossing will not take the cheque free from defects. So if a person is giving a cheque for goods which may be defective, he should cross his cheque 'Not negotiable' so that no one, not even a holder in due course, can sue him for the full price if the goods turn out to be defective and the cheque is stopped.

It was *held* in *Redmond* v *Allied Irish Banks plc* [1987] FLR 307 that a bank is not under a duty to warn a customer of the danger of accepting a cheque crossed 'Not negotiable' *when he pays it in*. If he turns out to have no title and the bank is sued in conversion by the true owner or voluntarily reimburses him, the bank can obtain an indemnity from the customer. The bank would seem to be under a duty of care to a customer, however, who actually asked for advice about the nature of not negotiable cheques.

The crossing 'A/C Payee' is not provided for in the 1882 or other Act. It is an instruction to the collecting banker, addressed to him by a person who has no contract with him, and it would be negligence in a banker if he collected the money for some other account, for a person with no title. The crossing has no effect on a paying banker since it merely states what is to happen to money after receipt. The crossing does not prevent the cheque from being transferred or indeed from being negotiable (*National Bank* v *Silke* [1891] 1 QB 435). Obviously, no banker would normally collect the money for an endorsee but the drawer would remain liable on the instrument and would have to pay the amount of the cheque to an endorsee.

Bankers will sometimes collect a cheque crossed 'A/C Payee' for someone other than the payee, particularly if the cheque is for a small amount and the customer is one of long standing.

If a cheque is issued uncrossed a holder can cross it generally or specially, and if it is issued crossed generally a holder may turn the crossing into a special crossing. In addition, a holder may also add the words 'Not negotiable' to a crossing. This would only affect those who took the instrument after the crossing had been added. Section 81 provides that only where a person *takes* a crossed cheque marked 'Not negotiable' shall he not get a better title to it than the person who transferred it to him. A cheque cannot be uncrossed except by the drawer.

The safest crossing is a combination of 'Not negotiable, A/C Payee only'. The 'Not negotiable' crossing takes the cheque out of the category of negotiable instruments with the advantage to the drawer which has already been outlined. The 'A/C Payee' crossing warns the collecting banker that if he collects the cheque for someone other than the payee and that person is not entitled to it, the banker may be liable in damages to the true owner.

A crossing on a cheque is not a complete protection in view of the fact that the person who misappropriates it can try, and may succeed, in opening a bank account in the name of the payee (*see*, for example, *Marfani & Co* v *Midland Bank* (1968) at p. 487).

Examples of crossings on cheques are given in Fig. 18.1.

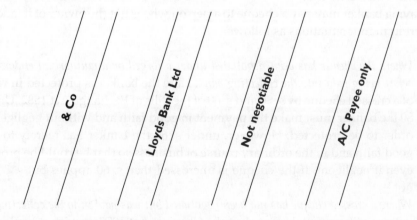

Fig. 18.1 Examples of crossings on cheques

STATUTORY PROTECTION OF THE PAYING BANKER

Section 60 of the Bills of Exchange Act 1882 and s. 1 of the Cheques Act 1957 provide some protection to a paying banker who pays a cheque to a person who is not the owner of it. In the absence of this statutory protection the banker would be liable in conversion to the true owner. It should be noted that these statutory protections do not apply where the banker pays out a cheque on which his customer's signature as a drawer is forged. The banker will not be allowed to debit the cheque to the customer's account unless the customer is estopped from denying that the forged signature is his, as in *Greenwood* v *Martins Bank* [1933] AC 51 where a husband who knew his wife was forging his signature did not tell the bank.

It should be noted that a banker who honours a cheque upon which the drawer's signature has been forged does not thereby impliedly represent the signature to be genuine and can recover the money paid thereunder from the recipient. Thus, in *National Westminster Bank* v *Barclays Bank International* [1974] 3 All ER 834. A stole a cheque from B and forged B's signature in order that C (the payee) could obtain money from B's account as part of a fraudulent scheme to acquire sterling. It was held that although the bank could not debit B's account with the amount of the cheque which it had paid, it could recover the money from C on the grounds that it was paid under circumstances of mistake of fact.

The main purpose of the Cheques Act 1957 was to make it unnecessary for the payee of a cheque or a subsequent endorsee to endorse the cheque before paying it in to his own bank account. Endorsement of a cheque is still necessary to effect the negotiation of an order cheque and it is the practice of banks to require an endorsement when cashing uncrossed cheques across the counter.

The Cheques Act merely amended the law in certain respects and in the absence of consolidating legislation there is at the present some overlapping between the statutory provisions that give the paying banker his protection when paying someone who has no title.

A paying banker may pay a cheque to a person who is not the owner of it (and thus convert it) in four situations as follows.

(a) *Where the cheque has been negotiated under a forged or unauthorized endorsement before being paid into the collecting bank.* Here the banker is protected in respect of a crossed cheque by s. 80 and s. 60 of the Bills of Exchange Act 1882. Under s. 80 the banker must make the payment in good faith and without negligence in order to be protected. However, under s. 60 the banker has merely to act in good faith and in the ordinary course of business so that he could be protected even if negligent. If the cheque is uncrossed then s. 60 applies but s. 80 does not.

(b) *Where a crossed cheque has not been negotiated but was paid in to the collecting bank without endorsement.* Here s. 1 of the Cheques Act 1957 protects a banker who pays in good faith and in the ordinary course of business.

(c) *Where an uncrossed cheque has been paid over the counter on a forged endorsement.* Here a banker who pays in good faith and in the ordinary course of business would be protected by s. 60 of the Bills of Exchange Act 1882.

(d) *Where an uncrossed cheque has been paid over the counter on an irregular endorsement*, as where the payee's name and the endorsement do not match. Here the banker would be protected by s. 1 of the Cheques Act 1957 provided he paid in good faith and in the ordinary course of business.

Where these protections apply the banker is entitled to debit his customer's account with the amount of the cheque.

It should also be noted that a banker can plead the contributory negligence of his customer under s. 47 of the Banking Act 1979 in order to reduce the damages payable by the banker, as where one director signs cheques in blank before going on a business trip and leaves the cheque book in an unlocked drawer so that the signature of another director is forged by a clerk and the cheques paid. Although the banker would have paid out contrary to the mandate, the amount of compensation he was liable to pay to the company whose funds are converted could be reduced in such a case by the contributory negligence of the director concerned.

STATUTORY PROTECTION OF THE COLLECTING BANKER

At common law a banker who collects a cheque for his customer in circumstances where that customer has no title to it is liable in conversion to the true owner. Statutory protection is, however, given to the collecting banker by s. 4(1) of the Cheques Act 1957, provided:

(a) he collects for a customer. It is clear from the cases that a person who has handed in a cheque for an account to be opened is immediately 'a customer' within the meaning of s. 4. It should also be noted that s. 4 applies to protect a banker even where he has allowed his customer to draw against the cheque before it was cleared so that in effect when he collects the cheque he is collecting it for himself and not for a customer. Nevertheless s. 4 applies;

(b) he acts without negligence. Broadly, whenever the terms of a cheque would raise a doubt in the mind of a bank cashier of ordinary intelligence and care as to whether the customer has a good title to it, the bank owes a duty to make inquiries as to the customer's title. The application of this principle can be seen in *Lloyds Bank* v *Savory & Co* (1933) (*see below*), *Bute (Marquess)* v *Barclays Bank Ltd* (1954) (*see below*) and *Underwood* v *Bank of Liverpool* (1924) (*see below*), in which the bank was found negligent and *Orbit Mining and Trading Co* v *Westminster Bank Ltd* (1962) (*see* p. 453), and *Marfani* v *Midland Bank Ltd* (1968) (*see below*), where the bank was found not negligent.

The main areas of a collecting banker's negligence are as follows.

(a) Failure to obtain references or follow them up on opening an account (*Lumsden & Co* v *London Trustee Savings Bank* [1971] 1 Lloyd's Rep 114.

(b) Failure to obtain the name of the customer's employers (*Lloyds Bank Ltd* v *E B Savory & Co* (1933) (*see below*)). It would appear, however, from the case of *Orbit Mining & Trading Co Ltd* v *Westminster Bank* (1962) (see p. 453) that the bank need not update this information.

(c) Failure to obtain the name of the husband's employers when an account is opened for a married woman (*Lloyds Bank Ltd* v *E B Savory & Co* (1933) – *see below*).

(d) Collecting for the private account of a partner or a director cheques payable to the firm or to the company (*Underwood* v *Bank of Liverpool* (1924) – *see below*).

(e) Collecting for an employee cheques payable to his employer or drawn by his employer (*Lloyds Bank Ltd* v *E B Savory & Co.* (1933) – *see below*).

(f) Collecting for the private account of an agent cheques which he receives only as an agent (*Bute (Marquess)* v *Barclays Bank Ltd* (1954) – *see below*).

(g) Collecting cheques payable to a limited company for an account other than that of the company (*London & Montrose Shipbuilding and Repairing Co Ltd* v *Barclays Bank Ltd* (1925) 31 Com Cas 182). However, the matter is not beyond doubt because in *Penmount Estates Ltd* v *National Provincial Bank* (1945) 173 LT 344 a bank in a similar situation successfully defended itself in an action in conversion. However, it can be said that a bank would not collect a cheque payable to a limited company for an account other than that of the company without very strict inquiry. This makes it very difficult to endorse over to an endorsee cheques payable to a company.

(h) Collecting account payee cheques for someone else.

The following cases can now be introduced by way of illustration.

Lloyds Bank Ltd *v* E B Savory & Co [1933] AC 201

Two clerks, Perkins and Smith stole bearer cheques from Savory & Co, their employers who were stockbrokers, and paid them into branches of Lloyds Bank – Perkins into an account at Wallington, and Smith into his wife's account at Redhill and subsequently at Weybridge. The clerks paid in the cheques at other branches, using the 'branch credit' system, with the result that the branches in which the accounts were kept did not receive particulars of the cheques. Neither bank made inquiries concerning the employers of Smith and Perkins. The frauds were discovered and Savory & Co brought an action against the bank for conversion. The bank pleaded s. 82 of the Bills of Exchange Act, and denied negligence, since the 'branch credit' system was in common use by bankers. At first instance judgment was given for the bank, but this was reversed on appeal and the bank then appealed to the House of Lords. *Held* – The appeal should be dismissed as the bank had not been able to rebut the charge of negligence. With regard to the defence under s. 82, the court *held* that, although the branch credit system had been in use for 40 years, it had 'an inherent and obvious defect which no reasonable banker could fail to observe'. Lord Wright said: 'Where a new customer is employed in some position which involves his handling, and having the opportunity of stealing, his employer's cheques, the bankers fail in taking adequate precautions if they do not ask the name of his employers. . . . Otherwise they cannot guard against the danger known to them of his paying in cheques stolen from his employer.' This was not the ordinary practice of bankers but that did not acquit them of negligence. Such inquiries should be made on the opening of an account even though they could turn out to be useless if the customer changed his employment immediately afterwards.

Bute (Marquis) v Barclays Bank Ltd [1954] 3 All ER 365

A Mr McGaw in his capacity as manager of farms belonging to the Marquis of Bute made applications to the Department of Agriculture for Scotland for Sheep Hill Subsidies. McGaw left the Marquis's employment and subsequently warrants drawn by the Department (similar in effect to cheques) were sent to McGaw in satisfaction of his applications. Each warrant was payable to 'D. McGaw (for the Marquis of Bute)'. McGaw applied to a branch of the defendant bank for permission to open a personal account with the warrants and the bank did so, collecting the amounts of the warrants for McGaw's newly opened personal account. The court *held* that the defendant bank was liable in conversion to the Marquis and could not claim statutory protection because it had not discharged the onus of proving that it had acted without negligence. McNair J pointed out that the warrants clearly indicated that McGaw was to receive the money as an agent and it is elementary banking practice that such documents should not be credited to the personal account of the named payee without inquiry.

   Comment: There was obvious negligence here because there was an agent paying cheques clearly intended for his principal into his own account. Some have argued that he could be regarded as an agent for collection, but this would still have involved negligence because he was paying into a private, and not an agency, account.

Underwood v Bank of Liverpool [1924] 1 KB 775

A cheque was made payable to a one-man company and it was held negligent for a bank to collect it for the private account of the 'one man' who was also the managing director.

Marfani & Co v Midland Bank [1968] 2 All ER 573

The managing director of the plaintiff company signed a cheque for £3,000 drawn by the office manager Kureshy payable to Eliaszade and gave it to Kureshy for despatch. However, Kureshy opened an account with the cheque at the Midland Bank by falsely representing that he was Eliaszade and that he was about to set up a restaurant business.

   The bank asked for references and Kureshy gave the names of two satisfactory customers of the bank, and one of these references indicated, while on a visit to the bank, that Kureshy, whom he knew as Eliaszade, would be a satisfactory customer. The second referee did not reply to the bank's inquiry. Kureshy then drew a cheque for £2,950 on the account and absconded. It appeared that the bank did not ask to see Kureshy's passport and his spelling of Eliaszade was inconsistent with the spelling on the cheque. Further the bank officials did not notice the similarity in handwriting between the cheque and the endorsement. The plaintiff company sued the bank for conversion and it was *held* that the bank had not fallen short of the standard of ordinary practice of careful bankers and was protected by s. 4 of the Cheques Act 1957.

BANK AS A HOLDER FOR VALUE OR HOLDER IN DUE COURSE

Section 2 of the Cheques Act provides that a banker who gives value for a cheque payable to order which the holder delivers to him for collection without endorsing it has such (if any) rights as he would have had if upon delivery the holder had endorsed it in blank making it a bearer cheque.

This concept is useful to a banker where, for example, he has allowed a customer to have an overdraft and the customer pays in a cheque which the banker uses to reduce that overdraft because, should the cheque which the banker uses to reduce that overdraft not be met and the customer be unable or unwilling to sue upon it, the bank can itself take action against the drawer in the hope of reducing the overdraft by bringing an action under s. 2 of the Cheques Act 1957 instead of the customer.

However, before an action can be brought the bank must show that it is at least a holder for value and under s. 2 value must be given by the bank itself. Value could be given, for example, where the bank could prove that it had reduced the customer's overdraft and had charged interest for a period of time only on the overdraft as reduced by the cheque. It is much more likely, however, that the bank will show that it has given value by allowing a customer to draw against a cheque before it is cleared because the customer is using the bank's money and not his own at that stage. It would be necessary for the bank to show that it was a holder for value in order that a successful action could be maintained on a cheque which had no defects. However, if there is a defect on the cheque the bank would have to prove that it was a holder in due course and could only do this:

(a) if it had no knowledge of the defect and took the instrument in good faith;
(b) the bank's title did not depend upon a forged endorsement; and
(c) there were no irregularities on the face of the cheque.

Illustrations of the use of s. 2 of the Cheques Act 1957 by a bank can be seen in the following cases.

Westminster Bank Ltd v Zang [1965] I All ER 1023

Mr Zang, having lost heavily at seven-card rummy, drew a cheque for £1,000 payable to 'J. Tilley or order', receiving from Mr Tilley £1,000 in cash to pay part of his gambling debts.

The £1,000 cash belonged to Tilley's Autos Ltd, a company of which Tilley was managing director. Tilley took Zang's cheque to his bank, asking them to credit the account of the company, which was overdrawn. Tilley did not endorse the cheque before paying it in. The cheque was dishonoured and the bank returned it to Tilley so that he could sue Zang. The action was commenced but discontinued and the cheque was returned to the bank who sued Zang as holder in due course or holder for value of the cheque. The bank failed in its claim. The reasons given in the Court of Appeal were as follows.

(a) As the payee (Tilley) had asked the bank to credit the cheque to the account of a third party (Tilley's Autos), the cheque had not been received for collection within the meaning of s. 2 and as the cheque was not endorsed the bank were not 'holders' (per Denning MR).

(b) The cheque had been received for collection but the bank had not given value, so that s. 2 did not apply (per Salmon LJ).

(c) The cheque had been received for collection but the bank in returning the cheque to Tilley lost their lien and consequently the protection of s. 2 (per Danckwerts LJ).

In the House of Lords in 1966 their Lordships unanimously *held* that the cheque had been received for collection, but the bank had not given value.

The company's account was overdrawn, but it was hard to see how, by crediting the cheque to the account and reducing the overdraft, the bank gave value for it, because in fact interest had been charged on the original amount of the overdraft unreduced by the cheque. There was no agreement express or implied to honour the cheques of Tilley's Autos before they had been cleared, and consideration could not, therefore, be established in this way.

Barclays Bank Ltd v The Astley Industrial Trust Ltd [1970] 1 All ER 719

Mabons Garage Ltd were motor dealers who banked with the plaintiffs and arranged hire-purchase transactions with the defendants. In November 1964, the plaintiffs gave Mabons a temporary overdraft up to £2,000 and on 18 November when the account was £1,910 overdrawn cheques for £2,673 drawn by Mabons were presented for payment. The bank manager agreed to pay them only after receiving an assurance from the directors of Mabons that cheques for £2,850 in favour of Mabons and drawn by the defendants would be paid into the account the next day. On 19 November when Mabons' overdraft stood at £4,673 two further cheques for £345 drawn by Mabons were presented for payment and the bank manager refused to pay these until he had received the defendants' cheques for £2,850. On the 20 November the defendants stopped their cheques which it appeared they had been induced to draw by the fraud of Mabons' directors. In an action by the bank claiming to be holders in due course of the cheques the defendants alleged that the bank had not taken them for value. *Held* – by Milmo J – that the bank was a holder in due course since:

(a) a banker who takes a cheque as agent for collection can also be a holder in due course under s. 2 of the Cheques Act 1957;

(b) the bank was a holder in due course. They were holders because they had a lien on the cheques and were entitled to hold them pending payment of the overdraft. The value was the overdraft of £4,673. An antecedent debt would support a bill of exchange.

The bank was entitled to recover the amount of the cheques from the defendants.

Regarding the decision in *Westminster Bank Ltd v Zang* (1965) (*see above*) Milmo J said, 'I should mention that *Westminster Bank Ltd v Zang* was strongly relied upon by the defendants, but I do not consider that it established their contentions. The facts were materially different from those in the present case and in particular there was no question of the bank having a lien such as there admittedly was in the present case'.

Comment: The bank appears to have obtained the benefit of the antecedent overdraft by virtue of their banker's lien.

BANKING OMBUDSMAN

In January 1986 19 banks combined to set up and fund an Ombudsman. His role is to provide an independent body which will receive and resolve complaints by customers about the banking practices of the banks involved, which include all the big English and Scottish clearing banks.

The Ombudsman can make an award of up to £50,000 to customers who sustain a complaint. The award binds the bank provided the customer is willing to accept it in full and final settlement of the claim.

Complaints can be made about most aspects of personal banking: this includes the insurance and trustee services which the banks provide. However, complaints about refusal of an overdraft or loan would appear to be excluded by the scheme, as would complaints about charges. The reports of the Ombudsman indicate that cashcard machines are causing more complaints than any other banking service.

GRADED QUESTIONS

Essay mode

1. (a) (i) What is the purpose of crossing a cheque? What forms may a crossing take?
   (ii) What do you consider to be the most suitable form of crossing from the point of view of the drawer?
   (b) Arnold transferred the following cheques to Brian:
   (i) an uncrossed cheque payable to Charles whose endorsement had been forged by Arnold;

(ii) a cheque crossed 'not negotiable' payable to Arnold which Arnold had obtained by fraud;

(iii) a cheque crossed 'account payee' payable to Arnold and endorsed by him.

Brian had no knowledge of the history of the cheques at the time of transfer and gave Arnold value for all of them.

Advise Brian whether he has a good title to any of these cheques.

(The Institute of Company Accountants. Law Relating to Business. November 1989

2. (a) What is the effect of the following words written within the crossing of a cheque:

(i) 'Not negotiable';

(ii) 'And Co';

(iii) 'Account payee'?

(10 marks)

(b) H sold goods to J and received a cheque as payment. J changed his mind about the purchase and instructed his bank, the Z Bank, not to pay the cheque. H presented the cheque for payment and the Z Bank having overlooked the stop order, paid it. J is now seeking to recover the money paid to H from the Z Bank.

Advise J.

(10 marks)

(20 marks)

(The Chartered Association of Certified Accountants. Paper 1.4(E). June 1988)

3. 'At the present day I think it may be asserted with confidence that a banker's duty of non disclosure of his customer's affairs is a legal one arising out of contract and that the duty is not absolute but qualified.' If, as the statement says, the duty is not absolute, but qualified, when may a banker disclose information about a customer's affairs? *(Author's question)*

Objective mode

1. On 1 August, Arthur lent Bruce £120 to be repaid by monthly instalments of £20 each and received a cheque from Bruce for £20 postdated to 1 September. Arthur presented the cheque for payment on 11 September, but it was returned by the bank since there was no money in Bruce's account and he had no permission to overdraw.

Bruce then persuaded his fiancee's sister Catherine to draw an open cheque for £20 in favour of Arthur dated 14 September. Bruce took the cheque to Arthur's home, but he was away on business so Bruce left it with Arthur's wife, together with a note which said: 'This one is okay.'

Arthur returned on 17 September and found Catherine's cheque and the note. In the meantime, Bruce and his fiancee had quarrelled and broken off their engagement with the result that on 18 September, before Arthur had presented

Catherine's cheque for payment, Catherine telephoned Arthur and told him that she intended to stop payment of it immediately.

Arthur thereupon altered Catherine's cheque to £120, the cheque being drawn in such a way as to enable this to be done without detection. Arthur then presented the cheque for payment at Catherine's bank and received the money before Catherine managed to inform the bank that the cheque should be stopped.

Catherine's bank has debited her account with £120 and she is wondering what right, if any, the bank has to do this. She is also interested to know what right, if any, she might have to recover the money from Arthur.

An examination of the legal position is required.

(a) One of the following legal concepts is relevant to any claim which Catherine might make on the bank.

Select:
A Conversion.
B Negligence.
C Fictitious payee.

(b) From the following list select one decision which you think represents Catherine's position in regard to the bank:

A The bank can debit her account with £120.
B The bank can debit her account with £20.
C The bank cannot debit her account with any amount.

(c) One of the following legal concepts is relevant to any claim which Catherine might make against Arthur.
Select:

A *Non est factum.*
B Accord and satisfaction.
C Estoppel.
D Consideration.

(d) From the following list select one decision which you might think represents Catherine's position in regard to Arthur.

A Catherine can recover £120 from Arthur.
B Catherine can recover £100 from Arthur.
C Catherine cannot recover anything from Arthur.

2. X who is a customer of the Y Bank Ltd, has a deposit of £400 with no permission to overdraw. X draws up a cheque payable to Z for £600.
   The bank may:

A Pay £400 only.
B Pay £600.
C Refuse payment altogether.

3. X draws a cheque on the Y Bank Ltd payable to Z. Z, on receipt of the cheque, crosses it generally. The cheque is then stolen by T who opens an account at the U Bank Ltd in the name of Z. The U Bank presents the cheque to the Y Bank Ltd which pays in good faith and without negligence.

The Y Bank is not liable to Z. TRUE/FALSE

Answers to questions in objective mode appear on p. 551.

19 | Agency and the partnership contract

The OBJECTIVES are to explain the relationship between principal and agent from its formation to its termination with special emphasis being placed on the agency of directors of companies and partnerships.

GENERAL PRINCIPLES OF AGENCY

Agency is a relationship existing between two parties called principal (P) and agent (A), the function of A being to create a contractual relationship between P and a third party (T). The agent is merely the instrument used to form the contract. He need not have contractual capacity. The principal must have contractual capacity.

Appointment of agent

An agent is normally appointed by a contract between himself and his principal. The agent must have capacity to contract if *his* contract with the principal is to be enforceable, otherwise agent and principal may not be able to enforce the rights and duties arising under the contract of agency. The appointment may be:

(a) *Express*. No particular form of agreement is required but if A is to be authorized to contract under seal his appointment must be by deed (a power of attorney). It should be noted that an agent who is appointed orally may bind his principal by a written contract or a contract which requires writing, e.g. an agreement concerning land.

(b) *By ratification*. Where an agent makes an unauthorized contract on behalf of his principal, though purporting to act for him, the principal may afterwards ratify or adopt the contract.

Where ratification of a contract is validly effected it is retrospective in its operation, i.e. the parties are put in the position they would have occupied if the professed agent had when the contract was made, the authority he purported to possess;

Ratification is only possible if:

(i) The principal had contractual capacity when the contract was made. Thus a prospective agent cannot enter into a contract on behalf of a company before incorporation and the company cannot ratify the contract after its incorporation. In such a case the prospective agent is considered to have contracted as a principal and is liable to the other party on the contract and not merely for breach of warranty of authority (s. 36(C) of the Companies Act 1985).

(ii) The contract is within the principal's power, e.g. it is not in the case of a company *ultra vires* (*see Ashbury Railway Carriage Co* v *Riche* (1895) at p. 76).

A leading case on ratification appears below.

Bolton Partners v Lambert (1889) 41 Ch D 295

The plaintiffs claimed specific performance of an agreement under which the defendant was to take a lease of the plaintiffs' premises. Preliminary negotiations had taken place between Lambert and a Mr Scratchley, who was a director of the plaintiff company. As a result of these negotiations, the defendant wrote to the plaintiffs on 8 December 1887, offering to take the lease. On 9 December, Scratchley wrote to Lambert to say that the offer would be placed before the board, and on 13 December 1887 Scratchley wrote to the defendant stating erroneously that the directors had accepted his offer. On 13 January 1888, the defendant wrote to the plaintiffs alleging that he had been misled as to the value of certain plant and machinery on the premises, and stated that he withdrew all offers made to the plaintiffs in any way. Evidence showed that Scratchley had no authority to bind the company when he wrote the letters of 9 and 13 December. The matter had not been put before the board but merely a works committee which had no authority to bind the company. The board did ratify Scratchley's acts but not until after 13 January 1888. *Held* – The acceptance by Scratchley would have constituted a contract in all respects except for his lack of authority. However, once that authority was given, it was thrown back to the time when the act was done by Scratchley and prevented the defendant from withdrawing his offer because it was then no longer an offer but a binding contract.

(c) *By operation of law – agency of necessity.* This arises without any agreement where A is forced by some emergency to act on behalf of P. The situation usually arises where A is in possession of property belonging to P and has to act to preserve that property. It should be noted, however, that the agent can only act where it is impossible to obtain instructions from the principal. **Illustrations from case law appear below.**

Great Northern Railway Co v Swaffield (1874) LR 9 Ex 132

The defendant sent an unattended horse by the plaintiffs' trains from King's Cross to Sandy, Bedfordshire. The horse arrived at Sandy at 10.08 p.m. but there was no one to meet it. The officials at Sandy station did not know the defendant or his address and accordingly the station master directed that the horse be put into a livery stable near to the station. Shortly afterwards the defendant's servant arrived to collect the horse and was told that it was in the livery stable and that he could have it for a charge of 6d. He refused to pay, as did the defendant when informed of the situation. The dispute over the charges went on and the horse was eventually delivered to the defendant four months later, the plaintiffs having paid £17 for stable charges. They now sued to recover this sum of money. *Held* – They could recover it. The plaintiffs were agents of necessity to incur expense in looking after the horse which they could not deliver.

Springer v Great Western Railway Co [1921] 1 KB 257

The defendants agreed to carry tomatoes for the plaintiff from Jersey to Covent Garden market. The ship was late in arriving at Weymouth, and when it did arrive the defendants' employees were on strike. When the cargo was unloaded by casual labour some of the tomatoes were good and some were bad. However, the defendants' traffic agent decided to sell the whole consignment locally because he felt that they could not be taken to Covent Garden in time to arrive in saleable condition. He did not communicate with any of the consignees, the plaintiff being one. The plaintiff claimed damages in conversion based on the market price of the goods at Covent Garden, and since the strike had caused shortages, this price was high. The defendants claimed that in the circumstances they must be considered as having a right to sell. The plaintiff said that if he had been informed of the position he could have got lorries to transport the goods to London. *Held* – The plaintiff was entitled to damages because the defendants were not in the position of agents of necessity so long as they could communicate with the owner and get his instructions.

(d) *By estoppel – holding out or apparent authority.* In this case there is really no appointment at all. It arises where P holds out a person as his agent for the purpose of making a contract with a third party and the third party relies on that fact. In such a case P is estopped from denying the fact of agency. **The following case shows this point**.

Dodsley v Varley (1840) 12 A & E 632

The defendant's agent W occasionally employed B to purchase wool on behalf of the defendant. B's previous purchases from the plaintiff had always been ratified by the defendant. In June 1839, the defendant wrote to B saying that he did not wish B to make any further purchases for him. In July 1839 B bought wool from the plaintiff which the defendant refused to pay for and the plaintiff now sued for the price. *Held* – The plaintiff succeeded. B was the defendant's agent by *apparent authority*, and although there was some doubt as to whether the revocation of authority was notified to the plaintiff, the jury found as a fact that the plaintiff did not have such notice when he sold the wool.

Authority of agent

The agent may bind his principal in contract by reason of *actual authority* or *usual authority*.

(a) *Actual authority*. The principal is bound by any act which he has expressly authorized A to do on his behalf.

(b) *Usual authority*. This may increase A's powers beyond that of his actual authority unless, of course, T is aware of the lack of authority. **The following is the leading case**.

Watteau v Fenwick [1893] 1 QB 346

For some time prior to 1888 the Victoria Hotel, Stockton-on-Tees, had been owned by a Mr Humble. In 1888 he sold the hotel to the defendants but remained in the hotel as manager, his name remaining on the door and the licence continuing in his name. The defendants had forbidden Humble to buy cigars on credit, but he bought a supply from the plaintiff who gave credit to Humble personally since he did not know of the existence of the defendants. When the plaintiff discovered what the true situation was, he brought this action against the defendants for the price of the cigars. *Held* – The cigars were articles which would usually be supplied to and dealt in at such an establishment, and Humble was acting within the scope of his *usual authority* as the manager of such a house. The defendants were bound by the contract made by Humble and could not set up secret instructions to him as a defence to the plaintiff's action.

Comment: If the third party knows of the agent's lack of authority he does not obtain a contract with the principal.

Relationship of principal and agent

The duties of an agent

These are as follows.

(a) To carry out the terms of the agency, and:
   (i)   to carry out his work with reasonable care and skill;
   (ii) to disclose any personal interest in the contract to P. This derives from the agent's fiduciary duty;
   (iii) not to delegate his authority unless this is *authorized by the principal*, or is *customary* (thus it is the practice of country solicitors to employ town agents in the matter of litigation so that delegation of their authority in this way would be acceptable) or *necessary*, e.g. as where the agent is ill. It should be noted that if a delegation of authority is validly effected the agent still remains personally liable to the principal for the proper performance of the contract.

(b) To account for all money and other property received for the principal and to keep proper accounts of all transactions.

(c) Not to make any secret profit out of the agency nor to take a bribe from a third party. If the agent takes any secret profit or bribe the principal has all the following rights:

(i) to dismiss the agent without notice;

(ii) to refuse the agent his remuneration or commission or to recover it if paid;

(iii) to recover the bribe – from the agent if he has received it; or from the third party if it has not been paid but only promised;

(iv) the principal, rather obviously, may repudiate the contract with the third party whether or not the secret payment had any effect on the agent;

(v) the principal may prosecute the agent and the third party under The Prevention of Corruption Act, 1906 with the consent of the Attorney General or Solicitor General.

The following cases illustrate the above legal principles.

Keppel v Wheeler [1927] 1 KB 577

The plaintiff sued the defendants, who were estate agents at Walham Green, for damages for breach of duty whilst acting as his agents. The plaintiff had instructed the defendants to sell a block of flats of which he was the owner. The flats were valued at £7,000 but the plaintiff was desirous of a quick sale, and when the defendants introduced a purchaser, E, who was prepared to offer £6,150, the plaintiff instructed the defendants to go ahead, and an agreement to sell 'subject to contract' was made. This agreement was not, of course, binding on the parties. Before contracts were exchanged, another purchaser, D, offered to pay £6,750 but the defendants told him that the flats were sold, and instead of communicating with the plaintiff they put D in touch with E. Contracts were exchanged between the plaintiff and E at a price of £6,150, and later between E and D for £6,950 which was the price eventually agreed between E and D. The plaintiff heard of the transaction between E and D and sued the defendants. *Held* – The defendants were under a duty to tell the plaintiff of D's offer because at the time he was not bound to E. The defendants were therefore liable in damages. The measure of damages was the difference between the two offers, i.e. £600, but the defendants were entitled to commission on the offer of £6,150 and also on the damages, and since the agreement provided for one and a half per cent commission which had already been paid on the £6,150, the plaintiff recovered £591.

McPherson v Watt (1877) 3 App Cas 254

The respondent was a Scottish solicitor advising certain trustees. The trustees wished to sell the trust property and were about to advertise it when the respondent promised to find a purchaser. The respondent's brother made an offer for the trust property which the trustees accepted. The sale to the brother was a mere sham because the intention was that the respondent would get the property via the brother, and they had an arrangement to this effect. The trustees were ignorant of the arrangement, and when they discovered the true state of affairs, they brought this action to set aside the sale. *Held* – The sale could be set aside, and it was immaterial that the contract was a fair one.

Andrews v Ramsay & Co [1903] 2 KB 635

The plaintiff was a builder and the defendants were auctioneers and estate agents. The plaintiff instructed the defendants to find a purchaser for certain property belonging to the plaintiff, the price to be £2,500 and the agreed commission £50. A month later the defendants wrote to the plaintiff saying that a person named Clutterbuck had made an offer of £1,900 for the property, but the plaintiff would not sell. Later Clutterbuck offered £2,100 and as the defendants said they could not get more, the plaintiff agreed to sell. Clutterbuck paid the defendants a deposit of £100 and the defendants paid £50 to the plaintiff and retained £50 as commission. After the sale had been completed the plaintiff discovered that the defendants had received a commission of £20 from Clutterbuck. The plaintiff recovered the £20 in the county court and now sought to recover the £50 commission because of the defendants' breach of duty whilst acting as agents. *Held* – He could do so. Where an agent takes a secret commission, the principal can recover that commission and also any commission which he himself has paid to the agent.

Shipway v Broadwood [1899] 1 QB 369

The defendant wished to buy a pair of horses and asked a veterinarian named Pinkett to find him a pair. Pinkett suggested that the defendant should buy a pair of horses which was being sold by a Worcester horse dealer. The defendant agreed to buy them if Pinkett passed them as sound. Pinkett gave the defendant a certificate of soundness and the horses were delivered to the defendant who sent a cheque to the dealer. On delivery the horses were found to be unsound, and the defendant returned them and stopped the cheque. The dealer now sued on the cheque, and the defence was that there had been total failure of consideration and that the plaintiff had warranted the horses sound. The plaintiff succeeded at first instance, the judge finding that no warranty had been given and that the defendant had simply agreed to buy if Pinkett certified the horses sound, as he had done. Evidence showed that Pinkett had received a commission from Shipway, but the judge gave no ruling as to the effect of this on Pinkett's judgment. It was *held*, by the Court of Appeal, that no such ruling was necessary. It was possible to find for the defendant merely on the evidence that a commission had been paid. It was not necessary to inquire whether Pinkett had been biased by receiving it.

Rights of the agent against his principal

These are as follows.

(a) *To be remunerated for his services.* The remuneration is generally specified in the agreement and may take the form of salary or commission, or both. If no remuneration is specified the court will imply a reasonable remuneration where the relationship is a commercial one and payment is usual. The agent loses his right to remuneration if he is in breach of one of the duties which he owes to his principal or if he acts without authority.

(b) *To be indemnified by the principal for any expenses properly incurred.* The agent may, in the course of his duty, make a payment of money for the principal, e.g. an insurance premium and he has a right to be indemnified by the principal and recover any money paid.

(c) *To a lien on any goods of the principal.* This is a special right under which the agent may retain the principal's goods which are in the agent's lawful possession where the principal has not satisfied his liabilities to the agent. The power is to retain in the hope of a settlement; there is not in general a power to sell. A lien may be of two kinds:

    (i)   *a general lien.* Under a general lien the agent may retain goods of the principal, even though the principal does not owe the agent money in respect of those goods but in respect of other goods the agent has dealt with; or

    (ii) *a particular lien.* Under such a lien the agent is only entitled to retain a particular article until the principal pays him what he owes in respect of it.

The law does not favour general liens and such a lien will only arise, either by express agreement of the principal and agent; or by judicially recognized custom, e.g. a customary general lien is possessed by bankers (*see* p. 489). Thus an agent's lien will in most cases be a *particular lien.*

Agent's liability

If the agent indicates to the third party that he is contracting as an agent, whether he names his principal or not, the contract is between the principal and the third party and the agent will not normally be liable on it. The agent may be liable, however, in certain circumstances which are set out below.

(a) *Bills of exchange.* The general rule is that an agent is liable on a bill of exchange if he signs it without making it clear that he is signing on behalf of a named principal. This could occur, for example, where the agent signs his name without making it clear that he is signing 'for and on behalf of' a named principal.

(b) *Contracts by deed.* Where the agent enters into a deed on behalf of the principal it is the agent who must sue and be sued. Thus, where an accountant entered into an agreement by a deed as liquidator of a company it was *held* that because the agreement was in the form of a deed the defendant accountant was personally liable on it (*Plant Engineers (Sales) v Davies* (1969) 113 SJ 484). In such a case the agent would have a right of indemnity against the principal.

(c) *Third party insistence.* There may be cases where the third party has insisted that the agent also accepts liability before he will make the contract. If the agent has agreed to this he will be liable along with the principal. In other cases the agent may have agreed to be the principal's guarantor.

Unauthorized acts of the agent

Two situations may arise as follows.

(a) If the agent, although not in fact authorized, acts within his usual authority, the principal is liable on the contract and the agent is not, though the agent may be liable to the principal for breach of duty (*see Watteau* v *Fenwick* (1893), p. 498).

(b) If the act is outside the agent's actual and usual authority the principal is not liable but the agent is liable to the third party for *breach of warranty of authority* and this is so even though the agent acted in good faith believing that he had authority (*see Yonge* v *Toynbee* (1910) *below*).

   The action seems to be based on quasi-contract, for the agent is not liable on the contract as such and cannot be required to carry it out. However, the measure of damages awarded against the agent will include compensation for the loss of the bargain with the principal and damages will be awarded in the same way as if the third party had been suing the principal for breach of contract.

Termination of agency

The contract between the agent and the principal may be terminated as follows:

(a) *By mutual agreement* on terms acceptable to both parties.

(b) *By complete performance of the contract*, i.e. the completion of the business for which the agency was created. Thus an agent who is employed to sell a house terminates his agency on selling it.

(c) *By expiration of time* where the agency is entered into for a definite period.

(d) *Frustration*, which may arise by impossibility of performance as where the subject matter of the agency is destroyed. Thus if an agent is employed to sell a house the agency terminates if the house is destroyed by fire.

(e) *By death of either party*. Obviously the death of the agent will terminate the contract since it is one of personal service. Similarly the agent's authority is terminated by the death of the principal and this is so whether the agent or third party knows of the principal's death or not. Where the agent purports to contract on behalf of his principal after the principal's death there is no contract with the principal's estate and the agent can be sued for breach of warranty of authority.

(f) *By insanity*. When the principal has become insane the agency itself is automatically terminated, and the same is true where the agent becomes insane. Where the agent purports to contract on behalf of his principal after the principal's insanity there is no contract with the principal's estate and the agent can be sued for breach of warranty of authority. However, in regard to the mental incapacity of the principal, the Enduring Powers of Attorney Act 1985 should be noted. This Act provides for the creation of an Enduring Power of Attorney which continues in force in spite of the donor's mental incapacity.

The Enduring Power must be registered with the Court of Protection. Once registered the donor (principal) cannot revoke it but the court can if an application is made to it or by or on behalf of the donor, as where, for example, the donee (agent) has become mentally incapacitated or is guilty of some fraud.

The above provisions should enable a donee who is a solicitor or accountant or a relative with business experience to administer the affairs of elderly people who have become senile or otherwise mentally incapacitated without too much trouble or expense.

Two important cases (*Re K, Re F* [1988] 1 All ER 358) decide that an enduring power of attorney is not rendered invalid merely because at the time the power was executed (signed) the person giving it (the donor) was incapable of managing his property and affairs because of mental disorder. Such a power is valid if, at the time of execution, the donor understood the nature and effect of the power. The donor does not have to be in a position to perform all the acts authorized by the power.

In both cases there was evidence that Miss K and Mrs F fully understood the nature and effect of the power but, because of recurrent mental disability, they could not be said to be capable of managing and administering their property. Mr Justice Harman nevertheless allowed registration of the power despite objections from certain relatives.

The following case deals with termination of agency by insanity.

Yonge v Toynbee [1910] 1 KB 215

The plaintiff alleged that the defendant had written and published a letter which was a libel on her and proceeded to bring an action against him. The defendant instructed a firm of solicitors, W and Sons, to act for him in the matter. Before the action commenced the defendant was certified as being of unsound mind. However, W and Sons, not knowing of this, entered an appearance in the action for the defendant after his insanity and also delivered a defence. Various other interlocutory proceedings took place but the action was not in fact tried, and the plaintiff's solicitors asked that all proceedings be struck out, and that W and Sons, who had acted for the defendant after his insanity, should be personally liable to pay the plaintiff's costs because they had acted without authority. *Held* – by the Court of Appeal – that W and Sons had impliedly warranted that they had authority to act when they had not, and that they were personally liable for the plaintiff's costs.

Comment: Remember, however, that where there is an enduring power of attorney, under the Enduring Powers of Attorney Act 1985, in existence the authority of the agent (donee) continues in force despite the principal's (donor's) mental incapacity.

(g) *By bankruptcy*. The principal's bankruptcy terminates the authority of the agent but the agent's bankruptcy does not of itself give the principal the right to dismiss him unless the insolvency affects the agent's fitness to act. For example, the viability of an agent whose duties did not involve the handling of the principal's money or property, as would be the case where the agent merely took orders for goods, would not be brought to an end by the agent's bankruptcy.

(h) *Revocation of the agent's authority by the principal*. The principal may terminate the agent's actual authority at any time. No special formalities are required and even an appointment by deed is revocable by parol notice. However, this may not terminate the contract of employment and the agent may have an action for damages for wrongful or unfair dismissal. It should be noted that the agent's apparent authority continues until third parties with whom he has had dealings are notified of the agent's lack of authority.

The power of the principal to revoke the agent's authority is limited in some cases and, for example, the principal cannot revoke *where the agency is coupled with an interest*. The interest of the agent must be more than a mere right to salary or commission and must amount to a form of security as where the principal gives his creditor a power to collect the principal's debts and pay himself out of the proceeds. Such an agency is not terminated by revocation, death or other incapacity of the principal or agent.

(i) *By renunciation*. The agent may renounce his authority and thus terminate the agency, but again the contract of employment cannot be arbitrarily broken. The agent must give his principal the specified or customary or reasonable notice and if he does not do so the principal may sue the agent for breach of contract. The agent's apparent authority continues until third parties with whom he has had dealings are on notice of the agent's renunciation and if the agent does make a contract on behalf of his principal after renouncing his authority the principal will be bound to the third party but will have an action against the former agent.

PARTICULAR AGENTS

The mercantile agent (or factor)

The Factors Act 1889, using the term mercantile agent for what is also known as a factor, defines him as follows: 'A mercantile agent having in the customary course of his business as such agent authority either to sell goods, or to consign goods for the purpose of sale, or to buy goods, or to raise money on the security of goods' (s. 1(1)).

The following points arise from the definition.

Mercantile agent

An agent is a factor if, and only if, it is in the customary course of his business as such agent:

(a) to sell goods; or
(b) to consign goods for sale; or
(c) to buy goods; or
(d) to raise money on the security of goods.

A person who is not normally a factor may become one if he satisfies one of these four requirements, and a person may be a factor even though he acts for one principal only, or where he acts as a factor for the first time. Conversely a person who is normally in business as a factor will not be one for any transaction outside the scope of these four categories. The term factor does not, however, include carriers, wharfingers, warehousemen or other mere bailees nor does it include a person who is selling goods on behalf of himself and not for another. **The following cases illustrate a one principal factor and other aspects of the definition.**

Lowther v Harris [1927] I KB 393

The plaintiff wished to sell certain antiques and he arranged with a Mr Prior that Prior should find purchasers. Prior was an antique dealer in a small way of business. Among the articles to be sold were certain tapestries called the Aubusson and the Leopard tapestries. To facilitate the sale of the articles, the plaintiff took a house near to Prior's shop and stored the antiques in the house. Prior lived in a flat on the top floor of the house, and used a sitting room on the floor below. People who were taken to view the antiques were not in general told that Prior was an agent. Prior claimed that he could sell the Aubusson tapestry for £525 to a purchaser who did not in fact exist, and the plaintiff allowed him to take it away and Prior later sold it to the defendant for £250. Prior also sold the Leopard tapestry to the defendant but was never given authority to sell or remove that tapestry. The plaintiff now sued the defendant for damages for detinue or conversion. *Held* – Prior's authority was limited and he was not acting for other principals; yet he could still be a mercantile agent and was one in this case. He was in possession of the Aubusson tapestry with the consent of the plaintiff and gave a good title to the defendant under the Factors Act 1889. Regarding the Leopard tapestry Prior was never in possession of it with the plaintiff's consent; thus he did not give a good title and the plaintiff could recover its value.

Staffordshire Motor Guarantee Ltd v British Wagon Co Ltd [1934] 2 KB 305

A Mr Heap, who was a dealer in motor cars at Stoke-on-Trent, made an agreement with the defendants under which he sold to them a motor lorry, of which he was the owner, and they let it out to him on hire. Later Heap, representing himself as still the owner, sold the lorry to a Mr Pettit, the lorry being taken on hire-purchase and sold to the plaintiffs who hired it out to Pettit. Heap allowed his payments to fall in arrear and the defendants repossessed the lorry and now refused to deliver it up to the plaintiffs. The plaintiffs sued for damages for detention of the lorry and for its return. *Held* – Heap was not in possession as a mercantile agent for the purpose of the Factors Act 1889, s. 2(1). He was merely a bailee and the sale by him to the plaintiffs was not rendered valid by the Act.

Kendrick v Sotheby & Co (1967) 117 New LJ 408

The plaintiff bought a statuette which he later left with X to arrange for a photograph of the statuette to be taken and signed by the sculptor's widow. X handed the statuette to the defendants, who were auctioneers, with instructions to sell it. The defendants gave him an advance. *Held* – The plaintiff was the true owner. The defendants had been unable to establish a defence under the Factors Act 1889 that X was a mercantile agent and were ordered to deliver the statuette to the plaintiff. X was ordered to repay the advance paid by the defendants and also to pay all the costs.

Customary course of business

An agent may be a factor although he is not normally in business as a factor, nor a known kind of commercial agent. For example, a man who normally sells second-hand furniture which he has previously bought on his own account becomes a factor if he undertakes to sell a bedroom suite for a principal.

He must be authorized to sell the goods in his own name without saying that he is an agent

Thus in *Rolls Razor* v *Cox* [1967] 1 All ER 397 the defendant was a self-employed door-to-door salesman of washing machines. The plaintiff company supplied him with stock and a van. The company went into liquidation owing the plaintiff money for commission on goods sold. He wished to keep the company's goods until he was paid in full rather than prove in the liquidation. He alleged he could do this by exercising a factor's right of general lien (*see* p. 501). He needed to do this because the company did not owe him money on the goods in his hands but on goods already sold. The Court of Appeal said that he was not a factor and not entitled to a factor's lien. Lord Denning said: 'The usual characteristics of a factor are these. He is an agent entrusted with the possession of goods of several principals, or sometimes only one principal, for the purpose of the sale in his own name without disclosing the name of his principal and he is remunerated by a commission. These salesmen lacked one of those characteristics. They did not sell in their own names but in the name and on behalf of their principals the company. They are agents pure and simple and not factors'.

Goods

This term includes all forms of merchandise, but does not include stocks and shares and negotiable instruments.

Title

The Factors Act 1889, s. 2(1), makes an important amendment to the common-law rule *nemo dat quod non habet* (no one can give what he has not got) as regards agents who may properly be called factors. The section provides that:

Where a mercantile agent is, with the consent of the owner, in possession of goods or of the documents of title to goods, any sale, pledge, or other disposition of the goods, made by him when acting in the ordinary course of business of a mercantile agent, shall, subject to the provisions of this Act, be as valid as if he were expressly authorized by the owner of the goods to make the same; provided that the person taking under the disposition acts in good faith, and has not at the time of the disposition notice that the person making the disposition has not authority to make the same.

The main points of interest in the same section are as follows.

(a) *The mercantile agent must be in possession of the goods or documents of title in his capacity as a mercantile agent.* Thus the owner of a car who leaves it for repair at a garage does not consent to possession by the garage as a dealer. The garage cannot therefore confer a good title if they sell it, even though they might from time to time sell cars.

(b) *The consent of the owner.* Consent is presumed in the absence of evidence to the contrary (s. 2(4)). Even where the mercantile agent obtains the goods by false pretence or fraud he has usually obtained them with the consent, however mistaken, of the owner, and will give a good title to a purchaser from him. Where, however, the agent had obtained the goods by the old offence known as larceny by a trick, he was not normally regarded as having the real consent of the owner, but the better view was that he could still give a good title (*Pearson* v *Rose & Young Ltd* (1951) – *see below*). Many modern cases on consent have arisen in connection with the sale of motor vehicles by fraudulent agents. From these cases it seems clear that the owner must consent not only to the agent's possession of the vehicle but also to his possession of the vehicle registration document and ignition key, because the sale of a vehicle without these items is not a sale in the ordinary course of business. Since the passing of the Theft Act 1968, the offence of larceny by a trick has disappeared from English law and it is likely that deceptions of the kind practised in *Pearson* and similar cases will no longer be regarded as preventing the consent of the owner, the new offence of obtaining property by deception being more akin to false pretences. Thus it may be easier to obtain a good title from the deceiver.

Pearson v Rose & Young Ltd [1951] 1 KB 275

The plaintiff was the owner of a motor car and entrusted it for the purpose of sale to a Mr Hunt who was the managing director of a firm of car dealers. It was admitted that Mr Hunt was a mercantile agent. There was at the time a system whereby purchasers of new cars agreed not to sell them for a certain period of time and, in order to convince Hunt that this car could be sold without being in breach of a covenant not to sell, the plaintiff showed Hunt the registration book as proof of the date of its first registration. Hunt, who had formed the intention to defraud the plaintiff, then asked him to give Mrs Hunt a lift to a local hospital, thus diverting the plaintiff's attention from the registration book. The plaintiff left without it and forgot it, but later the same day Hunt sold the car to a person named Little, who then sold to a Mr Marshall, who then sold to the defendants. The plaintiff now sued the three purchasers in conversion and they claimed a good title under s. 2(1) of the Factors Act 1889. *Held* – The plaintiff consented to Hunt's possession of the car as a mercantile agent, but did not consent to his possession of the registration book as a mercantile agent. The sale of a car without its registration book was not a sale 'in the ordinary course of business' for the purposes of s. 2(1). Further, the consent required to pass a good title here was consent to possession of the car and the registration book. The plaintiff succeeded, as the defendants had not obtained a good title.

Comment: the point was made in the case that if the mercantile agent had obtained the car by deception (see s. 15, Theft Act 1968), e.g. by giving a worthless cheque, or by coming to view the car and representing himself to be another reputable dealer (as in *Cundy* v *Lindsay* (1878) – see p. 89) he would nevertheless be in possession of the car 'with the consent of the owner' for the purposes of s. 2(1) of the Factors Act 1889.

Stadium Finance Ltd v Robbins [1962] 2 All ER 633

The defendant, wishing to sell his Jaguar car, left it with a car dealer, Palmer, with a view to sale. Palmer was to inform him if inquiries were made. The defendant did not leave the ignition key but by accident left the registration document in the glove compartment which was locked. Palmer obtained a key, opened the glove compartment and took possession of the registration document. Palmer sold the car to one of his salesmen, Grossman, who bought it on hire-purchase, the deal being financed by the plaintiffs. Grossman defaulted on his payments and the plaintiffs sought to take possession of the car. However, the defendant, having discovered what had happened, had already retaken possession of the car. The question of title now arose. *Held* – The car was 'goods' for the purposes of s. 2(1) of the Factors Act 1889 even without the ignition key. However, the sale of the car by a mercantile agent who had not been put into possession of the registration document or key was not a sale in the 'ordinary course of business' for the purposes of s. 2(1). Further, since Palmer was not given the registration document or key by the defendant, he was not in possession of the vehicle with the 'consent' of the owner for the purposes of s. 2(1).

George v Revis (1966) 116 New LJ 1544

The plaintiff offered his car for sale and X, a fraudulent person, agreed to buy it subject to a satisfactory engineer's report. The plaintiff allowed X to drive the car away in order to obtain an engineer's report but he did not allow X to take the registration document. However, X managed to steal the registration document before leaving with the car. Later X sold the car to the defendant, who was an innocent purchaser. The plaintiff now claimed damages for conversion of the car and it was *held* – by Megaw J – that since X did not obtain possession of the registration document with the plaintiff's consent and since the document was of great importance in the sale of a car, the defendant did not acquire a title under the Factors Act 1889 and was liable in damages.

(c) *Regarding pledge.* The factor's power to pledge goods is statutory: there was no such power prior to the Factors Act. In order to obtain the protection of the section, the pledge must be for valuable consideration.

The principal can, of course, redeem the goods pledged by paying to the pledgee the amount of any loan or other consideration, e.g. goods given to the agent under the pledge. Where the consideration is goods and not money, the principal cannot be required to pay more than the value at the time of the pledge, even if the goods which formed the consideration have since appreciated in value. Whatever the principal has to pay to redeem the goods pledged he may recover from the agent, subject to an offset by the agent for any rights he had over the goods pledged, e.g. for a lien he may have had over the goods for his charges when he pledged the goods.

(d) *Acting in the ordinary course of business.* The factor must make the sale, pledge or other disposition, within business hours and at some place of business, and generally in circumstances which do not give rise to suspicion. As we have seen above the sale of a vehicle without the registration document and ignition key is not a sale in the ordinary course of business.

A sale or pledge by a mercantile agent through a clerk or other person authorized in the ordinary course of business to make contracts of sale or pledge on behalf of the mercantile agent, is considered to be an agreement with the mercantile agent (s. 6).

(e) *Regarding notice and good faith.* The person taking from the factor must prove that he did so in good faith and without notice of lack of authority. This probably means actual knowledge, though there may be circumstances where the third party is put on inquiry, as where a car is sold without a vehicle registration document. If in such circumstances the third party fails to make further inquiries he may be fixed with notice of the factor's lack of authority.

Del credere agents

In return for an extra commission, called a *del credere* commission, a *del credere* agent promises to guarantee the principal if the third party introduced by the agent fails to pay for the goods delivered to him, or if the third party becomes insolvent. As the contract with the *del credere* agent is part of the wider contract of agency no memorandum is required. This derives from the fact that a *del credere* agent is not totally unconnected in an economic sense with the transaction he is underwriting, as a guarantor must be. He receives some benefit from it by reason of the commission. The *del credere* agent is not liable for any other breach by the third party, e.g. where the third party refuses to take delivery of the goods.

Directors as agents

If the board acting together (or collectively) or one director acting on his own, has *actual authority* to make a particular contract on behalf of the company and that contract is within the company's powers (or, if not, is protected by s. 35 of the Companies Act 1985 – *see* p. 77) then the contract when made will be binding on the company.

However, where the directors act together, or as individuals, beyond their powers the position is as set out below.

Collective acts of the board

There are the following possibilities.

(a) *Companies Act 1985 (as amended)*. Section 35 provides that in favour of a person dealing with a company in good faith, the power of the board of directors to bind the company shall be deemed to be free of any limitation under the company's constitution, and a person shall not be regarded as acting in bad faith just because he knows that an act is beyond the powers of the directors. Therefore, if the above requirements are met, a transaction entered into by the board beyond its powers will bind the company.

(b) *The rule in Turquand's case*. This rule is best explained by looking straightaway at the facts of the case.

Royal British Bank v Turquand (1856) 6 E & B 327

The articles of the company gave the directors the power to exercise the company's borrowing powers if they first obtained approval of the members by ordinary resolution in general meeting.

The directors borrowed money for the company but did not get the ordinary resolution and the question whether the loan was valid or not arose.

The court said it was. The bank could sue the company to recover its loan even though the directors were not, as it happened, authorized to borrow. The bank was an outsider and was entitled to assume that an ordinary resolution in general meeting had been passed.

Comment: This case succeeded because the ordinary resolution involved did not have to be filed with the Registrar of Companies. Therefore, there was no constructive notice of it. During the period when there was constructive notice of a company's memorandum and articles and the contents of its file at the Registry it was decided that *Turquand* could not apply where the resolution required was a special or extraordinary resolution because these had to be filed and an outsider would have constructive notice that they had not been. The relevant decision is *Irvine v Union Bank of Australia* (1877) 2 App Cas 366.

Since the 1985 Act (as amended) in general abolishes the rule of constructive notice *Turquand*'s case should now apply to situations where special and extraordinary resolutions are required. The effect is to widen the rule.

(c) *Relationship between s. 35 and the rule in Turquand's case.* Section 35 gives the same protection as *Turquand* where correct internal procedures were not followed.

On the other hand, *Turquand*'s case would appear to be wider in some respects than s. 35 because it was applied in *Mahoney* v *East Holyford Mining Co* (1875) CR 7 HL 869 where the directors who made the transaction had never been appointed at all, and in *Davis* v *R Bolton & Co* [1894] 3 Ch 678 where the directors made a transfer of shares without a quorum at the meeting. The transfer was *held* valid.

Although s. 35 has not been fully interpreted by the courts, it seems logical to suppose that it would not apply in the circumstances of *Mahoney* and *Davis* because the court will presumably expect that when an English statute says 'the power of the board of directors to bind the company' it means directors who are properly appointed and have a quorum at the relevant meeting.

(d) *The proper purpose rule.* As we have seen, directors must use their agency powers for the proper purpose, that is for the benefit of the company. If they do not do so, the transactions they have entered into, while not *ultra vires* themselves or the company, can be avoided by the company provided that the person with whom the directors dealt was aware of the improper use of the power (*see* again the *Rolled Steel* case on p. 79).

Acts of individual directors and other officers of the company

To what extent will a company be bound by a transaction entered into by an individual director or other officer, e.g. the company secretary, who has no actual authority to enter into it?

There are the following possibilities.

(a) *Companies Act 1985 (as amended).* This states that, in favour of a person dealing with a company in good faith, the power of the board to authorize other persons to bind the company shall be deemed free of any limitation under the company's constitution. Therefore, an individual director, company secretary, employee or other agent authorized by the board to bind the company will do so even if he exceeds the powers given to the board or other agents of the company by the articles. Once again knowledge of lack of power is not bad faith.

(b) *The rules of agency law – usual authority.* Where a director or other officer of a company has no actual authority or authorization under s. 35 to enter into a transaction an outsider may be able to regard the company as bound by it if it is usual in the company context for a director or officer to be able to enter into a transaction of the kind in question. Since it is usual to delegate wide powers to a managing director and executive directors an outsider will normally be protected if he is dealing with a person who is a managing director or other executive directors, e.g. sales director, or who has been held out as such by the company.

Thus in *Freeman & Lockyer* v *Buckhurst Park Properties Ltd* [1964] 1 All ER 630 a managing director without express authority of the board, but with their knowledge, employed on behalf of the company a firm of architects and surveyors for the submission of an application for planning permission which involved preparing plans and defining boundaries. It was *held* that the company was liable to pay their fees. The managing director had bound the company by his acts which were within the usual authority of a managing director.

Where, however, the outsider deals with a non-executive director or officer, who has not been authorized under s. 35 his position is much less secure. An ordinary director and other officers of the company have little usual authority to bind the company.

Once one gets below the director level the position becomes even more of a problem. There is little, if any, usual authority in the executive of a company to make contracts on its behalf without actual authority, though it would appear that a company secretary has authority to bind the company in contracts relating to day-to-day administration.

Thus in *Panorama Developments* v *Fidelis Furnishing Fabrics* [1971] 3 All ER 16 the secretary of a company ordered cars from a car hire firm representing that they were required to meet the company's customers at London Airport. Instead he used the cars for his own purposes. The company did not pay the bill so the car hire firm claimed from the secretary's company. It was *held* that the company was liable for its secretary had usual authority to make contracts such as the present one which was concerned with the administrative side of the business.

Partners as agents

The power of a partner, including a salaried partner, to make himself and his partner liable for transactions which he enters into *on behalf of the firm* (not on his own behalf) is based on the law of agency. Each partner is the agent of his co-partners.

Section 5 of the Partnership Act 1890 makes this clear. It says that every partner is the agent of the firm and of his co-partners for the purpose of the business of the partnership.

Partners' powers

A partner's authority to enter into transactions on behalf of the firm and his co-partners may be set out under the following headings.

Actual authority

If a partner is asked by his co-partners to buy a new van for the firm's use and makes a contract to purchase one, the firm is bound. Section 6 deals with authorized acts and says that the firm will be liable for the authorized acts of partners and also employees of the firm.

Apparent authority

If a partner enters into a transaction on behalf of the firm without authority, the person the partner deals with may, if he or she does not know of the lack of authority, hold the firm bound under the provisions of s. 5 which gives partners some apparent authority.

However, s. 5 says that *the transaction must be connected with the business*. If there is a dispute about this the court will decide what can be said to be 'connected', regardless of what the partnership agreement may say. **The following case illustrates the point**.

Mercantile Credit Co Ltd v Garrod [1962] 3 All ER 1103

Mr Parkin and Mr Garrod had entered into an agreement as partners for the letting of garages and the carrying out of motor repairs, but the agreement expressly excluded the buying and selling of cars. Parkin, without Garrod's knowledge, sold a car to Mercantile for the sum of £700 but the owner of the car had not consented to the sale. The finance company did not, therefore, become owners of the car and wanted its money back. The court *held* that the firm was liable and that Mr Garrod was liable as a partner to repay what the firm owed to Mercantile. The judge dismissed the argument that the transaction did not bind the firm because the agreement excluded the buying and selling of cars. He looked at the matter instead from 'what was apparent to the outside world in general'. Parkin was doing an act of a like kind to the business carried on by persons trading as a garage.

Comment: The point of the case is that although the buying and selling of cars was expressly forbidden by the partnership agreement, the firm was bound. This is a correct application of s. 8, which provides that internal restrictions on the authority of partners will have effect only if the outsider deals with a partner, but with actual notice of the restrictions. In this case Mercantile had no such knowledge of the restrictions and, of course, there is no constructive notice of the contents of partnership agreements as there used to be of the objects of companies as set out in the memorandum (*see further* p. 79).

Also the transaction must be carried out *in the usual way of business*. In other words, it must be a *normal* transaction for the business. An example can be seen in *Goldberg* v *Jenkins* (1889) 15 VLR 36 where a partner borrowed money on behalf of the firm at 60 per cent interest per annum when money could be borrowed at between six per cent and ten per cent per annum. He had no actual authority to enter into such a transaction and the court *held* that the firm was not bound to accept the loan. The firm did borrow money but it was not usual or normal to borrow at that high rate.

Finally, s. 5 says that *the outsider must know or believe that he is dealing with a partner in the firm*. Because of the requirements of the Business Names Act 1985 as regards the display of the names of the owners of the firm on various documents and in various places a *dormant partner* is now more likely to be known as a partner to an outsider. So if a dormant partner makes an unauthorized contract in the ordinary course of business in the usual or normal way, the outsider should now be able to say that he knew or believed the dormant partner to be a partner. If so, a dormant partner can enter into an unauthorized transaction which will bind the firm under s. 5. If the outsider does not know the dormant partner is a member of the firm, as where the 1985 Act is not being complied with, then the firm will not be bound. A dormant partner would be since he made the contract.

Situations of apparent authority as laid down by case law

Section 5 does not say what acts are in the usual course of business. However, the courts have, over the years, and sometimes in cases heard before the 1890 Act was passed codifying the law, decided that there are a number of definite areas in which a partner has apparent authority. These are set out below.

All partners in all businesses

Here there is apparent authority to sell the goods (but not the land) of the firm, and to buy goods (but not land) on behalf of the firm, to receive money in payments of debts due to the firm and give valid receipts. So if A pays a debt due to the firm to B, a partner, who gives A a receipt then fails to put the money into the firm's funds, A is nevertheless discharged from payment of the debt. Partners can also employ workers but once they are set on they are employees of *all* the partners so that one partner cannot discharge an employee without the consent of the others. Partners also have an insurable interest in the firm's property and can insure it. They may also employ a solicitor to defend the firm if an action is brought against it. The authority of an individual partner to employ a solicitor to bring an action on behalf of the firm seems to be restricted to actions to recover debts owing to the firm.

All partners in trading partnerships

Partners in trading firms have powers *which are additional* to those set out above. Thus partners in a firm of grocers have more powers than partners in a professional practice of, for example, law or accountancy. There does not seem to be any good reason for this but it has been confirmed by many cases in court and cannot be ignored.

In *Wheatley* v *Smithers* [1906] 2 KB 321 the judge said in regard to what was meant by the word 'trader': 'One important element in any definition of the term would be that trading implies buying or selling'. This was applied in *Higgins* v *Beauchamp* [1914] 3 KB 1192 where it was decided that a partner in a business running a cinema had no implied power to borrow on behalf of the firm. The partnership agreement did not give power to borrow and because the firm did not trade in the *Wheatley* v *Smithers* sense there was no implied power to borrow. If a firm is engaged in trade, the additional implied powers of the partners are: (a) to draw, issue, accept, transfer and endorse promissory notes and bills of exchange, including cheques if connected with the business and in the usual way of business. *A partner in a non-trading business only has apparent authority to draw cheques in the firm's name on the firm's bankers.* If the cheque is stopped a payee, or someone he has indorsed it over to, can sue the firm on it; (b) to borrow money on the credit of the firm even beyond any limit agreed on by the partners unless this limit is known to the lender. Borrowing includes overdrawing a bank account; (c) to secure the loan, which means giving the lender a right to sell property belonging to the firm if the loan is not repaid.

Situations of no apparent authority

No partner, whether in a trading firm or not, has apparent authority in the following situations.

(a) A partner cannot make the firm liable on a deed. He or she needs the authority of the other partners. This authority must be given by deed. In English law an agent who is to make contracts by a deed must be appointed as an agent by a written document stated to be a deed.

(b) A partner cannot give a guarantee, e.g. of another person's debt, on which the firm will be liable.

(c) A partner cannot accept payment of a debt at a discount by, for example, accepting 75p instead of £1, nor can he or she take something for the debt which is not money. A partner cannot, therefore, take shares in a company in payment of a debt owed to the firm.

(d) A partner cannot bind the firm by agreeing to go to arbitration with a dispute. Going to arbitration with a dispute and having it heard by, say, an engineer, if the dispute relates, for example, to the quality of engineering work done under a contract is a sort of compromise of the right to go first to a court of law and have the case heard by a judge. A partner cannot compromise the legal rights of the firm.

(e) As we have seen, a partner has no apparent authority to convey or enter into a contract for the sale of partnership land.

A partner's liability for debt and breach of contract by the firm

If because of actual or apparent authority, a partner (or for that matter another agent such as an employee) makes the firm liable to pay a debt or carry out a contract, as where goods are ordered and the firm refuses to take delivery, the usual procedure will be to sue the firm in the firm's name. If the court gives the plaintiff a judgment and the firm does not have sufficient assets to meet it, the partners are liable to pay it from their private assets. Under s. 3 of the Civil Liability (Contribution) Act 1978 each partner is liable to pay the amount of the judgment in full. The partner who has actually paid the debt on behalf of the firm will then have a right to what is called a contribution from co-partners.

Before the 1978 Act contribution was equal. Thus if A paid a partnership debt of £300 he could ask partners B and C for a contribution of £100 each.

This rule of equal contribution is taken away by s. 2 of the 1978 Act which provides that the amount of any contribution which the court may give is to be what it thinks is 'just and equitable' so that it need not in all cases be equal, but most often will be.

The effect of the above rules is that a partner can be required to pay the firm's debts from private assets. From this we can see that only if *all* the partners are unable to pay the firm's debts will the firm be truly insolvent. Under s. 9 of the Partnership Act 1890 the estate of a deceased partner is also liable for the debts of the firm which were incurred while the deceased was a partner.

DEFINITION AND NATURE OF A PARTNERSHIP

The Partnership Act 1890 sets out the basic rules which apply to this type of business organization. All section references are to that Act unless there is a reference to some other named Act.

Definition

A partnership is defined as 'The relation which subsists between persons carrying on a business in common with a view of profit' (s. 1).

Explanation and consequences of the definition

(a) *The relation which subsists is one of contract.* A partnership agreement is a contract. However, it is not enough just to agree to be partners; you must also be *in a business which has started.*

Thus, if Jane and John decide that they *will* run a shop as partners, they are not partners in the eyes of the law until the shop is actually operating.

While they are preparing to open, as by ordering goods and starting a bank account, they are *not* partners, and contracts in the 'preparing' stage are *not* partnership contracts. If they are made they are made only by the person who actually enters into them. **The following case illustrates this point**.

Spicer (Keith) Ltd v Mansell [1970] 1 All ER 462
Mr Mansell (M) and Mr Bishop (B) lost their jobs. They agreed to go into business together and form a limited company to run a restaurant. While they were forming the company and before it had received its certificate of incorporation from the Registrar, Mr B ordered some goods from Spicer's for the business. They also opened a bank account in the name of the company.

The company was eventually formed but was not bound by the contract which Mr B had made because it was not in existence at the time. It was a pre-incorporation contract. These contracts do not bind the company when it comes into being.

Mr B went bankrupt before Spicer's had been paid. So, rather than prove in a bankruptcy, Spicer's sued Mr M on the basis that he was a partner of Mr B, and since partners are jointly and severally liable for the debts of the firm, Mr M, they said, should pay and then get a contribution from Mr B (though it was not too likely that he would).

The Court of Appeal decided that Mr B and Mr M were not partners. They were not carrying on a business together in partnership. They were preparing to carry on a business as a company as soon as they could. They were company promoters, not partners.

Comment: The case illustrates the importance of the relationship of partners and, indeed, its possible terrible consequences. Each partner makes the other his agent for the purpose of making contracts for him and, provided those contracts were within the scope of the partnership business, he is liable to perform all such contracts as if he had made them himself. Fortunately, for Mr Mansell in this case the court did not accept that the parties were partners so that Mr Bishop was liable on his own for the debt to Spicer's.

(b) *A partnership is 'between persons'*, but a company, being a legal person (*see* p. 75) can be a partner with a human person. The members of the company may have limited liability while the human person has not.

Two or more limited companies can be in partnership, forming a consortium as an alternative to merging one with the other.

(c) *Partners must be carrying on a business*, and for this reason a group of people who run a social club would not be a partnership.

Under s. 45 a business includes 'every trade, occupation, or profession', but this does not prevent a particular profession from having rules forbidding members to be in partnership, e.g. a barrister is not allowed to be in partnership with another barrister, at least for the purpose of practice at the Bar.

The importance of being in business together as partners is also shown by *Spicer v Mansell* (1970) *above*.

(d) *Partners must act in common*, and the most important result of this is that unless the agreement says something different, every general partner must be allowed to have a say in management, as s. 24(5) also provides.

A partner who is kept out of management has a ground to dissolve the firm unless there is something in the agreement which limits the right to manage.

(e) *There must be a view of profit*, and so it is unlikely that those groups of persons who have got together to run railway preservation societies are partnerships.

(f) *The sharing of gross returns*, by A and B will not normally indicate a partnership between A and B.

Partners share net profits, i.e. turnover less the outgoings of the business. Section 2 says that the sharing of gross returns does not, of itself, provide evidence of partnership. The following case illustrates this point.

Cox v Coulson [1916] 2 KB 177

Mr Coulson had a lease of a theatre. A Mr Mill was the employer/manager of a theatre company. Mr Coulson and Mr Mill agreed to present a play called *In Time of War*. Mr Coulson was to provide the theatre and pay for the lighting and advertising and get 60 per cent of the money which came in at the box office – the gross takings.

Mr Mill paid those taking part in the play and provided the scenery and the play itself and got 40 per cent of the gross takings.

Mrs Cox paid to see the play. As part of the performance an actor had to fire a revolver with a blank round in it. Because of alleged negligence a defective cartridge was put in the revolver and when the actor fired it Mrs Cox, who was sitting in the dress circle, was shot and injured. She wanted to succeed in a claim for damages against Mr Coulson. He had more money than Mr Mill. However, the actor was employed by Mr Mill and he alone was liable vicariously for the actor's negligence unless Mrs Cox could convince the court that Mill and Coulson were partners. The court decided that they were not; they were merely sharing the gross returns. Only the actor and Mr Mill were liable.

Comment: (i) The sharing of profits suggests a partnerlike concern with the expenses of the business and its general welfare. Sharing gross returns does not produce an *implied agreement* of partnership.

(ii) If there is an *express agreement*, oral or written, and in it the partners agree to share gross returns, then there would be a partnership.

(g) *Joint ownership* according to s. 2 does not of itself make the co-owners partners. That means that there is no joint and several liability for debt between the co-owners, say A and B. So if A and B are joint owners of 12 Acacia Avenue and A cannot pay a debt, say for a carpet which he has had fitted in his bedroom, B cannot be made liable as a partner. Co-owners are not agents one of the other as partners are.

(h) *Formalities*, that is, writing, is not required for a partnership agreement. However, to make quite sure what has been agreed by the partners there should be a written agreement.

The sharing of profits as evidence of partnership

At one time the sharing of profits was almost conclusive evidence of partnership. During this period a number of everyday business transactions could give rise to a partnership, though the parties did not want this because of the possibility of incurring liability for another's debts. The position was eventually clarified in regard to the business transactions set out below by s. 2(3) of the Act of 1890.

(a) *Partners can pay off a creditor by instalments out of the profits of the business.* **This comes from the following case which was decided before the 1890 Act.**

Cox v Hickman (1860) 8 HL Cas 268

A trader had got into debt and his creditors decided that instead of making him bankrupt and getting only a proportion of what he owed them, they would let him keep the business but supervise him in the running of it and take a share of the profits each year until their debts were paid in full.

An attempt was made in this case to make one of the supervising creditor/trustees liable for the trader's debts as a partner. But was he a partner? The court said he was not. He was a creditor being paid off by a share of profits.

Comment: (i) There was, in addition, no mutual participation in trade here, but a mere supervision of the business. Of course, if creditors assume an active role in management they may well become partners.

(ii) The more modern approach would be for the creditors to ask the court for the appointment of a receiver to run the business. Obviously, he would not be regarded as a partner.

(b) *Partners can pay their employees or agents by a share of profits.* It has long been the practice of some organizations to pay employees in part by some profit-sharing scheme. The Act makes this possible without putting the employees at risk of being regarded as partners and liable for the debts of the firm if the true partners run into money trouble.

The provision is also important to the true partners because the giving of labour is sufficient to form a partnership: the putting in of money by way of capital is not essential. So this provision makes sure that the employees themselves cannot claim to be partners just because they are sharing profits under an employees' scheme.

(c) *Partners can pay an annuity* (which is a sum of money paid at intervals during the lifetime of the person who is due to receive it) *by a share of profits to the widow or child of a deceased partner.* These annuities are common in partnership agreements.

This provision prevents those who receive these annuities from being regarded as partners by creditors of the firm merely because they have a share of profits. Once again, however, it is important that the persons receiving the annuity do not take part in the management of the firm.

Annuities payable to male widowers are covered (*see* s. 6(b)), Interpretation Act 1978: 'Words importing female gender include masculine gender unless a contrary intention appears'). There is no contrary indication here.

(d) *Partners can pay interest on a loan by a share of net profits provided that the contract of loan is in writing and signed by all the parties to it.* This provision will protect a lender if a creditor tries to make him liable for the debts of the firm he has lent the money to, as where the creditor argues that the lender is really a dormant partner.

However, the lender must not take part in the running of the business. Remember also that the lender will not need the protection of this provision if he is paid a fixed rate of interest on his loan, e.g. ten per cent per annum instead of ten per cent per annum of the profit. If he is paid ten per cent per annum interest he is clearly a creditor and not a partner.

Do not think that because there is no written contract that a lender will

always be a partner. It is still a matter for the court to decide if it is argued that
he is. Normally a properly drafted written contract should persuade the court
that the lender is not a partner.

(e) *Partners can pay for goodwill by a share of profits.* If A sells his business to partners
B and C, and B and C pay in cash for the tangible assets of A's business, e.g. the
plant and machinery, A, B and C may agree that the goodwill of A's business
should be paid for by giving A a share of the profits for a period of time. A will
not be regarded as a partner unless, of course, he takes part in the management
of the business.

The application of the section is illustrated by the case set out below.

Pratt v Strick (1932) 17 Tax Cas 459

A doctor sold his practice, including goodwill, to another doctor, it being agreed that the
selling doctor would, for three months, live in the house from which the practice was
carried on and introduce his patients to the purchasing doctor, being entitled to half the
profits and liable for half the expenses during that three months. Mr Strick, an Inspector of
Taxes, raised an assessment on the selling doctor under the Finance Act 1929 under which
the selling doctor was said to be liable to tax as a partner with the purchasing doctor on
three-twelfths of the annual profit, not merely the profit he took in the three months he was
introducing patients. The court said that there was no partnership and the practice was the
purchasing doctor's from the date of sale. Mr Strick's assessment was not valid.

Comment: This provision recognizes that one way of paying for goodwill is out of the
profits it is said to create. In addition, the contract is, of course, a contract of sale of a
business so it is hardly likely that it could be regarded as a contract of partnership.

Deferred creditors – generally

Under s. 3 those receiving money from the firm under headings (d) and (e) above are
deferred creditors if the partners go bankrupt during their lifetime or die insolvent.

Lenders and sellers of goodwill will not get any of the money owed to them until
all other creditors have been paid £1 in the £.

Thus the lender of money and the seller of goodwill do not get the best of both
worlds. Section 2 provides that they do not become partners and liable for debts but
s. 3 makes them deferred creditors if the partners are insolvent.

Deferred creditors – lenders with security

A lender who becomes a deferred creditor because of the partner's insolvency is in a
better position if he has taken a security over an asset or assets of the firm.

The court decided in *Re Lonergan, ex parte Sheil* (1877) 4 Ch D 789 that a deferred
lender can enforce a security by selling the asset or assets taken as security because
the first right to claim the debt (which is deferred by s. 3) and the second right to
enforce the security are independent rights, and the second right is not deferred by
s. 3.

TYPES OF PARTNER

Partners are of different types in law as set out below.

The general partner

This is the usual type of partner who, under s. 24, has the right to take part in the management of the business unless there is an agreement between himself and the other partner(s) that he should not. For example, the partnership agreement may say that some junior partners are not to order goods or sign cheques. We have seen, however, that in spite of restrictions of this kind, if a junior partner ordered goods on behalf of the firm, though he had no authority to do so, the contract would be good and the seller could sue the partners for the price if they did not pay.

However, by ignoring the partnership agreement and making unauthorized contracts in this way, the junior partner could give his co-partners grounds to dissolve the firm and exclude him from their future business operations.

The dormant partner

The 1890 Act does not mention this type of partner but in fact he is a partner who puts money (or other form of capital) into the firm but takes no active part in the management of the business. If he does take part in management he would cease to be a dormant partner and become a general partner.

The salaried partner

It is quite common today, at least in professional practices of, for example, solicitors and accountants, to offer a young assistant a salaried partnership without the assistant putting any capital into the firm as the general partners do.

Normally, these salaried partners are paid a salary just as an employee is with tax and national insurance being deducted from it. They are not partners for the purpose of dissolving the firm. If they want to leave they do so by serving out their notice or getting paid instead.

However, because they usually appear on the firm's letterheading as partners, they could, according to the decision in *Stekel* v *Ellice* [1973] 1 All ER 465 be liable to pay the debts of the firm as a partner by estoppel (*see below*).

Because of this case a salaried partner should get a full indemnity, as it is called, from the general partners in case he is made to pay the firm's debts. In practice this will not happen unless the firm has not paid its debts. Liability as a partner is joint and several so that if A is a full partner and B a salaried partner, and the debt £2,000, either A or B could be made to pay it all and then claim only a contribution, which would often be one half, from the other partner. Thus if B pays the £2,000 he is entitled to £1,000 from A. However, if B gets an indemnity from A, then if B has to pay the £2,000 he can recover *all* of it from A.

The partner by holding out (or by estoppel)

The usual way in which this happens in practice is where a person allows his or her name to appear on the firm's letterheading, whether that person is or is not a full partner (*see Stekel v Ellice* (1973)). It can also happen on the retirement of a partner if the partner retiring does not get his name off the letterheading.

Under s. 14 everyone who by words, spoken or written, or by conduct, represents himself, or knowingly allows himself to be represented as a partner in a particular firm, is liable as a partner to anyone who has, because of that, given credit to the firm.

Thus, although such a person is not truly a partner, he may be sued by a creditor who was led to believe that he was as if he was in fact a partner.

However, to become a partner by holding out (or estoppel, as it is also called) the person held out must *know* that he is being held out as a partner and consent.

The following case is an example.

Tower Cabinet Co Ltd v Ingram [1949] 2 KB 397

In January 1946 Ingram and a person named Christmas began to carry on business in partnership as household furnishers under the name of 'Merry's' at Silver Street, Edmonton, London. The partnership lasted until April 1947 when it was brought to an end by mutual agreement. After the dissolution of the firm Christmas continued to run 'Merry's and had new notepaper printed on which Ingram's name did not appear. In January 1948 Christmas was approached by a representative of Tower Cabinet and eventually ordered some furniture from them. The order was confirmed on letterheading which had been in use before the original partnership was dissolved and Ingram's name was on it, as well as that of Christmas. Ingram had no knowledge of this and it was contrary to an agreement which had been made between him and Christmas that the old letterheading was not to be used. Tower Cabinet obtained a judgment for the price of the goods against 'Merry's' and then tried to enforce that judgment against Ingram as a member of the firm. The Court decided that since Ingram had not knowingly allowed himself to be represented as a partner in 'Merry's' within s. 14 of the Partnership Act 1890, he was not liable as a partner by holding out (or estoppel).

Comment: As the case shows, a partner who has retired will not be liable if after retirement his name appears on the firm's letterheading if the other partners agree before he retires that the stock of old letterheading will be destroyed, or that his name will be crossed out. If old notepaper is used in spite of the agreement, the ex-partner is not liable: there is no duty in law to stop people telling lies! However, something should be done to show lack of consent if it is known that old letterheading is being used. This could be, for example, a recorded delivery letter to the continuing partners expressing dissent.

A partner who intends to work with the firm, perhaps part-time, after retirement, can avoid the above problems by describing himself on the firm's letterheading as a 'consultant'.

The person who is held out is liable to a creditor who has relied on him being a partner. That is all s. 14 says. However, in *Hudgell Yeates & Co v Watson* [1978] 2 All

ER 363 the court said that the true or actual partners could also be liable to such a creditor if they themselves were responsible for the holding out or knowingly allowed holding out to take place.

Finally, s. 14 provides that the continued use of a deceased partner's name will not make his estate (that is, the property he has left on death) liable for the debts of the firm.

DISSOLUTION

A partnership is usually dissolved without the help of the court though sometimes the court is brought in.

Non-judicial dissolution

Any of the following events will normally bring about a dissolution of a partnership.

(a) *The ending of the period for which the partnership was to exist.* Section 32(a) states that a partnership for a fixed term is dissolved when the term expires. A partnership for the joint lives of A, B and C ends on the death of A, or B, or C.

(b) *The achievement of the purpose for which the partnership was formed.* By reason of s. 32(b) a partnership for a single undertaking is dissolved at the end of it. In *Winsor v Schroeder* (1979) 129 NLJ 1266 S and W put up equal amounts of cash to buy a house, improve it, and then sell it at a profit which was to be divided equally. The court decided that they were partners under s. 32(b) and that the partnership would end when the land was sold and the profit, if any, divided.

If in partnerships of the type set out in (a) and (b) above, the firm continues in business after the period has expired, without any settlement of their affairs by the partners, an agreement not to dissolve will be implied. Unless there is a new agreement to cover the continuing partnership, it is a partnership at will. Section 27 applies to it so that the rights and duties of the partners are the same as before the original partnership ended. However, since it has now become a partnership at will, any partner can give notice to end it.

(c) *By the giving of notice.* Under s. 32(c) a partnership which is not entered into for a period of time or for a particular purpose can be dissolved by notice given by *any partner*, but not a limited partner.

The notice must be in writing if the partnership agreement is in the form of a deed (s. 26(2)). If not, oral notice will do.

The notice takes effect when all the partners know of it or from any later date which the person giving the notice states as the date of dissolution (s. 32(c)). No particular period of notice is required. Withdrawal of the notice requires the consent of *all* the partners (*Jones v Lloyd* (1874) LR 18 Eq 265) otherwise the dissolution goes ahead and the court will, if asked by a partner, order the other partners to wind up the firm with him. The court said in *Peyton v Mindham* [1972] 1 WLR 8 that it could and would declare a dissolution notice to be of no effect if it was given in bad faith as where A and B dissolve a partnership with C by notice in order to exclude C from valuable future contracts.

Dissolution by notice depends on what the partnership agreement says. If as in *Moss* v *Elphick* [1910] 1 KB 846 the partnership agreement says that dissolution is only to be by mutual consent of the partners, s. 32(c) does not apply.

(d) *Death of a partner.* Under s. 33(1) the death of a partner (but not a limited partner) dissolves the firm. The share of the partner who has died goes to his personal representatives who are usually appointed by his will. They have the rights of a partner in a dissolution. Partnership agreements usually provide that the firm shall continue after the death of a partner so that the dissolution is only a technical one. A deceased partner's share is paid out to his personal representatives, although partnership agreements do sometimes provide for repayment of capital by instalments, or by annuities, e.g. to a spouse or other dependent. Of course, there is bound to be a dissolution of a two-partner firm when one partner dies since if the other carries on business, it is as a sole trader.

(e) *Bankruptcy of a partner.* By reason of s. 33(1) the bankruptcy of a partner (not a limited partner) dissolves the firm. The partnership agreement usually provides that the business shall continue under the non-bankrupt partners, which means that the dissolution is again only a technical one, and the bankrupt partner's share is paid out to his trustee in bankruptcy. The agreement to continue the business must be made before the partner becomes bankrupt (*Whitmore* v *Mason* (1861) 2 J & H 204).

(f) *Illegality.* Under s. 34 a partnership *is in every case* dissolved by illegality. There can be no contracting-out in the partnership agreement.

There are two types of illegality.

(i) *Where the business is unlawful,* for example where the objects are unlawful because, as in *Stevenson & Sons Ltd* v *AK fur Cartonnagen Industrie* [1918] AC 239 the English company, Stevenson, was in partnership with a German company as a sole agent to sell the German company's goods. This would obviously involve day-to-day trading with an enemy in wartime and the partnership was therefore dissolved on the grounds of illegality; and

(ii) *where the partners cannot legally form a partnership to carry on what is otherwise a legal business,* as in *Hudgell, Yeates & Co* v *Watson* (1978) (*see above*) where a firm of solicitors was regarded as dissolved when one partner had made himself unqualified to practise as a solicitor by mistakenly failing to renew his annual practising certificate.

(g) *Charge.* Section 33(2) says that if a partner's share in the partnership (not a limited partner's share) is charged to pay a private debt, the firm may be dissolved, *not automatically*, but at the *option* of the other partners (including, this time, limited partners). There is no indication in the Act as to whether the option is exercisable by any partner or by a majority or by all unanimously. Since it seems similar to expulsion it may require the unanimous consent of the other partners.

The charge is a form of *involuntary assignment* of a partner's share. A private creditor of a partner who has been to court and got a judgment for debt cannot take the assets of the firm so as to pay it. He can, however, apply to the court under s. 23 for a charging order against the debtor-partner's share of the assets and profits of the firm.

The court may appoint a receiver under s. 23 to help the creditor to collect the share and under the same section the other partners can pay off the creditor and take over the charge which they can then enforce gradually against the partner, e.g. by taking some part only of his share of profit until he has paid off the debt.

Judicial dissolution

Dissolution by the court (normally the Chancery Division of the High Court) is necessary if there is a partnership for a fixed time or purpose and a partner wants to dissolve a firm before the time has expired or the purpose has been achieved *and* there is nothing in the partnership agreement which allows this to be done.

There must be grounds for dissolution. These are set out below.

(a) *Partner's mental incapacity.* This is a ground under the Mental Health Act 1983. The petition for dissolution is in this case heard by the Court of Protection which sits to look after the property of people who are of unsound mind or under some other disability. The partner concerned must be unable, because of mental disorder, of managing his property and affairs.

   A petition may be presented on behalf of the partner who is under the disability or by any of the other partners.

(b) *Partner's physical incapacity.* This is a ground under s. 35(b). The incapacity must be permanent. In *Whitwell* v *Arthur* (1865) 35 Beav 140 a partner was paralysed for some months. He had recovered when the court heard the petition and it would not grant a dissolution.

   Partnership agreements often contain express clauses which allow dissolution after a stated period of incapacity. In *Peyton* v *Mindham* (1972) (*see above*) a clause allowing a fixed-term partnership to be dissolved after nine months' incapacity was enforced.

   Section 35(b) states that the incapacitated partner cannot petition. It is up to his co-partners to do so otherwise he continues as a partner.

(c) *Conduct prejudicial to the business.* Section 35(c) provides for this. The conduct may relate to the business, as in *Essell* v *Hayward* (1860) 30 Beav 158 where a solicitor/partner misappropriated trust money in the course of his duties as a partner. This was a ground for dissolving a partnership for a fixed term, i.e. the joint lives of the partners.

It may, of course, be outside conduct. This will usually justify a dissolution if it results in a criminal conviction for fraud or dishonesty.

Moral misconduct is not enough unless, in the view of the court, it is likely to affect the business. In *Snow v Milford* (1868) 18 LT 142 a partner's 'massive adultery all over Exeter' was not regarded by the court as sufficient grounds for dissolution under s. 35(c).

Section 35(c) forbids a petition by the partner in default.

(d) *Wilful or persistent breach of the agreement or conduct affecting the relationship.* This is covered by s. 35(d). It includes, for example, refusal to meet on business or keep accounts, continued quarrelling and exclusion of a partner from management. However, as the court said in *Loscombe v Russell* (1830) 4 Sim 8, the conduct must be 'serious'. Thus occasional rudeness or bad temper would not suffice.

'Wilful' means a serious breach inflicting damage on the firm. Less serious breaches are enough if 'persistent'. In *Cheesman v Price* (1865) 35 Beav 142 a partner failed 17 times to enter small amounts of money he had received in the firm's books. The court ordered dissolution. The essential trust between the partners had gone.

Again, s. 35(d) forbids a petition by the partner in default. *No partner can force a dissolution by his own default.*

(e) *The business can only be carried on at a loss.* This is provided for by s. 35(e). It is hardly surprising as a ground for dissolution in view of the fact that partners are in business together with a view of profit, as s. 1 states. Therefore they must have a means to release themselves from loss.

Section 35(e) is not available if the losses are temporary. In *Handyside v Campbell* (1901) 17 TLR 623 a sound business was losing money because a senior managing partner was ill. He asked the court for a dissolution. The court would not grant it. The other partners could manage the firm back to financial prosperity.

The court will not, however, expect the partners to put in more capital (*Jennings v Baddeley* (1856) 3 K & J 78). *Any partner may petition.*

(f) *The just and equitable ground.* Under s. 35(f) the court may dissolve a partnership if it is just and equitable to do so. Although there is no direct authority on s. 35(f), it appears to give the court wide powers to hear petitions which could not be made under the other five heads that we have considered.

In *Harrison v Tennant* (1856) 21 Beav 482 a judicial dissolution was ordered where a partner was involved in long and messy litigation which he refused to settle. A similar order was made in *Baring v Dix* (1786) 1 Cox Eq Cas 213 where the objects of the firm could not be achieved. The firm was formed to work a device for spinning cotton but the device did not operate properly.

It appears from *Re Yenidje Tobacco Co Ltd* [1916] 2 Ch 426, a company dissolution based upon the fact that the company was in reality a partnership, that deadlock between the partners is enough for dissolution, even though the business is prospering.

All partners may petition. The court is unlikely, however, to dissolve a firm on the petition of a partner committing misconduct unless the other partners are doing so as well.

Creditors cannot petition the court to dissolve a firm of fewer than eight partners. They must proceed against the partners individually under the bankruptcy laws if the firm is not paying its debts.

If there are eight or more partners the firm can be wound up as an unregistered company under the Insolvency Act 1986. Under the provisions of the 1986 Act creditors can petition on certain grounds which are available in a company winding up, for example if the firm cannot pay its debts.

COMPANIES AND PARTNERSHIPS COMPARED

General

The following areas should be noted.

(a) A company is a persona at law. A partnership firm is not a persona at law. Thus a company continues to exist in spite, for example, of the death of any of its members, whereas this event will bring about the dissolution of a partnership.

(b) In a company the shares of the members are freely transferable, whereas no partner can transfer his share without the consent of the other partners, because this would involve the admission of a new partner on which the Partnership Act 1890 requires all partners to agree.

(c) A shareholder is not an agent for the company, but each general partner is an agent of the firm to make contracts which will bind himself and his other partners.

(d) The members of a company have no power to manage its affairs whereas, unless the partnership agreement otherwise provides, all partners have a right to take part in the management of the firm.

(e) The liability of each shareholder may be limited either by shares or by guarantee, but the liability of partners for the debts of the firm is unlimited, except in the case of a limited partner.

(f) The affairs of a registered company are closely controlled by the Companies Act 1985 and it must in general trade within the objects as set out in its memorandum. Partners may enter into any business they please and may make any arrangements they choose regarding the running of the firm, so long, that is, as they stay within the general limits of the law.

Advantages and disadvantages of incorporation

The *main* advantages put forward by professional advisers for the conversion of a business into limited companies can be summarized as follows.

(a) Perpetual succession of the company despite the retirement, bankruptcy, mental disorder or death of members.

(b) Liability of members for company's debts is limited to the amount of their respective shareholding.

(c) Contractual liability of the company for all contracts in its name.

(d) Ownership of property vested in the company is not affected by a change in shareholders.

(e) The company may obtain finance by creating a floating charge with its undertaking or property as security yet may realize assets within that property without the consent of the lenders during the normal course of business until crystallization occurs. *No other form of business organization can use such a charge.*

It is generally thought that the above advantages outweigh the *suggested* disadvantages of incorporation, which are:

(a) public inspection of accounts;

(b) administrative expenses, in terms, for example, of filing fees for documents;

(c) compulsory annual audit.

GRADED QUESTIONS

Essay mode

1. (a) Explain, giving illustrations, the duties which are owed by an agent to his or her principal. What remedies are available to a principal for breach of these duties?

   (b) Principal is in business as a manufacturer and supplier of office equipment. He appoints Angus for the period of five years as his sole agent to sell his equipment in the United Kingdom. Angus works on a commission basis and on the strict understanding that he will sell only at Principal's current list price and that he will not deal in the products of Principal's competitors. Since Principal's products are in short supply, Angus has been selling them above the list price and not accounting for the difference. He has also been supplying the products of one of Principal's competitors and earning an additional commission from the competitor. Principal now seeks your advice.

   Advise Principal.

   (The Institute of Chartered Secretaries and Administrators. English Business Law. June 1988)

2. In what circumstances will a principal be bound by a contract made by an agent on his behalf but without his actual authority?

   (The Institute of Company Accountants. Law Relating to Business. May 1989)

3. (a) In what ways may the authority of an agent come to an end?

   (12 marks)

   (b) Bright, a partner in a firm of consultants, intends to retire in the near future. Advise him of the extent to which he may still be liable for the firm's debts after retirement and of any measure he may take to avoid this liability.

   (8 marks)
   (Total: 20 marks)

   (The Chartered Institute of Management Accountants. Stage 1: Business Law. May 1989

4. (a) Explain the proposition that 'in relation to the business of the partnership all the partners are agents of each other and of the firm'.

   (10 marks)

   (b) In what way may a partnership be dissolved? Who owns the property of the partnership on dissolution?

   (10 marks)
   (20 marks)

   (The Chartered Association of Certified Accountants. Paper 1.4(E). June 1989)

Objective mode

1. Arthur, a well-known philanthropist who is concerned regarding the rise in house prices, put one of his properties on the market at £14,000, though its true market value was in the region of £16,000. He engaged Bob, an estate agent, to deal with the sale. Bob made an arrangement with his brother-in-law Charles, under which the house was to be purchased in Charles' name and later conveyed to Bob. After signing the contract of sale Arthur learned of the arrangement between Bob and Charles and now refuses to complete.

   Delete and complete the following as appropriate in order to produce a correct statement of the legal position:

   Arthur CAN/CANNOT be required to convey the property to Charles because Bob IS NOT/IS in breach of the duty of _____ which exists between principal and agent.

2. Complete the following definition:

   The Factors Act 1889, using the term mercantile agent for what is commonly known as a factor, defines him as a mercantile agent having in the customary course of his business as such agent authority either to _____ goods, or to _____ goods for the purpose of _____ or to _____ goods, or to raise _____ on the _____ of goods.

3. On Saturday, Alexander, an estate agent sold William's house to John for £30,000 'subject to contract' under an agreement between himself and William providing for commission at two per cent. The following Tuesday Alexander received an offer of £31,000 for William's house from Donald. Alexander said the house was sold and the sale to John has now been completed. William is now suing Alexander for damages and has refused to pay commission.

Complete the following in order to produce a correct statement of the legal position:

William will succeed in his claim because Alexander was in breach of his duty to exercise proper _____ and _____ .

4. Able and Baker are solicitors in partnership in Barchester. Charles is a solicitor employed by Able and Baker at a salary of £5,000 per annum. Charles does not take a share of profits or a payment contingent on or varying with profits, though his name appears, with his consent, on the firm's stationery along with the names of Able and Baker.

(a) Delete as appropriate so that the following statement is correct.

Charles IS/IS NOT liable to pay the firm's debts should the firm at any time be unable to do so.

(b) Which *one* of the following statutory provisions is relevant:

   (i)   Limited Partnerships Act, s. 1;
   (ii)   Companies Act 1985, s. 121;
   (iii) Partnership Act 1890, s. 14;
   (iv)   Factors Act 1889, s. 1.

5. Wyre and Watt were in partnership for twenty years dealing in electrical goods under the firm name of 'Sparks Electrical Supplies'. The partnership was dissolved by agreement on 1 January when Wyre retired. No announcement of the dissolution was made either in the *London Gazette* or in any other way. Watt carried on the business under the name of 'Sparks Electrical Supplies' as agreed and new letter-heading, order forms and invoices were prepared showing Watt as the sole proprietor of the business. Four months after Wyre had left the firm, a new typist ordered goods from Super Electrics (who had supplied goods to the old firm) and Modern Electrics (who had not supplied goods to 'Sparks' before and did not know or believe Wyre to be a partner) on old order forms showing the names of Wyre and Watt as proprietors. The goods were supplied but before payment was made Watt, who had always been a gambling man, went bankrupt and both Super Electrics and Modern Electrics obtained a judgment against Sparks Electrical Supplies. The firm's assets are not sufficient to pay the judgment and Super Electrics and Modern Electrics are intending to enforce the judgment against Wyre as a partner in 'Sparks'.

Note the following provisions of the Partnership Act 1890:

(i)   Every one who represents himself, or knowingly allows himself to be represented as a partner is liable to creditors of the firm who have relied on the representation (s. 14(1)).

(ii) A retired partner is not liable for debts incurred with new firms after his retirement unless they knew or believed him to be a partner (s. 36(3)).

(iii) A person who has had previous dealings with a firm can treat former partners as members unless he has notice of a change (s. 36(1)).

Now delete and complete by inserting (i), (ii) or (iii) as appropriate in order to produce correct statements.

(a) Wyre IS/IS NOT liable to pay the judgment obtained by Super Electrics because _____ .

(b) Wyre IS/IS NOT liable to pay the judgment obtained by Modern Electrics because _____ .

Answers to questions set in objective mode appear on p. 551.

20 | Negligence – generally and the business application

The OBJECTIVES of this chapter are to explain the legal concept of negligence and to deal in particular with the tort of negligence as it affects business professionals.

NEGLIGENCE GENERALLY

In ordinary language negligence may simply mean not done intentionally, e.g. the negligent publication of a libel. But while negligence may be one factor or ingredient in another tort, it is also a specific and independent tort and with this we are now concerned.

The tort of negligence has three ingredients and to succeed in an action the plaintiff must show:

(a) the existence of a duty to take care which was owed to him by the defendant;
(b) breach of such duty by the defendant; and
(c) resulting damage to the plaintiff.

The duty of care

Whether a duty of care exists or not is a question of law for the judge to decide. Since the decision of the House of Lords in *Donoghue* v *Stevenson* (1932) (*see* p. 267) the test has become objective and is based on the foresight of the reasonable man. This derives from Lord Atkin's 'neighbour' test which he formulated in the following words: 'You must take reasonable care to avoid acts or omissions which you can reasonably foresee would be likely to injure your neighbour. Who then is my neighbour? The answer seems to be persons who are so closely and directly affected

by my act that I ought reasonably to have them in contemplation as being affected
when I am directing my mind to the acts or omissions which are called in question.'
As we have seen the test is objective, not subjective, and the effect of its application is
that a person is not liable for every injury which results from his carelessness. **There
must be a duty of care, as the following case illustrates.**

Hay (or Bourhill) v Young [1943] AC 92

The plaintiff, a pregnant Edinburgh fishwife, alighted from a tramcar. While she was removing
her fish-basket from the tram, Young, a motor cyclist, driving carelessly but unseen by her,
passed the tram and collided with a motor car some fifteen yards away. Young was killed.
The plaintiff heard the collision, and after Young's body had been removed, she approached
the scene of the accident and saw a pool of blood on the road. She suffered a nervous shock
and later gave birth to a stillborn child. The House of Lords *held* that her action against
Young's personal representative failed, because Young owed no duty of care to persons
whom he could not reasonably anticipate would suffer injuries as a result of his conduct on
the highway.

Lord Atkin's 'neighbour' test has extended to monetary loss caused by careless
misstatements. This has produced a special area of negligence which is referred to as
professional negligence. This is considered in detail at p. 537.

Breach of the duty

If a duty of care is established as a matter of law whether or not the defendant was in
breach of that duty is a matter of fact. Since juries are not normally present in
negligence cases this again is a matter to be decided by the judge but on the basis of
fact, not law. If the defendant is not in breach of the duty to take care he will not be
liable (*see Daniels* v *White & Sons Ltd* (1938) at p. 269).

Resulting damage to the plaintiff

It is necessary for the plaintiff to show that he has suffered some loss since
negligence is not actionable *per se* (in itself). Thus I may believe that the man in front
of me is driving his car too fast and in that sense negligently but he would not be
liable unless he hit somebody or something and caused damage. Damage would not,
of course, be necessary for a criminal prosecution for dangerous driving but it is
essential to a civil action. It will have been noted also that damage is not necessary in
contract where nominal damages will be awarded even for a technical breach.

Mere economic loss

The 'neighbour' test of Lord Atkin does not extend to all kinds of damage and in
particular it should be noted that there is in general no liability where the
defendant's act causes mere economic or monetary loss to the plaintiff unless the

economic or monetary loss arises out of or is accompanied by foreseeable physical injury to the plaintiff or damage to his property. We have already noted that where the defendant's misstatement, as distinct from his act, causes monetary loss, then this is actionable (*Hedley Byrne* v *Heller & Partners* (1963), p. 115). This is the basis of professional liability which is considered further at p. 537. **An example of parasitical damages appears below**.

Spartan Steel and Alloys Ltd v Martin & Co Ltd [1972] 3 All ER 557

While digging up a road the defendants' employees damaged a cable which the defendants knew supplied the plaintiffs' factory. The cable belonged to the local electricity board and the resulting electrical power failure meant that the plaintiffs' factory was deprived of electricity. The temperature of their furnace dropped and so metal that was in melt had to be poured away. Furthermore, while the cable was being repaired the factory received no electricity so it was unable to function for some 14 hours. The Court of Appeal, however, allowed only the plaintiffs' damages for the spoilt metal and the loss of profit on one 'melt'. They refused to allow the plaintiffs to recover their loss of profit which resulted from the factory being unable to function during the period when there was no electricity. Lord Denning MR, chose to base his decision on remoteness of damage rather than the absence of any duty of care to avoid causing economic loss. However, he did make it clear that public policy was involved. In the course of his judgment he said: 'At bottom I think the question of recovering economic loss is one of policy. Whenever the courts draw a line to mark out the bounds of duty, they do so as a matter of policy so as to limit the responsibility of the defendant. Whenever the courts set bounds to the damages recoverable – saying that they are, or are not, too remote – they do it as a matter of policy so as to limit the liability of the defendant.'

Res ipsa loquitur

Although the burden of proof in negligence normally lies on the plaintiff there is a principle known as *res ipsa loquitur* (the thing speaks for itself) and where the principle applies the court is prepared to lighten the plaintiff's burden. In some cases it is difficult for the plaintiff to show how much care the defendant has taken and it is a commonsense rule of evidence to allow the plaintiff to prove the result and not require him to prove any particular act or omission by the defendant. Before the principle can apply the thing causing the damage must be shown to be under the control of the defendant and the accident which happened must be one which does not normally occur unless negligence is present. On proof of this situation negligence in the defendant will be assumed and he will be liable unless he can explain the occurrence on grounds other than his negligence. The explanation must of course be convincing to the court and it is not enough to offer purely hypothetical explanations. For example, if a tile falls off Y's roof and injures X who is lawfully on the highway below, this would probably be a situation in which *res ipsa loquitur* would apply. But if Y can show that at the time an explosion had occurred nearby and this had probably dislodged the tile and the court is impressed by this explanation of the event, the burden of proof reverts to X. **Illustrations appear below**.

Byrne v Boadle (1863) 2 H & C 722

The plaintiff brought an action in negligence alleging that, as he was walking past the defendant's shop, a barrel of flour fell from a window above the shop and injured him. The defendant was a dealer in flour, but there was no evidence that the defendant or any of his servants were engaged in lowering the barrel of flour at the time. The defendant submitted that there was no evidence of negligence to go to the jury, but it was *held* that the occurrence was of itself evidence of negligence sufficient to entitle the jury to find for the plaintiff, even in the absence of an explanation by the defendant.

Pearson v North-Western Gas Board [1968] 2 All ER 669

The plaintiff's husband was killed by an explosion of gas which also destroyed her house. It appeared from the evidence that a gas main had fractured due to a movement of earth caused by a severe frost. When the weather was very cold the defendants had men standing by ready to deal with reports of gas leaks, but unless they received reports there was no way of predicting or preventing a leak which might lead to an explosion. *Held* – by Rees J – that assuming the principle of *res ipsa loquitur* applied, the defendants had rebutted the presumption of negligence and the plaintiff's case failed.

Contributory negligence

Sometimes when an accident occurs both parties have been negligent, and this raises the doctrine of contributory negligence. At common law it was broadly true to say that if the plaintiff was to blame at all for the accident he would receive no damages. Now, however, under the Law Reform (Contributory Negligence) Act 1945 liability is apportionable between the plaintiff and defendant. The claim is not defeated but damages may be reduced according to the degree of fault of the plaintiff.

It should be noted that in *Froom* v *Butcher* [1975] 3 All ER 520 Lord Denning produced an additional definition of contributory negligence so that there are two, namely:

(a) to contribute to the accident, which is the old view of contributory negligence; and

(b) to contribute to the resulting damage, which is a more recent concept in the seat-belt cases.

Furthermore, in *Froom*, Lord Denning laid down a rather precise formula for contributory negligence in regard to seat-belts by saying that if failure to wear a seat-belt would have made no difference, then nothing should be taken off the damages. If it would have prevented the injuries altogether damages should be reduced by 25 per cent and if the injuries would have been less severe the damages should be reduced by 15 per cent, though exemptions would be made, said Lord Denning, for pregnant women and those who were very fat.

PROFESSIONAL NEGLIGENCE

At p. 267 we considered the scope of a manufacturer's liability for defective products which he puts into circulation and the way in which a consumer can take direct action against a manufacturer in negligence. The law of negligence also applies to the provision of services. In particular we are concerned with the position of those whose work involves giving professional business advice.

The background and development

Liability for negligent statements is an important area of the law, and the number of claims continues to increase. Negligent *statements* are now a more potent cause of actions at law than negligent *acts*. This state of affairs has had, and will continue to have, a major influence on the cost of indemnity insurance arrangements.

It was not always so. For example, in *Candler v Crane Christmas* [1951] 2 KB 164 Mr Ogilvie, the owner of a number of companies, was anxious to obtain an investment in them from Mr Candler. The defendants, a firm of accountants, prepared financial statements for Mr Ogilvie, *knowing* that they were to be shown to Mr Candler as a basis for his investment decision. Mr Candler did invest some money but a liquidation followed and he lost it.

He sued the defendants for damages, alleging negligent preparation of the financial statements. It was claimed that the defendants included freehold cottages and leasehold buildings as corporate assets without obtaining ownership evidence.

It was further claimed that the cottages were, in fact, owned by Mr Ogilvie, and that the title deeds were deposited with his bank to secure a personal overdraft. The leasehold buildings, it was alleged, did not belong to the company, but to Mr Ogilvie, and in any case, they had been forfeited, it was said, for non-payment of rent.

To succeed Mr Candler had first to establish, *as a matter of law*, that the defendants owed him a duty of care. If they had indeed been negligent in the preparation of the accounts this could then give rise to liability. The majority of the Court of Appeal decided that there was no duty of care in such circumstances, and so the accountants were not liable to Mr Candler, and would not have been, even if it had been proved that the financial statements were prepared negligently. There was no further appeal.

However, Lord Denning dissented from the majority view, being of the opinion that the accountants did owe a duty to Mr Candler, even though he was not a client. In his judgment, he said:

I think the law would fail to serve the best interests of the community if it should hold that accountants and auditors owe a duty to no one but their client. There is a great difference between the lawyer and the accountant. The lawyer is never called on to express his personal belief in the truth of his client's case, whereas the accountant, who certifies the accounts of his client, is always called on to express his personal opinion whether the accounts exhibit a true and correct view of his client's affairs, and he is required to do this not so much for the satisfaction of his own client, but more for the guidance of shareholders, investors, revenue authorities and others who may have to rely on the accounts in serious matters of business. In my opinion, accountants owe a duty of care not only to their own clients, but also to all those whom they know will rely on their accounts in the transactions for which those accounts are prepared.

However, although Lord Denning was prepared to widen the liability of accountants to encompass a person who was not a client, he does appear to have restricted that liability to persons who it is *known* will rely on the accounts, as the last sentence of the above extract from his judgment clearly reveals. But he was alone in his view of the case, and the expansion of the liability of the accountants (and others) for negligent statements had to wait for more than a decade.

As we have seen in *Hedley Byrne & Co Ltd* v *Heller & Partners* (1963) (*see* p. 115), the House of Lords overruled the majority judgment of the Court of Appeal in *Candler*, and approved the dissenting judgment of Lord Denning. The *Hedley Byrne* case, we may remind ourselves, arose from an advertising campaign which Hedley Byrne were to undertake for a company called Easipower. Hedley Byrne went to the company's bankers, Heller's, for reference, and later alleged that the reference provided was negligently prepared and gave a false picture of Easipower's financial position, so that Hedley Byrne were unable to recover their fees and expenses in the subsequent liquidation of Easipower.

The House of Lords decided that Heller's did owe a duty of care, *even though Hedley Byrne were not customers of the bank*. However, their Lordships were not able to proceed further because Heller's had inserted a disclaimer in the reference as follows: 'For your private use and without responsibility on the part of this bank or its officials.' This was adequate to avoid liability even if Heller's had been negligent, as was alleged.

The decision in *Hedley Byrne* widened the liability of all professionals (including, of course, accountants), but the House of Lords refrained, as a matter of public policy, from imposing the even wider test of *foresight* formulated by Lord Atkin in *Donoghue* v *Stevenson* (1932) (*see* p. 267). That case, as we have seen, related to negligence actions for *physical injury* arising from negligent *acts*, e.g. liability for a negligently manufactured product which causes physical injury to a consumer. Liability under that test extended to anyone who might reasonably be foreseen as suffering injury.

The need for a special relationship – knowledge of victim

Instead the House of Lords decided that in the negligent *statement* cases, there had to be a 'special relationship' between the maker of the statement and the person injured by it. Obviously, this need not be a contractual client relationship. Although their Lordships did not draw up a list of special relationships, comments made by them in their judgments suggest that the duty in regard to a negligent statement would be owed only to those persons whom the maker of the statement knows will rely on it, and not beyond that to those whom he might *foresee* relying on it. Thus the test for negligent statements causing monetary loss (knowledge) was narrower than that for negligent acts causing physical injury (foresight), though, in all honesty, it was difficult to see why liability as such should depend upon the nature of the damage.

Indeed, during the decade following *Hedley Byrne* there have been a number of judicial decisions which have suggested that the foresight test propounded in *Donoghue v Stevenson* could be appropriate in the negligent statement situation thus potentially widening liability.

One major development in this direction is the judgment of Lord Reid in *Home Office v Dorset Yacht Club Co Ltd* [1970] 2 All ER 294. This was an action by the owner of a yacht which was damaged by runaway Borstal boys who escaped while the three officers in charge of them were, contrary to instructions, in bed. In holding that the Home Office owed a duty of care to the owner of the yacht, Lord Reid made the following general comment regarding duty of care. '*Donoghue* v *Stevenson* may be regarded as a milestone . . . It will require qualification in new circumstances. But I think that the time has come when we can and should say that it ought to apply unless there is some justification or valid explanation for its exclusion.'

Further progress along these lines came in *Anns v London Borough of Merton* [1977] 2 All ER 492. In that case, the plaintiffs held a lease of a block of flats built in 1962. Later, considerable settlement caused cracks and the tilting of floors. The plaintiffs blamed the builders and also the local council because, it was alleged, the council had not inspected the flats during building as the by-laws required, so their shallow foundations were not detected. Their Lordships found that the local authority had a duty of care to the plaintiffs and made general comments on the duty of care.

Lord Wilberforce, in particular, took the remarks of Lord Reid (as mentioned) a stage further when he said:

> . . . the position has now been reached that in order to establish that a duty of care arises in a particular situation, it is not necessary to bring the facts of that situation within those of previous situations in which a duty of care has been held to exist. Rather the question has to be approached in two stages.
>
> First, one has to ask whether, as between the alleged wrongdoer and the person who has suffered damage there is a sufficient relationship of proximity or neighbourhood such that, in the reasonable contemplation of the former, carelessness on his part may be likely to cause damage to the latter, in which case a prima facie duty of care arises.
>
> Second, if the first question is answered affirmatively, it is necessary to consider

whether there are any considerations which ought to negate, or reduce or limit the scope of the duty or the class of person to whom it is owed or the damages to which any breach of it may give rise.

From knowledge to foresight

Lord Wiberforce's view that judges should consider broad principle rather than slavishly follow relevant previous decisions enabled Mr Justice Woolf to break out of the *Hedley Byrne* strait-jacket of 'special relationships' in *JEB Fasteners Ltd* v *Marks, Bloom & Co* [1981] 3 All ER 289. In April 1975, the defendants, a firm of accountants, prepared an audited set of accounts for a company called BG Fasteners Ltd for the year ended 31 October 1974. The company's stock, which had been bought for some £11,000, was shown as being worth £23,080, that figure being based on the company's own valuation of the net realizable value of the stock.

The accountants nevertheless described the stock in the accounts as being 'valued at lower of cost and not realizable value.' On the basis of the inflated stock figure, the accounts showed a profit of £11.25p. If the stock had been shown at cost, with a discount for possible errors, the accounts would have shown a loss of more than £13,000.

The defendant auditors were aware when they prepared the accounts that the company faced liquidity problems, and was looking for outside financial support from, amongst other people, the plaintiffs, JEB Fasteners, who manufactured similar products and were anxious to expand their business. The accounts which the defendants had prepared were made available by the directors of BG to the plaintiffs, who, although they had some reservations about the stock valuation, decided that they would take the company over in June 1975 for a nominal amount, because they would in so doing obtain the services of the company's two directors who had considerable experience in the type of manufacturing which the plaintiffs, JEB, carried on.

There were discussions between the plaintiffs and the defendant auditors during the takeover, but the auditors did not inform the plaintiffs that the stock had been put into the accounts at an inflated figure. The merger of the companies was not a financial success, and the plaintiffs brought an action for damages against the defendants.

The plaintiffs alleged that the defendants had prepared the company's accounts negligently, and that they relied on the accounts when buying BG Fasteners, and would not have bought the company had they been aware of its true financial position. It was contended on behalf of JEB that an auditor when preparing a set of accounts owes a duty to all persons whom he ought reasonably to have foreseen would rely on the accounts. The defendant auditors argued that if a duty of care existed, it could only be to persons who had made a specific request for information.

Woolf J decided that the defendant auditors did owe a duty of care to the plaintiffs, but that they were not liable in damages, since their alleged negligence was not the cause of the loss. The overriding reason for the takeover had been to obtain the services of two of BG's directors. On the balance of probabilities, the takeover would have gone ahead even if the accounts had shown the true position.

The judge said that, but for the statement of Lord Wilberforce in *Anns* (as mentioned), Marks, Bloom would not have owed a duty of care to those who took over BG because the foresight test could not have been applied, and a 'special relationship' would not have existed (it was admitted that at the time the accounts in question were audited, Marks, Bloom did not know that they would be relied on by the plaintiffs, or even that any takeover was contemplated).

Furthermore, Woolf J, having found a duty of care, said that following the Wilberforce test in *Anns*, he could find no considerations which he felt ought to exclude it in the circumstances of the Jeb case.

As regards the foreseeability issue, the judge said:

> As Mr Marks was aware of the financial difficulties of BG Fasteners Ltd, and the fact that they were going to need financial support from outside of some sort, I am satisfied that Mr Marks, whom I can treat as being synonymous with the defendants, ought to have realized the accounts could be relied on until the time that a further audit was carried out by the commercial concerns to whom BG Fasteners were bound to look for financial assistance. When he audited the accounts, Mr Marks would not know precisely who would provide the financial support, or what form the financial support would take, and he certainly had no reason to know that it would be by way of takeover by the plaintiffs.
>
> However, this was certainly one foreseeable method, and it does not seem to me that it would be right to exclude the duty of care merely because it was not possible to say with precision what machinery would be used to achieve the necessary financial support. Clearly, any form of loan would have been foreseeable, including the raising of money by way of debenture and, while some methods of raising money were more obvious than others, and a takeover was not the most obvious method, it was certainly one method which was within the contemplation of Mr Marks.

The judge went on to decide that the events leading to the takeover of BG were therefore foreseeable.

There was an appeal by JEB to the Court of Appeal, which upheld Woolf J's finding that there was a lack of causal connection between Jeb's loss and the auditors' alleged negligence. Thus they were not liable.

However, the Court of Appeal went on to say that it was not necessary in order to decide the appeal to determine the scope of an auditor's liability for professional negligence. Thus Woolf J's ruling on this matter retains some authority, but the law is still a little uncertain and in a state of development.

Further developments

Note should be taken of developments in the courts of Scotland, where the law of negligence is the same. The judgment of Lord Stewart in *Twomax Ltd and Goode* v

Dickson, McFarlane and Robinson and *Gordon* v *Dickson, McFarlane and Robinson* (1982) SC 113, delivered on 5 March 1982, in the Court of Session, is of interest.

Twomax acquired a controlling shareholding in a private company called Kintyre Knitwear Ltd. Dickson, McFarland and Robinson were the auditors of Kintyre. Messrs Goode and Gordon, the other plaintiffs, bought smaller holdings soon afterwards. All three plaintiffs (or pursuers as they are called in Scotland) said that in purchasing their interests in Kintyre they had relied on accounts prepared by the defendants, especially those for the year ended 31 March 1973 which showed a move away from a previous loss of £12,318 to a profit of £20,346. Subsequently, however, Kintyre went into receivership and then liquidation, and all three plaintiffs lost their entire investment.

The plaintiffs claimed that the accounts were false and misleading, that the auditors had prepared them negligently, and that if they had known the true position, they would not have invested in Kintyre at all.

The profit figure for 1973 was incorrect. The profit of £20,346 should have been £16,779 because of two errors, one of £3,200 in the accrual for commission, and another in the understatement of doubtful debts of £367.

Lord Stewart found for the plaintiffs and awarded them the amount of their investment plus interest at 11 per cent from the date of the investment. In reaching this decision, he also accepted the plaintiffs' claim that the accounts for the year ended March 1975 were negligently prepared because they showed a trading loss of £87,727, whereas such a loss could not have occurred in one year and must therefore result from undetected errors in previous years, so that the profit for the year ended 31 March 1973 must have been even more overstated.

Oddly enough, no actual errors could be identified. This suggests, therefore, that it is enough to found a successful claim against an accountant if the plaintiff can show a mere probability that the accounts were wrong together with some evidence of surrounding negligence. It is not, it seems, necessary to show in what particular respects the accounts were wrong.

An additional point in establishing the negligence of the accountants was that they did not attend stocktaking, even though there was no evidence that the stock was incorrect.

The judge also accepted that it was reasonable to invest in a company by relying solely on the last audited accounts. He also accepted that the auditors did not know the specific intention of the plaintiffs to invest at the time of the audit, but nevertheless *held* that they were liable. He was impressed by, and used, the Jeb foresight test which, he said, applied in this particular case. Although the auditors did not know of the specific intention of the plaintiffs when they did the audit, they were aware that Kintyre needed capital, and that the accounts were normally available to lenders because they were, as the auditors knew, lodged with the company's bank.

The auditors were also aware, apparently, that one of the directors wished to sell his shares. They also knew clean audit certificates were often relied on by lenders and investors as well as shareholders.

It should be noted that the Privy Council in *Yuen Kun Yeu* v *A G of Hong Kong* [1987] 2 All ER 705 and the House of Lords in *Curran* v *Northern Ireland Co-Ownership Housing Association* [1987] 2 WLR 1043 pointed out the danger of assuming that the comments of Lord Wilberforce in *Anns* lead to a rule that foreseeability of itself and automatically leads to a duty of care and that a defendant with objective foresight is therefore liable unless there are reasons, e.g. public policy, why he should not be so.

Woolf J's judgment does not seem in fact to take this view of *Anns*. He seems to have been saying that Mr Marks had a duty of care only towards those who might be called upon to supply the company with funds, e.g. a lender, a major investor, and of course, a takeover bidder. Suppose A prepares the accounts of Boxo plc in a negligent fashion and overstates the worth of the company so that it is not such a good investment as might appear from its accounts. The accounts are filed at the Companies Registry. C, who is thinking of doing business with Boxo plc, gets a search of Boxo's file and is so impressed by the negligently prepared accounts that he makes an investment in Boxo and subsequently loses his money when the shares fall in value. Would A be liable in negligence to C? Almost certainly not: if *Anns* is taken to its extreme, no doubt it is just about foreseeable that someone would do what C did and invest. However, in more recent times the courts have made it clear that mere foresight is not enough. There must be some 'relationship' or 'proximity' or 'neighbourhood' between the parties. This is likely to restrict liability to within reasonable bounds and close the floodgates to a wide variety of claims by plaintiffs *unless they are known to be the users of professional statements and, further, that the professional concerned knows of the use to which they will be put.* Given such a situation a duty of care will exist.

From foresight back to knowledge – the retreat from *Anns*

The following two cases show how in recent times the courts have drawn away from the foresight principle to a position of knowledge of user and use.

Caparo Industries plc v Dickman and Others [1990] 2 WLR 358

The facts were, briefly, that Caparo, which already held shares in Fidelity plc, eventually acquired the controlling interest in the company. The group later alleged that certain purchases of Fidelity shares and the final bid were made after relying on Fidelity's accounts, which had been prepared by Touche Ross & Co, the second defendants.

The accounts, Caparo alleged, were inaccurate and misleading in that an apparent pre-tax profit of some £1.3m should in fact have been shown as a loss of £400,000. It was also alleged that, if the supposed true facts had been known, Caparo would not have made a bid at the price it did and might not have made a bid at all.

The Court of Appeal decided that while Touche Ross did not have a duty of care towards members of the public in regard to the Fidelity accounts, it did owe a duty of care to Caparo because Caparo was already a shareholder in Fidelity when it made the final purchase of shares and the bid.

The two main judgments in the House of Lords provide an interesting contrast: Lord Bridge concentrates more on the case law and in particular on the dissenting judgment of Lord Denning in *Candler v Crane Christmas* [1951] 1 All ER 426, where Lord Denning thought that the defendant accountants should have a duty of care to Candler because they had prepared allegedly negligent financial statements on the basis of which they knew Mr Candler might invest in the company concerned; and the judgment of the House of Lords in *Hedley Byrne & Co Ltd v Heller & Partners Ltd* [1963] 2 All ER 575, where a bank supplied an allegedly negligent reference as to the creditworthiness of a company called Easipower which they knew would be used by Hedley Byrne as a basis for extending credit to the company, which then went into liquidation.

A salient feature of both those cases, said Lord Bridge, was that the defendant giving advice or information was fully aware of the nature of the transaction the plaintiff was contemplating, knew that the advice or information would be communicated to him, and knew that it was likely that the plaintiff would rely on that advice or information in deciding whether or not to engage in the transaction in contemplation.

The situation was quite different where the statement was put into more or less general circulation and might foreseeably be relied on by strangers for any one of a variety of different purposes which the maker of the statement had no specific reason to anticipate.

Lord Bridge felt that it was one thing to owe a possibly wider duty of care to avoid causing injury to the person or property of others, but quite another to owe a similar duty to avoid causing others to suffer purely economic loss.

His Lordship concluded that auditors of a public company's accounts owed no duty of care to members of the public at large who relied on the accounts in deciding to buy shares in the company. And as a purchaser of additional shares in reliance on the auditors' report, the shareholder stood in no different position from any other investing member of the public to whom the auditor owed no duty.

Lord Oliver was concerned with establishing the purpose of an audit under the Companies Act 1985. He went on to say that in enacting the statutory provisions Parliament did not have in mind the provision of information for the assistance of purchasers of shares in the market, whether they were already the holders of shares or other securities or people with no previous proprietary interest in the company.

The purpose for which the auditors' certificate was made and published was that of providing those entitled to receive the report with information to enable them to exercise the powers which their respective proprietary rights in the company conferred on them and not for the purposes of individual speculation with a view to profit.

The duty of care was one owed to the shareholders as a body and not to individual shareholders.

Comment: The decision represents a further retreat from the judgment of Lord Wilberforce in *Anns v Merton London Borough Council* [1977] 2 All ER 492. There was a view taken of that judgment that a person should owe a duty of care in negligence to anyone allegedly injured by his conduct, including those suffering economic loss, unless there was any good reason or ground of public policy to prevent the duty being imposed. More recently, and particularly in this case, the courts have shown that there is a real need for proximity and so have gone a long way to reducing the fear of ever increasing potential professional liability.

It now seems that knowledge as to the user of the statement concerned and, seemingly, also as to the purpose or probable purpose for which it will be used, is required to establish the necessary proximity in these cases where allegedly careless misstatements result in economic loss. It seems unlikely that there will now be any further movement towards foresight of the user and use which had begun to show itself in *JEB Fasteners* v *Marks Bloom & Co* [1983] I All ER 583.

Morgan Crucible Co plc v Hill Samuel Bank Ltd and Others, *Financial Times* Law Reports, 30 October 1990

The crucial events in the case were as follows. On 6 December 1985, Morgan Crucible (MC) announced a proposed unsolicited offer to acquire the entire share capital of First Castle Electronics plc (FC). When the announcement was made, FC's most recent published financial statements were the reports and audited accounts for the years ended 31 January 1984 and 1985.

On 17 December 1985, MC published a formal offer document which was addressed to FC shareholders. Morgan Grenfell advised MC and Hill Samuel advised FC. The directors of FC, acting on its behalf, sent their shareholders a number of circulars. They were also issued as press releases by Hill Samuel and copies were supplied to MC's advisers.

Two days later, a circular was sent out by the directors of FC, comparing MC's profit record unfavourably with FC's and recommending refusal of the bid. In subsequent circulars reference was made to the published financial statements, and one circular of 31 December 1985 stated that they could be inspected.

An FC circular to its shareholders, issued on 24 January 1986, forecast an increase in profits before tax in the year to 31 January 1986 of 38 per cent. A letter from the auditors, Judkins, was included, saying that the profit forecast had been properly compiled. Included also was a letter from Hill Samuel stating that in its opinion the profit forecast had been prepared after due and careful inquiry.

On 29 January, MC increased its bid; on 31 January, FC's board sent another letter to shareholders recommending acceptance of that increased bid; on 14 February, the bid was declared unconditional; and on 27 February, a further recommendation to accept the bid was sent by FC to its shareholders.

Later, MC alleged that the financial statements (audited and unaudited) issued prior to the bid, the profit forecast of 24 January, and the financial material contained in the circulars and recommendation documents were prepared negligently and were misleading. MC asserted that if the true facts had been known the bid would not have been made or completed. MC issued a writ on 6 May 1987 joining as defendants Hill Samuel, Judkins, and FC's chairman and board. It alleged that the board and the auditors were responsible for circulating the financial statements; that they and Hill Samuel were responsible for the profit forecast; that all of them owed a duty of care to MC as a person who could foreseeably rely on them; that the statements and forecasts were negligently prepared; and that MC relied on them in making and increasing its offer and thereby suffered heavy loss.

In dealing with the allegations and the House of Lords judgment in *Caparo*, Lord Justice

Slade said, first, that in *Caparo* all of the representations relied on had been made before an identified bidder had come forward, whereas in this case some of the representations had been made after a bidder had emerged and indeed because a bid had been made. They were clearly made with an identified bidder in mind, i.e. MC. MC had therefore applied for leave to amend its statement of claim to representations made after the bid and as part of the takeover battle. This could then distinguish MC's case from the situation in *Caparo*.

The issue before the court was whether MC's allegations as amended disclosed a reasonable cause of action. On the assumption that the allegations were true, was there a duty of care to MC? The judge went on to say, on the assumed facts, that the defendants could have foreseen that MC would or might suffer financial loss if the representations were incorrect; but that foreseeability in itself was not enough for liability to arise – there had to be a sufficient relationship of proximity between the plaintiff and defendant. In addition, it must be just and reasonable to impose liability on the defendant.

The fatal weakness in the *Caparo* case, the judge said, was that the auditors' statement, i.e. the annual accounts, had not been prepared for the purpose for which the plaintiff relied on it. It was therefore arguable that this case could be distinguished from *Caparo*.

On the assumed facts, the directors of FC, when making the relevant representations, were aware that MC would rely on them for the purpose of deciding to make an increased bid and, indeed, intended that they should. MC did rely on them for that purpose. It was therefore arguable that there was a sufficient proximity between the directors of FC and MC to give rise to a duty of care.

For the same reasons, it could be argued that Hill Samuel and Judkins owed MC a duty of care in terms of their representations involving the profit forecast and the audited accounts.

Leave was given to amend the statement of claim. MC's amended case should be permitted to go forward to trial.

Comment: So, some reliance can be placed on financial statements and other representations in a takeover after all. If, during the conduct of a contested takeover and after an identified bidder has emerged, the directors and financial advisers of the target company make express representations with a view to influencing the conduct of the bidder, then they owe him a duty of care not to mislead him negligently as was alleged.

Avoiding and excluding liability

The most practical suggestion that can be made in terms of avoiding liability is for an accountant to follow strictly the recommendations of the professional bodies in the field, e.g. the many accounting standards and other published material. If this is done the accountant will at least have the advantage of the judgment of McNair J in *Bolam v Friern Hospital Management Committee* [1957] 2 All ER 118. He said in connection with doctors: 'A doctor is not guilty of negligence if he has acted in accordance with a practice accepted as proper by a responsible body of medical men skilled in that particular art . . . merely because there is a body of opinion who would take a contrary view'. The statement is, of course, equally applicable to other professions, including accountants.

As regards ability to exclude liability by notice under s. 2(2) of the Unfair Contract Terms Act 1977 (*see* p. 155), this will work only if the clause is reasonable. It would seem that there are two factors of major importance in deciding the reasonableness or otherwise of limitations or exclusion of liability for professional negligence and these are: (a) insurance, and (b) the operation of a two-tier service.

As regards insurance, it would seem unreasonable for a professional person to try to exclude totally liability for negligence because that can hardly be regarded as best professional practice. On the other hand, it would probably be reasonable for him to limit his liability to a specified sum. In fact s. 11(4) of the 1977 Act states that if a person seeks to restrict his liability in this way the court must have regard to the resources which he would expect to be available to him for the purposes of meeting the liability and also how far it was possible for him to cover himself by insurance. It is thought, therefore, that a firm which takes out the maximum insurance cover which is reasonable in the circumstances, being one where the cover is not so great that the effect could be greatly to inflate the fees charged by the firm, then to limit liability to that sum would satisfy the requirement of reasonableness. There is judicial support for this argument in a number of cases, particularly *George Mitchell* v *Finney Lock Seeds* (1983) (*see* p. 159).

As regards a two-tier service, a professional person could offer a full service at a full price and a reduced service at a lower price. Again, it would seem so long as the user of the service is aware that the two-tier service is available and that he is accepting a reduced service at a reduced price without full liability, then the exclusion clause in a lower tier service ought to be regarded as reasonable.

It is, of course, worth bearing in mind in all of this that a limitation of liability for professional negligence is much more likely to be regarded as reasonable in a contract with a non-consumer, i.e. a business, than it is in a consumer contract. In fact we have already seen in *Smith* v *Eric S Bush* (1987) (*see* p. 116) that a disclaimer used by a professional person in a consumer situation was not effective.

It is also worth noting that as regards auditors engaged by a company to carry out a Companies Act audit, s. 310 of the Companies Act 1985 makes void any provision in a contract of engagement of the auditors which purports to exclude them from liability for negligence or breach of duty, though the company can now pay the premiums on an insurance policy both for auditors and directors.

Professional negligence insurance

Professional indemnity policies are available for a whole range of professional persons and experts, e.g. accountants, solicitors, company directors and insurance brokers. These policies carry an excess clause under which the insured bears the first part of the claim up to a fixed amount. The risk covered is variously described but there is now a tendency to cover 'full civil liability' followed by exclusions from cover of things such as libel. The policies usually cover loss caused to a client (i.e. by breach of contract), and to a non-client (i.e. in the tort of negligence).

GRADED QUESTIONS

Essay mode

1. Accountants owe a duty of care to their clients. They may also owe a duty of care in the law of torts to persons who are not their clients.

   What is the extent of potential liability of an accountant to a non-client where he gives negligent advice? To what extent can an accountant safeguard against this liability?

   (20 marks)

   (The Chartered Institute of Certified Accountants. Paper 1.4(E). June 1989)

2. John and Joe were on holiday together and had rented a caravan at Nurdsley Bay. The weather was poor and John had been complaining that he could not sleep at night because of the cold. Joe, being a generous sort of person, bought a hot water bottle from a local shop and gave it to John, refusing to take any payment from John for it. That night the hot water bottle burst and John was badly scalded. Joe was sleeping on the bunk below and some of the hot water splashed down his face, causing him injury.

   Advise John and Joe as to the sort of action, if any, which they may respectively bring and against whom, if anyone, the action will lie.   *(Author's question)*

3. Due to John's carelessness in allowing excessive electric current to develop in his generator the electricity supply in the locality was cut off for a few hours.

   As a result Joe's factory was at a standstill during this period and he lost £6,000 by way of profits from lost production.

   Advise Joe in regard to his rights, if any, against John.   *(Author's question)*

4. Over the last three years George, an accountant, has regularly consulted Arthur, a broker specializing in life assurance, about his investments. George received a large sum of money under his father's will and wished to invest it wisely. He consulted Arthur who advised him to take out a single premium policy with Long Life Ltd. Arthur received an introduction fee from Long Life Ltd and did not charge George for advice. Within six months of the transaction Long Life Ltd went into liquidation because it was in financial difficulties, having been unstable for three years.

   Advise George.

   Would your advice have been different, and if so in what respect, if it turned out that George had done some accountancy work for Long Life two years ago, and lying forgotten in his files were figures on which George had reached the opinion that Long Life might be in some financial difficulty?   *(Author's question)*

5. (a) In what ways may an agent acquire authority to bind his principal?

   (12 marks)

(b) Jack and Jill are partners and have a small garage where they sell petrol and carry out minor repairs and servicing of cars. They have expressly agreed that they will not buy and sell cars. One day, Jill, without Jack's knowledge, buys an expensive car on credit, sells the car for cash, and disappears with the proceeds. Explain whether Jack may be held liable to pay for the car.

(8 marks)
(Total: 20 marks)

(The Chartered Institute of Management Accountants. Business Law. May 1990)

Objective mode

1. To succeed in an action for negligence the plaintiff must show:

   (i) the existence of a duty to take _____ which was owed to him by the defendant, and

   (ii) _____ of such duty by the defendant

   (iii) resulting _____ to the plaintiff.

2. A, a college lecturer, obtained permission from the principal to use the college library on Sundays for research.

   One Sunday he let himself in and locked the main door behind him, proceeding to the library. He left his briefcase near the library door, taking two notebooks he was using into the research section. B, a student who had broken into the premises the previous night because his landlady had thrown him out, walked into the library, fell over the briefcase and fractured his skull. B has no claim against A or his employers.   TRUE/FALSE

3. A was carrying out repairs to his front bedroom and left a hammer on the outside sill. Having completed the repair, A slammed the window shut and the hammer fell off the sill striking B who was lawfully upon the pavement below. B is suing A.

   Complete and delete in the following order to produce a correct statement.

   B WILL/WILL NOT carry the full burden of proof in negligence because the principle of _____ DOES NOT/DOES apply.

4. A purchaser of a majority shareholding in Boxo plc has brought an action against the auditors of the company for negligence. The auditors were not aware at the time of the audit that the business was to be acquired. It was, however, in financial difficulties and this was known to the auditors. As regards the duty of care of the auditors which one of the following decisions is the court likely to make? Circle the correct answer.

   A The auditor owes a duty of care to his client in contract. The purchaser of the business is not owed a duty since duty in negligence does not extend to economic loss for careless misstatements. The auditor is not liable.

   B Liability in negligence for misstatements only extends to a particular person who should have been known to the defendant. In this case there is no such special relationship. The auditor is not liable.

C A duty of care for negligent misstatements extends to those people the defendant should have foreseen as being injured by his negligent acts or omissions. The auditor would be liable if his report was a factor in the decision to purchase.

D The duty of care for false statements is the same as that of a manufacturer. The defendant will be liable to persons who used the accounts on which he reported. The auditor will therefore be liable to the purchaser of the business on the same basis that the manufacturer of the ginger beer was liable to the consumer in *Donoghue* v *Stevenson*. The auditor will be liable.

Answers to questions set in objective mode appear on p. 551.

Answers to questions set in objective mode

Chapter 1
1 (C)
2 (A)
3 (C)
4 (B)
5 (D)
6 (C)
7 (C)
8 (D)

Chapter 2
1 (C)
2 (C)
3 (D)
4 (D) Assuming benefit so that *Williams* not *Stilk* applies.
5 (C)
6 (C)
7 (C)
8 (A)

Chapter 3
1 (A)
2 (A)
3 (A)
4 (C)
5 (D)
6 (D)
7 (B)
8 (C)

Chapter 4
1 (C)
2 (B)
3 (D)
4 (D)
5 (B)
6 (D)
7 (D)
8 (A)

Chapter 5
1 (A)
2 (B)
3 (B)
4 (D)
5 (D)
6 (B)
7 (D)
8 (D)

Chapter 6
1 (C)
2 (A)
3 (D)
4 (C)
5 (D)
6 (D)
7 (B)
8 (C)

Chapter 7
1 (C)
2 (C)
3 (B)
4 (C)
5 (D)
6 (A)
7 (D)
8 (C)

Chapter 8
1 (C)
2 (B)
3 (D)
4 (A)
5 (D)
6 (C)

Chapter 9
1 (A)
2 (D)
3 (A)
4 (D)
5 (B)
6 (A)

Chapter 10
1 (A)
2 (C)
3 (D)

4 (B)
5 (D)
6 (C)

Chapter 11
1 (B)
2 (B)
3 (C)
4 (B)
5 (C)
6 (B)

Chapter 12
1 (C) Original sale was at market price
2 (B)
3 (B)
4 (B)
5 (B)
6 (B)
7 (B)

Chapter 13
1 (A)
2 (B)
3 (C)
4 (C)
5 (B)
6 (D)

Chapter 14
1 (C)
2 (D)
3 (B)
4 (D)
5 (A)
6 (B)

Chapter 15
1 (B)
2 (B)
3 (D)
4 (D)
5 (C)
6 (D)

Chapter 16
1 genuine occupational qualification
2 False
3 False
4 *two*: automatically
5 Jane *can* claim constructive unfair dismissal
6 100: 90: 90: ten: 30: 30
7 one week: one month: two years: two weeks: one week: 12: 12
8 800: four months

Chapter 17
1 (a) False
  (b) True
2 A holder in due course
3 True
4 (a) True
  (b) False
  (c) False
5 True

Chapter 18
1 (a) (B)
  (b) (A)
  (c) (D)
  (d) (A)
2 (B) and (C) are correct.
3 True

Chapter 19
1 CANNOT: IS: fidelity
2 sell: consign: sale: buy: money: security
3 skill: care
4 (a) is
  (b) (iii)
5 (a) is: (iii)
  (b) is not: (ii)

Chapter 20
1 (i) care
  (ii) breach
  (iii) damage
2 True
3 will not: res ipsa loquitur: does
4 B

Index